PLANT TAXONOMY

Earl L. Core
Head, Department of Biology
West Virginia University

Englewood Cliffs, N. J. PRENTICE-HALL, INC.

LIBRARY OF CONGRESS
CATALOG CARD NO.: 55-10950

First printing .... July, 1955
Second printing .... April, 1959

PRINTED IN THE UNITED STATES OF AMERICA

68157

To FREDA

Preface

The oldest phase of botany—one of the most interesting and important—deals with the taxonomy of plants. The fascinating differences among the species of plants that inhabit the earth, and the uses to which man has put them, make the subject one of the most attractive and useful of the plant sciences.

Plant taxonomy is often not presented in the most effective possible manner. The taxonomist can become so involved in codes and systems that the plants themselves are almost forgotten. This book approaches the science of plant taxonomy from a historical viewpoint in Part One, discussing principles more or less in the order in which they were formulated. The ancients acquired knowledge of plants slowly; enthusiasm and great speed characterized the botanical exploration of the New World. From the first blundering attempts at the systematic arrangement of the plant kingdom, man progressed through the discovery of close evolutionary relationships, and has arrived in the twentieth century at a workable although not fully satisfactory method of classification.

Terminology in systematic botany is extensive, but this book regards it as a means of reaching an end, not the end itself. Many definitions, most with illustrations, appear in Chapters 12 and 13 and furnish ready reference. An index to terms appears at the end of the book, and, with the material in Chapters 12 and 13, functions as a glossary.

Part Two gives an account of the principal families of vascular plants, with significant information given in concise form.

In the preparation of a book of this sort, an author is dependent upon the work of a great number of people, so many that it is impossible to thank them all in print. Acknowledgment must be made here, however, of the valuable assistance given by Dr. P. D. Strausbaugh, Professor Emeritus of Botany, West Virginia University; Dr. Reed Rollins, Gray Herbarium, Harvard University; Dr. Ernst C. Abbe, Department of Botany, University of Minnesota; Dr. David Keck, New York Botanical Garden; and Dr. Aaron J. Sharp, Department of Botany, University of Tennessee, all of whom read the manuscript and offered numerous helpful comments.

Acknowledgment is also due to many others who aided in various ways in the preparation of this book. These include especially Thelma Grace Sullenberger and some of my other colleagues at West Virginia University, among whom may be mentioned William M. Leeson, C. G. Brouzas, Elizabeth Ann Bartholomew, Herald D. Bennett, C. H. Baer, Nelle Ammons, Leroy O. Myers, and Robert F. Munn; valuable assistance was rendered by L. F. Wilmott, of Sydney, Australia and Morgantown, W. Va.; H. de la Montagne, New York Botanical Garden; R. J. Rodin, California State Polytechnic College; Dr. George H. M. Lawrence, Bailey Hortorium, Cornell University; Dr. Frank E. Egler, American Museum of Natural History; Dr. J. C. Saha, Darjeeling Government College, Darjeeling, India.

The pen-and-ink drawings were prepared by William A. Lunk, University Museums, University of Michigan. Some of these illustrations have been redrawn and adapted from various sources, including the classic work of Engler and Prantl.

I shall welcome comment or criticism, and will appreciate having any errors called to my attention.

EARL L. CORE

Contents

Part One

Part Two

PART ONE

1

Introduction

Far down in the depths of time some man, somewhere, first gave a name to some plant and classified it as suitable for human food. Thus systematic botany, or plant taxonomy, began, because **taxonomy** is a **classification** of things, particularly of plants and animals, and any classification presupposes the existence of names. From that time to this the development of the subject has witnessed the coinage of a multitude of new names and the elaboration of more complete and exceedingly intricate systems for their classification.

Slowly and sometimes painfully primitive man, through trial and error, learned the uses of more and more plants, especially those that served for food. Seeds and grains, roots, leaves and shoots, fleshy fruits and nuts were added to his bill of fare, and were given names for ready reference. By similar experimental methods he discovered that other plants had remedial properties. Leaves, roots, and bark of some plants he made into brews for treatment of illnesses; poultices of parts of certain others he found to be astringent, able to stanch bleeding; others, he discovered, had purgative properties, while still others would relieve pain or induce sleep. In the steaming rain forest of Malaysia, the rich river valleys of China, on the vast arid plains of Turkestan, or the treeless, windswept summits of the Andes, man was detecting and utilizing serviceable plants and applying to them their distinctive names.

Probably many ages after the discovery of useful plants by prehistoric man came their introduction into cultivation. At first this involved merely the scattering of seeds about his home, for convenience in harvesting the crops; only much later did it come to include the preparation of the soil and the selection of better varieties. Practically all the important food plants of our own time were cultivated before the dawn of history, in many cases so long before that the very memory of their origin was lost in the mist of time and they were represented as gifts of the gods to the human race. Shen-nung, the Divine Plowman of China, first sowed the five kinds of grain; the goddess Cinteutl gave the *centli,* or maize, to the Toltecs; and Ceres, to the Romans, was the goddess of the growing vegetation. But in this period great advances were made in man's knowledge of plants, resulting in the accumulation of a mass of facts gained, it is true, by experience, but almost totally unorganized with respect to any relationship with each other.

Then, in the period of the ancient Greek civilization there began to be a searching for rational explanations of natural phenomena, to replace the fables and fairy tales of more primitive peoples. Discoveries of fundamental importance were made by the Greek philosophers in botany as

Figure 1. Planting rice in southeastern Asia. (Courtesy Chicago Natural History Museum.)

well as in mathematics, astronomy, physics, geography, zoology, and medicine. Theophrastus, a student of Plato and Aristotle, has justly received the title of "Father of Botany" and is recognized as one of the great botanists of all time.

But when Greek liberty was lost, the development of Greek science also ceased. The Romans, who inherited and absorbed their culture, were practical men, promoting agriculture and pharmacy, applied phases of botany. Pliny left a valuable legacy in his *Natural History,* compiling his information, he said, from 2000 ancient works, most of which have long since been lost. And Dioscorides prepared a *Materia Medica,* which the accident of history caused to be thumbed over for a thousand years and more. The eclipse of the human spirit in the centuries represented by the decline and fall of the Roman Empire affected the development of botanical study along with the other sciences and the arts.

After the long sleep of the Dark Ages, a new spirit of inquiry into natural philosophy began to be felt, faintly at first, about the thirteenth century. The invention of printing from movable type, around 1440, came at a time when men were becoming more inquisitive about the world of plant life. They roamed forest and field for plants, especially for those useful in the preparation of their homemade remedies. For that matter, all plants were deemed useful, could their virtues be disclosed. During the sixteenth century the chief botanical achievements were the printing

Figure 2. Planting potatoes in the high Andes. (Courtesy Chicago Natural History Museum.)

and wide circulation of books, called **herbals,** concerned chiefly with the medicinal properties of certain plants, and with the identification of these plants.

With the tremendous upsurge in the discovery and naming of new species of plants resulting from the great period of geographic exploration, the earlier methods of arranging them led to chaos and the need for a more convenient system of classification became accentuated. Faltering beginnings were made from time to time but it remained for the botanists of the eighteenth century to lay the foundations upon which our taxonomic systems of today have been constructed. Like the development of an embryo, the successive outlines of the plant kingdom came little by little to resemble more closely those of our own day, although even yet maturity has by no means been attained. The invention and improvement of the compound microscope, the discovery of thousands of new species, representing many families unknown in Europe, the tedious, piecemeal study and detailed descriptions of these plants resulted in the accumulation of a daily increasing body of facts which made possible the application of ever greater refinement to the elaboration of systems of organization.

In the twentieth century systematics or taxonomy has taken unto itself new aims and objectives, as well as vastly different fields of research. So true has this been that it is now customary to speak of the earlier style of descriptive taxonomy as the classical taxonomy, while the new style is concerned with investigations of living organisms, to detect evolution at work, to explain the origin of species, to reveal facts and principles of greater importance in general biology—in short, while continuing to aid in the naming and classification of species, to attempt at the same time an explanation of their diversity. This has been true in plant as well as in animal taxonomy.

Purposes of Taxonomy. With the changes that have taken place recently in the methods of systematists, there has arisen some doubt in the minds of many scientists as to the real purpose of taxonomy. Some students are of the opinion that the taxonomist should concern himself merely with the identification and proper pigeonholing of specimens. It is true that these are important tasks and are fundamental to an understanding of other branches of biology, but many systematists are not satisfied with such a limitation. It is impossible to predict what the future may bring in changes of points of view, but the present-day purposes of taxonomy may be summarized as follows:

Analytical phase. The primary objective of the plant taxonomist is the recognition of the exceedingly variable components of the mantle of vegetation that adorns the globe, with a terminology understood by all people. The plant taxonomist finds himself in a world in which there are countless numbers of individual plants. No two are exactly alike, although some are nearly so. By comparing the similarities and differences it has been possible, by painstaking study, to reduce the apparent confusion to some sort of systematic arrangement. The individuals that resemble each other most closely constitute a group known as a **species,** which is given a name to facilitate its subsequent recognition by workers throughout the world.

Synthetic phase. As noted above, the primary task of the systematist is the recognition and accurate description of species. But if he stopped there, he would soon face a chaotic accumulation of species descriptions. To prevent this, he must try to find an orderly arrangement of the species; he must devise a **classification.** This is the second objective of the taxonomist. Related species are placed together in categories of progressively higher rank, on the basis of their group relationships. Thus systematic botany provides the foundation for all the sciences and arts dealing with plants. When we consider that green plants afford man's principal means of utilizing energy from the sun and that plants furnish, directly or indirectly, most of his food, clothing, building materials, fuel, and medicine, we realize how essential it becomes to have an orderly classification recognized by civilized people around the world.

Experimental phase. The classification of the bewildering multitudes of organisms on the earth brings up many difficult problems, which have involved much speculation and theorizing. These problems have now led to a study of the factors of evolution, and this is the third task of the systematist. The taxonomist who studies the factors of evolution is trying to find out how species originate, how they are related to each other, what this relationship means. He thus studies species not merely as they are at present, but also as to their origin and their changes through the past. In this work it is possible for him to check his conclusions by experiments on living plants, instead of simply relying upon the implications of observed data. Furthermore, a satisfactory understanding of the intricate evolutionary phenomena can only be attained through a knowledge of other branches of biology such as ecology, geology, biogeography, paleontology, cytology, morphology, anatomy, physiology, genetics, and the like, so that this third phase provides the common ground on which these various disciplines may assemble their facts and draw their conclusions. A set of general principles applicable to the entire realm of living beings is beginning to develop from the convergence of these conclusions.

Whereas a few years ago taxonomy was looked upon by many as being a highly specialized, rather narrow branch of biology, it has now become one of the principal focal points of this science that concerns itself with the study of living things.

General View of the Plant Kingdom. Plants of one kind or another exist almost everywhere on the surface of the earth, in the air, the soil, the water, in very hot and very cold places, in very wet and very dry places. Most plants have their roots in the soil, but bacteria may float on dust particles in the air, and most algae live in the water. Some algae can grow in hot springs at a temperature of 179° F.; lichens endure heat and drought on the surface of a rock. Another alga forms the "red snow" of the Arctic, which is composed of millions of individuals of unicellular plants living on the surface of melting snow.

More than 300,000 species of plants are found in the world. These vary greatly in size, form, organization, color, distribution, ecology, life history. The largest plants now living are the giant sequoias of California, attaining a height of 272 feet and a diameter of 37 feet; the smallest known plants are the bacteria, a single individual of which may be 1/50,000 of an inch long. Plants may be trees, shrubs, herbs; vines climbing into trees or trailing on the ground; they may shed their leaves at the approach of unfavorable seasons, or they may bear foliage the year around. Most plants are **terrestrial,** having their roots in the soil, but some are **epiphytic,** growing perched upon other plants. Some are **aquatic,** floating on the surface of the water or submerged in the water. Most aquatics live in fresh water but some are marine, some live in brackish water, and some about salt lakes. Some plants produce flowers and seeds; others reproduce by spores alone; some are green and manufacture their own food; others are non-green and dependent upon other sources for a food supply. Some plants are found normally in cool Arctic or Alpine regions; others in hardwood or softwood forests; others in grasslands or deserts; others in tropical rain forests or savannas.

To arrange all these plants, so numerous and so various, into a natural system is a difficult task. Nevertheless, it is one of the important tasks to which the plant taxonomist has devoted himself.

References

Candolle, A. de, *L'origine des plantes cultivées.* Paris, 1883. Translated: *Origin of cultivated plants.* London, 1886.

Huxley, J. [Ed.], *The New Systematics.* London, 1940.

Hylander, C. J., *The world of plant life.* New York, 1947.

Mayr, E., *Systematics and the origin of species.* New York, 1942.

Reed, H. S., *A short history of the plant sciences.* Waltham, Mass., 1942.

Schery, R. W., *Plants for Man.* 564 pp. New York, 1952.

2

The Development of Taxonomy

The dependence of all peoples upon the plant kingdom is so great that no civilized nation of antiquity was without its writings on botanical subjects, at least upon the applied phases. A treatise on medicinal plants, a copy of which is extant, was said to have been prepared by the mythical Emperor Shen-nung of China; regardless of authorship, it is much older than the Christian era. A medical papyrus in Egypt was written before the time of Moses. An Assyrian herbal of the seventh century B.C. lists medicinal and other plants. In ancient India similar treatises were prepared while a botanical lore only slightly inferior to that of Europe was developed by the Aztecs in pre-Columbian days. These, however commendable within themselves, had little or no influence upon the development of our modern system of plant taxonomy. This had its beginning among the philosophers of ancient Greece.

The Father of Botany. Theophrastus, a student of the great Plato, was the founder of botanical science in Greece. He was born in 370 B.C., in Lesbos, and went to Athens at an early age to become a pupil of Plato, from whom it is presumed he first learned the principle of classification found in his extant literary works. Aristotle at this time was also a student, only fifteen years older than Theophrastus. When Plato died, in 347 B.C., Theophrastus became the pupil of Aristotle; since they had been fellow-students and the difference in their ages was not very great, they remained on nearly equal terms, and much attached to each other. At the death of Aristotle in 323 B.C., he left his favorite pupil his library, the largest assembled up to that time, and his garden on the grounds of the Lyceum.

In the garden of the Lyceum in Athens, then, botanical science came into being. Theophrastus did not travel far beyond the walls of the garden, but his life was nevertheless remarkably full and interesting. He enjoyed the personal friendship of two of the world's greatest thinkers and witnessed the careers of Philip of Macedon and his son Alexander, who had also been taught by Aristotle. To the followers of Alexander

Theophrastus owed his accounts of such exotic plants as cotton, banyan, pepper, cinnamon, myrrh, and banana. Under his direction the School had 2000 students; these brought him knowledge of the plants of Greece and nearby regions. His writings are full of phrases like "the people of Mount Ida say," "according to the Arcadians," "the Dorians call the tree . . ."; it may be assumed that these were reports contributed by students who came from the districts mentioned.

The writings of Theophrastus were most voluminous; a list of 227 treatises is given by an ancient writer, covering many topics. Only fragments of most of these are extant. His two botanical works, *Enquiry into Plants* and *The Causes of Plants,* are the principal ones that have survived. The style of these suggests that they may have been notes for lectures. "There is no literary charm; the sentences are mostly compressed and highly elliptical, to the point sometimes of obscurity" (Hort).

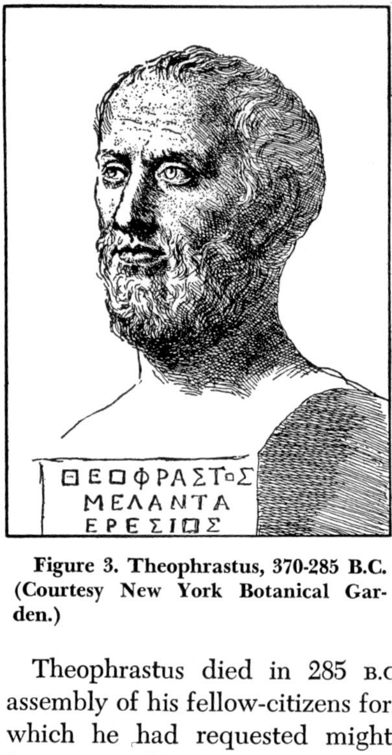

Figure 3. Theophrastus, 370-285 B.C. (Courtesy New York Botanical Garden.)

A simple nomenclature for plants already existed in the time of Theophrastus, recognized by farmers, carpenters, apothecaries, charcoal-burners. This nomenclature Theophrastus brought together in his books; the names of nearly 500 plants are given, and, because the books were so widely used, the names gained general recognition. Some of them still appear as generic names in modern classification, as Krataigos (*Crataegus*), daukon (*Daucus*), asparagos (*Asparagus*), and Narkissos (*Narcissus*).

Theophrastus died in 285 B.C., at the age of eighty-five. A great assembly of his fellow-citizens formed the funeral procession to his grave, which he had requested might be in some peaceful corner of the Lyceum garden.

The writings of Theophrastus contain a considerable amount of sound botanical information mixed with typical Greek speculative philosophy; for the next eighteen centuries the world produced little that was better.

The scholarship of the Greeks faded away as their freedom was lost. The great blaze of glory of the age of the philosophers faded to an ever-fainter glow as Hellenic culture spread to other lands but failed to find soil suitable for its growth.

Among the Romans no substantial science was built upon the foundation laid by Theophrastus. Agriculture and pharmacy, however, were fields of applied botany that received some development at the hands of the practical-minded citizens of Rome. Cato the Censor (234-149 B.C.) wrote *De Re Rustica,* the first agricultural book in Latin, mentioning 120 cultivated plants.

During the flowering of Roman culture in the first century A.D. two important books were produced which greatly affected botanical studies for a millennium and a half. These deserve special attention.

Pliny's Natural History. Caius Plinius Secundus was born in northern Italy in A.D. 23 and died while observing the eruption of Vesuvius in A.D. 79. This relatively short life-span was so crowded with intellectual activity that a favorite theme of historians of his time was his prodigious capacity for work.

Pliny moved to Rome while still a youth and studied under the grammarian Apion. He visited Africa, Egypt, and Greece, and later served in the army in Germany, where he was promoted to the command of a troop of cavalry. During his military career he traveled as far as the Baltic Sea and visited Belgic Gaul. In his twenty-ninth year he returned to Rome and applied himself to writing. After a period spent in Spain as procurator, he returned to Rome in A.D. 70 and was admitted to the intimate circle of the friends of the Emperor Vespasian. About A.D. 73 he was appointed prefect of the fleet at Misenum, near Pompeii. In A.D. 77 he published his *Natural History* (*Historia Naturalis*), dedicated to Titus.

While he was with the fleet at Misenum, 24 August A.D. 79, he observed the great cloud of smoke arising from the crater of Vesuvius. He at once went to sea in a small vessel to observe the phenomenon, eventually reaching the home of a friend, where he passed the night. Next morning, when it seemed likely the house would collapse, they took to the open air, with pillows on their heads as protection from the falling stones and ashes. As they were taking their flight, Pliny fell to the ground, the dense vapor of sulfurous fumes apparently having suffocated him.

Of all the works written by Pliny, only the *Natural History* has survived. This is a vast compilation of ancient knowledge and belief on almost every known subject. Pliny himself states that these matters were collected from about 2000 volumes (nearly all of which have now perished), and it has been determined that these works were the products of nearly 500 different authors. Until 1469 Pliny's work existed in manuscript only, but so great was the esteem accorded it in the Middle Ages that copies were made in great numbers; about 200 are known today. From the days of the Roman Empire almost to the beginning of the nineteenth century it had profound influence on students of biology. Cuvier says of it: "The work of Pliny is one of the most precious monuments that have come down to us from ancient times, and affords proof of an astonishing amount of erudition in one who was a warrior and a statesman. Despite the faults which we are obliged to admit in him when viewed as a naturalist we are bound to regard him as one of the most meritorious of the Roman writers."

Dioscorides and His *Materia Medica.* A contemporary of Pliny was Pedanios Dioscorides, a Greek born in Cilicia, the exact date unknown. Indeed, very little is known of the life of Dioscorides, in contrast to that of Pliny, save that he was a physician, that he traveled extensively to study plants, and that he obtained a considerable amount of information concerning their pharmaceutical properties. To record this information he published a *Materia Medica,* describing fairly accurately the roots, stems, leaves, and sometimes the flowers, of about 600 species of plants.

The *Materia Medica* is divided into five books, the first dealing with Aromatics, Oils, Ointments, Trees, the second with Living Creatures, Milk and Dairy Produce, Cereals and Sharp Herbs, the third with Roots, Juices, Herbs, the fourth with Herbs and Roots, the last with Vines and Wines, Metallic Ores. Written in Greek, the book gives the common names for the plants in that language, and adds in various cases names applied in the Latin, Egyptian, Gallic and other tongues. While the books and chapters have no taxonomic significance, as compared with modern systems, still it is remarkable that there are certain series of related plants. For example, in Book III, Chapters 31-47 deal with lavender, origanum, thyme, pennyroyal, dittany, *Marrubium, Ballota, Salvia, Mentha, Satureja,* and *Marjoram,* all members of the *Labiatae,* and Chapters 60-71 deal with *Echinophora, Bupleurum, Angelica, Tordylium, Sison,* anise, caraway, dill, cumin, *Ammi,* and coriander, all members of the Umbelliferae. It is apparent, therefore, that Dioscorides had some sense of actual relationships as we think of them today. A great many of the vernacular names coincide (at least with slight changes in spelling) with generic names as used today, for example, Zingiberi, Asphodelos, Skilla, Kapparis, Anemone, Chelidonion, Gentiane, Aristolochia, Dipsacon, Aloe, Linon, Phasiolos, Raphanis, and Aspharagos.

The book was illustrated with drawings of the plants and these gave it still greater significance. It is the first known book on plants to contain illustrations. Of course, since the books in those days could be reproduced only through copying by hand, the condition of the sketches would vary greatly with the different copies. The most famous of the manuscripts of Dioscorides was prepared for the Princess Juliana Anicia, daughter of the Byzantine emperor Flavius Anicius Olybrius, about the year A.D. 500. The illustrations in this manuscript were well done and most of them have been identified, although some were misplaced and some cannot be identified with certainty. The manuscript was acquired by the Imperial Library in Vienna about 1569.

It has been said that for 1500 years the *Materia Medica* was the alpha and omega of European botany and that it has been more attentively studied, word for word, and line for line, than any other book on botany ever written. During the Middle Ages no drug plant was recognized as genuine unless the *Materia Medica* had been used in its identification.

The Middle Ages. The decline and fall of the Roman Empire brought with it the loss of interest in literature and science. The laborious process by which each copy of a book had to be separately handmade kept the total number of copies relatively small. For a thousand years the producers of books scarcely held their own: ancient classics were probably lost at a more rapid rate than the few mediocre productions of the Middle Ages could take their place. Most people who concerned themselves about botanical science at all were content to follow the writings of Theophrastus, Pliny, and Dioscorides.

During this period came the extraordinary rise of Islam among the Arabians, who spread their culture from Spain to Bokhara. Islamic scholars themselves contributed notably to botanical science and they kept alive some of the ancient writings of the Greeks and Romans, protecting them from the destruction suffered in Europe. A Persian writer, Abu Mansur, wrote a book on medicinal plants reminiscent of Dioscorides but also containing references to Indian plants. Ibn Sina, or Avicenna (980-1037), also a Persian, compiled a *Canon of Medicine* with many references to medical plants. This book was very popular and was much copied, going through more than twenty editions in the sixteenth century.

At last European intellect, after its long sleep of the Middle Ages, began to show signs of awakening. Here and there came gropings toward experimentation and observation, instead of a slavish adherence to old authorities. But it was a long and tremendously costly struggle. Centuries passed before the full light of the Renaissance shone upon European scholars.

Albertus Magnus. Typical of the writers of the early Renaissance, and certainly the greatest who wrote in the field of botany, was Albert of Bollstädt, "Doctor Universalis," who was esteemed one of the most learned men of his age and received the title "Albertus Magnus" conferred on him during his lifetime by general acclamation. He has been called "the Aristotle of the Middle Ages."

He was born in southern Germany about 1193 and entered the University of Padua where he studied the philosophy of Aristotle, and came to have an extensive knowledge of geography, astronomy, medicine, botany, and zoology, as well as of ecclesiastical affairs. After teaching at several German schools, he expounded the philosophy of Aristotle in Paris from 1245 to 1248, where he had as one of his pupils Thomas Aquinas, later to become a saint as the "Angelic Doctor" who reconciled the teachings of Aristotle with the doctrines of the Christian Church. In 1259 he was appointed Bishop of Ratisbon by Pope Alexander IV, but retired in 1262 to devote the remainder of his life to study. He died in 1280.

His writings on all subjects fill twenty-one folio volumes. Although affected by many medieval ideas and superstitions, he realized the value of scientific investigation and advocated in his writings the importance of experimentation. The botanical portion of his writings, called *De vegetabilis,* comprises a very small part of his total work. He drew upon the writings of certain medieval scholars but his book contains a great deal of original matter. It is primarily a book of plant descriptions, with a limited amount of philosophical discussion. Unlike Dioscorides, he felt it was useless to concern himself with a catalogue of all species of plants, with their distinguishing characters. He did, however, work out a new system of general classification, using characteristics recognized today as significant, although designated by different names. He divided the plant kingdom into *Leafless plants* (Cryptogams, in part) and *Leafy plants* (mostly Phanerogams, with some Cryptogams), further dividing the leafy plants into *Corticate* (evidently Monocotyledons) and *Tunicate* (Dicotyledons), the Tunicate plants being subdivided into herbaceous and woody.

He was especially interested in cultivated plants of the field and orchard, giving descriptions of the plants and methods of culture. The walnut tree (*Juglans regia*), he points out, is unfavorable to certain plants around it on account of its "indwelling extreme toxic bitterness," a fact that many people believe to have been discovered only recently.

Albert's work deals mainly with plant descriptions and with practical matters of gardening and orcharding. In Book VI, for example, "de speciebus quarundam plantarum," he discusses several species, including *Abies,* "Arangus" (orange), "Arbor mirabilis" (Castor bean), "Arbor paradisi" (*Musa paradisiaca,* the banana), *Castanea, Fraxinus, Malus, Olea, Prunus, Quercus, Vitis,* etc. Spinach is mentioned for the first time in any European book. He named and described a great many common garden vegetables, such as turnips, radishes, carrots, cabbage, lettuce, cucumbers, parsley, and celery. *De vegetabilis* was widely distributed and read for the next 200 years, not only in the universities but also among the common people. In morphology it was probably not excelled for the next 400 years.

The Age of Herbals

Although there continued to be a gradual awakening of the scientific spirit, no great advances in botany were made for a long time. The invention of printing with movable type in Europe about 1440 greatly aided in the dissemination of ideas, by making books available to a wider audience. About this time men began to grow more curious concerning plants, particularly those from which medicines could be prepared. It was becoming increasingly evident that the *Materia Medica* of Dioscorides, which had been pored over so faithfully for so many centuries, was inadequate for the identification of all medical plants, especially those north of the Alps. So it came about that the first botanical books to be written after the invention of movable-type printing were descriptions of plants of medical value. These books represented a type that came to be known as the *herbal;* the root-diggers were called *herbalists.* The writing of such books reached a climax during the sixteenth century; as a matter of fact, they constituted the chief botanical accomplishments of that century, the great century of the Renaissance. Many of the herbalists were physicians, led to the study of botany by the need for plant remedies, although other learned men, including clergymen, were also among the herbalists. The Age of the Herbals, according to Arber, lasted from about 1470 to 1670, during which time botany made the most steady, rapid, and consistent advance recorded up to that time. Kurt Sprengel, in his *Geschichte der Botanik,* gave the honored title of "German Fathers of Botany" to the greatest of the Herbalists. The earliest of these was Otto Brunfels.

Otto Brunfels. The herbal of Brunfels, Sprague says, forms a link between ancient and modern botany, to be regarded as the end of the classical and medieval works on the one hand, and the beginning of modern taxonomy on the other. In some ways it may almost be said that modern systematic botany starts with Brunfels.

Brunfels was born about 1489 at Mainz. He received a good education and took the degree of Master of Arts by the time he was twenty-one. He then entered a monastery at Strasbourg where he remained until 1521, when, becoming a Protestant, he fled from the monastery and spent the next three years in various places as an evangelical pastor and theological writer. He contracted tuberculosis, which so affected his voice that he gave up preaching and returned to Strasbourg in 1524 to establish a boys' school. He continued his writings on education and theology, and began to apply himself to medicine and botany. His first publication was the *Herbarum vivae Eicones,* the first volume of which appeared in 1530. The second volume appeared in 1531 and the third was issued posthumously in 1536. He received the degree of Doctor of Medicine at the University of Basel about 1533 and was appointed town physician of Bern, a position he held until his death the following year. Plagued by sickness and theological dissensions, his life was evidently rather unhappy, but a new era in the history of botany began with the publication of his herbal.

The text of the *Herbarum* has been generally considered of little value, since it is chiefly made up of extracts from earlier writers—Theophrastus, Pliny, Dioscorides, and others. Brunfels had, apparently, no clear conception of plant classification, and in nomenclature he made no outstanding advance, using mostly the Latin names employed by the ancients, with common names in German. Many of the names, it is true, are familiar today, but, for that matter, as noted above, some of our present generic names go back to Theophrastus. A random sampling of names from Brunfels include *Plantago, Helleborus, Aristolochia, Asarum, Sanicula, Borago, Verbena, Narcissus, Viola, Urtica, Pisum, Brassica, Iris,* names in general applied to the same plants today. Many others occur that would not be recognizable today. Traces of medieval superstition are present in the *Herbarum,* for instance in his description of the blotch on the leaf of *Polygonum:* "This herb is also of two kinds, large and small, but both have a peach-like leaf which is blotched in the middle, just as if a drop of blood had dripped on to it, a mighty and marvellous sign which astonishes me more than any other miracle of the herbs."

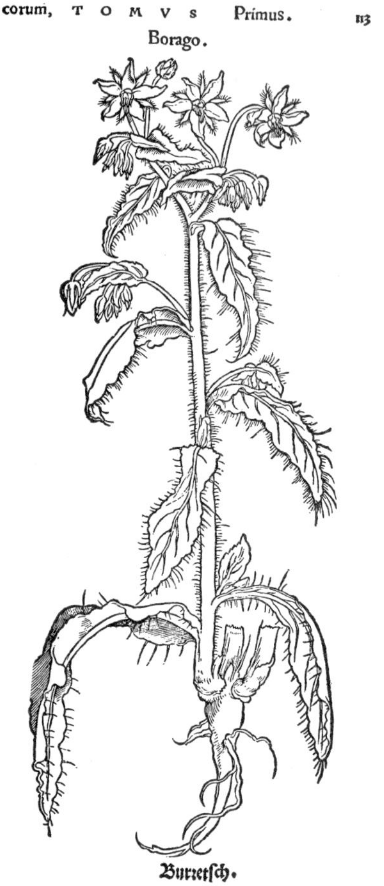

Figure 4. Borago. An illustration from Brunfels' *Herbarum vivae Eicones.* (Courtesy New York Botanical Garden.)

It is, however, upon the remarkable lifelike engravings that the value of the *Herbarum* depends (see Figure 4). They were prepared from living plants and were not copies of previous pictures. The book, therefore, in this respect, represents a return to nature. The illustrations are so good that most of the species represented in the figures can be identified. Some of these figures constitute the primary historical basis of a modern species name, as used later by Linnaeus.

Jerome Bock (Hieronymus Tragus). Bock, a contemporary and friend of Brunfels, is listed as the second of the "German Fathers of Botany." He was born at Heiderbach, Bavaria, in 1498. His parents planned a monastic life for him, but this was distasteful to him and, after passing through the university, he became a schoolmaster at Zweibrücken and overseer of the garden of a German count. Like Brunfels, he embraced Protestantism and later became a preacher at Hornbach, where he also practiced as a physician and pursued his botanical studies. Religious troubles arose, and he was forced to leave Hornbach, although, after various hardships, he was later able to return to resume his work as a preacher. He died in 1554.

In his botanical work Bock became acquainted with Otto Brunfels and provided various bits of material that were used in the *Eicones.* He conceived the idea of writing a herbal in the German tongue, a great innovation, since practically all scientific books from the days of Theophrastus and Pliny had been in either Greek or Latin, languages that had long since become obsolete except among scholars.

Bock's great work, the *New Kreüterbůch,* appeared in 1539. It contained no illustrations, but, in contrast to the *Herbarum,* its chief claim to distinction lies in its excellent first-hand descriptions. Bock noted the localities and habitats of the plants he described, so that his work showed some resemblances to a modern flora. He appears to have been a keen collector, tramping the woods and fields despite bad health, and apparently included only those plants that came under his personal observation. He noted flower parts as corolla, stamens, pistils, and apprehended something of natural relationships, although his arrangements were influenced by various considerations, which accounts for the fact that unrelated plants frequently stand together. He included 567 species, classified into herbs, shrubs, and trees, the first two parts of his book containing the herbs, the third and final part the shrubs and trees.

Leonhart Fuchs (Fuchsius). The third of the "German Fathers," regarded by many as the most meritorious of them all, was Leonhart Fuchs, born at Wemding, Bavaria, in 1501. He had a precocious development and a strong personality; he attended the University of Erfurt and is said to have taken a bachelor's degree at the age of thirteen. Later he went to the University of Ingolstadt, where he obtained a master's degree in 1521 and the degree of Doctor of Medicine in 1524. While at Ingolstadt he read the works of Martin Luther and became a Protestant.

After two years of private practice as a physician in Munich, he was appointed Professor of Medicine at Ingolstadt in 1526 and resigned in 1528 to become physician to the Margrave of Brandenburg at Ansbach, probably because there he could give free expression to his religious views. In 1529 he obtained a wide reputation by his successful treatment of a deadly epidemic known as the English Sweating Sickness. In 1533 he received a call to return to Ingolstadt but was prevented from taking up his duties there by religious antagonism and in 1535 he became Professor of Medicine at the newly organized Protestant University of Tübingen, where he remained for the last thirty-one years of his life. Here in spite of a strenuous academic and professional career, he found time to prepare his herbal, *De historia stirpium,* which appeared from the press in 1542. This work was in Latin but it was succeeded in 1543 by a German edition called the *New Kreüterbůch.* Both works were well illustrated with original engravings. Two other volumes were at least partly ready for the press at the time of Fuchs' death in 1566 but were never published.

Various opinions have been expressed as to the value of the work of Fuchs, as compared with the other herbals of the sixteenth century. It was his aim to identify and figure the medicinal plants known to Dioscorides and other ancient writers. The work is modeled after the *Materia Medica,* being divided into 344 *capita* (chapters) of which 267 correspond with those of Dioscorides.

Since he was so much under the spell of Dioscorides, it is not to be expected that much originality would be found in Fuchs' descriptions. However, in combination with the excellent figures, they assist, as did those of Brunfels, in identifying plants mentioned by medieval writers, and hence become the "historic types" of Linnean species. Fuchs' herbal includes figures of 487 species, of which 289 were known to the ancients, 64 to those of the Middle Ages, and 31 were first recorded by Brunfels. The remainder, 103, were first figured by Fuchs, although some of them had been described by Bock. Thus his work was of great value in giving a picture of what was known about medicinal plants in Germany in his day, summarizing the references of classical and medieval writers concerning them, and laying a foundation for further research.

Despite his veneration for the ancients, evidences are not wanting to indicate that Fuchs felt it was necessary to supplement their work. For instance, while most of the habitats of the species are copied from Dioscorides, these are sometimes supplemented or replaced by the actual habitats where Fuchs had seen the plants growing in Germany and, with reference to *Centaurium umbellatum,* he went so far as to observe: "Although Dioscorides writes that it grows in wet and damp places, yet everyone knows that with us it commonly grows in hard dry grassy fields and meadows."

A passage from his Dedicatory Epistle, quoted by Arber, gives some insight into the nature of the man: "There is no need for me to set forth to the multitude the pleasure and delight afforded by a knowledge of plants, since there is none but knows that there is nothing in this life more pleasant and delightful than to wander through woods and over mountains and fields wreathed and adorned with a variety of the choicest flowers and herbs, and to gaze on them attentively. This enjoyment and pleasure is in no small degree enhanced by a knowledge of their properties and powers: for real understanding doubles the charm and delight of vision."

In summary, it might be said of these three "German Fathers" that Brunfels brought out the first herbal with really good illustrations; Fuchs far surpassed him in number of figures, as well as in their methodical arrangement, while Bock felt that figures were useless, and was therefore incited to draw up those apt and pithy descriptions which made him a master in the field of botanical writing.

Valerius Cordus. One other name was included by Sprengel among the "German Fathers," a name for centuries comparatively little known—Valerius Cordus, whose tragic early death may have prevented him from becoming the greatest of all the herbalists. He was born in 1515, the son of Euricius Cordus, a physician and botanist. At sixteen he graduated from the University of Marburg and later became an expounder of Dioscorides at the University of Wittenberg. He traveled widely to observe plants and made a stay at Tübingen, so he was doubtless personally acquainted with Leonhart Fuchs.

Since he longed to see, in their native haunts, the plants about which Dioscorides had written, he undertook a long excursion into Italy, traveling partly on foot, partly on horseback. Travel was difficult in those days, and exposure and fatigue led to a tragic end. He was injured by a kick from a horse, and became quite ill, reaching Rome only with difficulty. He seemed to rally temporarily, then suffered a relapse and died in Rome in 1544, at the age of twenty-nine.

Cordus himself published none of his writings, but his most important work, *Historia plantarum,* was printed in 1561, edited by Konrad Gesner (1516-1565), professor of medicine at Tübingen. It is generally accepted as the most important of the early German herbals. The chief value of the work of Brunfels and Fuchs lies in their fine engravings, that of Bock in his concise descriptions. Cordus, who wrote in Latin, far surpassed Bock in the exactness of his descriptions and has been called the founder of modern botanical description. His book includes 502 species, of which about sixty-six were apparently new. They include not only German and Italian plants but numerous others imported from foreign countries. Tournefort (1700) said Cordus was the first to excel in plant description and Haller (1771) said he was the first to show how to describe plants from nature, instead of relying on the accounts of the ancients.

His close observations enabled him to describe with a remarkable degree of accuracy the movements of leaves, the circumnutation of twiners, the insectivorous habits of sundew, and the tubercles on roots of legumes. The reproduction of ferns, a mystery to many people both before and after his time, was no puzzle to him. "Trichomanes," he wrote, "grows abundantly on moist shaded rocks, although it produces no stem or flower or seed. It reproduces itself by means of the dust that is developed on the backs of the leaves, as do all kinds of ferns."

It was unfortunate that Gesner felt he should supply figures from various sources to illustrate the plants described so well by Cordus. In order to do this he had to identify the plants of Cordus in terms of names used by other botanists. Out of about 270 figures supplied, more than forty represent species now regarded as different from those described by Cordus. This led to mistakes by later authors, and to criticism of Cordus, although the errors lay in the incorrect association of the illustrations and not in the descriptions.

Pierandrea Mattiola (Matthiolus). Meanwhile in Italy on the soil of Pliny and Dioscorides, the herbal was likewise being developed. The plants here, many of them, were actually those of the classical writers and not so much ingenuity was required to make the descriptions fit the specimens.

Chief among the Italian herbalists was Mattiola (1501-1577), who was born at Siena. He was the son of a physician and his early interests led him also into the study of medicine. He practiced in various towns and was physician to the Archduke Ferdinand and to the Emperor Maximilian II. His interest in medicinal plants led him to collect data for a commentary on Dioscorides. Luca Ghini, who taught botany at Bologna and for a time at Pisa, was working on a similar commentary and turned over his material to Mattiola. Mattiola's masterpiece was *Commentarii in sex libros Pedacii Dioscoridis,* published in 1544. It immediately had a phenomenal success, was translated into numerous languages, and ran through countless editions. Although it claimed to be merely a commentary on Dioscorides, it actually included a great many more plants added by Mattiola himself. While some of the editions had beautiful figures, it is generally felt that his descriptions were not as good as those of some of the other herbalists.

Andrea Cesalpino. An Italian botanist, contemporary with Mattiola, who was very different from the other herbalists of the 16th century was Andrea Cesalpino of Arezzo (1519-1603). As a child he is said to have hated the assigned work in school so much that his parents and teachers finally despaired of educating him. Left to himself, he astonished them by becoming an outstanding scholar. He studied botany and medicine at Pisa under Luca Ghini, later becoming professor of botany and medicine at Bologna. In 1592 he went to Rome as physician to Pope Clement VIII. He prepared a herbarium of 768 well-mounted plants that is still in existence, one of the oldest known.

His famous work, *De plantis,* appeared in 1583. It consists of sixteen books, the first of which, only thirty pages in length, states his theory of botany and is the part upon which his fame rests. The other fifteen books contain descriptions of about 1520 plants, arranged as woody and herbaceous. He was essentially a philosopher of the school of Aristotle and sought a system of classification based on reasoning and not upon the utilitarian approach of the other herbalists. He carried out this classification by making a thorough study of the plants, particularly the fruits and seeds ("the final cause of plants consists in that propagation which is effected by the seeds," he wrote), but also of other parts and even of the activities of the plants, so that with him morphology, anatomy, physiology, and taxonomy are inseparably joined. His most outstanding conclusion was that the organs of fructification were more important in classification than the habit, which was contrary to the thought of his day; for this Linnaeus called him the first of the systematists.

The work of Cesalpino was not appreciated by his contemporaries, for it was in advance of the times, and lay almost unnoticed; only in the next century was it recognized for its true worth.

The Dutch "Big Three." In the Low Countries the herbal flourished exceedingly, chiefly through the zeal of a trio of botanical friends, and the remarkable collaboration of the "prince of publishers," Christophe Plantin of Antwerp, who developed printing as one of the fine arts.

Eldest of the trio was **Rembert Dodoens (Dodonaeus)**, who was born in Malines, Belgium, in 1517. He studied at Louvain and also in France, Italy, and Germany, eventually receiving the degree of Doctor of Medicine. He had a successful career as a physician, serving the Emperor Maximilian II and his successor, Rudolph III, and finally became professor of medicine at Leyden. His interest in medical plants induced him to prepare a herbal and, to illustrate it, he obtained the wood-blocks that had been used in Fuchs' book. This was published in Flemish in 1554, under the title *Crŭÿdeboeck*. He arranged the plants according to a system of his own and cited localities and flowering times for the Low Countries, an indication of his originality. The publisher, after the appearance of another edition in 1563, then parted with Fuchs' blocks, interposing difficulties in the plan of Dodoens to issue a Latin edition. At this point he met Plantin, whose interest in the project was so great that he employed artists and had new blocks engraved. The result was that the much-modified Latin edition, known as *Stirpium historiae pemptades sex sive libri triginta,* completed in 1583, was an outstanding artistic as well as scientific publication. Most of the figures were original. Some were borrowed from his two friends, l'Écluse and l'Obel. Dodoens died in Leyden in 1585.

Charles de l'Écluse (Carolus Clusius) arrived in Antwerp just as the *Crŭÿdeboeck* came from the press. He had been born in Arras, Flanders, in 1526 and studied at Louvain, Marburg, Frankfurt, Strasbourg, and Lyons. In 1551 he entered the University of Montpellier and became interested in botany from the teaching of Guillaume Rondelet, among whose other students were de l'Obel and Jean Bauhin. He obtained an M.D. degree in 1553 and then traveled through various countries, coming at last to Antwerp. He was much impressed by the herbal of Dodoens and immediately prepared, as his first major botanical activity, a French edition which appeared in 1557, under the title *Histoire des Plantes.* Dodoens himself supervised the production and added a few subjects.

His life seems to have been somewhat melancholy. He was converted to Protestantism and suffered persecution, some of his relatives actually being executed. His property was confiscated and much of his later life was troubled by poverty and poor health. He finally became a professor at the University of Leyden. He made several trips to England and was acquainted with Sir Francis Drake, who gave him American plants. An expedition to Spain and Portugal with two of his pupils resulted in the collection of 200 new species, which were described in a book printed by Plantin in 1576 and for which new wood-blocks were made, some of these also going into Dodoens' Latin herbal. In 1583 a second work ap-

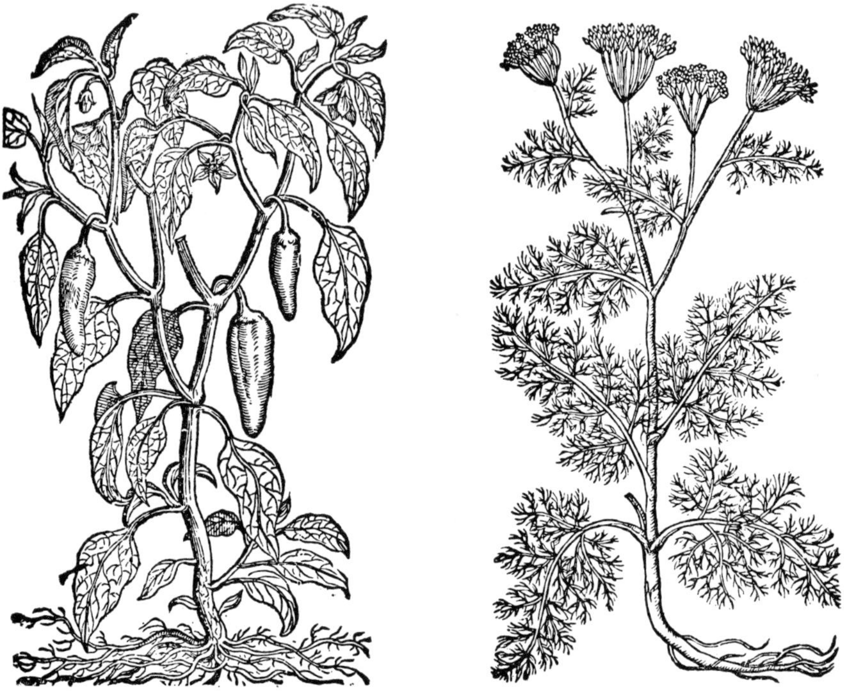

Figure 5. *Left,* chili pepper, *Capsicum frutescens; right,* dill, *anethum graveolens.* Drawings from L'Obel's *Crŭÿdeboeck.* (Courtesy Chicago Natural History Museum.)

peared, treating the plants of Austria and Hungary in the same manner. These were brought together and republished in 1601 as the *Rariorum plantarum historia.*

Clusius was a man of wide friendships and had an extensive botanical correspondence. He was much interested in gardens and, while director of the Botanical Garden in Vienna, introduced the potato into cultivation. He died in 1609.

The youngest of the three botanical friends was **Mathias de l'Obel (Lobelius)**, who was born at Lille, Flanders, in 1538, and studied at Montpellier under Rondelet, who bequeathed him his botanical manuscripts. His chief botanical work was the *Stirpium adversaria nova*, printed by Plantin in 1570. He apparently made a very conscious effort to work out a natural classification; one innovation of his book was a synoptic table of species which preceded each group of plants. In his preface, as quoted by Arber, he writes: "For thus in an order, than which nothing more beautiful exists in the heavens or in the mind of a wise man, things which are far and widely different become, as it were, one thing." His contemporaries quickly realized the superiority of his system over those already existing. He made a rough separation of the classes now known as Monocotyledons and Dicotyledons. In 1581 the book was translated into Flemish and appeared under the title of *Crŭijdeboeck*, with a dedication to William the Silent, whom he served as physician. Later Plantin brought out an album containing many of the engravings used in the works of Dodoens, l'Écluse, and l'Obel, now grouped according to the classification of l'Obel, which was regarded as the best. After the assassination of William in 1584 l'Obel went to England, attracted by the favor bestowed by Queen Elizabeth I upon arts and letters. He was well received in England and eventually received the title of Botanist to James I. He died in 1616.

The Father of British Botany. L'Obel found in England a relatively new herbal which had been completed in 1568 and had won for its author, William Turner, recognition as the founder of British botany. Turner was born in Northumberland about 1515 and educated at Cambridge as a clergyman, later taking an M.D. degree in Italy. Like many of the sixteenth century botanists, he was associated with the Reformation movement. He was imprisoned under Henry VIII for his caustic comments and, while his fortunes improved under Edward VI, during the reign of Queen Mary he was forced to flee the country. He traveled in Italy, Switzerland, Holland, and Germany and studied botany under Luca Ghini, collaborator of Mattiola and teacher of Cesalpino. He corresponded with Leonhart Fuchs. Under Elizabeth he returned to England but his theological views kept him in hot water even under her reign. He died in 1568.

An interest in botany that dated from his college days at Cambridge and had, as we have seen, developed during his exile, led Turner to undertake the preparation of an herbal that would do for England what had just been done for countries on the continent of Europe by the earlier herbalists. It is true that the *Grete Herball* (giving "parfyte knowledge and understandynge of the vertue of all maner of herbes and trees") had been printed in 1526 but it dealt so much with ancient and current superstitions and remedies derived from plants, while treating the plants themselves in such an indifferent manner, that it was not worthy of being compared with the work of the "German Fathers." Turner complains that he could get no information on plants, even from physicians.

His *Herball* was published in three installments, the first in London in 1551, the second (including the first) in Cologne in 1562, during his exile, and the third (with the two preceding parts) in 1568. The completed work was dedicated to Queen Elizabeth. He used other works for reference but his own work shows much originality. He wrote, as quoted by Arber: "They that have red the first part of my Herbal, and have compared my writinges of plantes with those thinges that Matthiolus, Fuchsius, Tragus, and Dodonaeus wrote in y[e] firste editiones of their Herballes, may easily perceyve that I taught the truthe of certeyne plantes, which these above named writers either knew not at al, or ellis erred in them greatlye . . . And because I would not be lyke unto a cryer y[t] cryeth a loste horse in the marketh, and telleth all the markes and tokens that he hath, and yet never sawe the horse, nether coulde knowe the horse if he sawe him: I went into Italye and into diverse partes of Germany to knowe and se the herbes my selfe." The plants are arranged alphabetically, with illustrations mostly taken from Fuchs' work. Many old superstitions concerning plants are swept out.

John Gerard. The name of John Gerard (1545-1612), English barber, surgeon, and physician, is better known than that of Turner but most scholars are of the opinion that his fame is undeserved. His reputation rests upon *The Herball or Generall Historie of Plantes,* printed in 1597. Arber relates that John Norton, the publisher, had commissioned a Dr. Priest to translate Dodoens' *Pemptades* into English, but Priest died before the work was quite finished, whereupon Gerard adopted Priest's translation, completed it, and published it as his own, altering the classification to that of l'Obel. There are about 1800 wood-cuts, secured mostly from a Frankfurt publisher, and which Gerard was unable to associate with their appropriate descriptions. One of the potato is new, and may have been the first figure of this plant to be published.

Thus upon the foundation laid by Theophrastus, Pliny, and Dioscorides men were at last building a superstructure. Bit by bit, a little here and a little there, the walls were slowly rising. The various artisans, each adding his own contribution, left the science of botany a bit more highly developed for the next worker, who took over where his predecessor left off.

The Doctrine of Signatures. It has been quite evident that the reawakening of interest in botany was largely the result of the search for more information concerning remedies to be derived from plants. Many of the beliefs concerning the efficacy of a remedy were based upon superstition or tradition inherited from the Middle Ages, yet the belief led to investigation and to the establishment of better ideas concerning its plant source. Furthermore, it was believed by some that many more plants might have medicinal properties, could they but be discovered.

An effort to find a formula for determining these led to the development of the curious *Doctrine of Signatures.*

According to this Doctrine, many medicinal plants are stamped with some clear indication ("signature") of their medical use. One of the foremost proponents of this theory was the mystical character, Philippus Aureolus Theophrastus Bombastus of Hohenheim, better known as Paracelsus (1493-1541). He was a physician and in 1527 was appointed professor at Basel but his disregard of convention and his eccentricities resulted in his leaving that post in a short time and for the remainder of his life he was a wanderer; he died in poverty in Salzburg. He became a legendary figure, being credited with magical powers for healing, probably largely inspired by his incredible boastfulness. His own explanation of the Doctrine of Signatures, as quoted by Arber, is: "I have ofttimes declared, how by the outward shapes and qualities of things we may know their inward vertues, which God hath put in them for the good of man."

Another botanist, Robert Turner (1664), states the Doctrine most clearly: "God hath imprinted upon the Plants, Herbs, and Flowers, as it were in Hieroglyphicks, the very signature of their Vertues."

Examples of signatures, as suggested by writers of the sixteenth century, include: the beliefs that long-lived plants will lengthen a man's life, while short-lived plants will abbreviate it; herbs with a yellow sap will cure jaundice; plants with flowers shaped like butterflies will cure the bite of insects; "the kernel [of a walnut] hath the very figure of the Brain" and will comfort the brain and head; a plant with a coiled inflorescence, like a borage, will cure a scorpion's sting; the maidenhair fern will prevent baldness; the adder's tongue will cure the bite of an adder; the lungwort and liverwort will cure diseases of the lungs and liver.

It is perhaps not necessary to state that the Doctrine of Signatures was repudiated by the best of the sixteenth century herbalists.

Herbals of Other Civilizations. We have dealt thus at length with the development of botany in Europe as a handmaiden of the medical sciences. But, while it was in Europe that botany developed into the form now recognized by all men everywhere, it is a remarkable fact that in some other civilizations, long isolated from the European culture, parallel developments had been under way. Since these, by the accident of history, had little to do with the formation of modern taxonomy, we need not spend much time with them, but a brief notice should be of interest.

China. The Oriental civilization is more ancient than the Occidental, and in some respects the Chinese progressed more rapidly than their European contemporaries. Printing from movable blocks, for instance, had begun in China by A.D. 1000, four centuries before it began in Europe. Furthermore, the Chinese had brought into cultivation far more plants than were being cultivated in Europe. Centuries of experience had given them a large store of facts concerning medicinal and food plants, and herbals for the dissemination of information were printed, as in Europe, but much earlier.

One of the greatest of these herbals was called *Cheng lei pen ts'ao,* written by T'ang Shen-wei, and printed in 1108. It went through many editions and was the authority in the field for 500 years. More than a dozen editions of this work are in the Library of Congress, including one printed in 1600, based on an edition of 1302. It comprises thirty-one books bound in twenty-four volumes, printed on bamboo paper.

This herbal was finally superseded by the *Pen ts'ao kang mu,* published in 1590 by Li Shi Chen, one of China's greatest natural scientists. Of the sixteen divisions of the book, five are on plants, namely: Herbs such as ginseng, iris, rhubarb, calamus, cattail; Grains such as barley, wheat, buckwheat, sesame, rice; Kitchen Herbs such as onion, carrot, spinach, beets, melons, mushrooms; Fruits such as plum, apricot, peach, apple, orange, date; Trees such as cedar, pine, camphor, elm, willow. It is said that he spent thirty years on the whole work, consulting about 800 authors. (Compare Pliny!) A remarkable fact is that the book contained a notice and illustration of maize, already introduced into China.

Another herbal is the *Pen ts'ao fa hui,* compiled by Hsu Yung-ch'eng, collated and revised by Hsueh K'ai about 1450. It contains quotations from former writers on various drugs, including one from Li Kao, a famous physician of about 1275, concerning *Ma huang* (*Ephedra,* the source of our drug ephedrine): "Ma huang masters apoplexy, colds, and headaches. It expels diseased influence from within the skin and causes perspiration. It opens up the nine passages, opens up the pores of the skin, cures coughs, and allays dyspnoea."

Swingle says that "Chinese literature is undoubtedly the best in the world as source material for the history of the utilization of wild plants and their domestication as cultivated crops."

India. The science of botany in India had its beginnings in a very remote age, with the development of agriculture in the country. Indians of the Vedic Period (2000 B.C.–800 B.C.) already cultivated crops such as wheat, barley, millet, dates, vegetables, melons, cotton; a knowledge of descriptive botany and rudimentary plant physiology was necessary for the successful cultivation and propagation of plants. In the Vedic literature there are many terms used in the description of plants and plant parts, both external features and internal structures, and there is furthermore evidence that fertilizing and rotation of crops were practiced for the improvement of the soil. Medical science and the collection of medicinal plants also had their beginnings in these very ancient times. The Atharva-Veda contains a wealth of details bearing on the subject of medicinal plants and the diseases against which they were applied.

One of the earliest works dealing with plant life from a scientific standpoint is the *Vrikshayurveda* (science of plants and plant life). A manuscript of this work, compiled by Parasara probably before the beginning of the Christian era, was discovered recently. This treatise was the basis of botanical teaching preparatory to medical studies in ancient India. The first of the eight chapters of the book outlines the morphology of plant members, discussing leaves, flowers, fruits, roots, bark, stem, heartwood, sap, excretions, spines, seeds, and shoots. The second chapter deals with the nature and properties of soil. In the third chapter names, descriptions, and distribution of the fourteen forest types of India are given. The fourth and succeeding chapters take up the morphology of plant members in detail. Some of these descriptions indicate that Parasara must have had a magnifying apparatus of some kind. In the internal structure of a leaf, he says, there are innumerable cells (*rasakosa*) that serve as storehouses of sap that has all the elementary properties derived from the earth. The soil solution is transported from the roots to the leaves by the transporting system (*syandani*), and is there digested with the help of chlorophyll (*ranjakena pacyamanat*) into nutritive substances and by-products. A system of classification was provided, based on a study of the comparative morphology of plants, which, Majumdar states, was more advanced than any developed in Europe before the eighteenth century. Numerous families (*ganas*) are so clearly distinguished as to be easily recognizable today. Flowers of the Samiganiyam are hypogynous, with five petals of different sizes, a gamosepalous calyx, and the fruit a legume with seeds on the sides (evidently the Leguminosae). The Svastika-ganiyam (Cruciferae), so-called "because the calyx resembles a Swastika," have a superior ovary, four free sepals, four free petals, and six stamens, two of which are shorter; two carpels are united and form a two-locular fruit. In the Tripusaganiyam (Cucurbitaceae) the flowers are epigynous, sometimes bisexual, with five sepals, five united petals, three stamens and a trilocular ovary with three rows of ovules.

Mexico. At the time of the discovery of America, the nations of Europe were not much superior in botanical lore to the Aztecs of Mexico, who had developed botanical gardens, operated apothecary shops, and extensively cultivated flowers for ornamental purposes. A large number of words in the language of the Aztecs have the suffix *-xochitl* (flower).

The existence of a large body of botanical knowledge is indicated by a remarkable herbal known as the Badianus Manuscript, written in 1552 by two Aztecs, and discovered in 1929 in the Vatican Library. In its foreword it is described as "A little book of Indian medicinal herbs composed by a certain Indian, physician of the College of Santa Cruz, who has no theoretical learning, but is well taught by experience alone." The book, of 118 pages, is richly illustrated with paintings of plants in brilliant colors. The drawings, although inferior to those being produced in

Europe at the same time, are yet about as good as those in the European herbals of the thirteenth and fourteenth centuries. The book shows no indication that its authors were influenced by European writings; it must be concluded that the science of botany was undergoing in the New World a development somewhat similar to its development in the Old World.

The two authors whose names appear with the manuscript were Martinus de la Cruz, the native physician, who composed the work in Aztec, and Juannes Badianus, who translated it into Latin. That these Indians had become Christians is indicated by their Spanish names.

The book is divided into thirteen chapters, each dealing with various types of diseases, giving the remedies prescribed and modes of treatment. Most of the remedies are of plant origin and many of these plants are illustrated on the pages where they are mentioned. Many of these figures are so good that the species they represent can be identified with certainty; others have been identified through a study of the Aztec names. Over 300 Aztec names are given, most of which refer to plants; about 175 plants have been identified at least as to genus or family. Of course no clues are furnished here from classical names, because these were not known to the authors. Among familiar plants illustrated are *Achillea millefolium, Polygonum persicaria, Theobroma cacao,* and *Vanilla fragrans.*

The following example (from Plate III) will suffice to illustrate the style: "When the milk flows with difficulty, the herb *Chichilticxiuhtontli*[1] which recalls the salad herb by its smallness, *tohmioxihuitl*[2] and a crystal are to be crushed in *octli* [pulque] and boiled. The potion is to be drunk frequently. Besides the herb *Memeyaxiuhtontli*[3] is to be crushed in *octli,* the juice of which the woman should also drink; she should enter a bath, where she is to drink another potion made of corn. Yet when she comes out she is to take as a drink the sticky water of boiled corn." It is of interest to note that the two plants illustrated, as increasing lactation, are plants with a milky juice, a usage which suggests the European belief in the Doctrine of Signatures, of the same period.

Toward an Improved Taxonomy

As the Age of the Herbalists wore on, we have seen botany rise from a position of dependence upon medicine to that of an independent science. Whereas at first classification was upon a utilitarian basis, the plants being arranged according to their uses to man, there came finally to be a growing effort to classify them according to their own natural relation-

[1] "Little red plant."

[2] "Hairy plant"—this plant is illustrated and appears to belong to the tribe Cichorieae of the Compositae.

[3] "Little milk plant"—this is also illustrated and appears to be a species of *Euphorbia.*

ships to each other. At the same time there gradually arose a desire for a more precise system of naming plants, to eliminate some of the confusion that has been noted.

The Bauhin Brothers. One of the students of Leonhart Fuchs at Tübingen was Jean Bauhin. He was born in Switzerland in 1541 and received a medical education, studying at the University of Basel before he went to Tübingen. After some travels he spent a period at the University of Montpellier as a student of Rondelet, who had also instructed l'Écluse. His Protestantism made his life there uneasy and he was obliged to return to Switzerland. He attempted a most ambitious work on plants, but unfortunately his death, in 1613, came before it had been completed. His son-in-law, J. H. Cherler, who had assisted him in its preparation, brought out a preliminary sketch in 1619, and the entire work was published in 1650-1651, under the name *Historia plantarum universalis.* It was a compilation from all sources, including descriptions of 5000 plants. There were more than 3500 figures.

Figure 6. Gaspard Bauhin, 1560-1624. (Courtesy New York Botanical Garden.)

It is, however, in the work of Jean's brother, Gaspard (Casper), that the culmination of the botanical work of the herbalists is reached. Here classification, nomenclature, and description attain their highest point before the start of the eighteenth century.

Gaspard was born in 1560 and was thus nineteen years younger than his brother. He studied at Basel, Padua, Montpellier, Paris, and Tübingen. Fuchs had died in 1566, so Gaspard missed the famous herbalist who had been his brother's teacher. After extensive travels in which he observed and collected widely, and became acquainted with many well known botanists, he was recalled to Basel in 1580 by his father's illness. He settled there and became professor of botany and medicine in the University.

He never collaborated with his brother, but Jean's example inspired him to start the compilation of a similar great work on plants, collecting, in a single book, all that had been previously written on plants and drawing up a concordance of all the names given by various writers to the same species. His early travels constituted a good preparation for the task and he formed a herbarium of 4000 specimens, including plants from Egypt and even the East Indies. He spent many years of labor on his work, but, like his brother, was not able to bring it to completion. It is regrettable that the two brothers, with almost identical objectives, could not have joined forces.

Gaspard, however, was fortunate enough to see the publication of three preliminary volumes of his work, the *Phytopinax* in 1596, the *Prodromos theatri botanici* in 1620, and, most important of all, the *Pinax theatri botanici,* in 1623. The *Prodromos* contained descriptions of 600 plants which the author regarded as new, together with 140 good figures, one of which represents the potato, which still bears the name *Solanum tuberosum,* given it by Bauhin.

The *Pinax* was divided into twelve books, each subdivided into a number of sections. In general, neither books nor sections have titles, but there are some exceptions. In Book IV is a section headed *Umbelliferae,* including eighteen genera. Truly natural groups are to be found in several sections. Book III, Section 6, contains six genera of composites; Book III, Section 2, includes six crucifers; and Book V, Section 1, includes four genera of the nightshade family, followed by three from the poppy family. Many other groups, of course, have no indication of natural relationship. It is perhaps not strange, considering the times, that he should place duckweeds among Cryptogams, water ferns among mosses, and unite corals and sponges with the seaweeds.

A point of great value is that Bauhin fully recognized the distinction between genera and species, a distinction we have seen to be lacking in the work of the earlier herbalists. For Bauhin every plant has a generic and a specific name, although it is true that the names are not always binomials, but often trinomials or quadrinomials. On the other hand, he does not describe the genera; it is only from the name that we know that several species belong to the same genus.

Still more importantly, the *Pinax* converted chaos into order so far as nomenclature was concerned, being so successful as to earn for the author the title *legislateur en botanique.* The word *Pinax* means a register and the book deserved its title, since it was a thorough concordance of the various names bestowed by different authors upon the same plant, with one name selected by Bauhin as the most suitable, as the result of his forty years of research. To quote from Sachs: "Dioscorides, Theophrastus, and Pliny either add no descriptions to the names of their plants, or they describe them in so unsatisfactory a manner, that it was a very difficult task for that day, as it is still for us, to recognize the plants of the ancient writers; hence arose such a confusion of names that the reader of a botanical work can never be sure whether the plant of one author is the same as that of another with the same name. . . . Kaspar Bauhin sought to put an end to this condition of uncertainty by his *Pinax,* in which he showed in the case of all species known to him what were the names given to them by the earlier writers, and he has thus enabled us to see our way through the nomenclature of the period of which we are speaking; the *Pinax* is in a word and for that time a completely exhaustive book of synonyms, and is still indispensable for the history of individual species—no small praise to be given a work that is more than 250 years old."

The great *legislateur en botanique* died in 1624, the year following the publication of his *Pinax.*

John Ray. The Age of the Herbalists was over and a new era in botany was beginning. Nevertheless, lethargy seemed to have followed the publication of the *Pinax* in the seventeenth century. It was only at the end of the century that great things began once more to be recorded. The principal advance in taxonomy was made by John Ray, who exemplified the highest ideals of scholarship and character.

Ray was born in Essex, England, in 1628. After a brilliant career at Cambridge University he was ordained as a minister in 1660. In 1662, when he had prospects of a distinguished career at Cambridge, he refused assent to the Act of Uniformity and was forced to resign his position. For several years thereafter he traveled in England, Scotland, France, Holland, Germany, Switzerland, and Italy, investigating the plant life as he went. He died in 1705.

His largest work, a *Historia plantarum* in three volumes, was published between 1686 and 1704. The plant kingdom was divided into herbs and trees (the system of Theophrastus thus reaches the start of the eighteenth century), but the herbs were again divided into Imperfectae, with mostly algae, fungi, mosses, and ferns, and the Perfectae, the seed plants, divided into monocotyledons and dicotyledons. The trees were also divided into monocotyledons and dicotyledons. In 1688 he published *Fasciculus Stirpium Brittannicarum,* a catalog of British plants arranged according to his scheme of classification. Subsequent editions of his *Historia* also had a somewhat improved classification. In the final system the herbaceous seed plants included twenty-five dicotyledonous classes and four monocotyledonous. Several of these were quite natural groups: for example, the Umbelliferae, Verticellatae (now Labiatae), Tetrapetalae (now mostly Cruciferae), Leguminosae, and Staminae (grasses). The work included all the plants made known by his predecessors and contemporaries.

The *Historia* was accepted immediately as the standard botanical work of the day; a hundred years later Sir James Smith wrote: "This vast and critical compilation is still in use."

Influenced by the philosophy of Cesalpino, classification was at last showing faint resemblances to that of our own day. Ray's arrangement was to influence Jussieu and Candolle, and so to abide as a basis for modern taxonomy.

J. P. de Tournefort. Joseph Pitton de Tournefort was born at Aix en Provençe, in 1656. His family intended him for the church and entered him in a Jesuit school, where he showed no interest in the curriculum. He did, however, develop very early an interest in natural science, which led him to "skip school to go a simpling* in the fields, and to study Nature instead of the Language of the ancient Romans" (Fontenelle's *Eulogium*). On one occasion, it is related, this brought him into serious trouble when he scaled a wall in search of plants and was taken for a thief. He came across copies of Dioscorides and Mattiola, which he studied avidly and which increased his interest. In 1678 he explored the mountains of Dauphiny and Savoy, collecting plants, and in 1679 he entered the University at Montpellier. Here he had for his professor Pierre Magnol (1638-1715), "a famous Botanist who would have been the first of the Age, had he not had M. Tournefort for his Contemporary" (Lauthier, *Life of Tournefort*). After collecting in the vicinity of Montpellier, he undertook a journey to Spain in 1681. In crossing the Pyrenees he fell among bandits, who stripped him of everything except his overcoat, which, fortunately, held some money which had slipped down into the lining and was overlooked. His botanical work in Spain turned out very well, but on the return trip, at Perpignan, the house where he lodged fell down during the night and he remained for a considerable time in the ruins, miraculously escaping death. Returning to Montpellier he continued his studies, afterwards going to Orange, where he received an M.D. In 1683 he was called to Paris as professor of botany in the Jardin de Roy (Jardin des Plantes, see p. 124) which gave him the incentive for travels in Spain, Portugal, England, and Holland, for the enrichment of the Garden. In 1694 he published his *Eléments de Botanique*, which was translated into Latin and published, with additions, in 1700, as *Institutiones Rei Herbariae*, in three quarto volumes, the first containing descriptions of plants, the other two their figures, from copper plates. Lauthier states: "In this work he found a Way to clear the main Difficulties of Botany, by reducing the Eight Thousand Eight Hundred Forty Six Species of Plants at that Time known, to Six Hundred Threescore and Thirteen Genera; and those Genera into Two and Twenty Classes . . . And as Dioscorides treated only of Six Hundred Sorts of Plants, M. de Fontenelle, in his History of the Academy of Sciences for the Year 1700, says with his usual Delicacy, that by the Labours of M. Tournefort we are now acquainted with more Genera of Plants, than Dioscorides knew Species." In 1700 he was commissioned by King Louis XIV to make a

* Collecting *simples*, or medicinal plants, from which *compounds* are made.

scientific expedition to the Levant, which he entered upon with much enthusiasm, since he would now have an opportunity "To examine upon the Spot whether what Theophrastus, Dioscorides, Matthiolus, and several other Authors, have written concerning Plants, were conformable to Truth." On this expedition he traveled through Greece and Asia Minor, to the boundaries of Persia. His account of this trip, *Voyage de Levant,* was published in 1717, after his death. In commendation of his system of classification, it was noted by his admirers that the 1356 plants he brought home with him were fitted into his arrangement with the addition of only twenty-five new genera. He was a correspondent of John Ray and M. Sarrasin, Royal Physician in Canada. He was elected to the

Figure 7. Joseph Pitton de Tournefort, 1656-1708. (Courtesy New York Botanical Garden.)

Academy of Sciences on the nomination of the Abbé Bignon. In 1708 he was mortally injured by a cart in the street and died within a few months; he left his collections to the King, his books to the Abbé Bignon.

Tournefort has been called the founder of the modern concept of genera. This statement requires some qualification. It is true that many of his generic names were validated by Linnaeus and remain well known today (examples are *Betula, Castanea, Fagus, Quercus, Ulmus*). Nevertheless, as we have seen, the establishment of the genus as a definite concept was accomplished by Gaspard Bauhin who, however, gave only the name of the genus, supplying the species with descriptions. Tournefort gave both names and descriptions to genera, but merely named the species. Sachs concludes: "Tournefort therefore was not the first who established genera; he merely transferred the center of gravity, so to speak, in descriptive botany to the definition of the genera."

His system of classification is in many ways inferior to Ray's. Did the *Institutiones* not bear the date 1700, Sachs remarks, we might conclude that it was written before the *Historia plantarum.* There is no distinction between Phanerogams and Cryptogams, nor between monocotyledons and dicotyledons. The arrangement of the book made it quite easy to identify a plant, and most botanists had no interest in a natural system although there was a growing eagerness to learn plants. For these reasons most works on systematic botany in France, Germany, Italy, and even England for the first half of the eighteenth century were founded upon the system of Tournefort.

Linnaeus: The End of an Era. The year before Tournefort died there was born in Rashult, Sweden, on May 23, 1707, a child who was to become the most widely known botanist of modern times, during whose lifetime an era would end, and a new direction in botany be taken. Carolus Linnaeus (afterwards Carl von Linné) was even born with a botanical name, for Linnaeus is the Latin form of the Linn, or linden, tree. He entered the University of Lund in 1727 to study medicine, after his father had given up his insistence to have his son enter the priesthood. At Lund he met Kilian Stobaeus and obtained lodging in his home. Having no money to buy books, Linnaeus found the library of Dr. Stobaeus a veritable treasure-mine. The only difficulty was in his lack of time for reading; he remedied this by persuading the assistant to loan the books in the evening, to be returned early in the morning. Thereafter Linnaeus sat up most of the nights reading. At 1:30 one morning, seeing the candle was still burning, Dr. Stobaeus entered the room to blow it out; to his surprise he found Linnaeus deep in study, surrounded by a pile of his own books. Instead of being angry, the professor was highly impressed and from that time on allowed him the use of his complete library and gave him free board. But since Lund was not a suitable place for studying medicine, he transferred the next year to the University of

Uppsala, which proved little better. The first year at Uppsala was not very happy for the poverty-ridden youth. In late April (1729) the aged Dean, Olaf Celsius, returning from a long stay in Stockholm, found Linnaeus sitting on a bench with flowers in his hand, writing descriptions. The unusual sight led to a recognition of the enthusiasm of the boy and to the receipt of a royal scholarship. He was sent on an expedition to Lapland in 1732, a trip that greatly widened his knowledge and left a lasting impression upon him. His first important publication was the *Flora Lapponica* (1737).

In 1734, on another expedition, to Dalecarlia, he met Sara Lisa Moraeus, eighteen-year-old daughter of Dr. John Moraeus, and fell in love with her. Since Linnaeus had yet to earn his M.D. degree, it was agreed that he would go abroad for two years and, if he was successful, the marriage would be consummated. So, in 1735, he went to Holland where, at Harderwijk, he received the degree in due time.

Figure 8. Carolus Linnaeus, 1707-1778. (Courtesy New York Botanical Garden.)

In Holland Linnaeus met some of the great naturalists of the day, including Jan Frederick Gronovius (1690-1762), who wrote one of the first books on North American botany, *Flora Virginica,* in 1739; and Hermann Boerhaave (1668-1738), one of the best-known scholars of Europe, who offered to send Linnaeus on an expedition to Africa or America. These opportunities Linnaeus declined.

Before returning to Sweden, Linnaeus visited England (in 1736) and met Johann Jacob Dillen (1687-1747), professor of botany at Oxford. At first Dillen, who had remarked "this is he who is bringing all botany into confusion," received him in a most unfriendly fashion, but they parted warm friends after a month together, Dillen offering to share his salary with Linnaeus if he would remain with him. Among others he visited in England was Sir Hans Sloane (1660-1753), president of the Royal Society. Both Dillen and Sloane were thereafter advocates of the Linnean system in England.

Returning to the continent he visited in Paris Bernard de Jussieu (1699-1777), botanist at the Royal Garden, and his brother, Antoine (1686-1758), also a botanist; Bernard himself was working on a system of classification, particularly for the plants in the Garden.

Back in Sweden late in 1738, after being honored abroad as *princeps botanicorum,* Linnaeus was but an inexperienced physician hoping to obtain a practice. This was not slow in coming—the Queen herself became one of his patients. The next year, having won the success demanded by Dr. Moraeus, he married Sara Lisa. In 1741 he obtained the post of professor of medicine and botany at the University of Uppsala, a position he had long desired. In a letter to a friend he said: "Should life and health be vouchsafed to me, you will, I hope, now see me perform something noteworthy in botany." Jackson adds: "He kept his word; during more than a third of a century, Uppsala became, through Linnaeus' activity, the central point for the study of natural history, especially botany."

Of the numerous writings of Linnaeus there is need to discuss only one, *Species plantarum,* a two-volume work of 1200 pages published in 1753 that contains the outline of his "sexual system." This work was hailed by his contemporaries as the beginning of a new epoch in botany; by later critics (including Sachs) it has been regarded as rather the end of an era. Either interpretation may be adopted, depending upon the vantage point. In many ways, Linnaeus, it is true, represented the last link of a chain, in which Cesalpino and Ray also figured prominently; he adopted the best of the seventeenth and eighteenth century work and built it into his system, just as Bauhin did with his predecessors. Sachs says "We learn to appreciate the contributions of Cesalpino and his successors in the 17th century, and even of Kaspar Bauhin for the first time in the works of Linnaeus; we are astonished to see the long-known thoughts of these writers, which in their own place look unimportant and incomplete, fashioned by Linnaeus into a living whole." Linnaeus recognized natural relationships but felt that only through an artificial arrangement could the multitude of species known be presented in a serviceable manner. As Jackson says, "just when all this material threatened to overwhelm the builder, the sexual system was produced, by which plants could easily be examined and thus determined." The strength of his system, then, lay in the fact that a plant unknown to the average person could be identified and named, not merely classified by it. The exhibition of natural affinities, he thought, must be sought by other means.

The system was simplicity in itself. All plants were grouped into twenty-four classes, sorted mostly on the basis of characteristics of the stamens. An outline follows, with some examples from each class.

Class	1.	Monandria	Stamens one, *Canna, Salicornia*
	2.	Diandria	Stamens two, *Olea, Veronica*
	3.	Triandria	Stamens three, many grasses
	4.	Tetrandria	Stamens four, *Protea, Galium*
	5.	Pentandria	Stamens five, *Ipomoea, Campanula*
	6.	Hexandria	Stamens six, *Narcissus, Lilium*
	7.	Heptandria	Stamens seven, *Trientalis, Aesculus*
	8.	Octandria	Stamens eight, *Vaccinium, Dirca*
	9.	Enneandria	Stamens nine, *Laurus, Butomus*
	10.	Decandria	Stamens ten, *Rhododendron, Oxalis*
	11.	Dodecandria	Stamens 11-19, *Asarum, Euphorbia*
	12.	Icosandria	Stamens 20 or more, on the calyx, *Cactus, Mesembryanthemum*
	13.	Polyandria	Stamens 20 or more, on the receptacle, *Tilia, Ranunculus*
	14.	Didynamia	Stamens didynamous (in two pairs of different lengths), many mints
	15.	Tetradynamia	Stamens tetradynamous (with four long stamens and two shorter), mustards
	16.	Monadelphia	Stamens monadelphous (united in one group), mallows, etc.
	17.	Diadelphia	Stamens diadelphous (united in two groups), legumes, etc.
	18.	Polyadelphia	Stamens polyadelphous (united in three or more groups), *Theobroma, Hypericum*
	19.	Syngenesia	Stamens syngenesious (united by their anthers), many composites
	20.	Gynandria	Stamens united to the gynoecium, orchids, etc.
	21.	Monoecia	Plants monoecious, *Carex, Morus*
	22.	Dioecia	Plants dioecious, *Salix, Juniperus*
	23.	Polygamia	Plants polygamous, *Acer, Nyssa*
	24.	Cryptogamia	Flowerless plants, *Pteris, Agaricus, Lichen*

The limitations of such a system would naturally be expected when only one set of organs is used, instead of deriving characters from all organs. But its convenience was so great that it may actually have retarded the progress toward a more natural arrangement, since many botanists were satisfied merely to catalogue new species in this simple manner. As noted above, Linnaeus himself recognized that a natural system should be sought, that his plan was only temporary, but he was able to accomplish very little in this direction. Sachs concludes ". . . this theory of Linnaeus is no precursor of our theory of descent, but is most distinctly opposed to it; it is utterly and entirely the fruit of scholasticism, while the essential feature in Darwin's theory of descent is that scholasticism finds no place in it." From this viewpoint we must look upon him as the end of an era.

The greatest significance of his work lay in his creation (more or less accidentally, perhaps) of a new and precise system of nomenclature. *Species plantarum* was intended to be a reference book on all plants known at the time, somewhat in the way of bringing Bauhin's *Pinax* up to date. For each plant Linnaeus gave the generic name, the *trivial* name (printed in the margin opposite each species), a polynomial descriptive phrase (intended by Linnaeus as the specific name), references to previous publications or his herbarium specimens, and the region where the plant was found (see Figure 9). The convenience of the use of the *trivial* name (or *specific epithet*) was so obvious that the combination of the generic and trivial name came to be generally employed, and resulted in the establishment of *binomial nomenclature,* although Linnaeus evidently did not regard this as an important phase of his book. He was not the first to use binomials; Dioscorides, as we have seen, had used a few eighteen centuries before; but he was the first to establish universal use of binomials. The book, *Species plantarum,* and the date, 1753, have been chosen by modern botanists as the starting point of present-day botanical nomenclature; from this viewpoint we must regard Linnaeus as opening a new epoch.

Linnaeus' students were numbered by the hundreds each term. The students were attracted by the wide fame of his publications, his sympathetic personality, and the famous botanical excursions which he instituted each summer: excursions organized with an Annotator to take notes, a Fiscal to maintain discipline, marksmen to shoot birds, and so forth. At the end of the trip, Jackson states, "they marched back to the town, the Professor at their head, with French horns, kettledrums and banners, to the botanic garden where repeated 'vivat Linnaeus' closed the day's enjoyment. This cheeriness, rejoicing and ardour among the young men, attracted not only foreigners but up-country people to share in these delights."

His students, filled with enthusiasm, set out to explore the world. Among them were Peter Thunberg, Daniel Solander, Adam Kuhn and Benjamin Jardel (the only two Americans), Peter Kalm, John Rotheram, the only Englishman and one of the two at Linnaeus' bedside when he died, Fredrik Hasselquist, who died in Syria, Petrus Löfling, his favorite pupil, who died in Guiana, Anton Martin, the first Swedish naturalist to explore the Arctic, Christopher Ternström, who died on his way to the East Indies, Pehr Forskål, who perished in Arabia. "The deaths of many whom I have induced to travel have made my hair gray," Linnaeus mourned, "and what have I gained? A few dried plants, with great anxiety, unrest, and care."

Linnaeus died in 1778 and his collections and post as professor of botany at Uppsala went to his son, Carl, who is generally regarded as far inferior to his father. When he died in 1783 the collections went to Sara Lisa, Linnaeus' widow, and her daughters, who sold them to the highest bidder, James Edward Smith, an English botanist, for the sum of 1000

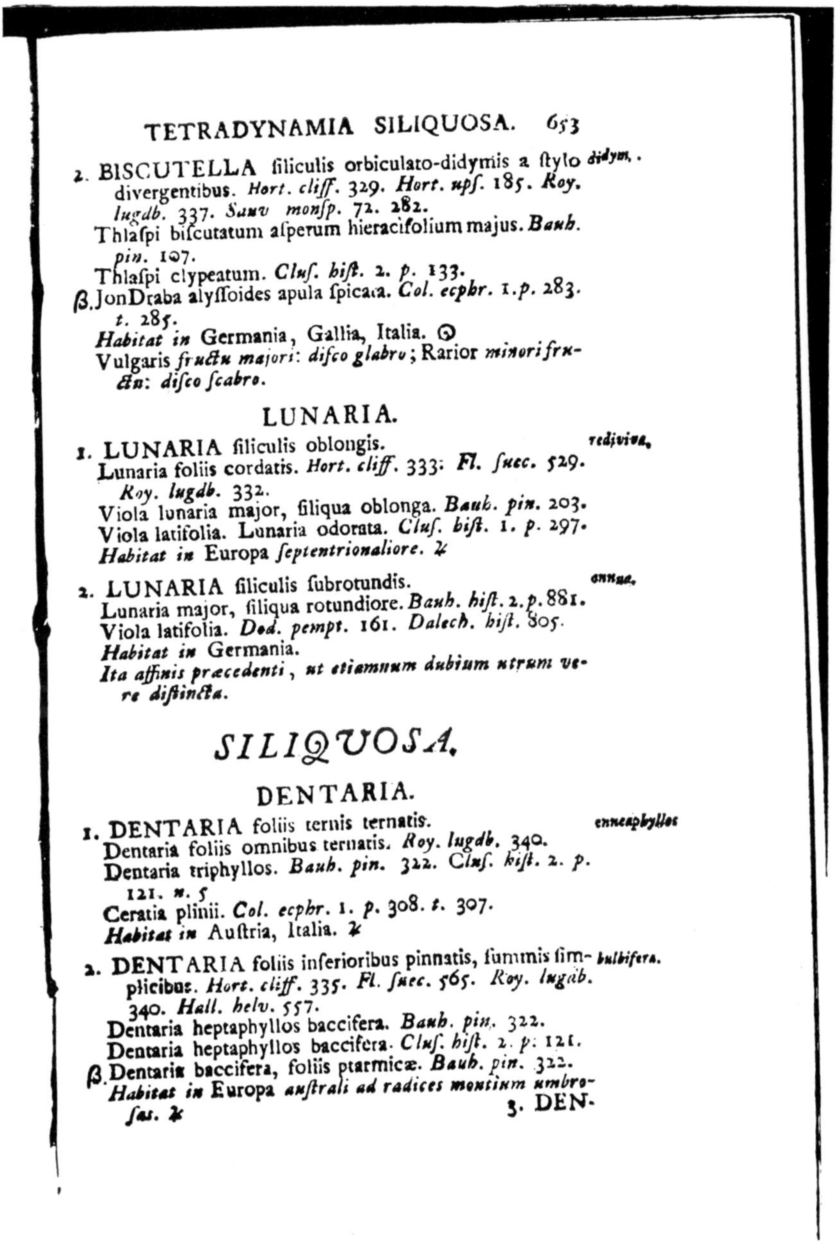

TETRADYNAMIA SILIQUOSA. 653

2. BISCUTELLA ſiliculis orbiculato-didymis a ſtylo divergentibus. *Hort. cliff.* 329. *Hort. upſ.* 185. *Roy. lugdb.* 337. *Sauv monſp.* 72. 282. *didym.*
Thlaſpi biſcutatum aſperum hieracifolium majus. *Bauh. pin.* 107.
Thlaſpi clypeatum. *Cluſ. hiſt.* 2. *p.* 133.
β. JonDraba alyſſoides apula ſpicata. *Col. ecphr.* 1. *p.* 283. *t.* 285.
Habitat in Germania, Gallia, Italia. ☉
Vulgaris *fructu majori: diſco glabro*; Rarior *minori fructu: diſco ſcabro.*

LUNARIA.

1. LUNARIA ſiliculis oblongis. *rediviva.*
Lunaria foliis cordatis. *Hort. cliff.* 333. *Fl. ſuec.* 529. *Roy. lugdb.* 332.
Viola lunaria major, ſiliqua oblonga. *Bauh. pin.* 203.
Viola latifolia. Lunaria odorata. *Cluſ. hiſt.* 1. *p.* 297.
Habitat in Europa *ſeptentrionaliore.* ♃

2. LUNARIA ſiliculis ſubrotundis. *annua.*
Lunaria major, ſiliqua rotundiore. *Bauh. hiſt.* 2. *p.* 881.
Viola latifolia. *Dod. pempt.* 161. *Dalech. hiſt.* 805.
Habitat in Germania.
Ita affinis præcedenti, ut etiamnum dubium utrum vere diſtincta.

SILIQUOSA.

DENTARIA.

1. DENTARIA foliis ternis ternatis. *enneaphyllos*
Dentaria foliis omnibus ternatis. *Roy. lugdb.* 340.
Dentaria triphyllos. *Bauh. pin.* 322. *Cluſ. hiſt.* 2. *p.* 121. *n.* 5
Ceratia plinii. *Col. ecphr.* 1. *p.* 308. *t.* 307.
Habitat in Auſtria, Italia. ♃

2. DENTARIA foliis inferioribus pinnatis, ſummis ſimplicibus. *Hort. cliff.* 335. *Fl. ſuec.* 565. *Roy. lugdb.* 340. *Hall. helv.* 557. *bulbifera.*
Dentaria heptaphyllos baccifera. *Bauh. pin.* 322.
Dentaria heptaphyllos baccifera. *Cluſ. hiſt.* 2. *p.* 121.
β. Dentaria baccifera, foliis ptarmicæ. *Bauh. pin.* 322.
Habitat in Europa *auſtrali ad radices montium umbroſas.* ♃

3. DEN-

Figure 9. A page from Linnaeus' *Species plantarum.* (Photograph by William M. Leeson.)

guineas. Later the collections became the property of the Linnean Society of London, which Smith and others founded in 1788.

Species plantarum went through many editions and remained the dominant system of classification until the beginning of the 19th century. One of the most important revisions was the fifth (1797-1805), by Karl Ludwig Willdenow (1765-1812), director of the Berlin Botanical Garden from 1801 to 1812. It was completely rewritten and greatly enlarged, published in four large volumes. Many American plants were described for the first time in this work.

References

Arber, A., *Herbals, their origin and evolution,* 2d ed. Cambridge, 1938.

Badianus Manuscript, An Aztec herbal of 1552. Translated and annotated by Emily Walcott Emmart. Baltimore, 1940.

Fontenelle, [M.], *Eulogium of M. Tournefort* (in Tournefort's *A Voyage into the Levant,* English translation. London, 1741).

Greene, E. L., *Landmarks of botanical history. Part 1. Prior to 1562 A.D.* Smithsonian Misc. Coll. Pt. of vol. 54, Publication 1870. 1909.

Jackson, B. D., *Linnaeus, the story of his life.* Adapted from the Swedish of T. M. Fries. London, 1923.

Lauthier, [M.], *The Life of M. Tournefort* (in Tournefort's *A Voyage into the Levant,* English translation. London, 1741).

Majumdar, G. P., *Genesis and development of plant sciences in ancient India.* 13th All-India Oriental Conf.: Technical Sciences 97-120. Calcutta, 1946.

Meyer, E. H. F., *Geschichte der Botanik.* Konigsberg, 1854-1857.

Nordenskiold, E., *The history of biology.* Translated from the Swedish by L. B. Eyre. New York and London, 1928.

Peattie, D. C., *Green Laurels. The lives and achievements of the great naturalists.* New York, 1936.

Reed, H. S., *A short history of the plant sciences.* Waltham, Mass., 1942.

Sachs, J. von, *History of botany (1530-1860).* Authorized transl. by H. E. F. Garnsey. Revised by I. B. Balfour. Oxford, 1890 (Original German edition, 1875).

Singer, C., *A history of biology,* 2d ed. New York, 1950.

Sprague, T. A., *The herbal of Otto Brunfels.* Jour. Linn. Soc. London 48: 79-124. 1928.

———, and E. Nelmes, *The herbal of Leonhardt Fuchs.* Jour. Linn. Soc. London 48: 545-642. 1931.

———, and M. A. Sprague, *The herbal of Valerius Cordus.* Jour. Linn. Soc. London 52: 1-113. 1939.

Sprengel, Kurt, *Geschichte der Botanik.* Altenburg und Leipzig, 1817-1818.

Swingle, W. T., *Notes on Chinese accessions on medicine and materia medica.* (In U. S. Library of Congress, Rept. by the Librarian, 1929-1930, pp. 368-379).

3

Modern Classification

When Linnaeus was in Paris in the spring of 1738 one of his principal objectives was to meet Antoine de Jussieu, professor of botany, and his brother Bernard, the demonstrator of plants in the Jardin des Plantes. The Jussieu brothers were natives of Lyons and both had studied under Pierre Magnol, the teacher of Tournefort; Antoine had succeeded Tournefort as director of the royal garden (see p. 33). Linnaeus was anxious to see the garden and he took part in some of B. de Jussieu's excursions with his students. Tradition relates that some fun-loving students "made up" a specimen from bits of several plants and presented it to the famous foreigner to see what he would call it, whereupon he demonstrated his fine sense of humor—and also paid a compliment to his friend—by replying that only God or Jussieu could name it. The incident serves to call attention to the fact that the two botanists evidently impressed each other greatly. The talented Jussieu started to arrange the plants in the garden according to the Linnean system, but the farther he progressed, the more changes he introduced; finally the system no longer bore resemblance to that of Linnaeus, but became the system of Jussieu.

Bernard de Jussieu, however, was never completely satisfied with his arrangement and never published it, except in the garden catalogue. His nephew, Antoine-Laurent (1748-1836), who came to Paris in 1765 to work with his uncle and later became professor of botany at the Jardin des Plantes, incorporated it with ideas of his own and published it in 1789 (the year of the French Revolution) in his book *Genera plantarum secundum ordines naturales disposita.* This book, although it did not attract much attention in an era of world-shaking events, may be said to have marked the beginning of the natural systems of classification.

Genera Plantarum. In Jussieu's system all plants were classed into one hundred "orders," each one carefully characterized. Nearly all of these "orders" (we would say families) are still recognized today. These were then grouped into fifteen classes, and the classes into three grand divisions. Although from that day to this the categories have been shuffled and reshuffled, most of them are still recognized as valid units. The system follows, in outline, with examples of some of the "orders" in each class.

	Class
Acotyledones (Fungi, Algae, Musci)	I
Monocotyledones	
Stamina hypogyna (Cyperoideae, Gramineae)	II
Stamina perigyna (Lilia, Narcissi, Irides)	III
Stamina epigyna (Musae, Orchideae)	IV
Dicotyledones	
Apetalae	
Stamina epigyna (Aristolochiae)	V
Stamina perigyna (Proteae, Lauri, Polygoneae)	VI
Stamina hypogyna (Amaranthi, Nyctagines)	VII
Monopetalae	
Corolla hypogyna (Labiatae, Solaneae, Borragineae)	VIII
Corolla perigyna (Rhododendra, Ericae)	IX
Corolla epigyna	
Antheris connatis (Cichoraceae)	X
Antheris distinctis (Rubiaceae)	XI
Polypetalae	
Stamina epigyna (Araliae, Umbelliferae)	XII
Stamina hypogyna (Ranunculaceae, Cruciferae)	XIII
Stamina perigyna (Rosaceae, Leguminosae)	XIV
Diclines irregulares (Amentaceae, Coniferae)	XV

Jussieu has, somewhat extravagantly, been called the founder of the natural system. Careful study of the pages of botanical history has indicated, however, that every pioneer has a great debt to those who have gone before him. Sachs states this most clearly: "It is not uninteresting to note here how Bauhin first provided the species with characters, and named the genera but did not characterize them, how Tournefort next defined the limits of the genera, how Linnaeus grouped the genera together, and simply named these groups without assigning to them characteristic marks, and how—finally—Antoine-Laurent de Jussieu supplied characters to the families which were now fairly recognized. Thus botanists learned by degrees to abstract the common marks from like forms; the groups thus constituted were being constantly enlarged, and the inductive process was thus completed which proceeded from the individual to the more general."

Reed says that the accomplishments in taxonomy during the eighteenth century outweighed all that had been done in preceding ages. "When the century ended there was established a binary system of nomenclature, based on the genus and species . . . and a system of classification which was essentially based on natural affinities."

Figure 10. Antoine Laurent de Jussieu, 1748-1836. (Courtesy New York Botanical Garden.)

As the work of Jussieu was founded upon that of his predecessors, so it in turn formed the basis upon which more refined systems were developed; before his death in 1836 he saw his natural system modified for use in a vast project conceived and executed by a family whose name has become a household word among botanists.

The Candolle Family. Augustin Pyrame de Candolle was born in 1778 in Geneva, where his family had for generations enjoyed a high reputation, and received his botanical training in Paris, where he spent the years 1798 to 1808. During this period he lived in close intercourse with Jussieu, Lamarck, Cuvier, Geoffroy St. Hilaire, and other naturalists of the city. From 1808 to 1816 he was professor of botany at Montpellier, during which time he made many botanical journeys in all parts of France and the neighboring countries, and wrote numerous monographs. His most important work of this period was the *Théorie élémentaire* (1813), in which he presented his views on the approach to plant classification. He introduced a new term, **taxonomy,** to designate the theory of plant classification. In emphasizing the need for classification he mentioned that 30,000 species of plants were known. From 1816 until his death in 1841 he resided once more in Geneva, where he did much to make that city a great center for botanical research.

The monumental work of Candolle's life was the *Prodromus systematis naturalis regni vegetabilis,* in which it was his intention to classify and describe every known species of vascular plants. This aim was similar to that of Linnaeus in his *Species plantarum,* except that it was on a much grander scale and based upon a natural system of classification. The plan of his system, as published in 1819, follows:

I. Vasculares (vascular plants, with cotyledons)
- Class 1. Exogenae (vascular bundles in a ring: dicotyledons)
  - A. Diplochlamydeae (both calyx and corolla present)
    - a. Thalamiflorae (polypetalous, hypogynous)
      - Orders (Families) 1 to 46, Ranunculaceae, Cruciferae, Malvaceae, etc.
    - b. Calyciflorae (perigynous or epigynous, polypetalous or sympetalous)
      - Orders (Families) 47 to 84, Rosaceae, etc.
    - c. Corolliflorae (gamopetalous, hypogynous)
      - Orders (Families) 85 to 108, Primulaceae, Labiatae, Scrophulariaceae, etc.
  - B. Monochlamydeae (calyx only present)
    - Orders (Families) 109 to 128, Chenopodiaceae, etc. (128 is Coniferae)
- Class 2. Endogenae (vascular bundles scattered: monocotyledons, etc.)
  - A. Phanerogamae (flowers present)
    - Orders (Families) 129 to 150, Liliaceae, Iridaceae, Orchidaceae, etc.
  - B. Cryptogamae (flowers absent, hidden, or unknown)
    - Orders (Families) 151 to 155, ferns, etc.

II. Cellulares (plants without vascular bundles, or cotyledons)
- Class 1. Foliaceae. Leafy; sexuality known
  - Orders (Families) 156, 157, mosses, liverworts
- Class 2. Aphyllae. Not leafy; sexuality unknown
  - Orders (Families) 158 to 161, algae, fungi, lichens

It will be noted that there are many resemblances to the system of Jussieu. Candolle accounted for 161 "orders" (families) as compared to the hundred of Jussieu. It should also be noted that he treats the ferns as coordinate with the monocotyledons. A further noteworthy feature was his inclusion of the gymnosperms among the dicotyledons. The "natural system," for plants, Candolle noted, can only be determined by studying the "ensemble" of their anatomical characters and arranging them according to their resemblances. For publication in a book it was necessary to treat the plants in a linear arrangement but he recognized that the plant kingdom should be represented naturally by a branching scheme and not in a simple series.

Year after year he continued work on the stupendous undertaking. Candolle himself published seven volumes, the first in 1824. His son, Alphonse de Candolle (1806-1893) continued the work, with many of the families treated by specialists, and, in all, ten more volumes appeared, the last in 1873. Refinements were made in the scheme of classification from time to time and the last edition of *Théorie élémentaire,* published in 1844 by Alphonse de Candolle, contained 213 families. The Candolle system dominated plant taxonomy until 1860, despite the fact that more than two dozen systems were proposed during the period 1825 to 1845 alone.

Still a third Candolle, Anne Casimir Pyrame (1836-1918), the son of Alphonse, enjoyed a reputation as a botanist.

Robert Brown. The first half of the nineteenth century was a period of tremendous activity in the field of taxonomy as new lands were explored, new plants discovered, and new schemes devised for their classification. Robert Brown (1773-1858) invented no new plan of classification but perhaps no one in Europe during this period contributed more than he to an understanding of the problems involved in plant classification. He was recognized as Britain's principal botanist of the period and was called by Alexander von Humboldt "facile Botanicorum princeps, Brittaniae gloria et ornamentum."

The son of a Scottish clergyman, Brown was born at Montrose. He studied medicine at Aberdeen and Edinburgh and later was stationed with the army in Ireland. When the British Admiralty dispatched a scientific expedition to Australia under Captain Matthew Flinders in 1801 he was appointed naturalist to the expedition, on the recommendation of Sir Joseph Banks. After landing the expedition, Captain Flinders was shipwrecked on his return to England and detained by the French, so that the naturalists were left in Australia until 1805. This gave Brown an opportunity to make a careful study of the plant life and he returned to England with a collection of 4000 species, most of them new to science. He observed that less than one-tenth of the Australian plants were found elsewhere in the world. In 1814 he published his *Botany of Terra Australis,* following in general the preliminary scheme of Candolle. In his writings he dealt a crushing blow to the Linnean system, which was dominant in England up to that time, not actually attacking it, as Harvey-Gibson notes, but simply ignoring it altogether.

Soon after his return to England he was made librarian of the Linnean Society and in 1827 became the first "keeper" of the Botanical Department of the British Museum; here Brown, for more than forty years, "sat spider-like at the centre of the botanical web." Collections from all parts of the world came to his attention and formed the basis for many monographs and papers on the taxonomy, morphology, and geographical distribution of various groups of the plant kingdom.

The Parade of Systems. It is impossible to mention here, much less discuss, all the systems of classification proposed during the first half of the nineteenth century. Noteworthy are the schemes of Stephen Endlicher (1805-1849) of Vienna, who divided the plant kingdom into thallophytes (algae, lichens, and fungi) and cormophytes (mosses, ferns, and seed plants), published in his *Genera plantarum secundum ordines naturales disposita* (1836-1840), treating 6835 genera; of Adolphe Brongniart (1770-1847), the founder of paleobotany, who applied his studies of fossils to plant classification; and of John Lindley (1799-1865), of England, who published in *The Vegetable Kingdom* (1846) a system based on physiological characters.

Kew Gardens: Bentham and Hooker. In 1759 Princess Augusta, the mother of George III of England, began developing a botanical garden on the grounds of Kew House, and placed William Aiton (1731-1793) in charge. She died in 1772 and the King moved into Kew House, combining with it the adjoining lands of Richmond Lodge to form the Kew Gardens of today. The King invited Sir Joseph Banks (1743-1820), President of the Royal Society, to assist him as unpaid director of the gardens, an association that continued until the death of both men. The Gardens became a rich depository of living plants from all parts of the world and in 1789 Aiton published a three-volume catalogue of the species grown there, as the *Hortus Kewensis.* Banks was responsible for sending Captain William Bligh of the *Bounty* to Tahiti, with the object of introducing breadfruit into the West Indies, an expedition which resulted in the famous mutiny on the *Bounty.*

The death of George III and Sir Joseph in 1820 resulted in the rapid disintegration of Kew as a scientific institution and its transformation into a royal pleasure garden. A report by John Lindley and others, in 1840, recommended that Kew be developed into a national botanical garden and a center of botanical research for the Empire. Parliament adopted the recommendation and made Kew a public institution; Sir William Jackson Hooker (1785-1865), in 1841, accepted the post as first director.

Hooker's botanical writings were voluminous, but were purely descriptive; he made no contribution of fundamental importance in the development of taxonomy. But, as Gilmour notes, "His real memorial is Kew."

In 1855 Joseph Dalton Hooker (1817-1911), the son of Sir William, was installed as assistant to his father. Thirty-eight years old, he had already won a reputation as one of the most colorful and talented botanists of Europe. His life story was an alternating series of explorations and critical expositions of the results. From the purely geographic standpoint his travels place him in the first rank of explorers. At the age of twenty-two he sailed on the *Erebus* with Sir James Ross to the Antarctic. Later came his famous travels in the Himalayas (1847-1851) and visits to Mount Lebanon (1860), the Atlas Mountains (1871), and the Rockies (1877), the latter with Asa Gray.

While still a youth Joseph Hooker came in touch with George Bentham (1800-1884), an "amateur" botanist who was seventeen years his senior. Bentham was personally acquainted with Robert Brown, John Lindley, and William Hooker; in 1830 he became friendly with Alphonse de Candolle and began to collaborate with him in the preparation of the famous *Prodromus.* In 1854 he presented his magnificent collection to Kew and was induced to go there to work, still as an "amateur," though

Figure 11. Alphonse de Candolle, 1806-1893. (Courtesy New York Botanical Garden.)

virtually a member of the staff. Here he began the preparation of the first of a series of floras of the British Colonies, a project which had for some time been contemplated by the Kew authorities. Bentham himself was responsible for a volume on Hong Kong (1861) and a seven-volume flora of Australia (1863-1878). As a "before-breakfast relaxation" he undertook the preparation of a *Handbook of the British Flora,* published in 1858.

Very quickly in the course of his monographic work Bentham found himself in difficulty as to the precise limitations of genera. This led him to undertake a vast work, *Genera plantarum,* in which he presently (about 1857) had the assistance of Joseph Hooker. This work appeared at intervals, the first part in 1862 and the final part in 1883. About two-thirds of it were written by Bentham, an accomplished Latin scholar. It is interesting to note that the system followed, like all systems up to that time, was based on the doctrine of the constancy of species, although the publication of the first part coincided with the appearance of Darwin's *Origin of Species.* Hooker, a close friend of Darwin, at that time favored a complete reorganization of their classification, but was opposed by Bentham, who did not then accept the principles of evolution, although he did so later.

It is natural that the Bentham-Hooker system should have been patterned closely upon that of Candolle, a close friend of Bentham. But it differs in many respects, as will be noted from the synopsis below:

DICOTYLEDONS

I. Polypetalae (Petals separate)
    Series 1. Thalamiflorae. Hypogynous ("Orders" 1-33)
        (Ranunculaceae, Cruciferae, Malvaceae, etc.)
    Series 2. Disciflorae. Receptacle expanded as a disc. ("Orders" 34-55)
        (Geraniaceae, Rutaceae, Anacardiaceae, etc.)
    Series 3. Calyciflorae. Perigynous, sometimes epigynous ("Orders" 56-82)
        (Rosaceae, Myrtaceae, Umbelliferae, etc.)
II. Gamopetalae (Petals united)
    Series 1. Inferae. Ovary inferior ("Orders" 83-91)
        (Rubiaceae, Caprifoliaceae, Compositae, etc.)
    Series 2. Heteromerae. Ovary usually superior, carpels more than 2 ("Orders" 92-103)
        (Ericaceae, Primulaceae, Ebenaceae, etc.)
    Series 3. Bicarpellatae. Ovary usually superior; carpels usually 2 ("Orders" 104-127)
        (Scrophulariaceae, Solanaceae, Labiatae, etc.)
III. Monochlamydeae (Perianth simple)
    Series 1. Curvembryeae. Embryo curved ("Orders" 108-134)
        (Nyctaginaceae, Amarantaceae, Chenopodiaceae, etc.)
    Series 2. Multiovulatae Aquaticae. Submerged herbs ("Order" 135)
        (Podostemaceae)

Series 3. Multiovulatae Terrestres. Terrestrial plants ("Orders" 136-138)
(Nepenthaceae, Aristolochiaceae, etc.)
Series 4. Micrembryeae. Embryo very small ("Orders" 139-142)
(Piperaceae, Myristacaceae, etc.)
Series 5. Daphnales. Ovary of one carpel, ovule 1 ("Orders" 143-147)
(Proteaceae, Lauraceae, Elaeagnaceae)
Series 6. Achlamydosporeae. Pistil 1-celled, ovules 1-3 ("Orders" 148-150)
(Loranthaceae, Santalaceae)
Series 7. Unisexuales. Flowers unisexual ("Orders" 151-159)
(Euphorbiaceae, Urticaceae, Juglandaceae, etc.)
Series 8. Ordines Anomali. Relationships uncertain. ("Orders" 160-163)
(Salicaceae, Empetraceae, etc.)

GYMNOSPERMAE ("Orders" 164-166)
(Gnetaceae, Coniferae, Cyadaceae)

MONOCOTYLEDONS

Series 1. Microspermae. Without endosperm ("Orders" 167-169)
(Orchidaceae, etc.)
Series 2. Epigynae. With endosperm; ovary inferior ("Orders" 170-176)
(Iridaceae, Amaryllidaceae, etc.)
Series 3. Coronarieae. Ovary superior ("Orders" 177-184)
(Liliaceae, etc.)
Series 4. Calycineae. Perianth sepaloid ("Orders" 185-187)
(Juncaceae, Palmae, etc.)
Series 5. Nudiflorae. Perianth lacking ("Orders" 188-192)
(Typhaceae, Araceae, etc.)
Series 6. Apocarpae. Carpels single or separate ("Orders" 193-195)
(Alismaceae, Naiadaceae, etc.)
Series 7. Glumaceae. Flowers in spikelets or heads ("Orders" 196-200)
(Cyperaceae, Gramineae)

A special feature was the addition of the Disciflorae, and a curious arrangement was the division of certain groups on the basis of aquatic or terrestrial characteristics. The system includes only the seed plants, which were considered to number 97,205 species.

The *Genera plantarum* was accepted at once in the British Empire and in the United States and to some extent on the continent of Europe; in the United States it remained dominant until the first part of the twentieth century and is even yet retained by many British botanists, affording the basis for the arrangement of plants in the Kew Herbarium.

Sir Joseph Hooker succeeded his father as director of Kew in 1865, during the preparation of the *Genera plantarum;* he resigned the post in 1885 to his son-in-law, Sir William Thiselton-Dyer (1843-1928). After his retirement he was responsible for another major work in the literature of systematic botany, the *Index Kewensis* (p. 148). At the centenary of

Darwin's birth, in 1909, Hooker was present, still vigorous, to do homage to his great friend.

The *Genera plantarum* was the last great work on plant classification to be based on the doctrine of the constancy of species. The publication of Darwin's *Origin of Species* in 1859 automatically closed this period and opened a new era in the history of taxonomy. The plant kingdom heretofore had been regarded as composed of more or less mechanical units, each specially formed by the Creator. "Darwin replaced this static picture by the dynamic one of a succession of sensitive, living beings, interacting constantly with their environment and, through this interaction, constantly evolving new forms in response to environmental changes" (Gilmour).

Charles Darwin and the *Origin of Species*. One of the important events in the history of mankind took place on July 1, 1858, although at the time it excited very little attention. The event was the reading before the Linnean Society in London of a joint paper by C. Darwin and A. R. Wallace, with the rather uninteresting title "On the tendency of Species to form Varieties; and on the Perpetuation of Varieties and Species by Natural Means of Selection." Sir Joseph Hooker, who was present at the meeting (Darwin himself was not) commented that "the subject was too novel and too ominous for the old school to enter the lists before armoring." The theory was more fully expressed in the book *Origin of Species* published the next year, and known to every educated man in the world at least by title. Simpson says, "The world has never been the same since . . . It is a plain fact that all currents of western thought have been profoundly influenced by even the most technical features of Darwinism."

Charles Darwin was born in Shrewsbury on February 12, 1809 (the same day as Abraham Lincoln), and died in 1882, after a life that, from the physical standpoint, with one exception, was quite uneventful. The single adventure was a voyage around the world on H. M. S. *Beagle* in 1831-1836. The story of this he related in a fascinating style in *The Voyage of the Beagle,* published in 1839, a travel book that still maintains a steady sale.

Intellectual adventure, of course, was always present. Darwin himself relates in his *Autobiography* how his theory came to mind. When he was on board the *Beagle,* he said, he believed in the permanence of species, but vague doubts occasionally flitted across his mind. On his return home he began to prepare his journal of the voyage for publication and then saw that many facts pointed to the common descent of species. Finally, in July 1837, he began keeping a notebook to record any facts which might bear on the question. In 1844 he wrote to his friend Joseph Hooker that he had read "heaps of books" and continued collecting facts. At last he began to see gleams of light and he became convinced, quite contrary to the opinion he started with, that species were not immutable ("it is like confessing a murder"). The problem that confronted him at this time was how to explain the tendency of organisms to diverge in character as time goes by. "That they have diverged greatly," he writes in his *Autobiography,* "is obvious from the manner in which species of all kinds can be classed under genera, genera under families, families under sub-orders and so forth." The solution, he thought, was that the offspring of dominant forms tend to become adapted to many and greatly diversified ecological niches.

Charles Lyell, whose *Principles of Geology* had influenced Darwin greatly in his college days at Cambridge, urged him finally (in 1856) to write out his voluminous notes for publication. He got about half through the work, but found his plans overthrown, for in 1858 Mr. Wallace, then in the Malay archipelago, sent him an essay, "On the Tendency of Varieties to depart indefinitely from the Original Type." This essay contained exactly the same theory as Darwin had been developing. Despite his disappointment, it was Darwin's proposal that Wallace's essay be published at once, ahead of his own work. Lyell and Hooker, however, urged him to present jointly the essay of Wallace with an abstract of his own manuscript. He was at first unwilling to consent, thinking that Mr. Wallace might consider his doing so unjust, "For I did not then know how generous and noble was his disposition." Even so, the joint presentations, on July 1, caused very little attention at the moment.

Darwin continued then to work on his manuscript, although on a scale not more than one-third as extensive as his original plan. He was often interrupted by poor health, but finally the copy was ready for the press. He confessed that the subject matter was rather stiff, and felt that only a few copies would be needed. It appeared from the press on November 24, 1859, and the edition, of 1250 copies, was sold before nightfall. Hooker himself said of the book, "It is the very hardest book to read to full profit, that I have ever tried." But its effect upon the world was immediate and astounding, and inspired the most violent controversies which raged for more than a half century. Without entering into these controversies, we might note simply that his work established the fact of evolution. It is true that many writers before his time had discussed evolution and had proposed theories to account for it. But these attracted very little interest on the part of other biologists and often sound ideas were associated with much nonsense. Darwin's own presentation was based upon so many facts, and was so logically arranged, that, from the scientific viewpoint (as contrasted with the irrational and emotional viewpoint), no doubt remained of the truth of evolutionary theory.

Phylogenetic Systems. The term **phylogeny** was invented by Ernst Heinrich Haeckel in 1866 to designate the science of genealogical development in phyla or in other plant and animal groups. The gradual acceptance of the concept of evolution stimulated an effort on the part of taxonomists to devise systems of classification that would indicate the actual relationships of the plants, from the evolutionary viewpoint. In general, these systems have attempted to classify plants beginning with the simplest and proceeding to the most complex. Several different schemes have been proposed but it is recognized that none clearly accounts for the true relationships. This is because not enough information is available on the evolutionary origin and development of the present plant kingdom; it may be expected that as more facts are revealed by research the systems will gradually be improved. After nearly a century, phylogenetic taxonomy is yet in its early stages. Much remains to be done. It should be noted that these "phlogenetic systems" do not show abrupt departures from the earlier nineteenth century "natural systems." This was for the simple reason that, even though the attempt might be made to place the most primitive plants at the base and the most advanced at the top of the scheme, there were still few criteria available for consideration other than the morphological resemblances and differences which had long been in use. It is quite obvious that we do not in fact know the actual descent of any plants, since this is a thing of the past. Therefore, as Turrill remarks, phylogeny continued to be based on natural classification, not classification upon phylogeny.

Julius von Sachs (1832-1897), professor of botany at Würzburg, was the first to abandon the old scheme and in 1868 substituted a new plan, which, however, was never generally accepted. He did later propose a classification of the algae and fungi attempting to bring out the evolutionary relationships of these groups, and to show how certain groups of fungi may have developed from certain groups of algae by a loss of chlorophyll.

Eichler. August Wilhelm Eichler (1839-1887), studying morphology in the light of the doctrine of evolution, proposed in 1883 a classification embracing the entire plant kingdom, which he divided into two groups, cryptogams and phanerogams. His system is briefly outlined below:

A. Cryptogamae
- I. Division Thallophyta
  1. Class Algae (Cyanophyceae, Chlorophyceae, Phaeophyceae, Rhodophyceae)
  2. Class Fungi
- II. Division Bryophyta
  1. Class Hepaticae
  2. Class Musci
- III. Division Pteridophyta
  1. Class Equisetineae
  2. Class Lycopodineae
  3. Class Filicineae

B. Phanerogamae
- I. Division Gymnospermae

II. Division Angiospermae
 1. Class Monocotyleae
 2. Class Dicotyleae
  1. Subclass Choripetalae
  2. Subclass Sympetalae

Features of this system include the new classification of the algae and the division of the seed plants, for the first time, into Gymnosperms and Angiosperms.

Die Natürlichen Pflanzenfamilien. Heinrich Gustav Adolf Engler (1844-1930), published a classification based upon that of Eichler, differing from it merely in detail. This system was so well publicized that it was adopted by a majority of the botanists of the world soon after the beginning of the twentieth century. It was first issued (in 1886) as a guide to the botanical garden of Breslau but soon began to appear in a greatly expanded form in a monumental work, *Die Natürlichen Pflanzenfamilien.* Even in this work, however, Engler did not regard his system as completely phylogenetic, but rather as one having the groups built up step by step to form a generally progressional morphological series.

Comparing this arrangement with the Bentham and Hooker system, it will be noted that Engler abolished the large artificial group, Monochlamydeae (flowers with only one whorl of the perianth present) and distributed its members among apparently related forms having separate petals, constituting a large series, the Archichlamydeae. He made but one other group of the dicotyledons, the Sympetalae, corresponding to Bentham and Hooker's Gamopetalae. In the subdivision of the Archichlamydeae Engler took the view that the most primitive flower consisted mainly of stamens and carpels protected by bracts, or perhaps rudimentary perianths. Evolutionary advance he traced through the Amentiferae and other plants with naked flowers to those with sepal-like perianths, and thence to flowers with both calyx and corolla. Hence the series started with the Piperales and ended with the Umbelliflorae. This concept, it will be observed, differed from the view held by Candolle and Bentham and Hooker, that the flowers of the Ranunculaceae represent the most primitive Angiosperms. The supporters of this last view reasoned that the evolution of the flower had proceeded very far before the origin of the Angiosperms, and that the flowers which Engler claimed as primitive were derived from plants with a perianth, by a process of reduction, or loss of parts.

A complete outline of Engler's system was published in his *Syllabus der Pflanzenfamilien,* which has now gone through numerous editions. The first volume (Bacteria to Gymnosperms) of a 12th edition, by Hans Melchior and Erich Werdermann, appeared in 1954. The general outline has changed little through the various editions, although the arrangement of some of the families has varied.

By this system, the plant kingdom was divided into fourteen major divisions (*Abteilungen*), as follows:

1. Schizophyta. Bacteria, blue-green algae
2. Myxomycetes. Slime molds
3. Flagellatae. Flagellates
4. Dinoflagellatae.
5. Heterocontae.
6. Bacillariophyta.
7. Conjugatae.
8. Chlorophyceae. Green algae
9. Charophyta.
10. Phaeophyceae. Brown algae
11. Rhodophyceae. Red algae
12. Eumycetes. Fungi
13. Archegoniatae. Bryophytes, pteridophytes
14. Embryophyta Siphonogama. Seed plants

The orders of seed plants were arranged as follows:

1. Subdivision Gymnospermae
- *1.* Class Cycadofilicales
- *2.* Class Cycadales (Cycadaceae)
- *3.* Class Bennettitales (Bennettitaceae)
- *4.* Class Ginkgoales (Ginkgoaceae)
- *5.* Class Cordaitales (Cordaitaceae)
- *6.* Class Coniferae (7 families)
- *7.* Class Gnetales (3 families)

2. Subdivision Angiospermae
- *1.* Class Monocotyledoneae
  - 1. Order Pandanales (3 families)
  - 2. Order Helobiae (7 families)
  - 3. Order Triuridales (Triuridaceae)
  - 4. Order Glumiflorae (Gramineae, Cyperaceae)
  - 5. Order Principes (Palmae)
  - 6. Order Synanthae (Cyclanthaceae)
  - 7. Order Spathiflorae (Araceae, Lemnaceae)
  - 8. Order Farinosae (13 families)
  - 9. Order Liliiflorae (9 families)
  - 10. Order Scitamineae (4 families)
  - 11. Order Microspermae (Burmanniaceae, Orchidaceae)
- *2.* Class Dicotyledoneae
  - 1. Subclass Archichlamydeae
    - 1. Order Verticillatae (Casuarinaceae)
    - 2. Order Piperales (3 families)
    - 3. Order Hydrostachyales (Hydrostachyaceae)
    - 4. Order Salicales (Salicaceae)
    - 5. Order Garryales (Garryaceae)
    - 6. Order Myricales (Myricaceae)
    - 7. Order Balanopsidales (Balanopsidaceae)
    - 8. Order Leitneriales (Leitneriaceae)
    - 9. Order Juglandales (Juglandaceae)
    - 10. Order Julianiales (Julianiaceae)

11. Order Batidales (Batidaceae)
12. Order Fagales (Betulaceae, Fagaceae)
13. Order Urticales (4 families)
14. Order Podostemonales (Podostemonaceae)
15. Order Proteales (Proteaceae)
16. Order Santalales (7 families)
17. Order Aristolochiales (3 families)
18. Order Balanophorales (Balanophoraceae)
19. Order Polygonales (Polygonaceae)
20. Order Centrospermae (10 families)
21. Order Ranales (19 families)
22. Order Rhoeadales (7 families)
23. Order Sarraceniales (3 families)
24. Order Rosales (17 families)
25. Order Pandales (Pandaceae)
26. Order Geraniales (21 families)
27. Order Sapindales (23 families)
28. Order Rhamnales (Rhamnaceae, Vitaceae)
29. Order Malvales (7 families)
30. Order Parietales (31 families)
31. Order Opuntiales (Cactaceae)
32. Order Myrtiflorae (23 families)
33. Order Umbelliflorae (3 families)

2. Subclass Metachlamydeae (Sympetalae)
   1. Order Diapensiales (Diapensiaceae)
   2. Order Ericales (4 families)
   3. Order Primulales (3 families)
   4. Order Plumbaginales (Plumbaginaceae)
   5. Order Ebenales (7 families)
   6. Order Contortae (6 families)
   7. Order Tubiflorae (22 families)
   8. Order Plantaginales (Plantaginaceae)
   9. Order Rubiales (5 families)
   10. Order Cucurbitales (Cucurbitaceae)
   11. Order Campanulatae (6 families)

The main reason for the widespread adoption of this plan was the elaborate form in which it was presented. For about thirty years Engler was professor of botany at the University of Berlin, and director of the Berlin Botanical Garden from 1889 to 1921. Like Candolle, and later Bentham and Hooker, he conceived the idea of executing a monumental work providing the details of his taxonomic system. With his associate, Karl Anton Eugen Prantl (1849-1893), the work was begun, with the plan of providing keys and descriptions for all families, from the algae to the Compositae. For each family there was given a summary of knowledge concerning the embryology, morphology, anatomy, geographic distribution, and so forth, with descriptions of the genera and a bibliography of pertinent literature. While the two associates did much of the work themselves, many sections were assigned to specialists in the different groups. Abundant illustrations were provided.

This vast work, *Die Natürlichen Pflanzenfamilien,* which Lawrence calls a "glorified genera plantarum," began to appear in 1887; it was completed, in twenty-three volumes, in 1915. Because of its great detail it was quickly adopted as a valuable reference work in most countries of the world except the British Empire (where the Bentham and Hooker system continued to be used); a vast literature developed, based upon this scheme, and plant specimens in many herbaria throughout the world were arranged according to the "Engler-Prantl sequence."

Figure 12. ***Left,*** **George Bentham, 1800-1884;** ***right,*** **Joseph Dalton Hooker, 1817-1911. (Courtesy New York Botanical Garden.)**

A second edition began to be prepared in 1924, and despite the death of Engler in 1930 and the interruption of World War 2, eight volumes have appeared. Ludwig Diels (1874-1945), who succeeded Engler as director of the Berlin Botanical Garden in 1921, later took over the editorship of the revised edition.

The Twentieth Century. Richard von Wettstein (1862-1931), an Austrian, originated a system that somewhat resembles that of Engler and Prantl, but is considered as more closely approaching phyletic realities. Unisexual, naked flowers are regarded as more primitive than bisexual flowers with a perianth. Wettstein differed from Engler and Prantl in regarding the dicots as more primitive than monocots; the latter he regarded as derived from Ranalian ancestors.

Charles Edwin Bessey (1845-1915), an American and a student of Asa Gray, prepared a scheme original in many respects, although with resemblances to the Bentham and Hooker outline. He considered that the Ranales were the primitive angiosperms, one branch giving rise to the monocots, the other to the dicots, which in turn bifurcated into the Strobiloideae, or plants with hypogynous flowers, and the Cotyloideae, with perigynous or epigynous flowers. The details of the arrangement are shown in the accompanying chart (Figure 14).

Hans Hallier (1868-1932), a German, presented a phylogenetic system which resembles that of Bessey, although the two were developed

Figure 13. *Left,* Adolf Engler, 1844-1930; *right,* Karl Prantl, 1849-1893. (Courtesy New York Botanical Garden.)

independently. He regarded the dicots as older and more primitive than the monocots. His classification is considered valuable not so much for its overall arrangement as for the realignment of genera and families.

John Hutchinson (1884-), a Briton, proposed a plan that, in its basic principles, somewhat paralleled that of Bessey. He regarded the angiosperms as monophyletic and derived from hypothetical proangiosperms. A departure in his system was the division of the angiosperms into the Lignosae (predominantly woody plants) and the Herbaceae (predominantly herbaceous). His treatment of the limitations of orders and families is considered excellent.

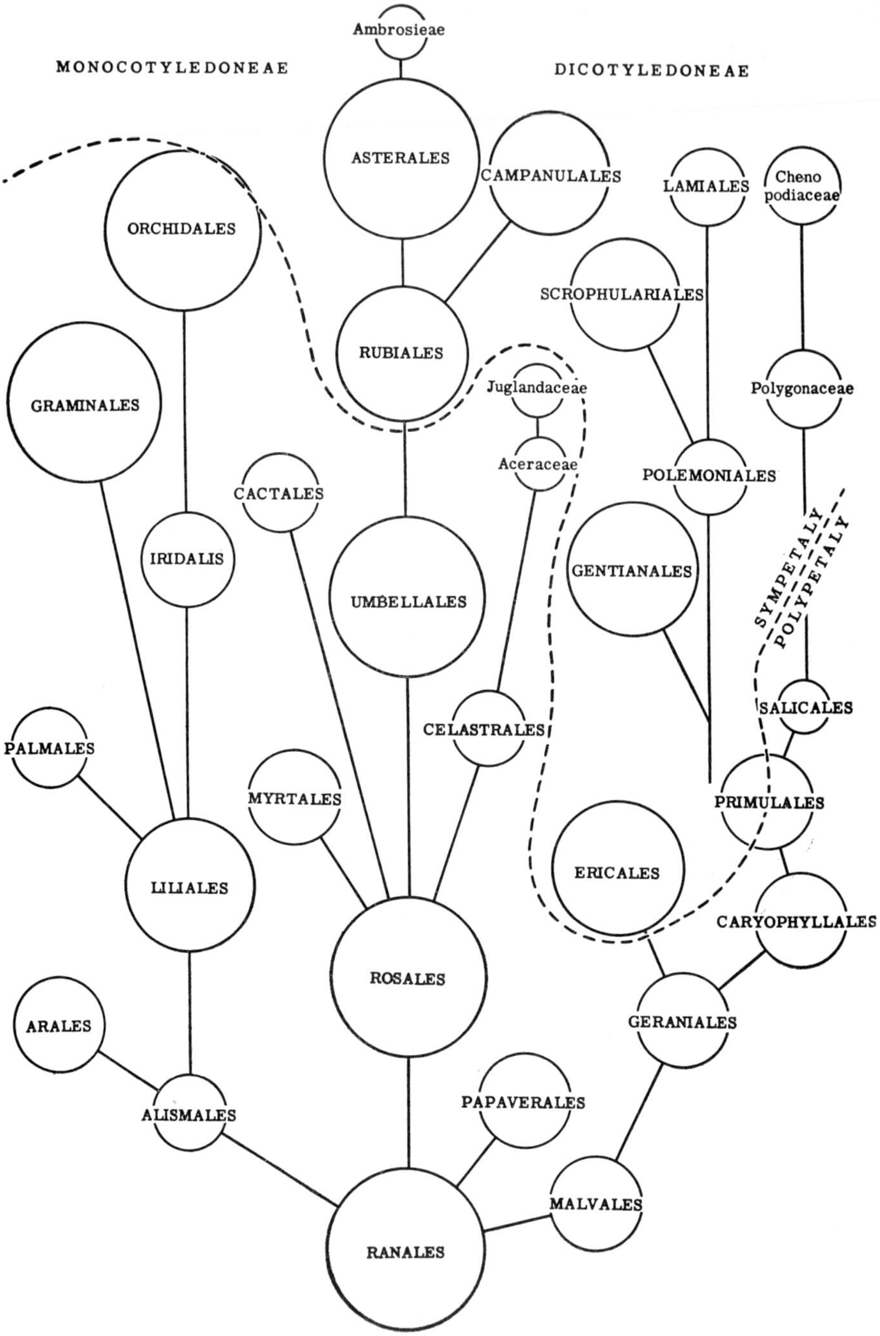

Figure 14. A classification of the angiosperms, following the Bessey system. Note the right-hand line of evolution comprised of hypogynous dicotyledons, the center line of perigynous and epigynous dicotyledons, and the left-hand line of monocotyledons. (Adapted by permission from Raymond J. Pool, *Flowers and Flowering Plants,* 2d edition, copyright 1941, McGraw-Hill Book Company, Inc.)

Carl Skottsberg (1880-), a Swede, devised a system that is a modification of the Engler classification. He interpreted the monocots as having been derived from an unknown primitive dicot. Apocarpy was regarded as primitive, with syncarpy as more advanced. Apetalous families were viewed to have been of polyphyletic origin and therefore were redistributed from positions given them by Engler.

August A. Pulle (1878-1955), of the Netherlands, published (in 1938) a modification of Engler's plan. He followed Engler in regarding the Spermatophyta as a division but treated it as composed of four subdivisions, Pteridospermae, Gymnospermae, Chlamydospermae (Gnetales), and Angiospermae. The Angiosperms were divided into monocots and dicots. The orders of dicots were arranged into eight series, in accordance with his opinion that the Monochlamydeae and Sympetalae are not natural groups.

Alfred Barton Rendle (1865-1938) published a classification resembling the Engler scheme, but differing from it in some minor features. The orders of dicots were arranged in three grades, the Monochlamydeae, Dialypetalae, and Sympetalae. His two-volume work is distinguished for the clarity of the descriptive material and the careful discussions of family relationships.

Schemes proposed by Gilbert Morgan Smith (1885-) for nonvascular plants in 1938 and by Arthur Johnson Eames (1881-) for vascular plants in 1936 were brought together in skeletal outline by Oswald Tippo (1911-) in 1942, into a phylogenetic system that is rapidly being adopted throughout the United States in general botany textbooks. This system, outlined below, emphasizes that the Pteridophyta is not a homogeneous group and that there is no distinct line of demarcation between "pteridophytes" and "spermatophytes." The relationships indicated are derived from a sound study of paleobotanical data and a comparison of these with data obtained through study of living plants.

Kingdom Plantae
- Subkingdom Thallophyta
  - Phylum Cyanophyta
  - Phylum Chlorophyta
  - Phylum Chrysophyta
  - Phylum Pyrrophyta
  - Phylum Phaeophyta
  - Phylum Rhodophyta
  - Phylum Schizomycophyta
  - Phylum Myxomycophyta
  - Phylum Eumycophyta
- Subkingdom Embryophyta
  - Phylum Bryophyta
    - Class Musci
    - Class Hepaticae
    - Class Anthocerotae

- Phylum Tracheophyta
  - Subphylum Lycopsida
    - Class Lycopodineae
      - Order Lycopodiales
      - Order Selaginellales
      - Order Lepidodendrales
      - Order Pleuromeiales
      - Order Isoetales
  - Subphylum Sphenopsida
    - Class Equisetineae
      - Order Hyeniales
      - Order Sphenophyllales
      - Order Equisetales
  - Subphylum Pteropsida
    - Class Filicineae
      - Order Coenopteridales
      - Order Ophioglossales
      - Order Marattiales
      - Order Filicales
    - Class Gymnospermae
      - Subclass Cycadophytae
        - Order Cycadofilicales
        - Order Bennettitales
        - Order Cycadales
      - Subclass Coniferophytae
        - Order Cordaitales
        - Order Ginkgoales
        - Order Coniferales
        - Order Gnetales
    - Class Angiospermae
      - Subclass Dicotyledoneae
      - Subclass Monocotyledoneae

The Engler-Prantl system still remains dominant in most of the large herbaria and the various published floras of the world. This, however, is largely because it is the most recent of the great monographs, as Bentham and Hooker was previously and the Candolle system before that. Changes in sequence of orders and families cannot, of course, be made every time a new treatment appears. But research continues, systems are still being refined, and doubtless after the passage of due time another monumental treatise will be produced and another chapter in the history of taxonomy will be begun.

References

Bentham, G., and J. D. Hooker, *Genera plantarum.* London, 1862-83.

Bessey, C. E., *Phylogenetic taxonomy of flowering plants.* Annals of the Missouri Botanical Garden, 2: 109-164, 1915.

Candolle, A. P. de, and others. *Prodromus systematis naturalis regni vegetabilis.* (17 vols., 4 index vols.) Paris, 1824-73.

Darwin, C., *Origin of Species.* London, 1859.

Darwin, F. (ed.), *Charles Darwin's Autobiography*. New York, 1950.

Eames, A. J., *Morphology of vascular plants. Lower groups.* New York, 1936.

Eichler, A. B., *Blüthendiagramme construirt und erlautert.* Leipzig, 1875-78.

Endlicher, S. L., *Genera plantarum.* Vienna, 1836-50.

Engler, A., *Führer durch den königlichen botanischen Garten der Universität zu Breslau.* Breslau, 1886.

———, *Syllabus der Pflanzenfamilien,* various editions. The first edition may be cited as: *Syllabus der Vorlesungen über specielle und medicinisch-pharmaceutische Botanik. Eine uebersicht über das gesammte Pflanzensystem mit Berücksichtigung der Medicinal und Nutzpflanzen.* Berlin, 1892.

———, K. Prantl, and others, *Die natürlichen Pflanzenfamilien.* 23 vols. Leipzig, 1897-1915; 2nd ed. (incomplete), 1924-1953.

Fuller, H. J., and O. Tippo, *College botany.* New York, 1940.

Gilmour, J., *British botanists.* London, 1944.

Green, J. R., *A history of botany, 1860-1900.* Oxford, 1909.

Hallier, H., *Phylogenetic system of flowering plants.* New Phytol. 5: 151-162. 1905.

Harvey-Gibson, R. J., *Outlines of the history of botany.* London, 1919.

Hutchinson, J., *The families of flowering plants.* 2 vols. London, 1926, 1934.

———, *British flowering plants.* London, 1948.

Jussieu, A. L. de, *Genera plantarum.* Paris, 1789.

Lawrence, G. H. M., Taxonomy of vascular plants. New York, 1951.

Lindley, J., *The vegetable kingdom.* London, 1846.

Pulle, A., *Remarks on the system of the spermatophytes.* Med. Bot. Mus. Herb. Ryks-Univ. Utrecht, 43: 1-17. 1937.

Rendle, A. B., *Classification of flowering plants.* 2 vols. Cambridge, 1904, 1925.

Simpson, G. G., *The meaning of Darwin,* in *Charles Darwin's Autobiography.* New York, 1950.

Skottsberg, C., *Vaxternas Liv.* Vol. 5. Stockholm, 1940.

Smith, G. M., *Cryptogamic botany.* Vol. 1. New York, 1938.

Takhtajan, A. L., *Phylogenetic principles of the system of higher plants.* Botanical Review 19: 1-45, 1953 (Transl. from the Russian; first publ. in Botanicheski Zhurnal, Vol. 35, 1950).

Tippo, O., *A modern classification of the plant kingdom.* Chronica Botanica 7: 203-206, 1942.

Turrill, W. B., *Taxonomy and Phylogeny.* Botanical Review 8: 247-270, 473-532, 655-707, 1942.

Wettstein, R., *Handbuch der systematischen botanik.* Leipzig, 1924.

4

Plant Exploration

Coincident with the reawakening of interest in the plants of Europe, there opened up, through a period of unparalleled geographical discovery, a vast new botanical horizon. Here were to be found plants of a diversity and number so marvelous, as compared with those known by Theophrastus, Pliny, and Dioscorides, or even by the "German Fathers," as to appear positively fantastic. The addition of these new species made more difficult the development of taxonomy, it is true, by adding a vast body of new facts before the old ones were fully known, but the preparation of a broader and more complete scheme of classification was at the same time made possible. Just as we have pointed out how botanical science in Europe gradually brought about a more accurate conception of the nature and relationships of plants, so we shall now note how the flora of the world gradually came to be known through botanical exploration. The story of a few botanical explorers must suffice as typical of the work of many.

The New World. With the discovery of the New World a vast, new, and marvelous vegetable realm was opened for exploration. The first European book of comprehensive scope dealing with the plants of America was by a Spanish physician, Nicolas Monardes (1493-1588), who never visited the western hemisphere, but wrote down travelers' tales, or descriptions of things brought to him. The first part of his book was published in 1569 and the second in 1571. In 1574 these were revised and combined in *Primera y segunda y tercera partes de la historia medicinal de las cosas que se traen de nuestras Indias Occidentales que sirven en medicina* (First and second and third parts of the medical history of the things brought from our West Indies that are useful in medicine). This work is very interesting reading, but full of great marvels recorded by the over-credulous author. In 1577 this work was translated into English under the title, *Joyfull Newes out of the Newe Founde Worlde, written in Spanish by Nicholas Monardes, physician of Seville, and Englished by*

John Frampton, merchant. This work contained a picture of the tobacco plant (*Tabaco*), perhaps the first ever published, and it is said that Indians and Negro slaves of the West Indies, after smoking it, "doe remaine lightened, without any wearinesse, for to laboure again: and thei dooe this with so greate pleasure, that although thei bee not wearie, yet thei are very desirous for to dooe it: and the thyng is come to so muche effecte, that their maisters doeth chasten theim for it, and doe burn the *Tabaco,* because thei should not use it" (quoted by Arber).

In 1688 a young physician, Hans Sloane (1660-1753), embarked from England for the British West Indies. He was well educated, having studied in London, Paris, and Montpellier and was said by Pulteney to have been "the first man of learning, whom the love of science alone had led from England, to the distant parts of the globe; and, consequently, the field was wholly open to him." He spent fifteen months studying the plants of Jamaica and, "having an enthusiasm for his object . . . returned home with a rich harvest" of 800 species new to science. Upon his return to England he published an account of them in his *Catalogus plantarum* (1696), following Ray's system where possible in their arrangement. He formed a scientific collection and library that later became the nucleus of the British Museum, first opened to the public in 1759.

Another English naturalist who investigated the plant life of the New World in these early days was Mark Catesby (1679-1749). Catesby landed in Virginia in 1712, remaining for seven years and sending back collections of plants with the assistance and encouragement of Sir Hans Sloane and others. In 1722 he returned to America, landing at Charleston. He spent three years studying the fauna and flora of the southeastern portion of North America. This study resulted in the publication of *The Natural History of Carolina, Florida, and the Bahama Islands;* the first volume appeared in 1731, the second in 1743, and an appendix in 1748. It was illustrated with 200 plates from Catesby's paintings.

Rumphius. Meanwhile, in the Orient, one of the world's great botanists was laying the foundations of knowledge of the immensely diversified flora of Indonesia. George Eberhard Rumpf (better known as Rumphius) was born in 1628 in Solms, Germany. In 1653 he was appointed to a commercial post by the Dutch East India Company and took up his residence on the island of Amboina, between New Guinea and Celebes, a region important for its spices. At once he undertook the task of collecting, describing, and illustrating the plants of Amboina and neighboring islands. In 1670 his work was nearly completed, but he wanted to take one more trip. This trip resulted in blindness that afflicted him the rest of his life. Aided by his wife, he continued to work, translating the Latin text of his work into Dutch. In 1674 this partnership was ended when a great earthquake occurred, in which his wife and oldest child were killed.

Figure 15. George Everhard Rumphius, 1628-1702. (Courtesy New York Botanical Garden.)

With such help as he could get from the Company staff he continued to work, but in 1687 his house and library were destroyed by a fire which also burned some of his manuscripts and illustrations. With incredible persistence in the face of such tremendous discouragements, he renewed his work and with the aid of his son and others replaced the lost material. In 1690 he completed his manuscript and sent it to Batavia for transmittal to Europe. Ill-fortune continued to follow him; the ship on which it was sent was destroyed by the French and the manuscript lost. A copy had been kept by Rumphius, from which the work was reconstructed, but the courageous botanist died in 1702, before it could be published. The final manuscript lay in the Company offices for many years before it was finally edited and published, as the *Herbarium Amboinense* (1741-1755), by J. Burmann of Amsterdam. This contained descriptions of about 1750 species, of which 1060 were figured. Succeeding authors adopted many of Rumphius' descriptions and figures as the types of binomials. E. D. Merrill says of Rumphius: "He has been well characterized as the 'Pliny of the Indies,' for he was one of the outstanding naturalists of all time."

The Linnean Age. The contagious enthusiasm of Linnaeus, as previously noted, stimulated his students "in high spirits and burning zeal" to criss-cross the earth at the risk of their lives to search in all climates for new and unusual plants. Great perils were then connected with such journeys, and only scanty equipment could be provided for the explorers. Many of these "apostles," as Linnaeus tenderly called them, suffered a martyr's death, but, as Jackson notes, "that did not prevent others from offering themselves to similar tasks, to the same hunger, the same struggle, the same death. . . ." (See Figure 30.)

The first of these was Christopher Ternström. Though married and a father, he set out for the East Indies at the beginning of 1746. Linnaeus charged him especially to procure a tea plant in a pot, or at least seeds. News came presently that he had died on December 5, 1746, on the way to the Orient. Linnaeus was much grieved and Ternström's widow accused him of having enticed her husband away.

Next, an ambassador was sent to North America to secure seeds of a mulberry which could endure the climate of Sweden, so that the silkworm industry might be established. Pehr (Peter) Kalm was selected for the trip, funds were secured, and he set out, reaching Philadelphia after a long journey on September 15, 1747. After extensive travels in the Appalachian Mountains, he returned to Europe in 1751, with a large collection of seeds and dried plants, among which may be mentioned the mountain laurel (*Kalmia*) and the Virginia creeper.

Soon after Kalm left for America, another expedition was in progress. Fredrik Hasselquist, "modest, polite, cheerful, and intelligent, but very poor," set out for Palestine in the summer of 1747, with funds raised personally by Linnaeus with much hard work. He landed in Smyrna, traveled inland, and the following May went to Egypt, where he stayed until March, 1751. During the year 1751 he explored Palestine, parts of Arabia, Syria, Cyprus, Rhodes, and Chio, then back to Smyrna, near which town "our beloved Dr. Hasselquist, like a lamp whose oil is consumed, died on the 9th of February, 1752, to the grief of all who knew him." His valuable collections and manuscripts were held for debts and were redeemed by the Queen of Sweden, eventually coming to the hands of Linnaeus.

Petrus Löfling was Linnaeus' most beloved pupil, "graced with virtue, pious, just, loving and quick at grasping nature's many secrets." In 1750 he went to Spain to investigate its flora, upon Linnaeus' complaint that "it is lamentable that a cultivated European land should remain in so barbarous a state as regards botany." Two years were spent there, with many collections sent to Uppsala; then Löfling was appointed botanist of an expedition to South America. The expedition reached Cumaná, Venezuela, in 1754 but nothing more was heard from Löfling until the news came that he had died of fever in Guiana on February 22, 1756.

Pehr Forskål sailed for the Near East on January 4, 1761. Clothed as a peasant to escape marauding Bedouins, he wandered over Egypt and made a good collection of plants. He then went to Arabia, discovering one hundred new species and thirty new genera, including *Forskolea* (Urticaceae). Stricken with the plague, he died there on July 11, 1761, his collections ultimately reaching his old preceptor.

An explorer whose story reads more pleasantly was Carl Peter Thunberg (1743-1828). Linnaeus said of him that he never benefited so much from any other traveler. Thunberg had the desire to study the plants of Japan, which land was then closed to all nations except the Dutch; to gain admittance, he joined the Dutch East India Company's service as a surgeon. He first traveled to the Cape of Good Hope, where he spent the years 1772-1775, discovering many new species of plants afterwards described in his *Prodromus Plantarum Capensium* (1794-1800), justifying his title as the "father of Cape botany." He then went on to Japan, staying until the end of 1776, with stops at Java on the way out and back. He kept up a correspondence with Linnaeus all this time and supplied him with innumerable specimens, many of which came to have Thunberg's name attached to them as memorials to the intrepid collector. He returned to Uppsala only in 1779, when Linnaeus had been dead fifteen months; before many years he succeeded the younger Linnaeus as professor of botany there, a position he held for forty-five years. His *Flora Japonica* was published in 1784.

Andrew Sparrman (1747-1820) traveled with Lieutenant (later Captain) James Cook on his first voyage around the world, in 1765-1766, botanizing in China and other lands. In 1772 he went to the Cape of

Good Hope; he met Thunberg at Cape Town and with him made large collections of the interesting plants of the neighboring region. In November of that year he joined Captain Cook on a voyage to New Zealand, returning to Cape Town in 1775. He then undertook a long journey, traveling by ox-wagon through the Cape region. His account of his travels provided a valuable contribution to the botany of South Africa and many of his species were quoted by Linnaeus' son in his *Supplement* (1781) to the *Species plantarum.*

So it went. Jackson concludes: "Each nation has had its heroic age in the world's history; and each science which has won development has had its chivalrous period. In botany it is the Linnean period which has left its mark."

Around the World with James Cook. Two zealous London naturalists, John Ellis and Peter Collinson, for whom Linnaeus named the genera *Ellisia* and *Collinsonia,* requested their great Swedish contemporary to send some of his pupils to England to encourage the study of natural history. For this purpose, Daniel Solander (1736-1782), regarded by Linnaeus as the best of his disciples after Löfling, was selected. He went to London in 1760 and became such a thorough Englishman that he never saw his native land of Sweden again. He received an appointment to the British Museum and in 1764 became librarian to Sir Joseph Banks.

On August 26, 1768 Solander and Banks sailed from England on the ship *Endeavour,* Lieutenant James Cook, commander, on one of the most famous voyages in the history of navigation. Solander was thirty-five, Banks twenty-five; to the young botanists the next three years were a succession of thrills, high adventure, and marvelous scientific discoveries. In Tierra del Fuego, in January, 1769, ascending a mountain in search of plants, they were exposed to such bitter cold that Solander almost perished, and two attendants actually died. At Tahiti they went ashore in April; Banks learned the native language, and saw the breadfruit tree, for which he later sent Captain William Bligh and the *Bounty;* some of the seaman, regarding the land as Paradise, deserted and tried to remain behind when the *Endeavour* sailed. In October a land appeared, with ranges of hills rising one above another, crowned by a mountain range of enormous height; landing two days later, Cook, Banks, and Solander were the first white men to set foot on New Zealand.

New Holland (Australia) came into sight on April 19, 1770; they anchored the next day in a bay near what is now Sydney, New South Wales, and in the next two weeks the naturalists collected nearly 1000 species of such remarkable plants that their anchorage was named Botany Bay; years later the high quality wool exported from this harbor gave the name Botany to some of the world's finest fabrics. Sailing across the Indian Ocean in January and February, 1771, almost the entire ship's company became ill of malaria; Banks was so sick that for some time there was no hope of his recovery; in all, thirty men were lost. On March 15 they arrived at the Cape of Good Hope, where a stop was made for convalescence, and on June 12 they landed in England, having completed the voyage around the world. Banks and Solander came back with a vast collection of specimens and a determination that the plant resources of the expanding Empire should be thoroughly explored; how well Banks succeeded has already been noted.

Exploration of North America. We mentioned previously that Spanish botanists began very early the exploration of their new possessions in Mexico. The temperate portions of North America had to wait a long time before their plant life came to be known. One of the fathers of botanical science in the British colonies was John Clayton (1693-1773), of Virginia.

Clayton was born in Kent, England, and came to Virginia in 1705 with his father, who was an eminent lawyer and later attorney-general of Virginia. Young Clayton became clerk of "Gloster County" (Gloucester County), holding the office for fifty-one years. His home was near Soles, in what is now Mathews County, about sixty miles east of Richmond. He early developed an interest in the plants of his region and eventually traveled over much of Virginia east of the Blue Ridge Mountains collecting plants and studying them. Presently he wrote descriptions of many of his herbarium specimens and sent the notes and specimens to J. F. Gronovius, of Leyden. With the assistance of Linnaeus, who was then in the Netherlands, the plants were named and the descriptions were published in 1739 in a 206-page book, *Flora Virginica.* These descriptions are quite accurate and little doubt exists in any case as to the precise species described. S. F. Blake said that this work of Clayton's afforded "the chief basis of perhaps the greater number of North American plants published in the *Species Plantarum*" of Linnaeus. To one plant Gronovius gave the name *Claytonia,* honoring its discoverer.

About the time Clayton was working on his *Flora Virginica,* Lord Petre, an English nobleman, asked his friend, Peter Collinson, for the name of someone in America who might collect natural history specimens for him. Collinson recommended John Bartram (1699-1777), of Philadelphia, whom Linnaeus later called "the greatest natural botanist in the world." Bartram was a farmer with a meager education who, tradition says, sat down and pulled a daisy apart; he became so impressed with a desire to learn more about plants that he went into town to get a book on botany, then started sending Pennsylvania plants to Collinson. With orders from England he set off on his first collecting trip down the Atlantic seaboard, coming back with specimens of sassafras, spice bush, tulip-tree, swamp rose-bay, and so on. The results of his trip brought more orders from England and correspondence with Sir Hans Sloane and others.

Bartram traveled from Ontario to Florida, collecting specimens, seeds, living plants. His most remarkable discovery was made along the Altamaha River in Georgia, a shrub with showy white flowers, related to the tea plant of China. Brought back to his Philadelphia garden for planting, it was named *Franklinia* in honor of his friend, Benjamin Franklin. Since the eighteenth century no one has ever found it in the wild, although gardens are still supplied with descendants of Bartram's collections.

Among visitors to the Bartram garden was André Michaux, of Charleston, S. C. Michaux was born in 1746 near Versailles, France, and grew up a farmer, but with a good education, studying botany under Bernard de Jussieu. The death of his young wife at the birth of their son, François, caused a restlessness that led him to leave his farm and enter the service of the King. He traveled in Persia, experiencing numerous adventures and becoming fluent in the native language. Finally, at the request of the King, he migrated to America in 1785, with his son, then fifteen years of age. He started a garden near Charleston and began to send plants to France, as Bartram sent them to England. His diary relates the story of his travels and adventures in the forests of the New World. He traveled to Grandfather Mountain and the Blue Ridge, along the Ohio in boats, into the prairies of Illinois, south to Florida and the Bahamas. For five years François traveled with him before going back to France for his education in 1790. He discovered many new plants but received very little money from the government and in 1797 returned to Europe, was shipwrecked off the coast of Holland and washed to shore unconscious. In Paris great honors came to him and he was sent to the tropics on a new expedition, but died of fever very shortly in Madagascar in 1802. His great work was the *Flora boreali-americana* (1803), containing long lists of American plants that he had discovered and described. One of his most remarkable discoveries was the famous *Shortia,* found in the North Carolina mountains in 1788, but not again seen until 1877, when it was rediscovered by George M. Hyams (1861-1932).

His son François (1770-1850) added lustre to the family name by his own travels and collections in America, which he visited twice after his early stay with his father. His classic work was the *Histoire des arbres forestiers de l'Amerique septentrionale* (1810-1813), with an English translation published as *Sylva of North America* in 1818-1819.

Numerous other botanists won distinction in this early day. Amos Eaton (1776-1842), of Troy, N. Y., published his *Manual of Botany,* in 1817. Frederick Pursh (1774-1820) was born in Grossenhain, Saxony, and came to the United States in 1799. After several years of botanical exploration he brought out his *Flora Americae Septentrionalis* in 1814. One of his interesting discoveries was the hart's-tongue fern (*Phyllitis scolopendrium* var. *americana*). Gotthilf Heinrich Ernst Muhlenberg (1753-1815), of Lancaster, Pa., made botanical explorations in Pennsylvania, publishing his *Index Flora Lancastriensis* in 1791 and the *Catalogus Plantarum Americae Septentrionalis* in 1813. Lewis David von Schweinitz (1780-1834), of Bethlehem, Pa., was the greatest American authority of the times on the lower plants. His synopsis of North American fungi, published in 1832, contained descriptions of 3098 species. Stephen Elliott (1771-1830), a resident of South Carolina, published his two-volume *Botany of South Carolina and Georgia* in 1821-1824.

An enigmatic character, ridiculed or ignored by many of his contemporaries, classed as a titan by some modern writers, was Constantine Samuel Rafinesque (-Schmaltz) (1773-1840). Born in Constantinople of French and Graeco-German parentage, he came to America in his twentieth year. Immediately upon his arrival he began the study of plants in the region of Philadelphia, returning to Europe after three years with a large herbarium which was later lost in a shipwreck (1815). At the age of thirty-two he came back to America and settled in New York, where he became one of the founders of the Lyceum of Natural History. In 1819 he took a position as professor at Transylvania University, Lexington, Ky., under President Horace Holley. Already he was the author of about 250 pamphlets and articles on natural history, all of which must have meant little to the frontier students in the university, the first institution of higher learning west of the Appalachians. He was a man of peculiar habits and was very eccentric. It is said that he lectured in a most entertaining fashion, to the great delight of his audience, often causing many of the students to laugh heartily. His extreme absent-mindedness and foreign ways made him seem very peculiar.

He was scorned by most of his contemporaries. Even John Torrey, one of the few to appreciate his genius, wrote, "Rafinesque has just started on a three-months expedition . . . you may imagine how many *new* discoveries he will make." Eaton said, "His name is absolutely becoming a substitute for egotism. Even the ladies here often . . . talk of the Science of Rafinesque; meaning the most fulsome and disgusting manner of speaking in one's own praise."

He died alone, in Philadelphia, in abject poverty "surrounded by the hopeless confusion of his precious specimens, and copies of his nine hundred and thirty books and pamphlets." Only a century later did his talents come to be fully appreciated by students of plants of the eastern United States.

It might be appropriate to allow the eccentric, often unhappy scholar to have the last word, as he describes the pleasure of discovering and naming a new species: "This peaceful conquest has cost no tears, but fills your mind with a proud sensation of not being useless on earth, of having detected another link in the creative power of God."

A new period of botanical exploration was now about to be ushered in. The purchase of the Louisiana Territory led to an active period of exploration of the vast unknown region to the west of the Mississippi River. Thomas Nuttall (1786-1859) was the first botanical explorer of western America, traveling, through a period of more than thirty years "to the banks of the Ohio, through the dark forests and brakes of the Mississippi, to the distant lakes of the northern frontier; through the wilds of Florida; far up the Red River and the Missouri, and through the territory of Arkansas; at last . . . across the arid plains of the far west, beyond the steppes of the Rocky Mountains, down the Oregon to the extended shores of the Pacific." He suffered great hardships in his journeys, experiencing fever, hunger, fatigue, and, often, danger from hostile Indians. He collected hundreds of new species, some of which were sent to Candolle for publication, some of which he published himself. His principal work was the botanical classic, *The Genera of North American Plants* (1818). It was said of him that no other North American botanical explorer made more discoveries.

Another botanical explorer of this period, who visited Thomas Nuttall in Philadelphia, was David Douglas. Born in Scotland in 1798, he early developed an interest in botany and enjoyed an intimate friendship with William Jackson Hooker, then professor of botany in Glasgow. In 1823 he was sent by the Horticultural Society of London on a collecting trip to the eastern United States, and in 1824 started on his most famous trip, by ship around Cape Horn to the Oregon country where he landed in April, 1825. The next two years he spent in the wilderness, sleeping on the ground, for weeks never seeing another human being, suffering from exposure and lack of food, from fatigue and sickness. Rain destroyed many of his specimens but never dampened his enthusiasm. When he returned to England he took seeds of many shrubs and perennials, including the red currant (*Ribes sanguineum*), which alone was said to have more than paid for the cost of the expedition (£400). He is credited with having introduced more plants into British gardens than any other individual. The trees, especially, of the region made a deep impression on the explorer. One of them, which he described as "remarkably tall, unusually straight," and which he hoped might become "an important addition to the number of useful timbers" is now called Douglas fir; it is the world's greatest producer of structural timbers (Figure 16). Douglas was also the first to record the sugar pine (*Pinus lambertiana*), which he named for his friend, A. B. Lambert, and he suggested the specific epithets of many other plants, including *Pinus ponderosa.* He made several other collecting trips and died in Hawaii at the age of thirty-six (1834).

Many of the collections of the early Western travelers found their way for study to two botanists whose reputation grew rapidly with the passing years: John Torrey (1796-1873) of Columbia College and Asa Gray (1810-1888) of Harvard. Their association caused the citation "T. & G." to become so familiar that it is today recognized as a standard abbreviation. Their tireless efforts, boundless enthusiasm, and sympathy for students brought about something of a re-enactment, so far as the United States was concerned, of the Linnean Age. The taxonomic aspect of botany became almost an obsession in colleges and universities of the country.

Among botanists whose collections came to the attention of Torrey and Gray were Dr. Edwin James (1797-1861) who first ascended Pikes' Peak, in 1820; George Engelmann (1809-1884), who migrated to St. Louis from

Figure 16. Douglas fir, *Pseudotsuga menziesii*. (U. S. Forest Service.)

Frankfurt-am-Main, and who rode horseback through Illinois, Missouri, Arkansas, and Louisiana, collecting plants; Adolph Wislizenus (1810-1889), a country physician of Illinois, who traveled with a company of immigrants along the Oregon Trail to Oregon Territory, returning through Colorado ("under daily hardships about 3000 miles, had slept on the bare ground in all kinds of weather"); later he explored in Texas and Chihuahua, during the Mexican War, and was interned by the Mexicans; Augustus Fendler (1813-1883), who collected plants from Fort Leavenworth to Santa Fe, in 1846-1847; John Charles Fremont (1813-1890), adventurer, soldier, scientist, who led several expeditions to California before the Mexican War, and who found time in the midst of hardships and danger to collect plant specimens; Charles Wright (1811-1886), who explored in Texas and New Mexico and was employed on the Mexican Boundary Survey; J. M. Bigelow (1804-1878), botanist on Lieutenant A. W. Whipple's expedition "to ascertain the most practicable and economical route for a railroad from the Mississippi River to the Pacific Ocean," in 1853-1854; and many others. Both Torrey and Gray, themselves, in their later years, made visits to the western part of the country. Botanists such as these, and many others, made possible the accumulation of material eventually published as *A Flora of North America . . . , north of Mexico.* This monumental work appeared in seven parts, comprising twelve volumes, between 1838 and 1842. Thereafter Gray gave a great deal of his time to the preparation of his *Synoptical Flora of North America,* the first part of which was published in 1878. He left his name forever associated with the botany of the northeastern states through the publication of his *Manual of Botany* (1848), the 8th edition of which appeared in 1950.

Figure 17. Asa Gray, 1810-1888. (Courtesy Gray Herbarium, Harvard University.)

In Canada, meanwhile, similar explorations were under way. In 1818 Sir John Franklin made the first of his famous exploring trips to Arctic America. As naturalist he had with him Dr. John Richardson (1787-1865). The expedition suffered great hardships from the extreme cold and starvation. The Arctic coast around the Coppermine River was explored and the party traveled overland to Hudson Bay in 1822 before returning to England. In 1825 Franklin and Richardson were back again and Richardson followed the coast from the Mackenzie to the Coppermine rivers. Franklin's last expedition, with 128 men, set out from England in 1845 and perished on King William Island in 1847, without leaving a single survivor. Expedition after expedition was sent in search of them, including one by Dr. Richardson in 1848 but it was not until 1859 that the relics and records of the expedition were found.

The name of John Macoun (1832-1920) is one of the most familiar in the history of Canadian botany. His *Catalogue of Canadian Plants* was published in three parts, Part One in 1883, Part Two in 1884, and Part

Three in 1886. Previous to that time he had explored southern Canada from the Atlantic to the Pacific, traveling in the prairie region in 1872, Vancouver Island and British Columbia to the western slopes of the Rockies in 1875, again in the prairie region and to the alpine summit of the Rockies in 1879, to the Peace River Valley in 1880-1881.

South America. The discovery of America, and the "Joyfull Newes" of delectable foods, spices, strange fruits, and marvelous drugs (and especially gold) caused the greatest mass hysteria in Europe since the days of the Crusades. Expeditions set out almost daily and those who could not go awaited with eager anticipation the gifts the New World would have to offer. South America, however, was under the control of Spain and Portugal and became a sort of forbidden land for explorers of other nations. Not until 1735 were the naturalists of other European countries allowed to see the wonders of tropical America.

On May 16, 1735, Charles-Marie de La Condamine (1701-1774) set out from France at the head of a scientific expedition sponsored by the Académie des Sciences. Joseph de Jussieu, brother of Antoine and Bernard (page 41), went along as botanist. The expedition landed in November at Cartagena, where they saw papayas, cherimoyas, groves of cacao trees, and the pineapple, which they felt well repaid them for the hardships of the journey. From Cartagena they sailed to Porto Bello and crossed the Isthmus of Panama through deep forests of buttressed trees knit together by a tangle of lianas; especially common was the tall, smooth-barked tree (*Sterculia*) called by the Indians *panamá,* which had given its name to the region. Early the next year they sailed down the West Coast to Ecuador. Through the rain, they crossed the hot coastal forests and ascended the Andes to the high páramos above timber line, coming at last to Quito. Hindered by the suspicions of the Indians and Spanish colonials, they carried on triangulation work at the equator. Joseph de Jussieu's entire collection of Andean plants, the results of grueling labor, was destroyed through the ignorance of a servant; Jussieu lost his reason and never fully regained it as long as he lived. At last, his mission accomplished, Condamine, leaving Jussieu behind, returned to Europe by way of the Amazon Valley. Here, in the vast unexplored forests he found the Indians intoxicating fish by throwing a plant into the water and became the first European discoverer of barbasco, the source of rotenone; he saw them shooting game with arrows dipped in curare; he stopped to investigate the rubber plant and carried samples of rubber articles with him to Europe, where he arrived early in 1745, after ten years in South America.

José Celestino Mutis (1732-1808), of Cadiz, Spain, a correspondent with Linnaeus, went to Bogotá in 1760 as a teacher of mathematics and astronomy, causing great excitement by expounding the principle that the earth revolved around the sun, a teaching regarded by many as heretical. In 1783 Mutis was appointed as director of the famous Expedición Botanica, charged with studying the plants of Northern South America from the equator to the Caribbean Sea. While the task was of such vast proportions that it could not be completed on the scale that had been planned, the botanical results were of great importance and at the death of Mutis there had been accumulated many manuscripts on plants, a herbarium of 20,000 specimens, and thousands of pictures of plants, most of which were later taken to the Madrid Botanical Garden. Far from being a mere "Expedición," the organization became a scientific institute and a center of learning.

About the same time another famous Expedición Botanica was engaged in the exploration of Peru and Chile. This expedition was in charge of the Spanish botanists, Hipolito Ruiz (1754-1815) and José Pavon (? -1844). They were in Peru from 1778 to 1788 except for a year and a half passed in Chile (1782-1783). In Peru they explored along the coast and repeatedly crossed the Andes to collect on the moist eastern slopes as far as Huanuco, Tarma, and Huancayo. In Chile they collected mostly around Concepción, but also about Santiago and Valparaiso. They had many disasters and lost much of what they gathered in fire and shipwreck but enough remained to form the basis of numerous works, including their *Florae peruvianae et chilensis* (1798-1802).

Alexander von Humboldt (1769-1859) landed in Cumaná, Venezuela, on the fifteenth of July, 1799. The son of a French mother and a German father, he had been educated in Germany. One of his favorite books was the story of Condamine's travels. He had met Joseph de Jussieu, who had returned to France in 1779, after forty-five years in the Andes, still wandering in his mind, but nevertheless able to instill an enthusiasm for South America. He had with him on his journey to America his close friend, Aimé Bonpland, a botanist who had studied under Antoine-Laurent de Jussieu. In Venezuela they drank milk from the cow-tree (*Brosimum galactodendron*) and noted that one Negro, after drinking too much, vomited rubber balls! Near the river Casiquiare, which they found joined the Orinoco and the Amazon River valleys, they saw the almost fabulous Mount Duida, "a mountain that presents one of the grandest spectacles in the natural scenery of the tropical world." In 1801 they arrived in Cartagena and ascended the Magdalena on the way to Bogotá, where they visited José Celestino Mutis, celebrated director of the Expedición Botanica. Francisco José de Caldas (1770-1816), the most promising pupil of Mutis, went along as the explorers continued toward Quito, passing through Popayán, where years later would be erected a monument to Caldas, who was executed by a Spanish firing squad during the Revolution, with the words, "Spain has no need of savants." The trip to Quito, over wind-swept páramos, was filled with terrible experiences, but in January 1802 they reached the land Condamine had explored. The party attempted the ascent of Chimborazo, giving up 3000 feet below its summit; Humboldt, the rest of his life, felt that "of all mortals I was the one who had risen highest in all the world." Finally they reached the Pacific on the arid coast of Peru. In an effort to determine why rain did not fall, though the days were continually clouded, Humboldt discovered the cold ocean current offshore that today bears his name. From Lima they took ship in 1803 for Acapulco and after an eleven-month exploration of Mexico, left for Cuba. Here he found a letter from Thomas Jefferson, inviting him to the United States, and the explorers spent three weeks at Monticello. The return to Europe in 1804 was a great triumph. Humboldt was hailed as the "second discoverer of America" and Bonpland's vast collection of dried plants formed the basis for *Plantae aequinoctiales* (1805-1818), followed in 1815-1825 by a seven-volume descriptive work, *Nova genera et species plantarum* . . . , with the collaboration of Karl Sigismund Kunth (1788-1850); this is one of the great classics of American botany. Citations to the many new species described therein are commonly abbreviated "HBK."

In 1844, Richard Spruce (1817-1893), of Yorkshire, went to Kew Gardens to meet Sir William Hooker and George Bentham to talk about a way to get to South America on a botanizing expedition. He had read and been inspired by Darwin's *Voyage of the Beagle,* as Darwin had been inspired by Humboldt, who, in turn, had been inspired by Condamine. Bentham suggested that he could finance the expedition himself by collecting and selling specimens, and offered to advance him a sum on account. After a few years of preparation, during which time he looked over the animal collections being sent back by Alfred Wallace and Henry Bates from the Amazon, he set out for Brazil in 1849; he did not see England again for fifteen years. He landed at Pará and set out by vessel up the Amazon. He was about to lay the foundation of our knowledge of the botany of this great valley. "Fancy if you can," he wrote, "two million square miles of forest. . . . The largest river in the world flows through the largest forest. . . . Here our grasses are bamboos, sixty or more feet high . . . violets are the size of apple trees." At Santarém he met Wallace and Bates, and spent a year collecting. He found cashews, palms, jacarandas, Brazil-nuts, and sent back to Sir William Hooker valuable information concerning rubber trees. In 1850 he continued up the river, coming at last to Manáos, where the dark waters of the Río Negro enter the yellow waters of the Solimoes. Here he spent eleven months, collecting and preparing for a journey up the Río Negro, setting out near the end of 1851. Day after day the small vessel ascended the river, through the unbroken lines of forest, bedecked with countless flowers. At last rapids began to interrupt the smooth waters of the stream. At a stopping place, Spruce sent back another shipment of plants; he was already becoming famous in the botanical institutions of Europe; Humboldt himself inspected some of the specimens. At the mouth of the Uaupes he came upon his friend, Wallace, very ill with malaria; with Spruce's care he recovered and was able to set out downstream. In the fall of 1852 he ascended the Uaupes, a succession of paddling and portaging. He found the coca plant and sent it to Europe, where it aided in the isolation of cocaine. He also found ipecac and often used it to combat dysentery. In 1853 he came to San Carlos, at the mouth of the Casiquiare, ascending the river to Mount Duida. Going down the Orinoco he was stricken by malaria and for thirty-eight days his life hung in the balance. He did not die and at last he was able to start the return trip to Manáos, reaching that city in 1854, after an absence of four years, to find it in the pandemonium of a great rubber boom. Unwittingly, Spruce, through his own studies, had helped bring the boom about.

Figure 18. Richard Spruce, 1817-1893. (Courtesy New York Botanical Garden.)

Spruce now set out by steamship (March 14, 1855) up the Solimoes to Iquitos. Fifty miles above the town he again took to the open canoe for the ascent of the Huallaga. In the little village of Tarapoto, Peru, at 1500 feet elevation, he made his headquarters for two years, collecting and sketching, regaining his health, befriending the courteous people. These days, he said, were "the most agreeably placed . . . in my South American wanderings." Here he received instructions from the British government to proceed to Ecuador to procure seeds and plants of the quinine tree to be grown in India. The trip was made up the Río Pastaza, the worst traveling he had in South America. At Banos, at the foot of the volcano Tunguragua, the thermometer was 48° F.; after his years in the tropics, he found the cold almost unbearable. Approaching Ambato he crossed the páramos in a piercingly cold driving rain. He established himself in Ambato near the end of 1858 and began to search for the "red bark" tree (*Cinchona*). The Ecuadorians met with suspicion Spruce's proposal to visit the cloud forests where the quinine grew, but at last he was able to secure 600 plants and over 100,000 ripe seeds. These were established in the British possessions in India. After three more years of collecting on the Peruvian coast, he took ship and returned to England in 1864. Unlike Humboldt, Spruce had no welcoming committee, nor did his return attract any great attention, except on the part of such men as Bentham, J. D. Hooker, Wallace, and Darwin, and he spent the remainder of his life in comparative poverty and poor health.

Karl Friedrich Philipp von Martius (1794-1868) arrived in Rio de Janeiro in July 1817 and remained in Brazil until June 1820. He collected widely from Rio de Janeiro to Pará and up the Amazon River to Alto Amazonas. After returning to Germany he started issuing publications on his collections, finally starting work on his comprehensive and monumental *Flora Brasiliensis,* "one of the most sumptuous of floras." The first part appeared in 1829, and, with the aid of many contributing authors, additional parts continued to appear for decades. It was not until 1906, many years after the death of Martius, that the great task was finally completed. Its fifteen folio volumes include more than 20,000 pages, 3805 plates, and account for 22,767 species.

Africa. The other tropical lands were similarly explored by enthusiastic botanists who risked their lives for the sake of learning. In Africa, the work of Michel Adanson (1727-1806) in the eighteenth century was especially noteworthy. He was a well-educated Frenchman who was acquainted with Bernard de Jussieu, and later with Cuvier. In 1748 he took a modest position with a commercial establishment in Sénégal. Cuvier comments, "The motives of his decision for Sénégal are curious. It is of all the European establishments, the most difficult to penetrate, the hottest and most unhealthy, the most dangerous in all respects, and, as a result, the least known to scientists." He reached Sénégal in May, 1749 and remained for more than four years, making an inventory of the natural resources of the country. He found that most of the plants and animals were unnamed and set out to study and classify them. The matter of establishing their relationships with the plants and animals of Europe was a difficult one in some respects, and it became necessary for him, little by little, to broaden the European systems of classification to accommodate the new organisms he had found in Africa. He corresponded with Jussieu, communicating to him the details of his system and after his return to France he published them in his *Histoire naturelle de Sénégal* (1757) and *Famille des Plantes* (1763). Rarely has the work of taxonomist, explorer, and systematist been so perfectly accomplished by one man.

Friedrich Martin Josef Welwitsch (1807-1872) was born in Carinthia but went to Portugal in 1839 and spent many years in studying the botany of that country and its colonies. In 1853 he went to Luanda, Angola, and explored the coastal region between the Quizembo and the Cuanza rivers. In 1854 he ascended the river Bengo to Golungo Alto, where he met David Livingstone, and spent some time with him. In all, he spent two years in the dense jungle before traveling to Pungo Andango and then returning to Luanda, having collected over 3200 species of plants. In 1859 he went to Benguela and in the desert near Cape Negro discovered the remarkable plant which has been given his name (*Welwitschia*). Hiern, his biographer, relates: "The sensations of the enthusiastic discoverer, when he first realized the extraordinary character of the plant he had found, were as he has said, so overwhelming that he could do nothing but kneel down on the burning soil and gaze at it, half in fear lest a touch should prove it a figment of the imagination." Asa Gray called this "the most wonderful discovery, in a botanical point of view," of the nineteenth century. Welwitsch returned to Lisbon in 1861, bringing with him what has been called the best and most extensive herbarium ever collected in tropical Africa.

Figure 19. ***Welwitschia mirabilis.*** **(Photograph by R. J. Rodin.)**

The flora of South Africa was studied by many early botanists, because the Cape of Good Hope was an important stopping place on voyages to the Orient, and because the plant life there was found to be of such a fascinating nature. Linnaeus, in his *Flora Capensis* (1759), the first book on South African botany, states, "African plants, especially from the Cape, have a rough appearance . . . so that learned botanists in gardens can distinguish at a glance African plants from others."

Lieutenant William Paterson (1755-1810) made numerous exploring trips in South Africa between 1777 and 1779, traveling by ox-wagon. On his first trip he crossed the Lange Bergen into the Great Karroo and was amazed at the change in the country, characterized by an abundance of curious species of *Mesembryanthemum.* On a second journey, in 1778, he reached the Orange River not far from its mouth, noting in the region huge Kokerbooms (*Aloë dichotoma*) twelve feet in circumference and twenty feet high. On the return trip he discovered, near the Bokkeveld Mountains, the interesting elephant's foot (*Testudinaria elephantipes*), the root of which was eaten by the natives. A third trip, in 1779, took him back to the Orange River, somewhat farther inland; here he found the beautiful *Pachypodium namaquanus* and noted the great abundance of Mimosa (*Acacia*) and its production of a gum used by the natives as food. It was said of him, disparagingly, that he "thought more of botanical collections than of extending the cords of British sovereignty."

William John Burchell (1782-1863) was another of the founders of South African botany, traveling there foı several years (1811-1815) with no other companions than Hottentots, covering about 4500 miles through regions "never before trodden by European foot," accumulating a collection of 63,000 objects of natural history and making about 500 drawings of landscapes, plants, and so forth. His travels were made by ox-wagon, the oxen "sometimes encouraged by good words, at other times terrified into exertion by the blows of the shambok, the loud crack of the whip, the smart of its lash, or the whoop and noisy clamouı of the boor and his Hottentots." Near the Roggeveld Mountains he became entangled in a hookthorn bush he was attempting to collect with the result that two of his men had to assist him to freedom: "In revenge for this ill-treatment, I determined to give the tree a name which should serve to caution future travelers against allowing themselves to venture within its clutches." The name he gave was *Acacia detinens* (detaining). Crossing the Orange River he reached Griquatown and made numerous botanizing trips in its environs, noting particularly the red-leaf (*Terminalia erythrophylla*), with beautiful autumnal coloration, the wit-gat boom (*Boscia albitrunca,* of the Capparidaceae), its trunks appearing as if whitewashed, and the remarkable *Elephantorrhiza elephantina* (Leguminosae), its roots a favorite food of elephants.

Another botanical explorer of South Africa was James Bowie (? -1853), a Kew gardener, who arrived at Cape Town in 1817 and spent the years until 1823 in long journeys. His name is commemorated by the curious *Bowiea.* It was said of him that he enriched the gardens of Europe with a greater variety of succulent plants than did any other man.

Australia. The botanical excursions of Cook, Banks, Solander, and Brown in Australia have already been noted. In 1817 Allan Cunningham (1791-1839) arrived at Sydney as a collector for the Kew Gardens. During that year he traveled about 1200 miles in New South Wales, collecting 450 species of plants. Returning to Sydney he accompanied an exploring expedition to the northern and northwestern coasts, spending the four years from 1818 to 1822 in that region, collecting many interesting plants. Subsequently he investigated the flora of Illawarra and the Blue Mountains. In 1836, after an absence of six years, he returned to Australia as Colonial Botanist and Director of the Botanic Gardens at Sydney.

In 1831 Sir Thomas Mitchell (1792-1855), then Surveyor-General of New South Wales, made expeditions into the interior of eastern Australia and into tropical Australia in the neighborhood of the Gulf of Carpentaria. Among notable plants he discovered were the Australian capertree (*Capparis mitchellii*), calomba (*Trigonella suavissima*), bottle-tree (*Brachychiton rupestris*), and batwing coraltree (*Erythrina vespertilio*).

Baron Sir Ferdinand Jakob Heinrich von Müller (1825-1896), of Rostock, Germany, emigrated to Australia in 1847, when threatened with tuberculosis. He began doing botanical work in South Australia, while working as a chemist, and in 1852, at the suggestion of Sir Joseph Hooker, he was appointed as first Government Botanist for Victoria. During that year he traveled about 1500 miles, to Beechworth, the Buffalo Mountains, Mount Buller, and the head of the Latrobe River. The next year he explored the Grampian Mountains, thence to the junction of the Murray and Darling rivers and then through the Australian Alps to the Snowy River, returning to Melbourne after traveling 2500 miles. A third great exploration took him through the Dandenong ranges to the Latrobe River, thence to the Avon River and Mount Wellington and on to Omeo and Mount Kosciusko, returning via Buchan and Cabbage Tree Creek to Melbourne, about 1000 miles. These expeditions added about 1000 species to the known flora of Australia. With such material at his disposal he began to think of publishing a work on the plants of Australia and eventually did collaborate with George Bentham in his great *Flora Australiensis* (1863-1878). Audas states that no one since Robert Brown had done so much for the advancement of Australian botany.

India. The Portuguese were the first Europeans to come to India and the first to begin the modern study of Indian plants. The first book concerning Indian flora published was in 1563 by Garcia d'Orta, entitled *Coloquios dos Simples e Drogas da India,* containing descriptions of a large number of drug plants. The next, *Tractado de las Drogas,* was by C. Acosta in 1578.

One of the earliest works of great scientific value was by Hendrik van Rheede (1660-1699), the Dutch governor of Malabar, an amateur botanist, who made a large collection of Indian plants about 1676 and published descriptions of them in the *Hortus Indicus Malabaricus,* of thirteen folio volumes and 794 plates; this was issued at Amsterdam in 1670-1703, under the editorship of Jan Commelyn. Other notable contributions were by John Burman (1707-1779), *Thesaurus Zeylanicus* (plants of Ceylon and peninsular India), in 1737; by Paul Hermann (1646-1695) whose collection of Ceylon plants was treated by Linnaeus in 1747 as *Flora Zeylanica;* and by Nicholaus Burman, whose *Flora Indica* appeared in 1768.

John Gerard Koenig (1728-1785), a Danish botanist, arrived in India in 1768. To promote the study of Indian botany he formed a society called "The United Brothers." Members of the brotherhood exchanged specimens among themselves and sent plants to Europe for study. In this way many Indian plants came to be described by A. J. Retz, A. W. Roth, H. A. Schrader, and other eminent botanists.

As noted elsewhere (p. 125), the Royal Botanic Gardens were founded at Calcutta in 1787 and Lieutenant Colonel Robert Kyd (1746-1793) became the first superintendent. After Kyd's death William Roxburgh (1751-1815) succeeded him. He has been described as "the Linnaeus of India." His first contribution was *The Plants of the Coast of Coromandel* (1795, 1798, 1819) in three folio volumes, with about 300 colored plates. His *Flora Indica,* issued in 1820-1824, was a monumental work in which a systematic account of Indian plants was presented for the first time. He left admirable colored drawings of 2533 plants native to India. Dr. Francis Buchanan (1762-1829) succeeded Roxburgh in 1814; he had made extensive tours in Nepal (1802) and elsewhere but returned to England in 1815; his collections were described by D. Don in 1825, in his *Prodromus Florae Nepalensis.* Nathaniel Wallich (1786-1854) was superintendent of the Gardens from 1815 to 1835; he organized collecting expeditions to Nepal, western Hindustan, Lower Burma, and made vast collections which were studied by Candolle, Kunth, Lindley, Bentham, and others. Wallich himself prepared a catalogue of the collections, published 1828-1849 and known to the botanical world as *Wall. Cat.* (Wallich, *Catalogue of Dried Specimens . . .*), listing 9148 species. In 1830, 1831, and 1832 he published his great *Plantae Asiaticae Rariores* (three vols., folio). Robert Wight (1796-1872) was active in investigation, chiefly of the Peninsular flora, during this period, and published a part of his work as *Icones Plantarum Indiae Orientalis* (six vols., 1838-1853), containing figures and descriptions of 2101 Indian plants. During his thirty-five years in India he described nearly 3000 species of Indian plants.

William Griffith (1810-1845) spent thirteen years in India and went on numerous long expeditions, to the Assam Valley, Burma, Bhutan, Sikkim, Central India, and Malacca. He collected 9000 species and described them in manuscripts published after his death. Between 1842 and 1847 Thomas Thomson (1817-1878) collected the flora of the Punjab and during 1847-1849 that of the Himalayas and Tibet. These collections were transferred to Kew and incorporated in the preparation of Joseph Dalton Hooker's *Flora of British India* (1876-1897).

Hooker himself visited in India in 1847-1851 and explored Sikkim and the Khasia Hills with his friend Dr. Thomson. In the Himalayas he discovered the magnificent rhododendrons of that region and prepared a monograph on them (1849).

Southeastern Asia. One of the most zealous explorers of the southeastern Asiatic flora in the eighteenth century was Juan de Loureiro (1715-1796). He was a Jesuit missionary of Portugal who located at Hue, Cochin China, in 1742 and gained so much influence that he eventually came to hold a position in the court of the king. He had a slight knowledge of medicine and searched for medicinal plants, thereby studying the flora of the country and accumulating a good herbarium, despite the fact that he was not a professional botanist. In 1780 he went to Canton and there continued his botanical studies for three years. Foreigners at that time were not permitted to travel beyond their stations, but he was able to hire a Chinese peasant who had some knowledge of medicinal plants to make collections for him, and to communicate to him the common names of the plants. These he was able to check in a good Chinese book on botany. In 1781 he sailed from Canton, stopping for three months on the island of Mozambique for further collecting before his return to Portugal. In 1790 he published his botanical work, *Flora Cochinchinensis,* in two volumes with a total of 744 pages, in which 1300 species were described, 630 of them new to science.

Karl Ludwig Blume (1796-1862) went to Java in 1817 as a physician in the Dutch service. His inquiries into native medicines led to a study of the plants of the region and he made a large botanical collection. About 1822 he was made director of the Botanical Garden at Buitenzorg, a post he held until 1826. He published in 1825-1826 his *Bijdragen tot de Flora van Nederlandsch Indië.*

One of the most thrilling discoveries in the history of botanical exploration was made near Bencoolen (Bangkahulu), Sumatra, in 1818. Sir Stamford Raffles (1781-1826), governor of the East India Company's establishments in Sumatra, later the founder of Singapore, was making his first journey into the interior, accompanied by Dr. Joseph Arnold, a distinguished naturalist. Dr. Arnold relates the discovery as follows: "But here I rejoice to tell you I happened to meet with what I consider as the greatest prodigy of the vegetable world. I had ventured some way from the party, when one of the Malay servants came running to me with wonder in his eyes, and said, 'Come with me, Sir, come! A flower; very large, beautiful, wonderful!' I immediately went with the man about a hundred yards in the jungle, and he pointed to a flower growing close to the ground under the bushes, which was truly astonishing. . . . I soon detached it and removed it to our hut. To tell you the truth, had I been alone, and had there been no witnesses, I should I think have been fearful of mentioning the dimensions of this flower, so much does it exceed every flower I have ever seen or heard of. . . . When I first saw it a swarm of flies were hovering over the mouth of the nectary. . . . It had precisely the smell of tainted beef. . . . Now for the dimensions, which are the most astonishing part of the flower. It measured a full yard across . . . and the weight of this prodigy we calculated to be fifteen pounds. . . . A guide from the interior of the country said, that such flowers were rare, but that he had seen several, and that the natives called them *Krubut* (Great Flower)." In honor of the two discoverers, Robert Brown named the Great Flower *Rafflesia arnoldi.*

Figure 20. ***Rafflesia arnoldi.*** **(Adapted from Figuier.)**

The Philippines. Pierre Sonnerat (1745-1814) was the first visitor to the Philippine Islands for the specific purpose of conducting research in natural history. The earliest great botanical collection was by Hugh Cuming, in 1836 to 1840; he collected 2200 numbers in the Philippines, with many duplicates that were widely distributed. M. Blanco published the first edition of his *Flora de Filipinas* in 1837, with a second edition in 1845 and a third, in four volumes, in 1877-1883. This last edition lists 4479 species for the Islands, but the work is not regarded as very trustworthy.

In 1902, after the American occupation, Elmer Drew Merrill (1876-) arrived in Manila as botanist of the Bureau of Agriculture, remaining until 1923. During this period remarkable botanical progress was made. A herbarium of 250,000 mounted specimens was accumulated, and 400,000 duplicates were distributed. The list of known Philippine species of flowering plants was extended from less than 2500 to 8120, while approximately 1000 species of lower vascular plants are known. Dr. Merrill himself described hundreds of new species.

China. After the travels of the memorable Marco Polo, China was for a long time forgotten in Europe and when the Portuguese arrived there, in 1516, it was regarded as a new discovery. Little was done for many years to acquire a knowledge of the general plant life of China and the first noteworthy European collector was James Cunningham, English naturalist and surgeon in the service of the East India Company at Amoy. He first went to China in 1698 and made a second voyage in 1700. He distributed his rich herbarium among his friends, including Leonard Plukenet (1642-1706), whose *Amaltheum Botanicum* (1705) contains descriptions of about 400 Chinese plants, most of them from Cunningham's collections.

Figure 21. Elmer Drew Merrill. (Foto Cuatrecasas.)

Around the middle of the century the Jesuit missionary, Pierre d'Incarville (1706-1757), sent interesting collections of plants of the Peking region to his *maître en botanique,* Bernard de Jussieu. Incarville joined the Chinese mission in 1740 and died in Peking seventeen years later. In his honor A. L. de Jussieu named the genus *Incarvillea* (Bignoniaceae), a beautiful scarlet-flowered plant of northern China. Among interesting plants introduced into the gardens of Europe by Incarville was *Ailanthus altissima.*

The travels and explorations of Robert Fortune (1812-1880) introduced a new era in the botanical history of China. He was sent by the Royal Horticultural Society to China in 1843 for the purpose of securing living plants, seeds, and herbarium specimens. In all, he visited China four times between 1843 and 1861 and explored widely in the provinces of Fukien, Chekiang, and Anhwei. His notes on Chinese plants and Chinese gardening possess a high interest. Among plants he introduced to Europe were bleeding-heart, Chinese cabbage, various camellias, kumquat (*Fortunella*), and numerous azaleas.

Another man who deserves a foremost place among the botanical explorers of China was Henry Fletcher Hance (1827-1890). He first arrived at Hong Kong when he was seventeen years old and resided there for many years in the service of the British government. In 1861 he was established at Whampoa, near Canton, where he lived for a quarter of a century and wrote the greatest part of his numerous papers on Chinese plants. Long before his death he had attained a world-wide reputation as an eminent botanist and his private herbarium eventually included over 22,000 specimens.

Francis Blackwell Forbes, an American, resided in China from 1857 to 1874 and from 1877 to 1882. He made important collections of Chinese plants and collaborated with William Botting Hemsley, of Kew, in the preparation of the *Index Florae Sinensis,* the first part of which appeared in 1886, the last in 1905.

Pére Armand David (1826-1900) contributed eminently to our knowledge of the natural history of Asia. In 1862-1865 he botanized extensively in northern China, while a Lazarist missionary, and in 1866 made a long exploring trip in South Mongolia. In 1868 he passed through Central Asia to Chungking, and finally reached the eastern border of Tibet, where he discovered (in 1869) the curious tree now called *Davidia involucrata.* Early in 1870 he came back to China and from 1872 to 1874 he traveled widely, from Peking through Honan, Shensi, and Hanchung to Hankow, thence into Kiangsi and then to Shanghai. He estimated that on his various trips he collected about 3000 species.

Augustine Henry (1875-1930) was one of the most successful of the explorers of the Chinese flora. He went to China in British customs service in 1881, remaining until 1900. He lived at Ichang, in Hupeh province, from 1882 to 1889, and in this region, botanically unknown, he made an enormous collection, extremely rich in new species. Later he collected in other parts of China, and in 1896 went to Mentze, Yunnan province, another very rich and interesting field for botanical exploration. He introduced to gardens *Lilium henryi* and other Chinese plants.

One of the most remarkable botanical discoveries of the twentieth century was made in China in 1941 by T. Kan, a Chinese botanist, at Mou-tao-Chi, in Szechuan province. Prof. Kan found a large deciduous conifer which was called by the natives *shui-sa* (water-fir). Specimens were later collected and identified by H. H. Hu as belonging to the fossil genus *Metasequoia,* recently described from Japan. Less than 1000 trees were found and the larger ones were being cut for wood, so that the tree was apparently on the verge of extinction. It is one of the few examples of a genus known first from fossils, later discovered to be represented by living individuals; these well deserve the title of "living fossils."

Central and Northern Asia. During the first half of the seventeenth century the whole of northern Asia, from the Urals to the sea of Okhotsk, was conquered by Russia, and gradually adjoining regions of Central Asia were added. The botanical exploration of this vast region was carried on at first by distinguished German naturalists in the Russian service.

Daniel Gottlieb Messerschmidt (1685-1730) was the first botanist to explore Siberia. It is said that Peter the Great, while visiting in Germany in 1716, asked for the assistance of an able naturalist to explore the natural resources of his empire and the name of Messerschmidt was proposed. He went to St. Petersburg in 1719 and from 1720 to 1727 traveled in Siberia, making vast collections. He also visited Mongolia and explored in the region of the Dalai Nor (lake) in western Manchuria.

Alexander von Bunge (1803-1890) was born at Kiev and studied botany at Dorpat (now Tartu, Estonia) under Carl Friedrich von Ledebour, author of the *Flora Rossica* (1842-1853). In 1826 he accompanied Ledebour and Carl Anton Meyer on an expedition to the Altai Mountains, an expedition that resulted in the publication of Ledebour's *Flora Altaica* (1829-1833), in which the genus *Halogeton* was first described. He remained for some time in Kolyvan and later transferred to Zmeinogorsk. In 1829 he met Alexander von Humboldt on his expedition to Siberia. In 1830 he was appointed botanist on a mission sent by the Academy of St. Petersburg to China; the mission proceeded to Urga, crossed the Gobi desert and finally arrived at Peking. In 1831 he botanized around Kalgan, in Mongolia, and in northern China, collecting several hundred specimens. He passed the winter in Irkutsk and then, in 1832, explored the eastern part of the Altai Mountains before returning to St. Petersburg. In 1836 Ledebour retired and Bunge succeeded him at Dorpat, which post he held until his retirement in 1867. Among his writings was his *Enumeratio Plantarum Chinae Borealis* (1832).

Another botanist who explored in this region was Porphyri Yevdokimovich Kirilov (1801-1864), who accompanied Bunge in 1830 on his mission to China and thereafter spent more than ten years in Peking, investigating the flora of the adjacent region. He secured a specimen of *Panax schinseng* from Manchuria, said to be still the only herbarium specimen of this famous plant, from its wild state.

Nikolai Stepanovich Turczaninov (1796-1863) studied at the University of Kharkov and early took a strong interest in botany. From 1828 to 1836 he explored the mountainous areas about Lake Baikal, as far as the border of China. In 1833 he became the first botanist to collect along the Amur River and there discovered *Lespedeza bicolor.* His great work, *Flora Baicalensi-Dahuria,* appeared in 1842-1856.

One of the most famous of the botanical explorers of Central and Eastern Asia was Carl Maximowicz (1827-1891). He was born at Tula and was educated at St. Petersburg and at Dorpat, where he studied botany under Bunge. In 1853 he was sent by the Botanical Garden at St. Petersburg as a botanical collector to the Amur valley and after his return wrote *Primitiae Florae Amurensis* (1859). In 1859 he was again sent to Eastern Asia, traveling by way of Irkutsk to Blagoveshchensk and the mouth of the Sungari River. Early in 1860 he arrived in Khabarovsk and then visited various ports along the Manchurian coast. Later that year he went to Japan, collecting extensively in the vicinity of Hakodate, and sending to St. Petersburg about 800 specimens of Japanese plants. Later he collected in many other parts of Japan and returned by ship to St. Petersburg in 1864 with seventy-two chests of herbarium specimens, 300 kinds of seeds and 400 living plants.

The illustrious explorer, Nicolai Mikhailovitch Przewalski (1839-1888), made numerous expeditions into Central Asia, visiting Mongolia and the Tangut country in 1870-1873, crossing the Tien-shan Mountains from Kuldja to Lob Nor in 1876-1877, traveling from Zaisan, at the Tarbagatai frontier, to Tibet and the upper waters of the Yellow River, in 1879-1880; while in his fourth great journey, in 1883-1885, he crossed the Gobi desert from Urga to Koko Nor, Lob Nor, and the Khotan River. Many interesting new plants were collected on these trips.

Vladimir Leontievich Komarov (1869-1946) of St. Petersburg traveled extensively in Asiatic Russia, particularly in eastern Siberia. In 1895-1897 he made an expedition into Manchuria, where the new Manchurian railway was being surveyed, and also into Korea. During these journeys he collected about 6000 specimens, including some 1300 species, many of them new to science. The fruits of this labor appeared as the *Flora of Manchuria* (three vols., 1901-1907) and the *Flora of Kamchatka* (1927-1930). He had the idea of preparing a vast flora of China and Mongolia, but, while publishing many monographs toward it, was not able to bring it to completion.

Conclusion. Exploration for plants still continues: local exploration leading to the writing of local floras; museum or university exploration in the preparation of regional floras; exploration in connection with monographic work; exploration for economic plants such as rubber, quinine, small fruits and grains. Outstanding among recent or contemporary plant explorers are Ernest H. Wilson (1876-1930), who introduced into cultivation more than 1500 species, mostly from China; Joseph F. Rock (1884-), who has collected widely in Burma, Assam, Siam, China, and Tibet; George Forrest (1873-1932) who collected over 30,000 specimens in China and Tibet; Niels Ebbesen Hansen (1866-), agricultural explorer for the United States government and the Soviet government in Russia, Transcaucasia, Siberia, China, and Turkestan; Merritt Lyndon Fernald (1873-1950), explorer and student of the systematic and geographic botany of eastern North America, especially from Virginia to Newfoundland; Alf Erling Porsild (1901-), student of Arctic botany, member of exploring expeditions to Alaska, Northern Canada, Greenland, and Lapland; Nicholas Polunin (1909-), who has explored extensively in Lapland, Spitzbergen, Greenland, and the Canadian Arctic; F. Kingdon-Ward (1885-), who explored extensively in China and Tibet, spending perhaps more time in the field than any other plant explorer; Reginald Farrer (1880-1920), who explored in

Burma and died there; David Fairchild (1869-1954), who collected in many parts of the world, mostly for the U. S. Department of Agriculture; Joseph Clemens (1862-1936) and his wife, Mary Strong Clemens, who botanized extensively in the Philippine Islands, Borneo, New Guinea, and neighboring regions; Francis Raymond Fosberg (1908-   ) and Harold St. John (1892-   ), who have explored the Pacific islands.

References

Audas, J. W., *The Australian Bushland.* North Melbourne, 1950.

Bretschneider, E., *History of European Botanical Discoveries in China.* London, 1898.

Brown, R., *An account of a new genus of plants, named* Rafflesia. Transactions of the Linnean Society 13: 201-234, 1822.

Call, R. E., *Life and writings of Rafinesque.* Louisville, 1895.

Ewan, J., *Frederick Pursh (1774-1820) and his botanical associates.* Proc. Amer. Phil. Soc. 96: No. 5, Oct., 1952.

Hagen, V. W. von, *South America called them. Explorations of the great naturalists.* New York, 1945.

Hiern, W. P., *Catalogue of the African plants collected by Dr. Welwitsch.* Part I. London, 1896.

Hutchinson, J., *A botanist in southern Africa.* London, 1946.

Jackson, B. D., *Linnaeus, the story of his life, adapted from the Swedish of T. M. Fries.* London, 1923.

Jenkins, C. F., *Asa Gray and his quest for* Shortia galacifolia. Arnoldia 2: 13-28, 1942.

Merrill, E. D., *An interpretation of Rumphius'* Herbarium Amboinense. Bur. of Sci. Publ. 9. Manila, 1917.

Peattie, D. C., *Green Laurels. The lives and achievements of the great naturalists.* New York, 1936.

Pennell, F. W., *Thomas Nuttall.* Bartonia 18: 1-51, 1936; 19: 51-54, 1938.

Pulteney, R., *Historical and biographical sketches of the progress of botany in England.* London, 1790.

Rodgers, A. D., *John Torrey, A story of North American botany.* Princeton, 1942.

———, *American Botany. 1873-1892.* Princeton, 1944.

Spruce, R., *Notes of a botanist on the Amazon and Andes . . .* London, 1908.

5

The Origin of Species

As has been noted, taxonomists through the centuries have been eminently successful in describing species, in exploring widely for the discovery of new species, in collecting material from all parts of the world, in distinguishing and naming groups of species, in drawing ever finer distinctions between species. In the earlier days species were regarded as static entities; Linnaeus ably presented this concept when he said (in 1751): "We number so many species as were created of diverse form in the beginning." Thus all the scientist had to do was to discover, as Mann (1952) puts it, "where God had drawn the line." Then, she adds, "over this mild landscape swept the tornado of evolution bringing a nightmarish fluidity, a welter of similar yet dissimilar forms, a distressing lack of separateness."

The New Systematics. "To hope for the new systematics," Julian Huxley remarks, "is to imply no disrespect for the old." Taxonomy had simply come to the point where it had to find new principles to "enable it to cope with the vast burden of its own data." Since 1859 the outlook has completely changed, slowly at first, then with great rapidity; today, instead of being a narrow, highly specialized branch of biology, systematics has become one of the focal points. The story of this change is a fascinating one and worthy of taking its place alongside accounts of the earlier "Heroic Age" of botany.

Mendel. While Darwin was laboring on the production of his great book, *The Origin of Species,* a monk in Brünn, Austria (now Brno, Czechoslovakia), named Gregor Johann Mendel (1822-1884), was engaged in a set of simple experiments concerning garden peas that he grew on the monastery grounds; his results were not regarded as spectacular and his associates must have felt he was wasting his time; nevertheless, his paper, which unlike *The Origin of Species* attracted no attention whatsoever at the time, is now ranked among the great biological classics, and was an approach toward an understanding of the practical aspects of evolution. He noted, for example, that certain distinctive characters of each of the several varieties of peas he studied remained constant from year to year. Some of the peas were higher than his head; some were dwarfs only knee-high. Some were white-flowered; some were red-flowered. On some the flowers were in terminal clusters; on others they were in axillary clusters. On some the pods were yellow, on others they were green. Some pods were inflated, others were constricted between the seeds. Some had all yellow seeds, in others the seeds were all green. In some the seeds were rough, in others they were smooth.

By artificial cross-pollination Mendel made crosses between the varieties, and kept a record of the appearance of all the hybrid plants. No matter how the crosses were made between any two pure-line plants, he found that certain of the characters in the pairs mentioned above dominated the others; for example, the progeny of a tall and a dwarf parent were all tall. When these hybrids bloomed, he allowed them to self-pollinate naturally. Again he kept careful records and planted the seeds the next season. He now noted that the characters were segregated generally in a three-to-one ratio, for example, three tall plants to each one dwarf plant. He further noted that each of the separate pairs of characters was inherited independently of each other. For eight years he continued his experiments, obtaining data on many thousands of progeny. It was evident that these hereditary potentialities must have been carried by certain units of matter which had been transmitted from parent to progeny. But there the matter rested for the time being and Mendel, who apparently lost his interest in botany, died in obscurity.

Figure 22. Gregor Johann Mendel, 1822-1884. (From W. Bateson, *Mendel's Principles of Heredity*, published by the Cambridge University Press. By permission of their American agents, the Macmillan Company.)

Cell Division. Meanwhile, another discovery was announced in 1875, although its connection with Mendel was not realized for many years. Eduard Strasburger (1844-1912), in his *Zellbildung und Zellteilung* for the first time elucidated the curious phenomena associated with cell division in plants, whereby the chromatin of the nucleus was converted into a number of *staves* (named **chromosomes** by W. Waldeyer in 1888).

This process was named **mitosis** by Walther Flemming (1843-1905) in 1882. In this process, it was noted, the nucleus did not merely divide into two equal parts, but became separated into a given number of bodies, the chromosomes. These bodies then appeared to divide lengthwise into two identical halves, one half going into each of the new cells. However, it was observed that in the formation of eggs and sperms, the chromosomes did not split; instead, they assembled in pairs and one of each pair migrated to opposite poles of the cell, to form the nuclei of the gametes, thus leaving only half as many chromosomes in each of the new cells as there were in the parent cell. This process has been named **reduction division** or **meiosis.** In the union of sperm and egg (**fertilization**), the original number of chromosomes becomes re-established.

Beginning of Genetics. In the beginning of the twentieth century three separate European workers in plant heredity, Carl Correns, Hugo deVries, and E. Tschermak, were working on experiments similar to those of Mendel and simultaneously pointed out the agreement between Mendel's observations and their own results. Mendel's name suddenly became one of the best known in biology, his fame competing even with that of Darwin.

In 1902 it occurred simultaneously to W. S. Sutton (1876-1916), a graduate student at Columbia University, and to Theodor Boveri (1862-1915), the great German cytologist, that the behavior of the chromosomes in meiosis and in fertilization resembled in a striking manner the behavior of the "factors" of inheritance, as noted in the experiments of Mendel and others. Upon the assumption that Mendel's "factors" were carried upon chromosomes, the science of **genetics** (from *genesis,* birth or origin) was established. The laws of genetics are, therefore, felt to be true, not because units representing the factors can actually be seen on the chromosomes, but because of the parallelism which is seen to exist between a concrete set of facts (chromosome behavior) and hypotheses advanced to explain another set of facts (dominance, segregation, independent assortment). Thus, the facts of inheritance indicate that factors occur in pairs and that one member of each pair is contributed by one parent of the individual and one by the other parent. This is precisely the case with respect to the chromosomes, as can be observed by actually counting them. Experiments made by Edmund Beecher Wilson (1856-1916), by Thomas Hunt Morgan (1866-1945), and by their students at Columbia University, quickly assembled a vast body of evidence in support of these assumptions. Concerning Morgan it has been said that he "discovered both the aim of this research work and the means of carrying it out, thereby providing the study of heredity with a wealth of material by way of detailed discoveries of far-reaching theoretical application, such as had never been found elsewhere" (Nordenskiold).

Cytogenetics. The known facts of genetics and cytology are now far too numerous to be restated here. Suffice it to say that the **factors** of Mendel are now regarded as located on the chromosomes; since there are far more factors than chromosomes, then each chromosome must bear numerous factors; the units of matter carrying the factors are called **genes.** Chromosomes are normally constant in number for each species. In the common horsetail (*Equisetum arvense*) there are 272 per cell, the largest number known for any plant, while in some fungi there are only four chromosomes per cell. If both genes of a pair (**alleles**) represent identical characters, as tallness, they are **homozygous;** if, on the other hand, one gene represents tallness and the other dwarfness, they are **heterozygous.** The paired chromosomes, bearing the alleles, are **allelomorphic.** The exact manner in which genes influence the development of plants is still far from being understood. Evidently they help bring about some complicated chemical processes in the cells. The gene itself may be a large protein molecule.

The solution of problems of plant relationships may thus be seen to involve the integration of cytology and genetics; the combination of techniques in these two fields is known as **cytogenetics.**

Genotypic Variation. As would be assumed, the factors possessed by a plant species would be "independently assorted" as Mendel found, only if they were carried on separate chromosomes. Those factors on the same chromosome would follow each other into the gametes; in other words, they are **linked.** All the factors in a single chromosome constitute one **linkage group.** However, in some cases, when the pairs of chromosomes are separating into the gametes, they may become so interwoven that they exchange segments with each other. Thus the factors come to be associated somewhat differently; this is called **crossing over.** Other chromosomal changes may also occur, such as loss of a gene or block of genes. Furthermore, there is evidence that the genes themselves are not always exactly duplicated. If a gene is a protein molecule, it might be in the form of a peptide chain, with hundreds of amino acids occupying positions in the chain. Since there are twenty different kinds of amino acids, there would be a very large number of different possible combinations. There is normally an exact duplication of each gene at each chromosome duplication, but it could hardly be expected that such a complex system would always be repeated without a slip. Some slight rearrangement of the amino acids in one gene would result in a change of the character of the gene; it would result in a **mutation,** or change, in the progeny, as compared with the influence that had previously been exerted by that gene.

As pointed out above, the chromosomes exist in *one set* in the gametes, and in *two sets* in the vascular plant itself. The one-set condition is referred to as the **haploid** condition (the n-number), while the two-set condition is the **diploid** (the $2n$-number). Under certain conditions (as, for example, if reduction division should not occur) the plant comes to possess more than two sets of the haploid number. This is **polyploidy.** If each of the chromosome sets has been derived from the same individual, the condition is **autopolyploidy.** This plant would not differ from its diploid ancestor in *kinds* of genes, but only in *number,* and hence is not markedly different morphologically, although sometimes more robust. For instance, if the diploid number is 8, and the chromosomes were doubled in polyploidy, the new number would be 16. Since this is four times the haploid number for that plant, the new individual is called a **tetraploid.** An individual with six times the haploid number would be an **hexaploid,** one with eight times the haploid number would be an **octoploid,** and so on. In many genera the species have related chromosome numbers, often in multiples of a basic number. Various species of *Crepis* in western America, for instance, have chromosome numbers of 22, 33, 44, 55, 77, and 88 in their vegetative cells.

Some polyploids, however, are of hybrid origin; these are called **allopolyploids.** If the haploid gametes of two different species unite, a hybrid plant is produced, but the chromosomes cannot mate in pairs, with the result that the hybrid is usually sterile. But if there should then be a doubling of chromosomes, as in the absence of reduction division, there comes to be a polyploid situation, with allelomorphic pairs of chromosomes and resulting fertility. As an example might be cited the classic case of *Raphanobrassica,* obtained in 1928 by Karpechenko from hybrids between radish, *Raphanus sativus,* and cabbage, *Brassica oleracea.* Both have 18 as the diploid chromosome number, and the offspring of the cross also have 18, nine from the radish and nine from the cabbage. These plants may live normally but at meiosis the chromosomes mostly fail to pair off, since they are not allelomorphic. Hence the gametes degenerate, making the hybrid nearly or quite sterile. However, if in some cells the chromosome complement should become doubled, then at meiosis allelomorphic pairs are present and normal gametes are produced. This leads to seed formation and to second-generation hybrids, which have thirty-six chromosomes, nine pairs of radish and nine pairs of cabbage chromosomes. Since the morphological characters of these hybrids are intermediate between radish and cabbage, they have been given the name *Raphanobrassica.*

Another famous case of the artificial synthesis of species is Müntzing's work with *Galeopsis.* He crossed *G. pubescens* and *G. speciosa,* both of which have 16 as the diploid chromosome number. A backcross of the hybrid on one parent, *G. pubescens,* resulted in a plant having thirty-two chromosomes, and indistinguishable from a wild species, *G. tetrahit,* with which it readily interbreeds. It may be assumed, then, that the artificial *G. tetrahit* is genetically identical with the natural species, and, hence, that the natural *G. tetrahit* arose through a cross in nature between *G. pubescens* and *G. speciosa* at some unknown time in the past.

Autopolyploids and allopolyploids are called **euploids,** since whole **genoms** (sets of chromosomes) have been doubled. There are many instances, however, in which only single chromosomes have been duplicated (or, in other cases, lost). Such plants are known as **aneuploids.** Related aneuploids have irregular chromosome numbers, instead of producing multiples. Euploids seem to be genetically stable, whereas taxonomic confusion prevails when the numbers are irregular. Thus, one section of the genus *Iris* has the species well defined—all with the chromosome number 10. Another section has the species also fairly well defined, with the chromosome numbers in a euploid series, 8, 12, 16, 20, and 24. In a third section the species are not clearly defined and great morphological variation exists, the so-called species representing an aneuploid series, 8, 10, 11, 12, 14, 16, 17, 19, 20, 21, 22, 36, 42, 43-44, and 54-56.

Methods in Experimental Taxonomy. Modern systematists use methods vastly different from the time-honored techniques of the past to provide information concerning the proper identification and classification of plants. These involve experimental cultivation, genetics, and cytology.

Growth in uniform or varied environments provides a means of observing the interaction between heredity and environment. Vegetative offspring (**clones**) can be separated from the parents and grown under different ecological conditions. By such experiments, plants thought to represent distinct genetic varieties or even species have been found, in some cases, to be only environmental forms, since they change, in response to the environment. On the other hand, plants that were previously thought to be only environmental forms are sometimes shown to be genuine varieties of species, since they breed true under a diversity of conditions.

Cytogenetical analysis involves such techniques as the determination of correlations between external morphology and chromosome differences; the crossing of selected forms to see whether seeds are produced, and, if so, what kinds of progeny are formed from them; the counting of chromosomes of various members of certain series, to determine their relationship to each other; and the analysis of the chromosomal homologies in hybrids, as determined at meiosis, as an indication of their degree of genetic relationship.

The Mechanisms of Evolution. Dobzhansky has outlined the evolutionary process as consisting of developments in three levels. At the first level, he states, changes in the genes (mutations) are the most obvious, but there are also changes of a mechanical sort, entailing rearrangements of the genes within the chromosomes, while reduplications (polyploidy) or losses of whole chromosome sets are also important as evolutionary forces. These mutations and chromosomal changes occur with a certain frequency and constantly supply the raw materials of evolution.

The second level of the evolutionary process involves the further fate of these mutations. Once they are injected into the genetic composition of the population they may be decreased in frequency and ultimately lost, or increased in frequency in succeeding generations. The influences of selection, migration, and geographical isolation mold the population into new shapes. Most of the new combinations probably have no survival value, but many others may be supposed to be harmonious with the various ecological niches of the environment. If the entire field of possible gene combinations is considered with reference to the adaptive value, there are seen to be "adaptive peaks" (characterized by large numbers of individuals), separated by "valleys" (with few or no individuals representing these combinations). The "peaks" are groups of related combinations that make their carriers fit for survival in a certain environment; the "valleys" are less favorable combinations. Each species or variety occupies one of the "peaks," separated from its nearest relatives by a "valley." A change in the environment may then make the old genic combinations less suitable than before, with the result that the population becomes reduced or the species may become extinct; however, the combination of genes may be reconstructed so that the species again comes to be in harmony with the environment. Thus the old "peak" becomes leveled off and some of the old "valleys" may become "peaks." Many genes, of course, have no adaptive values, but simply are inherited simultaneously in combinations with others that do have value.

The third level of the evolutionary process involves the fixation of the diversity already attained. Varieties and species may exist as separate entities only if they are kept from interbreeding with other groups of individuals. Unlimited interbreeding would result in an exchange of genes and a consequent fusion of the distinct groups into one. A number of mechanisms such as ecological isolation, sexual isolation, hybrid sterility, and the like, guard against such a fusion. This final stage, in which two populations develop interbreeding barriers and become distinct, may be called **speciation.**

What Is a Species? In pre-Darwinian days no great difficulty was felt in defining the species concept, nor in separating the various species from each other. Since each species was believed to have arisen from a distinct act of the Creator, it must necessarily be regarded as a definite fundamental unit; the only task of the taxonomist was to learn to distinguish between the various entities.

The situation, however, was completely changed by the development of the theories of evolution, whereby such concepts as variety, species, and genus came to mean only the degrees of separation in a process of gradual change from the ancestral stock. Even so, most biologists continued to feel there was something about a species that made it a definite entity. Many methods were proposed for recognition of a group of specific rank, as distinguished from one of varietal rank only; no satisfactory result has been attained, however, and some indifferent biologists have gone so far as to regard the entire concept as merely subjective, proposing that "a species is a man-made category for a group of individuals."

The cause of such a situation is not difficult to determine. It would be easy to define species only if they were, as once believed, separate acts of creation, or if they arose from each other by sudden changes, in a single step. The first concept is no longer held in modern science, the second apparently is realized only occasionally, as in the origin of species through allopolyploidy. The more usual method of species formation, in many groups apparently the only one, is through a slow process of accumulation of genetic changes (gene mutations, chromosomal changes, and so forth), whereby two or more varieties become more and more distinct and gradually approach the rank of separate species. The decision of a taxonomist as to just when this point has been reached can usually be only arbitrary. What the classical taxonomist studies at his time in history is a cross-section of the phylogenetic lines, the beginnings of which are lost in the dim past; the modern systematist sees these lines in constant change and attempts to comprehend the statics and dynamics of the change.

The different manners whereby various taxonomists have distinguished between certain species in nature are explained by the nature of their species concepts. Most of the species of Linnaeus and many later taxonomists are broadly delimited; such a large species has been called a **Linneon.** On the other hand, the naming of groups could be carried to an absurd extreme, to the finest recognizable units. These units, called by some **biotypes,** are regarded by others as species; they are sometimes called **Jordanons** (from Alexis Jordan). Taxonomists who make use of broad groups are sometimes called "lumpers," while those who emphasize minor differences are called "splitters."

In some cases, forms so distinct in appearance as to be generally regarded as separate species may cross freely when brought into contact, as when a woodland species migrates to the margin of a grassland. Intergrading forms called **hybrid swarms** are thus produced; sometimes these are of such distinctive appearance as to be regarded as constituting different species, and they may actually so become, through the action of natural selection. If one of two species is much more abundant than the other at the zone of contact, most of the crosses will take place between the commonest parent and the descendants of previous crosses. Such hybrids will thus appear merely as somewhat unusual examples of the common parent. This phenomenon, involving the "infection" of one species with genes of another, has been called **introgressive hybridization.**

In some genera offspring are often (even regularly) produced by development from unreduced unfertilized eggs, there thus being no fusion of male and female gametes. This process is known as **apomixis,** as contrasted to **panmixis,** the condition of free cross-reproduction. It is genetically homologous with methods of artificial reproduction such as grafting, whereby clones are formed. The perpetuation of apomicts in nature, often in limited geographical areas, has resulted in many of them being described as distinct species (as, for example, in *Rubus, Crataegus, Taraxacum*), even though they represent no more different morphological characteristics than are possessed by biotypes. Biotypes, however, are connected by innumerable intermediate types, whereas the nature of apomicts renders them more sharply marked from each other. Incidentally, it has been determined that apomicts are usually, perhaps always, aneuploids. The problem of naming and classifying them has been the subject of much discussion.

Conclusion. Dobzhansky describes an imaginary situation, a world in which all possible gene combinations are represented by equal numbers of individuals. Under such conditions no distinct groups of individuals could occur and no classification would be possible.

Clearly, the existing organic world is quite unlike this imaginary one. Only an infinitesimal portion of the possible number of combinations are now realized, or ever have been realized. Furthermore, these are not scattered at random but are grouped into "adaptive peaks." Between the peaks occur "adaptive valleys," corresponding to inharmonious gene combinations, most of which are nearly or quite lethal, so that their carriers do not develop. If they did develop, a mass of freaks would be expected.

Diversity in the organic world is not, therefore, either merely subjective (existing only in the mind of man) or merely superficial. On the contrary, it is the result of a fundamental discontinuity in the genetic make-up of organisms. Each species represents the aggregation of individuals about an "adaptive peak," and the fact that one group can be distinguished from related ones implies that the potential gene combinations between the peaks are rarely or never formed.

It is amazing and most reassuring to realize that, from a practical standpoint, the category of species, as treated by Linnaeus and other classical taxonomists, has undergone so little change in the twentieth century, despite the vastly different manner in which it is now being studied. A majority of the species of Linnaeus are still treated in the same way they were treated in 1753, and, furthermore, the agreement as to which individuals belong together in a species is normally universal. Only in certain "difficult" groups is chaos likely to reign. Thus it may be seen that the data accumulated by the classical taxonomists, far from having been discarded in the light of modern experimental studies, have actually afforded the basis upon which these studies have had their foundation, just as we may expect systematists of the future to build upon the increasingly complex structure existing today.

References

Anderson, E., *Introgressive Hybridization,* New York, 1949.

Dobzhansky, T., *Genetics and the origin of species.* New York, 1941.

Huxley, J., ed., *The new systematics.* London, 1940.

Karpechenko, G. D., *Polyploid hybrids of* Raphanus sativus *L.* × Brassica oleracea *L.* Zeitschr. ind. Abst. Vererb. 48: 1-83, 1928.

Linnaeus, C., *Philosophia botanica.* Stockholmiae, 1751.

Mann, P., *Systematics of flowering plants.* New York, London, 1952.

Mendel, G. J., *Versuche über Pflanzen-Hybriden.* Verh. Naturforschenden Verein Brünn 4: 3-47, 1866.

Müntzing, A., *The evolutionary significance of autopolyploidy.* Hereditas 21: 263-378, 1936.

Simonet, M., *Nouvelles recherches cytologiques et genetiques chez les* Iris. Ann. Sci. Nat. Bot. 10 ser. 16: 229-383, 1934.

Stebbins, G. L., Jr., *Asexual reproduction in relation to plant evolution* (A review of Gustafson's "Apomixis in higher plants"), Evolution 3: 98-101, 1949.

Strasburger, E., *Zellbildung und Zellteilung.* Jena, 1875.

6

The Evolution and Migration of Floras

It must be clear from the facts discussed in the previous chapter that the problems presented by the plants of today, including their taxonomy as well as their distribution, can only be understood by a knowledge of the conditions and plants of the past. In the course of time the vegetation of the earth has been gradually changed by the evolution and migration of floras. Theories concerning these processes involve a study of the hypothetical shapes of the land masses of the past, and the manner in which these were connected or separated in different ages. For example, the presence of members of the same genus or family in South America, Africa, and Australia seems to imply that at some time the plants were free to migrate from one to another of these continents, now widely separated by broad oceans. Two theories have been advanced to account for such migrations:

The continental masses have been connected by land bridges. By this theory it is suggested that the continents were connected by land which has now sunk beneath the sea. In general, this theory is not supported by direct evidence. It is regarded as practically certain that nearby lands, such as Alaska and Siberia, may have been connected, but it seems most unlikely that continents as remotely separated as Australia and Africa could have been connected by a land bridge across the vast expanse of the Indian Ocean.

The continents were once part of a single great mass and have since drifted apart. This hypothesis, known as the theory of continental drift, is based upon the postulation that the center of the earth is a viscous basaltic mass, upon which the platforms of continental masses actually float about, although so slowly that appreciable movement can be detected only over periods of great length. It is believed that this movement has centered on Africa and that this continent, and the main part of Eurasia, have retained their original position more or less unchanged, while America, Australia, and Antarctica have drifted away. The basic principles of this theory are becoming more generally accepted and would tend to provide explanations for many plant geographical problems, but it must be understood that this theory, too, is unsupported by direct evidence.

Areography

In plant geography, the term **area** is given to the region of distribution of any species or other taxonomic group. A consideration of the distribution of plant groups is most important in systematics and Cain has suggested the term **areography** to designate the science dealing especially with area.

Certain fundamental concepts may be recognized in any discussion of areas. For example, the *shapes* of areas of distribution of species tend at first to be circular, as a result of random dissemination of migrules in all directions, but this tendency is somewhat offset by the fact that the principal climatic zones extend farther from east to west than they do from north to south; areas, as a result, are often roughly oval in an east-west

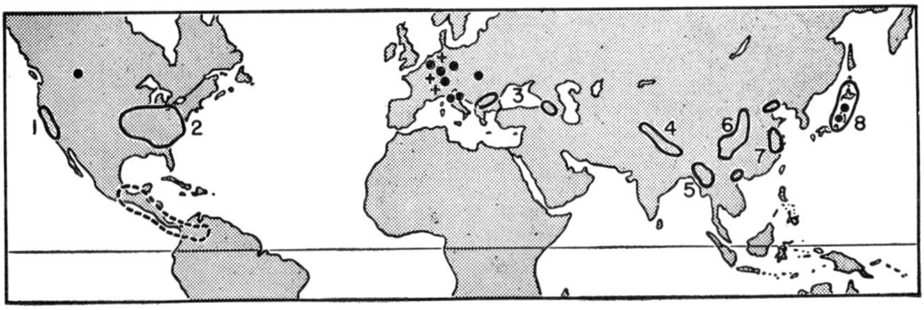

Figure 23. Map showing discontinuous relict areas in the family Hippocastanaceae. The dotted line indicates distribution of *Billia.* The numbers indicate ranges of *Aesculus* species: 1. *californica,* 2. *glabra, octandra, parviflora, pavia,* 3. *hippocastanum,* 4. *indica,* 5. *punduana,* 6. *wilsonii,* 7. *chinensis,* 8. *dissimilis* and *turbinata.* Disks and crosses show stations at which fossils of *Aesculus* have been found. (Adapted by permission from Stanley A. Cain, *Foundations of Plant Geography,* Harper & Brothers, 1944, p. 251.)

direction. Hultén notes, in his *Theory of Equiformal Progressive Areas,* that the chief feature of comparatively recent areas is their concentricity about the point from which they radiated. Plants with similarly shaped areas of different sizes have radiated from the same center and the center can be located satisfactorily if enough species are compared. Hultén's studies have been made in arctic and boreal regions, only relatively recently made available for plant occupation following the last glaciation. Areas range in *size* from the minute, when a species is known from but a single station, to cosmopolitan, when it is nearly world-wide in its distribution. Willis' famous *Age and Area Theory* is, in general, the hypothesis that the longer a species has existed, the greater will be the area of its distribution. Many factors, of course, affect the size of areas and this theory is not very highly regarded today. The *margin* of an area bears a relationship to barriers of various kinds. For instance, an expanding area tends to have a relatively continuous boundary, whereas a contracting area has a tendency to be relatively discontinuous and broken, just as water that once continuously covered a table-top, dries up gradually, becoming dissociated into separate areas. Larch, a tree that is withdrawing northwards following the last ice age, survives in isolated bogs far south of its general range, while beech, a tree advancing northwards, does not show such disjunct colonies. Such isolated colonies, as of the larch, are called **relict areas.** A relict area is always associated with a **refugium,** a locality which has not been changed climatically or otherwise as greatly as the region as a whole.

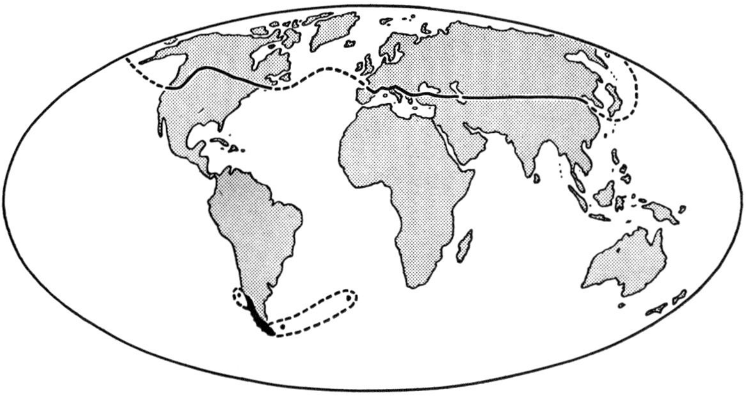

Figure 24. Map showing bipolar distribution of the genus *Empetrum*. (Adapted by permission from Stanley A. Cain, *Foundations of Plant Geography,* Harper & Brothers, 1944, p. 302.)

Discontinuous Areas. Many taxonomic groups (families, genera, species) have discontinuous areas, that is, the same group exists on widely separated parts of a continent, or of the earth. Such cases are of great interest to botanists because of the problems presented by the discontinuities. The solution of these problems involves most of the principles of dynamic plant geography. The condition in which a plant has more than one area is known as **polytopy;** such plants are **polytopic.** For example, the genus *Jeffersonia* includes one species in the eastern United States and another in Manchuria. These are called **vicarious species,** or **vicariads,** since each represents the genus in its own area (vicar is from the Latin *vicarius,* alternation, the place or office of one person being assumed elsewhere by another). One widely accepted hypothesis to account for polytopy is that intervening areas have been covered in the past by a continuous population, although not necessarily all at one time.

Endemism. Endemism is the situation in which a given species (or other group) has one restricted region of distribution. It should be noted that it is rather difficult to state just how restricted such an area must be in order to be regarded as endemic. Furthermore, the term endemic might refer to two different types of organism: those that are relatively youthful, just beginning to spread, and those that are relatively ancient, relict species, on the verge of dying out. Such relict species are often called **epibiotic,** leaving the term endemic, in a stricter sense, to youthful species, but in practice it is often difficult to determine if a species is endemic (in the strict sense) or epibiotic. Examples of local endemism may be seen on the *shale barrens* of the southern Appalachians, and, of course, they are abundant and well-known on oceanic islands, where they

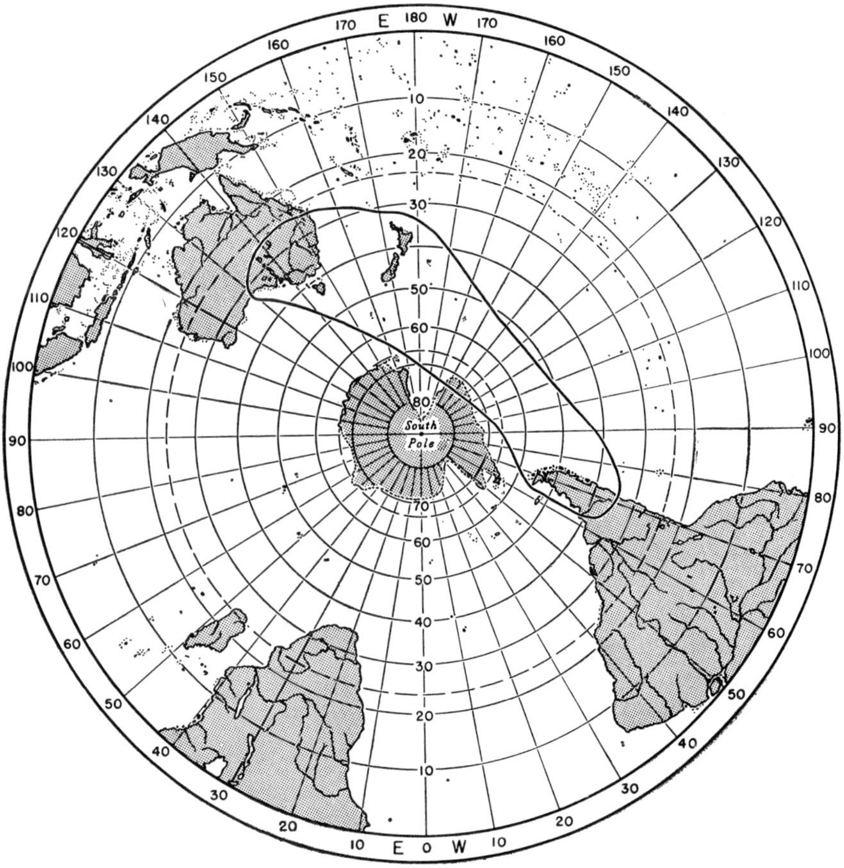

Figure 25. Map showing bicentric distribution of the genus *Nothofagus* in the southern hemisphere. (Adapted from Good's *Geography of the Flowering Plants,* Longmans Green & Co., Ltd.)

played an important part in the formulation of Darwin's ideas concerning the origin of species.

Centers of Area. Cain states that species in general have a center of origin, a center of variation, a center of frequency, a center of dispersal, and, "with the vicissitudes of change through a long history, may have one or more centers of survival and secondary centers of development." The genus *Magnolia*, for example, has two centers, in eastern Asia and in the eastern United States; *Empetrum* has two centers, in Arctic regions and in southern South America; and *Nothofagus* has two centers, one in Australasia, the other in southern South America. For a young species, its center of dispersal is its center of origin. However, for an older species that has experienced changing climates and subsequent migration, there may be one or more centers of dispersal far removed from the center of origin. Such secondary centers are often centers of preservation, from which the population may again spread following the improvement of climatic conditions; they may also be centers of evolution where polyploidy and hybridization bring about the origin of new species, with new centers of origin. The determination of these centers is often aided by paleobotanical data.

Species Senescence. There has been much discussion on the part of botanists as to the contrast between certain populations regarded as **senescent** (old, weak, unaggressive) and others regarded as **juvenile** (young, strong, aggressive). While there is by no means agreement among students concerning the concept of senescence, one theory has associated it with polyploidy. Thus, a group would exist first as a diploid, becoming polyploid as time goes by, with new species arising by natural selection. Stebbins states that since the polyploid members of a given complex of species (or varieties) "are more numerous and widespread than the diploids, one would naturally expect that as a polyploid complex becomes older and as conditions cease to be favorable for the type of plant represented by that particular complex," the diploid members would be the first to disappear. Later the polyploids also begin to die out, so that in the last stages of its existence the complex becomes simple once more, a single polyploid species without any close relatives. As examples Stebbins cites *Psilotum* and *Tmesipteris,* the only survivors of the Psilotales, the most ancient known order of vascular plants. These genera are both monotypic, and both plants have over one hundred chromosomes in their sporophytic cells. "They may represent," he says, "remnants of polyploid complexes which flourished hundreds of millions of years ago in the Paleozoic era." There seems to be some evidence that polyploids are more numerous than diploids at the periphery of the range of a given complex, and that polyploids are more numerous in areas that have recently been subjected to great climatic changes (as a region re-

Geologic Time Chart

GEOLOGICAL UNIT OF TIME		EVENTS
CENOZOIC ERA	*Pleistocene Epoch*	Widespread glaciation.
	Pliocene Epoch	Rise of herbs. Man appears.
	Miocene Epoch	Reduction of forests. Mammals at peak. Grazing types spread.
	Oligocene Epoch	World-wide distribution of forests. Mammals evolve rapidly.
	Eocene Epoch	Modern mammals appear.
	Paleocene Epoch	Archaic mammals dominant.
MESOZOIC ERA	*Cretaceous Period*	Rise of angiosperms. Gymnosperms dwindling. Dinosaurs, pterodactyls, toothed birds reach peak, then disappear. Small mammals.
	Jurassic Period	First known angiosperms. Conifers and cycads dominant and cordaites disappear. Dinosaurs and marine reptiles dominant.
	Triassic Period	Conifers and cycads dominate forests. Seed ferns disappear. Small dinosaurs. First mammals.
PALEOZOIC ERA	*Permian Period*	First cycads and conifers. Continental uplift and mountain building.
	Pennsylvanian Period (Upper Carboniferous)	Spore-bearing trees such as lepidodendron and calamites dominate forests. Extensive coal formation. Reptiles and insects appear.
	Mississippian Period (Lower Carboniferous)	Lycopods, horsetails and seed ferns abundant. Early coal deposits. Climax of crinoids and bryozoans.
	Devonian Period	First forests. Primitive lycopods, horsetails, ferns and seed ferns. First amphibians. Brachiopods reach climax.
	Silurian Period	First land plants. Algae dominant. Widespread coral reefs.
	Ordovician Period	Marine algae dominant. Invertebrates increase greatly. Trilobites reach peak.
	Cambrian Period	Algae abundant. Marine life only. First abundant fossils. Trilobites and brachiopods dominant.
PROTEROZOIC ERA		Bacteria and algae.
ARCHEOZOIC ERA		Presumptive origin of life. No fossils found.

(From Northen, *Introductory Plant Science*, p. 370. Courtesy The Ronald Press Co.)

cently freed from glaciation), whereas diploids tend to occupy older areas and more stable habitats.

Good summarizes these concepts in his *Theory of Generic Cycles* as follows: the genus at first is juvenile, monotypic, and endemic, becoming mature, polytypic, and continuous over a more or less wide area; finally, through extinction and radial evolution, it becomes senile and discontinuous, and may end by being relic-monotypic. It has been noted, however, that there are many exceptions to these conditions, and, while the theory does provide a basis for the interpretation of some situations, it does not apply in all instances.

History of Vegetation through Geologic Times. The floras of the various geologic eras are becoming gradually better known through the study of fossil remains and it is now possible to present a somewhat sketchy history of the development of vegetation through the ages. This development is of great interest to those who attempt to present phylogenetic schemes for the classification of living (as well as extinct) plants.

Figure 26. Restoration of a carboniferous swamp forest. A, *Calamites;* B, C, fallen trunks of *Lepidodendron;* D, E, *Sigillaria;* F, G, *Sphenophyllum;* H, a seed fern, with seeds hanging from the tips of fronds; I, *Cordaites.* (Courtesy Chicago Natural History Museum.)

It is to be noted that the earth's history is divided into five great eras, based chiefly upon the kinds of fossils found in each. The first era (Archeozoic) consists of the oldest rocks and these contain no fossils, probably because the life of the time was too simple to leave traces; it is estimated at 1,900,000,000 years ago. Next is the Proterozoic, 1,400,000,000 years ago, with a few fossils, but only of a primitive type. In the Paleozoic the plant remains are abundant but they all represent ancient groups of plants, as ferns, club mosses, and seed ferns. The Paleozoic is believed to have ended about 200,000,000 years ago. Next is the Mesozoic, about 100,000,000 years ago, during which gymnosperms came to be dominant, while, finally, the Cenozoic is the age of flowering plants. Each of these eras is divided into shorter time spans called periods.

Paleozoic Floras. No plants more complex than bacteria and algae have been detected in Cambrian and Ordovician rocks. But in the Silurian fossils of the first vascular plants appear. These plants are known as Psilophytes (Figure 90). The Psilophytes were upright, with branched stems and scale-like appendages, possibly representing primitive leaves. The sporangia were borne on the stem tips or at the bases of branches. Spores were produced in tetrads. Xylem and phloem were present in the stems. The modern *Psilotum* may be a descendant of these plants.

Primitive lycopods were also present in the Devonian, with tree species which became dominant plants in the Mississippian and Pennsylvanian. *Lepidodendron* and *Sigillaria* were two common genera, with narrow leaves and sporophylls in cones. Their closely packed leaf scars on the stems are among the most common and interesting fossils in the shales accompanying coal deposits. *Calamites,* the ancestor of *Equisetum* of the present day, was also present. Some species grew to a height of a hundred feet or more. The stems were jointed and the branches in whorls.

Ancient ferns were also present, many of them resembling the ferns of today, but often tree-like in size. Some were homosporous, some heterosporous. The latter, or perhaps their ancestors, gave rise to the first seed plants, the Pteridosperms, or seed ferns. These resembled ferns vegetatively but bore true seeds (Figure 95). They are found in the Devonian and reached their greatest development in the late Paleozoic, becoming extinct, along with the primitive lycopods and calamites, at the close of that era. Other primitive gymnosperms, such as *Cordaites,* were found in the late Paleozoic.

The vegetation of the Mississippian and Pennsylvanian (grouped into the Carboniferous, or coal-bearing period) was very luxuriant and indicates that the climate was moist and temperate, with slight changes in season. Trees and shrubs predominated and supplied the parent materials of our great Paleozoic coal beds (Figure 30).

The Permian was a period of great aridity and also of glaciation, accounted for by the elevation of mountain ranges such as the Appalachians. It was a period of much more scanty vegetation, and was marked by the extinction of many ancient forms. It was the end of an era.

Mesozoic Floras. The major groups of plants in the Triassic and Jurassic periods were the Cycadeoids, or Bennettitales, and the primitive cycads. The Bennettitales were gymnosperms with the leaves clustered in a large apical crown, bearing in their axils cones of sporophylls with both pollen sacs and ovules (Figure 95). The cycads were similar to these plants, but were dioecious. Both of these seem to have been derived from the seed ferns, while the cycadeoids were possibly the ancestors of modern flowering plants.

In the early Cretaceous period, the flora was dominated by conifers, ferns, and cycads. The conifers were probably derived from the Paleozoic *Cordaites,* as were also the ginkgos, which were widespread in the Mesozoic. The early Cretaceous likewise includes a large array of angiosperms, with many of the genera common today. Apparently angiosperms had been evolving on the earth for a long time, although no fossils are known before that time. Ferns and cycads declined rapidly in abundance, but conifers remained widespread and abundant, with species of *Pinus, Sequoia,* and other genera, some of which are now extinct.

In the upper Cretaceous the most significant fact is the amazing diversification and spread of the angiosperms. The genera were widespread over the northern hemisphere and included many familiar today, such as *Magnolia, Liriodendron, Aralia, Platanus, Sassafras, Quercus, Ficus,* and *Salix.* Monocotyledons, such as cattails, grasses, sedges, and palms, were present in smaller numbers. A remarkable feature was the uniformity in composition of the flora, with fossils from places as widely separated as Greenland and Texas representing the same species.

Cenozoic Floras. Early in the Cenozoic era mountain-building activities resulted in the break-up of the north temperate zone into areas with various amounts of rainfall, areas with varying degrees of temperature, and zonation of environment against mountain slopes. The Rockies, Andes, and Himalayas arose in this period. Some angiosperms migrated into the south temperate lands of South America, South Africa, Australia, and New Zealand. The previously uniform floras became differentiated into the arctic floras of the north, the temperate floras of the midlatitudes, and the tropical floras of the low latitudes.

The Pleistocene was characterized by a period of perhaps a million years of recurring glaciations, or ice ages. In North America there were four of these, known as the Nebraskan, Kansan, Illinoian, and Wisconsin. The ice of each of these ages, however, was not an unbroken sheet from the Atlantic to the Pacific, but developed independently in different centers, so that one glacier might be advancing while another was receding. In Europe there were likewise ice ages, perhaps simultaneous with those of North America, with the northern ice sheet spreading down into Central Europe and a separate glacier spreading from the Alps. In Asia the polar ice cap did not cover much of the continent, but vast glaciers spread out from the mountain centers. Later, as the ice fields slowly disappeared, the land was dotted with innumerable lakes produced by the impeded drainage. The smaller lakes were invaded and gradually covered by bog vegetation, so common in the north today.

From the Miocene onward the outstanding changes in vegetation have been the extinction of many genera and species, and the reduction of some genera to a single species, or but a few species, which survived in

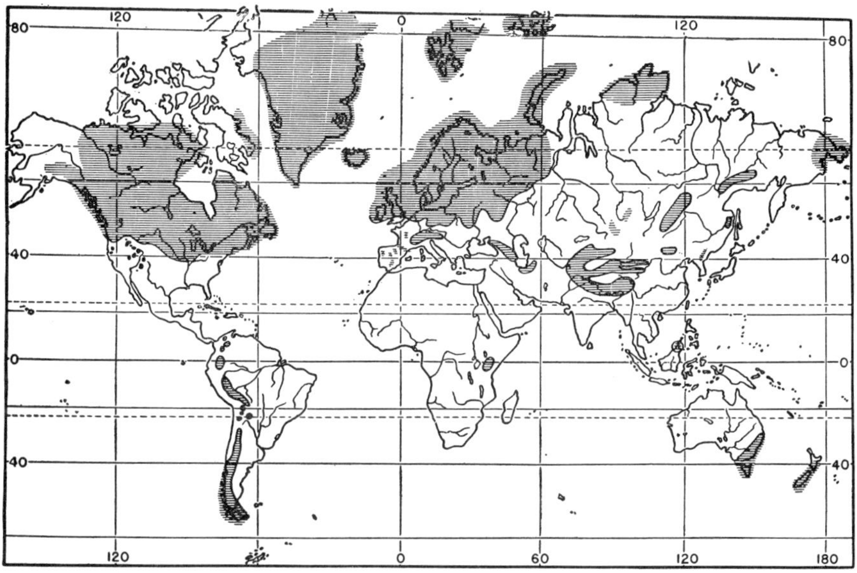

Figure 27. Map showing the maximum extent of Pleistocene glaciation. (Adapted by permission from a map by the Carnegie Institution of Washington.)

one or only a few, often widely separated, regions. Much of this extinction apparently took place before the end of the Pliocene, but many other species became extinct during the glacial period. Another outstanding change, in the United States, was the great extension of the grasslands from the southwest, which began in Eocene times as the Rockies were elevated, casting a "rain shadow" over west-central North America.

Good, summarizing the history of the angiosperms, says that from the time they first appeared, in the early Cretaceous, down to the middle or end of the Pliocene, the indication is that they developed and spread without encountering any serious difficulties such as rapid environmental changes. Throughout this long period the group gradually broadened and became differentiated by the multiplication of forms, coming to attain a more and more dominant position among the vegetation of the earth. The fossil record suggests that, at least in the northern hemisphere, there was one almost homogeneous flora. Then, during the Pliocene, this development was interrupted by a cooling of the climate of the higher latitudes, culminating in widespread glaciation and presenting problems never before encountered by the flowering plants.

These conditions continued into the Pleistocene. Many angiosperms were, as a result, faced with the necessity of adjusting themselves to the changing environments. The effects of the glaciation were intensified by the relative rapidity at which it came and by the accompanying series of alternating cold and warm periods. Good believes that in the early history of the angiosperms the speed of morphological evolution was "faster than and perhaps unrelated to climatic change," so that the plants changed "by the processes of evolution more rapidly than their surroundings." With the coming of the glaciation this relationship was completely reversed, and environmental change took place so rapidly that evolution was unable to keep pace with it; that is, "the environment was changing much more rapidly than its inhabitants." The result "was a state of stress between organism and environment such as may never have occurred before." Since pre-glacial conditions have not yet been restored, "the botanists of today are studying a world vegetation but lately subjected to a devastating disaster." Present-day plant geography, is, therefore, "the study of the consequences of this disaster."

As an example of an incident in this long and eventful period of change may be mentioned the fate of the Pliocene flora of Europe. This flora, as indicated by fossil remains, was closely allied to the present flora of eastern Asia and of North America. In the ever-increasing cold of the post-Pliocene, these plants were driven farther and farther south. For the eastern Asian and North American migration streams, the way to the south was open and the floras escaped, to move back northwards as the climate became milder. But in Europe the way was everywhere closed by impassable barriers of east-west ranges of mountains, of seas, and of deserts. Successive waves of migrants were driven against these barriers and perished, so that at last scarcely a trace of the Pliocene plants was to be found in Europe. In the northern hemisphere this has resulted in a remarkable discontinuity in the vegetation, revealed in the fact that many genera of eastern North America occur also in eastern Asia, but not in comparable latitudes in Europe. These include *Arundinaria, Buckleya, Boykinia, Cladrastis, Clethra, Chionanthus, Catalpa, Dicentra, Epigaea, Gymnocladus, Hamamelis, Jeffersonia, Liriodendron, Lindera, Liquidambar, Magnolia, Nyssa, Podophyllum, Philadelphus, Physocarpus, Panax, Phryma, Saururus, Shortia, Symplocarpus, Trillium, Wistaria, Xanthoxylon, Zizania,* and numerous others.

References

Babcock, E. B., *The genus* Crepis. *I. The taxonomy, phylogeny, distribution, and evolution of* Crepis. Univ. Calif. Publ. Bot. 21: 1-198. 1947. II. Systematic treatment. op. cit. 22: 199-1030, 1947.

Cain, S. A., *Foundations of Plant Geography.* New York, London, 1944.

Clausen, J., D. D. Keck, and W. M. Hiesey, *Experimental studies on the nature of species. I. Effect of varied environments on western American plants.* Carnegie Inst. Wash. Pub. 520, 1940.

Darrah, W. C., *Textbook of Paleobotany.* New York, London, 1939.

Good, R., *The Geography of the flowering plants.* London, 1953.

Hultén, E., *Outline of the history of Arctic and Boreal biota during the Quaternary period. Their evolution during and after the glacial period as indicated by the equiformal progressive areas of present plant species.* Stockholm, 1937.

Mason, H. L., *The principles of geographic distribution as applied to floral analysis.* Madroño 3: 181-190, 1936.

Stebbins, G. L., Jr., *The significance of polyploidy in plant evolution.* Amer. Nat. 74: 54-66, 1940.

Wherry, E. T., *Plants of the Appalachian shale barrens.* Jl. Wash. Acad. Sci. 20: 43-52, 1930.

Wulff, E. V., *An introduction to historical plant geography.* English transl. Waltham, Mass., 1943.

7

Climate and Natural Vegetation

Little by little, as a result of botanical exploration, the plant life of the earth came to be better known. It was discovered that, infinitely varied though it was, it could be fitted into a pattern the construction of which became gradually clearer. This pattern has been found to be closely correlated with the variations in temperature extremes, precipitation, length of day, drought periods, fogs—phenomena that can be summarized as climatic factors. Students of climates long ago recognized that vegetation patterns are the best indicators of climatic zones.

The principal species of plants will be discussed in a systematic manner in Part Two of this work, classified by orders and families. The present chapter provides supplementary information concerning the distribution of these species by indicating the patterns of the zones of natural vegetation in which they occur.

Like all other branches of science, the classification of climates has developed into a more nearly perfect system with the increase of knowledge. From the earlier primitive systems, in which temperature was the principal factor considered, there have developed the various modern systems, in which both temperature and rainfall are included, as well as evaporation, humidity, radiation, wind, and so forth.

One of the recent systems, prepared by Köppen, recognizes five major divisions of world climates, corresponding with the five principal vegetation groups proposed by A. de Candolle in 1874. These major plant groups are **megatherms,** plants that need continuously high temperature and abundant moisture; **xerophytes,** plants that tolerate dryness, but need at least a short hot season; **mesotherms,** plants that need a moderate amount of heat and moisture; **microtherms,** plants needing less heat and moisture; and **hekistotherms,** plants of the tundra beyond the limits of the forest.

Köppen's climatic divisions, corresponding to these vegetative groups are identified by capital letters, as follows: *A*, rainy climates with no

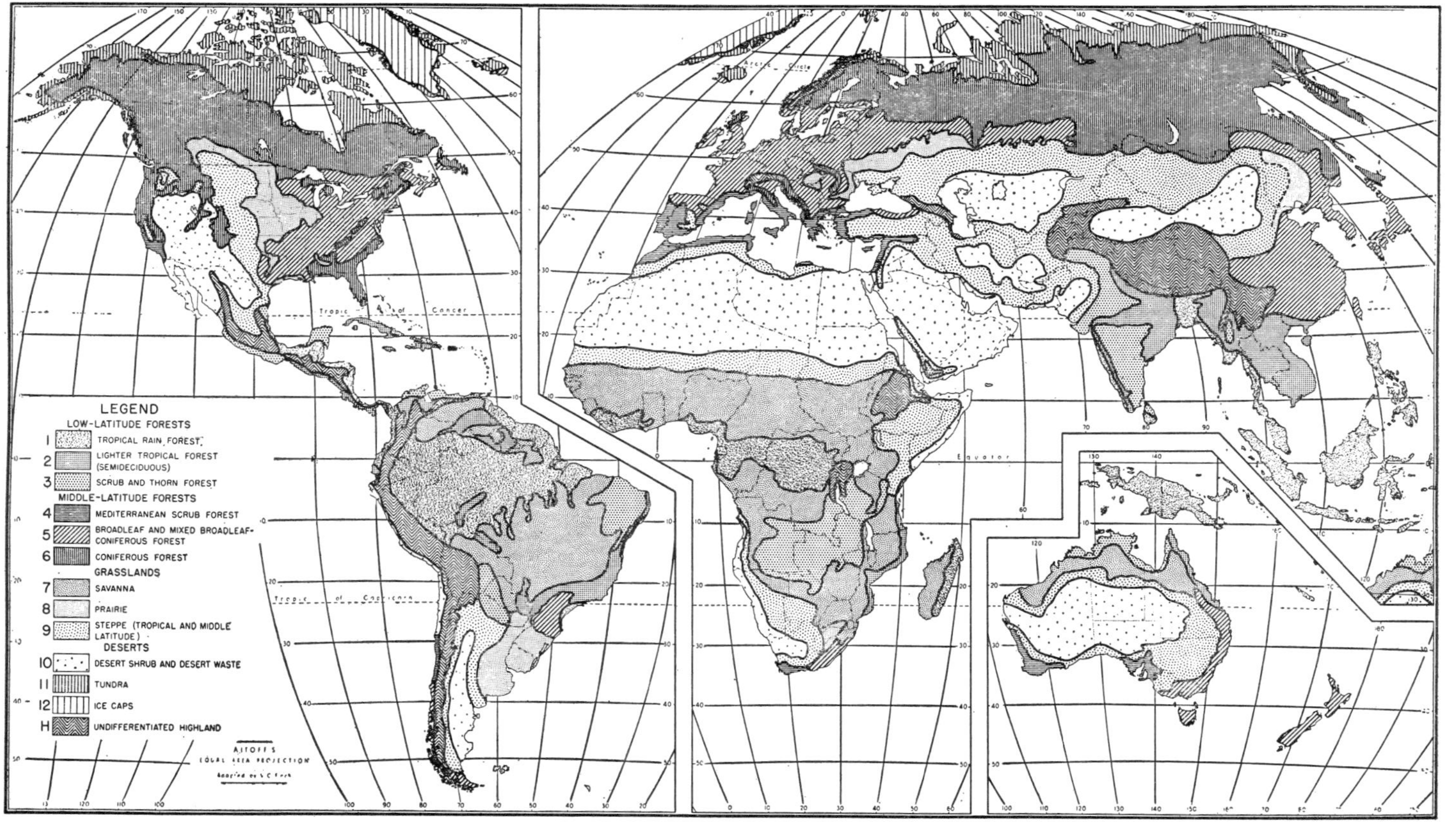

Figure 28. World distribution of existing virgin vegetation. (Courtesy U. S. Department of Agriculture.)

winters; *B*, dry climates; *C*, rainy climates with mild winters; *D*, rainy climates with severe winters; and *E*, polar climates with no warm season.

The various categories may be further subdivided. *A*, *C*, and *D* climates with no marked dry season are identified by the small letter *f* (German *feucht*, moist); those with dry seasons in winter by the small letter *w*; and those with dry seasons in summer by the small letter *s*. Thus an *Af* climate is a tropical climate with no dry season; a *Cs* climate is a warm-temperate climate with dry summers; and a *Dw* climate is a cold-temperate climate with dry winters. The *B* climates are divided into semiarid, *BS* (*S* is from Steppe, dry grassland), and arid, *BW* (*W* is from the German *Wüste*, desert). The *E* climates are divided into *ET* (*T* for Tundra), the tundra type, and *EF* (*F* for Frost), the continually frozen type. Still further subdivision could be made on the basis of other significant features of temperature and rainfall.

(A) The Tropical Climates. The general pattern of the tropical rain climates (*Af*) can be described rather simply. They occupy a belt about 20° wide on each side of the equator, typically on the eastern sides of the continents; this general position is modified in detail on each of the continents. The temperature is equable and high throughout the year, about 80° F., and the rainfall is regular and plentiful. No combination of physical conditions in the world is more favorable to vegetation and, Hardy says, "we may regard its luxuriance as the supreme effort of plant life at this period of the world's development." One of the tropical climate's most outstanding peculiarities is the remarkable variety of species included; as many as eighty to one hundred species of trees may be found on a single acre of ground. The trees are tall and straight, with the foliage mostly at the top. Little light reaches the forest floor, because of the thick canopy of broad, evergreen leaves, and, as a result, there is little color and little underbrush, although the space between the tree trunks is interlaced with an astonishing network of lianas. The rhythm of life is confused, each individual species going through the life processes in its own period. There are three chief areas of occurrence: in America, Africa, and the Indonesian region. The largest single area of tropical rain forest (**selva**) is in the Amazon valley of South America. Its westward extension is limited only by the Andes. The vegetation includes such a vast number of species that it is difficult to mention any special ones. Palms, however, are extremely numerous, while the Pará rubber tree (*Hevea brasiliensis*) and Brazil-nut tree (*Bertholletia excelsa*) are among the economic species. Epiphytic orchids and bromeliads are abundant. In Africa the situation is affected by complex wind movements resulting from the configuration and elevation of the continent, so that the east coast is drier than the corresponding parts of South America. But the Congo Valley and neighboring areas have forests only slightly less luxuriant than those of the Amazon. As in the Amazon, the species are extremely numerous and include many palms and an abundance of lianas. Rain forests occupy lowland areas of Indonesia and many small islands of the Pacific, as well as Ceylon and the Malabar Coast of India.

Both to the north and to the south of the *Af* climates are zones of *Aw* climates. These result from the apparent migration of the sun northward to the Tropic of Cancer and southward to the Tropic of Capricorn each year. Essentially this means that the rainy tropical climates are alternately extended farther north and farther south, as the sun spends six months in the northern hemisphere and six months in the southern. As a sort of crude illustration, this might be compared to a situation in which three men are sleeping together in a bed with a blanket too narrow to cover them. Alternately the man on the right and the man on the left have the blanket pulled from above them, while the man in the middle remains covered.

The selvas gradually change into woodland and scrub forests, with scattered trees in a dominant setting of tall grass (the **savanna**). The trees are small, often thorny, and spaced so far apart that the ground is little shaded, "giving the landscape the appearance of a poorly kept orchard." The variety of species is not nearly so great as in the selva. Among the most common trees are *Mimosa, Spondias, Zizyphus, Bombax,* and many palms, as *Attalea* and *Carnauba.* Cacti are abundant in the Americas, as are epiphytic bromeliads and orchids. During the rainy season the plants are a mass of foliage and brilliantly colored flowers, but during the dry season the leaves fall from the trees. In Brazil the grasslands are known as **campos** and are characterized by tall tufts of grass between the various shrubs, small trees, and liliaceous plants. The savanna represents one of the most widespread landscapes of Africa. Though the species of trees, shrubs, grasses, and herbs change from region to region, the main feature remains that of tall grasses interspersed with deciduous woody plants. Some kind of *Acacia* is always in sight. Larger trees standing alone include *Adansonia, Ceiba, Tamarindus, Butyrospermum,* and many palms as *Borassus, Elaeis, Hyphaene,* and *Raphia.* Elsewhere, in Somaliland, Rhodesia, and Angola, occur scrub forests. In Rhodesia these are termed **boschveld.** Flat-crowned, thorny acacias are abundant, along with the mopani-tree (*Copaifera mopani*). The savanna is also represented on the low plateaus of Siam and Laos, and to a lesser extent in Burma. In still drier regions the savanna passes into a more xerophytic type of vegetation known in Brazil as **caatinga,** or thorn forest.

In parts of Burma and some other sections of southern Asia **monsoon** climates (*Am*) result when winds which would normally blow from the northeast toward the equator turn to the north in summer because the land is heated more than the water. At Cherrapunji, in eastern India, 457 inches of rain falls annually, with 107 inches in July and only 0.3 of an inch in December. This produces a semideciduous forest with a very marked seasonal rhythm. Among the interesting trees are teak (*Tectona*), sandalwood (*Santalum*), and the horsetail-tree (*Casuarina*).

(**B**) **The Dry Climates.** In general the dry lands are found on the west coasts of the continents between about 20° and 30° north and south of the equator. As noted above, this is associated with the presence of cold ocean currents. Wind direction and the occurrence of mountain ranges also affect the distribution of these climates.

The basic fact concerning the climate of the dry lands is the deficiency in moisture. The most arid conditions result in the development of **deserts.** In most deserts rain falls only at infrequent intervals, many months or even years elapsing between showers. Temperatures, of course, vary with the latitude. In the poleward portions the winters are very cold, but at lower latitudes the highest air temperatures on earth are registered. Death Valley, California, has recorded 134° F. and even higher temperatures are known. At night the air cools rapidly and the greatest diurnal ranges of temperature are recorded in desert regions.

Desert plants usually grow some distance apart, the lack of a complete mat of vegetation being one of the distinguishing features of deserts. Other striking peculiarities are the brilliant colors and penetrating odors of the flowers. Some desert plants are ephemeral, evading drought by lying dormant as seeds in the long dry periods, then quickly completing their life cycles in the short, rare periods when water is available. Other desert plants are perennials that grow only in rainy periods and remain brown and dormant when little moisture is available. Still others are succulents, like cacti, which store water in their roots and stems.

There are five chief areas of dry climate. The largest of these begins at the west coast of Africa and extends completely across the continent, through Arabia and into the far interior of Asia. In South Africa the desert occupies the analogous position but is much less extensive. In North America the desert is found in the southwestern United States and northern Mexico. In South America it is involved with the Andes Mountains and occupies a very narrow strip. In Australia, because of the latitude, dry climates cover a large portion of the continent.

On the poleward side of each of the deserts, conditions become less rigorous and **steppes** (short-grass lands) result. These in turn merge into the taller grasses characteristic of the prairies, which are not included in *B* climates. Unlike the desert, the steppes are covered with a nearly continuous mat of vegetation. At maturity the grasses are only a few inches high and normally resemble a closely pastured meadow, resulting in a landscape of striking monotony.

(**C**) **The Mesothermal Climates.** The middle latitudes, from about 30° to about 40° from the equator, on a generalized continental mass, have forests (*Cf* climates) on their western and eastern coasts, with arid and semi-arid lands between. Rainfall is abundant and distributed throughout the year. The summers are hot, the winters relatively mild. Of course the configuration of the various land masses is quite different and as a result the pattern of forests is different but everywhere the mid-latitudes are characterized by forests that are a mixture of broad-leaved, mostly deciduous angiosperms and narrow-leaved, mostly evergreen, gymnosperms. Comparable forests of this type are found in the eastern United States, the Pacific coast of Canada, in western Europe and eastern Asia (the western and eastern coasts of Eurasia), on the eastern and western coasts of temperate South America, at the southern tip of Africa (a very small area), and in New Zealand and southeastern Australia. The general aspect of the forests is similar wherever they are found; the specific composition varies from continent to continent. The Pacific coast of Canada and southern Alaska produces a coniferous forest with a luxuriance unsurpassed in any part of the world; the dominant forms are *Picea, Abies, Pseudotsuga, Tsuga, Pinus,* and *Chamaecyparis.* In southeastern North America there are species of *Quercus, Juglans, Carya, Castanea, Betula, Salix, Populus, Ulmus, Magnolia, Liriodendron, Acer, Fraxinus, Pinus,* and so forth. In western Europe many of these genera reappear. In northeastern China species of many of these genera also appear, along with *Paulownia, Ailanthus, Sophora, Broussonetia,* and the like. In east-temperate South America are forests characterized by *Araucaria* and *Ilex.* In southern Chile are dense temperate rain-forests, analogous to those of the northwest coast of North America, with species of *Nothofagus, Drimys,* bamboos and tree-ferns, and a wealth of climbers and epiphytes. Southeastern Australia has a temperate forest with an aspect of its own, characterized by tall trees of *Eucalyptus,* with many lesser tree-ferns, arboreal Compositae, acacias, and Proteaceae. New Zealand has conifers like *Agathis* and *Podocarpus,* with evergreen species of *Nothofagus.*

At the edge of the forest, toward the arid climates, lies the **prairie.** This results from the *Cw* climate, with a reduced rainfall in winter. Unlike the grasses of the steppes, the prairie grasses are tall and have deep root systems. In their natural condition they were often above the head of a man on horseback. The landscape is well described by the expression *paja y cielo* (grass and sky), used by natives of the Argentine **pampas.** Besides the tall-grass lands of central North America, other comparable grasslands are found in the pampas of Uruguay and northern Argentina, in the Ukraine of southern Russia, and in the **veldt** of Orange Free State, Union of South Africa. The North American prairie originally included species of *Andropogon* and other grasses. In the pampas of South America are *Melica, Stipa, Aristida, Andropogon, Pappophorum, Panicum, Paspalum,* and others. In the European tall-grass lands *Stipa* and *Andropogon* occur, and they are also found in the veldt of South Africa.

The region about the Mediterranean Sea has an unusual type of climate that is designated *Cs* because of the dry summers. This results from the changes in convection currents of air from winter to summer. During the winter while the sun is on the south side of the equator, the westerly winds characteristic of mid-latitude lands occasionally swing farther south and carry rains over this region. In summer, with the sun on the north side of the equator, the belts are moved poleward and the storms

Figure 29. Eucalyptus forest in Australia. (Courtesy Australian News and Information Bureau.)

all pass north of these lands. These lands, then, are transitional between the deserts, on the side toward the equator, and the moist forest lands of the *Cf* climates. As one proceeds toward the poles, the length and amount of the winter rains increase; toward the equator the length of the summer dry period increases. These conditions produce an evergreen scrub forest of unusual character. Because the winters are not very cold, the sprouting of new leaves takes place in the fall when the rainy season starts, and the flowering and seed production occur in the spring. The summers are not long enough to enforce a period of rest, so the leaves do not drop. This type of climate is found on the western coasts of all the

Figure 30. Exploring for plants in the tropical rain forest. (*Silva primaeva montana chinantlensis,* by Liebman. Courtesy Chicago Natural History Museum.)

continents, at about 30° to 40° from the equator. The accident whereby a great arm of the ocean (the Mediterranean Sea) extends far inland at this latitude between Europe and Africa resulted in the development of an unusually large area of *Cs* lands in this region; for this reason the name **mediterranean** (spelled with a small initial letter) is sometimes applied to the climate wherever it appears. There are five such areas. Besides the region about the Mediterranean Sea, smaller areas are found in California, in Central Chile, in South Africa around Cape Town, and in Australia around Perth and Adelaide. Where conditions are most favorable the vegetation consists of an open evergreen woodland. Around the Mediterranean Sea are species of *Quercus, Pinus, Cupressus, Olea,* and *Laurus.* California also has species of *Quercus, Cupressus,* and *Pinus.* In Chile are species of *Quillaja* and *Escallonia,* which replace the oaks, while species of *Araucaria* replace the pines. In Australia species of *Eucalyptus* are prominent, and in South Africa there are *Leucadendron, Protea,* and *Widdringtonia.* Where conditions are less favorable, the forest degenerates into a dense tangle of low scrub, known in Europe as the **maquis,** in California as the **chaparral,** in Australia as the **Mallee scrub;** in the various areas the plants are similar in appearance although belonging to different species.

(D) **The Microthermal Climates.** Poleward of the megathermal climates a forested belt extends completely across the continents from ocean to ocean between about 50° and 70° from the equator. This is the boreal forest or **taiga,** composed principally of evergreen coniferous trees. Temperature is the most significant climatic element in this region. The winters are long and cold, the summers short and cool. Snowfall remains on the ground throughout the winter, but melts in the spring. The ground does not remain frozen through the summer. Especially in the interiors of the continents, away from the moderating influences of marine locations, very remarkable ranges in temperature between the warmest and coldest months occur. Minimum winter temperatures often drop to −75° F., and the maximum summer temperatures climb to 90 or 100°.

The boreal forest stretches from the Pacific to the Atlantic across North America, and in Eurasia a similar situation exists, with the conifers extending all the way across northern Europe and northern Asia, from the Atlantic to the Pacific. The principal genera include *Picea, Larix, Abies,* and *Pinus,* while species of *Populus* and *Betula* are associated. In the Southern Hemisphere the continental masses are so reduced in width in these latitudes that no boreal forests are developed.

(E) **The Polar Climates.** North of the boreal forest lies the **tundra,** a vast treeless expanse, with permanent ice just below the surface of the soil. The winters are cold and dark, the summers brief and cool, with freezing weather to be expected at any time. The soil, permanently frozen below, remains wet through the summer, from melting snows, fogs, and drizzling rains. The tundra of North America almost joins that of Asia and Europe, and a large number of the species are identical. Grasses, sedges, rushes, lichens, and mosses are common, as are many herbs, often with showy flowers. Shrubby species of *Vaccinium, Ledum, Empetrum, Salix, Betula,* and *Rhododendron* occur.

Poleward of the tundras are the permanent ice sheets; an example is that on the large island of Greenland. It would be proper to say that Greenland is still in the Ice Age. The same condition, even more extreme, is true of the vast continent of Antarctica, 5,000,000 square miles in area, where the land is also covered by an ice sheet, with, so far as is known, no surrounding fringe of tundra.

The Mountain Lands. Any consideration of the vegetative zones is complicated because of the presence of mountains, where higher altitudes produce conditions that bring about types of plant life different from those of adjacent areas. Temperatures and air pressures decrease with elevation, whereas length of day and seasonal phenomena resemble those of the surrounding lowlands. Vertical differentiation in plant zones is of course most easily observed in the tropics, ranging from "hot country" at sea level through "temperate country" and "cold country" to treeless alpine meadows (called **páramos** in the northern Andes) and, finally, permanent snow caps. On slopes especially exposed to moisture-laden winds there develop **cloud forests,** remarkable for the great abundance and wide variety of epiphytes, including mosses, liverworts, ferns, bromeliads, and orchids. Vertical differentiation remains a prominent feature in the middle latitudes but disappears entirely in the polar lands. It has been pointed out that a place at a considerable elevation in the tropics may have the same average temperature as a place at or near sea level in the middle or high latitudes. It must not be assumed, however, that these places have the same climate. There is not, for example, on tropical mountains the range of temperature from summer to winter found in higher latitudes.

The altitudinal limits of the various types of vegetation correspond to the pattern of vertical temperature distribution. In a general way, the same succession of types may be found in climbing a mountain near the equator as in traveling poleward on the continents. Tropical forests are on the lower slopes; mixed forests of broad leaved trees and conifers are higher up; still higher the conifers become more dominant. Above the forests are the **alpine meadows** which resemble somewhat the tundra regions. The zone of alpine meadows is widest in dry areas; some of these areas are very extensive and possess a most inhospitable climate; such are the cold deserts of Tibet and adjoining parts of Central Asia, and the cold dry **punas** of the central and southern Andes.

References

Blair, T. A., *Climatology. General and Regional.* New York, 1942.

Braun, E. L., *Deciduous forests of eastern North America.* Philadelphia, Toronto, 1950.

Candolle, A. de, *Géographie Botanique Raisonnée.* 2 vols. Paris, 1855.

James, P. E., *An outline of geography.* Boston, 1935.

Kendrew, W. G., *The climates of the continents.* 3d ed. Oxford, 1937

Köppen, W., *Gundriss der Klimakunde.* Berlin, 1931.

Richards, P. W., *The tropical rain forest; an ecological study.* Cambridge, England, 1952.

Schimper, A. F. W., *Plant geography upon a physiologicai basis.* English transl. Oxford, 1903.

Warming, E., *The Oecology of plants.* English transl. Oxford, 1909.

8

Gardens and Herbaria

Gardens

We have already noticed how gardens and gardening, from the days of Theophrastus to the present, have influenced the development of plant taxonomy. Gardens have not only contributed to supplies of human food and crude drugs, but the bringing together of many plants likewise gave a better opportunity for their scientific study. The botanical exploration of the world, indeed, was accelerated because of interest in the development of private and public gardens.

Long before the dawn of history man had begun to cultivate plants in gardens, to supply himself conveniently with food, to provide drugs, or to grow beautiful flowers. Even very primitive tribes engage in vegetable gardening and often, surprisingly, flower gardening. In the ancient Mediterranean civilization gardens were prominent features of the grounds of temples or palaces, as well as of the homes of the nobility. The number of plants cultivated by the ancient Egyptians was a source of wonder to neighboring peoples. The "Hanging Gardens" of Babylon are counted among the wonders of the ancient world. From conquered lands the Romans brought plants; they were successful in assembling more plants in Italy than had ever been brought together before in one country. Apples, pears, plums, apricots, peaches, were brought from Armenia, Persia, and other countries of western Asia; olives, figs, and almonds came from Syria. As the years went by and the Empire extended farther, more new species were introduced.

Other civilizations likewise were interested in gardening. In China and India, where famines were recurrent, gardening for food was a most laudable enterprise. The Aztecs, as we have seen, were great lovers of flowers and cultivated these in their gardens, for ornament as well as for drugs, while the palace grounds of the Incas at Yucay, according to Prescott, "were stocked with numerous varieties of plants and flowers that grew without effort in this *temperate* region of the tropics. . . ."

During the Middle Ages, with the general lapse in learning, it is not surprising that little attention was given to the introduction of new plants; people of that day were fortunate if they did not lose the plants they had inherited. Monasteries and other religious houses, noted as responsible for the preservation of many classical manuscripts, were likewise responsible for the cultivation of many kinds of fruits, vegetables and drugs and for their introduction from the Mediterranean countries into northern and western Europe, to provide food and employment for the members. Spinach and "good-Henry" were grown for greens; other food plants included dill, beets, onions, garlic, parsnip, cabbage; other "herbs" were lilies, roses, mints, fenugreek, sage, rue, cummin, and gladiolus.

With the Renaissance and the widening of men's horizons, the art of gardening prospered as a result of new enthusiasm. Bizarre and valuable plants from the newly discovered lands brought a new zest for plant introduction. The sixteenth century herbalists, as we have seen, acquainted the world with hundreds of plants, many of them growing in gardens. A mounting interest in the growing of flowers for beautification of grounds around homes led to the introduction of species from all parts of the world. The tulip, first figured in a European publication in 1559, became very popular in Holland and in 1634 a craze of wild speculation reached such a pitch that government intervention was necessary to stop the "tulip mania."

The interest in learning that led to the establishment and development of the great universities resulted likewise in the establishment of botanical gardens in connection with the schools. The first of these is said to have been that of the University of Padua. There, in 1533, Francis Bonafede, a professor of medicine, secured a "professorship of simples" (Lectura Simplicium), the first professorship of botany in Europe. In this connection he developed a garden of simples, financed by the Venetian Senate, which later, on June 29, 1545, officially established the Botanic Garden ("Orto Botanico"). Bonafede felt the need of illustrative material for the enrichment of his lectures, and the garden was established primarily to meet this need, being the first garden to be founded for didactic purposes. It has at present an area of about five acres, and besides the plantations a large herbarium and a library of over 18,000 volumes, including P. A. Saccardo's personal mycological library and one of the largest known collections of portraits of botanists (more than 600).

Almost as old (some say older, depending on the date accepted for the Padua Garden) is the botanic garden at Pisa, located on Via Luca Ghini. It was apparently established in 1543, with Luca Ghini as the first director, after Leonhart Fuchs had refused the position. Andrea Cesalpino was the second director (1554-1558). The garden at Florence may have been the third such garden to be established; Luca Ghini was assigned the task of its foundation in 1545. In Rome, gardens had existed in ancient times; the first garden for instruction was the Vatican Garden, established about 1566 by Michele Mercati, a student of Cesalpino.

Other prominent universities established botanic gardens within a period of relatively few years. One of the earliest was at Bologna, in 1567. There, as noted on page 20, Luca Ghini, the great teacher of botany, had lectured on simples from 1534 to 1544, but, as Meyer states, "without the help of a garden." Ulisse Aldrovandi was the first director (1567-1605). The botanical garden of the University of Leiden (Hortus Botanicus Academicus Lugduno-Batavus) was established in 1587. Clusius is said to have been the first to do planting in this garden, which by 1594 contained over 1000 species and varieties. Of the trees he planted, a laburnum was still standing in 1935. It is said that the first greenhouse was established here, in 1599, "for the protection of some plants introduced from the Cape of Good Hope, Geraniums, Mesembryanthemums, etc." One of the earliest botanical gardens in France was the "Jardin des Plantes de l'Université de Montpellier," founded in 1593. In 1626 Louis XIII of France authorized the establishment at Paris of a royal garden "to contain all kinds of medicinal herbs . . . for the instruction of the students of the University of Medicine"; the purchase of the site was confirmed in 1635 and it was opened to the public in 1640 as the "Jardin du Roy." This name came to an end in 1793, when it was changed to the "Museé National d'Histoire Naturelle," although still known under the popular name "Jardin des Plantes." Tournefort and the Jussieus were connected with this garden, and a new Arboretum, acquired in 1927, is known as the Jardin de Jussieu. The Oxford University Botanic Garden, the first in Great Britain, was established by the Earl of Danby in 1621; John Jacob Dillen (Dillenius), who entertained Linnaeus, was its director from 1734 to 1747; the first greenhouse in England was erected in this garden in 1734. The Botanic Garden at Cambridge University was established in 1762.

Several other great gardens were also founded in the seventeenth century. In Berlin, the Botanischer Garten, one of the world's great gardens, was established in 1646; among its famous directors have been J. G. Gleditsch (from 1744 to 1786), K. L. Willdenow (1801-1812), A. W. Eichler (1878-1887), Adolf Engler (1889-1921), and L. Diels (1921-1945); it has been located in the suburb of Dahlem since 1909. At Uppsala, Olaf (Olaus) J. Rudbeck founded a botanic garden in 1655; Olaf O. Rudbeck was its director in the student days of Linnaeus; in his turn Linnaeus was the director from 1742 to 1777 and Carl Peter Thunberg from 1784 to 1828; the original garden is now maintained as a memorial to Linnaeus, with the principal University garden on a different site. At Edinburgh the Royal Botanic Garden was founded in 1670, the second oldest garden in Great Britain; James Sutherland was the first "Regius

Keeper." In Japan the Botanic Gardens of Tokyo Imperial University were established in 1684, one of the first in the Far East.

Early in the eighteenth century two great gardens were founded in Russia, that of the University of Moscow in 1707 and Peter the Great's "Druggist's Garden" at St. Petersburg (now Leningrad) in 1713. Dr. Friedrich E. L. von Fischer (1789-1854) was the first director of the latter, which has been reorganized at various times and is now known as the V. L. Komarov Botanical Institute of the Academy of Sciences of the U.S.S.R. Its herbarium, said to include 5,000,000 specimens, is one of the largest in the world. One of the publications sponsored is the vast *Flora of the U.S.S.R.* (see page 159). In 1755 the Jardin Botanico de Madrid was founded; one of its famous directors was Antonio J. Cavanilles, noted for his "Icones" (illustrations) of American plants (1794). The "Hortus Botanicus" of the University of Budapest was founded in 1771, while in Portugal one of the oldest gardens, at Coimbra, dates from 1772. One of the great botanical gardens of the world, and one of the first to be established in the tropics, was founded at Calcutta in 1787 by Lieutenant Colonel Robert Kyd "not for the purpose of collecting rare plants (although they also have their uses) as things of mere curiosity or furnishing articles for the gratification of luxury, but for establishing a stock for disseminating such articles as may prove beneficial to the inhabitants." The large gardens (273 acres) contain representative collections of the world's tropical plants. The second director was William Roxburgh (1794-1814), "the Father of Indian Botany," who founded the herbarium, now one of the largest in Asia. The original name, Royal Botanic Garden, was changed to Indian Botanic Garden, in 1947.

Throughout the world during the nineteenth century the foundation of great gardens continued to provide institutions for the enrichment of botanical instruction. The Jardin Botanico do Rio de Janeiro, Brazil, was founded in 1808. In Norway the oldest garden is the Universitets Botaniske Have, at Oslo, founded in 1814; the oldest in Australia are the Botanic Gardens of New South Wales, at Sydney, founded in 1816. At Geneva, in 1817, the Conservatoire et Jardin Botaniques de Geneva were established; the first director was Augustin-Pyramus de Candolle, who had been professor of botany at Montpellier; the establishment of a botanic garden was a tacit condition of his accepting the professorship at Geneva. Under his directorship (1817-1835) and that of his son Alphonse (1835-1849) Geneva became one of the leading botanical centers of the world. The great tropical garden of Buitenzorg (Bogor), Java, was founded in 1817; it has an area of 205 acres, with an additional 150 acres in the Mountain Garden. The Royal Botanical Gardens, at Kew, were officially opened in 1841, with Sir William J. Hooker as first director; reference to the history of Kew has been made numerous times above; with the development of the British Empire in the nineteenth century, it came to be called the "botanical capital of the world." The herbarium contains 5,000,000 specimens, the arboretum 7000 species and varieties; about 13,000 species and varieties are under glass, while 8000 herbaceous species are grown out of doors. In Cape Town a botanic garden was laid out in 1848, while in Kingston, Jamaica, the Government Botanic Gardens were founded in 1857; included are the Hill Gardens, or "Government Cinchona," of several thousand acres, where the Cinchona tree was introduced into cultivation about 1870. The Singapore Botanic Gardens were established in 1859. The same year (1859) was the date of the opening of the first great garden in the United States, at St. Louis;

Figure 31. Main Building, The New York Botanical Garden. (Courtesy New York Botanical Garden.)

founded by Henry Shaw, who gave the original buildings and grounds to the public, it was at first (and is still, locally) called "Shaw's Gardens"; officially it is the Missouri Botanical Garden. In Copenhagen the present Universitets Botaniske Have was founded in 1871, although an early garden, later discontinued, was started in 1600. The Arnold Arboretum of Harvard University was founded in 1872; it owes its origin to Mr. James Arnold, who died in 1868, bequeathing $100,000 for the advancement of horticulture; in 1934 more than 6500 species and varieties of woody plants were being grown, said to be the largest number assembled in any one place in America. The first director was Charles Sprague Sargent (1872-1927) who started the famous Crataegus Collection, numbering 1300 species, varieties, and forms. The New York Botanical Garden, one of the greatest in America, was chartered in 1891;

Nathaniel Lord Britton was its first director. In Argentina the Jardin Botanico Municipal was founded in Buenos Aires in 1892.

The development of botanical gardens has continued into the twentieth century until virtually every university has its teaching garden. Noteworthy gardens founded since 1900 are the Brooklyn Botanic Garden, in 1910, with Charles Stuart Gager as first director; and the Botanic Garden, National Museum of Natural History of Peiping, in 1930. The Hortus Botanicus Arcto-Alpinus Stationis Kolaensis, at Kirovsk, Kola Peninsula, founded in 1932, is said to be the first botanical garden north of the Arctic Circle. The Jardin Botanique de Montréal, one of the leading gardens of Canada, was opened in 1936, with Frère Marie-Victorin as the first director.

These "gardens," of course, are far more than merely gardens, in the usually accepted sense of the word. They are usually *botanical institutions,* in which the outdoor garden is but one portion of an *ensemble* including the greenhouse, the herbarium, the library, and the research laboratory.

Herbaria

Most of the great botanical gardens have in connection with them collections of dried and pressed plants arranged in systematic order and available for reference or study. Such a collection is known as a **herbarium,** a name first applied by Linnaeus. The modern herbarium, according to Fosberg, "is a great filing system for information about plants, both primary in the form of actual specimens of the plants and secondary in the form of published information, pictures, and recorded notes."

Some of the great herbaria of the world, with approximate number of specimens in each, are listed in the following table:

Royal Botanical Gardens, Kew	5,000,000
V. L. Komarov Botanical Institute, Leningrad	5,000,000
British Museum (Natural History), London	4,000,000
Berlin-Dahlem,* Botanischer Garten	4,000,000
Paris, Jardin des Plantes	3,500,000
Harvard Univ. (combined herb.),† Cambridge	3,200,000
Geneva, Conservatoire et Jardin Botaniques	3,000,000
Calcutta, Indian Botanic Garden	2,500,000
U. S. National Herbarium, Washington	2,250,000
New York Botanical Garden, New York	2,241,000
Edinburgh, Royal Botanic Garden	1,500,000
Melbourne, National Herbarium	1,500,000
Missouri Botanical Garden, St. Louis	1,500,000
Uppsala, Botaniska Tradgard	1,300,000
Chicago Natural History Museum	1,246,000
Zurich, Botanischer Garten	1,125,000
Brussels, Jardin Botanique	1,100,000
Vienna, Botanischer Garten	1,000,000
Academy of Sciences, Philadelphia	1,000,000

* Almost totally destroyed in an air-raid bombing, March 1, 1943.
† Including the Gray Herbarium, 1,325,000 specimens.

Important herbaria located elsewhere include Cape Town, Pretoria, Buenos Aires, Tucumán, Buitenzorg, Brisbane, and Wellington. Seventy or more herbaria in the United States have more than 50,000 specimens each.

The Preparation of Herbarium Specimens. The equipment necessary for collecting and preparing specimens for the herbarium is relatively simple. Even makeshift materials may serve, although those who go on long expeditions or who do a great deal of collecting will want a more serviceable set of apparatus.

A **field notebook** is an indispensable item. Someone has said that memory is a treacherous ally; the field conditions that seem so fresh in mind at the time of the collection soon become vague and uncertain in the memory of the collector. It is very important that valuable field data be recorded *at the time,* not even waiting until evening. Dates, details of the habitat, abundance, size, color of flowers, and other features of interest should be included in the field notebook record.

For making the collections a strong **trowel** or plant digger is necessary to secure roots, rhizomes, tubers, bulbs, or other underground parts. A sharp knife is needed to remove specimens from trees or shrubs and to cut up the stems of even herbaceous plants. Stems broken off leave unsightly ends that reduce the attractiveness of the specimens.

Some kind of container must be available for temporary handling of the specimens when they are collected. Best results are likely to be secured by use of a **vasculum,** a metal collecting can into which the plants may be placed for carrying and which will prevent rapid wilting. A convenient form is oval in cross-section, about twenty inches long by eight inches wide and ten deep. Such cases can be secured from biological supply houses, although it may be desirable to have them made to order by local tinsmiths. The case should have a large lid, hinged on one edge and provided with a fastener that will keep it securely closed. A ring or buckle at each end of the case provides for the attachment of a strap, so that the vasculum may be suspended from the shoulder. It is also desirable to have a handle on the side, to provide a substitute method for carrying. If such a container is well made plants will remain fresh in it for a day or so, if necessary.

Some collectors make use of a **portable press,** in place of a vasculum. Such a press should be about twelve inches wide and eighteen inches long, made of thin boards and bound together somewhat in the manner of the covers of a book by means of straps or cords. Included in the press should be a few sheets of blotting paper, newspapers, and ventilators—to be described later. The portable press has an advantage over the vasculum in that the plants may be placed directly into it and thus avoid a certain amount of rumpling of the leaves, or closing of the flowers. Where a large amount of collecting is to be done, however, it cannot entirely supplant the vasculum.

Specimens for collection should be selected with considerable care. They should show complete leaves of various forms and sizes, and if possible, roots, rhizomes, and other underground parts of herbaceous plants. Flowers, fruits, and seeds are important, since most keys depend upon the reproductive features for certain identification. The specimens naturally should not be so large that the ends will extend beyond the press.

The transfer of the material from the vasculum to the press involves a careful technique. Foreign material should be washed or shaken from the roots and leaves. The leaves should be untangled and flattened out. The specimens should be trimmed to fit the press.

Many different devices for pressing and drying plants have been used with success. These vary all the way from two flat boards, with a big rock for a weight, to a very elaborate electric drier. A very satisfactory press may be made by using two plywood boards about twelve inches wide by eighteen inches long, or by nailing together a frame of light slats. The press may be "locked up" by means of leather straps or stout cord.

The **fillers** for the press consist of three types of items that may be designated as **folders, blotters,** and **ventilators.** The purpose of the folder is to receive the specimen and to serve as its container while in the press. It also serves as a temporary file for storage of the specimen until it is mounted. Newspaper stock or old newspapers may be used for these folders. The folder must be no larger than about twelve by eighteen inches in order to avoid making specimens too large for mounting on a standard mounting sheet. An ordinary newspaper folded in half is usually about the right size without any cutting. The blotters are the absorbent elements. These are furnished by dealers in botanical supplies and are generally of heavy gray or blue felt paper, of various weights, but cut in the standard size of twelve by eighteen inches. Thickness of the blotting material is largely a matter of individual choice. Ventilators may be sheets of corrugated cardboard or corrugated aluminum, cut to fit the press. Originally corrugated cardboard surfaced with paper on one side only was used; there are advantages, however, in using double-faced cardboard. Aluminum ventilators are still more efficient but of course are more expensive. These are not faced and may be nested together in storage. The function of the ventilator is to provide air passage through the press for the movement of dry warm air, and for the removal of water vapor.

The *placing of specimens in the press* is a matter of great importance, because the appearance of the permanent specimen will depend on how it is pressed and dried. Each specimen should be arranged so that it will look as natural as possible. Leaves should not be crowded or piled on top of each other. Bulky organs may be reduced by slicing off the back in such a manner as not to affect the exposed surface. Flowers with inflated corollas, like the lady's slipper, may be kept from being crushed by inserting a wad of cotton within the corolla. Pads of paper or cotton batting are helpful around bulky portions of some specimens, since they aid in keeping nearby foliage flat. Some flowers, like irises or spiderworts, require special drying with single layers of absorptive tissue above and beneath them. Some leaves should be turned over, in order that examples of both surfaces will be visible in the final specimen. *Temporary labels* should be added for each specimen, after which the folder is closed and placed in the press, with a blotter underneath and above it and with a ventilator underneath and above these.

Drying involves two possible techniques, either with or without artificial heat. *Drying without heat* was customary in most countries until relatively recently. In this process the press is locked up for about twenty-four hours and then opened for examination of the specimens and insertion of dry blotters. This gives an opportunity for such rearrangement of the plant parts as may be desirable. At this time the parts are somewhat flaccid and it is easy to straighten out leaves, petals, and so forth. The appearance of the finished specimen is often dependent upon the attention given to it at this stage. The press is then locked up again for another twenty-four hours, when the process of replacing the moist blotters is repeated. This goes on as long as necessary, although after three or four days some of the specimens should be ready for removal. Most of them should be completely dried in about a week. *Drying with artificial heat* is now a widely used method. By this method the specimens are placed in a field press for twenty-four hours to "sweat," then the press is opened and the specimens rearranged and put into the drying press for heating. The most convenient source of heat is through the use of electricity, with incandescent light bulbs. In the field where electricity is unavailable kerosene lanterns have been used effectively. Gasoline stoves may also be used. Any of these heat sources are potential sources of danger and many a collection has been lost through fire. The length of time required for drying with heat varies, of course, with the intensity of the heat and with the nature of the plant specimens. Twelve hours or less is considered by most collectors too-rapid drying. After twenty-four hours the press is opened, the dry specimens removed and the drying continued for the more succulent specimens.

Mounting the Specimens. Permanent filing of herbarium specimens requires their *mounting*, or attachment, to sheets of **mounting paper.** These are of standard size, eleven and one half by sixteen and one half inches. and should be of a good quality. Some curators use one hundred per cent rag paper, but this is quite expensive and paper of a lower rag content is more generally used. Various methods have been employed for the process of mounting but the most satisfactory is to glue the plant to the paper. In some institutions the specimens are attached by narrow strips of adhesive linen. Other curators employ a combination of the glue (for the flat leaves) with the gummed strips (for the heavier stems). The preferred technique of applying the glue is to use a piece of plate glass about fourteen by twenty inches in size, spreading the paste thinly over the surface, then dropping the plant, face upwards, upon the glue, making certain that all parts of the under surface come in contact with the glue. The plant may then be transferred to the sheet of mounting paper. The label should be pasted on the lower right-hand corner. The mounted sheet may then be replaced within the pressing folder and stacked up between blotters with a light weight. When the glue has

Figure 32. A mounted herbarium specimen. (Photograph by William M. Leeson.)

solidified the pressing folders are discarded and the specimens are ready for filing in the cases.

Herbarium labels are important parts of the finished specimen. An appropriate printed heading, such as *Flora of the Appalachian Mountains, Flora of Alaska, Flora of Tasmania,* is a desirable feature. All other data may be added by typewriter or in longhand; if hand-written, however, great care should be exercised to make the writing easily legible and permanent. The label should give the scientific name of the plant, the place collected, the date, and the name of the collector, as minimum requirements. For specimens gathered in the mountains a statement as to the altitude is important. Such items as the habitat and relative abundance may also be noted. For large plants, when only a small portion appears on the sheet, it is important to state the total height; this is especially desirable when collecting in regions little known botanically, in which case the specimen may represent an undescribed species. The label, however, should not be crowded with information, nor should it be too large. About two and one half by four inches is the customary size. Usually the sheets are stamped with the name of the institution, to designate ownership.

Filing the specimen is the next process. The large herbarium is arranged by families according to one of the well-known systems of classification. These families are usually numbered consecutively and an index card is displayed in the herbarium, with the family numbers indicated. Specimens of each genus are filed in a folded manila **genus cover,** sixteen and five eighths by twelve inches in size (when folded), with the family name and number, and the name of the genus, printed at the lower left corner. The genera may be filed under the families in alphabetical order (the most convenient) or according to some phylogenetic sequence, such as the Dalla Torre and Harms number (see p. 154). Sheets representing the various species may be filed in separate genus covers, or those of each species placed together in a **species cover,** of lighter weight and slightly smaller dimensions than the genus cover, within which it is placed. Species may be arranged within the genus in alphabetical order, or according to some phylogenetic sequence given in a monograph of the group. In a large genus this would require the use of an index card accompanying the first cover of the genus. Special treatment is necessary for bulky materials such as cones, capsules, and the like, which are too large to attach to the specimen sheets. These may be stored in boxes designed to fit on the shelves of herbarium cases.

The modern **herbarium case** is of welded and reinforced steel construction with tiers of pigeonholes each usually nineteen inches deep, thirteen inches wide, and about eight inches high. The cases should be dust-tight and insect-proof. Many old cases were made of wood and often were not insect-proof.

Preservation of specimens from insect depredations is essential, otherwise irreparable damage will be done. Notable among these insect pests are the herbarium beetle, the drugstore beetle, and the book louse. The herbarium beetle is the most destructive and passes its entire life cycle within dried specimens; the life cycle may be completed in seventy to ninety days, with the larval stage thirty-five to fifty days in length. A collection left unattended for a few months may be largely destroyed, and constant vigilance is necessary. Combined use of insecticides and repellents is most effective.

Insecticides include cyanide gas, paradichlorobenzene (PDB), carbon disulfide gas, or dichlorodiphenyltrichloroethane (DDT). Cyanide gas is the most effective, but it is very poisonous and should be used only by specially trained workers. Use of PDB is common, but more often as a repellent; however, if used in sufficient quantities it will kill insects. Carbon disulfide is a commonly used insecticide in herbaria, but it is highly inflammable and must be used with great care. A light sprinkling of DDT on the specimens will kill all insects present but it is not a permanent insecticide and loses its toxic property within a year or two. Another insecticide is a mixture of three parts ethylene dichloride with one part carbon tetrachloride, which may be used like carbon disulfide but has the advantage of being non-inflammable. Bichloride of mercury is often applied to the specimens before they are mounted, either by brushing the material upon the specimens, or by dipping the plants in the poison. While it is an effective stomach poison, it is not permanent and does not kill the insect unless eaten.

Repellents are substances that repel but do not necessarily kill the insects. The two principal repellents are naphtha flakes and paradichlorobenzene. Most effective use is said to be secured from a mixture of two parts of the former with one part of the latter, placed in small muslin bags within each case.

Type specimens, as noted on page 148, are specimens on which the name of some taxon has been based. For this reason type specimens are the most valuable specimens in any herbarium. They are, therefore, accorded special care by many curators, sometimes being kept in separate cases to avoid unnecessary handling. In some institutions they are also placed within a large envelope. If the entire herbarium is not fireproof, the type specimens are sometimes stored in a special building. During World War II about 60,000 types of the New York Botanical Garden were stored on the campus of West Virginia University to escape damage from possible air raids. Millions of specimens, including tens of thousands of types, were lost in the destruction of the Berlin herbarium from allied air raids in 1943. Seven American herbaria have been destroyed by fire since 1900.

References

Fosberg, F. R., *The Herbarium.* Scientific Monthly 63: 429-434, 1946.

Gager, C. S., *Botanic Gardens of the World. Materials for a history.* Brooklyn Botanical Garden Record 27: 151-406. 1938.

Jones, G. N., and E. Meadows, *Principal institutional herbaria of the United States.* American Midland Naturalist 40: 724-740. 1948.

Lanjouw, J., and F. A. Stafleu, *Index Herbariorum.* Part I. *The herbaria of the world.* Regnum Vegetabile 2: 1-179, 1954.

Reed, H. S., *A short history of the plant sciences.* Waltham, Mass., 1942.

Wyman, D., *The Arboretums and Botanical Gardens of North America.* Chronica Botanica 10: 395-494. 1947.

9

The Principles of Taxonomy

Plant taxonomy is a science concerned with the identification, nomenclature, and classification of the various kinds of plants composing the mantle of vegetation covering the earth. It should be noted that the terms plant taxonomy and systematic botany are used synonymously throughout this work. Identification is the determination that a particular individual is similar to some other known individual. Nomenclature is concerned with the application of the correct name to these individuals or groups of individuals. Classification is the disposition of these individuals or groups of individuals into categories according to some particular plan. Because of the inherent nature of the subject matter, whereby no two individuals are exactly alike, although often nearly so, these tasks constitute problems which as yet have been only imperfectly resolved.

Descriptive Taxonomy. The formulation of the principles of taxonomy began with descriptive taxonomy which had its main period of development in the nineteenth century (Chapters 2 and 3). This work was concerned with the observation of the similarities and differences, usually in terms of gross morphology, of the thousands of kinds of plants being discovered in all parts of the earth. The classification schemes devised in the earlier part of this period were called "natural systems," since they were based on man's understanding of nature at the time. Later the rapid acceptance of the theory of evolution led taxonomists to endeavor to classify plants on the basis of actual genetic and ancestral relationships, since the existing forms of life were regarded as the descendants of earlier forms. These schemes are known as "phylogenetic systems" (see p. 51); the fact that numerous systems of this type have been proposed but no one generally accepted is evidence of the fact that a true system is yet to be formulated.

Experimental Taxonomy. In Chapter 5 we noted how, in the twentieth century, there has developed a new sort of taxonomy, whereby, through experimental studies with living plants, an attempt is made objectively to reach the same goals that were sought by the earlier taxonomists, namely, the delimitation of biotic units and their classification in categories of an ascending order of magnitude. This involves such techniques as chromosome study, hybridization, transplanting from one habitat to another, and so on.

The modern taxonomy makes use of data assembled not only from the old fields of ecology, geography, and morphology, but also from the newer fields of genetics, cytology, and physiology.

Phylogeny. All modern taxonomic studies are founded on the tendency to make phylogeny (evolutionary development) the basic principle of taxonomy. However, phylogeny is not a tangible subject that may be studied independently and the results applied to taxonomy. Even though it be granted that present-day plants are descended by evolution from plants of the past, we do not in fact know the origin of more than a few species. In many cases we do not know the nearest living relatives. We do not actually know the phylogenetic history of any group of plants, since it lies in the unwritten past; hence our only recourse is to make use of criteria that seem to be pertinent. These criteria are those which have been the subject matter of descriptive and experimental taxonomy—morphology, ecology, cytology, and related sciences. For practical purposes morphology is still the most widely used means of identification and classification. This was true before the days of Darwin and it remains true today. The experimental method throws light on the mechanism of evolution, but requires much time for its operation. Fortunately, it has been discovered that genetic relationships are usually reflected in similarities and differences in morphological structure, which are readily detected by the eye, usually on brief examination.

Morphological Criteria. Individual plants or groups of plants resemble certain others in some respects, but in other respects resemble different ones. One might, for example, imagine a species resembling, and differing from, several others to the same degree but in different ways. There is no absolute rule that says which features should be regarded as most important, but a few "laws" or general principles have taken form. These are often called Besseyan principles, because in their original form they were stated by Charles E. Bessey in 1915. As examples of these may be mentioned the following:

Life has usually advanced from the simple to the complex (progressive evolution) but sometimes it has been simplified by degeneration or loss of parts (regressive evolution).

The simpler forms of life now existing are usually more like their ancestors than the complex ones.

Evolution is irreversible; that is, a product of evolution never goes back exactly to an ancestral condition.

In most groups of plants the woody habit is more primitive than the herbaceous habit.

Perennials are more primitive than biennials, and biennials more primitive than annuals. In some groups, however, the reverse seems to be true.

Terrestrial forms, in general, are more primitive than aquatics, epiphytes, saprophytes, or parasites.

In the flowering plants simple leaves are usually more primitive than compound leaves.

Bisexual flowers, among Angiosperms, preceded unisexual flowers.

The monecious habit is more primitive than the dioecious.

The solitary flower is more primitive than the cluster of flowers.

Polypetalous flowers are more primitive than sympetalous ones, the latter having been derived from the former by union of the petals.

The many-parted flower is the more primitive, the type with few-parted flowers being derived from it; apetaly is an advanced type.

Actinomorphic flowers are more primitive than zygomorphic flowers.

Hypogynous flowers are more primitive than epigynous flowers.

Separate carpels represent a more primitive condition than united carpels.

The primitive seed contains endosperm while the advanced type contains little or no endosperm.

Separate stamens are more primitive than joined stamens.

A simple fruit is more primitive than a compound fruit.

Anatomical Criteria. Differences in the anatomy of stems have long been recognized. These include differences in the arrangement of the bundles, differences in leaf traces, differences in the details of secondary growth. Histological differences in the xylem have also been observed, tracheae in the angiosperms replacing the tracheids of more primitive stems. These anatomical studies have proceeded to the point where the identification of wood is now possible by microscopic examination, without reference to external morphological characters.

Physiological Criteria. Certain groups of plants differ more or less in their physiology, and physiological or chemical reactions have been used in identifications, especially among the bacteria, fungi, and lichens. Another important physiological indicator is the serum diagnosis, developed by Karl Christian Mez (1866-1944), of the University of Königsberg. By this method a protein extract is made from a given kind of plant and injected into the body of an animal (usually a rabbit). After the rabbit's blood has had time to react to the protein, some of its blood is removed and the serum mixed with the protein extract of a different kind of plant. The formation of a precipitate indicates relationship. The degree of relationship is indicated by the abundance of the precipitate or by the degree of dilution of the serum and extract at which precipitation occurs.

Ecological Criteria. The effects of the environment upon plants have been widely studied by ecologists and now are coming to offer explanations concerning taxonomic relationships. One type of experiment involves growing different varieties of the same species side by side in a garden under uniform conditions. Under such conditions the hereditary differences will stand out, since differences caused by unlike environments are eliminated. Another sort of experiment involves growing the same plants under different environmental conditions; the differences that develop will thus be seen to be the result of ecological factors and not heredity.

Paleobotanical Criteria. The study of existing forms of plants gives a very incomplete knowledge of phylogeny because most of the ancestral forms have long since disappeared. A few of these vanished forms have been preserved as fossils in rocks. Some fossils are merely imprints, others consist of plant parts in which the organic material has been replaced bit by bit with minerals, thus preserving the cellular structure, often very faithfully. Unfortunately, these fossil records are very fragmentary and, while they have yielded much of value, they have left much more unrevealed.

Categories Used in Taxonomy. It may be seen that the taxonomy of today is founded upon the hypothesis that phylogenetical relationships exist between plants, that the plants of today are the more or less modified descendants of the plants of the past. As evolutionary processes progress, closely related ancestors come to have offspring of increased structural complexity, less and less closely related. It is, then, desirable to place plants in categories indicative of their supposed genetic relationships. The term **taxon** (plural taxa) is used to designate any category, of whatever rank, as species, genus, family, order. The basic unit of taxonomic work has been considered to be the species. This taxon had its origin in the ancient civilizations. A taxon including one or more species is a genus. The genus, too, is of long standing, especially among certain plants. The present concept of the genus, however, has developed only in the last two or three centuries. Nomenclaturally, genus and species are the taxa upon which the binomial system has been established.

A group of genera having uniform characteristics is a family. Some families are readily recognized as natural taxa, since the genera have definite characters binding them together. Others are not such natural groups. Furthermore, families are of no particular size; a family may be composed of one genus or 400 genera. As a rule, family names are terminated by the ending *-aceae.* Most family names are taken from the name of a genus in the family as Fagaceae, from *Fagus.* Some family names are from generic names used before Linnaeus, but now nonexistent, as Aquifoliaceae, from *Aquifolium,* the ancient name of the holly but now used as the name of a species of *Ilex* (*I. aquifolium*). Eight family names of long standing are excepted from this general practice: these are Palmae, Gramineae, Cruciferae, Leguminosae, Guttiferae, Umbelliferae, Labiatae, and Compositae. Even for these, alternative names, ending in *-aceae,* are given and may be used if desired. The category next in line, including one or more families, is the order. An order possesses less taxonomic unity than a family. Conventionally, Latin names of orders are taken from the name of one of their families, with the ending *-ales*, thus, Fagales. The class is the next taxon above the order. Classes usually have the ending *-ae;* they include one or more orders. The highest category in the plant kingdom is the division, including a varying number of classes.

The principal categories used in the classification of plants may be summarized thus:

Division (*e.g.*, Trachaeophyta)
  Subdivision (*e.g.*, Pteropsida)
    Class (*e.g.*, Angiospermae)
      Subclass (*e.g.*, Dicotyledoneae)
        Order (*e.g.*, Fagales)
          Family (*e.g.*, Fagaceae)
            Genus (*e.g.*, Fagus)
              Species (*e.g.*, F. sylvatica)

When the groups are very large, they are often subdivided for convenience. Thus, there may be a suborder, ending in *-ineae* (*Rosineae*), a subfamily, ending in *-oideae* (*Caesalpinoideae*), a tribe, ending in *-eae* (*Pomeae*), a subtribe, ending in *-inae* (*Rosinae*), the last three being subdivisions of a family, and a subgenus, as *Eugeum,* or section as *crus-galli,* subdivisions of genera. Categories below the rank of species are also sometimes given, as subspecies (abbreviated ssp.), variety (var.), subvariety (subvar.), form (f.), and clone (cl.).

It should be emphasized that no one of these categories is subject to precise definition; their delimitation varies from botanist to botanist; each is more or less subjective in nature.

References

Bessey, C. E., *The Phylogenetic taxonomy of the flowering plants.* Ann. Mo. Bot. Gard. 2: 109-164. 1915.

Pool, R. J., *Flowers and flowering plants.* New York, 1929.

Swingle, D. B., *A textbook of systematic botany.* New York, 1928.

10

Nomenclature

Common Names. Nomenclature is the application of names to plants. It is perhaps unnecessary to state that plants themselves have no names; the names by which we know them are the names we have applied to them. Such names serve two important purposes; first, and originally, they are for convenience in referring to them, and second, they indicate relationships. Individual plants, of course, very seldom receive individual names; the names applied are collective names, applying equally to all individuals of one kind. All languages and dialects have **vernacular** or **common names** for the important plants growing in the regions where the various languages are spoken, but in all lands the rare or less important plants have no common names. To botanists, who are interested in all plants without respect to their economic importance, this is most inconvenient.

Furthermore many of the well known and widely distributed plants have a large number of common names. Moldenke calls attention to the fact that the pansy has about fifty common English names, as well as approximately as many in German, French, and Spanish, and probably also names in Russian, Hebrew, Chinese, Japanese, and other languages. Gerth's *Dictionary* lists for the broad-leaf plantain forty-six English names, eleven French names, seventy-five Dutch names, and one hundred and six German names.

Thus it can be seen that common names are unsatisfactory, because many plants have *no* common names and some have *too many.*

Scientific names, however, have been given by botanists to all known plants. These are published and used in accordance with established practices, which means that the names are the same in all languages and therefore provide an international means of referring to the plants. These were not suddenly adopted arbitrarily, however, but came gradually into use. It has been noted that many of our present *scientific* names had their origin as *common* names used widely in ancient Greece and recorded by

Theophrastus. Some of these were rendered into Latin by Pliny and other Roman authors, who also added many Latin words for other plants. Among present-day *scientific* names originating as Latin common names are *Salix* (willow), *Populus* (poplar), *Corylus* (hazelnut), *Ostrya* (hornbeam), *Betula* (birch), *Alnus* (alder), *Fagus* (beech), *Quercus* (oak), *Ulmus* (elm), *Ficus* (fig), *Morus* (mulberry), *Urtica* (nettle), *Rumex* (dock), *Pyrus* (pear), *Rubus* (bramble), *Rosa* (rose), *Prunus* (plum), *Viola* (violet), and *Plantago* (plantain).

Common names, of course, were used by the common people and recorded in botanical books by the Chinese, Hindus, Aztecs, and other peoples. It is only historical circumstance that has resulted in *scientific* names having their foundation in Latin rather than Chinese, Aztec or some other language. After the disintegration of the Roman Empire, Latin continued to be used by educated people throughout Europe, because the languages of modern Europe were still in the formative stage and could not be used for precise writing; furthermore, they were, of course, of limited circulation as compared with Latin. As time went by Latin itself gradually evolved into Italian, French, Spanish, Portuguese, and was no longer spoken as in the days of Pliny; spoken Latin, in other words, became a "dead language."

We have noted how the classical names came to be adopted by the herbalists of the sixteenth century. A problem, however, arose when a single Latin word covered several kinds of plants, as, for instance, numerous species of oaks, roses, or violets. It then became necessary to apply adjectives to distinguish between the species. Sometimes several adjectives were necessary, so that the name of a plant became a long and cumbersome descriptive phrase as *Caryophyllum saxatilis, foliis gramineus, umbellatis corymbis* (the Caryophyllum that grows in rocky places, with grass-like leaves and flowers in umbellate corymbs), used by Bauhin, and *Lychnis alpina linifolia multiflora, perampla radice* (the Lychnis of the high mountains, with leaves like flax, many flowers and a very large root) used by Tournefort. We have also noted how the later writers attempted to shorten the names so they could be used with greater convenience, and how at last, Linnaeus, without actually intending to do so, established the usage of *binomial nomenclature*—the use of only *one* descriptive word *with* the Latin name. This practice proved so convenient that it was at once adopted by botanists, and, in establishing the proper *scientific name,* it was decided not to go back of Linnaeus' book, *Species plantarum,* published in 1753. Actually, of course, many of his names were copied from previous writers and we have seen how some of them were inherited from Theophrastus himself. But for practical purposes we regard the date 1753 as the beginning of our present system of *scientific nomenclature.*

Generic Names. It is perhaps needless to say that the same generic name should not be used for more than one group of plants, nor the same specific word for two different species within the same genus. The generic name is always spelled with a capital letter; most specific words (by some botanists *all* specific words) are spelled with small letters.

The vast majority of the members of the plant kingdom, of course, were outside the boundaries of the Roman Empire, and, being unknown to the Romans, naturally had no Latin name. In order for the system to have universal application, therefore, it became necessary to invent generic names for these plants, and to give the names a Latin appearance by slightly revising their spelling or adding a suffix. These names have come from many sources.

(1) Many new genera have been named in commemoration of some person, usually a botanist, or a patron of botany or horticulture. A whole history of botany could be written by reference to such names. There is a *Theophrasta* for the Father of Botany; a *Dioscorea* for the author of the great *Materia Medica;* a *Brunfelsia, Fuchsia, Tragia,* and *Cordia* for the "German Fathers"; a *Matthiola* and a *Caesalpinia* for the two great Italians; a *Dodonaea, Clusia,* and *Lobelia,* for the Dutch "Big Three"; a *Turnera* for the founder of British botany; a *Gerardia* for the British herbalist; a *Tournefortia* and a *Linnaea. Bauhinia,* a plant with conspicuously two-lobed leaves, honors the two Bauhin brothers. *Magnolia* memorializes Pierre Magnol, Tournefort's professor at Montpellier, and *Bignonia* the Abbé Bignon, his patron in Paris; *Sarracenia,* the physician Michel Sarrasin, of Quebec, with whom he corresponded. The friends of Linnaeus are immortalized on page after page of the *Species plantarum* and later books: *Rudbeckia,* for Olaf Rudbeck, under whom he went to Uppsala to study; *Moraea,* for his father-in-law; *Dillenia,* for his friend at Oxford; *Jussieua,* for Bernard de Jussieu; *Kalmia,* for Pehr Kalm, who found the plant in America; *Kuhnia,* for Adam Kuhn, of Philadelphia, one of his two American students; *Ternstroemia,* for his student, Christopher Ternström, who died on his way to the East Indies; *Thunbergia* for his student, C. P. Thunberg, the first botanist of Europe to explore Japan. Likewise there is a *Candollea,* a *Lindleya,* a *Banksia,* a *Benthamia,* a *Hookera,* a *Rumphia.* There is a *Claytonia,* for John Clayton, a *Jeffersonia,* for Thomas Jefferson, a *Nicotiana* for Jean Nicot, who introduced tobacco into Europe; a *Wistaria* for Casper Wistar, a distinguished anatomist of Philadelphia; a *Monarda,* for Nicolas Monardes, author of the first European book on American plants; a *Blighia,* for Capt. William Bligh, of the *Bounty;* an *Avicennia* for the Arabian physician, Ibn-Sina, or Avicenna; a *Burchellia,* for William J. Burchell, a *Warscewiczia,* for J. von Warscewicz, a Pole; a *Karwinskia,* for W. F.

Karwinski, a Hungarian; a *Maximowiczia,* for Carl Maximowicz, who explored Siberia; a *Tsoongia,* for K. K. Tsoong, a Chinese; a *Matsumuria* for J. Matsumura, a Japanese. *Lewisia* and *Clarkia* honor Meriwether Lewis and William Clark, of the Lewis and Clark Expedition. *Einsteinia* is for Albert Einstein, *Gaylussacia* for the famous chemist, J. L. Gay-Lussac; *Victoria* for Queen Victoria; *Parkia* for Mungo Park, the African explorer; *Merrillia,* for Elmer D. Merrill, American botanist.

(2) Many other generic names are formed by combination of two or more Greek or Latin words, usually expressive of some feature of the plant. Examples are *Phytelephas,* "plant-elephant," the generic name for the vegetable ivory palm; *Liriodendron,* "lily-tree," from the shape of the flowers of the tuliptree; *Gymnocladus,* "naked-club," from the long, little-branched stems of the Kentucky coffeetree; *Leucadendron,* "silver-tree," from the silvery leaves of the silvertree; *Xanthoxylum,* "yellow-wood," from the color of the wood of the prickly-ash; *Xanthorhiza,* "yellow-root," from the color of the roots of the shrub yellowroot; *Callicarpa,* "beautiful-fruit," from the fruits of the beauty-berry; *Oxydendrum,* "sour-tree," from the acid leaves of the sourwood; *Anigozanthos,* "unequal-flower," from the irregular flowers of the Kangaroo-paw; *Fagopyrum,* "beech-wheat," from the shape of the grains of buckwheat, resembling beechnuts. Some words are of "hybrid" origin: *Liquidambar,* for example, is from the Latin *liquidus* (liquid) and the Arabic *ambar* (amber); this is not, however, regarded as good usage.

(3) In many cases, when common names for plants existed in the lands in which they were discovered, these names from the native languages were converted into Latin generic names. Among these may be mentioned *Tsuga,* from the Japanese; *Ailanthus,* from the Moluccan; *Asimina* and *Catalpa* from the American Indian; *Nelumbo,* from the Ceylonese; *Ravenala,* from the Madagascarian; *Ginkgo,* from the Chinese; *Puya,* from the Araucan; *Pandanus,* from the Malayan.

(4) Another type of generic names includes those of fanciful, mythological, or poetic origin. Some of these, of course, were applied by the ancient Greeks and Romans themselves, others have been applied by modern botanists. *Nymphaea,* water lilies, refers to the beautiful water-nymphs; *Circaea,* the enchanter's-nightshade, alludes to Circe, the enchantress, and *Calypso* refers to the sea-nymph of that name, both of them concerned in the story of Ulysses; *Dodecatheon* (twelve gods) was a name given by Pliny to a plant believed to be under the care of the principal gods; *Theobroma* (god's-food) was applied to the chocolate plant.

Of course these are only examples and there are many other types of origin of generic names.

The Specific Epithet. The second part of the scientific name, called by

Linnaeus the "trivial name," is now known as the **specific epithet;** it likewise may be derived from many sources.

(1) Since it was originally suggested by the descriptive adjective applied in classical days, it might be expected that this would continue to be the commonest form of the specific epithet, as indeed it is. These may be indicative of color as *rubra* (red), *alba* (white), *flava* (yellow), *nigra* (black), *fusca* (brown); they may indicate the size, shape, or habit of the plant, as *nana* (dwarf), *gigantea* (giant), *alta* (tall), *crassa* (thick), *tenuis* (thin), *scandens* (climbing), *natans* (swimming), *repens* (creeping), *pendulus* (hanging); they may indicate the plant's relative abundance, as *vulgaris* (common), *rara* (rare); they may designate the plant's habitat, as *arvensis* (in fields), *palustris* (in swamps), *arenicola* (in sand), *saxatilis* (among rocks), *aquatica* (in water), *sylvatica* (in woods), *muralis* (on walls); they may describe the plant's uses, as *sativus* (sown for crops), *officinalis* (sold in apothecaries' shops), *hortensis* (grown in gardens), *esculentus* or *edulis* (edible); they may indicate other characteristics, as *foetida* (ill-scented), *fragrans* (fragrant), *spinosa* (spiny), *tomentosa* (woolly), *vernalis* (of spring), *aestivalis* (of summer), *autumnalis* (of autumn), *hiberna* (of winter), *acuminata* (long-pointed), *biennis* (biennial), *rostrata* (beaked), *religiosa* (religious), *toxicaria* (poisonous); or they may indicate the region where the plant was found, as *canadensis* (Canadian), *virginica* (Virginian), *noveboracensis* (of New York), *noveangliae* (of New England), *chinensis* (Chinese), *gallica* (French), *anglicus* (English), *zeylanica* (Ceylonese), *japonica* (Japanese), *novogranatensis* (Colombian, that is, of New Granada), *canariensis* (of the Canary Islands), *allegheniensis* (of the Allegheny Mountains), *saximontana* (of the Rocky Mountains), *capensis* (from the Cape of Good Hope), *nepalensis* (of Nepal), *australiana* (of Australia). A glossary of common Greek and Latin roots appears on page 429.

(2) Another type of specific epithet is a descriptive adjective formed by combining two or more Greek or Latin words and thereby making reference to some distinctive feature or characteristic of the plant, as *latifolia* (broad-leaved), *angustifolia* (narrow-leaved), *grandiflora* (large-flowered), *cordifolia* (with heart-shaped leaves), *quadrilocularis* (four-celled).

(3) A third type of specific epithet is formed from a noun, with a suffix indicating some resemblance or relationship, as *bignonioides* (resembling *Bignonia*), *quercifolia* (with leaves like *Quercus*), *amaranthoides* (resembling *Amaranthus*), *zinniaeflora* (with flowers like *Zinnia*).

(4) A very common type of specific epithet is the commemorative name, in honor of some famous botanist or other person, usually someone who had an intimate connection with that species. Since these were

proper names they are often spelled with capital letters, unlike most specific epithets. These may be written in two ways: as a noun in the possessive case, for example *Thunbergii* (*Berberis Thunbergii,* Thunberg's barberry), *Muehlenbergii* (*Quercus Muehlenbergii,* Mühlenberg's oak), *Dillenii* (*Desmodium Dillenii,* Dillen's tick-trefoil), *Rafinesquii* (*Viola Rafinesquii,* Rafinesque's violet), *Gronovii* (*Cuscuta Gronovii,* Gronovius' dodder), *Willdenowii* (*Carex Willdenowii,* Willdenow's sedge); or as a possessive adjective, as *Gesneriana* (*Tulipa Gesneriana,* Gesner tulip), *Grayana* (*Crataegus Grayana,* Gray hawthorn), *Muelleriana* (*Eucalyptus Muelleriana,* Müller stringybark).

(5) A fifth type of specific epithet is a noun itself, rather than an adjective, often an old Latin or Greek word for some plant, and therefore a word that might have become a generic name, and sometimes did, but which is now reduced to a position within some other genus. Examples may be seen in *Pyrus Malus* (*Malus* was the old Roman word for the apple), *Prunus Cerasus* (*Cerasus* was the Roman word for the sour cherry), *Alisma Plantago-aquatica* (*Plantago-aquatica* was the ancient term for the water-plantain), *Lychnis Flos-jovi* (*Flos-jovi* was the Greek name for the flower of Jove), *Capsella Bursa-pastoris* (*Bursa-pastoris* was the classical word for the shepherd's purse). Other words of this type include names for plants taken from some vernacular or aboriginal language, as *Ipomoea Batatas* (*Batatas* was used for the sweet potato by the Tainos, aborigines of the West Indies), *Theobroma Cacao* (*Cacao,* the chocolate, is from an Aztec name), *Nicotiana Tabacum* (*Tabacum* is from the Taino word for tobacco). These names, like those of a commemorative nature, are often spelled with capital initial letters. Many botanists are coming to believe, however, that all specific epithets, regardless of their origin, should be spelled with small initial letters. There seems to be no good reason why this should not be done. Some conservative botanists insist that the origin of the epithet is likely to be lost if this is done, but botanists long ago stopped spelling the geographical adjective (as *americana*) with an initial capital and the meaning is still clear. The latest "Rules" provide for the use of the small initial letter, although stating that authors desiring to use capital initial letters for particular epithets may do so.

Specific epithets, when adjectives, must agree grammatically with the generic name, which is always in the singular number and in the nominative case. The generic names do, however, differ in gender, being either masculine, feminine, or neuter. The rules governing the gender of Latin nouns are too complex to be noted here, but the gender of a generic name can usually be determined by noting the form of the specific epithets. The following examples show the forms assumed by some common adjectives to indicate gender.

Masculine	*Feminine*	*Neuter*
albus	alba	album
niger	nigra	nigrum
tener	tenera	tenerum
viridis	viridis	viride
acer	acris	acre
repens	repens	repens
altior	altior	altius
bromoides	bromoides	bromoides
japonicus	japonica	japonicum
virginicus	virginica	virginicum
vulgaris	vulgaris	vulgare
chinensis	chinensis	chinensis
scandens	scandens	scandens
pubescens	pubescens	pubescens

Genitive (possessive) names always end in -i or -ii, regardless of the gender of the generic name, if the person honored was a man, as is usually the case (Baileyi, Nuttallii). If the person honored was a woman, then the proper ending in all genders, is -ae, as *Margaretae, Vernae, Mariae, Jonesae,* while if two or more persons were being honored (as two brothers or man and wife) the ending would be -orum, as *Davisiorum.*

Generic names ending in -a are usually feminine, those ending in -um are neuter, and those ending in -us are usually masculine, except for the names of many trees, which are feminine (*Quercus, Populus, Fagus, Pyrus*).

A noun used as a specific epithet is equivalent to a noun in apposition and does not necessarily agree in gender with the generic name (for example *Pyrus Malus, Allium Cepa*).

Organized Nomenclature. As long as most botanists of the world were followers of the various editions of Linnaeus' *Species plantarum,* his binomial system was relatively simple in its operation. But as increasing numbers of new plants were discovered in the newly explored parts of the world and more botanists were publishing new names for these plants, discrepancies in practice soon became apparent. There were no widely accepted rules governing nomenclature. In general, priority of publication was recognized and most authors tried to avoid giving different names to the same species, or the same names to different species. However, names were increasing too rapidly and nomenclature began to be confused. There were no indexes or abstracting services and botanists of one country could not keep up with names that had been proposed by those of other countries.

In 1813 Augustin de Candolle published his *Théorie élémentaire de la botanique,* giving explicit instructions on nomenclatural procedure; the first detailed set of rules was contained in this work, and many botanists adopted the suggestions. In 1821 Ernst Gottlieb Steudel (1783-1856) published his *Nomenclator botanicus,* a list of the Latin names of all plants then known, the first such index since the time of Linnaeus. A revised edition appeared in 1840; both editions, in their day, were widely used.

But in different countries nomenclature followed different patterns, set by botanists of considerable prestige and influence. National and personal jealousies further complicated the situation and the need for an international accord became increasingly apparent. At last the Swiss botanist Alphonse de Candolle called for an assembly of botanists to outline a new system of rules. This, the First International Botanical Congress, met in Paris in 1867. About 150 botanists from Europe and America were invited to attend and each was sent a copy of Candolle's *Lois de la nomenclature botanique.* When the Congress assembled, a few days were spent in study of the *Lois* and they were adopted with only slight revision.

These laws were to a considerable extent the revision and interpretation of earlier rules, with a few new proposals. Attention was given to the matter of author **citation.** The person who first properly publishes the name of a species, genus, or other taxonomic group is said to be the **author** of that group, and in formal citations the author's name, often abbreviated, is placed after the name of the group (for example, *Trillium erectum* L., a plant named by Linnaeus). The names of well known authors are abbreviated, for convenience, and the better known the author the more his name can be abbreviated. Linnaeus, a name which is very familiar, is abbreviated to L., but few others can be so greatly shortened. Different persons with the same name require initials or other designation. W. J. Hooker and his son, J. D. Hooker are usually distinguished by abbreviating the first as Hook. and the second as Hook. f. (*filius*). Augustin de Candolle is abbreviated DC., Alphonse, A. DC., and Casimir, C. DC. Robert Brown is usually given as R. Br., André Michaux as Michx., Willdenow as Willd. In case a name is proposed but not published by one author and is subsequently published by another author, the name of the latter is added, with the Latin preposition *ex* (from) as a connecting word, thus *Hypoporum virgatum* Nees ex Martius, *Flora Brasiliensis.* When a taxon is transferred from one genus to another as in the transfer of *Hypoporum virgatum* to the genus *Scleria,* the name of the first author must be cited in parentheses—*Scleria virgata* (Nees) Steud. Likewise, if a taxon is altered in rank, as, for example, being changed from a species to a variety but retaining its previous epithet, the name of the original author must be cited in parentheses.

Thereafter the Paris Code (or "de Candolle Rules") governed to a considerable extent the taxonomic activity in most countries, although it soon became apparent that numerous defects were present. Various schools of thought put into practice their own interpretations of the

Rules, with the result that the international aspect began to be lost. One of the principal variations was the so-called "Kew Rule" which stated, contrary to some belief at that time, that if a species was transferred to another genus, the specific epithet need not be transferred to the new genus, but that the author of the new combination was free to use whatever epithet he chose.

Index Kewensis. The most comprehensive index to the scientific names of seed plants that has yet been compiled began to appear in 1893. This was the *Index Kewensis plantarum phanerogamarum,* inspired and made financially possible by a gift from Charles Darwin to the Royal Botanic Gardens through his friend, Joseph Dalton Hooker. Under the direction of Hooker, the vast amount of clerical work was accomplished by Benjamin Daydon Jackson (1846-1927) and a staff of assistants. The original work, published in 1893-1895, consisted of an alphabetical list of the genera published from the time of Linnaeus down to 1885. Under each generic name was given, in alphabetic order, every species epithet known to have been published for a member of that genus, each entry being followed by the name of the author, the place of publication, and the native country of the plant. About 375,000 entries were included. Ten supplements were published, up to 1947, each covering the literature of a five-year period. An eleventh supplement appeared in 1953, covering the literature published from 1940 to 1950. This work has become an indispensable reference for all plant taxonomists, and is always consulted in monographic studies.

New Codes. In the United States a group of botanists under the direction of Nathaniel Lord Britton (1859-1934), first director of the New York Botanical Garden, met at Rochester in 1892 and formulated a set of rules based on modifications of the Paris Code. These rules are generally referred to as the Rochester Code. Among their recommendations were the following: that each new species published was to be based upon a designated herbarium specimen, filed in a certain herbarium, to be known as the **type specimen** for the new binomial; a species transferred from one genus to another must carry its epithet with it, unless that epithet had already been given to a species in the new genus; all binomials resulting from such a transfer must be accepted, even if the specific epithet repeats the generic name, as *Sassafras Sassafras;* this type of binomial is known as a **tautonym.**

The first truly international botanical congress was held in Vienna in 1905. At this congress advocates of the Rochester Code attempted to have their basic principles included in the proposed revision of the international code. The new rules, however, did not include these proposals and in some cases even were exactly opposite to them, as in the banning of tautonyms. Another provision of the new code concerned **nomina generica conservanda,** whereby generic names having a wide use would be "conserved" over names that had priority but were less well known. For example, *Carya,* as the generic name for the hickories, was published in 1818 and was therefore antedated by *Hicoria,* published in 1817. But *Carya* had been much more widely used than *Hicoria,* and so by this special dispensation the law of priority was suspended. Another requirement was that names of new groups be accompanied by a Latin **diagnosis** (description).

Most of the American adherents of the Rochester Code, dissatisfied with the results of the Vienna Congress, refused to accept the new International Rules and published a slight revision of the Rochester Code in 1907 under the name of the American Code. This created two opposing schools of thought among American botanists, one headed by Dr. Britton and his students, advocating the American Code and the other headed by the students of Asa Gray, who followed the International Rules. This difference of opinion was greatly emphasized, to the perplexity of amateur botanists, by the publication of the seventh edition of Gray's *Manual of Botany* in 1908 (by B. L. Robinson and M. L. Fernald, of Harvard University) and the second edition of Britton and Brown's *Illustrated Flora* in 1913 (by N. L. Britton and Addison Brown of the New York Botanical Garden).

Another International Botanical Congress was held in Brussels in 1910, it having been decided to hold the meetings at five-year intervals. Little action of a significant nature was taken, however, and World War I prevented the holding of the meeting scheduled for 1915. The next Congress assembled at Ithaca, N. Y., in 1926, where no matters of nomenclature were brought to a vote, but did receive considerable discussion and were referred to a committee for further study.

Finally, at the Cambridge, England, Congress in 1930 (the Fifth International Botanical Congress), accord among the major factions was at last reached. Determined efforts were made to harmonize the differences between the Vienna Rules and the American Code. As a result of these efforts the new rules were the product of an agreement between both parties. Lawrence says, "For the first time in botanical history, a code of nomenclature came into being that was international in function as well as in name." Among provisions which had been under dispute, but which now were agreed upon, were the following: the type concept was accepted; tautonyms were ruled as inadmissible; Latin diagnoses were to be required after January 1, 1932; agreement was reached upon a list of **nomina generica conservanda.** As a result of this accord, the American Code, theoretically, at least, came to an end. There was, of course, no immediate way to prevent use of the many books prepared in the United States on the basis of this Code. It was only through the publication of the eighth edition of *Gray's Manual of Botany* in 1950 (by M. L. Fernald) and the third edition of the *Illustrated Flora* in

1952 (by H. A. Gleason of the New York Botanical Garden) that harmony was brought about between the two principal botanical reference books in use in the Northeastern United States.

The Sixth International Botanical Congress met at Amsterdam in 1935 but few major changes were made in the rules. A proposal for a selected list of **nomina specifica conservanda** was defeated by an overwhelming vote. The Congress scheduled for 1940 was again postponed by world war, and the Seventh International Botanical Congress, in Stockholm, was not held until 1950. A feature of the meeting was a pilgrimage to the home of Linnaeus, whose book published 197 years before, had marked the simple beginning of a system which was now governed by Rules so complicated that more than seventy articles were required for their presentation. The Eighth International Botanical Congress met in Paris in 1954, the one hundredth anniversary of the founding of the Société Botanique de France.

Selected Provisions from the Rules. While it is unnecessary in a work of this scope to introduce a full discussion of the International Rules of Botanical Nomenclature, as revised in 1950, the inclusion of a few important items will be helpful and will give some idea of the nature of the Code.

Provisions are made for the nomenclatural treatment of **apomicts.** The term **apomixis** (away from intermingling) refers to the many types of reproduction in which the male and female gametes do not fuse (p. 98). Groups such as *Rubus* and *Hieracium,* having a large number of apomicts, are likely to have these named as species by taxonomists, with the result that an enormously long list of species accumulates. These, however, should not be considered as homologous with sexually-reproducing species and the new rules suggest that they may be distinguished by inserting the abbreviation *ap.* (apomict) between the generic name and the specific epithet (*Rubus ap. eriensis*).

The dates accepted as starting points for nomenclature in various taxa were set as 1753 for algae, lichens, liverworts, and vascular plants, while 1801 was set for mosses and some fungi, and 1821-1832 for other fungi, since these groups were imperfectly known and incorrectly treated by Linnaeus.

When a species is transferred from one genus to another the original specific epithet must be retained, unless there is already the same epithet present in the new genus, or unless the new combination results in a tautonym. Thus, Linnaeus in 1763 described the hemlock under the name *Pinus canadensis.* Carrière in 1855 recognized that it was not a pine and transferred it to the genus *Tsuga,* resulting in the proper combination, *Tsuga canadensis* (L.) Carr. But, on the other hand, the botanist Du Roi, in 1771, described the American larch under the name *Pinus laricina,* and Michaux, recognizing that it was not a pine, transferred it, in 1803, to the genus *Larix* as *Larix americana* (Du Roi) Michx. This is not in accordance with the Rules, so Karl Koch, in 1873, corrected the situation by making the proper combination, *Larix laricina* (Du Roi) K. Koch.

The name of any plant must, of course, not duplicate a name previously used for a different plant. Such duplicate names are called **homonyms** and the later homonym must be replaced by a new name. Many such homonyms have been published, usually because some botanist, studying a plant he believed to be new, published for it a name which seemed appropriate but which, unknown to him, had already been used. For example, in 1810 Poiret described a grass as *Agrostis arachnoides.* Elliott, in 1816, described a different grass under the same name. These names, thus, were *homonyms,* and the later one is illegitimate under the International Rules. Schultes in 1824 renamed Elliott's plant *A. elliottiana* and this name is the correct designation for it, even though not the earliest name applied to it.

A somewhat humorous instance of homonyms concerns a collection of specimens of *Scleria* made by Schiede in Mexico. These were described in 1845 by Schlechtendahl and published in the *Botanische Zeitung,* Vol. III. One species was described on page 489 of that work, under the name S. *schiedeana.* On page 494 of the same work a different plant was inadvertently described under the same name, resulting in the unusual situation whereby homonyms appeared in the same paper. Schlechtendahl corrected his mistake in an obscure note appearing in *Linnaea* in 1847, renaming the second plant S. *scabriuscula.* Steudel, however, in preparing his work on the Cyperaceae, published in 1855, failed to observe the correction and, jestingly, published the name S. *homonyma* for the second S. *schiedeana.* His joke backfired, however, for his own binomial was an illegitimate synonym, since an earlier usable name existed.

The name of any taxon should not be used if it is a source of error or uncertainty such as would result from its use by different authors in various senses. For example, Linnaeus (1753) described a North American oak as *Quercus rubra,* but the material on which he based his species apparently represented at least two different species, as recognized today. In 1771 Du Roi applied the name *Q. rubra* to the red oak, using the name *Q. falcata* Michx. f. for the southern Spanish oak. In 1915 Sargent, after studying Linnaeus' material, tried to establish the name *Q. rubra* L. for the Spanish oak and *Q. borealis* Michx. f. for the red oak (Rhodora 17: 39, 40. 1915). As a result, confusion reigned, because some botanists followed the new interpretation and some the old. Hence, Rehder proposed that *Q. rubra* be regarded as a **nomen ambiguum** (ambiguous name) and be completely rejected from use for any plant. However, not all botanists agreed that the name was ambiguous and Fernald (1950) in the eighth edition of *Gray's Manual* continued the use of *Q. rubra* in its older sense, for the northern red oak.

From time to time much disaffection is registered among botanists because research continually brings changes in nomenclature to various taxa of plants. These changes are particularly disturbing when they apply to familiar plants with well known names. Such complaints, however, do not take into account the fact that systematic botany is a living science, dealing with a living subject matter, and that fluidity in nomenclature is not only a necessary corollary but even a desirable one, if progress is to continue.

The remarks of A. de Candolle,* one of the earliest students of the laws of botanical nomenclature, are still pertinent: "There will come a time when all the plant-forms in existence will have been described; when herbaria will contain indubitable material of them; when botanists will have made, unmade, often remade, raised or lowered, and redefined several hundred thousand groups from classes to mere varieties, and when synonyms will have become much more numerous than accepted groups. Then science will have need of a great revision of its formulae. This nomenclature which we now strive to improve will then appear like an old scaffolding, laboriously patched together and encumbered by the debris of rejected parts. The edifice of science will have been built, but the rubbish incident to its construction not cleared away. Then perhaps there will arise something wholly different from Linnaean nomenclature, something so designed as to give certain and definite names to certain and definite groups.

"That is the secret of the future, a future still very far off."

References

Candolle, A. de, and others, *Lois de la Nomenclature botanique, adoptées par le Congrès International de Botanique tenu à Paris en aout,* 1867. Geneve, 1867. English transl. London, 1868.

Gerth van Wijk, H. L., *A dictionary of plant names.* 2 vols. The Hague, 1911-1916.

Hitchcock, A. S., *Methods of descriptive systematic botany.* New York, 1925.

Moldenke, H. N., *A brief course in elementary systematic botany for gardeners.* Lithoprinted. New York, 1947.

* Translated by C. A. Weatherby, Amer. Jour. Bot. 36: 7. 1949.

11

The Literature of Systematic Botany

A complete bibliography of taxonomic literature would fill many volumes. Taxonomy is basically descriptive in its nature; its literature is necessarily voluminous. Furthermore, this literature is to be found in all sorts of publications—in whole volumes devoted to certain subjects, in small pamphlets, and in articles published in a wide variety of periodicals. Every civilized nation has had taxonomists, and this literature may be found in many languages. There is at present a tendency to write in one of the leading languages, such as English, French, German, Spanish, or Russian, and of course some literature, especially original descriptions, is still written in Latin. Even so, taxonomy is truly international in its character and it must be recognized that studies of broader than purely local nature involve the use of many different languages. It is for these reasons that indexes, such as the *Index Kewensis* are so essential in this field.

The following list is intended to include some of the more important works of a world-wide scope. It will be realized how incomplete it is when stated that the bibliography for a single state would run into hundreds of items.

General Indexes

Index Kewensis plantarum phanerogamarum. 2 vols. 11 suppls. Oxford, 1893-1953. The history of this work, so essential to any study of the taxonomy of flowering plants, has already been related.

Index filicum. Copenhagen, 1906, with suppls. to 1933. This deals with the Filicineae (true ferns) in somewhat the same manner that the *Index Kewensis* treats the flowering plants.

Gray Herbarium Card Index. Cambridge, Mass. This covers the flowering plants and ferns of the western hemisphere and is an index to names of all taxa published since 1873. Approximately 260,000 cards have been issued.

Genera siphonogamarum. Berlin, 1907. This work by C. G. Dalla Torre and H. Harms is a list of orders, families, and genera of seed plants, arranged according to the Engler-Prantl system. The genera are arranged systematically and numbered consecutively from 1, *Cycas* to 9629, *Thamnoseris*, and these numbers are used by some curators as the sequence for filing material in the herbarium.

Index Londinensis to illustrations of flowering plants, ferns and fern allies. Oxford, 1920-1941. An alphabetical index to illustrations appearing from 1753 to 1935 (the index proper covers the period 1753 to 1920, and a supplement includes literature to 1935).

Thesaurus literaturae botanicae. G. A. Pritzel. 547 pp. 1847-1851; ed. 2. 576 pp. Leipzig, 1872. Very important for early botanical literature.

Guide to the literature of botany; being a classified selection of botanical works, including nearly 6000 titles not given in Pritzel's Thesaurus. B. D. Jackson. 626 pp. London, 1881.

A bibliography of eastern Asiatic botany. E. D. Merrill and E. H. Walker. 719 pp. Jamaica Plain, 1938.

The Classics

Many of the works which have been landmarks in the development of systematic botany have been described in the preceding historical chapters. They include the works of Theophrastus, Pliny, Dioscorides, T'ang Shen-wei, Albertus Magnus, Brunfels, Bock, Fuchs, Cordus, Mattiola, Cesalpino, Dodoens, l'Ecluse, l'Obel, Turner, Gerard, de la Cruz, Badianus, Hsu Yung-ch'eng, Li Shi Chen, the Bauhins, Ray, Tournefort, and Linnaeus. Although they exerted a powerful influence in their day, these books are now principally of value from the historical standpoint.

Works of a Broad Scope

There is no single world flora, accounting for every *species* on earth. There are, however, numerous works treating of the *families* or even *genera* known throughout the world. Some of the better-known of these are:

Baillon, H. *Histoire des plantes*. 13 vols. Paris, 1867-1895. A comprehensive work treating all known families and genera of vascular plants, copiously illustrated and with extensive bibliographic references.

Bentham, G. and Hooker, J. D. *Genera plantarum*. 3 vols. London, 1862-1883. One of the great reference books of all time. The descriptions were prepared from the plants themselves.

Bessey, C. E. *The phylogenetic taxonomy of flowering plants*. Annals of the Missouri Botanical Garden, 2: 109-164. 1915. An outline based upon a revision of the Bentham-Hooker system.

1084 HABENARIA.

HABENARIA:—
lucida, Wall. ex Lindl. Gen. et Sp. Orch. 319.—Burma.
lutea, Benth. in Journ. Linn. Soc. xviii. (1881) 354 = Perrottetiana.
macilenta, Reichb. f. in Flora, xlviii. (1865) 180.—Guiana.
macrandra, Lindl. in Journ. Linn. Soc. vi. (1862) 139.—Afr. trop.
macrantha, Hochst. ex A. Rich. Tent. Fl. Abyss. ii. 294.—Abyssin.
macroceras, Spreng. Syst. iii. 692 = seq.
macroceratilis, Willd. Sp. Pl. iv. 44.—Costa Rica.
macrophylla, Goldie, in Brewst. Edinb. Phil. Journ. vi. (1822) 331.—Am. bor.
macrostachya, Lindl. Gen. et Sp. Orch. 307.—Ind. or.
maculosa, Lindl. l. c. 309.—Am. trop.
malacophylla, Reichb. f. Otia Bot. Hamb. 97.—Afr. austr.
Mannii, Hook. f. in Journ. Linn. Soc. vii. (1864) 222. —Afr. trop.
margaritacea, Linden, in Illustr. Hortic. xxix. (1882) 52, nomen.—N. Granat.
marginata, Colebr. in Hook. Exot. Fl. t. 136.—Ind. or.
martialis, Reichb. f. Otia Bot. Hamb. 99.—Afr. trop.
mascarenensis, Spreng. Syst. iii. 690.—Ins. Mascar.
maxillaris, Lindl. in Hook. Journ. Bot. i. (1834) 5.—Am. trop.
Mechowii, Reichb. f. in Flora, lxv. (1882) 532.—Afr. trop.
megaceras, Rodrig. Orch. Nov. i. 161 = obtusa.
Melvillii, Ridl. in Journ. Bot. xxiii. (1885) 170.—Bras.
membranacea, Lindl. Gen. et Sp. Orch. 313.—Afr. trop.
mesodactyla, Griseb. Fl. Brit. W. Ind. 644.—Ind. occ.
mexicana, Linden, in Illustr. Hortic. xxix. (1882) 52, nomen.—Mexic.
Michaeli, Greene, in Bull. Calif. Acad. i. iv. (1885) 281.—Am. bor. occ.
Michauxii, Nutt. Gen. Am. ii. 189.—Am. bor.
micrantha, Hochst. ex Seub. Fl. Azor. 25.—Ins. Azor.
micrantha, Reichb. f. in Flora, xlviii. (1865) 180 = arenaria.
micrantha, Wall. ex Lindl. Gen. et Sp. Orch. 302 = cubitalis.
microceras, Hook. f. in Journ. Linn. Soc. vii. (1864) 221.—Afr. trop.
microstylina, Reichb. f. Xenia Orch. iii. 17.—Bolivia.
Miersiana, Champ. ex Benth. in Hook. Kew Journ. vii. (1855) 37.—Hongkong.
Milnei, Reichb. f. Otia Bot. Hamb. 96.—Afr. austr.
minutiflora, Ridl. in Journ. Linn. Soc. xxi. (1885) 503.—Madag.
misera, Ridl. l. c.—Madag.
modesta, Dalz. in Hook. Kew Journ. ii. (1850) 262. —Ind. or.
modestissima, Reichb. f. in Linnaea, xxii. (1849) 811. —Am. trop.
montana, A. Rich. in Ann. Sc. Nat. Sér. II. xv. (1841) 73 = longicornu.
montana, Rodrig. Orch. Nov. i. 154.—Bras.
montana, Wight, Ic. t. 1714, partim = decipiens.
montevidensis, Lindl. Gen. et Sp. Orch. 314.—Urug.
montevidensis, Spreng. Syst. iii. 692.—Urug.
muricata, Rodrig. Orch. Nov. ii. 255.—Bras.
muricata, Vidal, Phan. Cuming. Philipp. 80, 82, 83, 151.—Ins. Philipp.
mutica, Span. in Linnaea, xv. (1841) 477.—Ins. Timor.
mystacina, Lindl. Gen. et Sp. Orch. 312.—Bras.
nasuta, Reichb. f. & Warm. in Otia Bot. Hamb. 80.—Bras.
natalensis, Reichb. f. l. c. 97.—Afr. austr.
nemorosa, Rodrig. Orch. Nov. i. 160.—Bras.
neuropetala, Miq. Ann. Mus. Bot. Lugd. Bat. ii. 207. —Japon.
nigra, R. Br. in Ait. Hort. Kew. ed. II. v. 192.—Europ.
nivea, Spreng. Syst. iii. 689.—Am. bor.
novemfida, Lindl. in Benth. Pl. Hartw. 94.—Guatemala.
Novo-Ebudarum, F. Muell. Phyt. New Hebr. 22.—N. Hebr.
nuda, Lindl. Gen. et Sp. Orch. 312.—Bras.
nutans, Ridl. in Journ. Linn. Soc. xxi. (1885) 507.—Madag.
nyikana, Reichb. f. Otia Bot. Hamb. 100.—Afr. trop.

HABENARIA:—
obsoleta, Spreng. Syst. iii. 689.—Am. bor.
obtusa, Lindl. Gen. et Sp. Orch. 315.—Bras.
obtusata, Richards. in Frankl. Narr. 1st Journ. 750. —Am. bor.
occultans, Welw. ex Reichb. f. in Flora, xlviii. (1865) 178.—Afr. trop.
ochroleuca, R. Br. Prod. 313.—Austral.
odontopetala, Reichb. f. in Linnaea, xviii. (1844) 407. —Mexic.
odoratissima, Franch. Fl. Cher-et-Loire, 578.—Europ.
Oerstedii, Reichb. f. in Bonplandia, iii. (1855) 213.—Nicaragua.
orangana, Reichb. f. Otia Bot. Hamb. 101.—Afr. austr.
orbiculata, Hook. Exot. Fl. t. 145 = Hookeriana.
ornithoides, Rodrig. Orch. Nov. i. 162.—Bras.
ornithopoda, Reichb. f. in Linnaea, xx. (1847) 696 = laevigata.
ovalifolia, Wight, Ic. t. 1708.—Ind. or.
Paivaeana, Reichb. f. Xenia Orch. iii. 17.—Bolivia.
paludosa, Lindl. in Journ. Linn. Soc. vi. (1862) 139. —Afr. occ.
paludosa, Reichb. f. in Flora, xlviii. (1865) 178 = Protearum.
paludosa, Rodrig. Orch. Nov. i. 153.—Bras.
papillosa, Ridl. in Journ. Linn. Soc. xxi. (1885) 504. —Madag.
paranaënsis, Rodrig. Orch. Nov. ii. 249.—Bras.
parvidens, Lindl. Gen. et Sp. Orch. 317.—Peruv.
parviflora, Lindl. l. c. 314.—Bras.
pauciflora, Reichb. f. in Bonplandia, ii. (1854) 10, sub n. 3.—Bras.
pauciflora, Rodrig. Orch. Nov. i. 157.—Bras.
paucifolia, Lindl. Gen. et Sp. Orch. 310.—Chili.
pectinata, D. Don, Prod. Fl. Nep. 24.—Reg. Himal.
pedicellaris, Reichb. f. Otia Bot. Hamb. 100.—Abyss.
pedicellata, S. Wats. in Proc. Am. Acad. xii. (1877) 276.—Am. bor. occ.
pelorioides, Par. & Reichb. f. in Trans. Linn. Soc. xxx. (1874) 139.—Burma.
peltastes, Reichb. f. Otia Bot. Hamb. 99.—Afr. trop.
pentadactyla, Lindl. Gen. et Sp. Orch. 307.—Reg. Argent.
peramoena, A. Gray, Bot. N. U. St. ed. V. 503.—Am. bor.
perbella, Reichb. f. Otia Bot. Hamb. 98.—Abyss.
peristyloides, A. Rich. in Ann. Sc. Nat. Sér. II. xiv. (1840) 270.—Abyss.
peristyloides, Wight, Ic. v. 18. t. 1702 = stenostachya.
Perrottetiana, A. Rich. in Ann. Sc. Nat. Sér. II. xv. (1841) 74.—Ind. or.
petalodes, Lindl. Gen. et Sp. Orch. 316.—Bras.
petromedusa, Webb, in Hook. Niger Fl. 180.—Ins. Cap. Virid.
physoplectra, Reichb. f. in Linnaea, xlii. (1877) 17.—N. Hebrid.
picnostachia, Rodrig. Orch. Nov. ii. 250.—Bras.
Pinguicula, Benth. in Journ. Linn. Soc. xviii. (1881) 355.—China.
plantaginea, Lindl. Gen. et Sp. Orch. 323.—Ind. or.
Platanthera, Reichb. f. in Linnaea, xli. (1877) 55.—Urug.
platyanthera, Reichb. f. l. c. xxii. (1849) 860.—Abyss.
platyphylla, Spreng. Syst. iii. 690.—Ind. or.
plectomaniaca, Reichb. f. & S. Moore, in Journ. Bot. xvi. (1878) 136.—Afr. trop.
pleistadenia, Reichb. f. in Journ. Linn. Soc. xxi. (1885) 404.—Afr. trop.
polypodantha, Reichb. f. Otia Bot. Hamb. 97.—Afr. austr.
ponerostachys, Reichb. f. in Bonplandia, iii. (1855) 213.—Ins. Philipp.
praealta, Spreng. Syst. iii. 691.—Ins. Borbon.
pratensis, Reichb. f. in Linnaea, xxii. (1849) 813.—Bras.
procera, Lindl. Gen. et Sp. Orch. 318.—Afr. trop.
promensis, Lindl. in Wall. Cat. n. 7033 = marginata.
propinquior, Reichb. f. Beitr. Syst. Pfl. 53 = xanthantha.
Protearum, Reichb. f. Otia Bot. Hamb. 57.—Bras.
Pseudostylites, Reichb. f. & Warm. l. c. 79.—Bras.
psychodes, Spreng. Syst. iii. 693 = fissa !
psycodes, A. Gray, Man. Bot. N. U. St. ed. V. 502 = fissa !
pterocarpa, Thw. Enum. Pl. Zeyl. 309.—Zeylan.
pubescens, Lindl. Gen. et Sp. Orch. 322.—Reg. Himal.
pumila, Poepp. Fragm. Syn. 21.—Chili.

HABENARIA:—
purpurea, Thou. Orch. Isles Austr. Afr. t.
pusilla, Reichb. f. Otia Bot. Hamb. 33.—
pyramidalis, Lindl. in Ann. & Mag. N (1845) 386 = strictissima.
quadrata, Lindl. Gen. et Sp. Orch. 316.—
Quartiniana, A. Rich. in Ann. Sc. Nat. (1840) 271.—Abyss.
racemosa, Rafin. Ann. Nat. 15.—Am. bo
radiata, Spreng. Syst. iii. 693.—Japon.
rariflora, A. Rich. in Ann. Sc. Nat. Sér. 70.—Ind. or.
reflexa, Blume, Bijdr. 403.—Java.
Reichenbachiana, Rodrig. Orch. Nov. i. 1
repens, Nutt. Gen. Am. ii. 190.—Am. bor
replicata, Hochst. ex A. Rich. Tent. Fl. —Abyss.
replicata, A. Rich. Fl. Cub. Fanerog. ii. 2
retusa, Riddell, Suppl. Cat. Ohio Pl. 17.-
retusa, Rodrig. Orch. Nov. ii. 253.—Bras.
rhodocheila, Hance, in Ann. Sc. Nat. (1856) 248.—China.
rhynchocarpa, Trim. Cat. Pl. Ceyl. 91.—
Richardiana, Wight, Ic. t. 1713.—Ind. or.
robusta, N. E. Br. in Gard. Chron. (1885) Bonatea.
robusta, Welw. ex Reichb. f. in Flora, l. (Afr. trop.
rodeiensis, Rodrig. Orch. Nov. ii. 256.—B
rostellifera, Reichb. f. Otia Bot. Hamb. 8
rostrata, Wall. ex Lindl. Gen. et Sp. Burma.
rotundifolia, Lindl. Gen. et. Sp. Orch. flora, Lindl.
rotundifolia, Richards. in Frankl. Narr 750; Spreng. Syst. iii. 692.—Am. bor.
Rumphii, Lindl. Gen. et Sp. Orch. 32 boina.
rupestris, Poepp. Endl. Nov. Gen. et Peruv.
rupicola, Rodrig. in Rev. Engenh. iii. (montana.
Rutenbergiana, Kraentz. in Bremen, Ab 258.—Madag.
sagittifera, Reichb. f. in Bot. Zeit. iii. (Japon; Manchur.
salaccensis, Blume, Bijdr. 403. t. 13.—M
santensis, Rodrig. Orch. Nov. ii. 253.—B
Sartor, Lindl. in Hook. Lond. Journ. 662.—Bras.
Saundersiae, Harv. Thes. Cap. ii. 29.—Af
sceptrodes, Reichb. f. in Bonplandia, iv. —Hab. ?
Schimperiana, Hochst. ex A. Rich. Tent. 295.—Abyss.
Schiechmareffiana, Cham. in Linnaea, iii. Herminium congestum.
Schisochilus, J. Grah. Cat. Pl. Bomb. 25
Schomburgkii, Lindl. ex Benth. in Journ. Bot. ii. (1843) 673.—Guiana.
Schwackii, Rodrig. Orch. Nov. ii. 254.—
Schweinfurthii, Reichb. f. Otia Bot. Hamb
secunda, Lindl. Gen. et Sp. Orch. 307.—
secundiflora, Rodrig. Orch. Nov. ii. 252.—
setacea, Lindl. Gen. et Sp. Orch. 312.—
seticauda, Lindl. ex Benth. in Hook. Bot. ii. (1843) 673.—Guiana.
setifera, Lindl. in Ann. Nat. Hist. iv. (Mexic.
Sieboldiana, Miq. Ann. Mus. Bot. Lugd. —Japon.
Sigillum, Thou. Orch. Afr. t. 20.—Ins. M
simense, Reichb. f. in Linnaea, xxii. (184 trop.
simillima, Reichb. f. Xenia Orch. iii. 18.-
simplex, Kraentz. in Bremen, Abh. vii. —Madag.
sochensis, Reichb. f. Otia Bot. Hamb. 100
socotrana, Balf. f. in Proc. Roy. Soc. Edi 96.—Ins. Socotra.
sparsiflora, S. Wats. in Proc. Am. Aca 276.—Am. bor. occ.
spathacea, A. Rich. & Gal. in Ann. Sc. iii. (1845) 29.—Mexic.
spathulata, Benth. in Journ. Linn. Soc. 355.—Reg. Himal.
spatulaefolia, Par. & Reichb. f. in Tran xxx. (1874) 140.—Burma.

Figure 33. A page from the *Index Kewensis*. (Photograph by William M. Leeson.)

Candolle, A. P., A., and C. de, *Prodromus systematis naturalis regni vegetabilis.* 17 vols. and 4 index vols. Paris, 1824-1873. This vast work, although entitled a Prodromus (forerunner) actually attempts to account for all species of dicotyledons. The first seven volumes were written by Augustin Pyramus de Candolle, and the remaining volumes were edited by his son Alphonse, and written by about thirty-five monographers, including Casimir de Candolle, son of Alphonse.

Engler, A., *Das Pflanzenreich.* Leipzig, 1900- . A compendious work in many volumes, dealing with genera and species of plants of the world.

Engler, A., and L. Diels, *Syllabus der Pflanzenfamilien.* 11th ed. Berlin, 1936. A condensation of the Engler system of classification.

———, and K. Prantl, editors. *Die naturlichen Pflanzenfamilien.* 23 vols. Leipzig, 1887-1915; 2nd ed., 8 vols., 1924- (incomplete). Keys, descriptions, and illustrations are given for the families and genera of all plants (except bacteria). A summary of knowledge concerning embryology, morphology, anatomy, and paleobotany is included, with references to selected bibliography.

Gunderson, A., *Families of Dicotyledons.* Waltham, Mass., 1950.

Hallier, H., *Provisional scheme of the natural (phylogenetic) system of flowering plants.* New Phytologist 4: 151-162. 1905.

Hutchinson, J., *The families of flowering plants.* Arranged according to a new system based upon probable phylogeny. I, Dicotyledons. 328 pp. London, 1926. II, Monocotyledons. 243 pp. London, 1934.

Jussieu, A. L. de, *Genera plantarum secundum ordines naturales disposita.* Paris, 1789.

Lindley, J., *An introduction to the natural system of botany, or a systematic view of the organization, natural affinities, and geographical distribution of the whole vegetable kingdom, together with the uses of the most important species in medicine, the arts, and rural or domestic economy.* London, 1830.

Pulle, A. A., *Remarks on the system of the spermatophytes.* Mededeelingen Botanisch Museum en Herbarium Rijksuniversiteit Utrecht, 43: 1-17. 1937.

Rendle, A. B., *The Classification of flowering plants.* 1, Gymnosperms and Monocotyledons, 403 pp. Cambridge, 1904. 2, Dicotyledons, 636 pp. Cambridge, 1925.

Schaffner, John H., *Phylogenetic Taxonomy of Plants.* Quarterly Review of Biology, 9:129-160. 1934.

Skottsberg, C., *Oversikt av vaxtriket,* in *Vaxternas Liv.* 5: 137-699. Stockholm, 1940. This is a modification of the classification of the entire plant kingdom, representing to a degree a compromise between the Bentham-Hooker and Engler-Prantl systems.

Wettstein, R., *Handbuch der systematischen Botanik.* 4th ed., 1152 pp. Leipzig and Vienna, 1935. A system of classification based on a revision of the Engler-Prantl scheme.

Floras

A descriptive flora is a systematic arrangement of the species of a given area, with keys and descriptions and often illustrations, by the use of which a student may determine the names and characteristics of the wild plants of the area. A flora covers a country, a section of a country, a state, a valley, or a county or vicinity of a city. Examples are Bentham's *Handbook of the British Flora,* Britton's *Manual of the Flora of the Northern States and Canada,* Black's *Flora of South Australia,* MacMillan's *Metaspermae of the Minnesota Valley,* Muir's *Vegetation of the Riversdale Area, Cape Province.* Distinctions are sometimes attempted between floras and manuals but in actual practice these terms are essentially synonymous.

The student of taxonomy should be familiar with the manuals or floras covering his own region and should know about some of the more important floras covering other regions. There are, of course, no reference works that cover in detail all plants known to exist; even if such reference works were available, they would be too cumbersome for ordinary use. It is in the regional flora, then, that the student finds available the details of the plant life of his immediate environment.

In some parts of the world, local floras have been studied and revised for so many years that few, if any, new species are likely to be found. But in many other regions, manuals are not available or are so antiquated and incomplete as to be of little general value. There is still a great need for carefully prepared floras, not only for Africa, Asia, and South America, but even for parts of the continents of Europe, North America, and Australia, which are by far the best known.

Of course, thousands of books and articles have been written and may be considered as local lists or regional floras, some covering only a very small area, some an entire country. There is naturally great variation in the dates and degree of completeness of such floras as exist. Extensive lists of floras of various states and countries may be found in Blake and Atwood's *Geographical Guide to Floras of the World.*

North America. Most parts of the United States are covered by regional manuals or floras.

For the northeastern states (also including southeastern Canada) Gray's *Manual of Botany* has been the standard reference work for a century. The eighth edition, by M. L. Fernald, appeared in 1950 and is a work of 1632 pages. Another flora, with illustrations of each species, is Britton and Brown's *Illustrated Flora,* a three-volume work, the third edition of which, by H. A. Gleason, appeared in 1952.

For the southeastern states the principal work is J. K. Small's *Manual of the southeastern flora,* published in 1933, essentially the third edition of Dr. Small's earlier *Flora.* This work, jokingly referred to as the "big Small" (it is a book of 1554 pages), reflects the liberal viewpoints of the author, and much of the nomenclature differs strikingly from that used in the northeastern floras.

The most extensive flora of the central states is P. A. Rydberg's *Flora of the prairies and plains.* This work, of 969 pages, covers the grasslands of Central North America, and was published in 1932.

For the Rocky Mountain region the most recent extensive flora is Rydberg's *Flora of the Rocky Mountains and adjacent plains;* the second edition, of 1144 pages, appeared in 1922. An earlier work was J. M. Coulter and A. Nelson's *New manual of Rocky Mountain botany,* published in 1909.

The Pacific states are covered by a comprehensive work, *An illustrated flora of the Pacific States,* by L. Abrams. This was modeled somewhat on Britton and Brown's *Illustrated Flora,* and includes 4 volumes. These were published in 1923, 1944, and 1951, with the fourth volume still in preparation. An illustration is provided for each species.

State floras exist or are in preparation for each of the states of the United States and most of the Canadian provinces are at least partially covered. For Alaska a most important work is E. Hultén's *Flora of Alaska and Yukon,* published in 10 parts from 1941 to 1950.

No complete modern floras exist for the countries south of the United States, although many valuable works have been published and numerous floras are in preparation. Three volumes of Hermanos Leon and Alain's *Flora de Cuba* have appeared (1946, 1951, 1953). Likewise, 2 volumes of C. Conzattis' *Flora taxonomica mexicana* have been published (1939, 1943-1947). P. C. Standley has written voluminously on the plants of Mexico and the Central American countries; some of these works include his *Flora of Yucatan* (1930), *Flora of Costa Rica* (an annotated list of species, 1937-1938), *Flora of Guatemala* (with J. A. Steyermark, 1949, incomplete), and *Flora of the Panama Canal Zone* (1928).

South America. Of the South American countries only a few have modern lists of species and there are no modern floras, in the usual sense of the word. One of the more recent works is H. Descole's *Genera et species plantarum argentinarum,* of which 4 volumes have been published (1943-1948) and many others planned. Other works include J. F. MacBride's *Flora of Peru* (1936-1949, incomplete); H. F. Pittier's *Genera plantarum venezuelensium* (1939), a key to the genera of plants of Venezuela; A. A. Pulle's *Flora of Surinam* (4 vols., 1932-1940, incomplete); and K. F. Reiche's *Flora de Chile* (6 vols., 1896-1911).

Europe. Europe, because of the long period in which it has been under investigation, is botanically the best known of all the continents. Hundreds of floras have been published, covering the various countries or portions of countries. Among some of the classical works are H. Coste, *Flore descriptive et illustrée de la France* (3 vols., 1900-1906), A. X. P. Coutinho's *Flora de Portugal* (1913), A. Fiori's *Nuova flora analitica d'Italia* (2 vols., 1923-1929), G. Hegi's *Illustrierte Flora von Mittel-*

Europa (13 vols., 1906-1931), J. Lid's *Norsk flora* (1944), C. A. M. Lindman's *Svensk fanerogamflora* (2d ed., 1926), H. M. Willkomm and J. Lange's *Prodromus florae Hispanicae* (3 vols., 1861-1880), and E. de Halacsy's *Conspectus florae Graecae* (3 vols., 1901-1904). The most recent *Flora of the British Isles* is by A. R. Clapham, T. G. Tutin and E. F. Warburg (1952).

Asia. The largest of the continents is the most lacking of all in modern floras. Japan and China, despite intensive botanical activity, have no true national floras and but few regional floras. The principal flora of India, by J. D. Hooker (see page 82), is long out-of-date. The plants of most countries of southwestern Asia are not included in any recent floras, except for Palestine, which, in sharp contrast, has been more fervently studied than that of any other part of the world with comparable area. Some outstanding works are in preparation, such as C. G. G. J. van Steenis' *Flora Malesiana,* including the area of Indonesia and surrounding regions. The great *Flora of the U.S.S.R.* (*Flora Unionis Rerumpublicarum Sovieticarum Socialisticarum*), by V. L. Komarov and others, will adequately cover both European and Asiatic Russia. The first volume appeared in 1934 and 23 volumes had been published by 1955.

Africa. The occupation of most of Africa by the European powers has resulted in intensive exploration and the preparation of numerous important floras, although these by no means adequately cover the continent. Noteworthy are J. Hutchinson and J. M. Dalziel's *Flora of west tropical Africa* (2 vols., 1927-1929), D. Oliver and others, *Flora of tropical Africa* (10 vols., 1868-1937, incomplete), and R. S. Adamson and T. M. Slater's *Flora of the Cape peninsula* (1950).

Australasia. The region of Australia and New Zealand has been well studied botanically and each political sub-division has one or more floras. Among these may be mentioned L. M. Bailey's *The Queensland Flora* (6 vols., 1899-1902), J. M. Black's *Flora of South Australia* (1922-1929), W. A. Dixon's *Plants of New South Wales* (1906), A. J. Ewart's *Flora of Victoria* (1930), L. Rodway's *The Tasmanian Flora* (1903) and T. F. Cheesman's *Manual of the New Zealand flora* (1906, 2d ed. 1925).

Monographs and Revisions

A *monograph* of a group of plants, such as a family or genus, is a treatise including all significant information of a morphologic or taxonomic nature concerning the group. Strictly speaking, a monograph should cover the group as it exists throughout the world; actually, however, the term is loosely used and often made to apply to treatments restricted to a continent or smaller area. For this sort of treatment the term *revision* should be used. Furthermore, a revision may be based only on herbarium studies, whereas a monograph should cover the cytology, morphology, anatomy, genetics, paleobotany, and ecology of the group, along with its taxonomy. Monographs are relatively few in number; revisions are numbered by the thousands.

Books on Trees and Shrubs

The interest and economic importance attached to woody plants has led to the publication of a large number of works on this subject. Books or bulletins on trees and shrubs have been issued for most of the states, and for many countries or other geographical areas. A sampling of such books appears below. The names of many others may be found in Harlow and Harrar's *Textbook of Dendrology,* 3d edition, 1950.

Bean, W. J., *Trees and shrubs hardy in the British Isles.* 4th ed., 3 vols. London, 1950.

Benson, L., and R. A. Darrow, *The trees and shrubs of the southwestern deserts.* 437 pp. Tucson and Albuquerque. 1954.

Brown, H. P., *Trees of the Northeastern United States.* Boston, 1937.

Coker, W. C., and H. R. Totten, *Trees of the southeastern states.* Chapel Hill, 1934.

Harrar, E. S. and J. G., *Guide to southern trees.* 712 pp. New York, 1946.

Kirkwood, J. E., *Northern Rocky Mountain trees and shrubs.* Stanford University, 1930.

Kraemer, J. H., *Trees of the Western Pacific Region.* 436 pp. illus. West Lafayette, Ind., 1951.

Mathews, F. S., *Fieldbook of American trees and shrubs.* New York, 1915.

Millard, N. D., and W. L. Keene, *Native trees of the Intermountain region.* U. S. Forest Service, Ogden, Utah, 1934.

Morton, B. R., *Native trees of Canada.* Forest Branch, Department of the Interior Bulletin 61. Ottawa, 1917.

Preston, R. J., *Rocky Mountain trees.* 285 pp. Ames, Iowa, 1940.

Rock, J. F., *The indigenous trees of the Hawaiian Islands.* Honolulu, 1913.

Sargent, C. S., *The silva of North America.* A description of the trees which grow naturally in North America exclusive of Mexico. 14 vols. New York, 1891-1902.

———, *Manual of the trees of North America exclusive of Mexico.* New York, 1926.

Standley, P. C., *Trees and shrubs of Mexico.* Contributions of the U. S. National Herbarium, Vol. 23. 1920-1926.

Sudworth, G. B., *Forest trees of the Pacific Slope.* U. S. Department of Agriculture Forest Service. 441 pp. 1908.

Taylor, R. F., *Pocket guide to Alaska trees.* U. S. Department of Agriculture Miscellaneous Publication 55. 1929.

Trelease, W., *Winter Botany.* 2d ed. 396 pp. 300 figs. Urbana, 1925.

Van Dersal, W. R., *Native woody plants of the United States.* Miscellaneous Publication 303, U. S. Department of Agriculture, 1938.

Popular Books on Wild Flowers

There is a constant demand for books of a "popular" nature, particularly concerning the more attractive "wild flowers." These books are written in somewhat simpler language than the more extensive floras and are usually well illustrated. A disadvantage is that they are usually incomplete and do not include all the plants of a given region. Almost every part of the United States is covered by such popular works. An extensive list of such works can be found in a *Guide to Popular Floras of the United States and Alaska,* by S. F. Blake, published in 1954. Only a few regional works are listed here.

Armstrong, M., and J. J. Thornber, *Field book of western wild flowers. A guide to the commoner wild flowers west of the Rocky Mountains.* New York, 1915.

Clements, F. E. and E. S., *Rocky Mountain flowers.* 3d ed. 390 pp. New York, 1928.

Dana, W. S., *How to know the wildflowers. A guide to the name, haunts, and habits of our native wildflowers.* New edition. New York, 1919.

Greene, W. F., and H. L. Blomquist, *Flowers of the South.* Chapel Hill, N. C., 1953.

Harned, J. E., *Wild Flowers of the Alleghenies.* 2d ed. 675 pp. Oakland, Md., 1936.

Hausman, E. H., *Beginner's Guide to Wild Flowers.* 376 pp. New York, 1948.

House, H. D., *Wild Flowers.* 362 pp. illus. New York, 1934.

Jennings, O. E., and A. Avinoff, *Wild Flowers of Western Pennsylvania and the Upper Ohio Basin.* 2 vols. Pittsburgh, 1953.

Mathews, F. S., *Field book of American Wild Flowers.* Rev. ed. 587 pp. New York, 1927.

Moldenke, H. N., *American Wild Flowers.* 453 pp. New York, 1949.

Sharples, A. W., *Alaska wild flowers.* Stanford University, 1938.

Wherry, E. T., *Wild Flower Guide.* 202 pp. Garden City, N. Y., 1948.

Books on Cultivated Plants

The literature on cultivated plants is, of course, much more extensive than that concerning the wild plants but most of it deals with methods used in the culture of plants. A few works of a descriptive nature are listed here.

Bailey, L. H., *Standard Cyclopedia of Horticulture.* 6 vols. New York, 1914-1917.

———, *Manual of cultivated plants.* ed. 2. 1116 pp. New York, 1949.

Candolle, A. de, *L'origine des plantes cultivées. Paris,* 1883. Transl. *Origin of cultivated plants.* London, 1886.

Grey, C. H., *Hardy bulbs, including half-hardy bulbs and tuberous and fibrous-rooted plants.* 3 vols. London, 1937-1938.

Hedrick, U. P., *Cyclopedia of hardy fruits.* New York. ed. 1. 1922; ed. 2. 1938.

Neal, M. C., *In gardens of Hawaii.* Bernice P. Bishop Museum Special Publication 40. Honolulu, 1948.

Popenoe, W., *Manual of tropical and subtropical fruits, excluding the banana, coconut, pineapple, citrus fruits, olive, and fig.* New York, 1920.

Rehder, A., *Manual of cultivated trees and shrubs, hardy in North America except in the subtropical and warmer temperate regions.* New York, 1940.

Schery, R. W., *Plants for Man.* 564 pp. New York, 1952.

Vavilov, N., *Studies on the Origin of Cultivated Plants.* Bulletin of the Institute of Applied Botany and Plant Breeding. Vol. 16. Leningrad, 1926.

Dictionaries

Dictionaries and glossaries are invaluable in a subject matter with so large a vocabulary as that of botany. A glossary is an alphabetical list of difficult terms, with their interpretations. A botanical dictionary may list and describe all known genera of certain plant groups.

Kelsey, H. P., and W. A. Dayton, *Standardized Plant Names.* 2d ed. American Joint Committee on Horticultural Nomenclature, Harrisburg, Pa., 1942.

Jackson, B. D., *A glossary of botanic terms: with their derivation and accent.* 4th ed. London, 1928. The standard botanical glossary.

Lemee, Albert, *Dictionnaire descriptif et synonymique des genres de plantes phanerogames.* 8 vols. Brest, 1929-1943. An encyclopedia of vascular plants.

Willis, J. C., *A dictionary of flowering plants and ferns.* 6th ed. Cambridge, 1931. Accounts for families and genera of flowering plants, with many botanical terms.

Botanical Periodicals or Serials

A great deal of botanical literature appears in serial publications of learned societies, educational institutions, and so forth. *Serials* may appear at regular or irregular intervals. Those published at regular intervals may be properly called *periodicals*. It is estimated that there are approximately 1000 serials regularly containing articles on plant taxonomy. Lists of the more important ones may be found in various reference books, such as Lawrence's *Taxonomy of Flowering Plants*.

References

Blake, S. F., and A. C. Atwood, *Geographical guide to the floras of the world*. An annotated list with special reference to useful plants and common plant names. Part 1. U. S. Department of Agriculture Miscellaneous Publication 401. 1942. Part 1 covers Africa, Australia, North America, South America and Oceanic islands; Part 2 is in preparation.

Hitchcock, A. S., *Methods of descriptive systematic botany*. New York, 1925.

12

Vegetative Morphology

The readers of this book, it is assumed, have studied the structure of vascular plants, but, since a knowledge of the details of plant structure is essential to a proper understanding of the principles of taxonomy, a brief summary is presented here. Those desiring a more complete treatment are referred to any good current textbook in general botany.

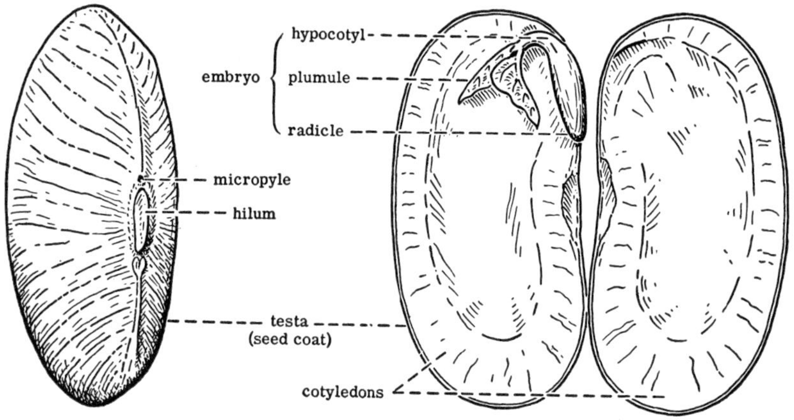

Figure 34. External and sectional view of seed of the garden bean, *Phaseolus*.

The Seed. It is clear that the seed provides the natural starting point for a study of plant structure. Everyone is familiar with a seed such as, for instance, the kidney bean. The bean seed is covered with a coat, or **testa;** a scar, the **hilum,** indicates the point where it broke from its attachment in the bean pod. In the space within the testa there is present an immature plant, or **embryo** (Figure 34). When the bean is soaked in water for several hours, the testa can be removed and the central mass opened up, somewhat like a book, into two thick halves, the **cotyledons.** These are large and swollen with the stored food supply of the seed. The cotyledons are hinged together by a small structure, the **hypocotyl,** which is conical on one end, forming the **radicle,** or embryonic root, while on the other end there are two or more tiny leaf-like structures: these, with a tiny **bud,** or growing point, constitute the **plumule,** or embryonic shoot. If the seed is kept in moist soil or sand for a few days, it germinates, that is, the structures within swell and tear the testa, whereupon the radicle elongates, forcing its way out and downwards to develop the roots, while the upper end of the axis also elongates, carrying the two cotyledons,

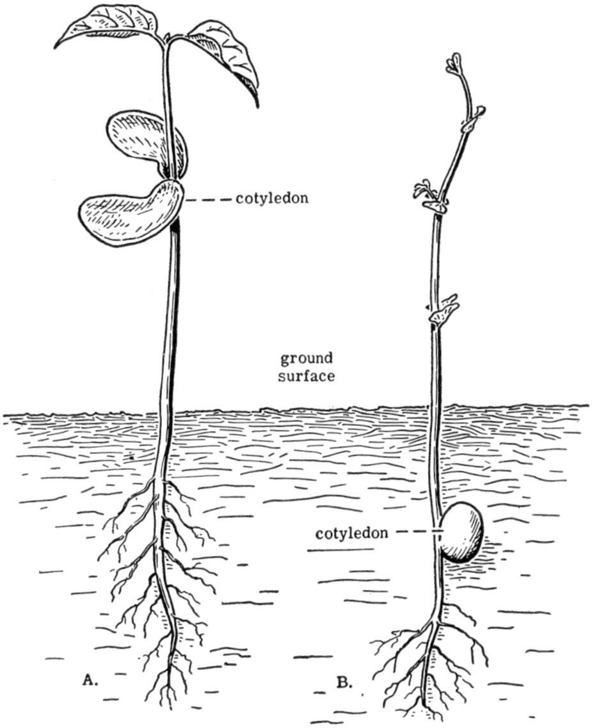

Figure 35. Seedlings showing: A, epigeal germination of the bean; B, hypogeal germination of pea, *Pisum*.

with the plumule, into the light, where they become green. After the plumule has enlarged and produced the first leaves, the cotyledons presently fall off, their store of reserve food having become exhausted.

The seed of the garden pea is very similar in construction to that of the kidney bean. However, in germination, the cotyledons of the pea seed remain within the soil while their food reserve is transferred into the developing young plant. A type of germination, like that of the bean, in which the cotyledons emerge from the ground, is known as **epigeal** (above thc earth), while that in which the cotyledons remain in the soil is called **hypogeal** (below the earth) (Figure 35).

When, on the other hand, the seed of a castor bean is opened, it will be found that the arrangement is quite unlike that of the bean or pea. Here the hypocotyl is not actually attached to the two halves of the thick mass, as in those seeds, but to two thin cotyledons, which are closely appressed between the two fleshy halves. With the aid of a lens, a very

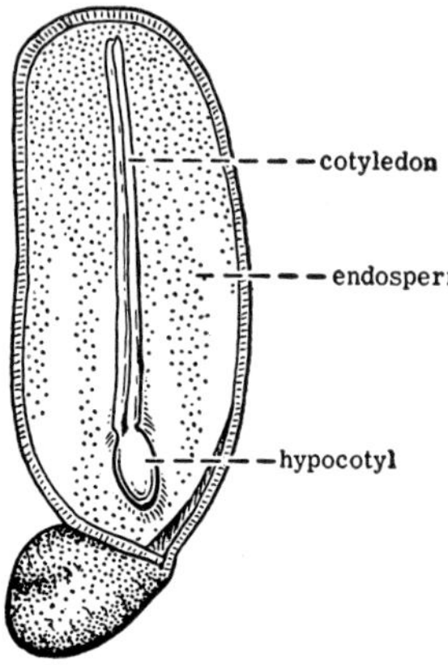

Figure 36. Section of seed of castor bean, *Ricinus communis*. (Adapted by permission from Johnson, *Taxonomy of the Flowering Plants*, copyright 1931 by Appleton-Century-Crofts, Inc.)

minute plumule may be observed between the two cotyledons. Here little or no food is stored in the cotyledons, but the food supply is present in the mass that surrounds the cotyledons. This external food supply is known as the **endosperm** (Figure 36). Seeds having the food supply external to the embryo are called **endospermic** (formerly **albuminous**);

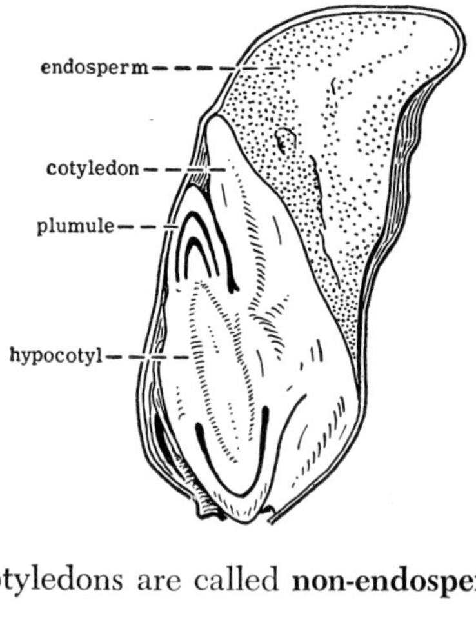

Figure 37. Section through grain (caryopsis) of maize, *Zea mays*. (Adapted by permission from Johnson, *Taxonomy of the Flowering Plants*, copyright 1931 by Appleton-Century-Crofts, Inc.)

those having the reserve food in the cotyledons are called **non-endospermic** (formerly **ex-albuminous**).

If a grain of maize (Indian corn) is examined, one of the flat surfaces will be noted to have an oblong whitish area. If a soaked grain is cut so as to pass through this area longitudinally, it is found to be sharply delimited from the remainder of the material in the grain (Figure 37). When a drop of iodine is placed on the grain, the small dense region changes only slightly in color, while the remainder of the grain turns dark blue or black, showing the presence of starch and consequently suggesting that this is a region of food storage. This is, in fact, the endosperm. On the other hand, the light area presents definite structures: the

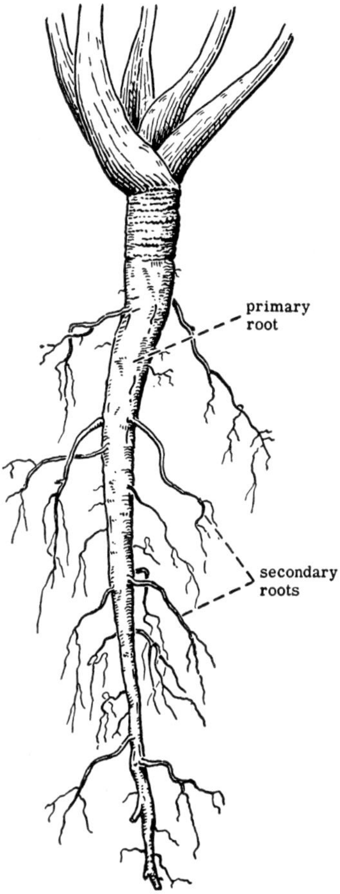

Figure 38. Primary and secondary roots of dandelion, *Taraxacum officinale*.

conical radicle can be found, pointing toward the sharp end of the grain, while the plumule, just above it, as usual, is composed of rudimentary leaves twisted around each other. Both radicle and plumule are separated from the starchy area by a shield-like structure that joins the axis of the embryo between the plumule and the radicle. This is a single cotyledon. Thus we have here the essential parts found in such seeds as the bean, the pea, or the castor bean, but with only one cotyledon instead of two. Plants having one cotyledon in their seeds are called **mono-**

cotyledons; those with two cotyledons are **dicotyledons.** Seeds of monocotyledons, like those of dicotyledons, may be endospermic (maize) or non-endospermic (water-plantain), and their germination may be hypogeal (grasses) or epigeal (onion).

In germination the seedling normally develops into two active growing regions, the underground root and the aerial shoot; this last can usually be divided into stem and leaf. These vegetative organs are useful as diagnostic features in the classification of plants and a distinct terminology has been developed.

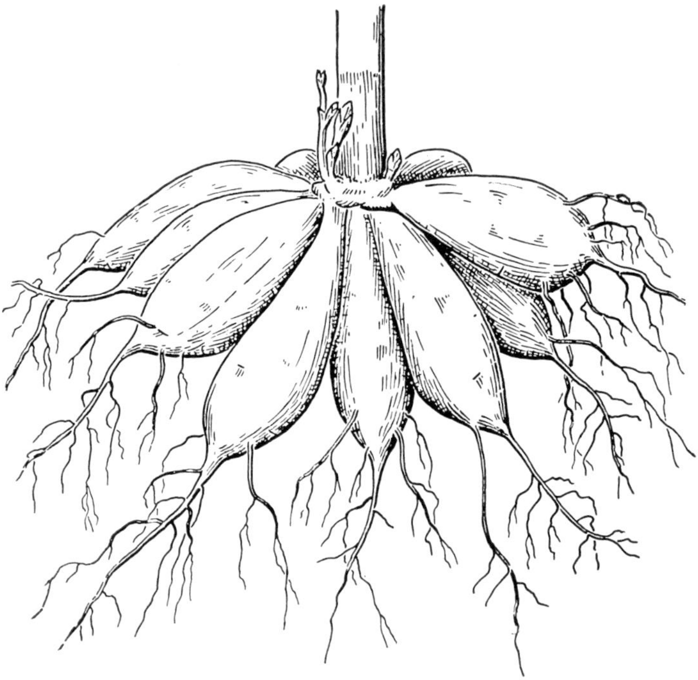

Figure 39. Fascicled, tuberous roots of *Dahlia*. (Adapted from Bergen and Caldwell, *Practical Botany*.)

Roots. The extension of the radicle forms the **primary root;** all branches are **secondary** (Figure 38). If the primary root persists and grows straight downward it is known as a **taproot,** as in carrot and dandelion. A taproot notably enlarged by the formation of a storage tissue is a **fleshy** or **tuberous root.** Fleshy roots are sometimes grouped in a spreading cluster and are termed **fascicled roots,** as in dahlia (Figure 39). In many plants the primary root is of short duration, being succeeded by a secondary root system that arises from the hypocotyl. This may be composed of numerous long, slender roots of about the same diameter. These are **fibrous roots** (Figure 40). Roots which arise from stems or leaves are called **adventitious.** These include **prop roots,** as in maize, where the roots grow from the stem above the ground and enter the soil, giving mechanical support (Figure 41); also included are **aerial roots,** as in poison-ivy, which aid in climbing, or in many epiphytes, where they absorb water and minerals directly from the rain (Figure 42). **Aerating roots** extend vertically out of the soil in plants of bald-cypress swamps (Figure 43).

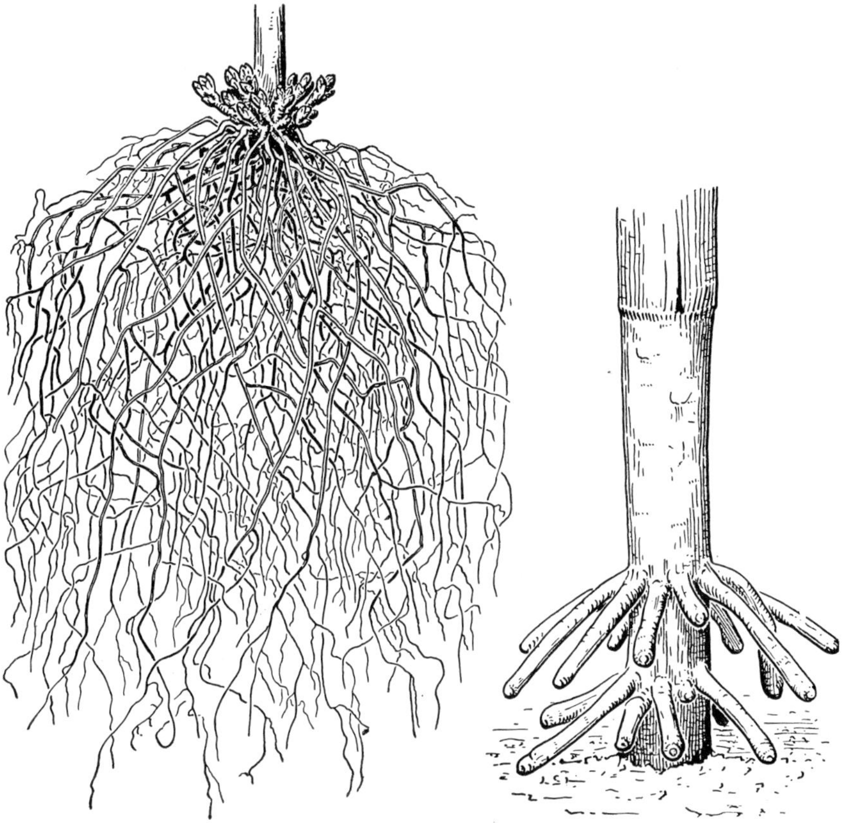

Figure 40-41. ***Left,*** **a fibrous root system. (Adapted by permission from Johnson,** ***Taxonomy of the Flowering Plants,*** **copyright 1931, Appleton-Century-Crofts, Inc.)** ***Right,*** **prop roots of maize,** ***Zea mays.***

Many tropical trees have **buttress roots,** with planklike extensions on their upper sides (Figure 44). Root-like absorbing organs, called **haustoria** are produced by some parasites, such as dodder (Figure 45).

With respect to their duration, roots may be classed as **annual, biennial,** or **perennial.** A plant that lives only one season is an annual and its roots are **herbaceous.** Some plants may develop as **winter annuals.** These are normally or often annuals, but if the seeds germinate in the fall the plants may live through the winter, growing slowly or not at all, resuming

Figure 42. Aerial roots of poison-ivy, *Rhus radicans*.

Figure 43. Bald-cypress, *Taxodium distichum*, in swamp, showing cypress "knees."

Figure 44. Buttress roots of a tropical tree. (Adapted from Brown, *The Plant Kingdom,* Ginn and Company.)

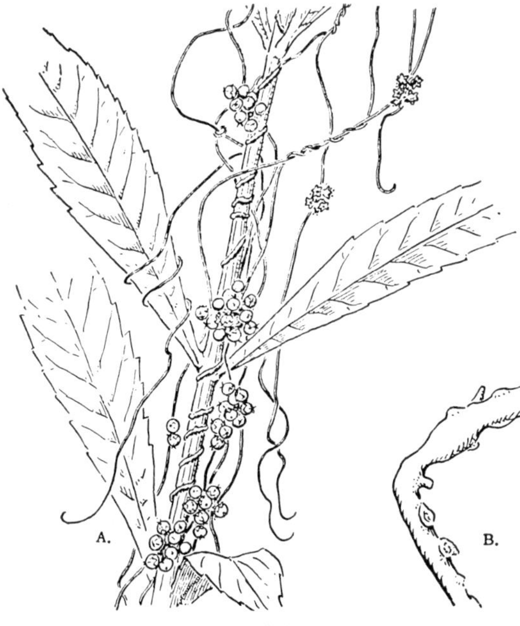

Figure 45. A, Dodder, *Cuscuta,* twining about a host plant; B, enlarged section, to show haustoria.

rapid growth in the spring and producing flowers and fruits. Biennials require two full seasons for their development. The seeds germinate the first year and a good root system is produced with, usually, a **rosette** of leaves (Figure 46). The roots are supplied with a rich store of food which is then used the second year to produce a vegetative shoot and form its flowers and fruits, after which the entire plant dies. Perennials live for several years. Some plants, **herbaceous perennials,** produce a new aerial shoot every year but die to the ground at the end of the season, living over from year to year in the underground parts. In trees and shrubs the

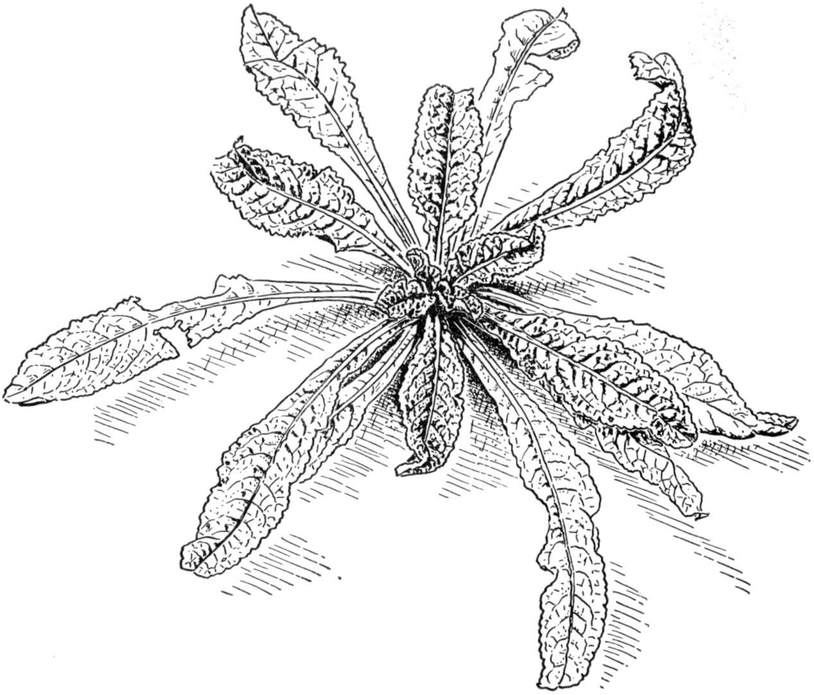

Figure 46. Basal rosette of leaves of wild teasel, *Dipsacus sylvestris*.

main root and its branches live several or many years, become thickened and hardened and may be called **woody roots.**

Other Underground Parts. Stems may under certain conditions also develop underground. An underground stem can be distinguished from a root by the presence of scale-like leaves, with buds in their axils; both leaves and buds are lacking in roots. A slender horizontal elongated underground stem is a **rhizome,** or **rootstock** (Figure 47, A). From the rhizome there arise aerial shoots and adventitious roots. Many kinds of flowering plants produce rhizomes, among them grasses, sedges, cattails, and bananas.

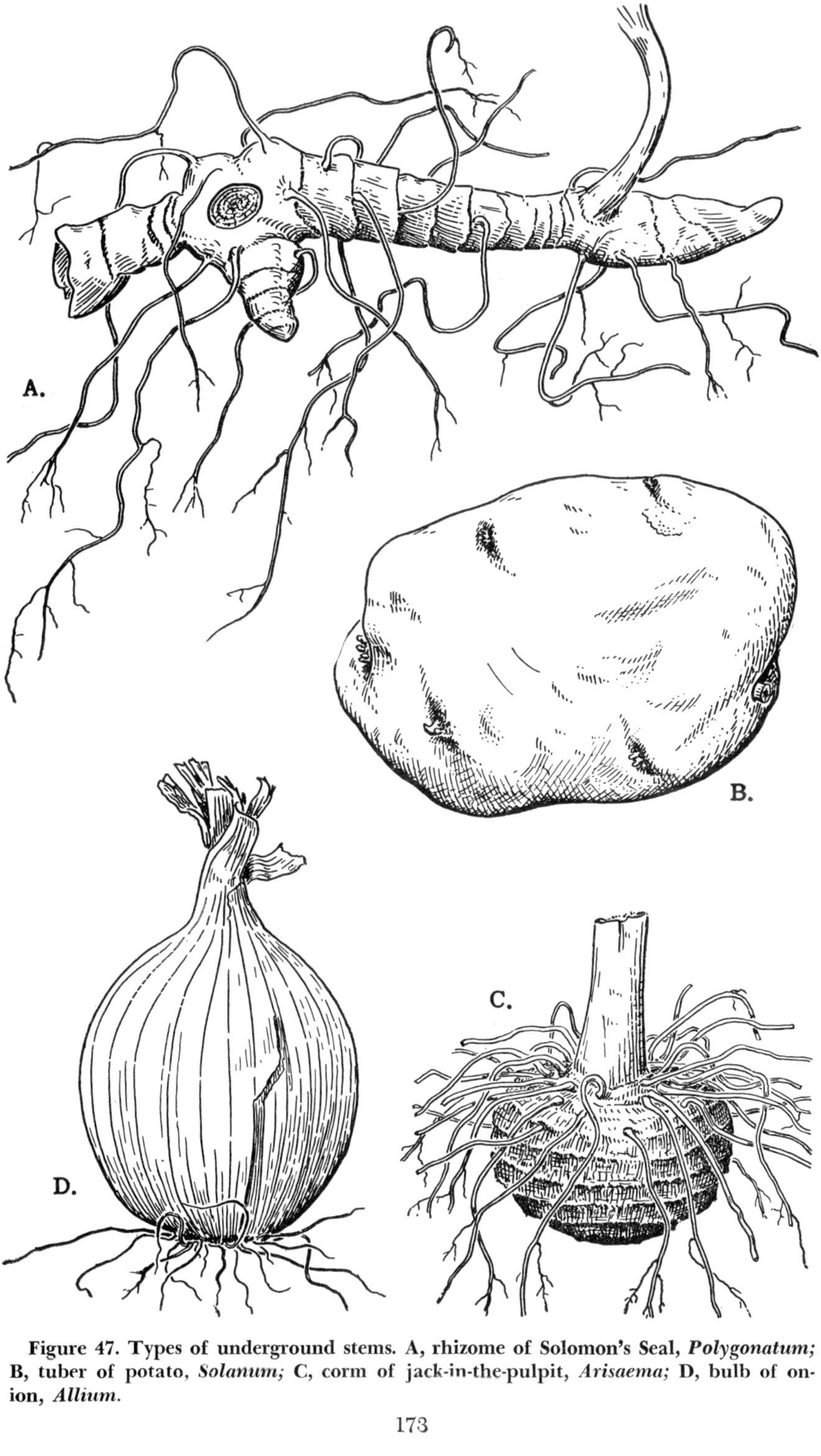

Figure 47. Types of underground stems. A, rhizome of Solomon's Seal, *Polygonatum;* B, tuber of potato, *Solanum;* C, corm of jack-in-the-pulpit, *Arisaema;* D, bulb of onion, *Allium.*

A shortened, greatly thickened underground stem is known as a **tuber** (Figure 47, B). These may form at the end of rhizomes, as in potato, or they may be in a series along a rhizome, like a string of beads, as in groundnut. The "eye" of a potato tuber is really a cluster of buds, the "eyebrow" a greatly reduced leaf.

An underground stem that is vertical rather than horizontal, with a shortened axis and a few thin, dry scale-like leaves is known as a **corm** (Figure 47, C). A tuft of adventitious roots is produced at the lower

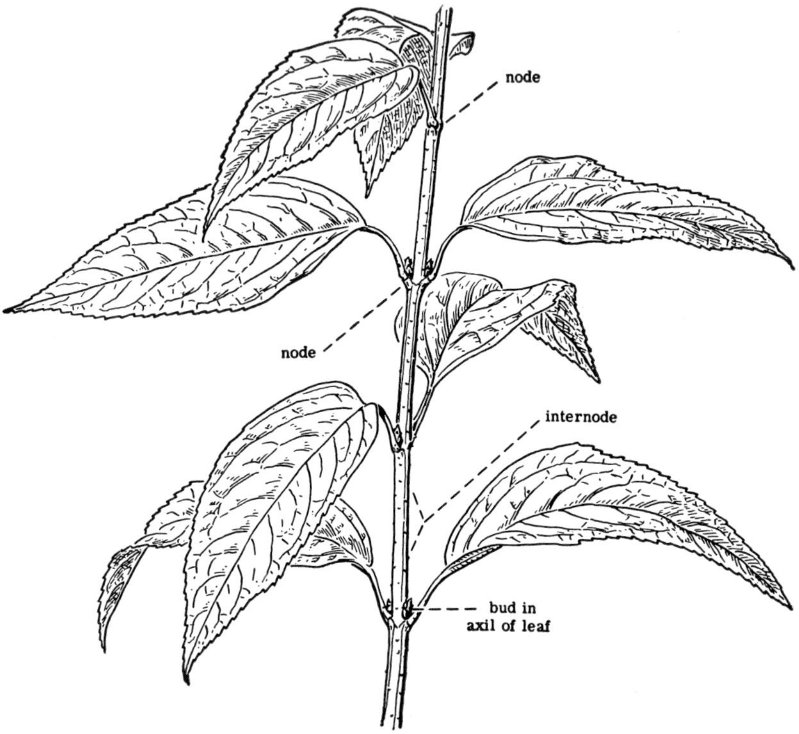

Figure 48. Section of stem of golden bells, *Forsythia*, showing nodes and internodes.

surface. Because the corm is so greatly shortened, the intervals between the leaves are scarcely discernible. Examples are crocus, gladiolus, and dasheen.

A **bulb** resembles a corm in being vertical and shortened, but differs in having prominent fleshy leaves that constitute the dominant feature, as in onion, lily, and tulip (Figure 47, D). A terminal bud produces the aerial stem, whereas from axillary buds new bulbs develop.

Stems. The stem displays the green leaves to the light in such a manner as to favor their photosynthetic activities. This is accomplished in such different ways in the different species of plants that the appearance is extremely variable. Such variations are of great value in plant classification.

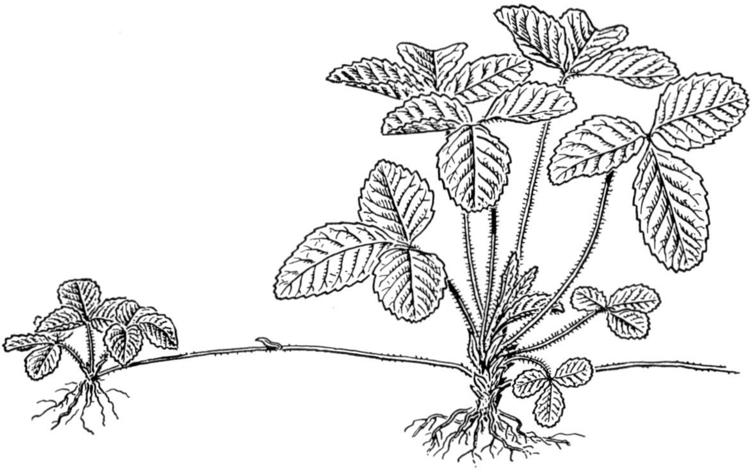

Figure 49. Runner of strawberry, *Fragaria,* with a young plant at the tip.

Figure 50. Garden bean, *Phaseolus,* a counter-clockwise twiner.

Typically, stems have **nodes** (joints where leaves and branches originate) and **internodes** (intervals between the joints), in contrast to roots (Figure 48). This is true, as indicated above, whether the stems are above ground or below ground. Buds (embryonic shoots) appear at the tips of the branches or at the nodes. As to duration, stems may be classified as **annual, biennial,** or **perennial,** as noted above for roots. As to position, they may be **aerial** or **subterranean.** The aerial stem is usually

Figure 51. False climbing buckwheat, *Polygonum,* a clockwise twiner.

more or less erect, but may be **prostrate** or **decumbent,** lying on the ground. A prostrate stem having the leaves conspicuously reduced is a **runner,** as in strawberry (Figure 49). It might be compared to a rhizome, with its position just above the soil instead of within the soil. Some stems, like black raspberry, currant, or gooseberry, bend over to the ground and take root, forming new plants; such stems are called **stolons.** Some stems that grow erect are slender and weak but are able to cling to some support, if it is available; these are **climbing stems.** Woody climbing stems, or **lianas,** may ascend high into crowns of trees. Climbers may hold themselves upright by **twining** around a support; this twining is characteris-

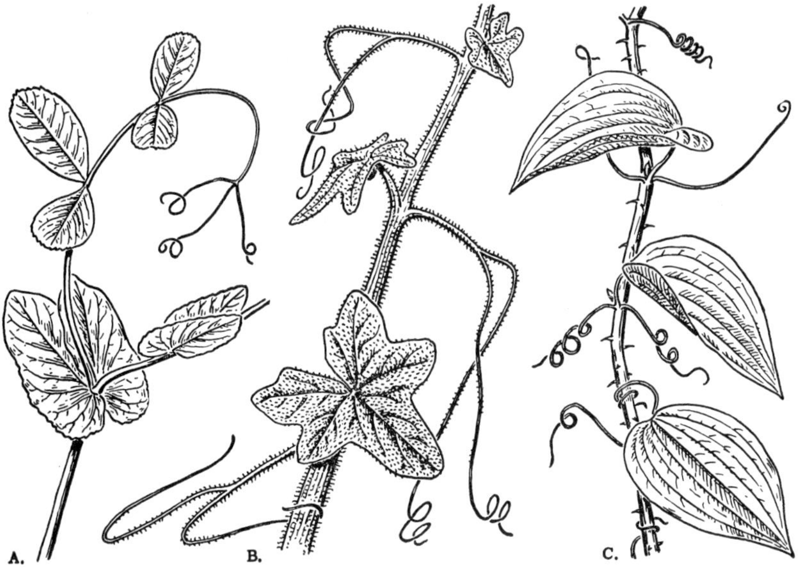

Figure 52. Types of origins of tendrils: A, modified leaflets of garden pea, *Pisum;* B, modified shoots of wild cucumber, *Echinocystis;* C, modified stipules of greenbrier, *Smilax.*

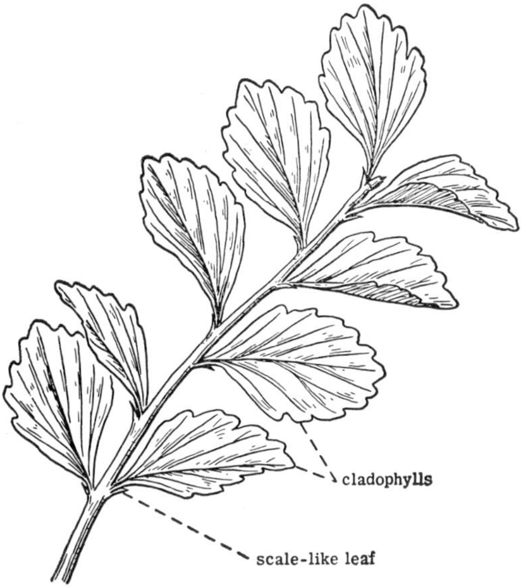

Figure 53. Cladophylls (phylloclades) of celery pine, *Phyllocladus.*

tically **counter-clockwise,** as in the lima bean (Figure 50), or **clockwise,** as in wild climbing buckwheat (Figure 51). Other climbing plants depend upon **tendrils,** slender branches of the shoot that are extremely sensitive to contact stimuli (Figure 52). Tendrils may be modified branches (cucumber), leaves or leaflets (pea), or stipules (greenbrier). The tip of the tendril may be thread-like, twisting around slender branches for support, or expanded in the form of an adhesive disk (Boston ivy), permitting the plant to support itself against tree trunks or walls.

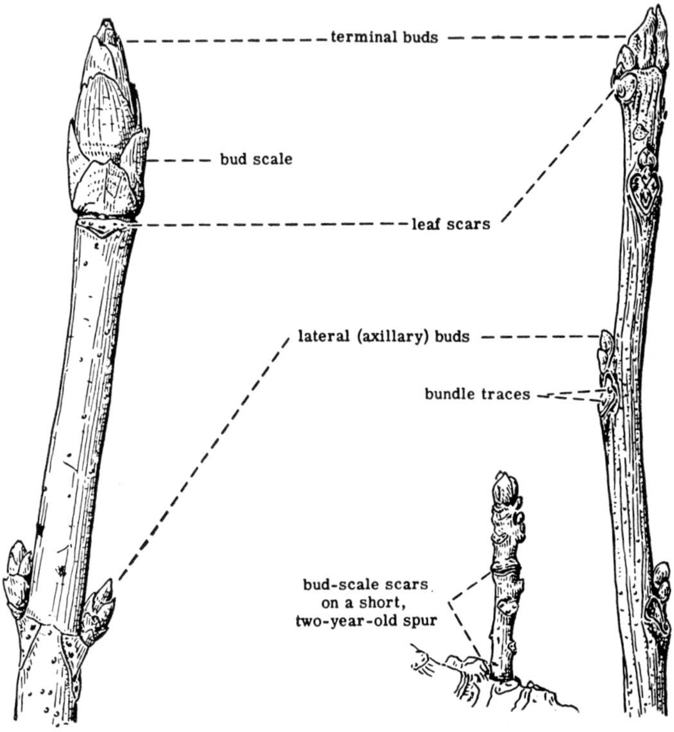

Figure 54. Winter twigs. ***Left,*** **buckeye,** ***Aesculus; right,*** **black walnut,** ***Juglans nigra.***

Stems may also be modified into strong, sharp-pointed structures, **thorns,** which may be unbranched, as in osage-orange, or branched, as in honey-locust. Other stems are modified into flattened, leaf-like structures called **cladophylls** (*klados,* sprout + *phyllon,* leaf), or **phylloclades,** which may easily be mistaken for true leaves, as in asparagus, acacia, or celery-pine (Figure 53).

The protective covering of woody plants is known as **bark.** In many species this is quite distinctive and hence of taxonomic value. The experienced lumberman recognizes trees and even logs by their bark alone. The appearance of the bark must be learned, however, by experience, since there is no accurate terminology for describing the bark of various trees. The bark, furthermore, varies greatly in the same species from youth to old age.

Twigs in Winter. A branch of a woody stem is known as a **twig** (Figure 54). These have taxonomic features that are of great value in identification of the plant in winter, when the leaves of many plants have fallen. **Winter buds** are the dormant growing points, usually covered by **bud scales,** which are modified leaves. These buds are of two types, the

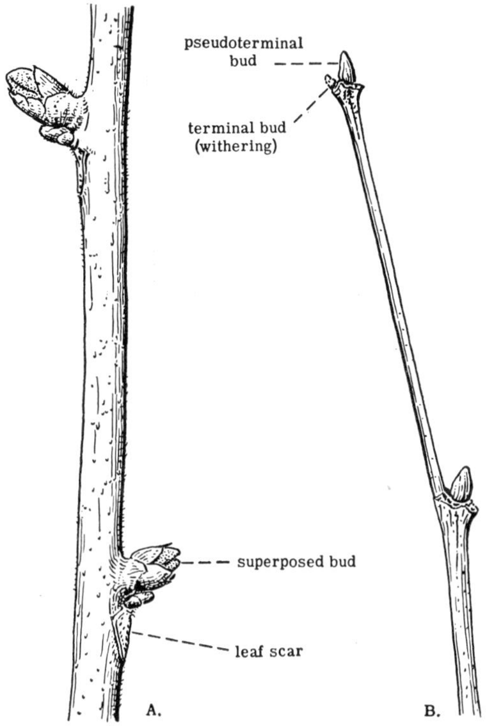

Figure 55. Winter twigs. A, hickory, *Carya,* showing superposed buds; B, sycamore, *Platanus,* showing pseudoterminal bud.

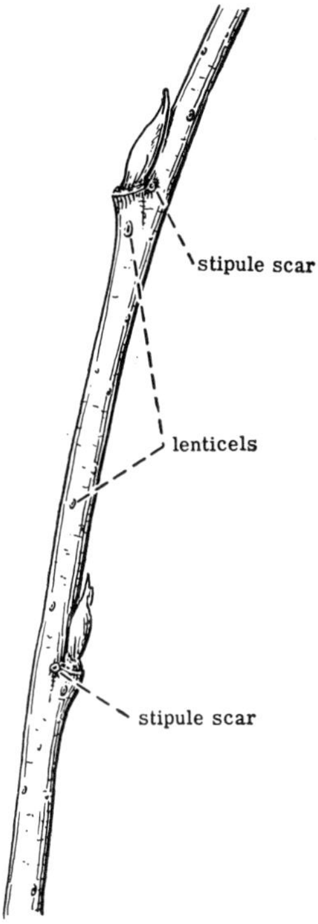

Figure 56. Winter twig of willow, *Salix,* showing stipule scars and lenticels.

terminal buds at the tip of the shoot and its branches, and the **lateral buds,** along the sides of the twigs. The lateral buds are called **axillary** if they arise in the **axils** of leaves, as they usually do. The axil is the distal angle formed by the petiole of the leaf with the shoot. Extra buds produced to the right or left of the axillary buds are called **accessory.** These may be **flower buds,** whereas the axillary bud might be a **leaf bud.** Lateral buds produced just above the axillary buds are said to be **superposed** (Figure 55, A). In some cases no terminal bud is formed, since the upper part of the twig is neatly dropped at the end of the growing season, leaving a smooth **terminal bud scar.** Often the uppermost axillary bud then becomes enlarged and may function like a terminal bud; it is, of course, only a lateral bud but may be called a **pseudoterminal bud** (Figure 55, B). Buds differ greatly in their size and shape, as well as in the number, arrangement, color, size, shape, and surface nature of the

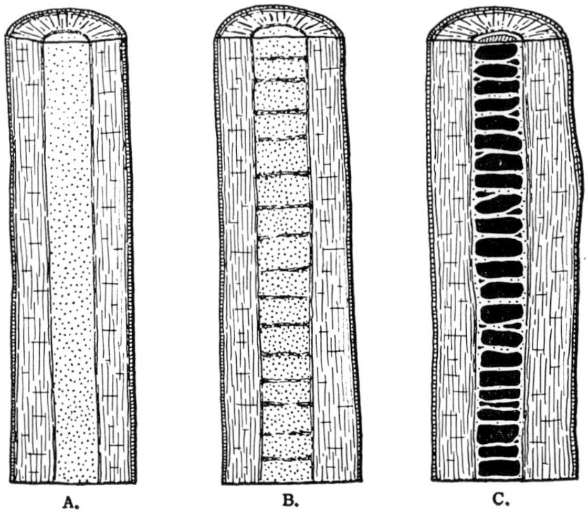

Figure 57. Types of pith in branchlets. A, continuous; B, diaphragmed; C, chambered.

bud scales; all these are valuable taxonomic features. When the scales of a bud fall as spring growth begins, they leave on the twig a ring of **bud scale scars.** A series of such scars indicates several years' growth.

Other distinctive features on winter twigs are the **leaf scars,** which indicate the point of attachment of the leaves. These are quite variable in

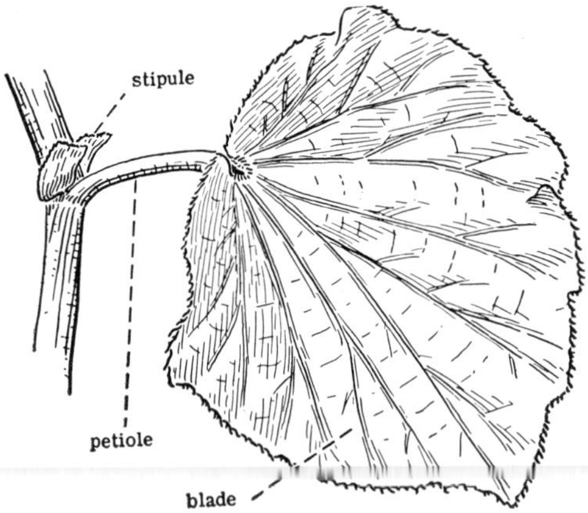

Figure 58. Leaf of *Begonia*, showing principal parts.

shape, and are of further taxonomic value because of the variation in number and arrangement of the **bundle scars** (or **traces**), which indicate the broken ends of the vascular bundles that passed from the stem into the leaves. Tiny **stipule scars** (Figure 56) may also be present, one on each side of the leaf scar, or the modified stipules themselves may be present as **prickles** (black locust), bud scales (magnolia), or tendrils (greenbrier) (Figure 59). **Lenticels** are spots on the surface of twigs, composed of loose tissues that aid in the aeration of cells beneath the bark. These are likewise of distinctive size, color, and form.

Figure 59. Types of modifications of stipules. A, leaf-like stipules of rose, *Rosa canina;* B, prickles of black locust, *Robinia pseudoacacia;* C, tendrils of greenbrier, *Smilax herbacea;* D, ocreae (sheathing stipules) of smartweed, *Polygonum.*

The nature of the pith is another useful taxonomic feature (Figure 57). The pith of different species varies greatly in color, relative size, and texture. It is usually **continuous,** but may have firmer cross-plates at intervals; this condition is called **diaphragmed.** If the tissue between the plates has disappeared, the pith becomes **chambered.**

Twigs also vary widely in diameter, odor, color, surface characteristics, and so on. The identification of woody plants in winter has a well-developed technique of its own.

Leaves. Leaves are the most varied of all the vegetative parts of the plant and therefore of the greatest value as taxonomic features. Many seed plants may be readily recognized by their leaves alone.

Typical leaves are composed of the **petiole,** or leaf stalk, the **blade,** or expanded portion, and the **stipules,** outgrowths one on each side at the base of the petiole (Figure 58). A leaf without a petiole is **sessile;** one

Figure 60. Types of phyllotaxy. A, alternate, weeping willow, *Salix babylonica;* B, opposite, red osier, *Cornus stolonifera;* C, whorled, Indian cucumber-root, *Medeola virginiana;* D, decussate, mock-orange, *Philadelphus;* E, distichous, starry plumelily *Smilacina stellata.*

without stipules is **exstipulate.** The stipules are usually green and leaf-like, but as noted above, they may be modified as prickles or tendrils, or they may sheath the stem, forming an **ocrea,** as in smartweed (Figure 59). Stipule-like structures called **stipels** may appear at the base of leaflets of compound leaves. The petiole sometimes has a cushion-like enlarged base, the **pulvinus** (as in sensitive plant), which may serve as the seat of irritability.

Leaves are arranged on the stem in a definite regular manner known as **phyllotaxy** (Figure 60). Usually only one leaf appears at a node and

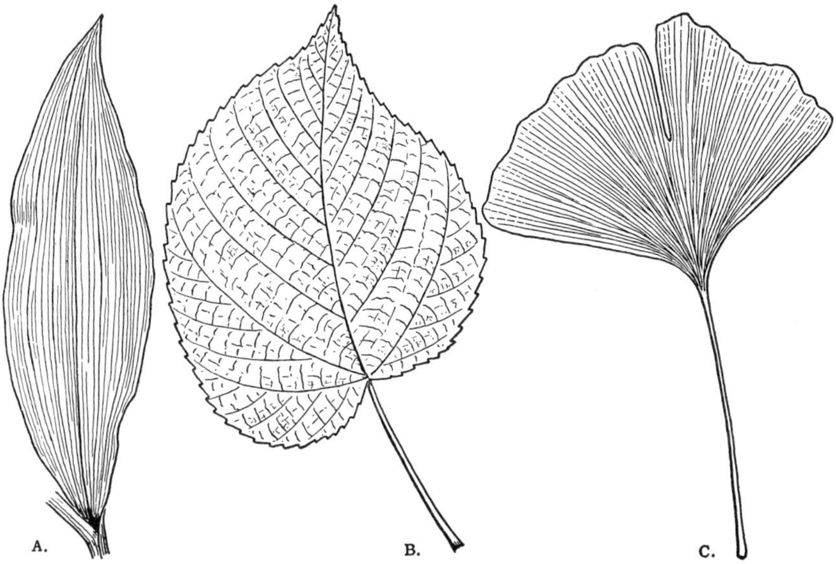

Figure 61. Types of venation. A, parallel, plumelily, *Smilacina racemosa;* B, netted, basswood, *Tilia;* C, dichotomous, ginkgo, *Ginkgo biloba.*

the leaves are then arranged in a spiral order and are said to be **alternate.** In many cases they are **opposite;** that is, there is a leaf on opposite sides at each node. In such a case, each pair of leaves is usually placed at right angles to the pairs above and below; such an arrangement is **decussate.** If there are only two rows the arrangement is **distichous.** In other species there are three or more leaves at a node; these are **whorled** or **verticillate.** Leaves may also be classed as **basal** or **radical,** arising from the base of the plant, and **cauline,** borne on the stem. Sometimes the bases overlap and the leaves are said to be **equitant** ("riding" one another) as in iris (Figure 105).

The arrangement of the vascular bundles or **veins,** of a leaf is termed **venation** (Figure 61). In monocotyledons the venation is usually **parallel** —the principal veins extend from the base to the tip of the leaf in a more or less parallel manner. In dicotyledons, on the other hand, **net venation** is the rule, the veins forming an irregular network. Net-veined leaves may be **pinnately veined,** when there is a prominent **midrib,** with more or less equal branches, or **palmately veined,** when a midrib is lacking and the principal veins radiate from a point near the base of the leaf. A third type of venation is **dichotomous,** or **forking,** in which the veins may appear parallel but actually fork at intervals; this type is common in ferns.

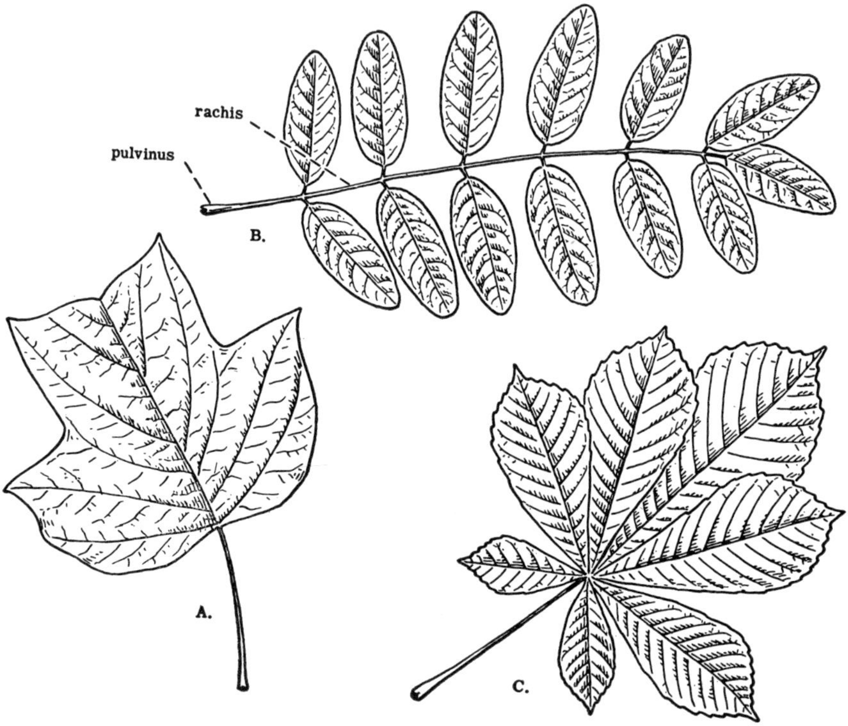

Figure 62. Simple and compound leaves. A, simple leaf of tulip tree, *Liriodendron tulipifera;* B, pinnately compound leaf of black locust, *Robinia pseudoacacia;* C, palmately compound leaf of horse-chestnut, *Aesculus hippocastanum.*

Leaves may be **simple,** having but one blade, or **compound,** having the blade divided into two or more individual parts called **leaflets** (Figure 62). If the leaflets arise from the sides of the **rachis** (the continuation of the petiole), the leaf is **pinnately compound.** If the leaflets, in contrast, diverge from a common point at the end of the petiole, the leaf is **palmately compound.** The divisions of a pinnately compound leaf may themselves be compound; the leaf will then be **bipinnate, tripinnate** and so on.

As to duration, leaves may be **fugacious,** falling almost as soon as formed, **deciduous,** falling at the end of the growing season, **marcescent,**

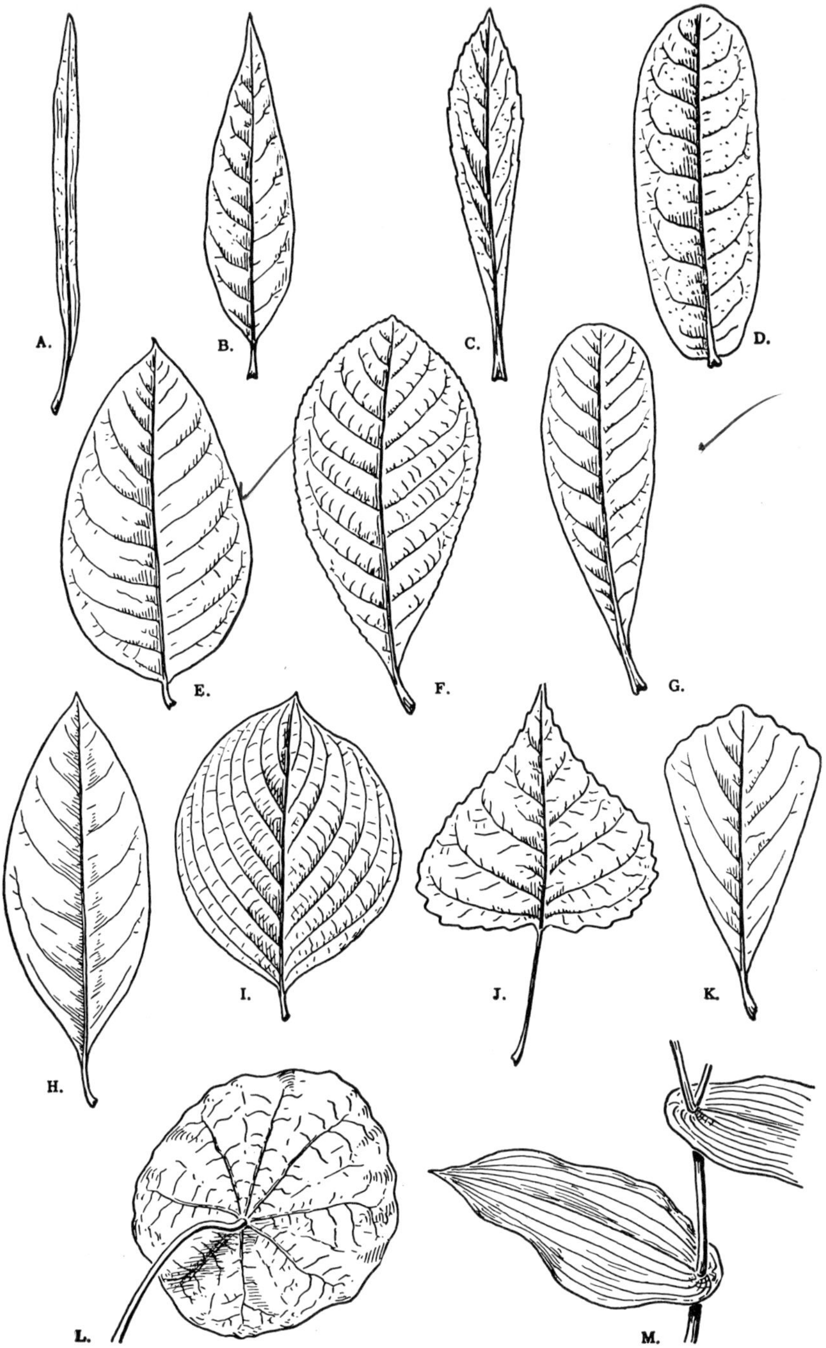

Figure 63. Shapes of leaf blades. A, linear, *Claytonia;* B, lanceolate, *Asclepias;* C, oblanceolate, *Solidago;* D, oblong, *Hypericum;* E, ovate, *Apocynum;* F, obovate, *Alnus;* G, spatulate, *Pittosporum;* H, elliptical, *Kalmia;* I, orbicular, *Cornus;* J, deltoid. *Populus;* K, cuneate, *Crataegus;* L, peltate, *Tropaeolum;* M, perfoliate, *Uvularia.*

withering at the end of the growing season but not falling until toward spring, or **persistent,** remaining on the stem for more than one season, the plant thus being **evergreen.**

The **shapes** of leaves are among their most variable characteristics, and suggest some of the commonest terms in systematic botany (Figure 63). A **linear** leaf is very narrow with nearly straight sides; a **lanceolate** leaf is narrow but tapers from the base toward the apex; an **oblanceolate** leaf is narrow, but broadest at the apex, tapering toward the base; an **oblong** leaf is somewhat rectangular, with nearly straight sides, although with rounded base and tip; an **ovate** leaf is egg-shaped, broadest below the middle; an **obovate** leaf has the broadest portion above the middle; an **elliptical** leaf is broadest at the middle, tapering more or less equally to the base and tip; an **orbicular** leaf is nearly circular in outline; a **spatulate** leaf is spoon-shaped, broad and rounded at the tip, tapering toward the base; a **deltoid** leaf is triangular; a **cuneate** leaf is wedge-shaped; a **peltate** leaf has the petiole attached to the under surface of a leaf like the handle of an umbrella; a **perfoliate** leaf is sessile and clasps the stem, which appears to extend through it.

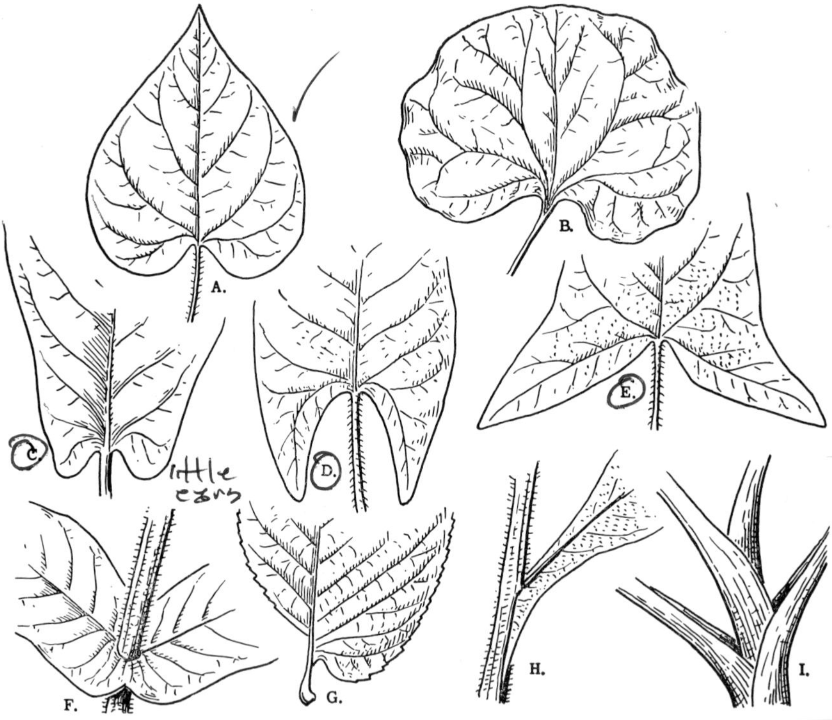

Figure 64. Types of bases of leaf blades. A, cordate, *Ipomoea;* B, reniform, *Asarum;* C, auriculate, *Magnolia fraseri;* D, sagittate, *Polygonum sagittatum;* E, hastate, *Polygonum arifolium;* F, connate, *Triosteum;* G, oblique, *Ulmus;* H, decurrent, *Symphytum;* I, sheathing, *Nephthytis* (Araceae).

The **base** of the blade may be **cordate,** heart-shaped, with a basal **sinus** and two rounded **lobes; reniform,** kidney-shaped, broader than long; **auriculate,** with **auricles,** or "ears" formed by the two projecting sides of the base of the blade; **sagittate,** arrow-shaped, with the auricles turned inwards; **hastate,** halberd-shaped, with the auricles turned outwards; **oblique,** the two sides of the base unequal; **decurrent,** the base of the blade appearing to run down the stem; **connate,** in which the bases of two opposite leaves seem to have fused around the stem; **sheathing,** in which the base of the petiole, more or less expanded, surrounds the stem (Figure 64).

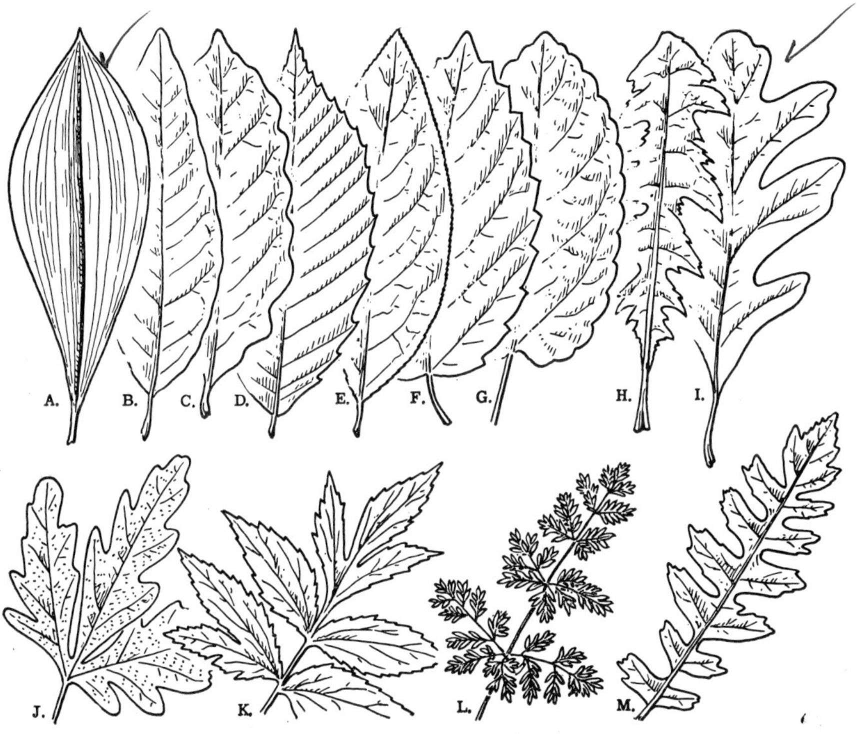

Figure 65. Types of margin of leaf blades. A, entire, *Medeola;* B, undulate, *Asclepias;* C, sinuate, *Quercus;* D, serrate, *Fagus;* E, serrulate, *Vaccinium;* F, dentate, *Viburnum;* G, crenate, *Coleus;* H, incised, *Taraxacum;* I, lobed, *Quercus;* J, parted, *Hibiscus;* K, divided, *Hydrophyllum;* L, dissected, *Daucus;* M, pinnatifid, *Capsella.*

The **margin** of a leaf may be **entire,** that is, even, not indented; **undulate** or **repand,** with shallow, wavy indentations; **sinuate,** with deeper but still wavy indentations; **serrate,** with teeth like a saw, pointed forward; **serrulate,** with very small or fine teeth pointing forward; **dentate,** with fine or coarse teeth pointing outward; **crenate,** scalloped, with broad rounded teeth; **incised,** cut into irregular or jagged teeth; **lobed,** cut more deeply into angular portions (lobes), with sinuses between; **parted,** cut so deeply that the sinuses extend almost to the midrib; **divided,** cut entirely to the midrib, forming a compound leaf (Figure 65). When the divisions are numerous and more or less fine and narrow, the leaf may be called **dissected.** A pinnately parted leaf may be called **pinnatifid.** If the divisions are themselves compound, the leaf is **decompound.**

The **tip** (or **apex**) of the leaf may be **acuminate,** gradually tapering to a long sharp point; **acute,** tapering more broadly to a sharp point; **obtuse,** blunt-pointed; **aristate,** ending an an **awn** (or bristle); **cuspidate,** ending in a sharp, rigid point, or **cusp; truncate,** seeming to be cut off square or nearly so; **retuse,** with a shallow notch; or **emarginate,** more deeply notched. A **mucronate** tip is essentially the same as a cuspidate tip. Leaves of some plants of tropical rain forests have long **drip tips** (Figure 66).

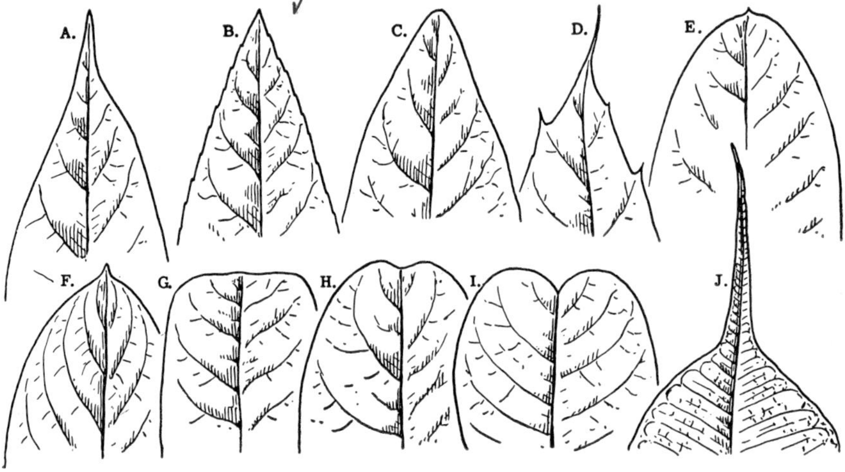

Figure 66. Types of apices of leaf blades. A, acuminate, *Aster;* B, acute, *Aster;* C, obtuse, *Apocynum;* D, aristate, *Quercus;* E, mucronate, *Asclepias;* F, cuspidate, *Cornus;* G, truncate, *Asclepias;* H, retuse, *Galactia;* I, emarginate, *Asclepias;* J, drip tip, *Ficus religiosa.*

The **surface** of leaves may be smooth or provided with hairs, scales, or coatings of various kinds. A **glabrous** leaf is smooth, without hairs of any kind; a **glabrate** leaf is glabrous or tends to become glabrous at maturity. The types and degrees of hairiness are extremely variable and numerous technical terms have been used to designate them. **Pubescent** is with fine, soft hairs; **puberulent** is with very fine, down-like hairs; **canescent** indicates fine white hairs; **hirsute,** stiff hairs; **hispid,** or **strigose,** stiff, bristly hairs; **pilose,** soft, slender hairs; **sericeous,** silky hairs; **villous,** long, shaggy hairs; **floccose,** with tufts of soft, silky hairs; **tomentose,** with long, curled, matted hairs (woolly). Hairs arranged in a star-shaped cluster are **stellate.** A leaf rough to the touch is **scabrous.** A **glaucous** leaf is covered with a whitish or bluish waxy material or "bloom"; a **glutinous** leaf has a sticky surface; a **glandular** leaf has tiny secreting structures on the surface or on the ends of hairs; a **glandular-punctate** leaf is dotted with glands; a **pulverulent** leaf is covered with a fine powder; a **pruinose** leaf is covered with more coarse, granular material; a **scurfy** leaf is covered with scales. Some plants, as nettles, have **stinging** hairs, containing a liquid irritating to animal tissues. Many plants have glandular hairs, secreting oil, resin, or mucilage. Hairiness, of course, may be characteristic as well of the surfaces of certain other plant structures, as stems or flowers.

References

Bose, G. C., *A manual of Indian Botany.* London, Glasgow, 1945 (?).

Gray, A., *Structural botany.* 6th ed. New York, 1879.

———, *Lessons in botany.* Rev. ed. New York, 1887.

Johnson, A. M., *Taxonomy of the flowering plants.* New York, London, 1931.

McLuckie, J., and H. S. McKee, *Australian and New Zealand Botany.* Sydney, 1954.

Priestley, J. H., and L. I. Scott, *An Introduction to Botany.* London, 1938.

Trelease, W., *Winter botany.* Urbana, Ill., 1918.

13

Floral Morphology

Although vegetative characteristics provide important taxonomic data, it is in the reproductive organs that the most significant criteria are found. This is for the reason that features of the reproductive organs in general are more stable and presumably the results of more ancient evolutionary changes. These organs include the **flower,** a specialized shoot in which the processes of pollination and fertilization lead to the production of the **fruit** and **seed.** A flower arises, as shoots normally do, from the axil of a leaf; the leaf in this case, however, is usually reduced in size and is termed a **bract** (Figure 67). Sometimes two smaller bracts (**bracteoles**) are to be found on the flower stalk or **pedicel.**

The arrangement of the flowers on the plant is known as the **inflorescence.** The stalk of the inflorescence is the **peduncle.** If the stalk arises directly from the ground it is called a **scape** (Figure 68). In some cases (carrot) the inflorescence is subtended by a whorl of bracts, forming the **involucre.** A flower may be **solitary** on the end of the stalk; more often, several flowers may be grouped together in a cluster. These clusters are variable but fall within rather well-defined classes and hence are of taxonomic value. In general they belong to two broad types. In one type the growing axis of the cluster has the oldest flowers at the base with progressively younger flowers toward the tip. The whole inflorescence thus tends to become more and more elongated, with, perhaps, mature fruits at the base while at the tip there may be still unopened flower buds. This type of inflorescence is known as **indeterminate** since it results from indefinite growth of the axis. In the other type the first flower to open is at the end of the stem and the later or younger flowers appear progressively lower down; hence the tendency is for the stem not to elongate during flower production. The growth of the floral axis, therefore, is **determinate.** So far as the positions of the youngest and oldest flowers is concerned, these two types are seen to be direct opposites.

Many theories have been proposed to explain the relationships of the various kinds of inflorescences. One of the most modern (Rickett, 1944) sets forth the concept that the primitive inflorescence was a **dichasium,** with the first flower to open being terminal and situated between two younger flowers on lateral branches (i.e., determinate in nature). From this, by only slight structural modifications, there arose the various types of inflorescences exhibited by flowering plants, somewhat as shown by the accompanying diagram (Figure 69).

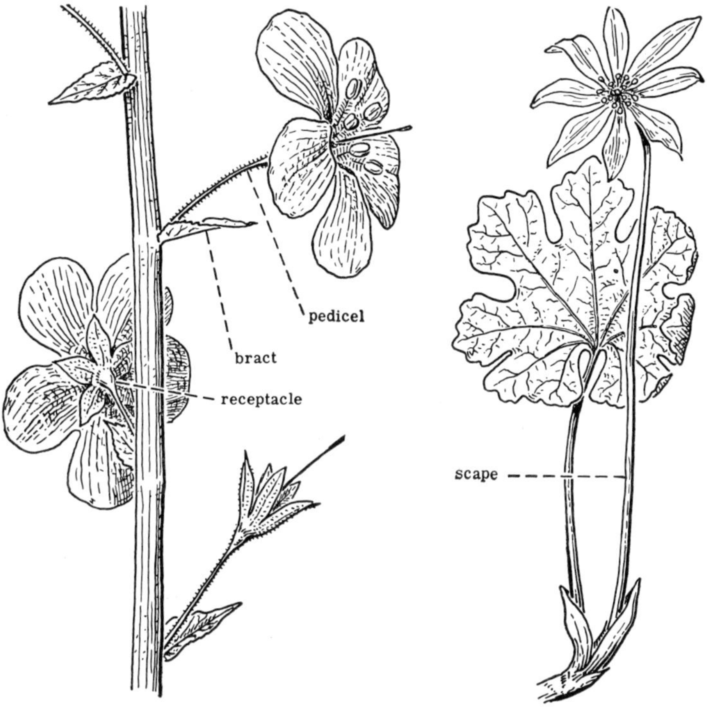

Figures 67-68. ***Left,*** **flower of moth mullein,** ***Verbascum blattaria. Right,*** **bloodroot,** ***Sanguinaria canadensis,*** **showing scape.**

By one line of development, there would be produced the **cyme** (as in pinks), a broad, more or less flat-topped cluster with the central flowers opening first. A **cymule** is a diminutive cyme. A **fascicle** or **glomerule** is a cyme with the flowers closely crowded. By reduction of the axes there would develop the **determinate umbel** (onion), with the pedicels of the individual flowers attached at virtually the same point, the central flowers opening first. Through suppression of the pedicels would be formed the **determinate head,** the individual flowers sessile. A **catkin,** or **ament** (birch) is a flexuous axis on which are produced dense clusters of reduced cymules (Figure 69). By another line of development, there would be produced a **helicoid** ("snail-like") **cyme** (heliotrope), the

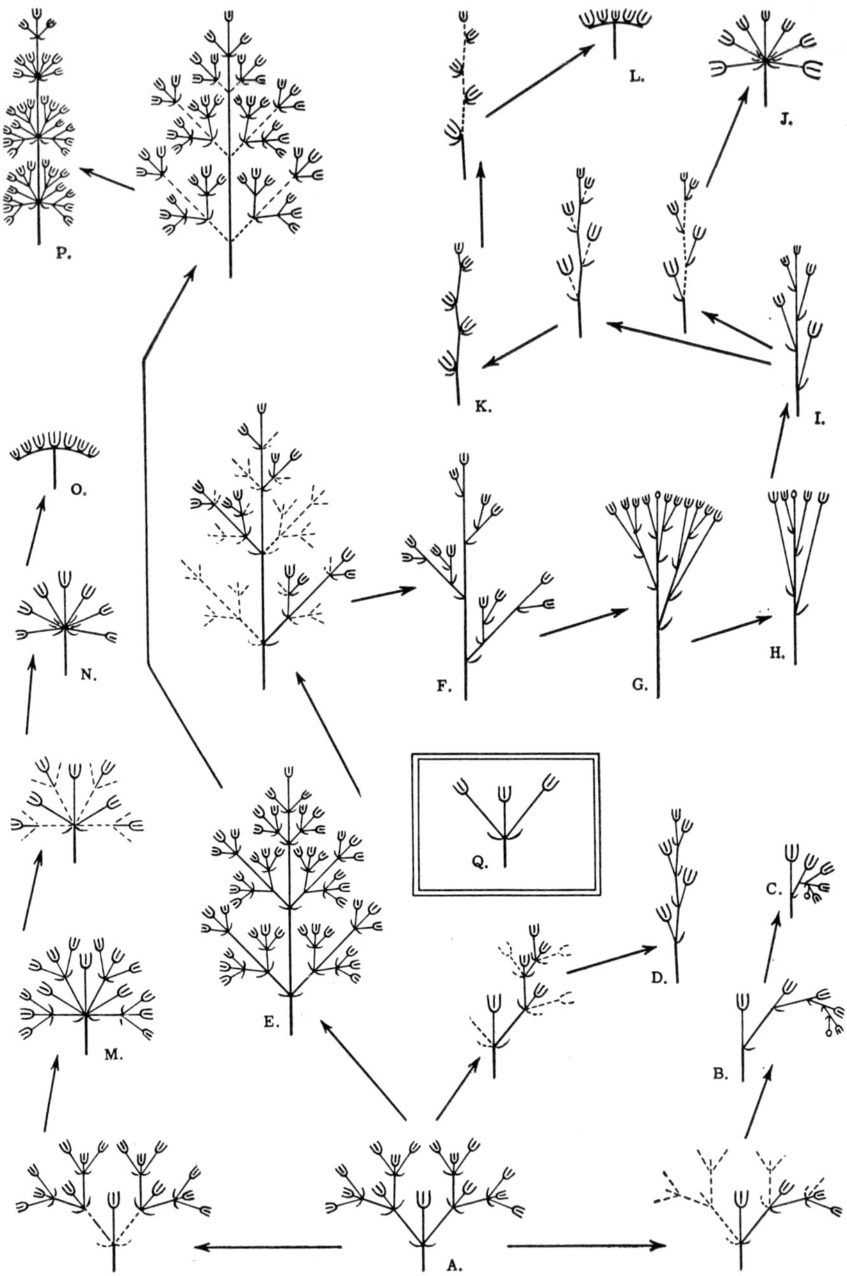

Figure 69. Diagram showing hypothetical evolution of types of inflorescence. A, compound dichasium; B, helicoid cyme; C, cincinnus; D, scorpioid cyme; E, thyrse; F, panicle; G, compound corymb; H, simple corymb; I, raceme; J, indeterminate umbel; K, spike; L, indeterminate head; M, cyme; N, determinate umbel; O, determinate head; P, verticillaster; Q, simple dichasium. (Redrawn from Lawrence, "Taxonomy of Vascular Plants," Copyright 1951 by The Macmillan Company, used by permission.)

branches developing on only one side of the axis. A **thyrse** (buckeye) has the main axis indeterminate and the lateral ones determinate. A **panicle** has all the branches indeterminate. A **corymb** (phlox) is somewhat like a panicle but with the lower branches (or pedicels) more or less elongated, giving the cluster a flat-topped appearance; the outermost flowers open first. Resembling a corymb, but with the lower pedicels not elongated, is the **raceme,** the lower flowers opening first. A **spike** resembles a raceme, but the pedicels do not develop and the flowers are sessile. A small spike may be called a **spikelet** (grasses; Figure 100). A **spadix** (calla lily) is a spike with a fleshy, thickened axis, usually produced in the axil of a large, more-or-less showy bract, the **spathe** (Figure 102). By suppression of the axis the spike becomes an **indeterminate head;** in the composites a modification of the head, known as a **capitulum,** is surrounded by an involucre of bracts called **phyllaries** (Figure

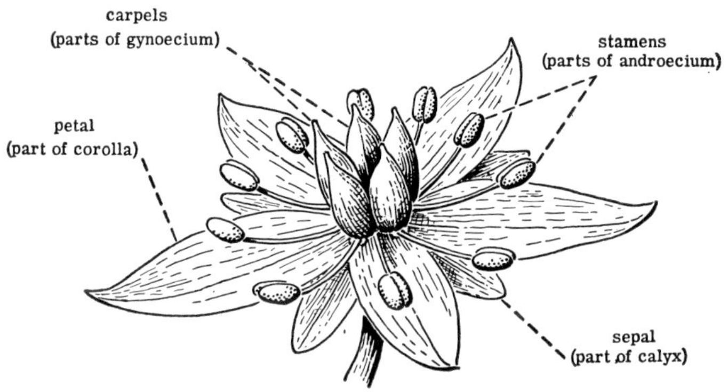

Figure 70. Flower of stonecrop, *Sedum ternatum,* showing principal parts.

125). An **indeterminate umbel** (carrot) with the outermost flowers opening first, differs from a raceme in having the main axis greatly shortened so that the several pedicels are attached at practically the same point. Thus it will be seen that heads and umbels, as generally understood, may be either determinate or indeterminate in structure.

Flowers. As noted above, a flower is a specialized shoot. The parts of a flower, then, represent specialized leaves, in which the degree of specialization might be regarded as indicative of the evolutionary position. Flower parts may be of short duration (**ephemeral** or **caducous**) or of longer duration. The flower parts are attached to the **receptacle,** the somewhat expanded upper end of the pedicel (Figure 67). In the least specialized flowers the receptacle is elongated and the floral parts are, therefore, **spirally** placed upon it in a manner somewhat resembling the attachment of ordinary leaves to the stem. But in more advanced flowers the receptacle is much shortened, so that it appears almost flat, and the floral parts seem to be whorled (**cyclic**).

The flower parts (modified leaves) normally occupy four or five whorls (Figure 70). Outermost is the **calyx,** the collection of **sepals,** usually green, enclosing the other parts in the bud. In composites and other families the calyx takes the form of bristles, scales, or teeth, and is termed the **pappus** (Figure 71, A). The **corolla** is the collection of **petals,** usually forming the showy part of the flower, commonly yellow, blue, white, or red. The **androecium,** the collection of **stamens,** produces the **pollen.** There are often two whorls of stamens. One or more of the stamens sometimes lose the normal function; such a structure is a **staminode** (Figure 72). The **gynoecium,** the collection of **carpels,** bears

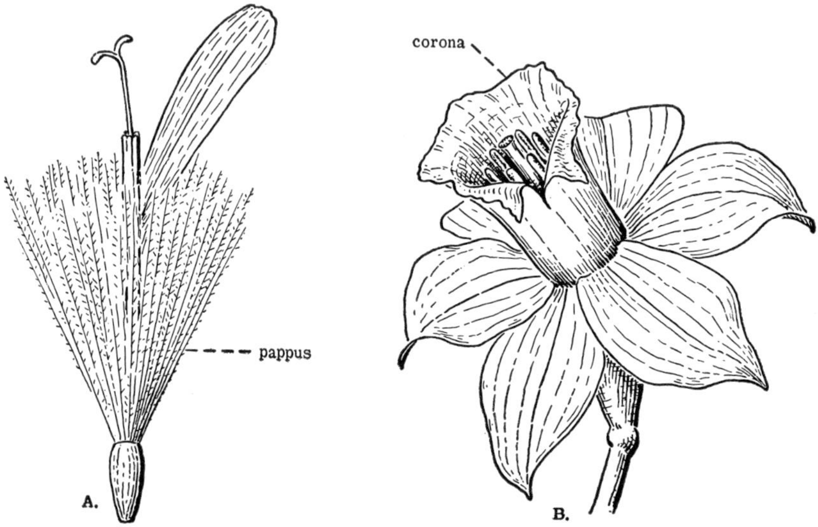

Figure 71. A, a composite flower showing pappus. B, flower of *Narcissus,* with corona (split to show pistil and stamens).

the **ovules,** bodies which, after fertilization, become the seeds (Figure 73). A **corona** or **crown** is found in some flowers (Figure 71, B). It is usually showy and may develop on the corolla (narcissus), or between the corolla and stamens, or from the whorl of stamens. The calyx and corolla together constitute the **perianth,** or floral envelope. These may be regarded as the **accessory parts** of the flower, while the stamens and carpels, directly responsible for the production of fruits and seeds, may be called the **essential parts.** Each stamen is composed of a slender stalk, or **filament,** and an expanded upper portion, the **anther,** composed of two 2-lobed halves joined by a **connective** (Figure 72). Each lobe normally forms a **pollen-sac,** within which the **pollen grains** are produced. Each pollen grain usually develops two male gametes or **sperm nuclei.** Each carpel bears, in its central cavity or **locule,** one or more ovules, each of which contains an **egg** or female gamete. The carpels may be separate from each other; more often, however, two or more are joined in a structure known as the **pistil,** which term, it is true, may also be applied to a single separate carpel as well. The pistil often has a bulbous base, the **ovary** (or **ovulary**), containing the ovules (Figures 73, 74) and a slender stalk leading upwards from the ovary, called the **style.** The tip of the style is often glandular and is known as the **stigma.** Each ovule is attached by a slender cord, the **funiculus,** to the **placenta** within each locule. The ovule is covered with one or two coats, the **integuments,** which

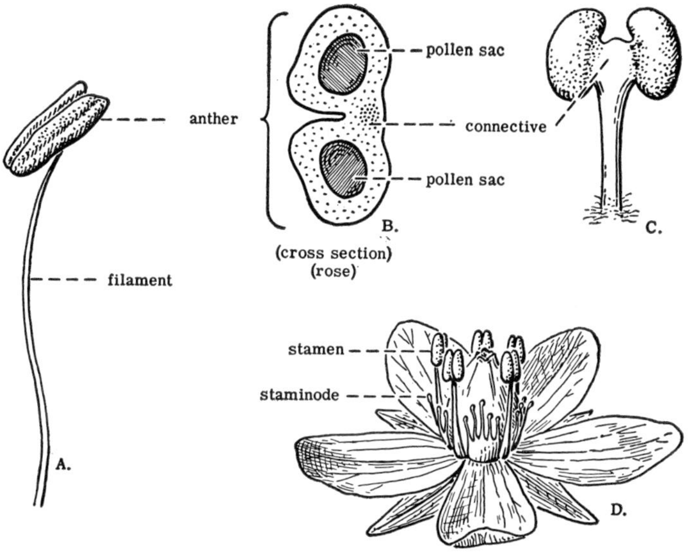

Figure 72. Stamens and staminodes. A, stamen of rose, *Rosa;* B, cross section of two-celled anther of rose (anthers of many plants are four-celled); C, apex of stamen of spiderwort, *Tradescantia;* D, flower of grass of Parnassus, *Parnassia,* showing staminodes.

incompletely close, leaving an opening, the **micropyle** (Figures 34, 84). The basal portion of the ovule is the **chalaza.** When the ovule lies in a straight line with its funiculus, it is described as **orthotropous,** but if the body of the ovule is bent or curved it is **campylotropous.** When it is bent over so far as to become fused with a portion of the funiculus, it is said to be **anatropous.** The fused portion of the funiculus appears as a ridge on the ovule, called the **raphe.**

Although the above description is generally true, flowers exist in an infinite variety of patterns which afford the basis for their classification into hundreds of families and thousands of genera. A discussion of some of these variations is now in order.

The number of parts in each whorl is quite variable and may be designated by the suffix **-merous,** as **5-merous.** Monocotyledons typically have 3-merous flowers, while those of dicotyledons are more often 4-merous or 5-merous. Flowers may be **complete,** having all four whorls of parts, or **incomplete,** lacking one or more whorls. When sepals and petals are lacking, the flower is **naked** (Figure 75); if only the petals are absent, it is **apetalous.** In apetalous flowers the calyx is often showy. A

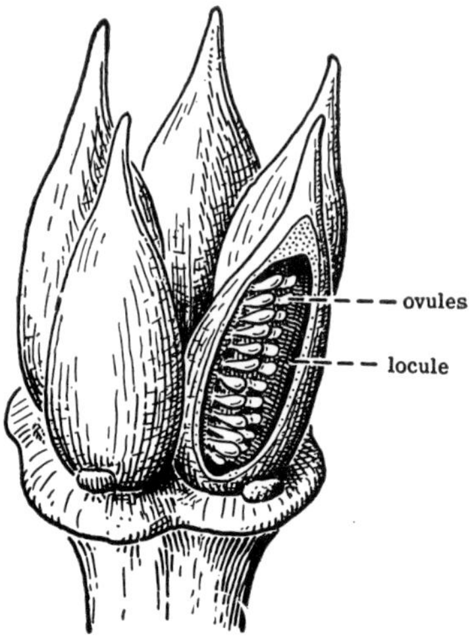

Figure 73. Gynoecium of stonecrop, *Sedum;* one of the carpels is cut open to show the ovules.

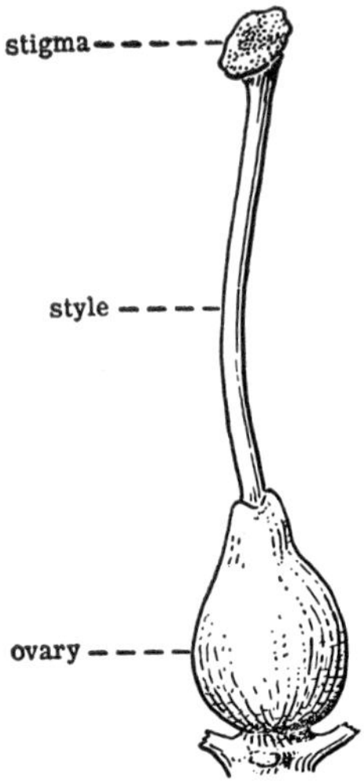

Figure 74. Pistil of plum, *Prunus.*

flower that has both whorls of essential parts is **perfect** (**bisexual, hermaphroditic**), regardless of whether sepals and petals are present; if either stamens or carpels are absent it is **imperfect** (**unisexual**). When stamens only are present, the flower is **staminate;** when carpels only are present, the flower is **carpellate,** or **pistillate.** Plants having both stamens and carpels in one flower are **monoclinous;** those with stamens and carpels in separate flowers are **diclinous.** Diclinous plants may be **monoecious,** that is, with both staminate and pistillate flowers produced on the same individual, or **dioecious,** with staminate and pistillate flowers produced on separate individuals. Some species have both perfect and imperfect flowers on the same individual; these are called **polygamous.** If perfect flowers and imperfect flowers of both types are found on a single plant, the species is **polygamo-monoecious,** but if perfect flowers are associated with staminate flowers on one plant and with pistillate on another, it is **polygamo-dioecious** (study Figure 70).

The Position of the Ovary. Great significance has been placed by phylogenists on the position of the ovary with respect to the other parts of the flower. These other flower parts may conveniently be referred to as the **androperianth** (that is, the androecium + the perianth). The basis for the grouping of families into orders takes this position into account, the ovary being referred to as **superior** (above the attachment of the other flower parts) or **inferior** (below the attachment of the other flower parts). Two theories have been proposed in explanation of the evolution of the ovary with respect to its position in the flower. By the **receptacular theory** it is asserted that the inferior ovary is surrounded by a cup of tissue developed from the receptacle. This theory has been widely held until relatively recently. The second theory, actually proposed by A. P.

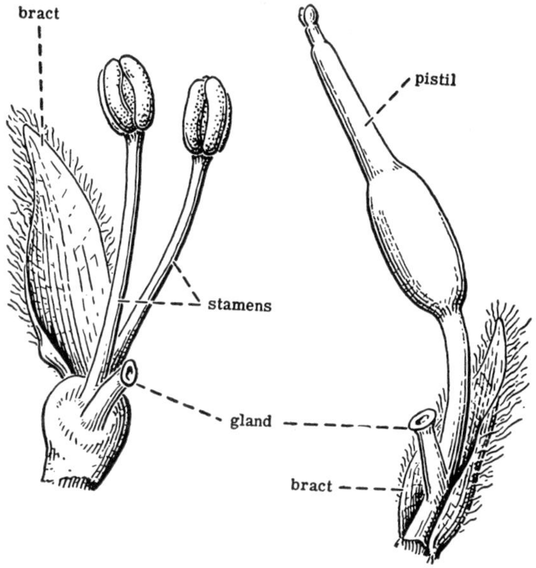

Figure 75. Naked flowers of willow, *Salix*. (Adapted by permission from Johnson, *Taxonomy of the Flowering Plants*, copyright 1931, by Appleton-Century-Crofts, Inc.)

de Candolle in 1827 but until recently not widely accepted, is the **appendicular theory.** This view holds that the tissue surrounding the inferior ovary is derived from the flower parts themselves (the **appendages** of the flower), and not from the receptacle. Recent anatomical studies indicate that only in a few cases, such as the Santalaceae, Calycanthaceae, and the genus *Rosa,* is this tissue receptacular in origin.

Egler (1950) has classified the principal types of floral pattern into six groups (Figure 77). While some flowers do not fit readily into one of these groups, they may at least be regarded as variations of them. In what is regarded as the most primitive type the sepals, petals, and stamens are attached to the receptacle at the base of the ovary (or ovaries). This type (Lily Type) has been called **hypogynous** (the other flower parts attached below the ovary); the ovary itself is **superior,** and **free.**

In a second type (Witch Hazel Type) the bases of the sepals, petals, and stamens form the **androperianth tube,** here only a **casing** tightly investing the ovary for a portion of its length; in such cases the ovary is more or less **half-inferior** or **half-adnate**—with the tube adnate or attached to it for half its length. The free parts of the calyx, corolla, and androecium thus arise at the summit of the casing, half-way up the ovary

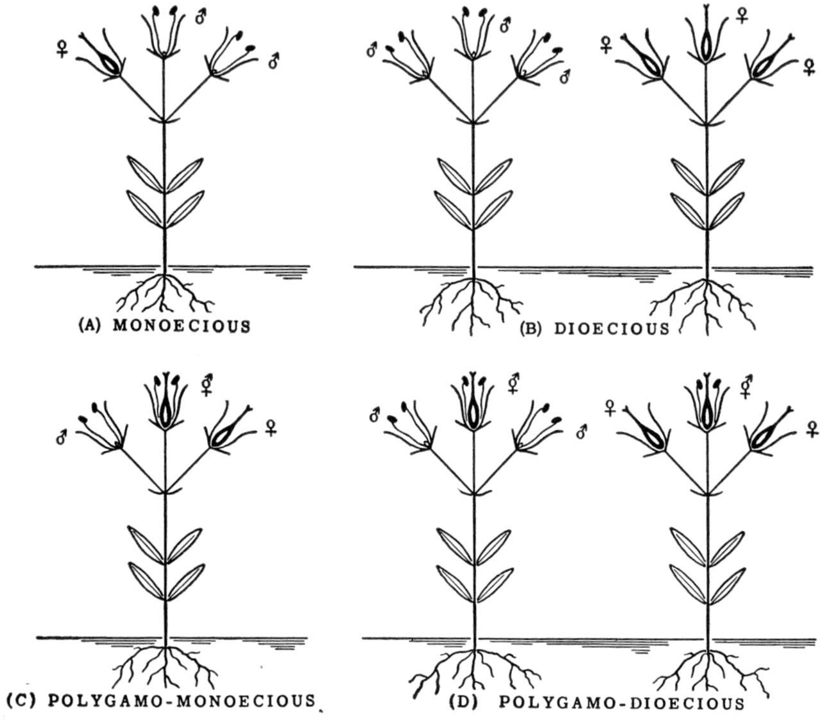

Figure 76. Diagrammatic sketch showing various relationships of diclinous flowers.

(or at various other levels). The androperianth tube has been erroneously called the **calyx tube;** actually, of course, much more than the calyx is involved. It has also been called the **hypanthium** (below the flower), a term which is unsatisfactory because of the implications with respect to its position.

In a third type (Carrot Type) the casing invests the ovary for its full length, with the free portions of the calyx, corolla, and androecium thus arising at the summit of the ovary. Such a flower is called **epigynous** (the free flower parts attached upon the ovary); the ovary itself is **inferior,** and **adnate.** Morphologically, it should be noted, the adnate and half-adnate ovaries actually have the other flower parts attached at their bases, just as do the free ovaries; the terms "superior" and "inferior," hence, should be used with some mental reservation.

A fourth type (Cherry Type) has the bases of the perianth and androecium united to form an androperianth tube, but the tube is not adnate to the ovary; such a tube has been called the **collar.** The free parts of calyx, corolla, and androecium arise from the summit of the hypanthium, *away from* the ovary, which is, itself, free. In a fifth type (Chokeberry Type) the androperianth tube is partially adnate to the ovary,

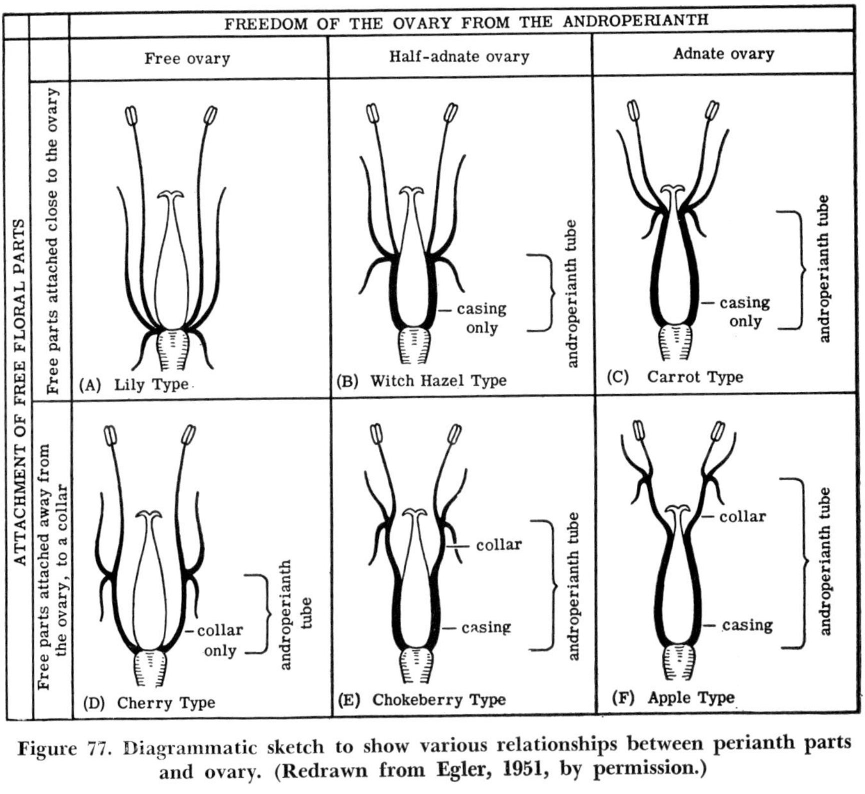

Figure 77. Diagrammatic sketch to show various relationships between perianth parts and ovary. (Redrawn from Egler, 1951, by permission.)

forming a casing, with the collar above this and the free parts of the perianth and androecium attached at the summit of the collar.

Finally, in a sixth type (Apple Type) the casing invests the ovary to its summit (the ovary is adnate), with the collar and the free parts of the perianth and androecium above that. This type, like the third type, may be regarded as epigynous.

It will be noted that two factors are involved in this classification, namely the freedom of the ovary from other parts, and the point of attachment of the free floral parts. Terms used in the past have been inadequate because they refer to only one or the other of these factors. For example, Types 4, 5, and 6 by various authorities have been called **perigynous** (the other flower parts attached around the ovary), although Type 4 might also be regarded as hypogynous, Type 5 as partly epigynous, and Type 6 as epigynous.

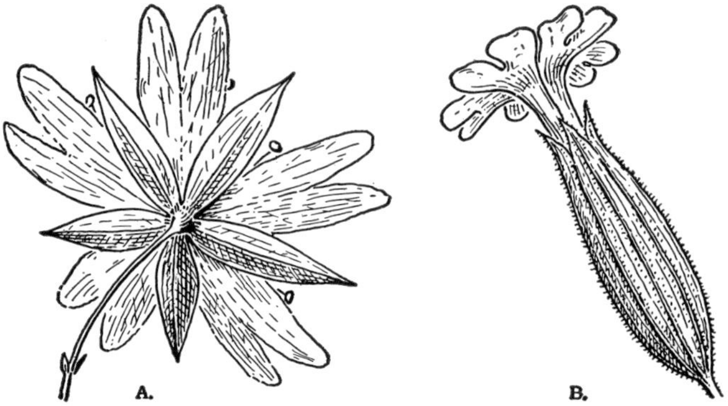

Figure 78. A, polysepalous calyx of chickweed, *Stellaria;* B, gamosepalous calyx of campion, *Lychnis.*

The parts included in each of the four whorls of the flower may be separate from each other or may be more or less united. (Of course the parts do not become united during their development, but the structure grows as a unit.) A flower having the sepals separate is called **polysepalous;** one with united sepals is **gamosepalous** or **synsepalous** (Figure 78).

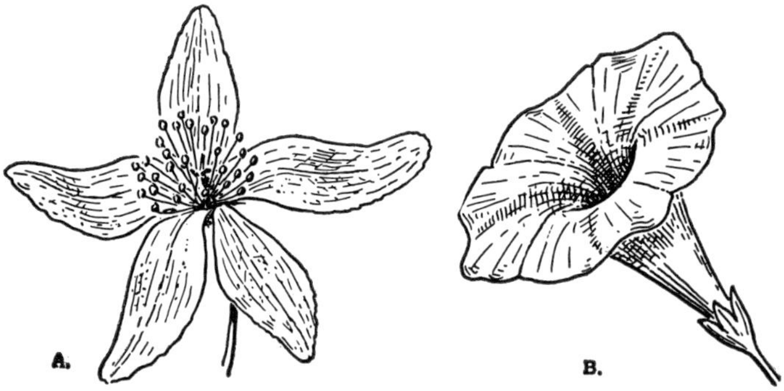

Figure 79. A, polypetalous corolla of St. John's-wort, *Hypericum;* B, gamopetalous (sympetalous) corolla of morning-glory, *Ipomoea.*

Similarly, a flower with separate petals is **polypetalous;** one with united petals is **gamopetalous** or **sympetalous** (Figure 79). The various types of sympetalous corollas are described as **urceolate, campanulate, labiate, funnelform, salverform, tubular, rotate,** terms which are suggested by the shape of the corolla. The united part of either calyx or corolla is the

tube; the rounded, free parts of the sepals or petals are the **lobes;** collectively they constitute the **limb;** when the lobes are so small as to be not apparent, they are said to be **obsolete.** Stamens, likewise, may be united (Figure 80); if the filaments are joined to form a hollow tube (or **column**) the condition is called **monadelphous** (one brotherhood); if they are united into two sets, the condition is **diadelphous** (two brotherhoods); if the filaments, on the other hand, are free, but the anthers are united into a tube, the stamens are said to be **syngenesious** (generation together, see Figure 125). In orchids, the stamens, style, and stigma are fused to form the **column** or **gynostemium.** As already noted, it is customary for the carpels to be joined to form a pistil; if the carpels are

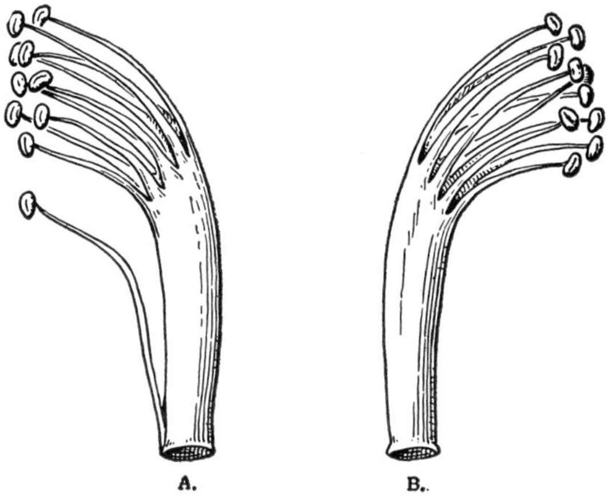

Figure 80. Types of union of stamens in the Leguminosae. A, diadelphous; B, monadelphous.

free from each other (the gynoecium **apocarpous**), each carpel constitutes a **simple pistil;** if two or more are united the pistil is **compound** (the gynoecium **syncarpous**). A compound pistil may have a separate stigma, style, locule, and placenta for each carpel, or these may be variously fused. Generally, however, it is assumed that each placenta represents a separate carpel (Figure 81). When there are separate locules for each carpel, with the placentas at the center, the **placentation** is **axile**—on the central axis. If, however, the partitions (**septa**) between the carpels are absent, resulting in a one-chambered ovary, with the placentas on the walls, the placentation is **parietal.** An ovary with but one carpel, also, may have parietal placentation. A compound ovary in which the septa are absent but the placentas are on a central stalk arising from the floor of the locule is said to have **free central placentation.** If the central stalk is greatly reduced or absent the placentation is **basal.**

Many flowers have the members of each whorl all alike and radially arranged; they may be called **regular** or **actinomorphic** (with **radial symmetry**). But others are **irregular** or **zygomorphic**, divisible into two equal halves along one plane only (with bilateral symmetry). These zygomorphic flowers exhibit a great variety of form and pattern; some of the most curious flowers are of this type. As examples may be mentioned the **papilionaceous** (butterfly-like) flower of beans and their relatives (Figure 82), and the **bilabiate** (two-lipped) flowers of mints (Figure 121).

A statement should now be made regarding the work of the flower. Ovules are the potential beginnings of seeds, and seed development

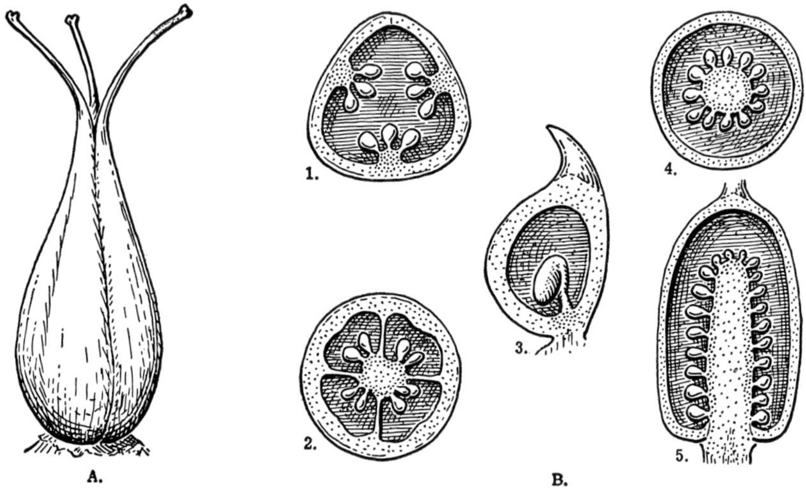

Figure 81. A, compound pistil of St. John's-wort, *Hypericum*. B, types of placentation: 1, parietal placentation of violet, *Viola;* 2, axile placentation of cranberry, *Vaccinium;* 3, basal placentation of buttercup, *Ranunculus;* 4-5, free central placentation of campion, *Lychnis*.

usually takes place only after the egg nucleus within the ovule has been fertilized by one of the two **sperm nuclei** within the pollen grain. The first stage in this process involves the movement of the pollen grain from the anther to the stigma; this is known as **pollination.** In some cases pollen grains merely fall upon the stigma of the same flower; this is **self-pollination** (**autogamy**). In **cleistogamous** flowers, the buds remain closed and self-pollination alone is possible (Figure 83). But many plants have adaptations that favor or insure **cross-pollination** (**allogamy**). The flowers of diclinous plants, of course, must be cross-pollinated. Furthermore, flowers of many monoclinous plants are unable to pollinate themselves because the stamens and carpels mature at different times, a phenomenon known as **dichogamy.** These flowers are called **protandrous** if the pollen matures first, and **protogynous** if the pistils mature first.

Pollen that must pass from plant to plant requires some agency for its transportation. In perhaps the most primitive type the pollen is scattered by the wind, some of it alighting accidentally upon the stigmas; plants of this type are called **anemophilous** (loving wind); in most of these the flowers are not showy. Many more species, however, have the pollen carried by animals that visit the flowers to secure food. The pollen grains adhering to their bodies are thus transported to another flower, where the pollen may be rubbed off against the sticky stigma. Although birds, bats, snails, and slugs are included among pollinating agents, insects,

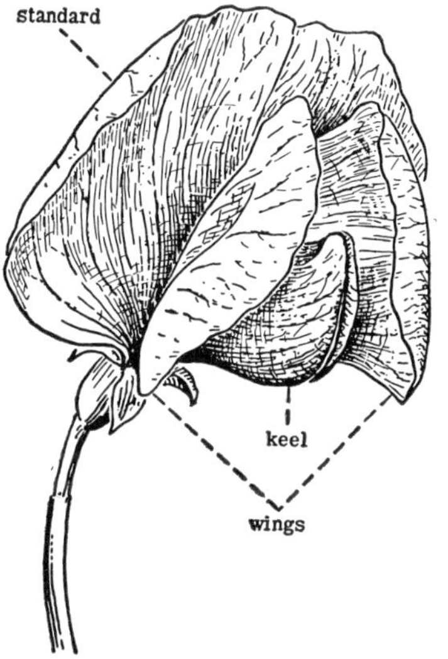

Figure 82. Papilionaceous flower of sweet pea, *Lathyrus*.

Figure 83. Violet, *Viola*, showing cleistogamous flowers.

especially bees, are by far the most important animals concerned here; plants pollinated by insects are called **entomophilous** (loving insects). Most insects visit flowers to secure a sweet fluid, **nectar,** secreted by glands known as **nectaries.** Nectar is used by bees in making honey. It is probable that insects are attracted to flowers by the showy corolla (or other parts) and by the various odors produced by different flowers. Flowers of some species of aquatic plants have the pollen carried by water.

When the pollen grains have alighted upon the stigma, each grain forms a **pollen tube,** which grows downward through the style, carrying the two sperm nuclei along (Figure 84). At last the sperm nuclei pass into the ovule, usually through the micropyle, one uniting with the egg to form the **zygote,** which initiates the embryo, the other uniting with two **polar nuclei** to form the **endosperm nucleus,** which is the beginning of the endosperm. This phenomenon, involving the functioning of both sperm nuclei, has been called **double fertilization.** From this point the ovule develops and enlarges to become the seed, with which we began our review of plant structures. But meantime the ovary, surrounding the ovule or ovules, has likewise been undergoing development and enlargement, to become the **fruit.** If fertilization does not occur, the entire flower usually withers, or, as is commonly said, fails to "set fruit." There are

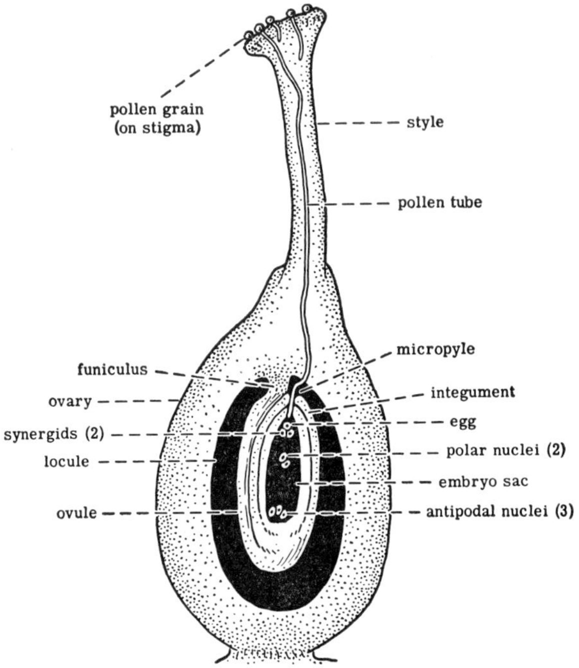

Figure 84. Longitudinal section (diagrammatic) of pistil of plum, *Prunus,* showing the pollen tube grown downward to the ovule.

usually fewer fruits on a plant than there were flowers. However, some plants, for example banana and pineapple, regularly produce fruits without fertilization. This condition is **parthenocarpy;** such fruits are **parthenocarpic.**

Fruits. Strictly speaking, a true fruit is a ripened ovary. It may, however, have various other structures associated with it, including the receptacle, calyx, and style; these are commonly included under the term fruit. Fruits are of great variety and are important taxonomic features.

The wall of the fruit, developed from the wall of the ovary, is called the **pericarp.** The pericarp may be **fleshy,** relatively soft and juicy, or **dry,**

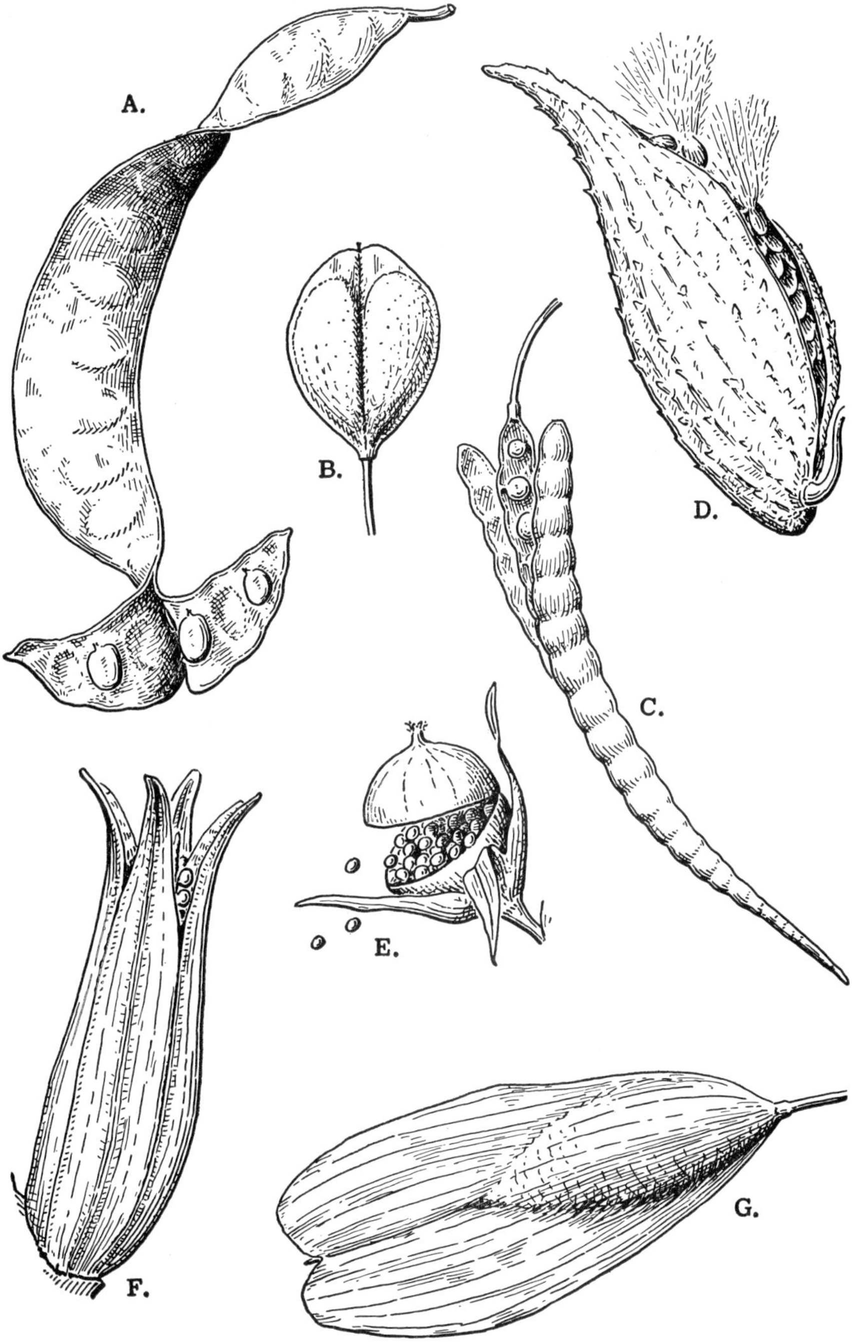

Figure 85. Types of dry fruits. A, legume of honey locust, *Gleditsia*; B, silicle of pepper-grass, *Lepidium;* C, silique of rock cress, *Arabis;* D, follicle of milkweed, *Asclepias;* E, pyxis of chaffweed, *Centunculus;* F, capsule of evening primrose, *Oenothera;* G, samara of ash, *Fraxinus.*

relatively hard and tough; of course all sorts of gradations exist between these two types.

Dry fruits may be classed as **dehiscent**—opening to permit the escape of numerous seeds—or **indehiscent**, where there is but one seed and therefore opening is not necessary, the entire fruit functioning as a single seed. Included among indehiscent fruits are the **achene**, in which the pericarp can be readily separated from the seed; the **caryopsis**, or **grain**, in which the pericarp is firmly united to the seed coat; the **utricle**, like an achene but with the pericarp bladdery-inflated; the **nut**, similar to an achene but larger and hard and bony; the **nutlet**, a small nut, sometimes indistinguishable from an achene; the **samara**, like an achene but provided with a wing which favors wind dispersal. Another type of fruit that may be classed as indehiscent is the **schizocarp** (splitting-fruit), which contains two seeds, but the entire fruit splits into two parts (**mericarps**), each part containing a single seed and thus resembling an achene. Still another fruit of this type is the **loment**, somewhat like a legume but constricted between the seeds; instead of dehiscing, it breaks into one-seeded segments.

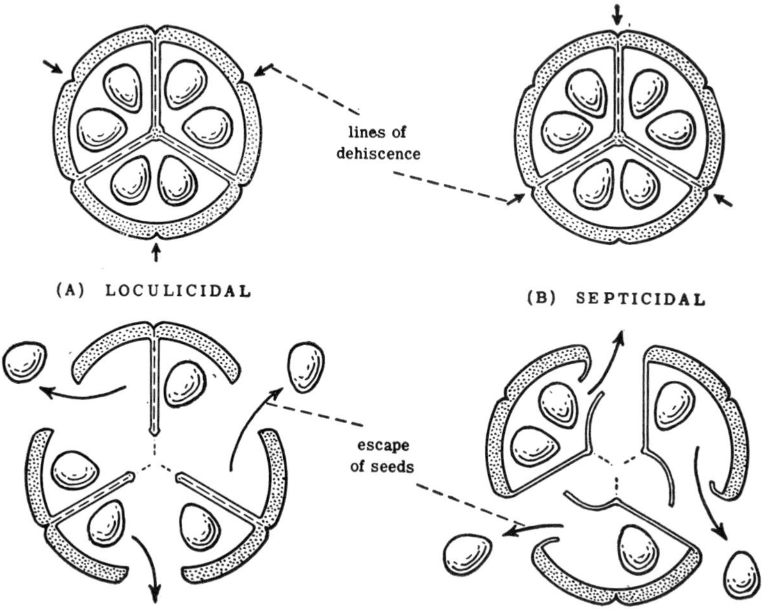

Figure 86. Types of dehiscence of capsules.

Dehiscent, dry fruits (Figure 85) include the **legume**, a fruit with one locule, but dehiscing along two sutures; the **follicle**, like a legume but dehiscing along one suture only; the **silique**, a long slender fruit of two carpels, the outer walls at maturity breaking completely away; the

silicle, like a silique, but short and broad; and the **capsule,** a dry fruit of two or more carpels, dehiscing into each locule. The mode of dehiscence is variable (Figure 86): **loculicidal** capsules split into the locules, more or less midway between the partitions, while **septicidal** capsules split at the partitions (septa). A **pyxis** is a type of capsule in which dehiscence cuts off the top like a lid.

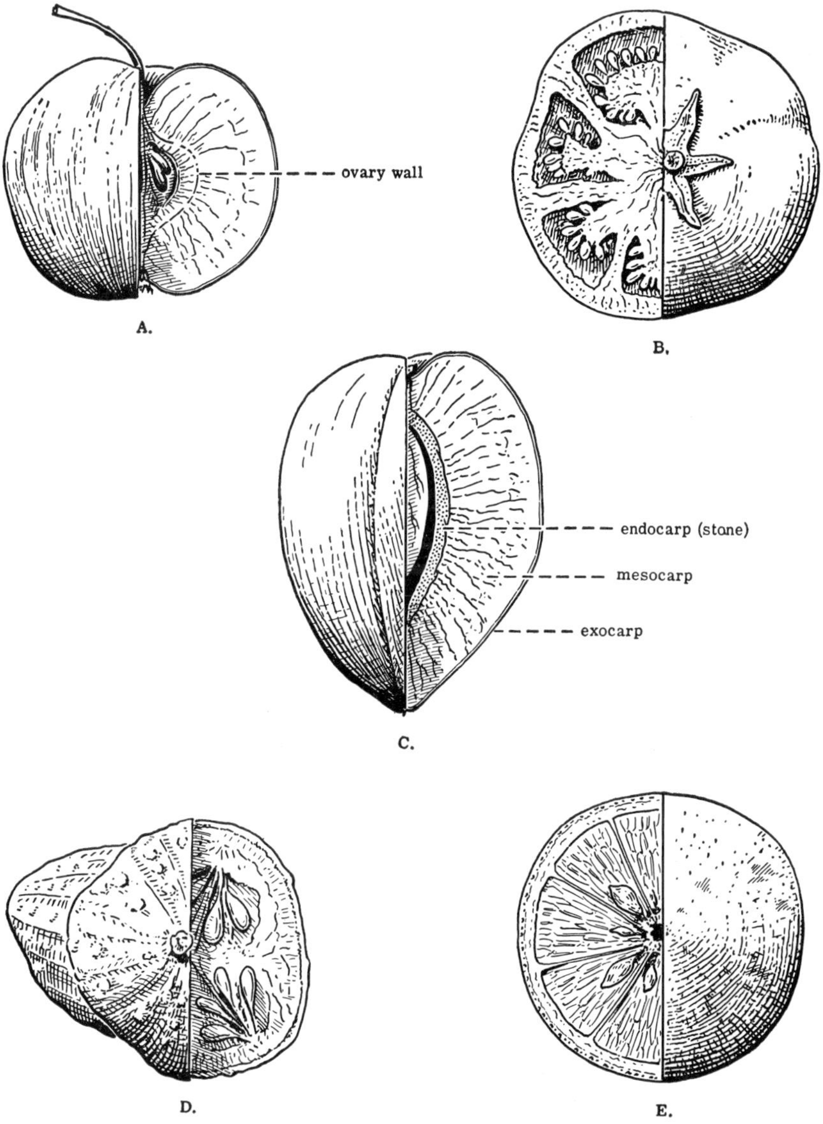

Figure 87. Types of fleshy fruits. A, pome of apple, *Pyrus;* B, berry of tomato, *Lycopersicon;* C, drupe of prune, *Prunus;* D, pepo of cucumber, *Cucumis;* E, hesperidium of orange, *Citrus.* A section is cut away in each case to show internal structure.

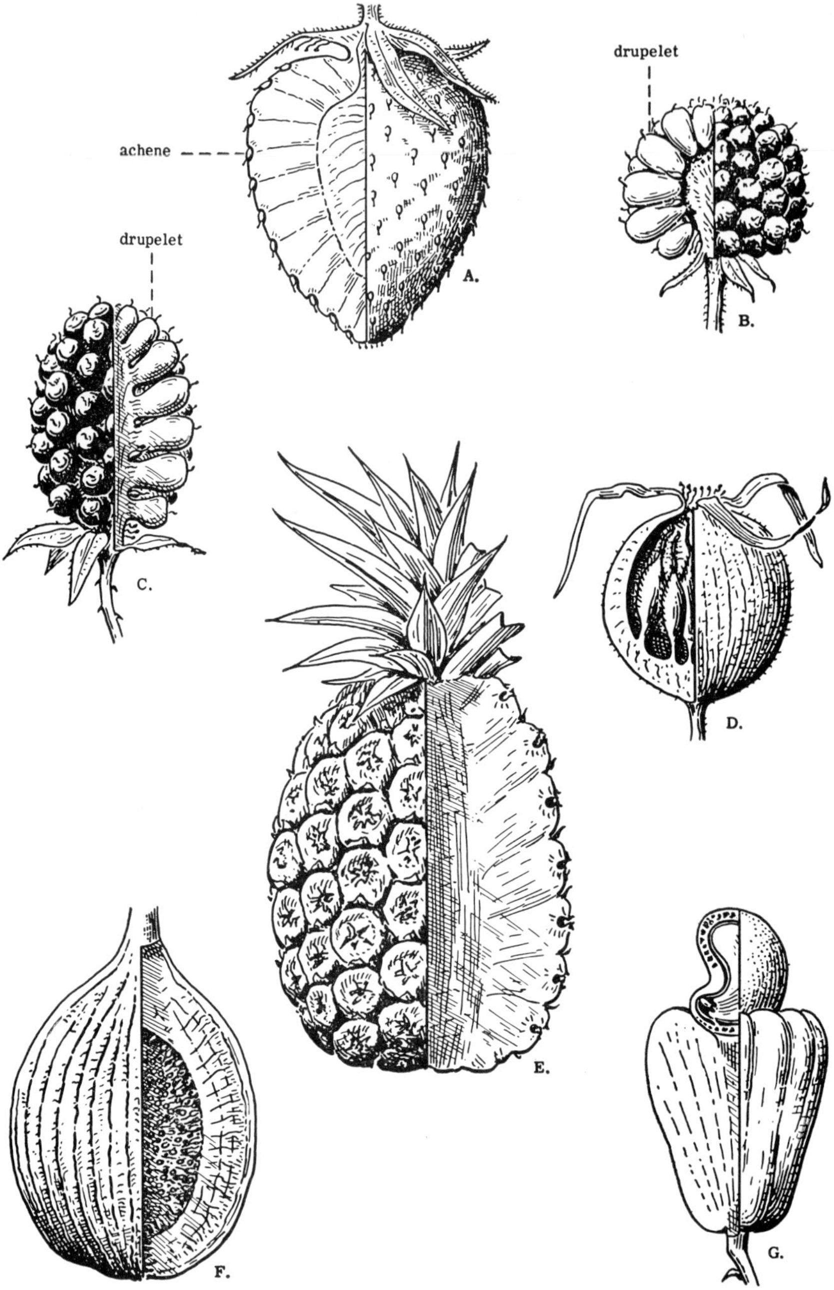

Figure 88. Types of aggregate, multiple, or accessory fruits. A, strawberry, *Fragaria,* with achenes upon a fleshy receptacle; B, raspberry, *Rubus,* with drupelets upon a dry receptacle; C, blackberry, *Rubus,* with drupelets upon a fleshy receptacle; D, hip of rose, *Rosa,* with achenes enclosed by a fleshy receptacle; E, syncarp of pineapple, *Ananas,* with fleshy fruits coalesced to each other and to the fleshy axis; F, syconium of fig, *Ficus,* with achenes enclosed by the fleshy axis; G, "double" fruit of cashew, *Anacardium.* Types A, B, C, D, and G are aggregate; types E and F are multiple. All of these (except B) may also be regarded as accessory, having *accessory* structures ripening along with the ovaries.

Fleshy fruits are all indehiscent, the fleshy tissue disintegrating in various ways to release the seeds (Figures 87, 88). There are three general groups, the first including fruits developed from (usually) a simple pistil, the second from a compound pistil, and the third from an aggregation of many pistils produced by one or many flowers. The **drupe,** usually developed from a simple pistil, has the pericarp consisting of three distinct layers, the **exocarp, mesocarp,** and **endocarp,** the endocarp taking the form of a hard **stone** surrounding the seed; fruits of this type are often called "stone fruits." Fruits developed from a compound pistil include the **pome,** which is developed from a several-carpelled, several-seeded, inferior ovary, the fleshy portion being a combination of pericarp and androperianth tube; the **berry,** developed from a several-carpelled, several-seeded ovary, either inferior or superior, having the seeds imbedded in a fleshy mass surrounded by a very thin covering; the **pepo,** like a berry, but having the outer wall of the fruit, developed from the androperianth tube, tough or firm and hard; and the **hesperidium,** like a berry, but having a thick leathery rind beset with many oil glands. In some berries the fleshy portion is an **aril,** an outgrowth from the funiculus, which more or less surrounds the seed. It should be noted that the term "berry," as commonly used, is often quite different from its botanical use. A third general class of fleshy fruits includes those developed from a combination of numerous separate carpels (pistils). An **aggregate** fruit is derived from the many carpels of a single flower; in this type of fruit the receptacle often becomes enlarged and fleshy, ripening with the carpels, as in blackberries and strawberries. The true fruits here may be of the nature of achenes (strawberry) or drupes (blackberry). In the blackberry the receptacle is fleshy and provides much of the edible portion of the aggregate fruit, while in the raspberry the receptacle remains dry and the aggregate fruit lifts off like a cap. The rose **hip** is an aggregate fruit that may be regarded as the opposite of a strawberry, having the individual achenes within a hollowed-out receptacle instead of on the outside of a "humped-up" receptacle. A **multiple** fruit is composed of the ripened ovaries (and associated structures) of many separate closely clustered flowers; in other words, this type of fruit is derived from a cluster of flowers instead of from a single flower. The ripened fruit includes sepals, bracts, pedicels, and floral axis, as well as the ovaries. The mulberry and pineapple are familiar examples. A special type of a multiple fruit is the **syconium** of a fig, in which the individual flowers are on the inside of a hollowed-out axis; this may be regarded as the opposite of the condition existing in the mulberry. In the cashew, in addition to the true fruit (the cashew-nut), a fleshy structure (the cashew-apple) develops from the flower stalk; the cashew, therefore, is popularly said to produce two kinds of fruits. In the case of the blue cohosh (*Caulophyllum*), on the other hand, it might be said that no fruit develops; the enlarging ovules burst the ovary, which then withers away, and the seeds, resembling drupes, continue to develop without a covering.

Seed Dispersal. The various types of fruits described above are adapted for dispersal of the seeds they contain. In some cases the fruits themselves may possess structural modifications that are important factors in their dispersal. The samara is easily carried by the wind. Some achenes are provided with woolly hairs or parachute-like tufts of hairs that favor wind dispersal. Some fruits are bladder-like and easily carried by water. Others are explosive and throw out the seeds for short distances. Many seeds produced in a capsule or other dry dehiscent fruit are provided

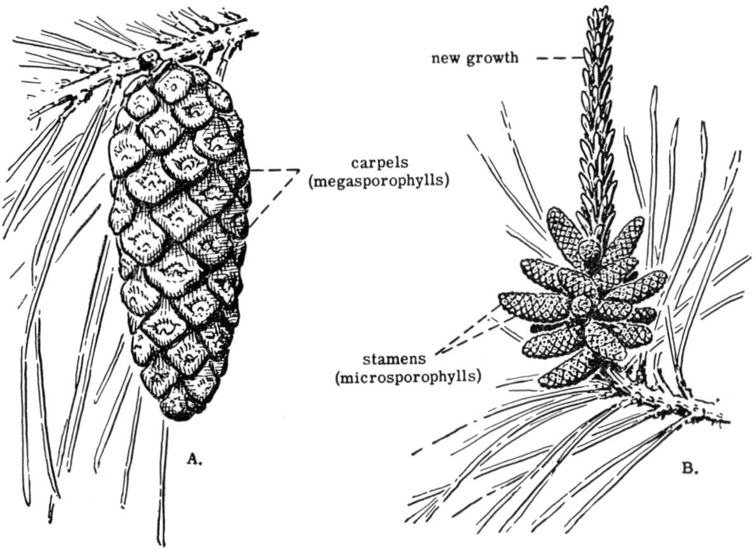

Figure 89. Cones of Scotch pine, *Pinus sylvestris*. A, ovulate or carpellate cone; B, staminate cones.

with hairs or wings. Some fruits, for instance the loment, are covered with hooks that attach to passing animals. Many fleshy fruits are eaten by animals, in which cases the seeds may be discarded or may pass uninjured through the animal's digestive tract. Nuts are carried away by rodents; some that are lost may germinate. Of all the animals, man, of course, is the greatest carrier of seeds. Some seeds, as those of the mangrove, germinate while still within the fruit and attached to the parent plant; this condition is **vivipary.**

Gymnosperms. The foregoing discussion has been applicable to the flowering plants, or **angiosperms** (plants with covered seeds). Not all seed plants, however, produce flowers, in the commonly accepted definition of the word. In the **gymnosperms,** the ovule is borne on the surface of the carpel, instead of being enclosed by it. Pollen grains are produced in small sacs borne on scales of various kinds, which may be called stamens, even though they do not resemble in appearance the conventional stamens of flowering plants. Fertilization results in the development of a seed borne exposed on the carpel, whence the name gymnosperm (naked-seed). Both carpels and stamens are often grouped in a structure called a **cone,** or **strobilus** (Figure 89). The staminate

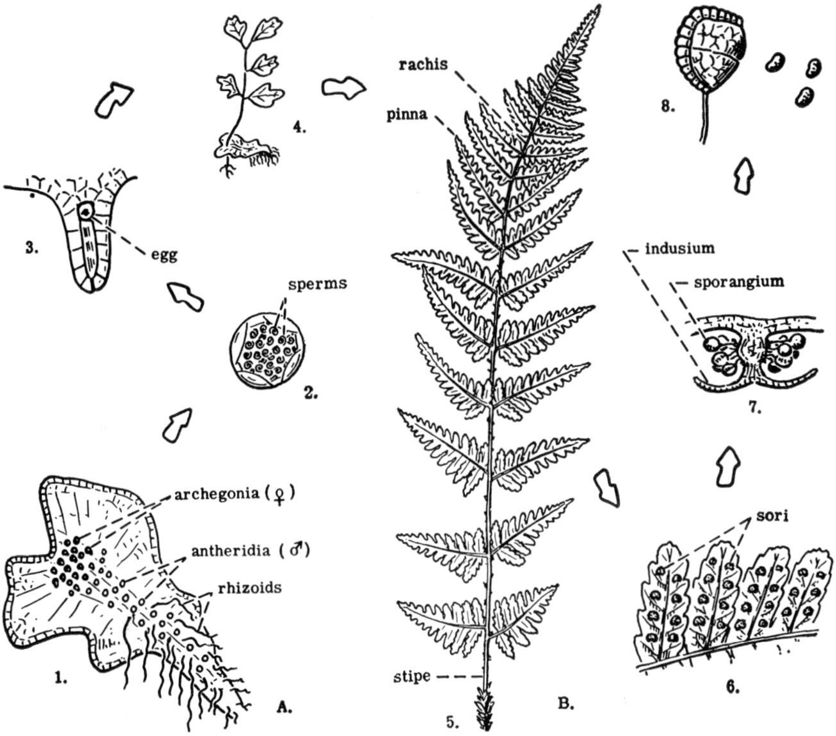

Figure 90. Stages in the life history of a fern. A, gametophytic generation; B, sporophytic generation. 1, lower side of prothallus; 2, antheridium with sperms; 3, archegonium with egg; 4, gametophyte with young sporophyte; 5, mature sporophyte; 6, sori on underside of fertile pinnules; 7, section through sorus; 8, sporangium and spores.

cones are of short duration, but the carpellate persist through the development of the seed and protect it somewhat as the seed of angiosperms is protected by the fruit. By some people these ripening carpellate cones are called fruits, but it may be readily seen that they do not correspond to the definition of the fruit as given above for angiosperms.

Other Vascular Plants. In addition to the seed-bearing plants, there are numerous other kinds of vascular plants—ferns, horsetails, clubmosses, and quillworts. These, like the seed plants, have roots, stems, and leaves, but do not produce flowers and seeds. Instead, their reproduction is by a unicellular body called a **spore,** produced in a **sporangium.** A plant producing spores is a **sporophyte.** The sporangia show almost every conceivable manner of arrangement on the plants, but are usually on modified or unmodified leaves. In ferns several sporangia often appear grouped in a **sorus,** sometimes protected by a flap of tissue, the **indusium** (Figure 90).

A spore germinates producing a **gametophyte,** or **prothallus,** ordinarily a small and inconspicuous thallus on the surface of the soil or beneath the soil (Figure 90). The gametophyte bears numerous sex organs, either male or female or both on the individual plant. Sperms are produced in an **antheridium** and a single egg in an **archegonium.** The egg is fertilized in the archegonium and the resulting zygote develops into the **sporophyte.** Many of these plants are **homosporous**—having the spores all alike—but some are **heterosporous,** bearing small **microspores** (produced in a **microsporangium**), which germinate to produce male gametophytes, and larger **megaspores** (produced in a **megasporangium**), which develop into female gametophytes (Figure 92).

When all phases of the life cycle are considered, these plants are not as different from seed plants as at first appears. The organ known as a seed probably originated, from an evolutionary viewpoint, in conjunction with heterospory in the primitive vascular plants. The structure from which the seed develops, as noted above, is the ovule and this is homologous with the megasporangium. In seed plants, however, the megaspore is permanently retained within the megasporangium and the female gametophyte thus develops within the old sporophyte tissue and not upon the ground. A seed may be defined as a matured ovule containing a young sporophyte, or embryo. Similarly, the microsporangium is the pollen sac, and the microspore is the pollen grain. The germinated pollen grain, containing the sperm nuclei and the tube nucleus, is, then, the male gametophyte.

References

Egler, F. E., *The terminology of floral types.* Biologia 2: 169-173, 1950-51.

Johnson, A. M., *Taxonomy of the flowering plants.* New York, London, 1931.

Lawrence, G. H. M., *Taxonomy of vascular plants.* New York, 1951.

———, *An introduction to plant taxonomy.* New York, 1955.

Pool, R. J., *Flowers and Flowering Plants* (2d ed.) New York, London, 1941.

Rickett, *The classification of inflorescences.* Botanical Review 10: 187-231, 1944.

Robbins, W. W., and T. E. Weier, *Botany. An introduction to plant science.* New York, London, 1950.

Swingle, D. B., *Textbook of systematic botany* (3d ed.) New York, London, 1940.

PART TWO

14

The Vascular Plants: Primitive Forms

The dominant plants of the mantle of vegetation now covering the earth's surface belong to the group known as the vascular plants—the Tracheophyta of the system of Tippo. All members of this group have tracheids or derivatives of tracheids, whence the name. These are produced in a vascular system, or stele, composed of xylem and phloem. The principal orders and families of these plants are discussed in the remaining pages of this work. In general they are arranged according to the latest revision of the Engler system, with the Tippo outline superimposed.

The family treatments have been made as uniform as possible, and include discussions of the roots, stems, leaves, and reproductive structures, in approximately the order named. Phylogenetical considerations are also included, with notes on the size and geographic distribution of each family. References are made to some of the interesting genera and species, particularly those of significant value to man. The number of species in each genus is usually indicated by figures in parentheses following the generic name.

The traditional system of classification that has been used in botanical textbooks for many years divided the plant kingdom into the Thallophyta, Bryophyta, Pteridophyta, and Spermatophyta. The last two groups are vascular while the Thallophyta and Bryophyta are non-vascular. Since in the Spermatophyta the reproduction, by flowers, was regarded as *open*—visible—these plants were formerly called **phanerogams** (*phaner,* manifest, *gamos,* marriage). Similarly, because the reproduction among the Thallophyta, Bryophyta, and Pteridophyta was more difficult to observe, these plants were called **cryptogams** (*crypto,* hidden). However, in another sense, the Pteridophyta and Spermatophyta could be grouped together, because both have a vascular system. The term vascular cryptogams, therefore, came to be applied to the Pteridophyta. Since most of the Pteridophyta are ferns, the entire group is sometimes inaccurately labeled ferns. An attempt to be somewhat more precise resulted in the phrase "ferns and fern-allies," the expression fern-allies being used to designate the lycopods, horsetails, and the like—all of the Pteridophyta except the ferns.

Modern morphological research, however, indicates that the Thallophyta is an artificial assemblage of quite unrelated forms, regarded by Tippo as members of ten separate "phyla." On the other hand, recent research has tended to break down the traditional distinctions between the Pteridophyta and the Spermatophyta. Since the discovery of the Seed-Ferns it has become apparent that the ferns are more closely related to the gymnosperms and angiosperms than to the fern allies, which term, therefore, becomes a misnomer.

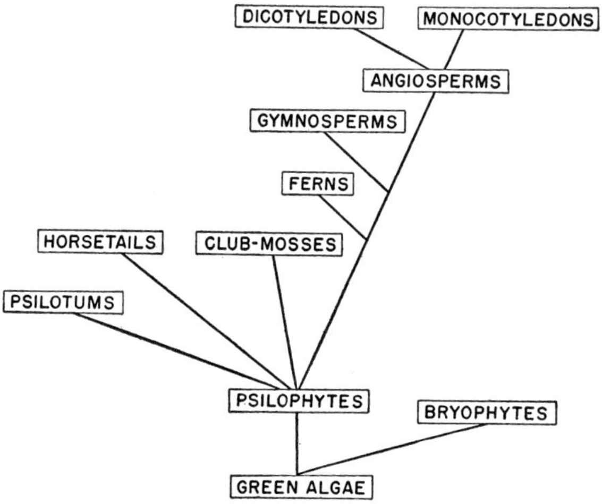

Figure 91. Diagram illustrating probable relationships of the principal groups of vascular plants. (Adapted from Henry T. Northen, *Introductory Plant Science*, copyright 1953 by The Ronald Press Company.)

The phylum Tracheophyta, following Fuller and Tippo, may be subdivided as follows (see Figure 91):

Subphylum Psilopsida
- Order Psilophytales
- Order Psilotales

Subphylum Lycopsida
- Order Lycopodiales
- Order Selaginellales
- Order Lepidodendrales
- Order Pleuromeiales
- Order Isoetales

Subphylum Sphenopsida
- Order Hyeniales
- Order Sphenophyllales
- Order Equisetales

Subphylum Pteropsida
- Class Filicineae
  - Order Coenopteridales
  - Order Ophioglossales
  - Order Marattiales
  - Order Filicales
- Class Gymnospermae
  - Order Cycadofilicales (Pteridospermae)
  - Order Bennettitales
  - Order Cycadales
  - Order Cordaitales
  - Order Ginkgoales
  - Order Coniferales
  - Order Gnetales
- Class Angiospermae
  - Subclass Monocotyledoneae
  - Subclass Dicotyledoneae

1. Subphylum Psilopsida

Members of the Psilopsida are the most primitive known vascular plants. The small plants have a dichotomously branching stem, but no real roots or leaves. The portion of the stem that is underground (the rhizome) bears **rhizoids,** hair-like appendages. The xylem consists only of tracheids. Reproduction is by spores, which are only of one type (homosporous). A spore germinates producing a minute gametophyte, a thallus on which are borne antheridia containing numerous sperms and archegonia, each with a single egg. Union of a sperm and egg results in a zygote that grows and produces another spore-bearing plant (sporophyte).

Order Psilophytales. In these plants the sporangia are always borne at the tips of the branches (Figure 93). Today they are known as fossils only, but they have a world-wide distribution in rocks of Silurian and Devonian age. The stele is a **protostele,** having a solid center of xylem (with no pith) completely surrounded by phloem. Our knowledge of this group began with the discovery of *Psilophyton* by Sir William Dawson in 1858. Other plants, *Rhynia, Horneophyton,* and *Asteroxylon* were discovered by R. Kidston and W. H. Lang at Rhynie, Scotland, in 1917. These plants were one to three feet high, although other forms were larger, six to nine feet high, resembling small trees with swollen stems. It should be noted that gametophytes have never been found on these fossil plants, although it is assumed that they possessed alternation of generations.

Order Psilotales. These are regarded by many botanists as the most primitive of living vascular plants. They have tiny emergences on the stems which may be regarded as primitive leaves. The sporangia are borne in the axils of these "leaves," instead of being terminal, as in the Psilophytales. The rhizome has a protostele, but the aerial branches have a pith; hence this stele is a **siphonostele.** Gametophytes are known and have been studied.

The order includes only one family, the Psilotaceae, regarded by many botanists as the most primitive of living vascular plants. The family is represented by two genera. *Psilotum* (2) is tropical and subtropical, reaching Florida, Bermuda, and Hawaii; the plants are often grown in greenhouses. *Tmesipteris* is mostly Australasian, extending north to the Philippine Islands.

2. *Subphylum Lycopsida*

Members of this subphylum have the sporophyte clearly differentiated into root, stem, and leaves. The leaves, mostly small, are regarded as evolutionary derivatives of the emergences of the Psilopsida. Usually the vascular system is a protostele, although in some plants it is a siphonostele. The sporangia are solitary on the upper surface of certain leaves called **sporophylls.** Often the sporophylls bearing sporangia are grouped at the ends of branches, forming cones or strobili. The subphylum is composed of five orders, two of which are now extinct. Its golden age was the Carboniferous; today there remain only four genera of rather insignificant plants.

Order Lycopodiales. This order is composed of one family, the Lycopodiaceae, including two living genera, *Lycopodium,* groundpine or clubmoss, with 180 species, and *Phylloglossum,* with one species. The sporophytes are herbaceous and the order presumably is derived from an herbaceous line which may go all the way back to the Devonian, although fossils are not known. The stems are mostly less than a foot high. The leaves are small, and evergreen, suggesting the name groundpine. The plants are homosporous and the strobili of several species borne on the ends of stalks resemble clubs, hence the name clubmoss (Figure 93). The vascular system of *Lycopodium* is a protostele, that of *Phylloglossum* a siphonostele. *Lycopodium* has a world-wide distribution, although it is most abundant in the tropics. *Phylloglossum* is found in Australia, Tasmania, and New Zealand.

Order Selaginellales. This order contains but one family, the Selaginellaceae, and one genus, *Selaginella,* the small clubmosses, with 700 species. These differ from the Lycopodiales in being heterosporous, and they are usually smaller and more delicate in appearance. The strobilus contains some sporangia (microsporangia) producing many small spores, or microspores, while other sporangia (megasporangia) produce only four relatively large spores, or megaspores (Figure 92). While still within the megasporangium the megaspore germinates, forming the female gametophyte, which is developed inside the megaspore, although the spore wall splits open. Meanwhile the microspore has developed into the male gametophyte, completely enclosed by the spore wall. This gametophyte produces a single antheridium containing numerous sperms, which, released by the rupture of the spore wall, swim to the female gametophytes lying within the megasporangia. Fertilization may take place either while the megasporangium is within the strobilus, or after it has escaped and fallen to the ground. The young sporophyte develops within the megasporangium. This behavior resembles the production of seeds, but the

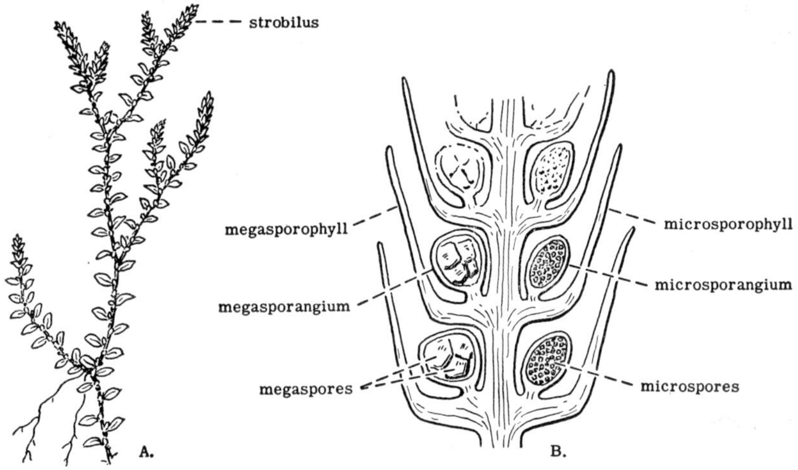

Figure 92. ***Selaginella apus. A,*** **habit sketch of plant;** ***B,*** **section through strobilus.**

structure in *Selaginella* corresponding to a seed lacks seed coats and has no definite dormant period.

Selaginella is widely distributed over the world, but is mostly tropical. Some species are grown in greenhouses. S. *lepidophylla,* resurrection plant, is sold as a novelty; when dry it closes up, resembling a bird's nest, but expands again when moistened.

Order Lepidodendrales. These plants, known as giant clubmosses, are represented by fossils only. They were all trees, some of them reaching a height of 135 feet and a diameter of six feet. They produced spores of two kinds and were, therefore, heterosporous. The microsporangia contained numerous small microspores, while in the megasporangia from four to sixteen relatively large megaspores developed. In some cases only a single megaspore matured in each megasporangium. A female gametophyte with its archegonia was produced in the megaspore while still retained within the megasporangium and, after fertilization, the entire structure was shed as a unit. This structure is very similar to a seed, although it cannot be called a true seed, since it had no ovule and, so far as fossil remains indicate, apparently no embryo.

These plants arose in the Devonian and reached their best development in the Carboniferous, being the dominant plants of the Coal Age and hence important in the formation of coal. They disappeared by the end of the Paleozoic, perhaps because they were unable to adapt themselves to the unfavorable climate of Permian times. Hundreds of species have been described. *Lepidodendron,* the scale-tree, had linear leaves, spirally arranged, which left characteristic scars when they fell off, suggesting the name (Figure 26). A related genus, *Sigillaria,* the seal-tree, had somewhat similar leaf scars.

Order Pleuromeiales. This is represented by a single fossil genus, *Pleuromeia,* from the Triassic. It was three to six feet high, unbranched, and had long grass-like leaves. The cones were heterosporous. *Pleuromeia* is regarded as intermediate between *Sigillaria* and *Isoetes.*

Order Isoetales. This order is composed of the single family, Isoetaceae, having only the genus *Isoetes* (60), the quillworts. These are small herbaceous, rush-like plants, mostly of wet places, and are found in cool climates throughout the world. The plants are heterosporous. The order, as noted above, may have arisen from the Triassic genus *Pleuromeia.*

3. *Subphylum Sphenopsida*

Members of this subphylum also have sporophytes with roots, stems, and leaves; the leaves were apparently developed from flattening of minor branches and occur in whorls at the nodes. The vascular system is a siphonostele (protostele in some extinct genera). The sporangia are borne on stalks called **sporangiophores.**

Order Hyeniales. This order consists of only two genera, *Hyenia* and *Calamophyton,* known only as Devonian fossils. These are in many ways intermediate between the other Sphenopsida and the Psilophytales; indeed, in some forms it is difficult to determine the subphylum to which they actually belong.

Order Sphenophyllales. This order includes only the fossil genus *Sphenophyllum,* the wedgeleaf, which is found from the Devonian to the Triassic, being most abundant in the Carboniferous. The wedge-shaped leaves were borne at the nodes in whorls of three, or some multiple of three. The strobili were either homosporous or heterosporous. The vascular system was a protostele.

Order Equisetales. Plants of this order possess jointed, ribbed, and furrowed stems, with the leaves and branches in whorls. The vascular system is a siphonostele and the strobili were either homosporous or heterosporous. The order includes two families.

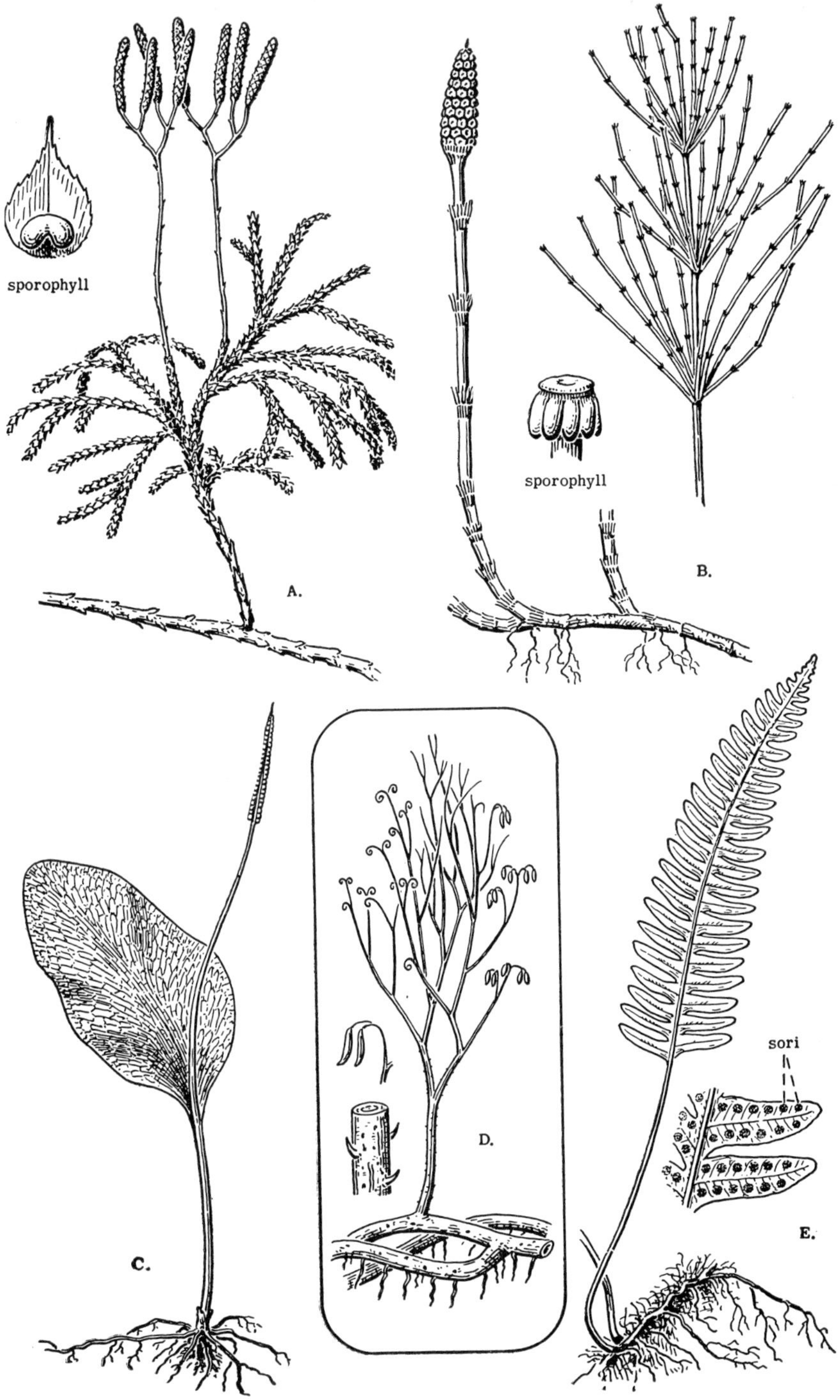

Figure 93. A, *Lycopodium complanatum;* B, *Equisetum arvense;* C, *Ophioglossum vulgatum;* D, restoration of *Psilophyton* (after Dawson); E, *Polypodium virginianum.*

Calamitaceae. Giant Horsetail Family. This family is composed of the fossil genus *Calamites,* the giant horsetail, which is found from the Devonian to the Triassic, reaching its climax in the Carboniferous (Figure 26). Some were sixty to ninety feet tall, possessing a cambium and secondary growth, but no growth rings. The strobili were either homosporous or heterosporous.

Equisetaceae. Horsetail Family. This family is represented by the single living genus, *Equisetum* (25); it is nearly world-wide in distribution, except for Australia and New Zealand. The species are herbaceous or shrubby, generally less than three feet high. The strobili are homosporous. The stele is a special type of siphonostele known as a **dictyostele,** having the vascular cylinder divided into a number of separate strands. *E. arvense,* common horsetail, is widely distributed over the world, often in dry habitats (Figure 93). *E. hyemale,* scouring rush, of North America and Eurasia, from its rough, siliceous texture, has been used by pioneers to scour pots, floors, and similar surfaces. *E. giganteum,* of the West Indies and tropical South America, grows up to thirty-six feet tall.

15

Pteropsida: Filicineae

The phylum Tracheophyta, as noted in the preceding chapter, contains all the vascular plants, and it has been divided into four subphyla, three of which have now been considered. Only about 2000 species of living plants are included in these three groups. All the remaining vascular plants, including over 200,000 species, are contained in the final subphylum, the Pteropsida. Here are placed the ferns, gymnosperms and angiosperms. The two last-named groups are the seed-bearing plants.

Earlier systematists separated the ferns and seed plants by placing them in separate divisions of the plant kingdom. Modern taxonomists believe that the importance of the seed habit as a phylogenetic character has been over-emphasized, this condition having been attained, or nearly attained, at various points in the evolution of plants. Among the fern-like fossils of the Paleozoic some have been found to be true ferns while others produced seeds, yet the other differences in structure were so slight that both seed-bearing and non-seed-bearing plants had been described by paleobotanists as members of the same genera. The presence of mesarch primary xylem (*cryptogamic wood*) in the stems of these ancient seed plants, together with their fern-like appearance, led to the suggestion that they were half fern and half gymnosperm.

The class Filicineae is composed of four orders, of which one is now extinct. About 175 genera comprising over 8000 living species are included. In general, these plants have large leaves, or **fronds**; they do not produce seeds; the sperm is motile in water; and both gametophytes and sporophytes are independent.

Order Coenopteridales. This group of ancient plants occurs only as fossils, from the Devonian to the Permian, most abundant in the Carboniferous when these ferns and their allies formed the dominant vegetation; thus that period was designated "The Age of Ferns." These plants resembled the psilophytes in that they bore the sporangia at the ends of the branches and the leaves were not well differentiated. In other features they resembled modern ferns, hence they may be regarded as intermediate between psilophytes and the ferns of today. The stele was of the protostele type. All species were homosporous.

Order Ophioglossales. These plants, usually conceded to be the most primitive of the living Filicineae, are included in one family, the Ophioglossaceae, with three genera including sixty species of herbaceous plants, generally widely distributed. They are **eusporangiate,** that is, several epidermal cells take part in the formation of each sporangium. The sporangia are borne on separate spikes arising from the leaves. *Ophioglossum* (28), adder's tongue fern, has a single simple oval leaf (Figure 93). *Botrychium* (23), grape fern or rattlesnake fern, includes plants with compound leaves; *B. lunaria,* moonwort, has crescent-shaped leaflets.

Order Marattiales. This order includes one family, the Marattiaceae, with seven genera comprising 150 species, principally of humid tropical forests. They are somewhat intermediate between the Ophioglossales and the Filicales, having the eusporangiate feature of the former, and the grouping of sporangia into sori characteristic of the latter. *Angiopteris* (60), of the Old World tropics, and *Marattia* (35), in the tropics of both hemispheres, are the chief genera.

Order Filicales. This is the principal group of living ferns and is regarded as the most highly specialized (Figure 90). The sporangium develops from a single epidermal cell, a type of origin known as **leptosporangiate.** Each sporangium has an **annulus,** a ring-like structure composed of heavy-walled cells concerned with dehiscence; this feature is lacking in the Ophioglossales. The leaves have **circinate vernation,** that is, they seem to unroll as they develop. This character is possessed by the Marattiales but not by the Ophioglossales. The stele may be a protostele, a siphonostele, or a dictyostele. If it is a siphonostele, the phloem may be on both the outside and inside of the stele (**amphiphloic**), or on the outside only (**ectophloic**). The primary xylem is commonly **mesarch,** that is, differentiation of the meristematic cells proceeds both centripetally and centrifugally. In many of the lower forms of vascular plants the xylem is **exarch**—differentiation proceeds from the periphery to the center of the axis (centripetally), whereas in the stems of seed plants the arrangement is **endarch,** with the differentiation centrifugal. The sporangia are borne in a cluster or sorus, there usually being many sori produced on the underside or margin of all or some of the leaves. In some species the sorus is more or less covered by an outgrowth of the leaf, known as the indusium. The gametophyte or prothallus is a small green thalloid structure rarely a fourth of an inch wide, with the sex organs borne on the under side.

The order Filicales consists of over 100 genera including about 8000 species, mostly of moist shady situations. These plants are most common in the tropics, where many occur as epiphytes on trees. About a dozen families are recognized, of which the following are the most common.

Osmundaceae. Flowering Fern Family. This is a group of mostly terrestrial ferns having compound, usually large leaves and no sori, the sporangia being scattered on differentiated portions of the leaf, or an entire leaf may be differentiated. These modified portions suggest the common name flowering fern, although they are by no means flower-like in structure. The annulus is incompletely formed.

The family, a primitive one among the order, includes three genera comprising twenty species, of temperate and tropical swampy regions. *Osmunda* (12) includes *O. regalis,* royal fern, *O. claytoniana,* interrupted fern, and *O. cinnamomea,* cinnamon fern, of North America and Eurasia.

Schizaeaceae. Curly Grass Family. These are terrestrial ferns of diverse habits, some being quite small and grass-like, whereas others are larger and climbing. The sporangia are mostly solitary, scarcely grouped into sori. The annulus is complete.

The family, regarded as a primitive one, includes four genera composed of about 160 species, mostly tropical. *Lygodium* (30), climbing fern, is a group of mostly tropical or subtropical plants, often grown as novelties. *Schizaea* (25) curly grass, includes small grass-like plants, mostly tropical, but occurring from Newfoundland to the Falkland Islands.

Gleicheniaceae. Gleichenia Family. These are terrestrial ferns with leaves that appear to be dichotomous because of repeated arrested development of the main divisions. The sporangia are in sori, but no indusium is developed.

This family, and the two preceding, have been regarded as the most primitive of the Filicales. By most botanists the Gleicheniaceae is regarded as composed of the single genus, *Gleichenia* (130), mostly of drier habitats in the tropics and subtropical portions of the southern hemisphere, a group of often weedy ferns.

Hymenophyllaceae. Filmy Fern Family. This is a family of small filmy ferns, the leaves being only one cell thick between the veins. The sporangia are in marginal sori enveloped by a cup-shaped indusium.

The family has been considered to be composed of two genera, including 750 species, mostly of tropical and warm temperate regions. *Hymenophyllum* (350), filmy fern, extends north to Norway and south to Cape Horn. *Trichomanes* (400), bristle fern, is mostly tropical and subtropical, extending to West Virginia, the Canary Islands, and western Ireland. By other authorities as many as thirty-three different genera are recognized.

Dicksoniaceae. Dicksonia Family. This is a family of tree ferns presumably evolved from ancestors related to the Schizaeaceae. The sori are bornc on the leaf margins at the tips of the veins and the leaf bases are hidden by a dense mass of wool. Tree ferns have neither cambium nor secondary tissue in their stems.

There are five genera including more than thirty species, mostly tropical, but with a distinctly disjunctive distribution. *Dicksonia* (20) occurs in tropical America, Juan Fernandez, St. Helena, and from Australia to Polynesia; *D. antarctica,* of southeastern Australia and New Zealand, is up to sixty feet tall. *Cibotium* (10), of tropical Asia, Hawaii, and Guatemala, includes plants often grown in tubs as ornamentals.

Figure 94. Tree ferns, *Alsophila,* in Mexico. (Photograph by C. J. Chamberlain, courtesy Chicago Natural History Museum.)

Cyatheaceae. Cyathea Family. These are also tree ferns and because of their size they were formerly grouped with members of the preceding family. However, it is now believed that they are not phylogenetically closely allied, but that the arborescent habit of the two groups has resulted from parallel evolution to the same level. The Cyatheaceae is regarded as derived from relatives of the Gleicheniaceae. Copeland regarded the family as having originated in the south temperate region, then migrating northwards along the Cordilleras to Mexico, also into Africa, Malaysia, and Polynesia.

The trunks are up to seventy-five feet or more tall, branching in some cases and often clothed with matted adventitious roots (Figure 94). The compound leaves are large, sometimes fifteen to twenty feet long, arranged in a terminal spreading crown and the stipes are often densely chaffy-scaly at the base.

Great differences of opinion exist as to the number of species, Diels recognizing 265 and Copeland more than 800. The number of genera is placed at three or more. *Alsophila* (200) is largely tropical, but ascends to nearly timber line in the Andes. *Cyathea* (200) is mainly tropical and subtropical; these ferns are a characteristic feature of the scenery of certain regions such as New Zealand; *C. medullaris* and *C. dealbata,* of that region, have a pulpy pith formerly eaten by the Maoris. *Hemithelia* (70) includes *H. smithii,* which extends south to the Auckland Islands (50° 40′, the record for tree ferns). Members of this family are often cultivated in tubs as ornamentals.

Polypodiaceae. Polypody Family. This, the largest family of ferns, includes plants of very diverse habit, mostly with compound (although sometimes simple) leaves arising from underground stems (rarely tree-like).

The family is composed of about 170 genera, including 7000 species that have a wide distribution, mostly in humid forests but also in deserts, extending from the equator to arctic and antarctic regions.

Woodsia (30) is found mostly in boreal and arctic regions, often on cliffs; *W. ilvensis* is circumboreal. *Cystopteris* (12), mostly boreal, includes *C. bulbifera,* bladder fern, of eastern North America, having on the under sides of the leaves bulblets that may give rise to new plants vegetatively. *Onoclea sensibilis,* sensitive fern, occurs in eastern Asia and eastern North America; the fronds are sensitive to early frost. *Dryopteris* (1150) of tropical and temperate regions, often has shield-shaped indusia, whence the common name shield fern; *D. filix-mas* is the male fern. *Polystichum* (300), mostly temperate, includes *P. acrostichoides,* the Christmas fern of North America. *Nephrolepis* (30), mostly of the tropics and subtropics, has some cultivated forms; the Boston fern is a variety of *N. exaltata. Asplenium* (300), spleenwort, is a genus of tropical and temperate regions; *A. ruta-muraria* is the wall-rue. *Camptosorus rhizophyllus,* walking fern, eastern North America, has elongated fronds that root at the tips, forming new plants. *Athyrium* (150), of tropical and temperate regions, includes *A. filix-femina,* lady fern. *Phyllitis* (10) has localized, disjunct areas of occurrence in Europe, North America, and South America; *P. scolopendrium* is hart's-tongue. *Blechnum* (150), of tropical and temperate regions, includes *B. magellanicum,* characteristic of the Chilean rain forest. *Gymnogramme* (80) is a genus of tropical and subtropical regions; *G. triangularis,* gold fern, of California, has the leaves white or golden beneath. *Adiantum* (120), of tropical and temperate regions, includes *A. capillus-veneris* and *A. pedatum,* maidenhair ferns. *Pteridium aquilinum,* brake or bracken fern, is a cosmopolitan weed. *Polypodium* (1200), polypody fern (Figure 93), is a genus of temperate and tropical regions; many species are epiphytic. *Platycerium* (8), stag-horn fern, of Africa, Malaya, and Australia, includes epiphytes of remarkable size.

Marsiliaceae. Water-Clover Family. This and the next family are often grouped in a separate order, the Hydropteridales, or water ferns. Recent studies indicate that both families should be considered as members of the Filicales. They are leptosporangiate ferns having their sporangia included in "fruiting bodies" called **sporocarps.** Members of this family are heterosporous, and the plants are monoecious, with both kinds of sporangia in each sporocarp. The leaf blades have two to four pinnae, somewhat resembling clover leaves.

The family has three genera including seventy-two species, almost cosmopolitan. *Marsilea* (65) includes *M. quadrifolia,* often grown in aquaria. *Pilularia* (6), pillwort, is a group of plants with grass-like leaves and pill-shaped sporocarps.

Salviniaceae. Salvinia Family. These are small floating aquatics not at all fern-like in appearance. Like *Marsilea,* they are heterosporous and bear sporangia in sporocarps, but only one kind of sporangium is borne in each sporocarp.

The family, consisting of two genera including about twenty species, is obviously closely related to the Marsileaceae. *Salvinia* (15) is tropical and temperate, including S. *natans* and others, much cultivated in aquaria. *Azolla* (4), of the same regions, is also grown in aquaria; it is our smallest fern.

16

Gymnospermae

The long ages of plant evolution have resulted in the development of the seed-producing plants as the present culmination of the evolutionary process. At the same time, these plants have come to form the dominant vegetation of the earth, and, in the Age of Man, they, almost alone, are the plants of economic significance.

The most primitive of the seed plants produce their ovules exposed, not enclosed by an ovary. These are called **gymnosperms** (naked-seeds), as contrasted to the **angiosperms** (covered-seeds). The gymnosperms, early in the Mesozoic, were the most advanced plants, from the evolutionary viewpoint, and formed the dominant vegetation, just as the angiosperms do today. Although reduced at present to a total of less than 1000 species, as compared to about 200,000 species of angiosperms, the gymnosperms are much more important than these figures indicate.

Gymnosperms, so far as known, are all woody plants; no herbaceous members occur. Some of them, as the big bald-cypress of Tule, and the giant sequoias of California, grow to enormous sizes and live for 3000 years or more. Nearly all of them are evergreen. Some form extensive forests of almost pure stands.

Order 1. Cycadofilicales. These are extinct plants but are well known in both the Old and New Worlds as fossils in rock mined as waste from coal mines. The fossils, often beautifully preserved, show roots, stems, leaves, seeds, and even pollen grains (Figure 26). They have a distinct fern-like appearance and for many years were thought to be ferns. About 1903 seeds were found connected with the leaves and stems; this sensational discovery resulted in their classification as a new order of gymnosperms. The structure of the seeds is quite similar to that of the seeds of modern cycads and the ginkgo, and therefore it is assumed that they possessed the swimming sperms that characterize those groups. The pollen grains also strongly suggest a life history similar to that of some modern gymnosperms. For these reasons there is no doubt that these fossil plants are properly classified with the gymnosperms, and their distinct fern-like appearance suggests that they may have formed a sort of connecting link between the ferns and the more modern gymnosperms; hence they may be regarded as the most primitive gymnosperms. They are popularly called seed-ferns.

Eospermatopteris, the oldest known seed-fern, was of tree size, thirty feet high, with a trunk three feet in diameter. *Lyginopteris* was a vine, climbing among the trees. *Medullosa* usually had a stem with three steles, as in pteridophytes, but with secondary wood like gymnosperms. Among

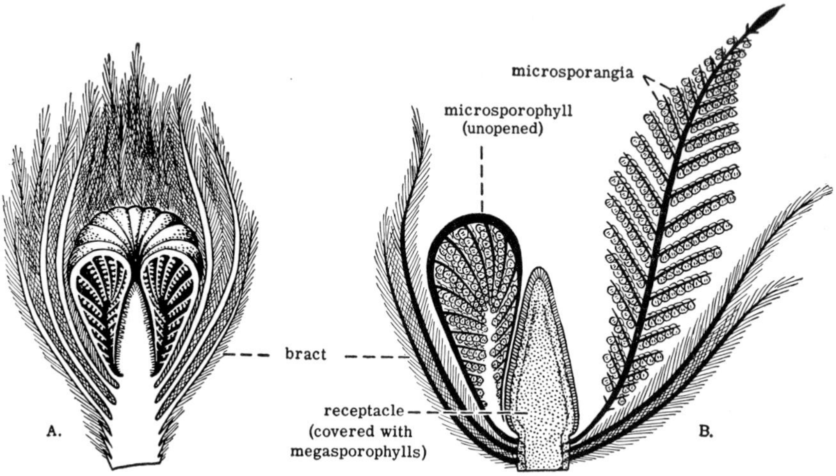

Figure 95. Bisexual strobili of *Cycadoeidea,* showing numerous basal bracts, several pinnate stamens (microsporophylls) each with many pollen sacs (microsporangia), and the elongated receptacle in the center, covered with carpels (megasporophylls). A, longitudinal section of young strobilus; B, older stage, with unfolded stamens. (After Wieland.)

the most highly advanced of the seed-ferns were *Eruplectopteris* and *Lescuropteris,* of the Permian.

The earliest fossils are from Devonian rocks, and they were very abundant in the Carboniferous periods but disappeared early in the Mesozoic.

Order 2. Bennettitales. These plants, which are called the cycadophytes, in reference to the similarity of their vegetative habit to that of the living cycads, were characteristic of the Mesozoic, "the age of cycadophytes." These plants apparently evolved from the seed-ferns, reached their culmination in the Jurassic, and became extinct in the Upper Cretaceous.

The cycadophytes were plants with a barrel-like stem, having the internodes shortened, usually with a crown of large compound leaves, with axillary unisexual or bisexual strobili, and ovules borne terminally (Figure 95). The inflorescence was somewhat flower-like in appearance, which has led to the suggestion that these plants were ancestral to the angiosperms; scholars who support this theory point to the resemblance, at least superficially, between the strobilus of cycadophytes and the flower of *Magnolia* (compare Figure 109).

Fossils of the genus *Cycadeoidea* were discovered in 1827. In this plant the terminal strobilus or "flower" had a central, ovule-bearing receptacle surrounded by a whorl of ten to twenty incurved, pinnatifid microsporophylls (stamens) each of which bore nearly one hundred pollen sacs. Another genus, *Williamsonia,* had mostly unisexual "flowers." Both of these plants were apparently unbranched, whereas in *Wielandiella* and *Williamsoniella* the stem was forking, and the flowers perfect. Fossils of cycadophytes have been found at many places in the northern hemisphere, indicating a wide distribution for the group.

Another fossil plant which seems closely related to the cycadophytes is *Caytonia,* tentatively placed in a separate order, the Caytoniales. This group, first described in 1925, had the seeds enclosed in cases suggesting carpels, with a berry-like "fruit." Furthermore, the presence of a stigma-like knob on the "fruit" suggests a possible bearing on pollination. Since these are angiosperm characters, *Caytonia* has been much discussed as a possible connecting link between the cycadophytes and the pro-angiosperms. Many botanists, however, are of the opinion that the "carpel" of *Caytonia* is different in its origin from the carpels of angiosperms.

Order 3. Cycadales. This order, of a single living family, the *Cycadaceae,* is an assemblage of greatly reduced survivors of a group that was world-wide in distribution during the Mesozoic. They are doubtless derived from the seed-ferns of the Paleozoic, and closely related to the cycadophytes of the Mesozoic. They are woody, more or less palm-like trees and shrubs found mostly in tropical regions. The stems are thick and tuberous, in some genera mostly subterranean, in others columnar and unbranched, all with a very large pith; they are very slow-growing. The leaves are alternate, persistent, pinnate or bipinnate. The plants are dioecious, bearing flowers in cones, the staminate with scattered pollen sacs and pollen grains (male gametophytes) with motile sperms, the ovulate with numerous ovules, often becoming very large; some cones weigh up to ninety-two pounds or more. The seeds are drupe-like, sometimes brightly colored. Only nine genera, including about one hundred species, are known. These have a wide but sporadic distribution, in the tropics and subtropics of both the Old and New Worlds.

Cycas (15) ranges from East Africa and Madagascar to southeast Asia, Australia, and Polynesia; *C. revoluta* occurs in southeastern China and southern Japan; the pith of *C. circinalis,* sago-palm, of Indonesia and the Philippines, yields sago starch. *Stangeria* is a monotypic genus of Natal, once thought to be a fern; *S. paradoxa* is known as Hottentot's-head. *Bowenia* includes two species of Queensland, with bipinnate leaves.

Dioon (3) is indigenous to Mexico. Plants six or seven feet high are estimated to be 1000 years old (Figure 96). In *D. edule* the starchy seeds are ground into a meal used for food. *Encephalartos* (15) is a genus of tropical and south Africa; these plants are xerophytic, with thick roots

Figure 96. *Dioon edule,* a cycad. (Courtesy Chicago Natural History Museum.)

and stems; the Kaffirs make a meal from the pith of *E. caffer,* Kaffir-bread, or Hottentot breadfruit, and other species. *Macrozamia* (15) is a genus of eastern Australia; *M. hopei* and *M. denisonii* are among the tallest cycads, growing to heights of sixty feet. *Zamia* (30), of tropical America, is the largest genus in the family; *Z. floridana,* coontie, and three other species found in Florida, are the only native cycads of the United States; the Seminoles used the starchy underground stem as a source of flour (Seminole bread plant). *Ceratozamia* (3) is a genus of southeastern Mexico, including *C. mexicana. Microcycas* is a monotypic genus restricted to western Cuba.

Order 4. Cordaitales. This group of extinct gymnosperms began its development, so far as the fossil evidence indicates, during the Devonian. The seed-ferns, cycadophytes, and cycads are all fern-like in habit, but the Cordaitales were not fern-like in appearance (Figure 26). From the cell structure, however, it has been assumed that they resembled the more primitive gymnosperms in having swimming sperms. In the structure of the secondary wood there is an approach to the Coniferales, and for that reason it has been suggested that they were ancestral to that group. The Cordaitales attained their maximum development during the Paleozoic and became extinct in the Mesozoic.

Cordaites was a tall forest tree with spreading spiral branches, bearing loose, unisexual cones. The leaves in some cases were a yard long, and six inches in width, with dichotomous venation. In some species the leaves were broad, spatulate, with a rounded apex. Other species had long, linear, grass-like leaves, while still others had broad lanceolate leaves with an acute apex. Superficially *Cordaites* resembled *Agathis,* of the Coniferales. *Pitys* is another genus of this group; one specimen has a stem forty-seven feet long and five feet in diameter. The stem of *Callixylon* may have exceeded 120 feet.

Order 5. Ginkgoales. Of this ancient order of seed plants, only one living representative, the maidenhair tree (*Ginkgo biloba*), remains; therefore it has been referred to as a "living fossil." It has been reported as growing wild in the forests of remote mountains in western China, but for centuries it was grown on grounds surrounding Chinese and Japanese temples and is now widely planted in America and Europe. It is quite desirable as a street and avenue tree, being tolerant of smoke and low water supply, and withstanding temperatures as low as 30° below zero (Fahrenheit).

The single species is a many-branched dioecious tree, growing to ninety feet in height. The leaves (Figure 61) are alternate and fan-shaped, often somewhat bifid, and dichotomously veined, like *Cordaites,* from which they may have been derived. The stamens are borne in a cluster resembling a catkin; each stamen has two anthers. The ovules are produced on short spurs, in pairs, each ovule being subtended by a small raised collar, which is possibly the vestigial remnant of the carpel, otherwise non-existent. The seed, often called a "fruit," is plum-like in appearance, with a fleshy outer layer surrounding an inner stony layer. At maturity the fleshy layer becomes very fetid and for this reason the staminate trees are more desirable for street planting. Fossils of various species of *Ginkgo* and other genera of the order are abundant in the northern hemisphere.

Order 6. Coniferales. This is the principal order of living gymnosperms and includes all the well-known and economically important gymnosperms forming large forests in the temperate zones. Not all of them bear the seeds in cones, but the cone (strobilus; see figure 89) is such a conspicuous feature of a large number of them that the name **conifer** (cone-bearer) has been applied to the entire group. Unlike the condition in the more primitive orders, the sperms are non-motile. The leaves are simple, mostly needle-like or lanceolate, not dichotomously veined.

The order may be treated as comprising 7 families, 48 genera, and about 520 species. The families are not large, and this fact, with the large number of monotypic genera, indicates great antiquity.

The families may be separated, in general, as follows:

a. Mostly dioecious; cone formation imperfect; seeds projecting beyond the carpels, with a fleshy aril or testa.
  b. Anther with 2 pollen sacs
    c. Foliage normal . . . . 1. *Podocarpaceae*
    c. Phylloclades present . . . . 2. *Phyllocladaceae*
  b. Anther with 3-8 pollen sacs . . . . 3. *Taxaceae*
a. Mostly monoecious; cone formation perfect; seeds concealed behind the scales; no aril or fleshy testa present.
  b. Leaves spirally arranged.
    c. Carpels with 1-2 ovules
      d. Carpels with 1 ovule . . . . 4. *Araucariaceae*
      d. Carpels with 2 ovules . . . . 5. *Pinaceae*
    c. Carpels with 2-8 ovules . . . . 6. *Taxodiaceae*
  b. Leaves opposite or whorled . . . . 7. *Cupressaceae*

Podocarpaceae. Podocarp Family. A family chiefly of the south temperate zone (also in Mexico and Central America), including five genera with about eighty species. They are mostly trees, growing to one hundred feet or more in height, with persistent, often broad leaves. They are dioecious, the stamens usually many in cones, and the ovule solitary, becoming a stony-coated seed partly enclosed by a fleshy aril. *Pherosphaera,* of Australia and Tasmania, is a shrub with scale-like leaves. *Microcachrys,* of Tasmania, has scale-like leaves and whorled carpels. *Saxegothaea conspicua,* from the southern Andes, is cultivated in northern climates as an ornamental tree. *Dacrydium* (20), of Malaya, New Zealand, Tasmania, and Chile, includes *D. franklinii,* Huon-pine, of Tasmania, and *D. cupressinum,* red-pine, of New Zealand, which produce good timber; *D. laxifolium,* pygmy pine, New Zealand, smallest of the conifers, produces cones when only eight centimeters high. *Podocarpus* (60) is the largest genus, distributed in Japan, southeastern Asia, Indonesia, Australia, New Zealand, South Africa, South America and Central America; some species are valuable timber trees.

Phyllocladaceae. Phyllocladus Family. This is similar to the Podocarpaceae, but the trees bear short shoots which are flattened, green, leaf-like structures (**phylloclades**). These structures, often lobed and dissected, suggest the common name celery-pine (Figure 53). The family includes a single genus, *Phyllocladus* (6), in Tasmania, New Zealand, Borneo, and the Philippine Islands. The timber is useful.

Taxaceae. Yew Family. These plants are apparently related to the Podocarpaceae, but produce three to eight pollen sacs on each stamen. The leaves are persistent, alternate, more or less two-ranked, linear or lanceolate, with pale green or glaucous lines on the under surface. The plants are dioecious or monoecious. The stamens are solitary or in cone-like clusters of three to fourteen stamens. The ovules are usually solitary, borne on a fleshy or rudimentary carpel. The seed is dry and nut-like, surrounded by a soft-fleshy, brightly colored aril.

The family includes about five genera and twenty species, with four genera found only in the northern hemisphere and the other an endemic genus of New Caledonia. *Taxus* is the largest genus, with about nine species of shrubs and small trees. Examples are *T. canadensis,* Canada yew, of east-central North America, *T. brevifolia,* Pacific yew, of the Pacific Coast of North America, *T. baccata,* English yew, of Europe, and *T. cuspidata,* Japanese yew. Several species are cultivated for ornament and the wood of some of them is used in cabinet work and for making bows in archery (*Taxus* is the classical word for bow). *Torreya* has three species in China and Japan, one in California (*T. californica,* California nutmeg) and one in Florida (*T. taxifolia,* stinking cedar). *Austrotaxus spicata* is endemic to New Caledonia. Two other genera (sometimes separated as the Cephalotaxaceae) are found in eastern Asia. *Cephalotaxus* has about six species of trees and shrubs, ranging from the Himalayas to Japan; *C. fortunei,* Chinese plum-yew, is cultivated as an ornamental. *Amentotaxus* is monotypic and endemic to western China.

Araucariaceae. Araucaria Family. This is a group of trees and shrubs, some of which grow to heights of 140 feet or more. The branches are symmetrical, often whorled; many of the secondary branches are deciduous. The leaves are evergreen, alternate, and of two forms, the juvenile being larger and differing usually from the adult leaves in shape; they persist for many years, clothing quite large branches. The trees are monoecious or dioecious, with the stamens numerous in rather large strobili, and the carpels numerous in cones which may become large and woody. The carpels each produce one ovule.

The family includes two genera, now mostly restricted to the south temperate zone, although fossils indicate members of the group were once abundant in the northern hemisphere; trees of the Petrified Forest of Arizona are classed in the fossil genus *Araucarioxylon*. The modern genus *Araucaria* includes about twenty-five species of New Guinea, New Caledonia, Australia, and temperate South America. Members of this genus are the dominant plants of the coniferous forests of Chile and

Figure 97. Brazilian pine, *Araucaria angustifolia*, in Paraná, Brazil. (After H. Schenck, *Südbrasilien Veget. Bilder*.)

southern Brazil, and all produce useful timber. *A. araucana*, of Chile, the monkey-puzzle tree, has short stiff leaves which completely cover the branches. *A. angustifolia*, Brazilian-pine, is a characteristic feature of the savanna forests of the southern Brazilian highlands (Figure 97). *A. excelsa*, Norfolk Island pine, is found on the island of that name, north of New Zealand. *A. bidwillii*, bunya-bunya pine, is found in Queensland, while *A. cunninghami*, hoop-pine, is also from Australia. *Agathis* (12) ranges from the Philippines to New Zealand. *A. australis*, of New Zealand, kauri-pine, is one of the largest commercial trees in the world; it is a good timber tree and also yields kauri copal. *A. alba*, of Indomalaysia, yields Manila-copal; it reaches a height of 180 ft.

Pinaceae. Pine Family. This is the largest and most important of the families of conifers. The members are nearly all trees, with whorled or opposite branches, and spiral or fascicled leaves. The leaves are mostly persistent, being deciduous in only a few genera. The plants are monoecious, with the stamens in small strobili and the carpels in cones that become woody at maturity. The carpels are flattened and distinct from the subtending bracts, which are usually shorter than the carpels. Each carpel typically bears two ovules. The seeds are winged.

Apparently the Pinaceae were more abundant in the middle Cenozoic era than now, but they have held their own better than most gymnosperms, perhaps because they have been able to adapt themselves better to the cold dry climates of post-glacial times. In many places they form forests of vast extent.

This is one of the most important of plant families. It produces far more lumber than any other family—perhaps more than all other families combined. Much of our paper pulp is secured from the Pinaceae. Turpentine and rosin are produced by pines. Many of the species are of ornamental value in landscape designs.

The family includes nine genera with about 210 species of wide distribution, especially in the north temperate regions.

Picea includes about forty-five species, the spruces, which constitute the world's most important sources of paper. The needles are angular in cross-section. *P. abies,* Norway spruce, is a valuable timber tree of Europe, often planted in North America. *P. obovata,* Siberian spruce, is found in the coniferous forests (taiga) of Russia and Siberia; other species, including *P. orientalis,* are found in the mountains of southern Europe from the Pyrenees to the Caucasus, and still others are found in the Himalayas. *P. jezoensis,* yeddo spruce, occurs in Manchuria and Japan; the plants are often grown as artificially dwarfed potted trees (*bonsai*). In North America, *P. glauca,* white spruce, and *P. mariana,* black spruce, characterize the boreal forest of Canada, while *P. rubens,* red spruce, is an Appalachian species. *P. sitchensis,* Sitka spruce, reaching 300 feet in height, is found near tidewater on the Pacific Coast, and *P. engelmanni,* Engelmann spruce, is found at high elevations in the Rocky Mountains; *P. pungens,* Colorado blue spruce, is a native of the Rocky Mountains, but much planted as an ornamental tree elsewhere.

Tsuga comprises about twelve species, the hemlocks. These characterize the forests of China, Japan, and North America, but are not found in Europe. The needles are flat, with two white lines beneath. *T. brunoniana* and others are found in Korea and northern Japan. *T. canadensis* is one of the most distinctive trees of the forests of the eastern United States, being associated with mesophytic hardwoods. *T. heterophylla* is one of the principal timber trees of the Pacific Northwest and is the largest member of the genus, up to 259 feet in height.

Pseudotsuga includes seven species of western North America and eastern Asia. The cones have distinctive three-lobed bracts. *P. menziesii*, Douglas fir, of western North America, is the leading timber-producing tree of the continent, at present producing more than six billion board feet annually. They are among the tallest trees known, with heights up to 385 feet (Figure 16).

Abies (40) includes the balsam firs, with numerous "blisters" on the trunk, filled with balsam. The cone scales and bracts are deciduous. The species are dispersed over Europe, Asia, and North America. *A. alba*, silver fir, is found in the mountains of southern Europe from the Pyrenees to the Caucasus; *A. sibirica*, Siberian fir, characterizes the taiga of northern Russia and Siberia; *A. veitchii*, veitch fir, of northern Japan, is a prominent member of the forests of that region. In North America the most widespread species is *A. balsamea*, characteristic of the boreal forests of Canada; in western North America, important species are *A. concolor*, white fir, and *A. lasiocarpa*, alpine fir, of the Rocky Mountains, and *A. grandis*, grand fir, *A. nobilis*, noble fir, *A. magnifica*, red fir, and *A. amabilis*, Pacific silver fir, of the Pacific Coast; *A. religiosa* is found in the mountains of Mexico and Guatemala.

Keteleeria (4) is restricted to China. The plants resemble *Abies*, but the cone scales and bracts are not deciduous.

Pinus (90) is the largest genus of the family, the plants characteristic of the north temperate zone and tropical mountains. The needles are of two types, the primary borne singly, in spirals, and the secondary mostly in fascicles of two to five; they are mostly much longer than those found in other conifers, sometimes over a foot long. The cones are also often quite large, sometimes twenty inches or more in length. Among five-needle pines may be listed *P. cembra*, stone pine, of the Alps and Carpathians; *P. strobus*, white pine, an important timber tree of the eastern United States, also in Mexico and Guatemala; *P. monticola*, western white pine, a valuable timber tree of the Pacific Coast of North America; and *P. lambertiana*, sugar pine, of California and Oregon, largest of all the pines, up to 245 feet in height. Other five-needle pines of western North America are *P. flexilis*, limber pine, *P. albicaulis*, white bark pine, and *P. balfouriana*, foxtail pine. Among two-needle pines are *P. sylvestris*, Scotch pine, of northern Eurasia from Scotland to Siberia, one of the most important timber trees of Europe; *P. montana*, mugo pine, of central and southern Europe, a dwarf species common in ornamental planting; *P. nigra*, Austrian pine, in southern Eurasia from Spain to Asia Minor; and *P. resinosa*, red pine, of eastern North America. Other two-needle pines are *P. banksiana*, jack pine, found throughout the boreal forest of Canada; *P. contorta*, lodgepole pine, widespread throughout the forests of western North America; *P. halepensis*, Aleppo pine, of the Mediterranean region; and *P. pinea*, stone pine, of the Mediterranean region, yielding edible seeds, pignolias. Among three-needle pines are *P. palus-*

tris, the longleaf pine, of the southeastern United States, with needles 12-14 inches long, important as a source of turpentine and one of the most valuable timber trees of the United States; *P. rigida,* pitch pine, of eastern United States; *P. taeda,* loblolly pine, of the southeastern United States; *P. echinata,* shortleaf pine, of the southeastern United States; and *P. elliottii,* slash pine, of Florida and Cuba. In western North America, *P. ponderosa,* ponderosa pine, is a valuable three-needle pine; it produces three billion board feet of lumber annually and in timber production is second only to Douglas fir in the United States; *P. jeffreyi,* Jeffrey pine, is a closely related species of California. One of the rarest pines of North America is *P. torreyana,* Torrey pine, restricted to San Diego County, California; *P. coulteri,* Coulter pine, of California, produces extremely heavy cones, up to five pounds; *P. attenuata,* knobcone pine, also of California, has prominent knobs on the cones; *P. radiata,* Monterey pine, of California, is much used in reforestation in New Zealand. Pines of the southwestern United States producing edible seeds (nuts) are *P. edulis,* piñon or nut pine, *P. monophylla,* singleleaf piñon, with solitary instead of fascicled leaves, *P. parryana,* Parry pine, usually with four needles in a fascicle, and *P. sabiniana,* Digger pine, so named from the Digger Indians of California.

The genus *Cedrus* includes about four species from the Mediterranean to the Himalayas, producing valuable lumber, but relatively scarce. *C. libanotica* is the cedar of Lebanon; it was used in ancient times in construction work, including Solomon's temple, and appears on the national flag of Lebanon. *C. atlantica,* Atlantic cedar, in Algeria and Morocco, also has valuable timber. *C. deodara,* deodar, is found in the Himalayas; the name is from the Hindu and means "timber of the gods."

Larix includes about ten species, the larches, of north temperate regions, differing from most conifers in having deciduous leaves. They are useful for wood or ornamental planting. *L. decidua,* European larch, is found in the Alps and Carpathians; it yields Venetian turpentine. *L. sibirica,* Siberian larch, occurs in the taiga of Russia and Siberia; *L. leptolepis,* Japanese larch, and *L. kurilense,* Kurile larch, are other species of eastern Asia. *L. laricina,* American larch or tamarack, is abundant throughout the boreal forest of Canada; *L. occidentalis,* western larch, of the northern Rocky Mountains, is one of the largest species of the genus, up to 210 feet in height.

Pseudolarix is a monotypic genus of China, resembling *Larix* in having deciduous leaves, but the cones disintegrate on ripening, as in *Abies; P. kaempferi* is known as the golden larch.

Taxodiaceae. Bald-cypress Family. These plants are somewhat similar to the Araucariaceae but the carpels bear two to eight ovules each. They are trees and shrubs with scale-like or needle-like, persistent or deciduous leaves which are solitary and in spirals, or connate in pairs and false whorls. The staminate strobili are small and clustered and the carpellate cones are woody, the bracts and scales partially or completely fused. The family includes nine genera with about sixteen species, mostly of the north temperate zone, but with one representative in the southern hemisphere.

Sciadopitys is a monotypic genus of Japan, having the branches in whorls; S. *verticillata,* parasol-pine or umbrella-fir, is much planted as an ornamental tree. *Cunninghamia* has one species in Formosa and one, *C. sinensis,* China-fir, in southern China and Indo-China. *Taiwania cryptomerioides* is endemic to Formosa (Taiwan). *Arthrotaxis* is the only genus of the south temperate zone; its three species are indigenous to Tasmania. *Sequoia* is a remarkable genus, now endemic to Oregon and California, but once, as indicated by fossil remains, widespread through the northern hemisphere. The two living species are among the largest trees on earth. S. *sempervirens,* the redwood, reaches 364 feet in height and twenty-seven feet in diameter; it is an important timber tree, with stands 80 per cent pure, yielding as high as 400,000 board feet to the acre. S. *gigantea,* the bigtree, is restricted to a small area in the Sierra Nevadas of California; it reaches a height of 293 feet and a diameter of thirty-seven feet; some trees may be 4500 years old. *Cryptomeria japonica,* Japanese cedar, yields good timber and is cultivated as an ornamental. *Metasequoia* is a monotypic genus endemic to western China; it attracted much attention because it was described and named from fossil remains several years before living trees (of *M. glyptostrobioides*) were found (page 86). *Taxodium* is another genus which, like *Sequoia,* was once apparently widespread but is now limited to three endemic species. *T. distichum,* bald-cypress, is an important timber tree of coastal swamps in the southeastern United States; unique features are the "knees" which project from the root system upwards above the water level (Figure 43). These are not formed when the trees grow in dry soil. *T. mucronatum,* the big cypress, of Mexico, is characterized by a vast girth; a large tree at Santa Maria del Tule, Oaxaca, is 112 feet in circumference and estimated to be 5000 years of age. *Glyptostrobus* (2) includes *G. pendulus* and *G. heterophyllus,* of China.

Cupressaceae. Cypress Family. These plants also resemble members of the Araucariaceae but have the leaves opposite or whorled, instead of spiraled. The species are trees and shrubs having scale-like or needle-like leaves, often dimorphic, with the juvenile leaves larger than the later ones. The plants are monoecious, or dioecious in certain genera. The pollen sacs are produced on more or less peltate stamens, while the ovules are produced on peltate carpels, 1-12 to each carpel. The mature cones are dry and woody, or fleshy and berry-like.

The family is world-wide in distribution, with fifteen genera and about 140 species. *Callitris* (20), cypress pine, occurs in Australia; some are shrubs in the bush region, others are trees yielding valuable timber and Australian sandarac, a resin used in varnish. *Tetraclinis articulata,* of southern Spain and northwestern Africa, is the source of Arar wood and African sandarac. *Widdringtonia* (5) occurs in tropical and South Africa; *W. juniperoides,* cedar, gives its name to the Cedar Mountains, in Cape Colony, where it grows in relict colonies in relatively inaccessible positions; it apparently had a much wider distribution in past geologic ages. *Fitzroya cupressoides,* alerce (larch), a large timber tree, is endemic to southern Chile and Patagonia. *Thujopsis dolabrata,* Hiba arborvitae, is endemic to Japan. *Libocedrus* (9) ranges along the western shores of North and South America, also in New Zealand, the East Indies, China, and Formosa, thus almost encircling the Pacific Ocean; *L. decurrens,* incense-cedar, is found in Oregon and California; *L. chilensis* is indigenous to the southern Andes; and *L. plumosa* occurs in New Zealand; most species yield valuable aromatic timber. *Thuja* (6) occurs in North America and eastern Asia; *T. occidentalis,* arborvitae, is found in eastern North America from Canada to Tennessee; *T. plicata,* western red cedar or giant arborvitae, is one of the important timber trees of the Pacific Coast of North America; it is the largest member of the genus, reaching a height of 250 feet; *T. orientalis,* of northeastern China and Korea, is often grown as an ornamental. *Fokienia* (3) is restricted to eastern China. *Cupressus* includes twelve species, the true cypresses, of the northern hemisphere. *C. sempervirens,* Mediterranean cypress, is characteristic of dry Mediterranean forests from Morocco to Crete and Iran; *C. macrocarpa,* Monterey cypress, is an endemic of southern California; *C. funebris,* the funeral cypress, of China, has a weeping habit and is planted as an ornamental. *Chamaecyparis* (6) is a genus of North America, Japan and Formosa; *C. nutkatensis,* Alaska yellow cedar or yellow cypress, is an important timber tree from Alaska to Oregon; *C. lawsoniana,* Port Orford cedar, or Lawson cypress, is a timber tree of Oregon and California; *C. thyoides,* Atlantic cedar, is a small tree of eastern North America; and *C. pisifera,* of Japan, is a commonly cultivated ornamental. *Juniperus* (60) is the largest genus in the family, the species distributed throughout the north temperate zone. The cones are fleshy and are known as juniper berries; a volatile oil extracted from some of them is used to flavor gin. *J. communis,* a circumboreal shrub, is an ornamental often planted; *J. sabina,* savin, is found from Spain to Central Asia; *J. chinensis* is a Chinese species grown as an ornamental. In eastern North America *J. virginiana,* eastern red cedar, is common; its wood is useful for making pencils; it is an alternate host for apple rust and its planting near large apple orchards is prohibited in some states. *Arceuthos drupacea* occurs from Greece to Syria.

Order 7. Gnetales. The Gnetales differ from the other gymnosperms by many characteristics, some of which are common to the angiosperms;

this has been interpreted by some students as indicating they may be a connecting link between the gymnosperms and angiosperms. However, no fossil Gnetales are found as far back as the Cretaceous and comparisons of the morphology and anatomy suggest that the various genera are only remotely related to each other and less so to the angiosperms or the other gymnosperms. As a matter of fact, the naked ovule is the only gymnosperm character. The wood contains vessels, not found in other gymnosperms, and lacks resin canals, which are present in other gymnosperms. Small structures at the base of the flowers have been regarded as primitive perianth parts. Three genera of woody plants have been placed in this order, but it is obviously a very artificial assemblage. Formerly these were grouped in one family, but the differences are so numerous and of such a fundamental character that each genus should represent a separate family and possibly even a separate order. About seventy-five species are recognized.

Ephedraceae. Ephedra Family. This is a family of small, much-branched, erect, decumbent or climbing shrubs. The leaves are opposite or whorled, mostly deciduous, usually reduced to thin sheaths, most of the photosynthetic activity being carried on by the stems. The staminate flowers are borne in compound strobili; each flower on a short stalk from a pair of bracts and composed of two thin scales ("perianth" of some botanists) and one to eight stamens. The ovulate flower is produced in a strobilus that has several pairs of bracts along the axis and a single terminal ovule with two integuments, the outer of four bracts ("perianth"), the inner of two similar bracts which elongate at flowering time and constitute the **tubullus.** The genus *Ephedra* (42) is of wide but sporadic distribution in arid regions of the Old World (from the Canary Islands to Iran, India, and China) and the New World, including both North America (in Texas, New Mexico, Arizona, Nevada, Utah, California, and Mexico) and South America (Bolivia and Argentina). The Asiatic species, especially *E. sinica* and *E. equisetina,* are the source of the medicinal alkaloid ephedrine (page 26). In the deserts of the southwestern states the plants are called Mormon tea and jointfir.

Welwitschiaceae. Welwitschia Family. This includes but one monotypic genus, *Welwitschia. W. mirabilis* is one of the most unusual plants in the world (see page 79 and figure 19). Found in the extremely dry deserts of Southwest Africa, it consists of a huge tuberous root, its crown just above the earth's surface, and two strap-shaped opposite leaves, the only ones produced by the plant in its entire lifetime of a century or longer; year after year they grow from the base, becoming torn and twisted at the tips. In the center of the crown are the flowers, the staminate with four "perianth parts" and six stamens, the ovulate with a tubular "perianth" and one ovule.

Gnetaceae. Gnetum Family. This family, composed of the single genus

Gnetum (15), is represented by shrubs or woody vines, in tropical or subtropical forests of both hemispheres (from the Himalayas to Queensland, West Africa, and tropical America). The staminate flowers have a tubular "perianth" and two stamens, while the ovulate have a tubular "perianth" and one ovule. The "perianth" surrounding the ripened ovule becomes fleshy and resembles a drupaceous fruit, being edible in some species, as *G. gnemon,* of Indomalaysia, which is sometimes cultivated.

17

Angiospermae. Monocotyledoneae

The angiosperms, as compared with the gymnosperms, are characterized in general by the presence of vessels in the wood, and by having the megasporangia or ovules enclosed by the folded megasporophyll, or carpel. This enveloping carpel forms a protective covering for the ovules and developing seeds, but fertilization is thereby rendered more complicated, and certain structural features appear as adaptations that facilitate pollination and fertilization. The megasporophyll or megasporophylls constitute the pistil, the basic element of the gynoecium. This has a terminal stigma to which pollen may become attached, and sometimes a more or less elongated style, which elevates the stigmatic zone into a more favorable position for the reception of pollen. The microsporophylls or stamens, likewise, constitute the basic elements of the androecium. Sterile leaves in whorls surrounding the carpels and stamens constitute the perianth, made up of sepals (calyx), or both sepals and petals, the latter collectively forming the corolla. This entire assemblage, comprising calyx, corolla, androecium, and gynoecium, is called the flower.

Angiosperms are often called **flowering plants,** as if the flower were purely an angiosperm structure. As we have seen, however, the gymnosperms possess stamens and carpels, and, in some instances, perianth-like structures, so that it is impossible to state definitely that the flower is restricted to angiosperms; a gymnosperm cone fits the ordinary accepted definitions of a flower.

Angiosperms are now the dominant plants upon earth, including approximately 300 families and about 200,000 species. Compared to other groups of plants, they are relatively youthful, since their fossils have not been found earlier than the Cretaceous, and their period of rapid expansion came after the period of dominance of gymnosperms and other lower plants.

Two lines of evolution characterized the development of the angio-

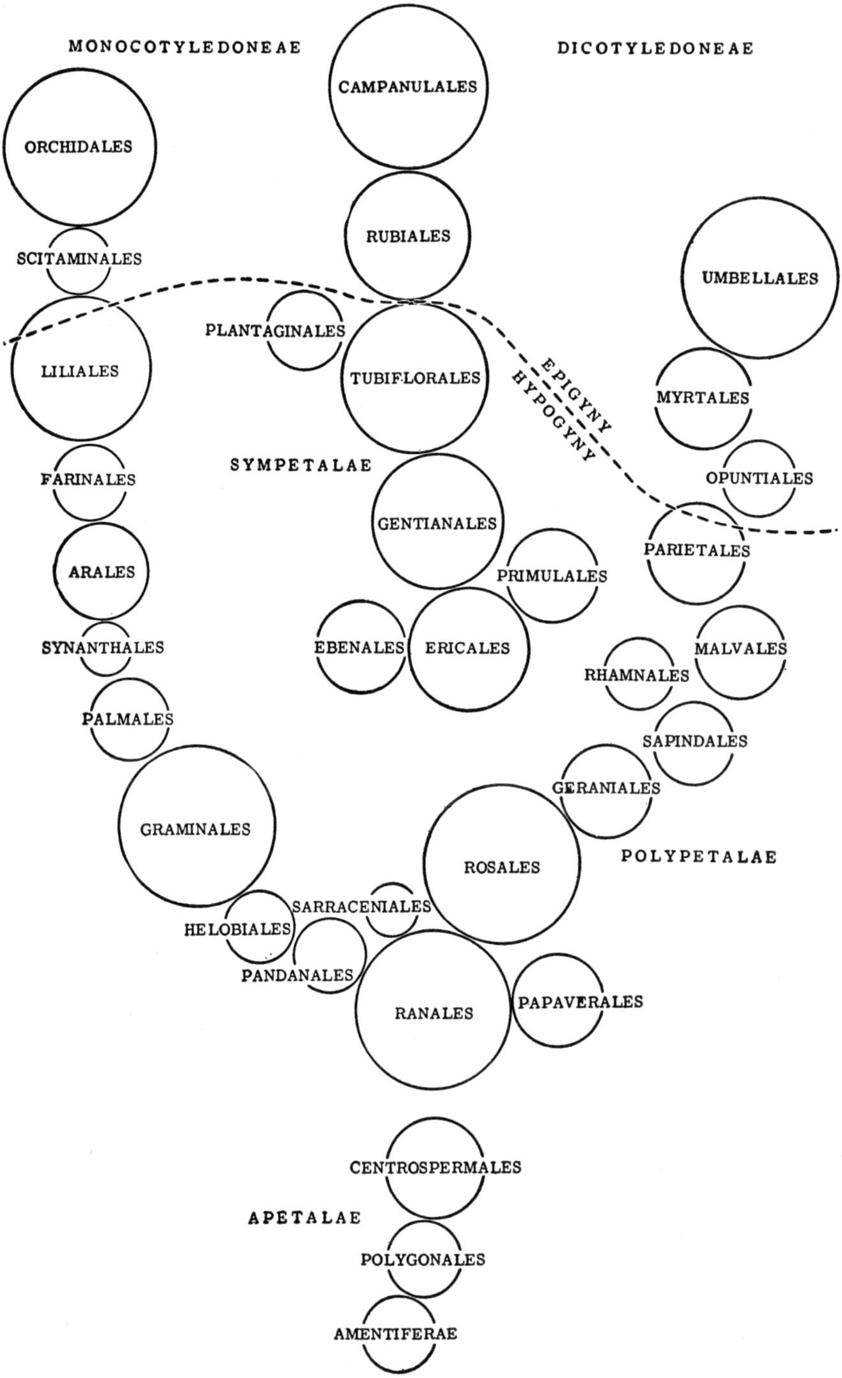

Figure 98. Chart showing hypothetical relationships of the principal orders of Angiosperms, following in general the Engler-Prantl sequence, (p. 56), except that here the presumed affinity of the primitive monocotyledons with the Ranales is indicated.

sperms, with the result that the group is readily divisible into two classes, the monocotyledons and the dicotyledons. It is now generally believed that the most primitive angiosperms were somewhat like the present-day Ranales (magnolias, buttercups, waterlilies), and that both the monocotyledons and the higher dicotyledons were derived from these. The evolution of most of the monocotyledons and the dicotyledons, therefore, was simultaneous, and in any treatment it is really quite immaterial which group appears first. Without any implication, therefore, respecting the relative ages of the two groups, we here treat the monocotyledons first, because they appear in that order in most keys and herbaria, following the Engler-Prantl scheme.

Subclass 1. Monocotyledoneae

These are commonly herbaceous plants (woody in palms and a few other families), the stems having the vascular bundles scattered throughout. The individual bundles are of the closed type (surrounded by a bundle sheath and not possessing cambium). The leaves are usually parallel-veined, with the margins typically entire. The flower parts are basically in threes or multiples of threes. The embryos have a single cotyledon.

Diels (1936) considered the monocotyledons to be composed of eleven orders, forty-five families, and more than 2000 genera. It is estimated that there are about 40,000 species already known, with many more being added each year.

The following key provides a synopsis of the principal distinguishing characters of the orders.

- a. Carpels 1 or more, usually distinct
  - b. Inflorescence not a true spadix
    - c. Perianth, if present, bristle-like or scale-like; endosperm present . . . . . 1. *Pandanales*
    - c. Perianth sepaloid or petaloid or none; endosperm none or very little
      - d. Plants with chlorophyll . . . . . 2. *Helobiales*
      - d. Plants without chlorophyll . . . . . 3. *Triuridales*
  - b. Inflorescence a fleshy spadix or dense glomerule
    - c. Leaves usually plicate, more or less split
      - d. Carpels free or united, 1-ovuled . . . . . 4. *Palmales*
      - d. Carpels united, many-ovuled . . . . . 5. *Synanthales*
    - c. Leaves not plicate . . . . . 6. *Arales*
- a. Carpels united into a compound ovary
  - b. Flowers much reduced, in the axils of dry chaffy scales, arranged in spikelets . . . . . 7. *Graminales*
  - b. Flowers usually showy, not in the axils of dry chaffy scales
    - c. Seeds with endosperm; ovary superior or inferior
      - d. Flowers regular or nearly so
        - e. Endosperm mealy; ovary superior . . . . . 8. *Farinales*

e. Endosperm fleshy or horny; ovary superior or inferior .... 9. *Liliales*
d. Flowers very irregular; ovary inferior .... 10. *Scitaminales*
c. Seeds without endosperm; ovary inferior .... 11. *Orchidales*

Order 1. Pandanales. This order consists of only the three families treated below. These families, regarded by Engler as primitively simple, are now generally felt to be simple through reduction of flower parts and to have been derived from lily-like ancestors.

a. Herbs with rhizomes
  b. Flowers in terminal spikes .... *Typhaceae*
  b. Flowers in axillary heads .... *Sparganiaceae*
a. Woody plants .... *Pandanaceae*

Typhaceae. Cattail Family.

Roots and Stems. Perennial herbs, with creeping rootstocks.

Leaves. Two-ranked, erect, with a long sheathing portion and a long narrow blade.

Inflorescences. Monoecious; inflorescence a dense spike, divided into two parts, the upper staminate and the lower pistillate.

Flowers. Naked, but surrounded by a number of hairs. Staminate flowers of 2-5 stamens; pistillate of 1 carpel.

Fruits and Seeds. Fruit an achene, covered with the hairs surrounding the flower, mentioned above, which aid in wind dispersal.

There is but the single genus *Typha,* the cattails, readily distinguished by the characteristic club-shaped spikes (Figure 99). This genus includes 12 species, found in marshes almost throughout the entire world.

Sparganiaceae. Burreed Family.

Roots and Stems. Perennial herbs with rootstock creeping in mud, the stems projecting above the water.

Leaves. Alternate, linear, sessile, sheathing, 2-ranked, erect or floating.

Inflorescences. Monoecious; flowers in spherical heads, the staminate uppermost in the cluster.

Flowers. Perianth of 3-6 small sepal-like parts. Staminate flowers of 3-6 stamens, pistillate with (usually) 1 carpel.

Fruits and Seeds. Fruit nut-like or drupe-like, indehiscent, with spongy exocarp and bony endocarp surrounding a single seed.

There is but the single genus, *Sparganium,* burreed, found in marshes and along shores throughout the northern hemisphere and also in Australia and New Zealand. The distinctive bur-like fruiting heads suggest the common name (Figure 99). There are about 20 species, of limited value as a source of food for wild life.

Pandanaceae. Screwpine Family.

Roots and Stems. Stems tall, woody, erect or climbing, often sup-

Figure 99. *A*, a sedge, *Carex grayi*, showing staminate and pistillate spikes, with a perigynium enlarged; *B*, cattail, *Typha latifolia; C*, burreed, *Sparganium eurycarpum*. (From Strausbaugh & Core, *Flora of West Virginia*, courtesy West Virginia University.)

ported by aerial prop roots, the plants sometimes palm-like in appearance.

LEAVES. Spiral, 4-ranked, linear, sessile, sheathing, tough, fibrous and leathery, keeled and canaliculate, spinose on the keel and margins; the stem often appears twisted, with the leaves in conspicuous spirals.

INFLORESCENCES. Plants dioecious; individual flowers are often crowded on the axis with neither bracts nor perianth and are difficult or impossible to distinguish from each other.

FLOWERS. The numerous stamens densely packed over the axis, scarcely distinguishable as separate flowers; pistils likewise scattered over the axis, sometimes several together or even somewhat united.

FRUITS. Fruit collective, each pistil developing into a more or less fleshy berry or drupe and the whole ripening as a multiple unit (**syncarp**).

The family includes 3 genera, and perhaps 400 species. The largest genus is *Pandanus* (180), the screwpines, found in the Old World from Africa through Indonesia to Australia. The conspicuously spiraled leaves suggest the common name. The fruits are edible, especially in *P. leram*, Nicobar breadfruit. Some species, as *P. candelabrum*, candelabrum tree (so-called because of its apparent dichotomous branching), are grown as ornamentals, sometimes in greenhouses in northern climates. *Freycinetia* (70) extends from Ceylon to Polynesia and New Zealand; they are usually climbing shrubs; fleshy, brightly colored bracts are eaten by bats, which incidentally effect pollination.

Order 2. Helobiales. This order is here treated as defined by Engler, but there is general agreement that it represents an unnatural assemblage of families. Beyond that, however, there is little agreement and various authors have arranged the families in different ways. Although regarded by Engler and others as being originally primitive, at least some of the families are thought by others to be simple by reduction, perhaps derived from the Liliales. The relationships of the various families to each other are not clear, and authorities differ in their interpretations.

a. Ovary superior
  b. Without latex; perianth, if present, calyx-like, or of only one whorl of parts
    c. Perianth, if present, calyx-like
      d. Perianth none, but with sepal-like appendages on the stamens; flowers perfect or imperfect . . . . *Potamogetonaceae*
      d. Perianth present
        e. Perianth-parts 2; flowers imperfect . . . . *Najadaceae*
        e. Perianth-parts usually 6; flowers perfect or imperfect . . . . *Juncaginaceae*
    c. Perianth corolla-like, of only one whorl of parts *Aponogetonaceae*
  b. Bearing latex; perianth composed of calyx and corolla

c. Ovules basal or nearly so .... *Alismataceae*
c. Ovules scattered over the inner surface of carpels .... *Butomaceae*
a. Ovary inferior .... *Hydrocharitaceae*

Potamogetonaceae. Pondweed Family.

ROOTS AND STEMS. Herbs with rhizomes creeping in mud; stems mostly submerged, jointed, the lower nodes bearing roots, the upper ones leaves.

LEAVES. Sheathing at base, the blades submersed or floating on the surface, 2-ranked.

INFLORESCENCES. With perfect flowers, or with the flowers imperfect, the plants then are either monoecious or dioecious.

FLOWERS. Perianth variable, the parts sepal-like, or lacking in some genera. Stamens 1-4. Pistil of 1-4 distinct carpels.

FRUITS AND SEEDS. Fruit an achene.

The family includes 9 genera, with approximately 125 species of almost exclusively submerged plants, distributed widely over the globe in salt water near the coasts, in brackish marshes, and in fresh water of streams, lakes, and bogs. The largest genus is *Potamogeton* (90), pondweed, most common in the north temperate zone, but found elsewhere. The flowers have 4 stamens, 4 carpels, and a pseudoperianth of 4 parts perhaps developed from the connectives of the stamens. Pollination is by wind, unusual in this family. Some of the species are important sources of food for wild life. *Zostera* (6), eelgrass or grasswrack, grows in salt water on gently sloping shores in most parts of the world; pollination is accomplished under water, by long thread-like pollen grains caught on large stigmas. *Ruppia maritima,* ditchgrass, is a cosmopolitan species of salt or brackish water; there are 2 stamens (and 2 sepal-like outgrowths) and 4 carpels. *Zannichellia palustris,* horned pondweed, is likewise cosmopolitan in fresh or brackish water; the plants are monoecious, the staminate flowers having 1 or 2 stamens, the pistillate 4 carpels. *Cymodocea* (7) occurs in tropical and subtropical waters; one species, *C. manatorum,* manatee-grass, is found in Florida. *Posidonia* (2) occurs in salt waters, *P. oceanica* in the Mediterranean and adjacent parts of the Atlantic Ocean, *P. australis* about Australia.

Najadaceae. Naiad Family.

ROOTS AND STEMS. Annual, submerged; stems much-branched, rooting from the nodes.

LEAVES. Linear, entire or toothed, often with prominent basal auricles (stipules), sessile, sheathing, opposite.

INFLORESCENCES. Plants monoecious or dioecious.

FLOWERS. Minute, either with or without a primitive perianth or bract. Staminate flowers with 1 stamen. Pistillate flowers with 1 carpel. Pollination under water.

FRUITS. Achenes.

The family includes a single genus, *Najas* (40), widely scattered in brackish or fresh water throughout the world. The simplicity of the flowers indicates that these plants are among the most primitive monocots.

Aponogetonaceae. Latticeplant Family.

ROOTS AND STEMS. Perennial, with tuberous rhizomes and fibrous roots.

LEAVES. Mostly basal, submerged or floating, long-petioled, the blades linear or oblong, netted-veined, with the tissue between the veins sometimes breaking up, leaving a network of veins with holes between (**fenestrate,** that is, window-like), whence the common name.

INFLORESCENCES. Simple, or with 2-8 spike-like branches.

FLOWERS. Perfect, projecting above the water. Perianth none or of 1-3 often petal-like parts, stamens mostly 6 or more; gynoecium of 3-6 separate carpels.

FRUITS. Follicles.

There is but a single genus, *Aponogeton* (22) extending from tropical and southern Africa to northeastern Australia and New Guinea. *A. fenestralis,* latticeplant, of Madagascar, is grown as an ornamental in aquaria and pools in the United States.

Juncaginaceae. Arrowgrass Family.

ROOTS AND STEMS. Perennial, from a rhizome that produces fibrous or tuberous roots; stems grass-like.

LEAVES. Flat, linear, sheathing.

INFLORESCENCES. Few-flowered racemes or spikes.

FLOWERS. Bisexual or unisexual. Perianth-parts 6, in 2 series; stamens 6; pistils 3-6, somewhat coherent at first, but separating at maturity.

FRUITS. Follicles.

The family includes 5 genera of marsh herbs, widely distributed. *Triglochin* (12), arrowgrass, is a genus of tufted herbs in fresh or salt water marshes or bogs of temperate and sub-arctic regions. *Scheuchzeria palustris* is found in cold sphagnum bogs and shores of the cooler part of the northern hemisphere. *Lilaea scilloides,* flowering quillwort, is a peculiar plant of alkaline lakes or muddy shores from British Columbia to Chile and Argentina, sometimes segregated in a separate family.

Alismataceae. Waterplantain Family.

ROOTS AND STEMS. Annual, or perennial from stout rhizomes; roots fibrous. Latex-bearing.

LEAVES. Basal, long-petioled, sheathing, the blades linear or ovate, the bases sometimes sagittate.

INFLORESCENCES. Racemes or panicles, the flowers perfect or imperfect, regular, often in whorls.

FLOWERS. Perianth in two series, the sepals 3, green, the petals 3, white, larger. Stamens 6 or more (rarely 3). Carpels 6 or more, separate.

The family includes 14 genera with about 75 species, of wide distribution, mostly in fresh water swamps and streams, and most common in the northern hemisphere. Phylogenetically the family is of much interest, since it is believed by many botanists to be one of the most primitive of living monocot families. The species resemble the Ranunculaceae and some of them differ primarily from members of that family only in possessing one cotyledon instead of two. The largest genus is *Sagittaria* (40), arrowhead; the submerged leaves are ribbon-shaped and the emersed ones arrow-shaped. The rhizomes of some species, notably *S. latifolia*, wapato, were eaten by North American Indians and are of value to water fowl. *Alisma* (6), waterplantain, includes the circumboreal *A. plantago-aquatica.*

Butomaceae. Flowering Rush Family.

Roots and Stems. Perennial, from a stout rhizome; roots fibrous. Usually latex-bearing.

Leaves. Sword-shaped, or petioled with orbicular or elliptic blades, netted-veined.

Inflorescences. Umbellate, or the flowers solitary.

Flowers. Perfect, regular, the perianth in 2 series, the outer of 3 usually green sepals, the inner of 3 larger, colored petals. Stamens usually 9 or more. Carpels 6 or more, separate or nearly so.

Fruits. Follicles.

The family includes 6 genera with 9 species, and is considered to be among the primitive monocots. *Butomus umbellatus*, flowering rush, a native of western Europe, has become naturalized in the St. Lawrence Valley and about the Great Lakes.

Hydrocharitaceae. Frog's-Bit Family.

Roots and Stems. Partially or completely submerged, rarely floating; roots in mud or floating in the water.

Leaves. Basal or cauline, the latter alternate, opposite or whorled, usually sessile, very variable, often ribbon-like.

Inflorescences. Flowers solitary or in umbels; bisexual or unisexual (the plants are then dioecious).

Flowers. Perianth-parts 6, usually in 2 series, the outer of three green sepals, the inner of three colored petals. Stamens 3-15. Gynoecium of a single pistil, with 2-15 united carpels, the ovary inferior.

Fruits. Berry-like, indehiscent or irregularly dehiscent.

The family is apparently closely related to the Butomaceae, differing in the inferior ovary and parietal placentation. There are 13 genera with about 90 species, found mostly in the warmer waters of the world. *Boottia* (20) is the largest genus, including dioecious plants of the Old World tropics. *Stratiotes aloides*, water soldier, or water-aloe, of Europe, has a short stem and aloe-like leaves; the plants float on the surface and bear dioecious flowers in summer, sinking in autumn, rising again in the spring. *Hydrocharis* (2) is found in Europe and Asia; *H. morsus-ramae*, frog's-bit, has orbicular floating leaves and dioecious flowers produced on the surface of the water. *Vallisneria* (3), watercelery, eelgrass or tape-grass, includes *V. spiralis* of the Old World and the similar *V. americana* of the New World. The plants are dioecious and submerged. The staminate flowers, borne on a short scape, break off and come to the surface, where they pollinate the pistillate flowers, borne on an exceedingly long scape which then curls in a spiral and drags the fruit to the bottom to ripen. *Elodea* (8), waterweed, is an American genus; *E. canadensis*, of North America, is often grown in aquaria.

Order 3. Triuridales. This is a small order of tropical saprophytes, including only the family Triuridaceae. The systematic status is doubtful. The leaves are small and scale-like, the small flowers are perfect or unisexual. The 3-8 perianth-parts are petal-like, often with long appendages, whence the name (*tri*, three, *oura*, tail). The stamens are 3, 4, or 6, the carpels numerous, separate. There are 4 genera with about 40 species. *Triuris* (25) is a tropical group including *T. hyalina*, ranging from Guatemala to Brazil.

Order 4. Graminales. Most botanists agree that this order is a very advanced group in which the apparently simple floral morphology really represents greatly reduced structures evolved from ancestors that are unknown but possibly of primitive liliaceous stock. The plants are characterized by prominent nodes, narrow leaves with sheathing bases, and small flowers borne in spikelets.

a. Culm mostly hollow, cylindrical or flattened; leaf-sheath split; fruit a caryopsis .... *Gramineae*
a. Culm mostly solid, triangular; leaf-sheath not split; fruit an achene .... *Cyperaceae*

Gramineae. Grass Family. The grass family is very large and economically the most important of all families of plants. For this reason, and because of its high degree of morphological specialization, there has been developed a terminology peculiar to the family (see Figure 100).

ROOTS AND STEMS. Roots are fibrous, rhizomes present or absent; stems (**culms**) erect, ascending, prostrate or creeping, typically hollow although sometimes solid, always closed at the nodes, these usually swollen, herbaceous or (among the bamboos) woody.

LEAVES. Alternate, 2-ranked, parallel-veined, of 2 parts, the **sheath** enveloping the culm, its edges usually overlapping and the **blade**, usually flat, linear or lanceolate; at the base of the blade, next to the culm, is a somewhat ringlike appendage, the **ligule.**

INFLORESCENCE. The inflorescence is composed of units called ***spikelets;***

these are aggregated in spikes, racemes, or panicles. A spikelet contains 1 or more **florets** (flowers), with subtending bracts. The axis of the spikelet is the **rachilla.** At the base of the spikelet are 2 bracts, the **glumes.** Above the glumes are attached the florets, varying in number from 1 to 50.

Flowers. Each floret bears normally 2 bracts, the **lemma,** somewhat resembling the glumes, and the **palea,** opposite the lemma, next to the rachilla. In the axil of the palea is the flower, usually bisexual, composed of a much reduced perianth represented by 2 (sometimes 3) **lodicules,** 3 (sometimes 6) stamens, and a pistil with 1 locule and 1 ovule, and 2 styles.

Fruit. A caryopsis or grain, rarely a nut, berry, or utricle.

This is the most widely distributed family of vascular plants. The grasses provide the vegetative climax in great areas of low rainfall, especially when there is a somewhat pronounced winter dry season; among these are the prairies and plains of North America, the savannas, campos and pampas of South America, the steppes of Eurasia, and the veldt of Africa (compare Chapter 7). Because of their abundance, the high nutritive value of the herbage, and because the growing point is located at the base of each internode, rather than at the apex of the stem, the plants are suitable for food for grazing animals; as a matter of fact, the grazing animals doubtless evolved simultaneously with the grasses. Man's own development was closely tied to the grasslands, where he pursued a nomadic life, following his domesticated cattle, and utilizing the concentrated food contained in the grains of some of the grasses. The best of these grasses were likewise domesticated for convenience in harvest and became his staple foods, the cereals. There are about 500 genera and approximately 4500 species of grasses.

Subfamily I. Panicoideae. Spikelets 1 (rarely 2)—flowered; articulation of the spikelets below the glumes.

Euchlaena mexicana, teosinte, of Mexico, is thought to be a relative of maize. *Zea* is a genus no longer known in the wild state; the single species, *Z. mays,* maize or Indian corn, originated in America. It is monoecious, having the staminate flowers terminal (forming the **tassel**), the pistillate axillary, forming a thick spike, the **cob,** with the long filamentous stigmas (the **silk**), hanging out at the end of the enveloping spathe-leaves (the **husk**). The fruit is an important cereal. There are numerous varieties, including var. *tunicata,* pod corn, with each kernel enclosed in a husk; var. *everta,* pop corn; var. *indurata,* flint corn; var. *indentata,* dent corn, the common field corn of the United States; and var. *rugosa,* sweet or sugar corn. *Coix* (6) is found in India and China; in *C. lachryma-jobi,* Job's tears, the sheath of the inflorescence bract is hollowed out and contains the 1-flowered pistillate spikelet, while the staminate spikelets project beyond the mouth; these bead-like sheaths

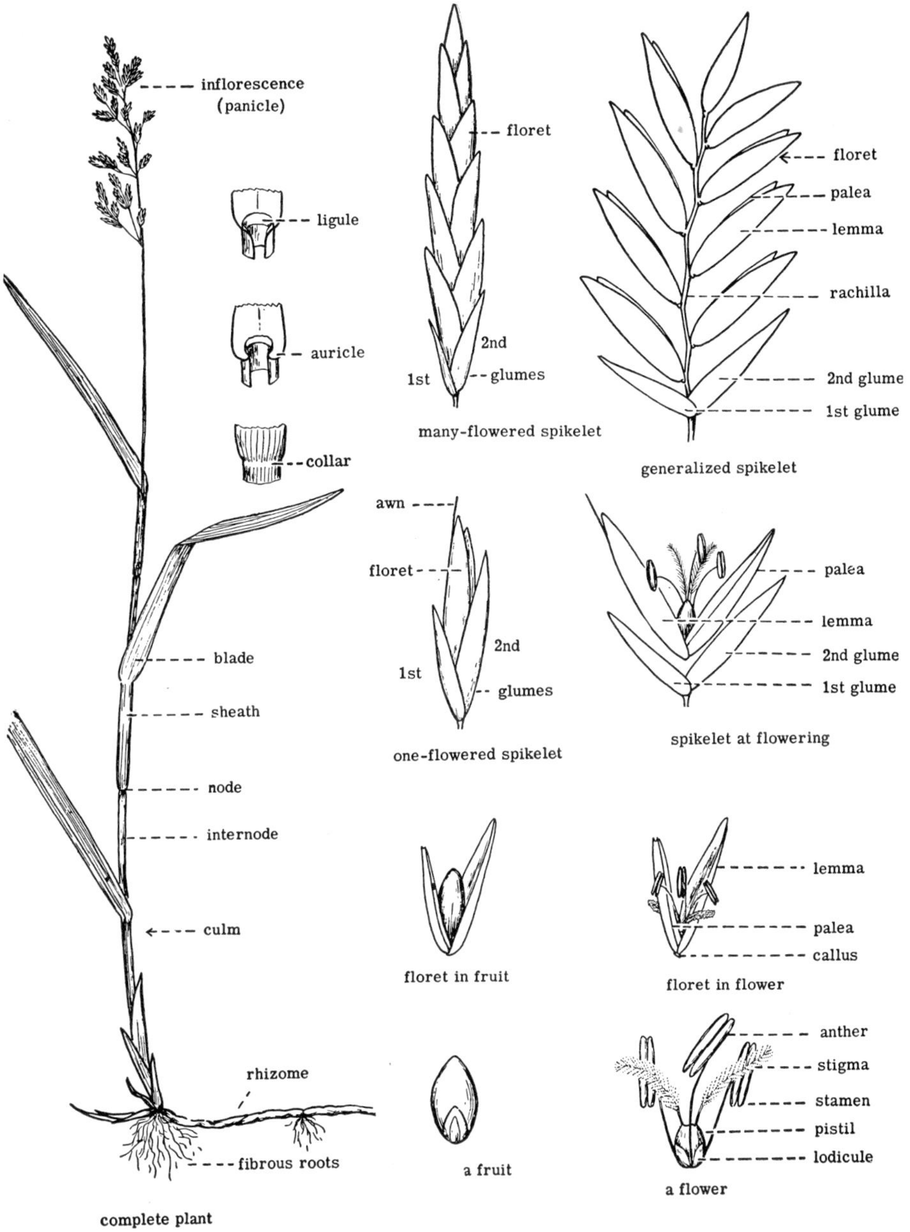

Figure 100. Diagrammatic sketch showing principal features of grasses. (Drawn by Nelle P. Ammons for Core, Berkley, and Davis, *West Virginia Grasses,* used by permission of West Virginia University.)

(tears) are used in rosaries and so forth, while some varieties are cultivated for food in southeastern Asia. *Tripsacum* (7), gama grass, is found in warm regions of North America.

Saccharum (12) is a tropical and subtropical genus. *S. officinarum*, sugar cane, is apparently a native of southeastern Asia, now widely cultivated. The canes are cut and crushed to extract the juice, which is then boiled down to yield molasses and sugar; the distilled fermented juice is rum. *Andropogon* (180) is a cosmopolitan genus; *A. gerardi*, big bluestem, and *A. scoparius*, little bluestem, were among the most important grasses of the North American prairie; *A. virginicus*, broomsedge, is a common weedy species of the eastern United States; some species are good forage grasses of the Mulga scrubland of Australia. *Cymbopogon* (60) is a genus of the tropics, some of the species characteristic of the savannas of tropical Africa. *C. nardus* yields oil of citronella, *C. citratus* lemon-grass oil, and *C. martinii* ginger-grass oil; *C. schoenanthus*, of North Africa, is camel-hay. *Vetiveria* (2), a related genus, of Indomalaysia, includes *V. zizanioides*, Khuskhus plant, which yields oil of vetiver from its aromatic roots. *Imperata* (6) is a genus of tall coarse grasses, including *I. cylindrica* and *I. exaltata*, cogon grasses, of the Philippine Islands, used in thatching. The genus *Sorghum* (13) yields numerous minor cereals, mostly tropical or subtropical. *S. vulgare* is guinea corn, cultivated as a cereal in the Mediterranean region. It has many varieties, including var. *saccharatum*, which yields sorghum molasses; var. *technicus*, broom corn, the long stiff rays of the panicle used in making brooms; var. *roxburghii*, shallu, a cereal of India; var. *durra*, durra, a North African cereal; var. *caffrorum*, Kaffir corn, of South Africa; var. *caudata*, feterita, of the Sudan; var. *sudanensis*, Sudan grass, a forage grass; and var. *nervosum*, kaoliang, a cereal of China. *S. halepense*, Johnson grass, is a weed of cultivated fields or a valuable forage grass; it was introduced into the United States by William Johnson.

Zoysia (3) extends from the Mascarenes to New Zealand; *Z. matrella*, Manila grass, is used for lawns in warm countries. Species of the genus *Paspalum* (200) form a large proportion of the pasture of the campos and pampas; they often grow in tall tufts; *P. scrobiculatum*, Kodo millet, is cultivated in India. *Panicum* (400) is the largest genus in the family; the widely distributed species are mostly weedy in the United States but important grasses in the campos and pampas. *P. miliaceum* is the true or proso millet, extensively cultivated in Russia; *P. miliare*, little millet, is grown in India; *P. maximum*, guinea grass, *P. barbinode*, Pará grass, and *P. molle*, Mauritius grass, are important for forage in warm regions. *Setaria* (30), the foxtail grasses, includes *S. italica*, Italian millet, cultivated as a cereal in the Near East and China. *Cenchrus* (15) is a genus of tropical and temperate regions, the sandburs; the spikelet is surrounded by an involucre of spines which becomes hard and prickly;

some species are troublesome to sheep-growers. *Digitaria* (100) includes *D. sanguinalis,* crabgrass, a cosmopolitan grass, often a pest in lawns. *Pennisetum* (50) is a tropical and subtropical genus, important in the Sudan semi-desert; *P. glaucum* is pearl or cattail millet, cultivated in India and the Sudan; *P. purpureum* is elephant grass, an important tropical forage grass. *Spinifex* (4), ranges from Australia to Ceylon and Japan; the plants are dioecious, and the pistillate spikelets are in heads, with long spiny bracts that stick in the sand when the fruits are blown away; it is one of the few grasses of the central desert of Australia.

Zizania (2), of North America and northeastern Asia, includes *Z. aquatica,* Indian rice, used as a cereal by North American Indians. The genus *Oryza* (6), a tropical group, includes *O. sativa,* rice, one of the leading food plants of the world (Figure 1), probably a native of southeastern Asia; it is cultivated in shallow water in most warm regions; the unmilled rice, whether growing or cut, is paddy; an intoxicating beverage made in Japan from fermented rice is sake. *Lygeum spartum,* of the Mediterranean region, yields esparto, used in making baskets. *Leersia* (6), of tropical and temperate marshes, includes *L. oryzoides,* rice cutgrass, the leaves of which have very sharp edges. *Echinochloa* (12) is mainly tropical; *E. frumentacea* is Japanese millet, cultivated as a cereal in the Far East; *E. crusgalli* is barnyard grass, a weed in the United States, but cultivated in some Asiatic countries.

Subfamily II. Poacoideae. Spikelets one- to many-flowered; articulation of the spikelet above the glumes. This subfamily may be divided in general into two groups, the herbaceous members, far more numerous, and the woody members, or bamboos.

Phalaris (20), of Europe and America, includes *P. canariensis,* canary grass, grown for birdseed, and *P. arundinacea,* reed grass. *Anthoxanthum* (6), of north temperate regions, includes *A. odoratum,* sweet vernal grass, which has a pleasant odor and taste derived from the large quantities of coumarin it contains. A related genus, *Hierochloë* (17), holy grass, of temperate and cold climates, is also fragrant; plants of *H. odorata* are placed on walks before church doors on saints' days in northern Europe.

The large genus *Aristida* (150) occurs in temperate and subtropical regions; the plants are called tripleawn grasses, in allusion to the 3-parted awn on the lemma; they are common on the plains of the western United States, in the Mulga scrubland of Australia, and on desert grasslands of northern Africa; *A. pungens,* drinn grass, is a favorite pasture of camels. *Stipa* (250) is also common in arid or semi-arid regions of tropical and temperate climates; *S. ichu,* ichu grass, is characteristic of dry, cold punas in the high Andes; *S. pennata,* feather grass, is common on the steppes of Eurasia and is often grown as an ornamental.

Phleum (10), is found in the north and south temperate zones; *P. pratense,* timothy, is one of the most valuable hay grasses of the United

States. *Sporobolus* (90), in warm regions of America and the Old World, is known as dropseed, in allusion to the fact that the grain readily falls from the spikelet when mature. *Polypogon* (16) is found in temperate and tropical regions; the spikelets, in a dense panicle, are covered with long silky awns, whence the name beardgrass. *Agrostis* (100) is a group of valuable forage grasses, especially *A. alba,* redtop; a form of this species, creeping bent, is cultivated on lawns and golf courses. *Calamagrostis* (150) is found in temperate and cold climates; *C. canadensis* is bluejoint grass; *C. cinnoides* is reed bent grass. *Ammophila* (40) is a genus of sand-loving grasses of the north temperate region, including *A. arundinacea,* marram, common on sandy coasts and useful as a sand-binder.

Holcus (8), of Europe and Africa, includes *H. lanatus,* velvet grass or Yorkshire fog; the entire plant is grayish-velvety-pubescent. *Aira* (9), hair grass, is mostly native of Europe; *A. caryophyllea, A. capillaris,* and *A. praecox,* have been introduced into America. *Deschampsia* (35) includes *D. caespitosa,* which is circumboreal and also appears on African mountains and in Tasmania and New Zealand; *D. flexuosa* likewise is circumboreal and appears in southern South America; *D. antarctica* is found in subantarctic America and South Georgia Island. *Melinis* (3) is a genus of tropical America and Africa; *M. minutiflora,* molasses grass, is a widespread fragrant grass of the tropics. *Trisetum* (55), of cool temperate and frigid regions about both poles, includes *T. flavescens* and *T. spicatum,* good forage grasses. *Avena* (70), of temperate regions, includes *A. sativa,* oats, a widely cultivated cereal of cool climates. *Arrhenatherum* (6), primarily of southern Europe, includes *A. elatius,* tall oat grass. *Danthonia* (100) is a genus of temperate and tropical regions, especially in South Africa, Australia and New Zealand; *D. racemosa,* mulga grass, is a valuable pasture grass of Australia; *D. spicata,* of eastern North America, is poverty grass or wild oat grass, common on pastures with poor soil. *Koeleria* (25) of temperate regions, includes *K. cristata,* June grass, widely distributed in North America.

Arundo (12) is a genus of tall woody grasses, resembling bamboo; the tropical and subtropical species include *A. donax,* reed, characteristic of the Mediterranean landscape; the stems are used for fishing rods. *Gynerium* (3), tropical and subtropical, includes *G. sagittatum,* caña-brava, of South America, used in construction; *G. argenteum,* pampas grass, forms tall hedges along water courses in the pampas. *Phragmites communis,* reed, cosmopolitan, forms hedge-like growths along ditches. *Cortaderia* (10), of South America, includes the ornamental *C. argentea,* pampas grass, of Brazil and Argentina.

Eragrostis (250) is widespread in warm climates; the name love grass is applied to some because the spikelets become attached to the hair of animals; *E. abyssinica,* teff, is a cereal grown in Abyssinia. *Eleusine* (10), tropical and subtropical, includes *E. coracana,* finger millet, ragi, or kurakkan, cultivated as a cereal in India and Africa; *E. indica,* yard grass, is a cosmopolitan weed.

Melica (80), melic grass, of the north and south temperate regions and tropical mountains, includes *M. mutica,* of North America; some are cultivated as ornamentals. *Briza* (20) is quake grass, the broad, slender-stalked spikelets shaking in the slightest breeze; the species are north temperate and South American in range. *Dactylis glomerata,* orchard grass, or cock's-foot, of the Mediterranean region, is a valuable pasture grass and has been introduced into many countries. *Cynosurus* (5), dog's tail grass, includes plants of temperate regions of the Old World; *C. cristata* is a valuable pasture and hay grass. *Poa* (250) is a genus of valuable grasses; *P. pratensis,* Kentucky bluegrass, is circumboreal, a very valuable pasture and lawn grass; *P. flabellata,* tussock grass, is characteristic of cold moors of southern Patagonia; *P. annua,* low spear grass, is a common cosmopolitan weed. *Glyceria* (36), mainly of North America, is a group of good pasture grasses of wet meadows; the grains have a sweet taste, whence the name manna grass. *Lolium* (8) is found in the Mediterranean region; *L. perenne,* darnel, English rye grass and *L. multiflorum,* Italian rye grass, are valuable pasture grasses. *Festuca* (80), a widespread genus, includes many good pasture grasses, especially *F. ovina,* sheep's fescue, *F. elatior,* meadow fescue, and *F. rubra,* red fescue. *Bromus* (100), brome grass, a genus of cool climates, is mostly of little value for pasture; *B. secalinus* is cheat or chess, a common weed; *B. inermis,* awnless brome grass, unlike most other members of the genus, is a valuable forage plant.

Cynodon (7), mainly of South Africa and Australia, includes *C. dactylon,* Bermuda grass, a sand-binder and pasture grass, as well as a weed in fields. *Spartina* (14), cordgrass, is a genus of temperate regions; the plants are mostly halophytes or marsh grasses. *Astrebla* (3), Mitchell grass, is one of the most important forage grasses of Australia. *Chloris* (60), is a genus of tropical and temperate regions; several are useful pasture grasses of Australia; from the digitate inflorescences, the plants are called finger grasses; *C. gayana,* South Africa, is Rhodes grass, cultivated for forage in dry regions. *Bouteloua* (40), ranging from Canada to Argentina, is mesquite grass, or grama grass; the species are very abundant on North American prairies, and form valuable hay. *Buchloe dactyloides,* buffalo grass, is a dominant grass on the plains of the western United States.

Nardus stricta, nard or mat grass, of Eurasia is common on dry moors.

Agropyron (60) is a genus of temperate regions; *A. repens,* quack grass or couch grass, is a troublesome cosmopolitan weed. *Secale cereale,* rye, is cultivated in Europe and elsewhere as an important cereal. *Triticum* (10), of southern Europe and central Asia, includes *T. sativum,* wheat, one of the world's most important staple foods; there are many varieties, as var. *dicoccum,* emmer, and var. *spelta,* spelt; *T. monococcum* is einkorn, one-grained wheat, one of the oldest in cultivation, but now little grown; *T. polonicum* is Polish wheat. *Hordeum* (25) is a genus of temperate regions; *H. vulgare,* barley, is cultivated as a cereal; beer is made from the sprouts; *H. jubatum,* squirreltail grass, is a troublesome weed in cool climates. *Elymus* (45), wild rye, lymegrass, includes plants of north temperate regions; *E. arenarius,* circumboreal, is a sand-binder.

Relatively few genera are included among the bamboos. *Chusquea* (70) ranges from Mexico to the West Indies and Chile; some species are climbers in Andean cloud forests, forming tangles. *Guadua* (30), of tropical America, includes *G. angustifolia,* a tall bamboo used in construction. *Arundinaria* (80), cane, of warm regions, includes *A. macrosperma* and *A. tecta,* which form cane brakes in the southern United States. *Dendrocalamus* (24), an Indomalaysian group, includes *D. giganteus,* giant bamboo, the largest known grass, forming great clumps and reaching a height of 120 feet; its growth is very rapid, as much as fifteen inches daily. *Bambusa* (75) is found in the Himalayas, Japan, Philippines, and Australia; its economic uses are very numerous, including construction materials, household articles, clothing, and food.

Cyperaceae. Sedge Family.

Roots and Stems. The plants are grass-like in appearance, with a solid, usually triangular stem (culm); roots fibrous, from a creeping or tuberous rhizome.

Leaves. Three-ranked, with a closed sheath and a narrow blade, the ligule usually absent.

Inflorescences. Spicate, racemose, paniculate, or umbellate, with a spikelet often as the basic unit, although this spikelet is quite different in structure from that of grasses; flowers unisexual or bisexual, when unisexual the plants usually monoecious.

Flowers. Minute, subtended by chaffy bracts; perianth represented by bristles, scales, or absent; stamens 1-6, usually 3; pistil 1, unilocular, with 2 or 3 style branches, the ovary superior.

Fruit. An achene or nutlet.

This is a very large family, of about 85 genera and over 3000 species, widely distributed throughout the world, but especially abundant in frigid and temperate regions, chiefly as marsh plants. Although the sedges have usually been regarded as closely allied with the grasses, there is growing evidence that the two families are not as closely related as they appear; the spikelets of sedges, for example, are not at all homologous with those of grasses. Unlike the grasses, the sedges are of slight economic importance. Several genera have in excess of 100 species each.

Subfamily I. Plants with bisexual flowers. *Scirpus* (200), bulrush, includes plants characteristic of wet moors, bogs, and marshes, mainly in cool climates. *Eleocharis* (150), spikerush, is a cosmopolitan genus; the species are denizens of wet places. *Eriophorum* (20), cotton grass, occurs in wet moors and bogs, in the north temperate zone; each pistillate flower has a perianth of bristles which grow out into long hairs.

Cyperus (600) is a genus of tropical and warm temperate climates; *C. papyrus* was used by the Egyptians as early as 2400 B.C. in paper-making; the word paper is derived from the classical name, papyrus; *C. esculentus,* chufa, is grown in Europe for its edible tubers, but is a troublesome weed in the southern United States; *C. alternifolius,* umbrella-plant, of Madagascar and the Mascarenes, is grown as an ornamental; *C. strigosus,* galingale, is a widespread weed in cultivated fields.

Oreobolus has a remarkable distribution, with 1 species in Australia, 3 in New Zealand, 1 in subantarctic America, 1 in Hawaii, 1 in Borneo and Sumatra. *Cladium* (50) is a genus of tropical and warm temperate regions, especially of Australia; *C. jamaicense,* sawgrass, occurs in the southern United States and in the West Indies. *Rhynchospora* (200), beakrush, includes plants of tropical and temperate regions.

Subfamily II. Plants with unisexual flowers. *Scleria* (200), nutrush, is mostly tropical and subtropical; the achene is often surrounded at the base by a disk or perianth-like structure, the **hypogynium;** some species are climbers in tropical forests, with sharp-edged leaves. *Uncinia* (25) is a genus mostly of the southern hemisphere, but north along the Andes to Mexico and the West Indies. *Carex* (1000) is one of the largest genera in the plant kingdom; the species are mainly of temperate regions, or on tropical mountains; the pistillate flowers are borne in a sac-like structure, the **perigynium,** possibly homologous with the hypogynium and representing a modified perianth.

Order 5. Palmales. This order includes only one family, the Palmae. These are woody shrubs, vines, or trees, a condition relatively rare among monocotyledons. The large size results, usually, from intense and protracted primary growth, not from secondary growth as in dicotyledonous trees.

Palmae. Palm Family.

ROOTS AND STEMS. Stems from very short, seemingly none, to 150 feet or more in height; the plants are often thick-stemmed, unbranched trees, but the stems may be long, slender, and flexuous. The principal tree family of the monocots.

LEAVES. Large, usually in a terminal cluster (**head**); petiole (**haft**) smooth or prickly, with a sheath at the base; blade either simple and palmate (in **fan palms**) or pinnately compound (in **feather palms**); alternately arranged in some climbing species.

INFLORESCENCE. Large, paniculate (sometimes called a spadix), below, among, or—rarely—above the foliage, subtended by one or more usually large bracts or spathes, sometimes very showy. In some genera the inflorescence is reported to contain over 200,000 flowers; in the talipot palm it is 20 feet high and weighs tons!

FLOWERS. Monoecious or dioecious, or sometimes bisexual; perianth of 6 small segments in 2 series; stamens mostly 6; carpels 3, free or united.

FRUITS AND SEEDS. Berries or drupes, exocarp fleshy, fibrous, or leathery. Endosperm relatively large.

Figure 101. Royal palm, *Roystonea regia*, the national tree of Cuba. (Photograph courtesy Hermanos Leon y Alain, Colegio de la Salle, Habana.)

To residents of the tropics this family is second only to the grasses in economic importance, providing food, shelter, clothing, and other necessities. The graceful trunks ending in a crown of large leaves are among the most characteristic features of tropical scenery. There are about 200 genera including perhaps 1500 species (or possibly many more, since they are poorly represented in herbaria because of their size). Phylogenetically they are usually regarded as allied to the Arales. The taxonomy is very difficult.

Phoenix (12) occurs in tropical Asia and Africa. *P. dactylifera*, the date palm, is characteristic of oases in North Africa and western Asia; it yields fruit, wine, sugar, and the pinnate leaves are made into hats, mats, thatch. Phoenicia is named from the abundance of these trees in that region.

Chamerops (2) is a genus of the Mediterranean region; *C. humilis,* dwarf palm, is the only palm in Europe, forming close thickets on waste lands. *Corypha* (6), of Ceylon and Indomalaysia, includes *C. imbraculifera,* talipot palm, 80 feet tall; the leaves are used as umbrellas. *Livistona* (25) is Indomalaysian; it includes *L. chinensis,* Chinese fan palm, used as an ornamental, the common tub fan palm. *Sabal* (10) and *Serenoa* (1), ranging from the sandy pinelands of the southern United States to Colombia, include the well-known palmettos of the southeastern United States. *Copernicia* (10), of tropical America, includes *C. cerifera,* wax palm or carnauba, of Brazil. It yields the hardest, highest melting commercial natural wax, which coats the leaves and is removed by drying and flailing the leaves. The tree suggests the name of the state of Ceará. *Washingtonia* (3), of California and Mexico, includes *W. filifera,* California fan palm, a favorite avenue palm.

Hyphaene (30) is a genus of Africa, Madagascar, and India; *H. thebaica,* is the doum palm in Egypt and the Sudan; it is often branched, a feature unusual among palms; the fruit has the flavor of gingerbread (hence gingerbread tree). *Borassus* (7), of the Old World tropics, includes the Palmyra palm, *B. flabelliformis;* its uses are many and varied; an old Hindu song enumerates 801, including timber, thatch, paper, brushes, mats, baskets, fruit, wine, and sugar; *B. aethiopica,* of the African savanna, is the deleb palm. *Lodoicea sechellarum,* double coconut, of the Seychelles, has one of the largest known fruits, weighing 30-40 pounds, and the largest seeds known, taking 10 years to ripen. The fruit was found floating years before the tree was discovered (in 1743), hence the French name *coco-de-mer.*

Mauritia (16) is a genus of tropical America, the buriti palms; these form stately groves in the Brazilian savanna, and supply wood, wine, fruit, and so forth.

Raphia (22) is a genus of tropical South America and Africa; *R. vinifera,* wine palm, of West Africa, yields West African piassava from fibers of the leaf-stalks; *R. ruffia,* of Madagascar, yields raffia, a strong fiber. *Metroxylon* (3), ranging from Siam to New Guinea, includes *M. rumphii* and *M. laeve,* sago palms; the pith yields sago starch. *Calamus* (300) includes plants of the Old World tropics, mostly leaf-climbers and growing, reportedly, to lengths of over 500 feet, making troublesome tangles; the stems are used for baskets, and other objects. *Daemonorops* (100) is another group of lianas, occurring in Indomalaysia; *D. draco,* climbing palm, yields dragon's blood, a red resin secreted on the surface of unripe fruits.

Arenga (12) is another genus of Indomalaysia; *A. saccharifera,* gomuti palm, yields palm sugar (jaggery), sago, fiber. *Caryota* (8), of Indomalaysia, includes *C. urens,* toddy palm, which yields toddy (sap), sugar, sago, Kitul fiber, wood. *Ceroxylon andicola,* of the northern Andes, produces a wax on the stem which may be scraped off and used commercially. *Roystonea* (6), is a group of Florida, the West Indies, and British Guiana; *R. oleracea,* cabbage palm, has a young head of edible leaves; *R. regia,* royal palm, of Florida and Cuba, is much planted along avenues. *Howea* (2), Lord Howe's palm, is restricted in its natural range to Lord Howe's Island. *Archontophoenix alexandrae,* Alexandra palm, is one of Australia's stateliest palms. *Areca* (40), of Indomalaysia, includes *A. catechu,* betel palm; the nuts are rolled in leaves of betel pepper and chewed by millions of people; it is the world's most widely used masticatory.

Elaeis guineensis, oil palm, of West Africa, yields a lubricating oil from the fruit. *Attalea* (70) occurs in South America and Africa; some species are characteristic of the Brazilian caatinga; *A. cohune,* of Central and South America, yields cohune nuts, a source of oil. *Cocos nucifera,* coconut, "man's most useful tree," is cultivated throughout the tropics. Food is obtained from the "meat" and "milk" of the fruit, while the leaves are used for thatching, mats, baskets, furniture; toddy and sugar are produced; the dried nuts, copra, yield oil, the resulting cake, poonac, is used for cattle feed; coir is an important fiber obtained from the husk of the fruit. *C. plumosa* is extensively grown as an ornamental. *Bactris* (160) is a group of usually very spiny plants of tropical America.

Phytelephas (12) is mostly in tropical America; the flowers are closely clustered and the fruit is composed of fused ovaries. The endosperm is very hard and is used as a substitute for ivory (vegetable ivory or tagua). *Nipa fruticans,* nipa palm, is very characteristic of brackish marshes on tropical coasts from the Moluccas to the Philippines; the fruits are woody, several combined into a dense head.

Order 6. Synanthales. This order, of palm-like climbers, epiphytes, or shrubs, includes only a single family. It seems to stand between the palms and the aroids in evolutionary advancement.

Cyclanthaceae. Cyclanthus Family. This is a tropical American family of 6 genera with about 50 species, including *Cyclanthus,* with 4 species from the Antilles to Amazonas and Peru. *Carludovica* (40) includes *C. palmata,* jipijapa, the leaves of which are gathered young, cut into strips, bleached, and made into Panama hats.

Order 7. Arales. Members of this order are characterized by the presence of a thickened spadix subtended by a single spathe. Engler regarded the group as derived from the palms by way of the Cyclanthaceae, but various other systematists have suggested numerous other interpretations, including a derivation from liliaceous ancestors.

a. Tuberous herbs (sometimes woody) .... *Araceae*
a. Minute floating thalloid aquatics .... *Lemnaceae*

Araceae. Aroid Family.

ROOTS AND STEMS. Plant habit exceedingly varied: herbs with aerial stems, tubers, or rhizomes, climbing shrubs, epiphytes with aerial roots, marsh plants, and so forth. The sap is often acrid, from the presence of **raphides,** needle-like crystals of calcium oxalate, in the cells.

LEAVES. Very variable, with parallel or netted venation.

INFLORESCENCE. A simple spadix subtended by a prominent and brightly colored spathe.

FLOWERS. Bisexual or unisexual, small, often fetid and attracting carrion flies, with or without a scale-like perianth of 4-6 parts; stamens 2, 4, or 8; carpel usually 1.

FRUITS AND SEEDS. Fruits generally berries, massed closely together on the spadix and often ripening together with it as a sort of multiple fruit; seeds with endosperm.

The family includes about 105 genera with 1500 species, mostly of tropical regions but also in temperate climates.

Pothos (60) occurs in Indomalaysia and Madagascar; they have climbing stems (hunters' rope) and adventitious roots. *Anthurium* (500) is the largest genus in the family, common in tropical American forests; many are epiphytes with aerial roots; the spathe is usually brightly colored; some species are ornamental, grown in greenhouses. *Acorus calamus,* north temperate, is sweet flag, or calamus, a marsh plant; the rhizome yields a drug.

Rhaphidophora (60) is Indomalaysian; the climbing stems have clasping and also pendulous roots; the cells contain raphides. *Monstera* (30), of tropical America, includes *M. deliciosa,* ceriman, of Mexico, cultivated for its edible fruits; the plants are climbing shrubs with round holes in the leaves.

Symplocarpus foetidus, skunk cabbage, has a strong skunk-like odor; it has a disjunct range, in eastern North America and eastern Asia. *Lysichiton* has 1 species in western North America, 1 in eastern Asia. *Calla palustris,* water arum, circumboreal, has a pure white spathe. *Orontium aquaticum,* golden club, occurs in eastern North America. *Peltandrum* (2) of eastern North America includes *P. virginica,* arrow arum.

Dracontium (10) is found in tropical America; the rhizome each year produces an enormous leaf and an inflorescence. *Amorphophallus* (90) of tropical Asia, is claimed to have "the world's largest flower"; in reality the allusion is to the inflorescence, the actual flowers being small. In *A. titanum,* of Sumatra, the spadix becomes 15 feet high, with a spathe 8 feet high; it has a lurid color and fetid odor, attracting carrion flies.

Philodendron (230) is the second largest genus, widespread in tropical America; the plants are shrubs, usually climbing, sometimes epiphytes with clasping and also pendulous roots that may eventually reach the soil. *Zantedeschia* (10), of South Africa, includes *Z. aethiopica,* the cultivated calla lily.

Colocasia (8), of Indomalaysia, is sometimes called by florists elephant's-ear; most important is *C. esculenta,* dasheen, and its var. *antiquorum,* taro, bearing large edible corms, important food items for people of Pacific islands and southeastern Asia. *Alocasia* (50), of the East Indies, includes *A. indica,* man-kachu, which produces edible rhizomes. *Caladium* (20) of tropical South America, is sometimes cultivated

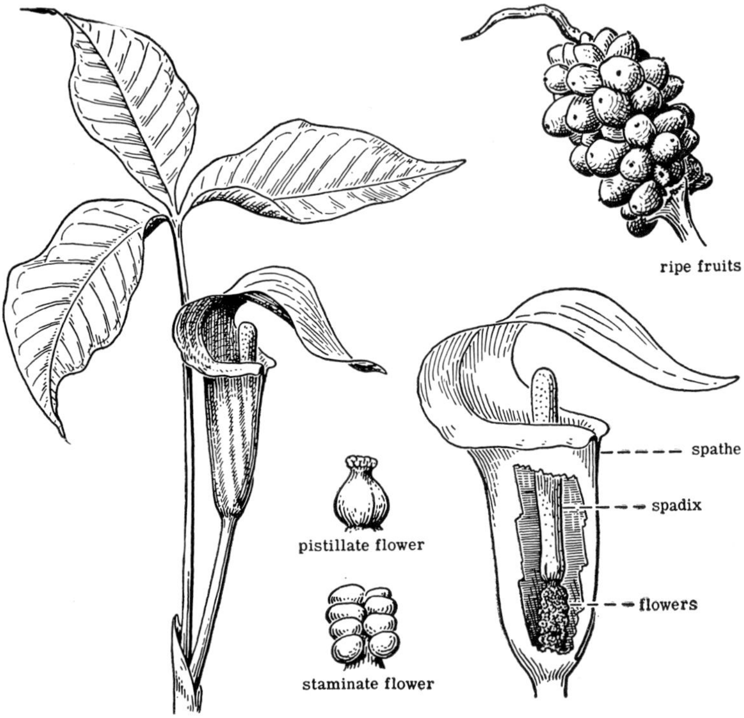

Figure 102. Jack-in-the-pulpit, *Arisaema triphyllum.*

for its large ornamental, often variegated, leaves. *Xanthosoma* (40), in tropical America, includes *X. sagittifolium,* yautia, cultivated for its edible corms and rhizomes.

Arum (12), of southern and central Europe, includes *A. maculatum,* cuckoo-pint, lords-and-ladies; the fetid odor attracts flies which enter the spathe and are held prisoner by rows of hairs that wither when the pollen is shed. *Arisaema* (110) occurs in Asia, Africa, and North America; it includes *A. triphyllum,* jack-in-the-pulpit, Indian turnip, of eastern United States; the corm (Figure 47) contains raphides, and is exceedingly acrid in taste.

Pistia stratiotes, water-lettuce, widespread in the tropics, is a floating monoecious aquatic, providing a link to the next family; the plants are often grown in aquaria.

Lemnaceae. Duckweed Family.

ROOTS AND STEMS. Free-floating water plants, with or without 1 or more roots hanging in the water.

LEAVES. The plants are leafless, each being composed of a small oval or oblong, flat or globose thallus which acts as a leaf.

INFLORESCENCES. Flowers unisexual, monoecious, solitary or in pairs, sometimes enclosed in a spathe.

FLOWERS. Staminate flowers usually of 1 stamen, pistillate of 1 carpel. The flowers, especially in the temperate zone, are rarely formed.

FRUIT. A utricle.

Most botanists agree that this family represents greatly reduced aroids, originating from *Pistia* or similar ancestral stocks. There are 4 genera, represented in fresh-water habitats throughout much of the world. *Spirodela* (2) includes *S. polyrhiza;* the shoots bear several roots. *Lemna* (10) is duckweed; the shoots have 1 root; the plants range from 3 to 20 mm. in length. *Wolffia* (12), watermeal, is rootless, with oval thalli; *W. arrhiza* is the smallest known flowering plant, being only 1 or 2 mm. in length.

Order 8. Farinales. Engler based this order of about a dozen families upon the single character of a mealy endosperm but later botanists are in general agreement that it is not a homogeneous group. Although the families have been redistributed by various authors, there is no uniformity in their treatments.

a. Perianth various, at least the outer whorl calyx-like
  b. Plants with basal, grass-like leaves
    c. Corolla yellow, rather showy .... *Xyridaceae*
    c. Flowers inconspicuous, in involucrate heads ..... *Eriocaulaceae*
  b. Leaves not usually grass-like
    c. Plants usually epiphytic .... *Bromeliaceae*
    c. Plants not epiphytic .... *Commelinaceae*
a. Perianth corolla-like, united .... *Pontederiaceae*

Eriocaulaceae. Pipewort Family.

ROOTS AND STEMS. Perennial, with grass-like habit; roots fibrous.

LEAVES. Mostly linear, basal, grass-like, crowded.

INFLORESCENCE. An involucrate head (somewhat resembling that of the Compositae).

FLOWERS. Inconspicuous, unisexual, regular or irregular; perianth in 2 series, differing in texture; staminate flowers with 4-6 stamens, pistillate with 2-3 united carpels.

FRUIT. A capsule.

The family includes 12 genera with about 1100 species, primarily in bogs and along wet shores, almost restricted to the tropics, but with a few species extending into temperate regions. Hutchinson placed this family in a separate order, the Eriocaulales, related to but advanced over the Xyridales. *Eriocaulon* (370), pipewort, hatpins, is mostly tropical but has some species in the Atlantic coastal plain of North America. *Syngonanthus* (175) is a genus of tropical America; the inflorescences of some are sold as "everlasting flowers." *S. flavidus,* shoe buttons, is in the southeastern United States. *Paepalanthus* (230) is mostly in tropical America, but with 1 species in Africa. *Lachnocaulon* (10), of tropical and subtropical America, includes *L. anceps,* hairy pipewort, in eastern United States.

Xyridaceae. Yelloweyed-grass Family. Tufted marsh plants, 2 genera, 200 species, tropical and subtropical, mostly in America; leaves basal, sheathing; flowers perfect, in spikes or heads; sepals 3; petals 3, mostly yellow; stamens 3; carpels 3, united. *Xyris* (190), yelloweyed-grass, is found in America (from Newfoundland to Uruguay), Africa, India, and Australia.

Commelinaceae. Spiderwort Family.

Roots and Stems. Roots fibrous, or sometimes thickened and tuber-like; stems herbaceous, annual or perennial, jointed.

Leaves. Sheathing, alternate, parallel-veined, entire.

Inflorescences. Cymose, terminal or axillary, or with only a single flower, sometimes subtended by a keel-like spathe.

Flowers. Bisexual; sepals 3, green; petals 3, colored, equal or unequal, mostly ephemeral and deliquescent; stamens typically 6, but sometimes reduced to 3 fertile and 3 aborted stamens (staminodes) or to 1 fertile stamen; carpels 3, united.

Fruit. A capsule.

The family is mainly tropical and subtropical, with 37 genera and about 600 species. Phylogenetically the family appears to have been derived from the Alismatales. *Commelina* (200) is the largest genus, including *C. communis,* dayflower, a widespread weed, sometimes cultivated as an ornamental.

Tradescantia (35), spiderwort, occurs in North and South America; the plants are often cultivated for ornamental flowers; the name refers to a mucilaginous material produced by the stems, which becomes silky and thread-like. *Zebrina* (3), of Central America, is wandering Jew; it is cultivated for the striped leaves.

Bromeliaceae. Pineapple Family.

Roots and Stems. Mostly short-stemmed epiphytes (sometimes terrestrial).

Leaves. Mostly basal, fleshy, often forming a pitcher-like rosette usually partially filled with water.

INFLORESCENCE. A terminal head, spike, raceme or panicle, the flowers often in the axils of brightly colored bracts.

FLOWERS. Bisexual, regular; sepals 3; petals 3, often brightly colored; stamens 6, carpels 3, the ovary superior or inferior.

FRUIT. A berry or capsule, sometimes (as in *Ananas*) joined in a multiple fruit (syncarp) (Figure 88, E).

The family is a very large one, with 65 genera including over 1500 species, almost entirely restricted to the New World, from Virginia to Chile. It is apparently related to but more advanced than the Commelinaceae. The plants are among the most conspicuous epiphytes of tropical rain forests.

Figure 103. *Tillandsia* sp., a subtropical epiphyte. (Photograph by Walter S. Chansler.)

Puya (80) is terrestrial, agave-like, common in the Andes, often above the timberline; *P. raimondii* reaches a height of 35-40 feet. *Pitcairnia* (170) is also mostly in the Andes; some are cultivated ornamentals; *P. feliciana* is native to French West Africa, the only species outside America. *Hechtia* (27) occurs in Florida, Texas, Mexico, and Central America. *Tillandsia* (400) is the most widely distributed genus in the family, ranging from Virginia to Argentina and Chile; some are epiphytes with pitchers, but others, as *T. usneoides,* Spanish moss, hang in long gray festoons from the branches of trees, like *Usnea* (a lichen). *Bromelia* (16) ranging from Central America to Argentina, includes *B. pinguin,* pinguin or wild pineapple, of the West Indies and Central America, and *B. serra,* of Bolivia, Paraguay and Argentina, characteristic of the Gran Chaco. Species of *Billbergia* (60), ranging from Mexico to southern Brazil, are sometimes cultivated as ornamentals. *Ananas* (5), ranges from Mexico to Paraguay; *A. sativus,* pineapple, is much cultivated, for example in Hawaii, for the edible fruit which develops from a mass of ovaries on a fleshy flower stalk.

Pontederiaceae. Pickerelweed Family. A family of aquatics, rooted or floating, 6 genera, 28 species, mostly tropical or subtropical; leaves usually opposite or whorled; flowers regular or irregular; perianth of 6 petal-like parts; stamens 6; carpels 3, united. *Heteranthera* (10), of African and American tropics, includes *H. dubia,* mud plantain, in eastern United States. *Eichhornia* (5) is a group of tropical American plants; these plants, like *E. crassipes,* water-hyacinth, float by large bladder-like petioles and become troublesome introduced weeds, clogging ponds and slow streams in Florida, Java, Australia. *Pontederia* (3), of tropical and temperate America, includes *P. cordata,* pickerel-weed, from Canada to Texas, and *P. lanceolata,* a coastal plain species, from Virginia to Florida and Texas.

Order 9. Liliales. This order, as set up by Engler, includes families separated from the Farinales by the fleshy endosperm. The conventional classification of families within the order stresses the ovary position, with an inferior ovary being derived from the superior.

a. Perennial herbs with calyx-like perianth
  b. Ovary superior .... *Juncaceae*
  b. Ovary inferior; climbing herbs .... *Dioscoreaceae*
a. Herbs, shrubs, or trees; perianth, at least the inner, usually corolla-like
  b. Ovary superior .... *Liliaceae*
  b. Ovary inferior
    c. Stamens 6
      d. Leaves linear, crowded .... *Velloziaceae*
      d. Leaves not as above .... *Amaryllidaceae*
    c. Stamens 3
      d. Stamens opposite the petals .... *Haemodoraceae*
      d. Stamens alternate with the petals .... *Iridaceae*

Juncaceae. Rush Family.

Roots and Stems. Grass-like herbs (rarely shrubs), often with fibrous roots, from a creeping rhizome.

Leaves. Basal or cauline, linear or filiform, flat or terete, sheathing basally, the sheath open.

Inflorescence. Flowers in cymes grouped in a panicle, corymb, or head, or the flowers solitary.

Flowers. Bisexual (rarely unisexual, the plants then dioecious), regular; perianth 6-parted, in two series, sepaloid; stamens 6 or 3; carpels 3, united.

Fruit. A capsule.

The family includes 8 genera with about 315 species in damp and cool places, in frigid and temperate regions and on tropical mountains; six genera, representing only 10 species, are restricted to the southern hemisphere. Although some authors regard the family as ancestral to the Liliaceae others believe it is a degenerate group reduced from lily-like ancestors. Hutchinson placed the Juncaceae in the class Glumiflorae, with the sedges and grasses. In superficial appearance the rushes closely resemble sedges and grasses, but differ in the 6-parted perianth.

Prionium palmita, palmiet, occurs in South Africa; it is a shrubby, aloe-like plant, about 6 feet high, the stem covered with fibrous remains of old leaves; it grows in abundance on edges of streams. *Juncus* (225), rush, has a world-wide distribution, with most species in the northern hemisphere; *J. tenuis,* path rush, is very common in little-used paths; *J. effusus,* common rush, is characteristic of wet meadows in Europe and America; *J. bufonius,* toad rush, is a cosmopolitan plant of ditches. *Luzula* (80), wood rush, includes chiefly north temperate and Arctic plants, mostly with hairy foliage, unlike members of the genus *Juncus.*

Liliaceae. Lily Family.

Roots and Stems. Mostly perennial herbs, from a rhizome, bulb, corm, or tuber; stems erect or climbing, sometimes modified into cladophylls.

Leaves. Basal or cauline, alternate or whorled, mostly with parallel veins.

Inflorescence. Scapose, racemose, paniculate, spicate, umbellate, often few-flowered, sometimes solitary-flowered.

Flowers. Mostly bisexual, regular; perianth 6-parted (rarely 4-parted), often large and showy, corolla-like, in 2 series, the segments sometimes united into a tube; stamens 6 (rarely 3, 4 or more) carpels 3, united.

Fruit. A capsule or berry.

This is a very large family, of 250 genera including 4000 species, widely distributed over the earth, especially abundant in warm temperate and tropical regions. Economically the family ranks very high in the number of important ornamentals. Phylogenetically the family is regarded by botanists today as representing basic monocot stock, from which many families formerly believed to be more primitive have been evolved by reduction. It is generally regarded as the most representative family of monocotyledons.

Tofieldia (18), false asphodel, of arctic and temperate regions, includes *T. palustris,* circumboreal, and *T. glutinosa,* eastern North America. *Narthecium* (4), bog-asphodel, includes *N. americanum,* of New Jersey and Delaware. *Veratrum* (50) is a genus of the north temperate region; *V. viride,* white hellebore, is in eastern North America. *Zygadenus* (10) is found in North America and Asia; *Z. venenosus,* death-camass, and others cause cattle poisoning. Monotypic genera of eastern North America are *Helonias* (*H. bullata,* swamppink) and *Amianthium* (*A. muscaetoxicum,* fly poison). *Xerophyllum* (3) of North America, includes *X. asphodeloides,* turkeybeard, of the Atlantic coastal plain, and *X. tenax,* beargrass, of the western mountains. *Chamaelirium* (2), of eastern North America, includes *C. luteum,* blazing star, devil's bit. *Uvularia* (5), of eastern North America, includes *U. grandiflora,* bellwort (Figure 63).

Colchicum (65) ranges from the Mediterranean to central Asia; *C. autumnale* is meadow saffron or autumn crocus; it yields an alkaloid (colchicine) used as a drug. *Gloriosa* (5), of tropical Asia and Africa, is cultivated for ornamental flowers; *G. superba* is climbing lily.

Asphodelus (12), asphodel, includes ornamental plants of the Mediterranean region. *Anthericum* (100) is found in Africa, America, and East Asia; *A. liliago* is St. Bernard's lily. *Bowiea volubilis,* of South Africa, is a xerophyte with a huge partly-underground corm giving off each year a much-branched climbing stem with small leaves which soon fall, photosynthesis being carried on by the stem. *Hosta* (8), plantain lily, East-Asiatic, includes *H. sieboldiana,* of Japan, ornamental. *Hemerocallis* (5), day lily, of Eurasia, includes plants cultivated as ornamentals. *Phormium tenax,* New Zealand hemp, is the only important hard-fiber plant of temperate countries; the leaves, from which the fibers are obtained, are sometimes 9 feet long. *Kniphofia* (75) is characteristic of South and East Africa and Madagascar; some species are cultivated as pokerplant or red-hot poker. *Aloe* (200) is a group, mostly of South Africa, especially in the Karroo Desert (page 79); the plants are shrubby or arborescent xerophytes, with the fleshy, waxy leaves in dense rosettes at the ends of the branches. *Xanthorrhoea* (12) is an Australian genus, including *X. hastilis,* grasstree or blackboy, a characteristic plant of the Australian desert; it is aloe-like, with a long spike of flowers.

Agapanthus (5), of South Africa, includes *A. umbellatus,* African lily, a cultivated ornamental. *Allium* (325) is a group of plants most of which have a strong odor and taste; *A. tricoccum* is ramps, of the Appalachian region; cultivated species are *A. sativum,* garlic, *A. cepa,* onion, *A. porrum,* leek, *A. ascalonicum,* shallot, *A. schoenoprasum,* chives. *Brodiaea* (50), of western North America and temperate South America, includes some cultivated ornamental flowers (spring starflower).

Erythronium (7) is a genus of attractive flowers of the north temperate zone; *E. dens-canis,* dog's tooth-violet, occurs from Europe to Japan; *E. americanum, E. albidum,* fawn lily, are found in eastern United States, *E. grandiflorum,* glacier lily, in western United States. *Tulipa* (50), tulip, is a well-known genus of the north temperate Old World, especially on the steppes of Central Asia. The cultivated tulips are regarded as varieties of *T. gesneriana;* the growing of the bulbs is an important industry, particularly in Holland (page 123). *Fritillaria* (50), of the north temperate zone, includes *F. meleagris,* snake's head (Central Europe), and *F. imperialis,* crown imperial (Iran), cultivated ornamentals. *Lilium* (60), of the north temperate zone, includes some of the most attractive ornamental flowers; some of them are *L. martagon,* Martagon (turban) lily, from Central Europe to Mongolia, *L. regale,* royal lily, China, *L. tigrinum,* tiger lily, East Asia, *L. croceum,* orange lily, southern Europe, *L. candidum,* madonna lily, southern Europe, *L. speciosum,* showy lily, Japan, *L. giganteum,* giant lily, eastern Himalayas and China, *L. superbum,* Turk's cap lily, eastern United States, *L. canadense,* Canada lily, eastern North America. *L. longiflorum,* white trumpet lily, Easter lily, is the most popular for greenhouses. *Calochortus* (40), mariposa lily, is a genus of western North America, including *C. nuttallii,* the state flower of Utah.

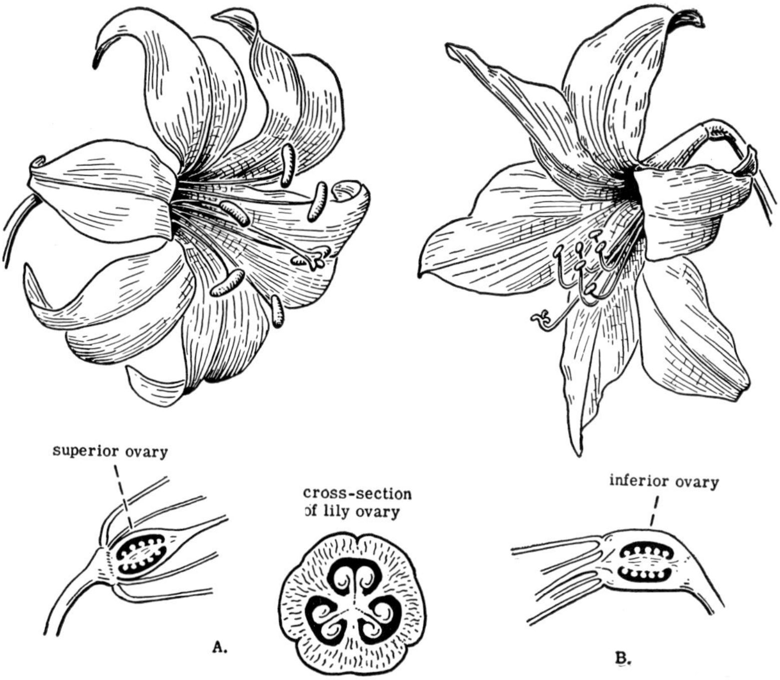

Figure 104. ***A,*** **flower of** ***Lilium; B,*** **flower of** ***Amaryllis.***

Scilla (100), squill, includes plants of the temperate Old World; the bulbs yield a glucoside used for rat poison; commonly cultivated as ornamentals are *S. sibirica,* Siberian squill, *S. hispanica,* Spanish jacinth, *S. verna,* sea-onion, and *S. nonscripta,* wood hyacinth. *Camassia* (4), quamash, includes plants of North America; the bulbs of some were used as food by American Indians; *C. scillioides* is wild hyacinth. *Ornithogalum* (100) is a genus of the temperate Old World; *O. umbellatum* is star-of-Bethlehem. *Chionodoxa* (4) is indigenous to Crete and Asia Minor; *C. luciliae,* glory-of-the-snow, is a cultivated ornamental. *Hyacinthus* (30), hyacinth, includes plants of the Mediterranean and South Africa; many forms are cultivated for their ornamental flowers, and their growing is associated with that of tulips in Holland. *Muscari* (40), grape hyacinth, of the Mediterranean region, is often cultivated for ornamental flowers.

Yucca (30), of southern North America, has an interesting type of pollination: a Pronuba moth collects pollen in a ball, stuffs it in the end of the hollow stigma, then lays her eggs in the ovary, the larvae eating some of the developing ovules, while other ovules become seeds; both the plant and the animal thus benefit. *Y. filamentosa,* eastern United States, Adam's needle, is a cultivated ornamental. *Y. aloifolia* is Spanish bayonet. *Y. arborescens* is Joshua tree, characteristic of deserts of southwestern United States, a striking object in the landscape. *Dasylirion* (15), sotol, of Texas and Mexico, is a genus of aloe-like xerophytes, with the dioecious flowers in an immense inflorescence. *Cordyline* (20), of the Old World tropics, occurs mostly on the Pacific islands, but has 1 species in South America; *C. terminalis,* India to Australia and Polynesia, is ti-palm. *Dracaena* (40), of the Old World tropics, is a genus composed mostly of trees. *D. draco,* dragon tree, Teneriffe, grows to height of more than 50 feet; one famous tree was 70 feet high, 45 feet in circumference and was estimated to be 6000 years old when it was blown over in 1868; resin from the trunk, dragon's blood, was collected formerly and used as varnish for the great Italian violins of the eighteenth century, *Sanseviera* (60), is a genus of the Old World tropics, mostly xerophytes with sword-like leaves, including *S. trifasciata,* and others, cultivated for ornamental striped leaves, and *S. zeylanicum,* bow-string hemp.

Smilacina (20), of the north temperate zone, includes *S. racemosa,* plumelily, or false Solomon's seal, and *S. stellata* (Figure 60), of eastern United States. *Maianthemum* (3), of north temperate regions, has the flower parts in 2's rather than 3's; *M. canadense,* Canada mayflower, is in eastern North America, *M. bifolium* in Europe and Siberia. *Streptopus* (5) is a genus of the north temperate zone, including *S. amplexifolius,* twisted-stalk, circumboreal. *Polygonatum* (30), Solomon's seal, a genus of the north temperate zone, includes *P. officinale,* of Eurasia, *P. biflorum,* of eastern North America, *P. multiflorum,* of Japan, and *P. verticillatum,* of the Himalayas; the plants produce a fleshy rhizome upon which the

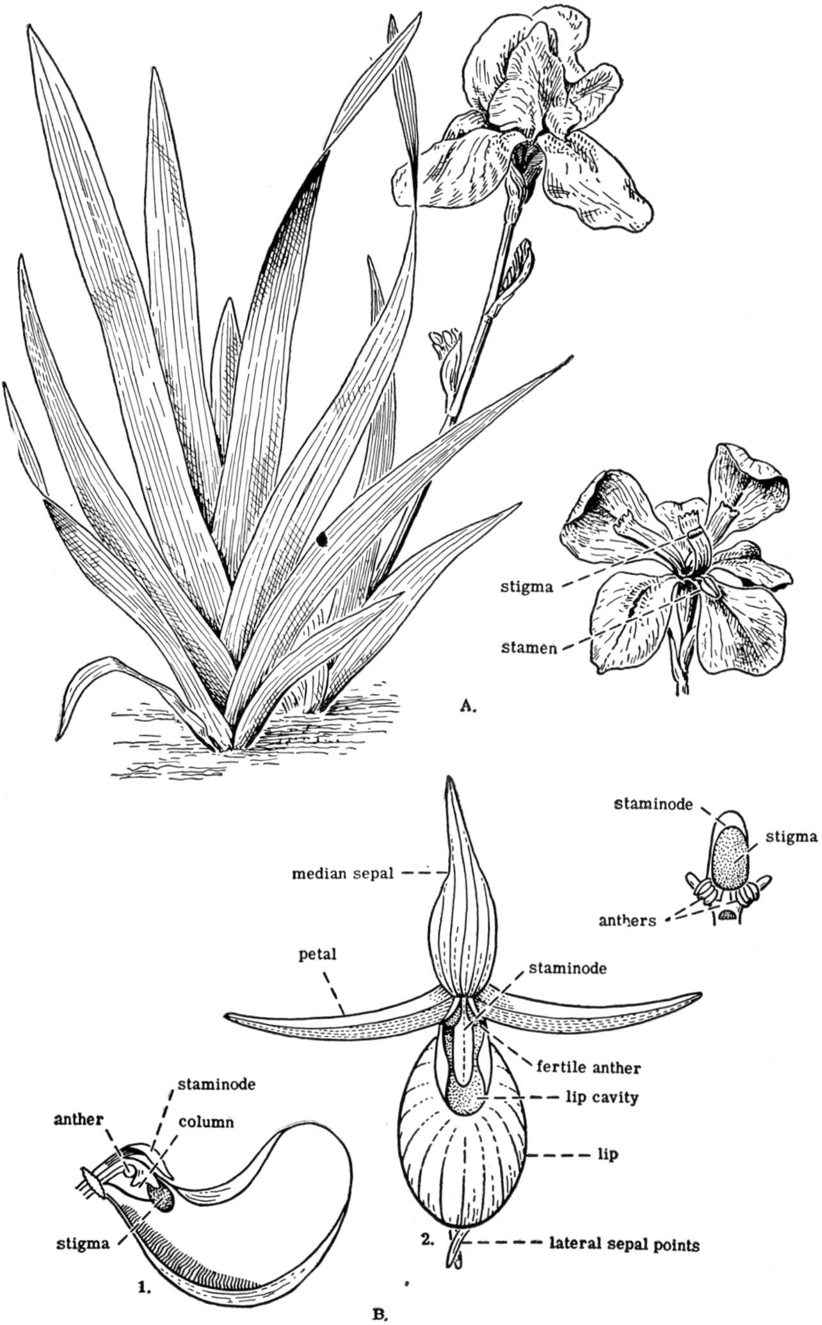

Figure 105. ***A, Iris,*** **showing plant with equitant leaves and structures of flowers;** ***B,*** **diagrammatic sketch of flower of lady's slipper,** ***Cypripedium,*** **showing:** ***1,*** **section through the slipper;** ***2,*** **general view of the flower; and** ***3,*** **apex of the column.**

annual shoots leave seal-like scars when they die (Figure 47). *Convallaria* (2), lily-of-the-valley, includes *C. majalis,* of Europe, a cultivated ornamental, and *C. montana,* a closely related species of the Appalachian Mountains. *Paris* (20), of Eurasia, includes *P. quadrifolia,* herb Paris or truelove, with leaves and flower parts in whorls of 4's (whence *herb paris,* from *par,* equal, pair). *Trillium* (30), wake robin or birthroot, is distributed in North America and eastern Asia; the net-veined leaves are in whorls of 3's, and the flowers are differentiated into a calyx and corolla; *T. grandiflorum* is in eastern North America. *Asparagus* (300), of the Old World, mainly Africa, has the leaves reduced to scales with small green shoots (phylloclades or cladophylls) in the axils; *A. officinalis* is cultivated for the edible young stalks; *A. plumosus* is the asparagus-fern of florists; *A. asparagoides* is smilax of florists. *Ruscus* (3), mostly Mediterranean, includes *R. aculeatus,* butcher's broom, a small shrub with leaf-like phylloclades in the axils of scale-like leaves; the dried sprays are dyed for decoration.

Lapageria rosea, Chilebells, of Chile, a climbing shrub with ornamental flowers and edible fruit, is Chile's national flower.

Smilax (300) is a genus mostly of tropical and subtropical regions; the species are mostly shrubs climbing by tendrils that are modified stipules (Figure 52), rare among monocotyledons; the leaves are net-veined, and the flowers dioecious; sarsaparilla is secured from roots of *S. medica* (Mexico), *S. officinalis* (Honduras), *S. ornata* (Jamaica); *S. rotundifolia* is greenbrier (*ronce verte* of French explorers), of eastern North America.

Haemodoraceae. Bloodwort Family. A family of herbs, 10 genera, 40 species, of Australia, South Africa, and America; flowers perfect, 6-parted; the roots often yield a bright red dye. Includes *Haemodorum,* 17 species of Australia, bloodwort, and *Lachnanthes tinctoria,* red-root or paint-root, of eastern North America.

Dioscoreaceae. Yam Family.

Roots and Stems. Climbing, herbaceous or woody, from a thick rhizome.

Leaves. Alternate, opposite or whorled, net-veined.

Inflorescence. A spike, raceme, or panicle; flowers unisexual and dioecious, or bisexual.

Flowers. Regular, small, inconspicuous; perianth 6-parted; stamens 3-6; carpels 3, united, inferior.

Fruit. A capsule or berry.

The family includes 10 genera with 650 species of tropical and warm temperate regions. Phylogenetically it appears to be derived from lily-like ancestors. The largest genus is *Dioscorea* (600), mostly in tropical America; the plants have twining annual stems from tubers or rhizomes that contain much starch; several are cultivated for food in the tropics; cultivated species include *D. alata,* white yam, the most common; *D. cayennensis,* negro yam or yellow yam, *D. trifida,* cush-cush or yampi, *D. bulbifera,* air-potato, *D. esculenta,* Chinese yam, *D. opposita* (*batatas*), cinnamon-vine. *D. villosa,* wild yam, occurs in eastern North America. *Tamus* (2), of the Mediterranean region, includes *T. communis,* black bryony, a climbing plant hibernating by tubers. *Testudinaria elephantipes,* elephant's foot, or Hottentot bread, of South Africa, has an enormous cork-covered edible tuber partly projecting out of the soil and giving rise to an annual slender climbing stem with large leaves (p. 80).

Velloziaceae. Treelily Family. A family of perennial arborescent xerophytes, with 2 genera including 175 species of tropical America and Africa; the lower parts of the stem are clothed with adventitious roots that absorb water from the atmosphere; flowers regular; perianth 6-parted; stamens 6 or more; carpels 3, united, inferior. *Vellozia,* treelily, with 75 species of tropical America, especially on campos, is cultivated in warm climates for ornamental flowers.

Amaryllidaceae. Amaryllis Family.

HABIT. Perennial, mostly scapose, from a rhizome, bulb, or corm.

LEAVES. Mostly basal, linear or strap-shaped, sometimes rigid and sword-shaped.

INFLORESCENCE. Umbellate, racemose, or paniculate, sometimes only a solitary flower.

FLOWERS. Perfect, regular or irregular; perianth-segments 6, free or united, petal-like; stamens 6; carpels 3, united, inferior.

FRUIT. A capsule or berry.

The family includes about 90 genera with 1300 species, mostly of tropical and subtropical regions. They are often xerophytes, coming into leaf in the spring or the rainy season. There are many cultivated ornamentals and several species yield fiber. Conventionally the family is regarded as related to and advanced over the Liliaceae, differing by the inferior ovary.

Haemanthus (60), cape tulip, includes plants of tropical and South Africa; some are cultivated ornamentals. *Galanthus* (9) is mostly Mediterranean, including *G. nivalis,* snowdrop, an early-blooming ornamental. *Leucojum* (9) is also mostly Mediterranean, including *L. vernum,* snowflake, an early-blooming ornamental. *Nerine* (15), of South Africa, includes *N. undulata,* Guernsey lily, of Cape Colony, a cultivated ornamental. *Amaryllis belladonna,* belladonna lily, of Cape Colony, is a cultivated ornamental. *Zephyranthes* (55), ranging from southeastern United States to Patagonia, includes *Z. atamasco,* Atamasco lily, from Pennsylvania to Florida. *Crinum* (130) is a genus of tropical and subtropical regions; several, including *C. asiaticum,* St. John's lily, are cultivated ornamentals. *Eucharis* (17), Eucharis lily, is a genus of tropical South America, including *E. grandiflora,* Amazon lily, of Colombia; they are cultivated as ornamentals. *Pancratium* (13), ranging from the Canary Islands through tropical Africa to tropical Asia, includes *P. maritimum,* sea daffodil, of the Mediterranean. *Hymenocallis* (40), spider lily, of tropical and subtropical America, has the appendages of the stamens united into a showy tube (**corona**); several are cultivated ornamentals. *Hippeastrum* (60) occurs in tropical and subtropical America; many of the species are cultivated ornamentals. *Sprekelia formosissima,* Jacobean lily, of Central America, is a greenhouse favorite. *Narcissus* (40), one of the best known groups of ornamentals in the world, is a genus mostly of the Mediterranean region; the flowers have a more or less well-developed corona developed from the perianth (Figure 71). *N. pseudo-narcissus* is daffodil; *N. poeticus,* poet's narcissus; *N. jonquilla,* jonquil; *N. incomparabilis,* narcissus; *N. odorus,* Campernelle jonquil; *N. tazetta,* polyanthus narcissus.

Agave (300) ranges from southern United States to northern South America, mostly in dry regions. *A. americana,* American aloe, century plant, or maguey, has a short stem and a rosette of waxy fleshy leaves, growing slowly for 5-100 years, then rapidly developing an enormous inflorescence sometimes 20 feet high; the fermented juice is pulque, a popular Mexican drink. Sisal hemp, for binder twine, and so forth, is from leaves of *A. sisalana;* henequen is from *A. fourcroydes,* which was used by the Aztecs; Tula istle is from *A. lophantha;* Salvador sisal is from *A. letonae;* Jaumave istle is from *A. funkiana. Furcraea* (*Fourcroya*) (20) is an *Agave*-like genus of tropical America, important as producers of hard fibers; *F. gigantea* is indigenous to Brazil (where called piteira), but grown commercially on island of Mauritius for Mauritius hemp; *F. macrophylla,* of Colombia, is fique, the fibers used for coffee bags; *F. cabuya,* of Ecuador, yields cabuya. *Polyanthes* (13), of Mexico and Central America, includes *P. tuberosa,* tuberose, a cultivated ornamental.

Bomarea (120) from Mexico to South America, is most abundant in the Andes; the plants are often climbing, and several, as *B. caldasii,* are cultivated ornamentals. *Anigozanthos* (8), kangaroo-paw, occurs in southwest Australia, the floral emblem of Western Australia. *Hypoxis* (100) is a genus of Africa and America; *H. hirsuta,* yellow stargrass, is in eastern North America.

Iridaceae. Iris Family.

HABIT. Usually herbaceous, from rhizomes, bulbs, or corms; stems solitary or several, or the plants scapose.

LEAVES. Mostly basal, generally equitant (Figure 105), linear or sword-shaped.

INFLORESCENCE. Racemose or paniculate, or the flowers solitary.

FLOWERS. Showy, bisexual, regular or irregular; perianth-segments 6, petal-like, united below; stamens 3; carpels 3, united, inferior.

FRUIT. A capsule.

This is a large family, of 58 genera with 1500 species, distributed over most of the earth except the coldest regions; South Africa and tropical America are the chief centers. Almost every genus contains species of value as ornamentals; over 10,000 named horticultural varieties, mostly of iris and gladiolus, are in the trade. Phylogenetically the family is related to the Amaryllidaceae, from which it may have been derived, or the two separately from the Liliaceae. Irises differ from lilies and amaryllids in having only 3 stamens.

Crocus (70) occurs mostly in the Mediterranean region; *C. luteus* and *C. vernus* are among the most popular ornamentals; *C. sativus,* saffron, is the source of a yellow dye. *Sisyrinchium* (75), blue-eyed grass, ranges from Canada to Patagonia, mostly in temperate regions. *Ixia* (25) occurs in South Africa; several are cultivated ornamentals. *Freesia* (3) is a group of South African plants, cultivated for ornamental perfumed flowers. *Tritonia* (50), mostly in South Africa, includes many cultivated ornamentals; *T. crocosmaeflora* (hybrid origin) is the montbretia of flower gardens. *Gladiolus* (250) ranges from South Africa to southern Europe; the species are among the most popular of cultivated ornamentals and include many varieties. *Tigridia* (12), extending from Mexico to northern Chile, includes *T. pavonia,* tigerflower, of Mexico and Guatemala, a cultivated ornamental. *Moraea* (90), a genus of South Africa and Australia, includes several cultivated ornamentals. *Iris* (200) is a genus of the north temperate zone, including a large number of species grown as ornamentals; *I. pseudacorus,* of Eurasia, is yellow flag; *I. sibirica,* from central Europe to Japan, is Siberian iris; *I. laevigata* is Japanese iris; *I. xiphium,* Spanish iris, is one of the oldest in cultivation; *I. germanica,* a hybrid, is fleur-de-lis; *I. foetidissima* is gladdon. The dried rhizome of *I. florentia* is orris root, a violet perfume. In the vernacular of the trade, the outer perianth parts are called "falls," their narrowed base the "haft," while the inner parts are "standards," narrowed to a "claw." *Belamcanda chinensis,* of eastern Asia, is a cultivated ornamental called blackberry-lily, from the cluster of large shining black seeds that remain for a time after the capsule walls split down.

Order 10. Scitaminales. This is a natural group of tropical families generally regarded as composed of highly advanced monocots, ancestral to or parallel with the Orchidaceae.

a. Staminode 1, not petaloid; anther-bearing stamens 5 . . . . . *Musaceae*
a. Staminodes 1 or more, some or all of them broad and petal-like
  b. Fertile stamen usually 1, bearing a 2-celled anther . . . *Zingiberaceae*

b. Fertile stamen 1, bearing a 1-celled anther
  c. Ovules many in each locule .... *Cannaceae*
  c. Ovules single in each locule .... *Marantaceae*

Musaceae. Banana Family.

HABIT. Mostly large herbs, often tree-like in appearance; stem stout, unbranched, sheathed by petioles.

LEAVES. Large, often enormous, alternate, entire (frequently with lacerations resulting from wind injury).

INFLORESCENCE. A spike or panicle, subtended by spathe-like bracts.

FLOWERS. Bisexual or unisexual (then monoecious, with staminate flowers above and pistillate below), irregular; perianth-segments 6, petal-like; stamens 5, with 1 staminode; carpels 3, united, inferior.

FRUIT. A berry, capsule or schizocarp.

The family includes 5 genera with 150 species of wide distribution in the tropics. Economically some of the species are of very great importance. Phylogenetically the family is the most primitive in the order. Some of the plants are among the largest of all herbs.

The genus *Musa* (75), "God's gift to the tropics," is a native of the Old World tropics. The plants are large tree-like herbs, sometimes more than 30 feet high. The inflorescence springs from the rhizome and is surrounded by the enveloping leaf-sheaths. The flowers are very numerous, in the axils of showy bracts, the lower fertile and giving rise to the "hands" of fruit. *M. paradisiaca* is the plantain or cooking banana, an important staple in the tropics, commonly eaten baked, boiled, or fried. *M. sapientum* is the banana imported in North America. Hundreds of varieties of these 2 species are in cultivation, some yielding as much as 240,000 pounds of fruits per acre. Leaf stalks of *M. ensete* are eaten in Abyssinia; the plant is 20-40 feet tall, with leaves up to 20 feet long, the largest known banana plant. Leaf stalks of *M. textilis* furnish Manila hemp, or abacá, the chief export of the Philippine Islands. *Ravenala madagascariensis*, traveller's-tree, of Madagascar, has water accumulated in leaf-bases which can be used for drinking; the fan-like aspect makes the plant an unmistakable object. *Strelitzia* (5), of South Africa, includes *S. reginae*, bird-of-paradise flower, a cultivated ornamental. *Heliconia* (50), of the West Indies and tropical South America, is platanillo or wild plantain.

Zingiberaceae. Ginger Family.

HABIT. Perennial herbs with fleshy rhizomes; aerial stem often short or none.

LEAVES. Basal or cauline, sheathing, alternate, 2-ranked, with a ligule at junction of blade and sheath.

INFLORESCENCE. Spicate or racemose, or the flowers solitary, subtended by conspicuous bracts.

FLOWERS. Bisexual, irregular; sepals 3, united; petals 3, usually different in color from the sepals; 1 stamen of outer whorl absent, the other 2 absent or present as large petal-like staminodes, the inner whorl having 1 fertile stamen, and the other 2 united to form a petal-like **labellum,** often the showiest part of the flower; carpels 3, united, inferior.

FRUIT. A capsule.

The family includes about 47 genera with 1400 species, distributed throughout the tropics, chiefly in Indomalaysia.

Hedychium (50), ginger-lily, garland-flower, or torchflower, is a genus of Madagascar and Malaysia; several are cultivated ornamentals. *Curcuma* (60) ranges from tropical Asia to Australia; tubers of *C. angustifolia* yield East Indian arrowroot; *C. longa* furnishes turmeric, a yellow dye and spice; tubers of *C. zedoaria* yield zedoary, a tonic and perfume. *Globba* (100) is a native of the East Indies, China, the Philippines, and New Guinea.

Zingiber (80) is a genus of tropical and subtropical Asia; *Z. officinale* yields ginger from rhizomes, the most important spice obtained from underground parts; *Z. cassumunar* yields cassumunar ginger; *Z. zerumbet* yields zerumbet, an East Indian spice. *Elettaria cardamomum,* true cardamom, of Indonesia has seeds used as an important spice in the Orient. *Amomum* (100) is a native of the East Indies and Australia; *A. cardamon,* of Java, yields aromatic seeds used as a substitute for true cardamon. *Aframomum* (50), in tropical Africa, includes *A. melegueta,* grains of paradise, Melegueta pepper, of West Africa, the seeds used as a spice. *Alpinia* (250), of the East Indies, Japan, Australia, and Polynesia, includes *A. officinarum,* of Hainan, and *A. galanga,* of the Moluccas, which yield rhizoma galangal, used medicinally; *A. speciosa,* shellflower, a striking plant, is ornamental. *Costus* (150), of the tropics of both hemispheres, includes many cultivated ornamentals.

Cannaceae. Canna Family. This family includes 1 genus, with 60 species, regarded by most authorities as restricted to America. The flowers are perfect, epigynous, irregular; there are 3 sepals and 3 united petals. The androecium is the most conspicuous part, with 1 petal-like stamen bearing half an anther, and 1-5 petal-like staminodes, one of which is the labellum. There are 3 united carpels, with a petal-like style. The genus *Canna* is native to tropical America, but widely introduced elsewhere. The rhizome of *C. edulis,* of Central America, is edible and known as Queensland arrowroot. Garden cannas are the result of hybridization and not referable to any species, but often treated as *C. generalis.*

Marantaceae. Arrowroot Family.

HABIT. Herbaceous perennials, from rhizomes, sometimes scapose.

LEAVES. Two-ranked, sheathing, mostly basal, often with a swollen pulvinus at the junction of the blade and sheath.

INFLORESCENCE. Spicate or paniculate, subtended and surrounded by spathe-like bracts.

FLOWERS. Perfect, irregular; sepals 3; petals 3; fertile stamen 1, often petal-like, with several petal-like staminodes; carpels 3, united, inferior.

FRUIT. A capsule.

This family is composed of 26 genera with 350 species, of the tropics of both the Old and New World. Most of the genera are American. Phylogenetically this is the most highly advanced family of the order.

Calathea (130), of the New World tropics, is the largest genus in the family; *C. allouia*, topee tampo, of the West Indies, is grown for edible tubers. *Maranta* (23) is a genus of tropical America; rhizomes of *M. arundinacea* furnish West Indian arrowroot, a food for children and invalids.

Order 11. Orchidales. Most systematists have regarded the Orchidales as the most highly developed group of monocots, although Hutchinson considered the grasses to be more advanced and other botanists have proposed other views. The group is characterized by the presence of very numerous, exceedingly minute seeds with an undifferentiated embryo and with little or no endosperm.

a. Stamens 3 or more; flowers regular or nearly so . . . . . . *Burmanniaceae*
a. Stamens 1-2, flowers irregular . . . . *Orchidaceae*

Burmanniaceae. Burmannia Family. A family of chiefly non-green saprophytes, 16 genera, 125 species, of tropical and subtropical regions. Perianth-parts 6, united; stamens 3-6; carpels 3, united, inferior. *Burmannia* (50) is mostly a tropical genus, with *B. biflora* ranging north to Virginia.

Orchidaceae. Orchid Family.

HABIT. Perennial herbs, terrestrial, epiphytic, or saprophytic, the terrestrial species with thickened roots, the epiphytic often with the stem swollen at the base to form a **pseudobulb** and with aerial pendulous roots invested by a layer of water-absorbing tissue (**velamen**).

LEAVES. Alternate, rarely opposite or whorled, simple, sometimes reduced to scales, sheathing basally.

INFLORESCENCE. Spicate, racemose, or paniculate, or the flowers solitary.

FLOWERS. Usually bisexual, zygomorphic, bracteate; perianth typically of 6 parts in 2 series, the outer of 3 green or colored sepals; the inner of 3 petals, of which the middle one (**labellum**) is larger than the others, and often very complex in structure, being frequently extended basally into a spur or sac with or without nectar; stamen 1 (sometimes 2), joined to the style in a central structure, the **gynandrium** or **column**, with 1 anther and 2 fertile stigmas, a beak (**rostellum**) representing the third stigma; pollen in mealy or waxy masses (**pollinia**); adaptations for pollination by insects many and very complicated; ovary inferior.

FRUIT. A capsule, with an immense number of exceedingly minute seeds.

This is an immense family, of 450 genera with perhaps 15,000 species, one of the largest families of plants, of wide distribution over the earth, but most abundant in tropical forests, where the majority are epiphytes. In most temperate and all arctic regions the genera are terrestrial. Economically they are important primarily as ornamentals.

Apostasia (16), of the Old World tropics, differs from most orchids in having 2 fertile stamens.

Cypripedium (30), of the north temperate zone, has the labellum slipper-like, so that insects getting in and out must brush against the anthers and stigmas; *C. reginae* is showy ladyslipper, *C. acaule,* stemless ladyslipper, or moccasin flower, *C. calceolus,* yellow ladyslipper (Figure 105).

Epipactis (20), of the north temperate zone, includes *E. latifolia* and *E. palustris,* of Europe. *Listera* (30), twayblade, of the north temperate zone, includes *L. ovata,* of Europe, and *L. cordata,* of North America, Greenland, Iceland, Europe, and Japan. *Neottia* (9), distributed in temperate Eurasia, includes *N. nidus-avis,* bird's-nest orchis, a leafless saprophyte with the roots forming a nest-like mass in humus. *Spiranthes* (200), ladies-tresses, is a genus mostly of north temperate and tropical Asia and America; the inflorescence is twisted, the flowers forming a spiral. *Goodyera* (80), is a genus of the north temperate zone; *G. repens,* rattlesnake plantain, is circumboreal. *Vanilla* (50) is a genus of tropical regions; the plants are climbers with fleshy leaves; the pods of *V. fragrans,* of Mexico, yield commercial vanilla. *Ophrys* (30), north temperate, includes *O. apifera,* bee-orchis, one of few self-pollinated orchids, *O. aranifera,* spider-orchis, and *O. muscifera,* fly-orchis, all of Europe. *Orchis* (80), of Europe, Asia, North Africa, and North America, includes *O. spectabilis,* showy orchis, of eastern North America. *Habenaria* (800), rein-orchis, is very widely distributed, and is one of the largest genera in the family; it includes *H. ciliaris,* yellow fringed-orchis, *H. fimbriata,* purple fringed-orchis, and *H. blepharoglottis,* white fringed-orchis, all of eastern United States.

Liparis (300), twayblade, is a genus of tropical and temperate regions, including *L. loeselii,* circumboreal. *Malaxis* (200), adder's-mouth, of tropical and temperate regions, includes *M. unifolia,* of North America. *Corallorhiza* (15), coralroot, is native of the north temperate region; the plants are saprophytes with much-branched fleshy rhizomes. *Calypso* is a circumboreal monotypic genus (*C. bulbosa*). *Epidendrum* (800) is a genus of epiphytes of tropical and subtropical America (called *pajaritos* in Latin America); the labellum is somewhat joined to the column; many are cultivated ornamentals. *Cattleya* (40), a genus of tropical American epiphytes, includes *C. trianae,* emblematic flower of Colombia, often represented on postage stamps; these plants are the most popular and showy of florist's orchids. *Laelia* (30) is another genus of very showy epiphytes, found in tropical America. *Dendrobium* (1000) is a very large genus of epiphytes, in Japan, tropical Asia, Australia, and Polynesia; many are cultivated ornamentals, including *D. nobile,* of southeastern Asia, and *D. phalaenopsis,* of Queensland. *Bulbophyllum* (1000), another very large genus, is found in tropical Asia and Africa; the plants are epiphytes with scale leaves, photosynthesis being performed by tubers; many are cultivated. *Masdevallia* (300) is a tropical American genus; the petals are small, and the sepals have very long slender extensions.

Stanhopea (40), ranging from Mexico to Brazil, has flowers of fantastic shapes; they are epiphytes with large pendulous flowers, the labellum forming a sort of a cage; many are cultivated, including *S. oculata* and *S. tigrina,* of Mexico. *Cymbidium* (60), mostly in tropical Asia, includes many cultivated plants. *Miltonia* (20) is a genus of epiphytes ranging from Mexico to Brazil, including *M. vexillaria,* Josefita, in Colombia. *Oncidium* (350) is a genus of tropical American epiphytes, some with flat tubers collecting humus; many are cultivated, including *O. pusillum,* mariposita del totumo, of Colombia, *O. varicosum,* of Brazil, and *O. papilio,* of Venezuela. *Odontoglossum* (100) is a genus of the tropical Andes; the plants are epiphytic and, with many other epiphytic orchids of Latin America, are called "parásitas." *Aerides* (40) is a genus of southeastern Asia, from India to Japan, with fleshy leaves. *Vanda* (45), of Indomalaysia, is a genus of epiphytes with fleshy leaves; some, including *V. coerulea* and *V. teres,* are cultivated. *Angraecum* (120) is a genus of tropical Africa, Madagascar, and the Mascarenes; *A. sesquipedale,* waxflower, a curious orchid of Madagascar, has a spur (nectary) over a foot long, pollinated by a moth with a tongue equally as long.

18

Angiospermae. Dicotyledoneae. Archichlamydeae

The dicotyledons constitute the vast majority of the angiosperms, including both herbaceous and woody members. The vascular bundles are arranged in a circle about the pith and through the activity of the cambium, lying between the xylem and phloem, secondary growth is produced. The leaves are typically net-veined. The flowers have their parts typically in multiples of 4's or 5's. The embryos have 2 cotyledons.

The principal distinguishing characteristics of the various orders are given in the key below. It should be borne in mind that these are quite broad statements concerning rather diversified groups and that exceptions to the general situation are not indicated.

The sequence of orders, by the Engler-Prantl system, may be noted by reference to the chart (Figure 98). At the bottom are the Apetalae, regarded as primitive because in these orders petals had not yet been developed, although in the order Centrospermales they begin to appear. The right-hand line of evolution includes the Polypetalae (having flowers with separate petals), evolving from the hypogynous Ranales to the epigynous Umbellales. The Apetalae and Polypetalae, by this system, are grouped as the Archichlamydeae. In the center line of evolution the chart shows the Metachlamydeae (or Sympetalae) with united petals, having the Ericales, with usually hypogynous flowers, at the bottom, and the Campanulales, with epigynous flowers, at the apex.

a. Petals separate or none (Archichlamydeae)
  b. Petals usually none (except in Centrospermales) (Achlamydeae, Monochlamydeae)
    c. Ovules with numerous embryo sacs . . . . . . 1. *Casuarinales*
    c. Ovules with only one embryo sac
      d. Perianth none, or bract-like
        e. Flowers mostly perfect, in spikes; carpels 1-4, free or united . . . . 2. *Piperales*

e. Flowers imperfect, at least the staminate in catkins; carpels united (Amentiferae)
  f. Ovary superior
    g. Fruit 4-many-seeded
      h. Fruit many-seeded . . . . 3. *Salicales*
      h. Fruit 4-seeded . . . . 5. *Balanopsidales*
    g. Fruit 1-seeded
      h. Stigmas 2 . . . . 4. *Myricales*
      h. Stigma 1 . . . . 6. *Leitneriales*
  f. Ovary inferior
    g. Leaves simple . . . . 8. *Fagales*
    g. Leaves pinnately compound . . . 7. *Juglandales*

d. Perianth present, sepal-like or petal-like
  e. Ovary superior
    f. Flowers perfect or imperfect; carpel 1 . . . . 10. *Proteales*
    f. Flowers mostly perfect; carpels 2 or more, united
      g. Carpels 3; leaves usually ocreate 13. *Polygonales*
      g. Carpels 2-many; leaves not ocreate
        h. Placentation basal or free central . . . . 14. *Centrospermales*
        h. Placentation mostly at apex of locule . . . . 9. *Urticales*
  e. Ovary usually inferior
    f. Stamens opposite the perianth-parts and adnate to them; plants often partially parasitic . . . . 11. *Santalales*
    f. Stamens alternate with the perianth-parts and free from them, or numerous; plants independent or sometimes parasitic . . . . 12. *Aristolochiales*

b. Both sepals and petals present, except in a few reduced forms (Polypetalae)
  c. Ovary usually superior
    d. Flower parts all separate and distinct . . 15. *Ranales*
    d. Some whorls of flower parts united
      e. Plants insectivorous . . . . 17. *Sarraceniales*
      e. Plants not insectivorous
        f. Placentation predominantly parietal; androperianth tube absent . . . 16. *Papaverales*
        f. Placentation predominantly axile or the ovules few or solitary in a single-celled ovary; androperianth tube often present
          g. Carpels solitary, or several and distinct, or united; ovary surrounded by an androperianth tube (the flower hypogynous, perigynous or epigynous) . . . . 18. *Rosales*

g. Carpels united; androperianth tube not present
h. Stamens usually not more than twice as many as the petals.
i. Stamens alternate with the petals, or of a different number
j. Ovules pendulous, the raphe toward the axis, or erect with the raphe outward . . . . 19. *Geraniales*
j. Ovules pendulous, the raphe away from the axis, or erect or ascending . . . . 20. *Sapindales*
i. Stamens opposite the petals . . . . 21. *Rhamnales*
h. Stamens usually very numerous
i. Placentas axile; sepals valvate . . . . 22. *Malvales*
i. Placentas parietal; sepals imbricate . . . . 23. *Parietales*
c. Ovary usually inferior
d. Succulent spiny xerophytes . . . . 24. *Cactales*
d. Not succulent or spiny
e. Ovules several in each locule; flowers usually not in umbels . . . . 25. *Myrtales*
e. Ovules 1 in each locule; flowers usually in umbels . . . . 26. *Umbellales*
a. Petals more or less united (Metachlamydeae. Sympetalae)
b. Ovary usually superior
c. Stamens mostly free from the corolla . . . . . 27. *Ericales*
c. Stamens borne on the corolla, as many as its lobes and opposite them, or more
d. Stamens usually in 1 whorl . . . . 28. *Primulales*
d. Stamens usually in 2-3 whorls . . . . 29. *Ebenales*
c. Stamens borne on the corolla, as many as its lobes and alternate with them, or fewer
d. Corolla not scarious; fruit not a circumscissle capsule
e. Ovaries 2, distinct, or sometimes united; flowers regular; stamens inserted near the corolla base . . . . 30. *Gentianales*
e. Ovary 1, compound; flowers regular or irregular; stamens mostly adnate to the middle of the corolla-tube or above . . . . 31. *Tubiflorales*
d. Corolla scarious; fruit a circumscissle capsule . . . . 32. *Plantaginales*

b. Ovary inferior
  c. Anthers distinct .... 33. *Rubiales*
  c. Anthers usually united .... 34. *Campanulales*

Order 1. Casuarinales. This order includes only the family Casuarinaceae.

Casuarinaceae. Casuarina Family. A group of trees with jointed green twigs (somewhat resembling *Equisetum*), often drooping, the leaves scale-like in whorls at nodes. Flowers unisexual, the staminate in spikes, the pistillate in dense spherical heads. They differ from other angiosperms in having numerous embryo sacs in each ovule. It is an isolated group, thought by Engler to be the most primitive of dicotyledons, and related to gymnosperms. Other systematists, however, have regarded the family as more specialized. There is only 1 genus, *Casuarina* (50), distributed in Australia, New Caledonia, Malaysia, the Mascarenes. In Australia the wood, valued for its hardness, is called beefwood and she-oak; the trees are also called South-Sea ironwood, Australian pine and horsetail tree. *C. equisetifolia, C. cunninghamiana,* are common in cultivation.

Order 2. Piperales. Although regarded by Engler as related to the Amentiferae, this group is believed by present-day botanists to be derived from the Ranales.

a. Stamens 1-10
  b. Carpels 1-4, united; 1 ovule in each locule .... *Piperaceae*
  b. Carpels 3-4, free or united; 2 or more ovules in each locule .... *Saururaceae*
a. Stamens 1-3 .... *Chloranthaceae*

Saururaceae. Lizard's-Tail Family. Perennial herbs with bisexual, naked flowers; stamens usually 6-8; carpels 3-4, free or united. There are 3 genera and 4 species, mostly of moist situations. The range is markedly disjunct, indicating great antiquity for the group. *Saururus* (2), lizard's-tail, includes *S. cernuus,* of eastern North America, and *S. loureirii,* of East Asia. *Anemopsis* is a monotypic genus of California and Mexico (*A. californica,* yerba mansa).

Piperaceae. Pepper Family.

Habit. Erect or climbing herbs, shrubs, rarely trees; vascular bundles more or less scattered, as in monocotyledons; nodes jointed or swollen.

Leaves. Alternate, rarely opposite or whorled, entire, often with a pungent taste.

Inflorescence. Dense fleshy spikes, the spikes sometimes arranged in umbels.

Flowers. Naked, bisexual or unisexual; stamens 1-10; carpels 2-5, united.

Fruit. A small drupe with a single seed.

The family includes about 12 genera with perhaps 1400 species in tropical regions of both hemispheres. Some of them have considerable economic value.

Piper (700) comprises representatives in both the Old and New Worlds. *P. nigrum* of Malaya, is pepper, the most important spice imported into the United States; black pepper is made by grinding the entire dried berry with its seed (the peppercorn), while white pepper is made from the seed alone. *P. betle* is betel pepper; the fresh leaves are chewed with betel nuts (p. 264) by natives of the East Indies. *P. methysticum,* of Polynesia, yields kavakava, an intoxicating beverage made from the roots and widely used. *P. cubeba,* cubebs, of the East Indies, is used in medicine as a stimulant, expectorant, and diuretic, while the inhalation of its smoke has a soothing effect in treatment of some respiratory diseases. *Peperomia* (500) is restricted to tropical and subtropical regions; many are epiphytes, with climbing stems, fleshy leaves, and adventitious roots; some are grown in hanging pots for their ornamental foliage.

Chloranthaceae. Chloranthus Family. Herbs, shrubs, and trees of tropical and subtropical regions. Leaves opposite, flowers small, bisexual or unisexual, sometimes with a calyx-like perianth; stamens 1-3, united; carpel 1, superior. There are 3 genera and about 36 species. *Chloranthus* (10) occurs in East Asia and the East Indies; *C. inconspicuus* yields chulan, used by Chinese to perfume tea.

Order 3. Salicales. This order includes only the family Salicaceae. The orders Salicales to Fagales, inclusive, have been grouped by some botanists in the super-order **Amentiferae** (*ament-* or catkin-bearing). Later botanists do not share this belief, feeling that these orders are neither closely related nor primitive groups. There is as yet, however, no uniformity in the various treatments. The plants have compound pistils, an advanced character.

Salicaceae. Willow Family.

Habit. Trees or shrubs, or suffruticose in some arctic species.

Leaves. Deciduous, simple, alternate, stipulate.

Inflorescence. Plants dioecious; flowers in erect or pendulous catkins.

Flowers. Naked; staminate flowers with 1-2 nectariferous glands and 2-30 stamens; pistillate flowers with 1-2 nectariferous glands and 1 pistil, with 2 united carpels and 1 locule (Figure 75).

Fruit. A capsule, with numerous hairy seeds.

The family is composed of 2 genera with about 340 species, almost world-wide in distribution, but with the main center in the north temperate zone.

Salix (300), willow, is found in many parts of the world, but mainly in the north temperate zone. Unlike other catkin-bearing plants, willows are sometimes insect-pollinated and the early flowers are a good source of nectar. The species freely hybridize. Important species include S. *nigra,* black willow, eastern United States, a timber tree to 100 feet high; S. *pentandra,* bay willow, Europe, a handsome ornamental; S. *amygdalina,* almond-leaf willow, Eurasia, the twigs much used in basketry; S. *fragilis,* crack willow, Europe; S. *alba,* white willow, Mediterranean, a timber tree and an ornamental, yielding salicin, a medicinal glucoside (an ingredient of aspirin); S. *babylonica,* weeping willow, China, an ornamental tree; S. *herbacea,* Arctic willow, a creeping circumboreal shrub, seldom over 2 in. high; S. *magnifica,* western China, remarkable for its large broad leaves; S. *caprea,* goat willow, Eurasia, a common ornamental, often called pussy willow, although this name is also applied to other species as well; S. *cinerea,* gray willow, Eurasia, a common ornamental; S. *sericea,* silky willow, eastern United States; S. *humilis,* prairie willow, eastern North America; S. *hastata,* halberd-leaf willow, Europe to Siberia and Kashmir; S. *irrorata,* Colorado to Arizona; S. *viminalis,* osier, Europe to Siberia and the Himalayas, twigs used in making baskets and furniture; S. *purpurea,* purple osier, Eurasia, with purple twigs in winter; S. *bockii,* western China, flowers in autumn; S. *sitchensis,* Sitka willow, Alaska to Oregon; S. *humboldtiana,* Humboldt willow, at high elevations in the northern Andes. S. *bracteosa,* of Korea, formerly represented the monotypic genus *Chosenia,* now included under *Salix.*

Populus (40), poplar, is also a genus of the north temperate zone. The wood is soft and is used for fuel and paper pulp. Formerly the trees were much planted along avenues because of their rapid growth, but they are undesirable for city streets because the roots clog sewers. Common species are P. *alba,* white poplar, abele, Eurasia, leaves white-felted beneath, often cultivated; P. *grandidentata,* large-tooth aspen, eastern North America; P. *tremula,* European aspen, Eurasia; P. *tremuloides,* quaking aspen, North America, with leaves that quake in breezes; P. *angustifolia,* narrowleaf cottonwood, Rocky Mountains; P. *balsamifera,* balsam poplar, Canada; P. *gileadensis,* balm-of-Gilead, a horticultural form, its origin unknown; P. *trichocarpa,* black cottonwood, Alaska to California, the largest poplar in America, attaining a height of 225 feet; P. *nigra* var. *italica,* Lombardy poplar, striking for its formal columnar habit; P. *eugenei,* Carolina poplar, a common horticultural form, its origin unknown; P. *deltoides,* cottonwood, eastern North America, to 175 feet high; P. *fremontii,* alamo (poplar), the only species in the deserts of the southwestern United States.

Order 1. Myricales. The order includes only the family Myricaceae. Present-day evidence leads to the belief that these plants are related to the Hamamelidaceae.

Myricaceae. Bayberry Family. Aromatic shrubs or trees, 2 genera, 40 species, of temperate and subtropical regions. Flowers naked, unisexual, the staminate of 2-20 stamens, the pistillate of 2 united carpels. The fruit is a small drupe, often covered with a whitish waxy coating, the source of wax for bayberry candles. *Myrica* (40) includes *M. gale,* sweet gale, in bogs of western Europe, northern Asia, and temperate North America; *M. cerifera,* bayberry, source of myrtle wax; *M. californica,* Washington to California. *Comptonia asplenifolia,* of eastern North America, is sweet fern; the pistillate catkins ripen as small "burs."

Order 5. Balanopsidales. The order includes only the family Balanopsidaceae, with the single genus, *Balanops,* a group of New Caledonian trees.

Order 6. Leitneriales. The order includes only the family Leitneriaceae. Lawrence regards the order as a much-reduced relic, not a primitive group, apparently not closely related to other orders.

Leitneriaceae. Corkwood Family. Dioecious trees and shrubs, the staminate flowers naked, with 3-12 stamens, the pistillate with a scale-like perianth and 1 carpel. There is 1 genus, *Leitneria,* and 1 species, *L. floridana,* corkwood, in swamps of the southern United States. Botanically it is interesting because it produces the lightest wood grown in the United States (specific gravity, 0.21).

Order 7. Juglandales. The order includes only the family Juglandaceae. There is little agreement among systematists as to the phylogenetic position of the order, except that it is much more highly advanced than indicated by Engler's treatment. It is not closely related to the Salicales nor to the Fagales.

Juglandaceae. Walnut Family.

HABIT. Deciduous trees or shrubs.

LEAVES. Alternate, pinnately compound, aromatic, exstipulate.

INFLORESCENCE. Plants monoecious; at least the staminate flowers in catkins.

FLOWERS. Staminate flowers with a varying number of bracts, a 3-6-parted perianth, and 3-100 stamens; pistillate flowers with a number of bracts, a 4-parted perianth and 2 united, inferior carpels; ovary with 1 locule, 1 ovule, and 2 stigmas; pollinated by wind.

FRUIT. A drupe-like nut with a dehiscent or indehiscent leathery or fibrous husk (exocarp) derived from the involucre and perianth, or sometimes a winged nutlet; seed 2-4-lobed, embryo very large, endosperm none.

This is a small family of 6 genera including 60 species, mostly of the north temperate zone, but also through Central America and the Andes to Argentina and through tropical Asia to Java and New Guinea. Economically it is of major importance for wood and nuts.

Juglans (15), walnut, is a genus of valuable timber and nut trees. *J. nigra,* black walnut, is a valuable timber tree of eastern United States. *J. cinerea,* butternut, eastern United States, is of less value. *J. colombiensis,* nogal (walnut), occurs in the tropical Andes. *J. regia,* English walnut, yields valuable nuts and useful wood known as Circassian, or Persian walnut; the tree is indigenous to western Asia (not

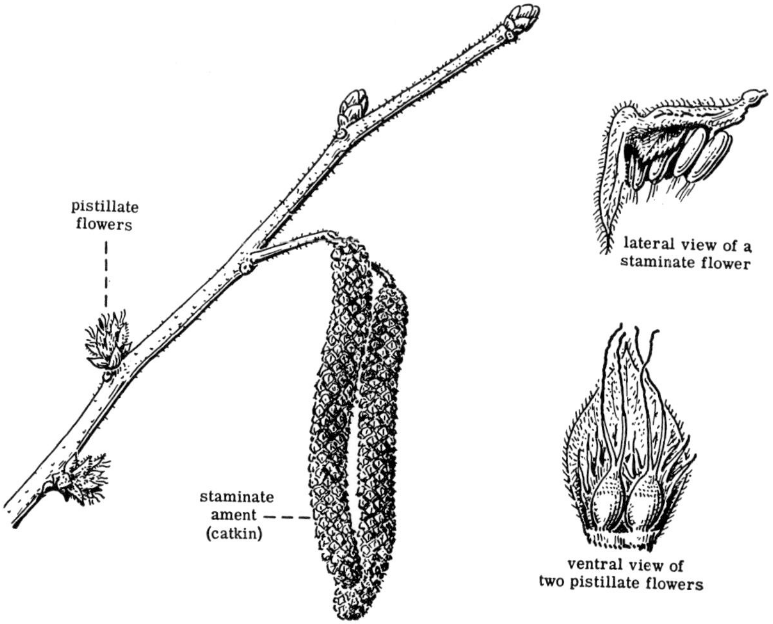

Figure 106. Flowers of hazel, *Corylus americana.*

England). *J. mandshurica* is Manchurian walnut, and *J. sieboldiana* is Japanese walnut. *Carya,* with 12 species of eastern North America and 1 of Indo-China, includes *C. ovata,* shagbark hickory, *C. laciniosa,* shellbark hickory, *C. tomentosa,* white hickory or mockernut, *C. glabra,* pignut, *C. pecan,* pecan, a valuable nut tree. *Pterocarya* (5), wingnut, ranges from Transcaucasia to eastern Asia. *Engelhardtia* includes 10 species in Indomalaysia and China and 1 in Central America; there are fossils in the United States.

Order 8. Fagales. Present-day systematists mostly agree that this order does not belong among the primitive dicots; many believe it to be related to the Hamamelidaceae.

a. Staminate and usually pistillate flowers in catkins . . . . *Betulaceae*
a. Staminate flowers in catkins, the pistillate subtended by an involucre which becomes a cup or bur in fruit . . . . *Fagaceae*

Betulaceae. Birch Family.

HABIT. Deciduous trees and shrubs.

LEAVES. Alternate, simple, stipulate.

INFLORESCENCE. Plants monoecious, both staminate and pistillate flowers in catkins.

FLOWERS. In much condensed cymules; staminate flowers naked or minutely 4-parted, stamens 1-4 in each flower (2-20 per cymule); pistillate flowers 2 or 3 in each cymule; carpels 2, united, inferior.

FRUIT. A small nut or samara, 1-celled, 1-seeded.

This is a family of shrubs and trees with 6 genera including 105 species, mostly of the northern hemisphere, but also in the tropical Andes and in Argentina. Some of them are important for hardwood lumber or for nuts.

Carpinus (20), of the north temperate zone, is a group of small trees. *C. betulus* is European hornbeam, *C. caroliniana,* American hornbeam or muscle-tree, *C. japonica,* Japanese hornbeam. *Ostrya* (7), hop-hornbeam, is a genus of small trees with hard wood (hence called ironwood), as *O. carpinifolia,* European hop-hornbeam, *O. virginiana,* American hop-hornbeam, and *O. japonica,* Japanese hop-hornbeam. *Ostryopsis* (2) is a genus of Chinese shrubs. *Corylus* (8) hazel, includes shrubs or small trees of the north temperate zone, with edible nuts; *C. tibetica,* Tibetan hazel, has fruit clusters resembling chestnut burs; *C. chinensis* is Chinese hazel; *C. americana* is American hazel (hazelnut in the United States); *C. maxima, C. avellana* and others, European hazel, filbert. *Betula* (40), a genus of the arctic and north temperate zones, includes several species of timber trees: *B. lenta,* black or sweet birch, eastern North America; *B. lutea,* yellow birch, eastern North America; *B. nigra,* river birch, eastern United States; *B. alba,* European white birch, Europe; *B. papyrifera,* canoe or paper birch, Canada. Dwarf birches of the arctic include *B. glandulosa* and *B. nana. Alnus* (20), alder, is a genus of the north temperate zone, extending south along the Andes. *A. glutinosa,* black alder, Eurasia, is used for making charcoal. *A. rugosa,* speckled alder, forms extensive swamp thickets in Eurasia and North America. *A. rubra,* red alder, is the largest of the alders, 130 feet high, the most important hardwood tree of Pacific North America. *A. ferruginea* is in the Andes of Colombia.

Fagaceae. Beech Family.

HABIT. Trees and shrubs.

LEAVES. Deciduous or evergreen, alternate, simple, stipulate.

INFLORESCENCE. Plants usually monoecious; the staminate solitary, in heads, or catkin-like racemes; pistillate solitary or few in a cluster.

FLOWERS. Staminate flowers with a 4-7-lobed perianth and 4-40 stamens; pistillate flowers solitary or in a 2-3-flowered cymule, with or without an involucre; perianth 4-6-lobed; pistil with 3-6 locules and as many styles; carpels united.

FRUIT. A 1-seeded nut.

This is a dominant family of 6 genera including 600 species, mostly of temperate and subtropical regions of the northern hemisphere; but also with 1 tropical and 1 south temperate genus. Economically the family is of great importance for its timber.

Fagus (10), beech, is distributed in the north temperate zone, including *F. grandifolia,* American beech, eastern United States, useful for clothespins; *F. sylvatica,* European beech, central and southern Europe, an important timber tree; *F. s.* var. *atropunicea,* purple or copper beech, an ornamental form with purple leaves. *Nothofagus* (16) is the beech of the southern hemisphere (see map, Figure 25), distributed in Chile, Patagonia, Tierra del Fuego, New Zealand, Tasmania, Australia, and the East Indies, forming large forests. *N. antarctica,* Chile, reaches 120 feet high; *N. cunninghami,* "myrtle tree," of Australia, is a good timber tree.

Castanea (10), chestnut, has usually 3 fruits together in a prickly involucre; the genus, characteristic of the north temperate zone, includes *C. sativa,* of the Mediterranean region, Spanish or Italian chestnut, with large edible nuts. *C. dentata,* American chestnut, was formerly an important timber and nut tree of eastern United States, but is now nearly exterminated by a blight (*Endothia parasitica*). *C. pumila,* southeastern United States, is chinquapin. *C. mollissima* is Chinese chestnut, and *C. crenata* is Japanese chestnut. *Castanopsis* has a burr like *Castanea* but the fruit requires 2 years to ripen; there are about 25 species in southeastern Asia; one species, *C. chrysophylla,* golden chinquapin, occurs in Oregon and California. *Lithocarpus* (100) is a group of evergreen trees and shrubs, mainly in southeastern Asia and Malaysia, but with 1, *L. densiflora,* tanoak, in Oregon and California; the flowers resemble those of *Castanea* but the fruit is an acorn. *Pasania* (100), of Malaya and Polynesia, is near *Quercus,* but often has 3 carpellate flowers in an involucre.

Quercus (300), of the north temperate zone and Polynesia, is the world's most important genus yielding hardwood timber. The involucre encloses only one pistillate flower, and the fruit ripens as an acorn. Representative species are *Q. phellos,* willow oak, southern United States, with lanceolate leaves; *Q. imbricaria,* shingle oak, eastern United States; *Q. falcata,* Spanish oak, southern United States; *Q. velutina,* black oak, eastern United States; *Q. kelloggii,* black oak, Oregon and California; *Q. coccinea,* scarlet oak, eastern United States, the leaves becoming scarlet in autumn; *Q. palustris,* pin oak, eastern United States; *Q. borealis,* red oak, eastern United States; *Q. aegilops,* Turkish oak, the acorns (valonia) used in tanning; *Q. cerris,* Turkey oak, an ornamental tree; *Q. coccifera,* kermes oak, Mediterranean, host of the kermes insect, which produces galls yielding red dye, the oldest known dyestuff; *Q. suber,* cork oak, Mediterranean, the source of commercial cork; *Q. ilex,* holly oak or holm oak, southern Europe, one of the hardiest of evergreen oaks;

Q. chrysolepis, California live oak; *Q. virginiana,* live oak, southeastern United States; *Q. infectoria,* Aleppo oak, western Asia and Cyprus, which produces insect galls used in ink-making; *Q. pubescens,* pubescent oak, southern Europe, western Asia; *Q. petraea,* durmast oak, Mediterranean, very valuable wood; *Q. robur,* English oak, Mediterranean; *Q. alba,* white oak, eastern United States, the most valuable oak in America; *Q. lobata,* valley oak, California; *Q. garryana,* Oregon oak, British Columbia to California; *Q. stellata,* post oak, eastern United States; *Q. macrocarpa,* burr oak, eastern North America, the acorn almost covered by a fringed cup; *Q. bicolor,* swamp white oak, eastern United States; *Q. michauxii,* basket oak, eastern United States; *Q. prinus,* chestnut oak, eastern United States; *Q. mongolica,* Mongolian oak, eastern Siberia, northern China, Korea, northern Japan; *Q. humboldtiana,* of the Colombian Andes, one of the southernmost oaks. Oak wilt has caused the destruction of many valuable timber trees in the United States.

Order 9. Urticales. This order has been variously treated by phylogenists but is now regarded by many authorities as related to and advanced over the Fagales. It is generally accepted as a natural group.

a. Fruit a samara, nut, drupe or multiple
  b. Sap not milky; fruit a samara, nut, or drupe ...... *Ulmaceae*
  b. Sap milky; fruit commonly multiple .... *Moraceae*
a. Fruit an achene
  b. Plants not aromatic, often armed with stinging hairs .. *Urticaceae*
  b. Plants aromatic, erect or twining .... *Cannabinaceae*

Ulmaceae. Elm Family.

HABIT. Trees or shrubs.

LEAVES. Simple, alternate, stipulate, often oblique at the base.

INFLORESCENCE. Solitary, cymose, or fasciculate; flowers bisexual or unisexual (the plants monoecious).

FLOWERS. Perianth of 4-8 somewhat united sepals; stamens 4-8, opposite the sepals; pistil 1, superior, of 2 united carpels, with usually 1 locule; styles 2.

FRUIT. A samara or drupe.

This family includes 15 genera with more than 150 species, tropical and temperate. It is not of major economic importance, although some species produce timber and several are grown as ornamentals.

Ulmus (30), elm, occurs mostly in the north temperate zone and on mountains of tropical Asia; the fruit is a samara. Several species produce timber or are grown ornamentally. *U. laevis* is European white elm. *U. americana,* American elm, has a wide-spreading crown, and is a valuable ornamental. *U. rubra,* slippery elm, eastern United States, produces a mucilaginous inner bark that is medicinal. *U. glabra,* Wych elm, north and central Europe and western Asia, is much cultivated; var.

camperdownii, Camperdown elm, has downwardly pointed branches. *U. campestris,* English elm, is widespread in Europe. *U. japonica,* Japanese elm, occurs in Japan and eastern Asia. *U. carpinifolia,* smooth-leaf elm, Mediterranean, has been long cultivated. *U. parvifolia,* Chinese elm, flowers in August, unlike most elms, which bloom in spring. Dutch elm disease, first discovered in Holland, has caused the destruction of many valuable trees. *Planera aquatica* is water-elm or planer-tree, of the southern United States. *Zelkova* (5) is a genus of temperate Asia, including *Z. carpinifolia,* a forest tree of the Caucasus. *Celtis* (60), hackberry, is a genus of the northern hemisphere; the fruit is a drupe. *C. occidentalis* is in eastern United States, and *C. australis,* nettle-tree, is a timber tree of the Mediterranean region.

Moraceae. Mulberry Family.

HABIT. Trees, shrubs, or herbs, with a milky juice.

LEAVES. Alternate, entire, stipulate, often lobed, evergreen or deciduous.

INFLORESCENCE. Flowers unisexual (plants monoecious or dioecious), in racemes, spikes, umbels, or heads, or on the inside of a hollow receptacle.

FLOWERS. Perianth usually of 4 sepals, free or united; stamens usually 4, opposite the sepals; pistil 1, the ovary superior or inferior, of 2 united carpels; locule and ovule usually 1; styles usually 2.

FRUIT AND SEED. Fruits basically drupes, often aggregated, sometimes united, with perianths and axes, in a multiple structure; or achenes within a fleshy receptacle.

This is a large family of 73 genera and 1000 species, mostly tropical and subtropical. It is characterized by the presence of a milky latex. Economically it is quite important for its many edible fruits.

Morus (12), mulberry, is a genus of north temperate regions; the edible fruits ripen as a mass. *M. alba,* white mulberry, of China, is grown for the leaves, fed to silkworms; *M. nigra,* black mulberry, of western Asia, is grown for its fruits. *M. rubra,* red mulberry, of eastern United States, also has edible fruits, while the timber is resistant to decay. *Maclura pomifera,* Osage-orange, bow-wood, of central United States, has the receptacle, perianths and pericarps of several flowers ripening into a large globular head; the thorny trees were formerly planted for hedges, and the wood is used for bows. *Chlorophora* (3), of tropical regions, includes *C. tinctoria,* tropical America, which yields fustic, the principal source of natural yellow pigments. *Broussonetia papyrifera,* paper mulberry, yields good fiber for paper from the inner bark, and it is widely grown throughout Polynesia for making tapa (or kapa) cloth. *Dorstenia* (80), a tropical genus, includes *D. contrayerva,* "counter-herb," an American herb yielding a drug used as a tonic and stimulant.

Artocarpus (40), of Indomalaysia, has the pericarps, perianths, and receptacle joined in a very starchy edible multiple fruit; *A. altilis,* breadfruit, is one of the important foods of the tropics; it is eaten baked, boiled, or fried; *A. heterophyllus,* jackfruit, is also eaten, often as a "poor man's bread." *Castilloa* (3), of tropical America, includes *C. elastica,* Panama rubber, formerly of some commercial importance. *Antiaris toxicaria,* the upas-tree, of Java, has extremely poisonous latex, and the tree has been the subject of fantastic legends that made its environment a desert because of the poisonous gas said to be given off by it. *Brosimum* (8), in tropical America, presents the opposite picture; the latex of *B. galactodendron,* cow-tree, milk-tree, of Venezuela, is edible (p. 75); *B. aubletii,* snakewood, is a valuable timber, the curiously streaked wood suggesting the name. *Ficus* (800) is a vast genus of tropical and subtropical regions; *F. elastica,* India, Java, is India-rubber plant, formerly a commercial source of rubber; *F. benghalensis,* East Indies, banyan, extends laterally indefinitely by aerial roots coming down from the branches and becoming trunks; *F. religiosa,* bo-tree, pipal-tree, or sacred fig, is the tree under which Gautama Buddha, at Buddh Gaya, received the heavenly light; *F. carica,* fig (Figure 88, F), western Asia, has been cultivated since prehistoric times for its edible fruits; *F. sycomorus,* sycomore, Mediterranean, also yields fruits, but inferior in quality; *F. laccifera,* India, yields shellac; *F. aurea,* strangling fig, of Florida, starts as an epiphyte, encircles its host and becomes a tree. *Cecropia* (50), in tropical America, includes *C. peltata,* trumpet-tree, which has a hollow stem occupied by fierce ants. It is an abundant tree in cut-over land in the northern Andes and one of the most distinctive trees in many areas, with conspicuous gray-green leaves.

Urticaceae. Nettle Family.

HABIT. Fibrous herbs, shrubs or small trees.

LEAVES. Alternate or opposite, simple, stipulate, sometimes with stinging hairs.

INFLORESCENCE. A cyme or head, or reduced to a solitary flower.

FLOWERS. Unisexual (the plants monoecious or dioecious), regular, minute, inconspicuous; perianth present or absent, when present of 4-5 free or united sepals; stamens mostly 4, exploding when ripe; pistil 1, of 1 carpel, the ovary superior or inferior.

FRUIT AND SEEDS. An achene or drupe.

The family includes 42 genera and 600 species, mostly tropical and subtropical. Stinging hairs are present in the first group below. Economically the plants are of slight importance.

Urtica (30), stinging nettle, includes species of temperate regions; the young tops of *U. dioica* and *U. urens,* of Eurasia, are eaten as greens. *Urera* (22) is a genus of tropical regions, with very powerful stinging hairs; the achene is enclosed in a persistent fleshy perianth, a pseudo-berry; *U. baccifera* is one of the most troublesome plants of Central American forests. *Laportea* (40) is a genus mostly of warm regions; the hairs sting severely. *L. canadensis,* wood-nettle, characterizes forests of eastern North America; *L. gigas,* nettletree, of Australia, grows to a height of 90 feet.

Pilea (200), mostly tropical, is the largest genus of the family. *P. microphylla,* artillery-plant, of tropical America, is cultivated as a curiosity; the ripe stamens explode, sending out puffs of pollen. *P. pumila,* clearweed, is common in forests of eastern North America.

Boehmeria (60) includes *B. nivea,* ramie, Chinagrass, of southeastern Asia, which yields the toughest and most silky fiber known but also the most difficult to prepare. *B. cylindrica,* false nettle, is found in eastern United States. *Parietaria* (7), pellitory, of temperate and tropical regions, has bisexual flowers, unlike other members of the family; *P. officinalis,* wall pellitory, is in Europe, and *P. pensylvanica,* in eastern North America. *Forskohlia* (5), named for a student of Linnaeus (page 66), ranges from the Mediterranean to India.

Cannabinaceae. Hemp Family. This is a small family of 2 genera with 3 species, sometimes united to the Moraceae. The plants are herbs or twining vines. The flowers are dioecious, the staminate in paniculate-racemose inflorescences, the pistillate in spikes. Sepals 5, stamens 5, carpels 2, united. *Cannabis* includes 1 species, *C. indica,* hemp, of Asia, cultivated in many temperate regions for its fiber. The resinous hairs yield hashish, which when inhaled or drunk, causes stupefaction, eroticism, and criminal fanaticism. It was long used by a sect, the Hashashīn (whence "assassins"), whose avowed purpose was to commit murder in order to enter paradise. The dried product (marijuana) may be smoked for similar effects. There are laws against its use in most countries. *Humulus* has 2 species, including *H. lupulus,* hops, Eurasia, the spikes of which are used to give flavor and sparkle to beer.

Order 10. Proteales. This order includes the single family, Proteaceae. It is generally felt that the group does not belong in the primitive position assigned it by Engler, but no agreement exists as to its proper position. Lawrence feels that it cannot be closely allied to any other known taxon.

HABIT. Trees and shrubs, rarely herbaceous.

LEAVES. Alternate, rarely opposite or whorled, simple, exstipulate.

INFLORESCENCE. A showy bracteate head, spike, or raceme.

FLOWERS. Usually bisexual, regular or irregular; perianth parts 4, united, petal-like, stamens 4, pistil 1, with 1 locule and style, the ovary superior.

FRUIT. A follicle, drupe, achene, or nut.

This is a dominant family of drier regions of the southern hemisphere, composed of 55 genera with 1200 species. About 475 species occur in South Africa and 700 in Australia. Other species occur in South America. The development of this family on lands now so widely separated from each other might be explained by the theory of continental drift (page 100). The vegetative habit is extremely variable, whence the name *Protea* (from Proteus, of Greek mythology, who readily assumed different shapes). The family is important for its ornamentals.

Protea (80) is found in South Africa, including *P. speciosa* and *P. mellifera;* the heads are showy, with colored bracts. *Leucadendron* (70) is another South African genus; *L. argenteum,* the famous silvertree has leaves covered with silvery-silky hairs, once much collected by tourists, now protected by law; the trees are grown ornamentally. Species of *Protea* and *Leucadendron* are characteristic of the maquis of Cape Colony.

Grevillea (170), of Australia, includes *G. robusta,* silky-oak, important for timber and as a shade tree; it is cultivated in the southern United States. *Hakea* (100) is a genus of Australian xerophytes with a hard woody fruit; *H. laurina,* sea-urchin, is an ornamental shrub with crimson flowers. *Roupala* (40), of the American tropics, Australia, and New Caledonia, includes *R. dariensis,* of Panama, "ratoncillo," with a skunk-like odor. *Macadamia* (5), of Australia, includes *M. ternifolia,* of eastern Australia, Queensland-nut, edible. *Guevina avellana,* of Chile, is "Chilean hazelnut"; the fruit is edible. *Telopea,* with 3 Australian species, includes *T. speciosissima,* waratah, ornamental. *Banksia* (50) is a genus of xerophytes of Australia, gorgeous-flowered shrubs of the eucalyptus forests, known as Australian honeysuckles. *Xylomelum* (4), wooden pears, in Australia, have pear-like fruits appearing edible but with woody tissue inside.

Order 11. Santalales. This order appears to be for the most part a natural taxon, but great diversity of opinion exists as to its proper phylogenetic position. Because of the presence of parasitic members, some authorities are led to the belief that it cannot be a primitive group.

a. Chlorophyll-bearing semi-parasites
  b. Ovules differentiated from the placenta
    c. Perianth-segments all alike, petaloid or sepaloid, with perigynous or epigynous disk .... *Santalaceae*
    c. Perianth-segments unlike, with distinct calyx and corolla .... *Olacaceae*
  b. Ovules usually not differentiated from the placenta; layer of viscin around seed; woody semi-parasites, usually on trees .... *Loranthaceae*
a. Non-green total parasites .... *Balanophoraceae*

Santalaceae. Sandalwood Family.

HABIT. Trees, shrubs, or herbs, some parasitic on roots or branches of trees.

LEAVES. Simple, usually opposite, entire, stipulate.

INFLORESCENCE. Usually a raceme, spike, or head, or the flowers solitary.

FLOWERS. Small, regular, bisexual or unisexual, the perianth sepaloid or petaloid, usually 4-5-lobed; stamens 4-5, opposite the perianth segments; pistil 1, with 3-5 carpels, 1 locule, 1 style, and, often, 3-5-lobed stigma; ovary inferior.

FRUIT. An achene or drupe. Seeds without testa.

This is primarily a tropical and temperate family, with 26 genera and 400 species. Economically it is of little importance.

Comandra (6), a genus of Europe and North America, includes *C. livida,* bastard toad-flax, widespread in Canada. The plants are herbaceous root-parasites. *Santalum* (17), of Indomalaysia, includes *S. album,* true sandalwood, ranging from Timor to India, valuable for its sweet-scented wood used in cabinet-making, perfumery, and so forth.

Thesium (220) is the largest genus in the family; it is especially well represented in Africa, both in Cape Colony and in the Mediterranean; 1 species extends to southeastern Asia, 1 is in Tasmania, 2 in Brazil. *Buckleya* has 4 species in eastern Asia, 1, *B. distichophylla,* in North Carolina and Tennessee. *Pyrularia* has 1 species, *P. pubera,* buffalonut or oilnut, from Pennsylvania to Georgia, and another, *P. edulis,* in the Himalayas. *Nestronia* is a monotypic genus endemic in southeastern United States.

Loranthaceae. Mistletoe Family.

HABIT. Herbs or shrubs parasitic on branches of trees, attached to the host by modified roots (haustoria), the stems branched.

LEAVES. Usually persistent, leathery, opposite or whorled, simple, entire, exstipulate.

INFLORESCENCE. A panicle, raceme, spike, or the flowers solitary.

FLOWERS. Bisexual or unisexual (the plants dioecious), green or brightly colored, small, the perianth parts in 2 series with 2 or 3 in each series, but both colored alike, the parts free or united; stamens as many as the perianth parts; pistil 1, with 1 locule; ovary inferior.

FRUIT AND SEEDS. Fruit a 2-3-seeded berry; a sticky substance (*viscin,* hence viscid, from *Viscum,* mistletoe) often surrounds the seeds; birds have difficulty in swallowing them and scrape the seeds off their beaks on tree branches, to which the seeds adhere and there germinate.

This is primarily a tropical family, with 30 genera including 1100 species. It is characterized by its usually aerial parasitic habit. It is of slight economic importance.

Nuytsia floribunda, of West Australia, differs from other members of the family in not being parasitic; it becomes a small tree. *Loranthus* (500) is the largest genus, characteristic of the Old World tropics.

Phoradendron (300) is a large genus of tropical and subtropical America, including *P. flavescens,* American mistletoe, of eastern United States. *Arceuthobium* (15), primarily American, is parasitic on conifers; *A. pusillum,* dwarf mistletoe, grows on spruce and larch in Canada, *A. oxycedri,* from the Mediterranean to the Himalayas, on *Juniperus,* and *A. minutissima,* of the Himalayas, on *Pinus excelsa. Viscum* (65) occurs mostly in Africa, but also in Europe, Asia, and Australia; *V. album,* true mistletoe, on many trees, but especially the apple, was used as a ceremonial plant by the Druids and other early Europeans, whence arose the modern custom of kissing under the mistletoe at Christmas. *V. minimum,* of South Africa, is parasitic on cactus-like plants of the genus *Euphorbia.*

Olacaceae. Malla-tree Family. A family of tropical shrubs and trees, with 25 genera including about 250 species. The flowers are small and bisexual, with a distinct calyx and corolla, and a superior ovary. *Ximenia* (12), a genus widespread in the tropics, includes *X. americana,* tallowwood, of South America, Africa, and Asia, used for carving. *Olax* (50), of the Old World tropics, includes *O. zeylanica,* malla-tree.

Balanophoraceae. Balanophora Family. This family represents the extreme of evolution in the order and comprises non-green total parasites on tree roots. They are fleshy, yellowish or reddish in color, and are nearly all tropical. Tuberous rhizomes are attached by haustoria to tree roots and from the rhizome develops the inflorescence, sometimes within it and breaking through, coming above the ground. The small flowers are unisexual, the staminate with 3-4 stamens, the pistillate with a 1-2-carpellate pistil, and an inferior ovary. There are 15 genera including about 110 species. Representative genera are *Balanophora* (70), of tropical Asia, Australia, and Polynesia; *Langsdorffia,* a monotypic genus ranging from Mexico to Brazil; and *Sarcophyte,* a monotypic genus of Cape Colony.

Order 12. Aristolochiales. It is generally felt today that this order is not as primitive as formerly believed, being simple by reduction, but there is lack of agreement as to its proper position.

a. Non-parasitic herbs or shrubs .... *Aristolochiaceae*
a. Parasitic herbs .... *Rafflesiaceae*

Aristolochiaceae. Birthwort Family.

HABIT. Low herbs, or woody, often climbing shrubs.

LEAVES. Alternate, simple, entire, exstipulate.

INFLORESCENCE. Axillary clusters or racemes, or the flowers solitary.

FLOWERS. Bisexual, regular or irregular; perianth of 3 petal-like, united sepals; stamens 6-36, free, or united to the style to form a **gynostemium;** pistil 1, of 4-6 united carpels, and 4-6 locules, the ovary inferior.

FRUIT. A capsule.

This is primarily a tropical family, although with a few temperate-zone representatives. There are 6 genera and about 400 species.

Asarum (60), of north temperate regions, is a genus of perennial herbs, self-pollinated (not by flies, as often claimed); *A. europaeum* is asarabaca, *A. canadense,* eastern North America, is wild ginger. *Aristolochia* (300) is the largest genus, an essentially tropical group of perennial herbs or twining shrubs. The curiously shaped irregular flowers are sometimes ornamental, as in *A. gigas,* pelican-flower. *A. clematitis,* birthwort, of Europe, was formerly used in medicine by midwives. *A. durior,* eastern North America, is Dutchman's pipe, or pipevine, climbing high into trees. *A. serpentaria,* eastern United States, is Virginia snakeroot, medicinal.

Rafflesiaceae. Rafflesia Family. A group of herbs parasitic on roots in tropical forests. The vegetative organs are reduced essentially to a mycelium, with a network of fine threads ramifying in the host tissue. The flowers are produced above ground, as adventitious shoots from the mycelium; they are unisexual, regular, from minute to very large; the perianth is 4-5-parted, the staminate flowers with numerous stamens, the pistillate with 4, 6, or 8 carpels, with an inferior ovary. *Rafflesia* (13) is a genus of Indomalaysia, parasitic on *Cissus; R. arnoldi* has flowers 18-36 inches across, weighing up to 20 pounds, the largest flowers known (page 83; figure 20). *Pilostyles* (20) occurs in Africa, Iran, and Mexico and southwestern United States.

Order 13. Polygonales. This order includes only the family Polygonaceae. It is generally believed that it is derived by reduction from the Centrospermales.

Polygonaceae. Buckwheat Family.

HABIT. Herbs, shrubs, or trees, sometimes twining; stems with swollen nodes.

LEAVES. Alternate, simple, usually with a stipular growth (ocrea) sheathing the stem at the base of the petiole (Figure 59).

INFLORESCENCE. Racemose, paniculate, spicate, or capitate.

FLOWERS. Usually bisexual, regular; perianth of 3, 4, 5, or 6 sepals; stamens 6-9; pistil 1, of 2, 3, or 4 carpels, 1 locule, and 2-4 stigmas; ovary superior.

FRUIT AND SEED. Fruit an achene, compressed or triangular, the seed with a copious mealy endosperm.

The family is characterized in general by swollen nodes, sheathing stipules, and a pungent acid juice. It is composed of 32 genera and 800 species, mostly of the north temperate zone. A few are important for food, some are ornamental and a number are noxious weeds.

Rumex (100) is a large genus, north temperate in distribution. The 3 inner sepals become enlarged on the fruit and often bear tubercles. *R. acetosa,* garden sorrel, is circumboreal. *R. acetosella,* sheep sorrel, a common and now cosmopolitan weed, is native of Europe. *R. crispus, R. obtusifolius,* and *R. conglomeratus,* dock, of Europe, are coarse weeds, the young shoots used as greens. *R. patientia* is patience dock, of Eurasia. *R. abyssinicus* is spinach-rhubarb. *R. hymenosepalus,* tanner's dock, yields canaigre, used in tanning. *Rheum* (40) is characteristic of temperate and subtropical Asia; *R. rhaponticum,* rhubarb, pieplant, is native of Central Asia; it is widely cultivated for the edible petioles; *R. officinale,* of Tibet and China, is medicinal. *Oxyria* has 2 species, 1 in the Himalayas, the other, *O. digyna,* mountain-sorrel, circumboreal and alpine. *Koenigia* is a remarkable genus, being monotypic and bipolar; *K. islandica* occurs in the Arctic, in the Himalayas, and in Tierra del Fuego. *Polygonum* (200) is the largest genus in the family, consisting of cosmopolitan herbs, including many weeds. *P. aviculare* is knotweed, a common weed. *P. viviparum,* bistort, is arctic and alpine; it often bears bulblets in place of flowers. *P. cuspidatum* and *P. sachalinense,* of eastern Asia, are soft-wooded shrubs. *P. convolvulus,* of Europe, black bindweed, is a common climbing weed. *P. orientale,* India, prince's feather, is grown as an ornamental. *P. hydropiper,* of Europe and North America, is waterpepper, and *P. acre,* of tropical and temperate America, is water smartweed. *P. sagittatum,* of Asia and North America, is tearthumb, the stems armed with saw-toothed prickles (Figure 64). *P. amphibium,* of Eurasia and North America, is amphibious. *Fagopyrum* (4), an Asiatic genus, includes *F. sagittatum,* buckwheat (cognate with *Buchweizen,* "beech-wheat," the grains shaped like beech-nuts), much grown for food, also a good honey plant.

Coccoloba (125), of tropical and subtropical America, includes *C. uvifera,* seagrape, of tropical beaches, with edible fruits. *Muehlenbeckia* (15), a genus of South America, New Zealand, and Australia, includes plants common in alkali swamps of the Mulga desert; *M. platyclados,* centipede plant, a vine of the Solomon Islands, has flat green phylloclades with transverse bands, often grown as a curiosity. *Antigonum* (4), of Mexico and Central America, includes *A. leptopus,* coralvine, grown for its pink flowers. *Triplaris* (12), of tropical America, includes *T. americana,* a myrmecophyte (that is, harboring ants in its hollow stems).

Eriogonum (170) is a large genus, mostly of arid regions in the western United States; it is one of the few genera which do not have ocreae; *E. alleni,* yellow buckwheat, is an endemic species on Appalachian shale barrens.

Order 14. Centrospermales. This order, regarded today as derived from ranalian ancestors, is in general characterized by basal or free-central placentation, to which the name makes reference.

a. Perianth bract-like
  b. Flowers bractless, or if bracted, the bracts not scarious; sepals green . . . . *Chenopodiaceae*
  b. Flowers bracted, the bracts and sepals mostly scarious . . . . *Amaranthaceae*
a. Perianth not bract-like
  b. Perianth not differentiated into calyx and corolla.
    c. Perianth-parts 5, united; carpel 1 . . . . *Nyctaginaceae*
    c. Perianth-parts 4-5, free or united; carpels usually more than 1, united
      d. Leaves thread-like or fleshy . . . . *Aizoaceae*
      d. Leaves neither thread-like nor fleshy . . . . *Phytolaccaceae*
  b. Perianth differentiated into calyx and corolla
    c. Sepals 2, petals 4-5
      d. Herbs or undershrubs; leaves fleshy . . . . *Portulacaceae*
      d. Twining herbs . . . . *Basellaceae*
    c. Sepals and petals 5, or petals sometimes none . . *Caryophyllaceae*

Chenopodiaceae. Goosefoot Family.

Habit. Annual or perennial herbs, shrubs, or rarely small trees, sometimes with fleshy jointed nearly leafless stems.

Leaves. Usually alternate, simple, sometimes very fleshy and terete or reduced to mere scales.

Inflorescence. Cymose, often bracteate.

Flowers. Bisexual or unisexual (the plants dioecious); perianth typically of 5 small united sepals, usually persistent in fruit; stamens as many as the calyx lobes and opposite them; pistil 1, with 2-3 carpels, 1-3 styles, and 1 locule; ovary superior or inferior.

Fruit. A nut or achene.

This is a family of 102 genera including 1400 species, cosmopolitan in distribution but centering in xerophytic and halophytic areas such as the Mulga of Australia, the pampas of Argentina, the alkali plains of southwestern United States, the shores of the Mediterranean, Caspian, and Red Seas, the steppes of Central Asia, and the South African Karroo. The family is of minor importance economically.

Chenopodium (100), goosefoot, of temperate regions, is perhaps the largest genus. *C. album,* lamb's quarters, is native to western Asia, but now a cosmopolitan weed. *C. quinoa,* quinoa, is a staple food of thousands of people of the high Andes; the seeds are cooked like rice. *C. bonus-henricus,* Good King Henry, is a common weed of Europe, sometimes used for greens. *C. ambrosioides,* tropical America, Mexican tea or wormseed, yields a vermifuge. *C. capitatum,* Europe and North America, is strawberry-blite, the ripe calyx becoming red. *C. botrys,* Europe, Jerusalem-oak or feather-geranium, is a widespread weed. *Eurotia* (2) includes *E. lanata,* winter fat, valuable winter forage in the Great Basin. *Atriplex* (100), orach, is a genus of temperate and tropical regions; *A. patula* is found in Europe and North America; several species, as *A. canescens,* wingscale, chamiso, *A. hymenelytra,* desert holly, are in southwestern U. S. deserts and some are members of the Australian salt-bush. *Spinacia* (3) is a genus of western and central Asia; *S. oleracea,* spinach, is widely grown for greens. *Kochia* (80) is found mostly in Australia; some species are ornamental, as summer cypress or belvedere; some constitute the "bluebush" of Australia's Mulga formation. *Beta* (12) is characteristic of the Mediterranean; unlike most of the family, its ovary is inferior; *B. vulgaris* is cultivated garden beet, also sugar beet, mangels, and Swiss chard; *B. perennis,* strand beet, occurs on coasts from the Atlantic through the Mediterranean. *Corispermum* (50), of southern Europe and Asia, is bugseed.

Salicornia (30), glasswort, samphire, is a group of succulent leafless herbs with jointed stems, on seacoasts; *S. herbacea* is widespread. *Sarcobatus* (2), of western North America, includes *S. vermiculatus,* greasewood, characteristic of alkali flats. *Suaeda* (100) is cosmopolitan on sea coasts and salt steppes; the plants are herbs with fleshy stems; *S. maritima,* sea-blite, is widespread. *Allenrolfea occidentalis,* iodine bush, is abundant in alkali deserts of southwestern U. S. *Salsola* (100) is also cosmopolitan in maritime situations or on salt steppes; *S. kali* is saltwort. *S. tragus,* Russian thistle, is a widespread weed of semi-arid lands of Eurasia and North America. *Haloxylon* (10) is a genus of the Mediterranean and Central Asia; *H. persicum,* from Iran to Mongolia, is saxual, a small tree, apparently leafless, characteristic of Turanian and Mongolian deserts. *Anabasis* (6), desert cauliflower, ranging from the Mediterranean to Central Asia, grows in dense tussocks or cushions in the Sahara, very characteristic. *Halogeton* (5), Central Asia, is halophytic; *H. glomeratus* was first noted in the United States (Great Basin) in 1936; it is very aggressive and causes great losses by poisoning livestock.

Amaranthaceae. Amaranth Family.

HABIT. Annual or perennial herbs, shrubs, trees, or vines.

LEAVES. Alternate or opposite, simple, usually entire, without stipules.

INFLORESCENCE. Flowers solitary, or in racemes or spikes, bracteate.

FLOWERS. Bisexual or unisexual (the plants polygamo-dioecious or dioecious); perianth of 3-5 free or united sepals; stamens usually 5, opposite the sepals; pistil 1, with 2-3 carpels, 1 locule and 1-3 styles, the ovary superior.

FRUIT. A utricle or nutlet, less frequently a berry, drupe, or circumscissle capsule.

The family is characterized by the presence of scarious bracts and a congested inflorescence. It is composed of 64 genera and 800 species, best represented in tropical regions, particularly of America and Africa. Economically it is of little importance.

Celosia (60), of tropical America and Africa, includes *C. aristata,* cockscomb, a cultivated ornamental, with hereditary fasciations. *Amaranthus* (60), of tropical and temperate regions, includes some cultivated ornamentals with colored leaves as love-lies-bleeding, Joseph's coat, and prince's feather; there are also many noxious weeds, as *A. retroflexus,* pigweed, tropical America, and *A. graecizans,* tumbleweed, North America. *A. caudatus,* jataco, achita, or quihuicha, of the Andes, has edible grains. *A. cruentus* and *A. frumentacea* are cultivated as cereals in tropical Asia by primitive tribes. *Ptilotus* (100) in Australia, is very characteristic, with colored sepals. *Charpentiera* (3), of Hawaii and Polynesia, is of interest because it includes trees up to 35 feet high. *Alternanthera* (170) is a genus mostly of tropical Asia; some species are cultivated for ornamental leaves. *Gomphrena* (100), globe amaranth, is a genus of tropical America; some members are cultivated for ornamental foliage. *Iresine* (70) is distributed in tropical and subtropical America; some species are noxious weeds and some (bloodleaf, Juba's bush) are grown for their deep-red leaves.

Basellaceae. Basella Family. A small family of mostly climbing herbs of tropical Africa, Asia, and America. A rhizome or tuber produces annually the climbing shoot. The flowers are often brightly colored. There are 2 sepals, 5 petals, 5 stamens, 3 united carpels, with a superior ovary. The family includes 4 genera with 20 species. *Basella* (3) is a genus of Africa and Asia; *B. indica,* Malabar-nightshade, is cultivated for the leaves, used as greens. *Ullucus tuberosus,* ullucos, of the high Andes of Colombia, Ecuador, Peru, and Bolivia, has lateral branches of rhizomes which swell into tubers like little potatoes, and are grown for food. *Boussingaultia* (14), of tropical Asia, includes *B. gracilis,* the Madeira-vine or mignonette-vine, Bermuda to Argentina; it has edible tubers, and is grown as an ornamental for the fragrant white flowers.

Phytolaccaceae. Pokeweed Family.

Habit. Herbs, shrubs, or trees, sometimes lianas.

Leaves. Alternate, simple, entire.

Inflorescence. Cymose or racemose.

Flowers. Usually bisexual, regular, small; perianth of 4-5 sepals, usually somewhat united; stamens 3-many; gynoecium of 1-16 distinct or united carpels, the ovary superior.

Fruit. A berry, drupe, schizocarp, utricle, or achene.

The family includes about 17 genera and 125 species, chiefly of the American tropics and subtropics. Economically it is of little importance.

Rivina (3), pigeonberry or rouge-plant, is distributed in tropical America; *R. humilis* is grown for the ornamental red berries. *Phytolacca* (35) is the largest genus; *P. octandra*, of Japan, has 8 stamens, whereas *P. americana* (*decandra*), pokeweed, of eastern United States, has 10; the young shoots are used as greens. *P. dioica*, ombu, is a solitary, umbrella-like tree of the pampas, very distinctive.

Nyctaginaceae. Four-o'clock Family.

HABIT. Herbs, shrubs, or trees.

LEAVES. Usually opposite, simple, entire, without stipules.

INFLORESCENCE. Cymose, usually with 1-5 leaf-like, often brightly colored bracts subtending each flower.

FLOWERS. Bisexual (rarely unisexual), regular; perianth of 5 united petal-like sepals (appearing like a corolla, since the bracts resemble sepals); stamens 1-30, usually 5; pistil 1, with 1 carpel and a superior ovary.

FRUIT. An achene.

The family includes 28 genera and 250 species, mostly of the tropics and subtropics. The plants are distinguished by the often colored sepal-like bracts and the petal-like calyx. It cannot be easily determined without microscopical examination that the calyx is not a corolla and therefore they are often erroneously keyed out among the Sympetalae. They are of little value except as ornamentals.

Mirabilis (60) is found in tropical Asia and America. *M. jalapa*, four-o'clocks, marvel of Peru, has flowers opening about 4 o'clock in the afternoon; the roots were formerly used as a source of the drug jalap. *Boerhaavia* (20), a tropical genus, includes *B. diffusa*, pantropical; some species are used medicinally. *Abronia* (33), mostly of southwestern North America, includes the sand-verbena, of deserts. *Bougainvillea* (13), of South America, has groups of 3 flowers each surrounded by 3 lilac or red persistent bracts; *B. spectabilis* is a widely cultivated ornamental vine. *Pisonia* (30) is a pantropical genus; *P. aculeata*, bagh-anchrha, is a straggling spiny shrub used for hedges in India. *Reichenbachia* is a monotypic genus of southern Brazil and Paraguay; the fruits have grappling hairs that adhere to animals. *Nyctaginea* is a monotypic genus of Texas and Mexico.

Aizoaceae. Carpetweed Family.

HABIT. Annual or perennial herbs or low shrubs, often xerophytic.

LEAVES. Alternate, opposite, or whorled, fleshy or scale-like.

INFLORESCENCE. Cymose, or the flowers solitary.

FLOWERS. Bisexual, regular; perianth of 5-8 united sepals; stamens 3-5 or indefinite, the outermost often sterile and petal-like (staminodes), resembling the rays of composites; pistil 1, of 3-5 carpels, 1-5 locules, and 2-20 stigmas; ovary superior or inferior.

FRUIT. A capsule.

This is a large family of 100 genera including perhaps 1100 species, particularly of South Africa, usually characterized by fleshy leaves. They are of little economic value except as ornamentals.

Mesembryanthemum (800) is the largest genus, comprising distinctive plants of South Africa; they are xerophytes of the most pronounced sort and the plants often assume fantastic shapes. The fruit of *M. edule,* Hottentot-fig, is edible. In *M. crystallinum,* iceplant, the leaves are densely coated with small glistening bladder-shaped hairs; it is grown as an oddity. *M. multiradiatum* is much planted in California and elsewhere. *Sesuvium portulacastrum,* sea-purslane, is a tropical seacoast halophyte. *Tetragonia* (50), of Chile, Cape Colony, Australia, and New Zea-

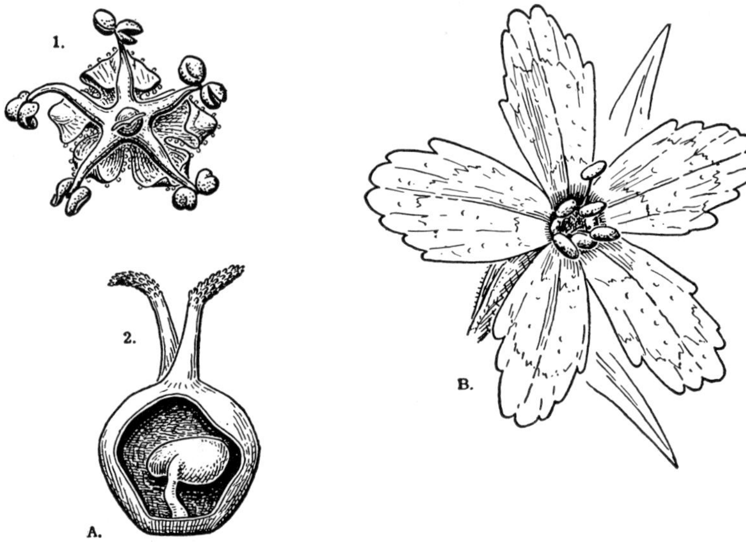

Figure 107. ***A,*** **goosefoot,** ***Chenopodium; 1,*** **flower,** ***2,*** **utricle, sectioned showing single seed with basal placentation;** ***B,*** **flower of a pink,** ***Dianthus armeria.***

land, includes *T. expansa,* New Zealand spinach, used as greens. *Mollugo* (12), a widely distributed genus, includes *M. verticillata,* carpetweed, of warm regions of America. *Aizoon* (3) occurs in Africa and Australia.

Caryophyllaceae. Pink Family.

Habit. Annual or perennial herbs, the stems typically with swollen nodes.

Leaves. Opposite, simple, mostly narrow.

Inflorescence. Cymose, or the flowers solitary.

Flowers. Bisexual, regular, perfect, the perianth of 2 series; calyx typically of 5 sepals, distinct or united into a tube (Figure 78); corolla typically of 5 petals, often notched or "pinked" (whence the English name of the family); stamens usually either the same number as the petals or twice as many; pistil 1, with 2-5 carpels, usually 1 locule, and 2-5 styles, the ovary superior; placentation free-central (Figure 81).

FRUIT. A capsule or an achene.

This is a large family of about 80 genera including 1800 species, primarily in the north temperate regions, but with a few characteristic of south temperate lands and tropical mountains; the Mediterranean area is the chief center. They are distinguished by their opposite leaves, free-central placentas, and notched petals (Figure 107, B). Many are grown as ornamentals. The older theory of the origin of the family claimed that it was derived from the Phytolaccaceae, by evolution of petals from the outer whorl of stamens. Later theories consider the family as derived from ranalian ancestors, giving rise by reduction to the amaranths and chenopods.

Corrigiola (10) is a genus of Europe, Africa, and the Andes. *Siphonychia* includes 7 species of southern United States. *Paronychia* (40), of temperate and tropical Europe, Africa, and America, includes *P. canadensis,* whitlow-wort, eastern United States. *Herniaria* (20) is a genus of the Mediterranean region, including *H. glabra,* rupturewort. *Scleranthus* (10), of Europe, Asia, Africa, and Australia, includes *S. annuus,* knawel.

Drymaria (70) is a genus of tropical and south temperate lands. *Holosteum* (6), jagged chickweed, is found in Europe and Asia. *Stellaria* (100), of widespread distribution, includes many common weeds, as *S. media,* chickweed. *Cerastium* (100), a genus of the north temperate region, includes many common weeds, as *C. vulgatum,* mouse-ear chickweed. *Spergula* (5), of temperate regions, includes *S. arvensis,* spurry, of Europe, now a nearly cosmopolitan weed. *Spergularia* (25) includes many widespread weeds, as *S. campestris,* sand spurry; *S. marina* is halophytic, in North America and Eurasia. *Arenaria* (160) is a genus of the north temperate zone, typically of sandy soil; *A. serpyllifolia,* sandwort, Europe, is now widespread. *Sagina* (25), of the north temperate zone with disjunct areas in the Himalayas and Andes, includes *S. procumbens,* pearlwort, of Eurasia and North America. *Colobanthus* (15) is a genus of south temperate lands; *C. crassifolia,* of subantarctic South America, Falkland Islands and South Georgia, is one of the southernmost of phanerogams. *Polycarpon* (7) is a cosmopolitan genus, including *P. tetraphyllum,* polycarp, or all-seed.

Agrostemma githago, corn-cockle, of Europe, is now a common weed in grainfields. *Lychnis* (10), of Europe and Asia, includes some cultivated ornamentals and some weeds, such as *L. chalcedonica,* Maltese cross; *L. flos-cuculi,* cuckoo-flower, ragged robin; *L. flos-jovis,* flower-of-Jove; *L. coeli-rosa,* rose-of-heaven; *L. coronaria,* mullein pink; *L. dioica,* red campion. *Silene* (400), campion, is the largest genus, mainly of the north temperate zone, especially in the Mediterranean, but also in Asia,

Africa, America, and Hawaii; *S. acaulis,* moss campion, is circumboreal; *S. virginica,* eastern United States, is fire-pink or catchfly; *S. noctiflora,* Europe, is night-flowering catchfly.

Gypsophila (90), of Europe and Asia, is characteristic of chalk outcrops; *G. paniculata,* baby's-breath, is a cultivated ornamental. *Dianthus* (300) is a large genus of Europe, Asia, and Africa; many are cultivated ornamentals, as *D. caryophyllus,* carnation, *D. chinensis,* Chinese pinks, *D. barbatus,* sweet william, *D. plumarius,* grass pinks. *Saponaria* (40), mostly of the Mediterranean, includes plants the juice of which forms a lather with water; *S. officinalis,* soapwort or bouncing Bet, is a widespread weed.

Portulacaceae. Purslane Family.

HABIT. Annual or perennial herbs.

LEAVES. Alternate or opposite, often fleshy, simple, usually stipulate.

INFLORESCENCE. Cymose, racemose, or the flowers solitary.

FLOWERS. Bisexual, regular, showy, the perianth of 2 series; calyx of 2 sepals; corolla of 4-6 petals; stamens as many as the petals or 2-4 times as many; pistil 1, with 2-3 carpels, 1 locule, and 2-5 styles, the ovary superior.

FRUIT. A capsule.

This is a family of 16 genera including 500 species, more or less cosmopolitan, but with 1 main center of distribution in western United States and 1 in southern South America. The plants are important chiefly as ornamentals.

Lewisia (15) is a genus of western North America; *L. rediviva,* bitterroot, has thick rhizomes and roots, with fleshy leaves, and survives over a year of drying; it is the state flower of Montana. *Portulaca* (100) is a group mostly of tropical and subtropical regions; *P. oleracea,* purslane, is a widespread weed; *P. grandiflora,* of Argentina, is garden portulaca or rose moss, an ornamental. *Calandrinia* (150), red maids, ranges from British Columbia to Tierra del Fuego and Australia, especially common in Chile. *Montia* (5), of temperate regions, includes *M. fontana,* blinks, or winter purslane, of Eurasia and North America. *Claytonia* (28) is a genus of north temperate and Arctic regions; *C. virginica,* spring beauty, is in eastern North America (p. 68).

19

Angiospermae. Dicotyledoneae. Archichlamydeae (cont.)

Order 15. Ranales. As mentioned previously in this work, the Ranales are thought by most systematists to represent some of the most primitive living angiosperms. The flower parts are numerous and distinct, mostly spirally arranged, and in general the perianth is not differentiated into calyx and corolla. A well-known theory suggests that they have been derived from the Bennettitales among the gymnosperms and that most other living angiosperms have descended from ancient ranalian stock (see page 231).

a. Aquatics
  b. Perianth absent; carpel 1; leaves finely dissected . . *Ceratophyllaceae*
  b. Perianth present; carpels usually numerous; leaves large . . . . *Nymphaeaceae*
a. Mostly terrestrial
  b. Oil cells absent
    c. Climbing shrubs
      d. Fruit a berry . . . . *Lardizabalaceae*
      d. Fruit a drupe . . . . *Menispermaceae*
    c. Erect shrubs or herbs
      d. Usually herbs; leaves often divided; carpels 1-many; fruit a follicle or achene . . . . . . *Ranunculaceae*
      d. Herbs or shrubs; leaves simple or compound; carpel usually 1; fruit a berry or capsule . . *Berberidaceae*
  b. Oil cells present
    c. Leaves alternate
      d. Flowers 3-merous . . . . *Annonaceae*
      d. Flowers not 3-merous
        e. Leaves simple, evergreen; flowers unisexual; seed arillate . . . . *Myristicaceae*
        e. Seed usually not arillate
          f. Fruit partially enclosed in a hollowed axis; leaves leathery; carpels 3, united . . *Lauraceae*
          f. Fruit not enclosed in the axis

g. Fruit winged .... *Hernandiaceae*
g. Fruit not winged
h. Stipules none
i. Carpel solitary, open along the ventral suture when young .. *Degeneriaceae*
i. Carpels usually more than 1, not open when young
j. Climbing or scrambling ... *Schisandraceae*
j. Not climbing .... *Winteraceae*
h. Stipules present .... *Magnoliaceae*
d. Leaves opposite
e. Flowers perfect .... *Calycanthaceae*
e. Flowers imperfect .... *Monimiaceae*

Ceratophyllaceae. Hornwort Family. A cosmopolitan family of floating water plants with 1 genus and 3 species. Plants monoecious, with sepaloid perianth; staminate flowers with about 12 sepals and 12-16 stamens; pistillate flowers with 9-10 sepals and 1 carpel; water-pollinated. *Ceratophyllum demersum* is hornwort, common in ponds and lakes, important as a shelter for aquatic animals.

Nymphaeaceae. Waterlily Family.

HABIT. Aquatic perennial (or annual) herbs with creeping or erect rhizomes.

LEAVES. Alternate, immersed, emersed, or floating, usually long-petioled, often peltate.

INFLORESCENCE. Flowers solitary.

FLOWERS. Bisexual, regular, often fragrant; sepals 3, 4, 5, or indefinite, petals 3 to indefinite, usually showy, the innermost "petals" sometimes really staminodes; stamens 3-6 or indefinite; carpels 3 to many, separate or united.

FRUIT. A follicle or berry, or aggregate.

The family includes 8 genera and about 90 species, in fresh waters of most parts of the earth, distinguished by its aquatic habit, long-petioled leaves, and long-peduncled flowers. They are of value primarily as ornamental plants of ponds.

Nelumbo includes 2 species, *N. lutea,* the yellow waterlily or lotus of eastern United States, and *N. nucifera,* sacred lotus, in tropical and subtropical Asia; it is sacred in India, Tibet and China. *Nymphaea* (7), of north temperate regions, includes *N. tuberosa,* white waterlily, in eastern United States. *Nuphar* (40) is a genus of tropical and temperate regions; *N. advena,* eastern United States, is cow-lily or spatter-dock. *Victoria* (3), is in the Amazon Valley; *V. amazonica,* giant waterlily, has floating leaves 6 feet across, turned up at the edges. *Cabomba* (4), fish-grass, occurs in warm parts of America; the leaves are much divided and submerged. *Brasenia schreberi,* water-shield, in North America, Asia, Africa, and Australia, has peltate leaves.

Ranunculaceae. Buttercup Family.

HABIT. Annual or perennial herbs, sometimes vines or shrubs.

LEAVES. Mostly alternate, usually palmately compound, without stipules.

INFLORESCENCE. Cymose, racemose, or paniculate, or the flowers solitary.

FLOWERS. Usually bisexual, regular or sometimes irregular; perianth generally colored, often composed of sepals alone, sometimes of sepals and petals both, the segments distinct and free; stamens usually many, distinct; carpels 3 to many, distinct, ovules 1 to many.

FRUIT. A follicle, berry, or achene.

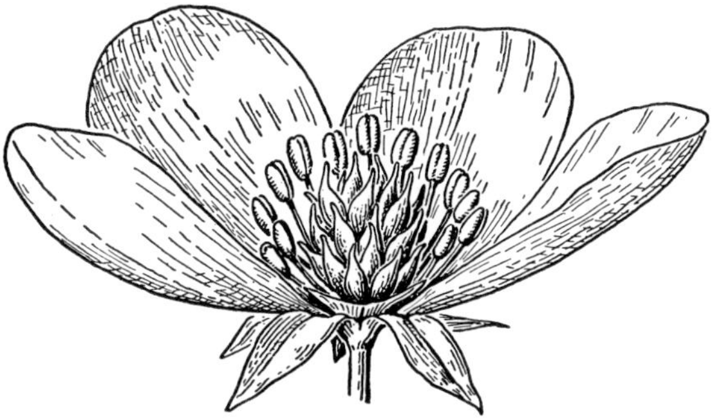

Figure 108. Flower of buttercup, *Ranunculus;* most of one petal and several stamens cut away to show the gynoecium.

A fairly large family, principally of the north temperate zone but also in the south temperate region, of about 35 genera including 1500 species. It is now generally recognized as among the most primitive of dicotyledons, because of the free and distinct flower parts (Figure 108). Economically the plants are most important as ornamentals.

Paeonia (30), of Europe and Asia, includes *P. officinalis,* peony, a cultivated ornamental, and *P. suffruticosa,* "tree" peony, of China and Japan.

Helleborus (22), is a genus of southern Europe; *H. niger,* Christmas-rose, and *H. viridis,* hellebore, are winter-blooming ornamentals. *Eranthis* (7) is distributed in the Mediterranean region; *E. hyemalis,* winter aconite, is an ornamental blooming in February. *Actaea* (12) is a genus of the north temperate region; the flowers have but 1 carpel, unlike most members of the family; *A. spicata,* Eurasia, *A. rubra, A. alba,* both of North America, are baneberries. *Xanthorhiza simplicissima,* of the Appalachians, is shrub yellowroot. *Aquilegia* (50), columbine, has petals with long spurs secreting nectar; it occurs mainly in the north temperate region. *A. vulgaris,* of Europe, is a cultivated ornamental; *A. canadensis* is found in eastern North America, *A. caerulea* is in the Rocky Mountains, the floral emblem of Colorado. *Caltha* (16), of the north temperate zone, includes *C. palustris*, marsh marigold, eastern North America. *Trollius* (12) is found in North America and Eurasia; *T. europaeus*, globe flower, is distributed from Central Europe to Siberia. *Aconitum* (75) is mostly north temperate; all the species contain a poisonous alkaloid, aconitin; *A. ferox* is Bikh poison, of Nepal; *A. uncinatum* is monk's-hood, of eastern United States; *A. napellus*, of Europe, is wolfbane, or aconite. *Delphinium* (200), of north temperate regions, has an irregular flower, with nectar in the single spur. *D. consolida*, field larkspur, is a native of the Mediterranean region. *D. ajacis*, rocket larkspur, of Europe, is a cultivated ornamental. *D. tricorne*, dwarf larkspur, is a spring flower of eastern United States. *D. grandiflorum*, bouquet larkspur, is a native of Siberia and China; many garden forms have been developed from it. *Nigella* (16) differs from most members of the family in having the carpels partly united, to form a several-celled capsule; a genus of the Mediterranean region, it includes *N. damascena*, love-in-a-mist, fennel flower, a cultivated ornamental.

Ranunculus (300) is the largest genus, distributed in the Arctic, north temperate, and alpine regions, also in the Andes and subantarctic South America and New Zealand. Unlike many members of the family, there is a well-marked calyx and corolla. *R. ficaria*, Eurasia, is lesser celandine; *R. aquatilis*, Europe, white water crowfoot; *R. cymbalaria*, Greenland, Eurasia, seaside crowfoot; *R. scleratus*, cursed crowfoot, North America and Europe; *R. abortivus*, eastern United States, small crowfoot; *R. repens*, North America, Europe, creeping buttercup; *R. acris*, tall buttercup, Europe, North America. *Myosurus* (7) is a genus of north and south temperate regions; *M. minimus*, Europe, North America, is mousetail. *Adonis* (25) includes plants of the Mediterranean region; *A. autumnalis*, Europe, is pheasant's eye.

Anemone (100) is a genus mostly of the north temperate zone and the Andes; several are cultivated ornamentals: *A. hepatica*, Europe; *A. nemorosa*, Europe; *A. ranunculoides*, Europe; *A. japonica*, Japan; *A. silvestris*, Central Europe and northern Asia; *A. coronaria* and *A. hortensis* of the Mediterranean. *A. virginiana*, eastern United States, is thimbleweed, *A. quinquefolia*, windflower. *A. pulsatilla* is the pasque-flower of Europe, while *A. patens* is the American pasque-flower. *Thalictrum* (10), meadow rue, includes plants of north temperate regions.

Clematis (230) is a large genus, more or less cosmopolitan, of mostly climbing shrubs. *C. alpina* is in the Apennines, Alps, Carpathians, and subarctic Eurasia. *C. vitalba*, southern Europe, is traveler's-joy. *C. jackmanni*, with large velvety purple flowers, is a hybrid. *C. virginiana*, eastern United States, is virgin's-bower, and *C. viorna*, also of the eastern United States, is leatherflower.

Lardizabalaceae. Lardizabala Family. A family of mostly climbing shrubs, with 7 genera including 15 species, from the Himalayas to Japan, and in Chile. The plants are monoecious or dioecious. The perianth is of 3 or 6 sepals, the stamens 3 or 6, the carpels 3 or more. *Decaisnea insignis,* in the Himalayas and China, has an edible fruit. *Akebia* (4), of China and Japan, is sometimes cultivated as a porch vine. *Lardizabala* includes 2 species of Chile.

Magnoliaceae. Magnolia Family.

HABIT. Trees or shrubs.

LEAVES. Alternate, simple, deciduous or evergreen, stipules present and enclosing the bud, then falling to leave a scar encircling the twig.

INFLORESCENCE. Flowers usually solitary.

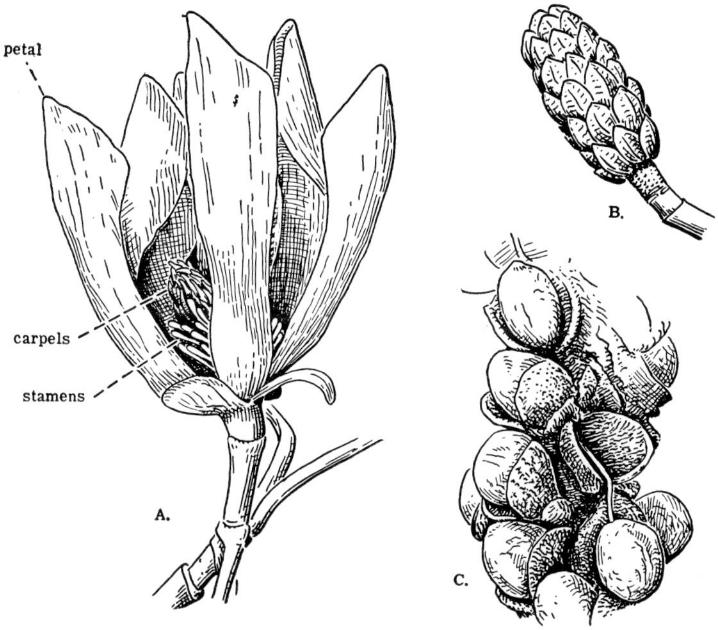

Figure 109. Flower and fruits of cucumber-tree, *Magnolia acuminata. A,* flower; *B,* young fruit; *C,* portion of mature fruit dehiscing.

FLOWERS. Bisexual, regular, large and showy; perianth of distinct sepals and petals, the sepals usually 3, the petals 6 to many; stamens numerous, spirally arranged on the elongated receptacle; carpels numerous, separate, spirally arranged on the upper portion of the elongated receptacle (Figure 109).

FRUIT. Aggregate, of follicles, samaras, or berries.

The family includes 10 genera with about 100 species. Many botanists regard this family to be one of the most primitive of all angiosperms, with possible relationships to the Mesozoic Bennettitales (page 231). Some of the trees yield useful wood and many are ornamental.

Magnolia (20) is characteristic of eastern Asia and North America; *M. acuminata,* cucumbertree, of eastern United States, yields timber. *M. grandiflora,* of southeastern United States, is a well-known ornamental. *M. soulangeana,* a hybrid of 2 Chinese species, is among the most gorgeous of early flowering shrubs. *Liriodendron,* a relic genus, includes 2 species, *L. tulipifera,* tuliptree (Figure 62), in eastern United States, and *L. chinense,* Central China. *Michelia* (15) occurs in tropical Asia and China; *M. champaca,* yields champaca oil, one of the most famous perfumes of India.

Schisandraceae. Schisandra Family. This family is composed of woody vines, with alternate simple exstipulate leaves, and unisexual regular flowers. The perianth is composed of a variable number of undifferentiated segments; the staminate flowers have a variable number of stamens, and the pistillate flowers have up to 300 distinct carpels. The fruit is aggregate and berry-like. There are 2 genera, *Schisandra* (7) and *Kadsura* (8), mostly of tropical Asia and Malaysia. Only S. *glabra* is American; it is a rare vine of the southeastern United States.

Winteraceae. Winter's Bark Family. This is a small family, mostly tropical or south temperate in its distribution, consisting of about 7 genera with 100 species. It is of considerable interest from phytogeographic and phylogenetic viewpoints, appearing to be one of the most primitive of living angiosperm families. *Illicium* (12) occurs in eastern Asia and in North America; *I. verum,* China, star-anise, yields a flavoring extract; this genus is sometimes separated as the Illiciaceae. *Drimys* (20) is found in the Cordilleras from Mexico to Tierra del Fuego and from New Zealand to Borneo; *D. winteri* is winter's bark, medicinal.

Degeneriaceae. Degeneria Family. This family includes only the remarkable *Degeneria vitiensis,* a tree discovered in Fiji by A. C. Smith in 1934. The stamens are not differentiated into filament and anther, but are merely broad microsporophylls. The single carpel, at anthesis, is not closed except in the basal portion. These features suggest that the family may be the most primitive taxon of existing angiosperms, representing retentions of structures that characterized the ancient ranalian stock.

Calycanthaceae. Calycanthus Family. A small family of aromatic shrubs, with 1 genus, *Calycanthus,* 6 species, in North America, Japan, China, and northeastern Australia. The perianth parts are variable in number and perigynous, the stamens 5 to 30, the carpels indefinite in a concave receptacle. Because of this last structure, some authors have regarded the family as allied to the Rosales. *C. floridus,* Carolina allspice or sweetscented shrub, is a cultivated ornamental.

Annonaceae. Custard-Apple Family.

HABIT. Trees, shrubs, or vines, aromatic.

LEAVES. Alternate, simple, entire, evergreen or deciduous, without stipules.

INFLORESCENCE. Flowers solitary, or in inflorescences of various types.

FLOWERS. Bisexual, regular; perianth of 3 sepals and usually 6 petals, distinct; stamens numerous, distinct; carpels numerous (or few), distinct, superior.

FRUIT. A berry, or the ripening pistils becoming united and adnate to the receptacle to form an aggregate fruit.

This is a family of 80 genera including 850 species, mostly in the tropics, especially of the Old World. They are of some importance in tropical regions as a source of edible fruits. There is general agreement that the family is related to the Magnoliaceae.

The genus *Asimina* (8), in eastern North America, is one of the few temperate zone members of the family; *A. triloba,* North American pawpaw, is a shrub or small tree. *Cananga* (3) ranges from tropical eastern Asia to Australia; *C. odorata,* ylang-ylang, yields Macassar oil, a perfume. *Xylopia* (80) is pantropical; *X. aromatica,* tropical America, and *X. aethiopica,* West Africa, have fruits used as peppers. *Annona* (100), of tropical America and Africa, is the most valuable genus; the fruits are aggregate, often very large, and edible; important species are: *A. cherimolia,* cherimoya, West Indies to Colombia; *A. squamosa,* sweet-sop or custard-apple, West Indies; *A. reticulata,* custard-apple, West Indies; *A. muricata,* soursop, guanabana, tropical America. *Uvaria* (100) distributed in the tropics of the Old World, is the largest genus; the plants are mostly lianas; *U. macrophylla,* of Bengal, has attractive red flowers.

Menispermaceae. Moonseed Family. A family of twining herbs and shrubs, including about 70 genera with 400 species, mostly of tropical regions. The flowers are unisexual, the plants mostly dioecious. There are 3-6 sepals, 3-6 petals, 3-6 stamens, and 3 carpels. A few are medicinal, containing drugs in their roots. *Menispermum* has 2 species, 1 in eastern Asia, 1, *M. canadense,* moonseed, in eastern North America. *Calycocarpum lyoni,* eastern United States, is cupseed. *Cocculus* (15), includes *C. carolinus,* Carolina moonseed, coral-beads, a vine with attractive red fruits.

Berberidaceae. Barberry Family.

HABIT. Perennial herbs and shrubs.

LEAVES. Alternate or basal, simple or compound, deciduous or evergreen.

INFLORESCENCE. In cymes or racemes, or the flowers solitary.

FLOWERS. Bisexual, regular; perianth of 4-6 sepals and 4-6 petals, the segments free and distinct; between the petals and stamens 1-2 series of petal-like nectaries ("honey-leaves") are often present; stamens 4-18, distinct, the anthers opening by flap-like, up-curling valves; pistil 1, with 1 locule.

FRUIT. A berry or follicle.

The family includes 10 genera with 200 species of north temperate regions. The species are apparently among the most primitive of angiosperms and their great antiquity is suggested by discontinuous ranges. The two sub-families treated below are not very closely related. Several species are cultivated as ornamentals.

Podophyllum has 1 species, *P. peltatum*, mayapple, in eastern North America, 4 others in Asia. *Diphylleia* has 1 species, *D. cymosa*, umbrella-leaf, in southeastern United States, 1 other in Japan. *Jeffersonia* has 1 species, *J. diphylla*, twinleaf, in eastern United States, 1 other in Manchuria. *Caulophyllum* has 1 species, *C. thalictroides*, papoose-root, in eastern United States, another in eastern Asia.

Berberis (175) is a large genus of the north temperate zone, primarily Asia, and the Andes of South America; many are ornamental shrubs, including *B. thunbergii*, of Japan. *B. vulgaris*, of Europe, is an alternate host of wheat rust. *Mahonia* includes 50 species of western North America and eastern Asia, often ornamental, as *M. aquifolium*, Oregon-grape. *Nandina domestica*, of China and Japan, is grown for its decorative red berries.

Myristicaceae. Nutmeg Family. A family of about 15 genera including 260 species of tropical regions of both the Old and New World. The simple evergreen leaves contain oil cells. The flowers are unisexual, with 3 united sepals, the staminate with 3-18 united stamens, the pistillate with 1 carpel. The fruit is fleshy and the seeds have a red aril. The principal genus is *Myristica* (100); *M. fragrans*, of the Moluccas, yields nutmeg from the seed, mace from the aril.

Monimiaceae. Monimia Family. A family of shrubs and trees with 32 genera including 350 species, mostly south of the equator; some species range north through South America into Mexico. The leaves are leathery and evergreen, often aromatic. The flowers are perigynous, mostly perfect, regular, with 4 to many sepals (or none), numerous (or few) stamens, and usually numerous carpels. The presence of a hollowed-out receptacle indicates a relationship with the Calycanthaceae. *Siparuna* (125), the largest genus, of tropical America, has a fig-like fruit. *Laurelia* has 1 species in New Zealand, *L. novae-zealandiae*, producing useful timber, and 2 in Chile, including *L. aromatica*, Peruvian nutmeg, the fruits used as a spice. *Monimia* (4) occurs in Madagascar and the Mascarenes.

Boldea boldus, boldo, of central Chile, has an edible fruit and the wood is used in cabinet making.

Lauraceae. Laurel Family.

HABIT. Trees or shrubs, the bark aromatic.

LEAVES. Mostly persistent, alternate, or opposite, entire, aromatic, without stipules.

INFLORESCENCE. Paniculate, spicate, racemose, or umbellate.

FLOWERS. Usually bisexual, regular, small; perianth in 2 series but the segments all mostly sepal-like, united into a tube at the base; stamens in 4 whorls of 3 in each whorl, or one or more whorls reduced to staminodes or absent; carpel 1, superior.

FRUIT. A drupe or berry, usually surrounded at the base by a cupule derived from the perianth tube.

This is a large family, with 45 genera including 1100 species, of tropical and subtropical regions in both hemispheres but mostly southeastern Asia. Presumably the family is related to the Magnoliaceae. Economically the plants are important for aromatic oils, for timber, and for edible fruits.

Cinnamomum (100) is a genus of Indomalaysia. *C. zeylanicum,* cinnamon, Ceylon, is cultivated in coppices for aromatic bark. *C. cassia,* southern China, cassia bark, is one of the oldest of spices, sometimes used to adulterate cinnamon. *C. camphora,* China, Japan, and Formosa, is camphor-tree; the camphor is distilled from young shoots or old trees cut into chips. *Persea* (12), in tropical America, includes *P. americana,* avocado or alligator-pear, grown for the edible fruit. *Nectandra* (100) in tropical America, includes *N. rodioei,* greenheart, British Guiana, with exceedingly hard strong wood, useful in marine construction. *Ocotea* (250) is the largest genus, distributed in the tropics of the Old and New World; some species yield good timber. *Umbellularia californica,* California laurel, is a woodland tree of Oregon and California. *Sassafras albidum,* eastern North America (Figure 32), yields oil of sassafras. *Lindera* (60) occurs mostly from Japan to Java, but has 2 species in the eastern United States, including *L. benzoin,* spice bush. *Laurus nobilis,* in the Mediterranean region, is the true laurel; the aromatic evergreen leaves were used as crowns for victors of ancient Olympic games. *Cassytha* (16) differs from other members of the family in its parasitic habit; the plants, of the Old World tropics, have the habit of *Cuscuta.*

Hernandiaceae. Hernandia Family. A small family of shrubs and trees, with 4 genera including 25 species, throughout the tropics. The flowers are bisexual or unisexual, regular, with 4-10 perianth parts, 3-5 stamens, and 1 inferior carpel. *Hernandia* (14) is the largest genus; *H. sonora,* jack-in-the-box, has a light fruit that rattles in the enclosing calyx.

Order 16. Papaverales. This order in general is distinguished from the Ranales by the cyclic arrangement of the flower parts and by the syncarpous gynoecium.

a. Flowers regular
  b. Gynoecium elevated on an elongate stipe (**gynophore**) .... *Capparidaceae*
  b. Gynoecium not elevated
    c. Sepals 2, stamens numerous, carpels 2 to many .. *Papaveraceae*
    c. Sepals 4, stamens 6, carpels 2 .... *Cruciferae*
a. Flowers irregular
  b. Flowers hypogynous
    c. Stamens and carpels on a somewhat elongated stalk (**androgynophore**)
      d. Androgynophore short, expanded into a disk on one side .... *Resedaceae*
      d. Androgynophore long and slender, not expanded into a disk .... *Capparidaceae*
    c. Stamens and carpels not elevated on an androgynophore .... *Fumariaceae*
  b. Flowers perigynous .... *Moringaceae*

Papaveraceae. Poppy Family.

Habit. Mostly herbaceous annuals or perennials, the sap usually milky or colored.

Leaves. Alternate, entire or cleft.

Inflorescence. Flowers mostly solitary.

Flowers. Bisexual, regular, showy, the calyx of 2-3 sepals, the corolla of 4-6 or more petals; stamens usually numerous; pistil of 2-many carpels, 1 locule, and 2-many parietal placentas, the ovary superior.

Fruit. A capsule.

The family includes 28 genera with 250 species, mostly of the northern hemisphere, with the milky or colored juice usually a distinguishing character. The economic importance is generally on the basis of ornamentals, but 1 species produces the drug opium.

Platystemon californicus, creamcups, of California, is ornamental. *Romneya* has 2 species in California, including *R. coulteri*, Matilija poppy. *Sanguinaria canadensis*, bloodroot, puccoon, of eastern North America, has red-orange juice (Figure 68). *Chelidonium* (5) ranges from Britain to east Asia; *C. majus*, celandine, has a yellow juice. *Macleya* has 2 species in eastern Asia, including *M. cordata*, plume poppy, of China. *Bocconia* (9), with apetalous flowers, occurs in Central and South America; *B. frutescens*, trompeto, is a distinctive shrub in the northern Andes. *Eschscholtzia* (15) is a genus of western North America; *E. californica*, California poppy, is a cultivated ornamental, the state flower. *Papaver* (100) is the largest genus, of Europe, Asia, South Africa, Australia, and North America. *P. somniferum*, opium poppy, of the Mediterranean, yields opium and morphine. Other species include *P. rhoeas*, corn poppy,

Europe, *P. nudicaule,* Iceland poppy, circumboreal, *P. dubium,* common poppy, Europe, and *P. orientale,* Oriental poppy, Armenia, Iran. *P. aculeatum,* South Africa, Australia, is the only poppy indigenous to the southern hemisphere. *Argemone* (9), in tropical and subtropical America, includes *A. mexicana,* prickly poppy. *Meconopsis* (40), of Eurasia, includes *M. cambrica,* Welsh poppy. *Stylophorum* (3) includes *S. diphyllum,* celandine poppy, eastern North America, and 2 other species in Asia.

Fumariaceae. Fumitory Family.

HABIT. Smooth weak herbs with a watery sap.

LEAVES. Alternate, basal or cauline, usually much-divided.

INFLORESCENCE. Usually racemose.

FLOWERS. Bisexual, irregular; sepals 2, minute; petals 4, in 2 series; stamens 6; pistil 1, with 1 locule and 2 parietal placentas; ovary superior.

FRUIT. A capsule or nut.

This is a family of 19 genera including 425 species, sometimes united to the Papaveraceae, but lacking the milky or colored juice of that family and its regular flowers. The species are most common in the north temperate zone and in South Africa. There are a few cultivated ornamentals.

Dicentra (15), in North America and Asia, includes *D. spectabilis,* bleeding heart, China, cultivated as an ornamental, *D. cucullaria,* Dutchman's breeches, and *D. canadensis,* squirrel corn, the 2 latter of eastern North America. *Adlumia fungosa,* of eastern North America, is climbing fumitory or Allegheny vine. *Corydalis* (300) of Europe, Asia, and North America, includes *C. cava,* Europe, *C. bulbosa,* Eurasia, *C. intermedia,* Europe, *C. flavula,* eastern North America. *Fumaria* (40), ranging from Europe to Central Asia, includes *F. officinalis,* fumitory, grown in flower gardens.

Cruciferae. Mustard Family.

HABIT. Annual, biennial, or perennial herbs.

LEAVES. Alternate, simple, without stipules.

INFLORESCENCE. Usually racemose.

FLOWERS. Bisexual, regular; sepals 4, petals 4, disposed in a cross (the flowers **cruciform**), stamens 6, with 4 of them longer than the other 2 (**tetradynamous**); pistil 1, with 2 carpels and 2 locules (Figure 110).

FRUIT. A silique (an elongated pod) or a silicle (a short broad pod) (Figure 85).

This is one of the most natural of families and, as noted elsewhere (page 27), was recognized as a group by the ancient Hindus. It is Linnaeus' Tetradynamia, the only class in his system that has retained its integrity in modern classification. It is a large family of 350 genera including 2500 species, distributed primarily in the north temperate zone, especially in the Mediterranean region. The plants are rich in sulphur compounds, yielding vitamin C, and a considerable number of them are food plants. Some are cultivated as ornamentals and many are widespread weeds, having been carried widely from their original homes.

Pringlea is a monotypic isolated genus of Kerguelen Island; *P. antiscorbutica* is Kerguelen cabbage. *Stanleya* (12), prince's plume, occurs in western North America.

Brassica (40) is the most important genus, mostly native to Eurasia. *B. oleracea* is the wild cliff cabbage, and its horiticultural varieties include var. *capitata,* cabbage; var. *botrytis,* cauliflower; var. *acephala,* kale; var. *gongolodes,* kohlrabi; var. *gemmifera,* Brussels sprouts; var. *italica,* broccoli, all grown as garden vegetables. *B. napus* is rape, a source of oil. Other food plants include *B. napobrassica,* rutabaga; *B. rapa,* turnip; *B. nigra,* black mustard, source of table mustard; *B. alba,* white mustard;

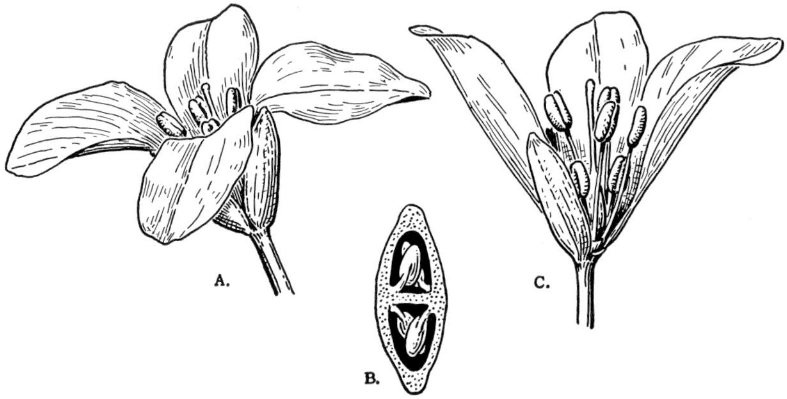

Figure 110. Toothwort, *Dentaria*. *A,* flower, showing cruciform corolla; *B,* cross-section of ovary; *C,* part of perianth cut away to show tetradynamous stamens.

B. pekinensis, pe-tsai, Chinese cabbage. *Eruca* (5) of the Mediterranean region, includes *E. sativa,* rocket salad.

Raphanus (8) ranges from Europe to Java; included are *R. raphanistrum,* Mediterranean, jointed charlock, and *R. sativus,* radish. *Crambe* (20) is a genus of Europe, tropical Africa and Central Asia; *C. maritima,* seakale, along the Atlantic and Baltic shores, has fleshy leaves blanched for food. *Cakile,* unlike other members of the family, has the pod transversely jointed; *C. maritima,* Mediterranean, and *C. edentula,* North America, sea-rocket, are strand plants.

Lepidium (130) is a cosmopolitan genus; *L. sativum,* of the Mediterranean, is garden cress; *L. virginicum,* North America, is wild peppergrass, a common weed. *Coronopus* (8), wart cress, swine cress, is a genus of widely distributed weeds, *Isatis* (30), ranging from southern Europe to central Asia, includes *I. tinctoria,* woad, formerly much used as a source of blue dye. *Iberis* (30) occurs mostly in the Mediterranean region; *I. amara,* candytuft, is a cultivated ornamental. *Thlaspi* (60), in temperate Eurasia and South America, includes *T. arvense,* penny cress, with orbicular fruits. *Capsella bursa-pastoris,* shepherd's-purse, is a cosmopolitan weed. *Cochlearia* (25) is a genus of Europe, Asia Minor, and China; *C. officinalis,* scurvy-grass, a boreal seaside plant, is used as an antiscorbutic. *Subularia* (2) occurs in Ethiopia, Europe, Asia, and North America; *S. aquatica,* awl-wort, grows at lake margins, usually submerged, one of the few aquatic annuals.

Anastatica hierochuntica, rose of Jericho, or resurrection plant, found from Morocco to Iran, rolls up when dry and may be blown to a moist place, where it expands. *Lunaria* (3), of Europe, has a silvery persistent septum of the fruit; *L. annua* is honesty, used for dry bouquets. *Alyssum* (100) ranges from Europe to Central Asia; *A. saxatile,* goldentuft, and *A. maritimum,* sweet alyssum, are cultivated ornamentals.

Draba (270) is a large genus, north temperate and arctic, with some in the Andes and subantarctic South America; *D. alpina,* arctic, subantarctic, extends north to latitude 82°; *D. verna,* Eurasia, whitlow grass, is a widespread weed. *Armoracia rusticana,* horseradish, of Europe and Siberia, is grown for the root used as a relish.

Cardamine (100), of the north temperate zone, includes *C. pratensis,* cuckoo-flower, circumboreal, *C. bellidifolia,* circumboreal, *C. pennsylvanica,* bitter cress, eastern North America. *Dentaria* (15) is a closely related genus of the north temperate zone, including *D. diphylla, D. laciniata,* toothwort, eastern North America. *Barbarea* (12), also of the north temperate zone, includes *B. vulgaris,* Eurasia and North America, winter cress, yellow rocket, a common weed. *Nasturtium* (50), of the temperate regions, includes *N. officinale,* watercress, Europe, cultivated in water for salad. *Aubrietia* (13), ranging from Italy to Iran, is grown as an ornamental in rock gardens. *Matthiola* (50) is found mostly in the Mediterranean and South Africa; *M. incana,* stocks, gilliflower, is a cultivated ornamental.

Hesperis (25), mostly of the Mediterranean, includes *H. matronalis,* dame's violet, "our lady of the evening," most fragrant in the evening. *Erysimum* (80) is a genus of Europe, western Asia, and North America; *E. cheiranthoides* is treacle mustard. *Cheiranthus* (10), is found in the Mediterranean region, China, and North America; *C. cheiri,* eastern Mediterranean, wall flower, is a cultivated ornamental. *Alliaria* (2), native in Europe, North Africa, and western Asia, includes *A. officinalis,* garlic mustard, with the odor of garlic. *Sisymbrium* (80) is both boreal and austral; *S. officinale,* hedge mustard, of Europe, is a widespread weed. *Arabidopsis* (16), of Europe, Asia, and West Africa, includes *A. thaliana,* mouse-ear cress, a common weed. *Camelina* (10), false flax, ranges from Europe to Central Asia. *Arabis* (220), rock cress, mostly north temperate zone, has some species cultivated as ornamentals.

Capparidaceae. Caper Family.

HABIT. Herbs, shrubs, or trees.

LEAVES. Alternate, simple or compound.

INFLORESCENCE. Generally racemose.

FLOWERS. Bisexual or unisexual, regular or irregular, sepals usually 4, petals 4-many (or absent), stamens 4-many; pistil 1, with 1 locule and 2 parietal placentas.

FRUIT. A capsule, berry, or nut.

This family is evidently closely related to the Cruciferae, but differs in having only 1 locule and in lacking tetradynamous stamens. It includes 46 genera with 700 species, distributed in the tropics of both hemispheres. They are of slight value economically.

Capparis (350), is a genus of warm climates; *C. spinosa,* capers, Mediterranean, is grown for the dried flower buds used in seasoning. *Koeberlinia* is a monotypic genus of southwestern United States and northern Mexico; *K. spinosa,* crucifixion thorn, is a leafless xerophyte with thorny twigs. *Cleome* (200) is especially abundant in tropical South America and Africa; *C. spinosa,* spider-flower, is a cultivated ornamental; *C. isomeris,* burro fat, is one of the commonest shrubs of southwestern U. S. deserts.

Resedaceae. Mignonette Family. A small family of xerophytic herbs, with 6 genera including 60 species, of Europe (chiefly Mediterranean), Asia, South Africa, and western North America. The flowers are racemose and irregular, with 4-8 sepals, 0-8 petals, 3-40 stamens, and 2-6 usually-united carpels. *Reseda* (50) is the chief genus, principally of the Mediterranean region; *R. odorata,* mignonette, is cultivated for fragrant flowers, and *R. luteola,* dyer's weed, was formerly used as a source of weld, a yellow dye.

Moringaceae. Moringa Family. A small family of trees, with 1 genus, *Moringa,* 3 species, ranging from the Mediterranean to India. The flowers are irregular, with the perianth and stamens on a cupule-like structure (hollowed receptacle), thus providing a connecting link to the Rosales. *M. oleifera,* horseradish-tree, is cultivated for edible fruits and for ben oil from the seeds, a non-drying oil used for lubricating watches.

Order 17. Sarraceniales. These three families of insectivorous plants are regarded by most systematists as constituting a natural group, although some authorities disagree.

a. Leaves modified as pitchers
  b. Low herbs of bogs and swamps .... *Sarraceniaceae*
  b. Climbing shrubs or herbs .... *Nepenthaceae*
a. Leaves not modified as pitchers, but the surfaces covered with glandular or sensitive hairs .... *Droseraceae*

Sarraceniaceae. Pitcher-Plant Family. A small family of insectivorous pitcher plants, with 3 genera including 14 species in America. The flowers are regular and bisexual, with 4-5 sepals, 0-5 petals, numerous stamens, and 3-5 united carpels. *Sarracenia* (7), pitcher-plant or side-saddle flowers (Figure 111), is in eastern North America; water collects in the pitchers and insects that fall in and drown are digested by enzymes secreted from the walls of the pitcher. *Darlingtonia californica* occurs in northern California and southern Oregon. *Heliamphora* has 4 species endemic on high mountains—for instance, Duida and Roraima, in Venezuela and British Guiana.

Figure 111. Pitcher plant, *Sarracenia purpurea.*

Nepenthaceae. Nepenthes Family. A small family of insectivorous herbs or shrubs, including 1 genus, *Nepenthes* (66), pitcher plants or monkeycups, in the tropics of the Old World from China to Australia, primarily in Borneo. The plants often climb by tendrils that are prolongations of the midrib of the leaf, the end of the tendril developing into the pitcher, in which insects drown and are digested. The flowers are unisexual, with 4 sepals, 4-16 stamens, and 4 united carpels.

Droseraceae. Sundew Family. A small family of 5 genera including about 100 species, of insectivorous herbs, with some representatives in most parts of the world. The flowers are perfect and regular, with 5 sepals, 5 petals, 5-20 stamens, and 3-5 united carpels. *Dionaea* is an interesting monotypic genus of North and South Carolina; *D. muscipula,* Venus-flytrap, has leaves that, upon stimulation, trap insects by the two halves of the blade closing like a book. *Aldrovanda vesiculosa,* widely distributed from Central Europe to Australia, is a rootless floating plant in which the leaves catch insects by closing upon them, after the manner of *Dionaea. Drosophyllum lusitanicum,* endemic to Portugal and northern Morocco, catches insects on the sticky leaves. *Drosera* (90), sundew, is the principal genus, represented on all the continents, but principally in Australia; the leaves have tentacles with knobs on the ends secreting a glistening viscous fluid that traps insects, whereupon the tentacles bend over, holding the insect against the leaf surface as it is digested; *D. longifolia* and *D. rotundifolia* are circumboreal, *D. intermedia* is in eastern North America. *Roridula* (2), in South Africa, has leaves like *Drosera,* but with no movement of the tentacles.

Order 18. Rosales. This order is characterized by having the ovary predominantly inferior or surrounded by an androperianth tube, although the flowers are sometimes hypogynous. It is a large, important, and very diversified order.

- a. Ovary superior
  - b. Flowers regular
    - c. Flowers hypogynous
      - d. Aquatics .... *Podostemonaceae*
      - d. Not usually aquatic
        - e. Plants succulent .... *Crassulaceae*
        - e. Plants not succulent
          - f. Insectivorous pitcher plants .... *Cephalotaceae*
          - f. Not insectivorous
            - g. Calyx and corolla minute or apparently none .... *Platanaceae*
            - g. Calyx and corolla usually present
              - h. Leaves mostly alternate
                - i. Leaves usually simple
                  - j. Leaves mostly deciduous .. *Saxifragaceae*
                  - j. Leaves evergreen .... *Pittosporaceae*
                - i. Leaves pinnate .... *Connaraceae*
              - h. Leaves opposite or whorled .... *Cunoniaceae*
    - c. Flowers perigynous
      - d. Fruit a legume .... *Leguminosae*
      - d. Fruit a capsule, achene, or drupe
        - e. Stamens numerous .... *Rosaceae*
        - e. Stamens 5 or 10 .... *Saxifragaceae*
  - b. Flowers irregular
    - c. Aquatics .... *Podostemonaceae*
    - c. Terrestrial
      - d. Carpels 2 or more, fruit a capsule .... *Saxifragaceae*
      - d. Carpel 1, fruit a legume .... *Leguminosae*

a. Ovary inferior
  b. Corolla none .... *Hamamelidaceae*
  b. Corolla present
    c. Leaves stipulate
      d. Stamens numerous; fruit a pome .... *Rosaceae*
      d. Stamens few; fruit a capsule .... *Hamamelidaceae*
    c. Leaves usually exstipulate .... *Saxifragaceae*

Podostemonaceae. Riverweed Family. This is a small family of remarkable plants living only in rushing water, on rocks in streams. The flowers open when the streams begin to dry up in summer, the seeds are shed on the rocks in the dry season, and germination occurs as the wet season begins again. There are about 43 genera including 140 species, mostly in tropical regions but with extensions in temperate regions. The flowers are naked, perfect, regular or irregular, with 1 to numerous stamens and usually 2, united carpels. *Podostemon* (12), mostly of tropical and subtropical regions, includes *P. ceratophyllum,* of eastern North America.

Crassulaceae. Orpine Family.

HABIT. Succulent annual or perennial herbs or shrubs.

LEAVES. Opposite, whorled, or alternate, simple, entire, fleshy.

INFLORESCENCE. Cymose.

FLOWERS. Bisexual, regular; sepals 4-30, generally distinct or nearly so; petals 4-30, distinct; stamens usually the same number as the petals or twice as many; carpels usually as many as the petals, distinct or united at the base.

FRUIT. A follicle.

A very natural family, of 33 genera with 1300 species, of wide geographical distribution, most abundant in arid regions, especially south-central Asia, northern Mexico and southwestern United States, South Africa, and the Mediterranean region. The plants are of economic importance only as ornamentals or novelties.

Crassula (300) is a large genus, located mostly in South Africa. Some are cactus-like in appearance, as *C. pyramidalis,* and some, like *C. arborescens,* are tree-like. *C. nemorosa* has vegetative reproduction through the formation of young plants in the inflorescence instead of flowers. *Kalanchoë* (150), mainly in tropical and South Africa and tropical Asia, has 1 species in tropical America. *Bryophyllum* (25), lifeplant, of the old world tropics, includes *B. pinnatum* (*calycinum*) and *B. tubiflorum.* In both of these adventitious buds arise in the notches of the leaves, giving rise to new plants. They are widespread weeds in warm regions. *Cotyledon* (40), mainly in South Africa, includes *C. orbiculatus,* and *C. reticulatus,* both of Cape Colony. *Umbilicus* (15), of the Mediterranean region, includes *U. pendulinus,* hanging on walls. *Sempervivum* (23), live-forever, ranges from the Pyrenees to the Caucasus. *S. tectorum,* houseleek, is planted on roofs of cottages, formerly thought to ward off lightning (often called thunderwort). Some species produce detached offsets and are known as hen-and-chickens. *Sedum* (500) is the largest genus, occurring mostly in the north temperate zone (Figures 70, 73). S. *telephium,* Eurasia, is orpine; S. *roseum,* roseroot, is circumboreal; S. *acre,* Europe, is mossy stonecrop; S. *ternatum,* eastern United States, is stonecrop; many are cultivated as ornamentals. *Echeveria* (150), of America, especially Mexico, also has decorative species, as *E. setosa* and *E. gibbiflora.*

Cephalotaceae. Cephalotus Family. A monotypic family including only *Cephalotus follicularis,* Australian pitcher plant, an insectivorous plant found in marshes of Western Australia. The lower leaves form pitchers in which insects drown, whereas the upper leaves are photosynthetic only. The flowers are perfect, regular, and apetalous, with 6 sepals, 12 stamens, and 6 free or united carpels.

Saxifragaceae. Saxifrage Family.

Habit. Herbs, shrubs, or small trees.

Leaves. Alternate or opposite, simple or compound, chiefly deciduous.

Inflorescence. Cymose, racemose, or paniculate.

Flowers. Bisexual, regular; androperianth tube sometimes present; sepals 4-5; often united, sometimes petal-like; petals 4-5, on the receptacle or androperianth tube, sometimes absent; stamens the same number as the petals and alternate with them, or twice as many; staminodes or nectar-glands often present; gynoecium of 2-5 separate carpels, sometimes united at base, or a single pistil with 1 carpel, or with 2-5 united carpels with axile placentation; ovary superior to inferior.

Fruit. A capsule or berry.

The family includes 80 genera with 1200 species. It is quite variable and with difficulty separated from related families, especially the Rosaceae. The distribution is cosmopolitan, but chiefly north temperate, with many arctic and alpine species and some xerophytes. They are economically important principally as ornamentals, although some yield edible fruits of minor importance.

Brexia is an isolated genus with 3 species, 1 in New Zealand, 1 in Madagascar, and 1 in Mauritius. *Escallonia* (50) is a genus of South America, especially in the Andes; the leaves are often leathery and glandular-dotted. *Itea* (11) occurs in eastern Asia and eastern North America; *I. virginica* is Virginia-willow, a white-flowered shrub.

Astilbe (30), of North America, the Himalayas, China, Japan, the Philippines, and New Guinea, includes *A. davidii,* of China, often cultivated. *Peltiphyllum peltatum,* Indian rhubarb, is in Oregon and California. *Saxifraga* (300), saxifrage, is the largest genus, mostly arctic and north temperate, but extending down the Andes to Tierra del Fuego. Some species are: S. *virginiensis,* eastern United States; S. *hirculus,* circumboreal; S. *aizoides,* circumboreal; S. *oppositifolia,* arctic and alpine, one of northernmost of flowering plants (83° 3′ on Ellesmere Island); S. *sarmentosa,* eastern Asia. *Tiarella* (4), a genus of North America, includes *T. cordifolia,* coolwort, false mitrewort. *Heuchera* (30), in North America, includes *H. americana,* alumroot; and *H. sanguinea,* coral bells, Arizona and New Mexico. *Mitella* (12), in North America, includes *M. diphylla,* eastern North America, mitrewort or bishop's cap. *Tolmiea menziesii* and *Tellima grandiflora* occur in western North America. *Chrysosplenium* (60) is a genus of the north temperate region, mostly in Asia, with 1 subantarctic; *C. americanum,* eastern North America, is golden saxifrage.

Parnassia (44) has a circumboreal range; the flowers have 5 staminodes nectar-secreting at their bases (Figure 72); *P. palustris,* grass-of-Parnassus, is circumboreal.

Francoa (2) occurs in Chile; *F. sonchifolia* is a perennial herb cultivated as wedding flowers.

Ribes (150), north temperate and Andean, includes shrubs with mostly edible berries. *R. vulgare,* Europe, and *R. rubrum,* Eurasia, red currants, are cultivated for their fruits; *R. sanguineum, R. aureum,* of western North America, are decorative; *R. nigrum,* northern Eurasia, is black currant; *R. grossularia,* Europe, gooseberry, is cultivated for edible fruits; *R. magellanicum* is in Patagonia and Tierra del Fuego.

Philadelphus (55) is a genus of north temperate shrubs, including *P. coronarius,* mock-orange, cultivated for its scented showy flowers. *Deutzia* (40) is found from the Himalayas to Japan and in the mountains of Central America; many, as *D. scabra,* are cultivated as ornamental shrubs. *Hydrangea* (80), of the northern hemisphere, includes *H. paniculata,* China, Japan, the common ornamental hydrangea, and *H. arborescens,* wild hydrangea, of eastern North America.

Pittosporaceae. Pittosporum Family. A family of trees, shrubs, or lianas, with 9 genera including 200 species, in tropical and subtropical regions of the Old World, principally Australia. The flowers are regular, perfect, with 5 sepals, 5 petals, 5 stamens and 2 or more carpels. The largest genus is *Pittosporum* (160), including *P. tobira,* of China and Japan, ornamental, and *P. eugenioides,* tarata, a white-barked tree of New Zealand; some species yield useful timber.

Cunoniaceae. Cunonia Family. A family of shrubs and trees with 26 genera including 250 species, mostly in the southern hemisphere. It is closely related to the Saxifragaceae. The flowers are small and usually perfect. There are 4-5 sepals, 4-5 petals (sometimes none), 8-10 or numerous stamens, and 2-5 carpels, separate or united. *Cunonia* (11) is chiefly in New Caledonia, but with 1 species in South Africa. *Weinmannia* (130) is the largest genus, ranging from Mexico and the West

Indies to Chile and from the Philippines to New Zealand; *W. pubescens,* encenillo, of the northern Andes, yields tannin. *Ceratopetalum apetalum,* lightwood, is a timber tree of New South Wales.

Hamamelidaceae. Witch-hazel Family.

HABIT. Trees or shrubs.

LEAVES. Alternate, simple, stipulate.

INFLORESCENCE. Axillary, capitate, or spicate.

FLOWERS. Bisexual or unisexual, regular or irregular; calyx mostly of 4-5 sepals united at the base, the corolla of 4-5 distinct petals (sometimes none); stamens 2-8, perigynous; pistil with 2 united carpels, 2 locules and a half-inferior or inferior ovary (Figure 77, B).

FRUIT. A capsule, often woody or leathery.

The family includes 23 genera with 100 species, mostly of Asia, but with other representatives in widely separated areas, including Africa, Australia, and eastern North America. The species are mostly of little importance except as ornamentals; a few yield gums or oils.

Hamamelis (6), witch-hazel, occurs in eastern Asia and eastern North America; *H. virginiana,* eastern North America, yields witch-hazel extract, used as a liniment; the flowers appear in autumn. *Corylopsis* (22), winter-hazel, of eastern Asia, is the largest genus; the flowers are surrounded by colored bracts and bloom in early spring. *Liquidambar* (4), distributed in Asia and North America, includes *L. orientalis,* Asia Minor, a source of storax, *L. styraciflua,* southern United States to Central America, redgum or sweetgum, a valuable timber tree, and *L. formosana,* of China. *Altingia* (5) ranges from China to Java; *A. excelsa* is large tree, with useful timber. *Fothergilla* (5), witch-elder, has a bicentric distribution in southeastern North America and Cashmir.

Platanaceae. Plane-tree Family. A family of trees, with 1 genus, *Platanus,* and 8 species, in the northern hemisphere. The leaves are alternate, with stipules encircling the twig, and the petiole base covering the bud. The flowers are unisexual (the plants monoecious) very small, in heads, with minute perianth-parts, the staminate with 3-4 stamens, the pistillate with 5-9 separate carpels, and a multiple fruit. *P. orientalis,* Mediterranean to Himalayas, is plane-tree; *P. occidentalis,* eastern North America, is sycamore; *P. acerifolia,* London plane, is supposed to be a hybrid between these two species; *P. racemosa* is California sycamore.

Rosaceae.

HABIT. Trees, shrubs, or herbs.

LEAVES. Alternate, simple or compound, stipulate.

INFLORESCENCE. Extremely variable, from solitary flowers to clusters of both racemose and cymose types.

FLOWERS. Usually bisexual, regular, generally perigynous, the calyx of 5 sepals united at the base, the corolla of 5 petals attached to the rim of the androperianth tube, stamens mostly numerous (sometimes 5 or 10); carpels numerous and distinct, or united into a compound pistil of 2-5 carpels.

FRUIT. An achene, follicle, pome, drupe, or aggregation of carpels, sometimes on an enlarged fleshy receptacle.

The Rosaceae is a large family of about 115 genera with 3200 species, widely distributed over most of the earth, especially abundant in North America, Europe, and eastern Asia. The members are in general characterized by the presence of the androperianth tube (see figure 77). The family is of very great economic importance, because of the large number of temperate zone fruits and the many cultivated ornamentals. The subfamilies are sometimes treated as independent families.

I. Fruit a follicle or capsule. *Spiraea* (80) is a genus of shrubs of the north temperate zone, mostly of central and eastern Asia; many are common in cultivation, as *S. vanhoutei,* a hybrid, a very popular ornamental, *S. prunifolia,* bridal-wreath, and *S. japonica,* with pink flowers. *Aruncus* (3), of the north temperate region, includes *A. silvestre,* Eurasia, and *A. dioicus,* North America, goat's-beard. *Gillenia trifoliata,* of eastern North America, is Indian physic. *Holodiscus discolor,* cream bush, occurs in western North America. *Physocarpus opulifolius,* ninebark, eastern United States, has bark that peels in many layers. *Quillaja* (3), in temperate South America, includes *Q. saponaria,* soapbark tree, of central Chile, the sap forming a copious lather. *Filipendula* (9), occurs in Eurasia and North America; *F. camchatica* is in northeastern Asia, and *F. rubra,* Queen-of-the-prairie, eastern United States. *Exochorda* includes 3 species of central and eastern Asia, often grown as ornamentals. *Rhodotypos kerrioides,* jetbead, of Japan, is a cultivated shrub. *Kerria* is a closely related genus of China; *K. japonica* is also cultivated as an ornamental shrub.

II. Fruit a pome (Figure 87, A). *Cotoneaster* (50), a genus of Eurasia, has many species grown as ornamentals. *Pyracantha* (3), firethorn, ranges from southern Europe to China; *P. coccinea,* eastern Mediterranean to Caucasus, is an ornamental shrub grown for its red fruits. *Mespilus germanica,* medlar, of southeastern Europe and western Asia, is grown for its edible fruit, eaten after frost when "bletting" (decay) has begun. *Crataegus,* hawthorn, is a genus variously estimated as comprising from 300 to 1000 species; many are probably apomicts (see page 98); some are ornamental, as *C. oxyacantha,* Europe, and *C. coccinea* and *C. macrantha,* North America; many are weed trees in old fields of eastern United States. *Cydonia oblonga,* quince, Central Asia, is widely grown for fruits which make fine preserves. A related genus, *Chaenomeles,* includes *C. lagenaria,* Japan, Japanese quince or "japonica," a cultivated ornamental. *Pyrus* (45) is a genus of Europe, Asia, and North America;

P. communis is pear, *P. malus,* apple, long cultivated for very important edible fruits; there are many other species grown for their ornamental flowers. *Sorbus* (80) is circumboreal in distribution; it includes *S. aucuparia,* rowan, Europe and northern Asia, *S. americana,* mountain-ash, North America, *S. aria,* whitebeam, Europe, and *S. torminalis,* service-tree, Denmark to North Africa. *Aronia* (3) is a North American genus; *A. arbutifolia* is chokeberry. *Eriobotrya* (10), in eastern Asia, includes *E. japonica,* loquat, Japan, China, grown for the edible fruit. *Amelanchier* (25), mainly in North America, includes *A. arborea, A. laevis,* service-berry, Juneberry, with edible fruits. Other related genera are *Stranvaesia,* with 5 species in Central Asia (including *S. davidiana,* ornamental) and *Heteromeles,* with a single species, *H. arbutifolia,* Christmas berry, California, used for Christmas decoration.

III. Carpels numerous, becoming achenes or drupelets and ripening as aggregate fruits (Figure 88, B, C). *Rubus* is a vast genus, variously estimated at 600 to 1000 species (mostly apomicts). The numerous pistils become drupelets in an aggregate fruit, often edible. Examples are *R. chamaemorus,* cloudberry, circumboreal; *R. arctica,* circumboreal; *R. saxatilis,* Eurasia; *R. idaeus,* red raspberry, circumboreal; *R. occidentalis,* blackcap raspberry, eastern North America; *R. phoenicolasius,* wine-berry, China, Japan; *R. odoratus,* purple-flowering raspberry, eastern North America; *R. deliciosus* is in the Rocky Mountains and *R. parviflorus,* thimbleberry, western North America. *R. canadensis, R. allegheniensis,* and so forth, eastern North America, are blackberries; *R. loganobaccus* is loganberry, a hybrid; *R. roribaccus,* trailing, is a dewberry, eastern United States. *Potentilla* (250) occurs chiefly in the north temperate and arctic; the fruit is an aggregate of achenes on a dry receptacle. *P. fruticosa,* shrubby cinquefoil, is circumboreal; *P. anserina,* silver-weed, north temperate; *P. canadensis,* cinquefoil, eastern United States; *P. palustris,* marsh five-finger, circumboreal. *Duchesnea* (2), of eastern Asia, is like *Fragaria,* but has the receptacle spongy, not juicy; *D. indica* is Indian strawberry. *Waldsteinia* (4), of the north temperate zone, is like *Potentilla,* but with fewer achenes; *W. fragarioides,* barren strawberry, occurs in eastern United States. *Fragaria* (10) has the carpels ripening as achenes on a fleshy edible receptacle (Figure 88, A). *F. vesca,* strawberry, is from Eurasia; cultivated varieties are derived from *F. virginiana* and *F. chiloensis. Sibbaldia* (8) has a wide distribution in boreal regions; *S. procumbens* is subantarctic. *Alchemilla* (70), lady's mantle, is a genus of the temperate regions and tropical mountains; the flowers are apetalous. *Rosa* (150), occurs in the north temperate zone and on tropical mountains. The carpels are enclosed in the cup-like receptacle (Figure 112). A large number of cultivated ornamentals have been derived from the wild species; some of them are *R. multiflora,* multiflora rose, China, Japan; *R. chinensis,* China rose; *R. wichuriana,* memorial rose, China,

Japan; *R. fragrans,* tea rose, China; *R. foetida,* Asia Minor; *R. gallica,* western Europe; *R. eglanteria,* eglantine, sweetbriar, western Asia; *R. canina,* dogrose, Eurasia; *R. cinnamomea,* cinnamon rose, Europe, western Asia; *R. odorata,* tea rose, China; *R. spinosissima,* Scotch rose, Europe, western Asia. *R. damascena,* damask rose, is the source of attar of roses (Bulgaria). *Agrimonia* (10), agrimony, is a genus of the north temperate zone, Brazil, and South Africa. The dry receptacle, covered with hooks, encloses the achenes. *Cercocarpus* (10), mountain mahogany, is a genus of evergreen shrubs of western North America from Oregon to Mexico. *Sanguisorba* (30), burnet, includes *S. officinalis,*

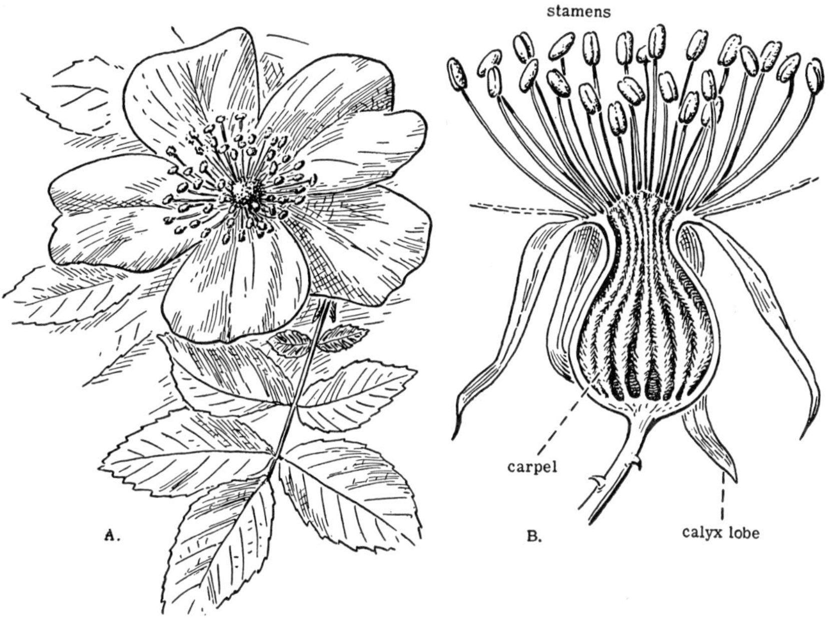

Figure 112. Perigynous flowers of rose, *Rosa*. *A*, general appearance; *B*, section, to show stamens and carpels.

Eurasia, and *S. canadensis,* North America. *Acaena* (120) ranges from Mexico to Tierra del Fuego, also in Polynesia; known as New Zealand burr. *Geum* (40) is a genus of the arctic, north temperate, Andes, and New Zealand; *G. rivale,* purple avens, and *G. urbanum* are circumboreal; *G. coccineum* is in the eastern Mediterranean; *G. vernum,* early avens, *G. canadensis,* white avens, and *G. flavum,* yellow avens, are in eastern North America. *Dryas* (3) is arctic and alpine; *D. octopetala* reaches the northern limit for flowering plants.

IV. Carpels ripening to drupes (Figure 87, C). *Prunus* (150) is a large and valuable genus of the north temperate zone. *P. spinosa,* sloe, Mediterranean, is grown for its ornamental blue fruits. Other species valuable for flowers or edible fruits are *P. armeniaca,* apricot, Central Asia; *P. institia,* damson plum, Asia; *P. domestica,* plum, prune, Asia; *P. amygdalus,* almond, central Asia; *P. triloba,* flowering almond, China; *P. persica,* peach, China; *P. cerasus,* sour cherry, Asia Minor; *P. avium,* sweet cherry, southern Europe; *P. mahaleb,* perfumed cherry, southern Europe; *P. serrulata,* Japanese flowering cherry, eastern Asia. *P. serotina,* wild black cherry, eastern North America is a valuable timber tree. *Nuttallia cerasiformis,* of western North America, is like *Prunus,* but with 2-5 drupes instead of 1.

V. Flowers irregular; fruit a drupe. *Chrysobalanus* (3), of tropical America, includes *C. icaco,* coco plum or icaco, an edible fruit.

Connaraceae. Connarus Family. A family of mostly twining shrubs, with 16 genera including 250 species of the tropics of both hemispheres. They are closely allied to legumes, but distinguished by the presence of more than 1 carpel. There are 5 sepals, 5 petals, 5-10 stamens, and 4-5 free carpels. *Connarus* (70) is the principal genus; *C. guianensis,* of tropical America, is zebrawood.

Leguminosae. Legume Family.

HABIT. Herbs, shrubs, and trees, of a great variety of forms, including aquatics, xerophytes, climbers. Some have roots bearing tubercles containing nitrogen-fixing bacteria. Many are thorny.

LEAVES. Alternate, usually pinnately (sometimes palmately) compound, occasionally simple, stipulate, sometimes scale-like; some exhibit **photeolic** (sleep) movements, or are sensitive to touch.

FLOWERS. Regular or irregular, usually papilionaceous (with a standard, wings, and keel (Figure 82); sepals 5, united at base; petals 5, free; stamens 10, free or united (monadelphous or diadelphous, Figure 80); carpel 1, superior.

FRUIT. A legume (Figure 85, A).

This is probably the second largest family of plants, with 550 genera including about 13,000 species, cosmopolitan in range, living in every soil and climate in a great variety of habitats. They are distinguished by the legume and the usually papilionaceous flowers. In economic importance the family is second only to the grasses. The genera can be divided into three sub-families, sometimes treated as separate families.

I. Mimosoideae. Flowers regular. *Inga* (200) is a genus of trees and shrubs of tropical America; *I. edulis,* guamo, has edible pods; the trees are used as shade for coffee in Colombia and Central America. *Enterolobium* (8) is a genus of tropical American trees; *E. cyclocarpum,* ear tree, conacaste, has coiled ear-shaped fruits and valuable timber. *Pithecolobium* (130) is a genus of tropical trees, mostly of America and Asia, including *P. dulce,* much planted along roadsides. *Samanea* (30), a genus of tropical plants, includes *S. saman,* rain-tree; the leaves fold together in cloudy weather and in darkness. *Albizzia* (50) is a genus of the Old World tropics. *A. julibrissin,* Asia, Africa, is ornamental, planted in southern United States as silktree or "mimosa." *A. lebbek,* East Indian walnut, or siris, yields good timber; it is called woman's-tongue-tree, from the rattling of the seed pods. *A. stipulata, A. molluccana,* are shade for tea in India. *Acacia* (500) is a vast genus of the tropics and subtropics, mostly trees, many xerophytic (p. 115). The leaves are pinnate, or the photosynthetic activity is carried on by phyllodes. The plants are especially numerous in the bush veldt of South Africa, their low, flattened crowns being characteristic features of the landscape; *A. horrida* is especially noticeable. In Australia the brigalow, *A. harpophylla* (and others), gives the name to the type of thorn forest of which it is the chief component, while the mulga, *A. aneura,* characterizes the bushy steppes known as the Mulga scrub. *A. sphaerocephala,* of Central America, has stipular thorns inhabited by ants (said to be the first case of myrmecophily discovered). *A. arabica,* babul, is almost the only tree in some arid parts of India. *A. senegal,* of the Sudan, yields gum arabic, which exudes from the branches during the blowing of dry desert winds. *A. decurrens,* black wattle, and *A. dealbata,* silver wattle, both of Australia, are used in tanning. *A. pycnantha,* golden wattle, its flowers very showy, is one of the most distinctive plants of Australia. *A. melanoxylon,* Australia, blackwood, has valuable timber. *A. armata,* Australia, is kangaroo-thorn. *A. greggii,* cat claw, is common in arid lands of the southwestern United States. *Mimosa* (350) is a large genus of tropical and subtropical America, Asia, and Africa; *M. pudica,* sensitive plant, with very sensitive leaves, is a common tropical weed. *Prosopsis* (30) is a genus of tropical and subtropical xerophytes; *P. juliflora,* mesquite, is a small tree widespread and exceedingly abundant throughout the southwestern United States, like *Acacia* in Africa and Australia. *Entada* (15) is a genus of tropical plants; *E. scandens,* nicker bean, has pods three feet long, sometimes carried to Europe by the Gulf Stream.

II. Caesalpinioideae. Flowers zygomorphic, but not papilionaceous. *Copaifera* (24), of tropical America and Africa, yields a resin, balsam of Copaiba. *C. mopani,* mopani-tree, is one of the most distinctive trees of the South African bush veldt, associated with *Acacia. Trachylobium* (3), in tropical Asia and Africa, includes *T. verrucosum,* yielding Zanzibar copal, the hardest of all resins except amber. *Hymenaea courbaril,* West Indian locust, yields a valuable wood and a resin, copal, found in lumps where it has accumulated under the trees. *Tamarindus indica,* tamarind, a native of tropical Africa, now widely grown, has an edible fruit; a beverage is made from the pulp around the seeds. *Amherstia nobilis,* of Burma, is a tree cultivated for its showy pink flowers. *Bauhinia* (200), a group of tropical trees and shrubs, includes *B. purpurea,* orchid-tree, of India, Burma, and Indo-China (see page 142). *Cercis* (5), of southern

Europe, East Asia, and North America, includes *C. siliquastrum,* Mediterranean, Judas tree, and *C. canadensis,* eastern North America, redbud. *Cassia* (450) is a large genus, in South Africa, Australia, New Zealand, and North America; *C. angustifolia,* East Africa, Arabia, is Indian senna, yielding a cathartic; *C. fistula,* India, is golden-shower, an ornamental tree; *C. nictitans,* eastern United States, is wild sensitive plant. *Koompassia* (2), of Malaya, is one of the tallest of tropical rain forest trees, reaching 330 feet. *Ceratonia siliqua,* carob tree, of the Mediterranean, has edible pods, St. John's bread; the seeds may be the original jeweler's carats. *Caesalpinia* (60) is a genus of the tropics and subtropics; *C. coriaria,* dividivi, is used in tanning; *C. pulcherrima,* Barbados-pride, peacock flower, is an ornamental shrub. *C. sappan,* India, is sappan or peach wood, called in Middle Ages bresel wood; the discovery of a similar species, *C. brasiliensis,* in America, gave the name Brazil to the country of its nativity. *Haematoxylon campechianum,* logwood, of tropical America, yields haematoxylon, a histological stain. *Gleditsia* (12), in tropical and temperate America and Asia, includes *G. triacanthos,* honey locust, with branched thorns. *Gymnocladus* is a related genus, with one species in China, and one, *G. dioica,* Kentucky coffeetree, in eastern North America. *Cercidium* (8), of arid regions, includes *C. floridum,* palo verde, southwestern United States, northern Mexico, with few small leaves and green bark. *Parkinsonia* (2) includes *P. aculeata,* also known as palo verde, common in cultivation in the southwestern United States. *Poinciana regia,* of Madagascar, flamboyant, royal poinciana, is cultivated for its gorgeous flame-colored flowers, one of the most beautiful of tropical trees.

III. Papilionatae. Flowers papilionaceous. *Cladrastis* has 1 species, *C. sinensis,* in eastern Asia and 1, *C. lutea,* yellow-wood, in eastern North America. *Sophora japonica,* Japanese pagoda-tree, China, Korea, is grown as an ornamental. *Myroxylon* (8), of tropical America, includes *M. pererae,* balsam of Peru, Salvador, and *M. balsamum,* balsam of Tolu, Venezuela, Colombia. *Baptisia* (12), of North America, includes *B. tinctoria,* wild indigo. *Crotalaria* (350) is a large genus of tropical and subtropical plants; *C. juncea,* Bombay hemp, or Sunn, yields a fiber, the earliest mentioned in Sanskrit. *Lupinus* (100) mostly in America, includes *L. texensis,* Texas bluebonnet, state flower of Texas, and *L. perennis,* eastern lupine, eastern North America. *Laburnum* (3), of Europe and western Asia, includes *L. vulgare,* golden-chain, an ornamental but poisonous tree. *Cytisus* (50), of Europe and the Mediterranean, includes *C. scoparius,* Scotch broom, with bright yellow flowers. *Genista* (100), of Europe, North Africa, and western Asia, includes *G. anglica,* needlegorse or whin, and *G. tinctoria,* dyer's greenweed. *Ulex* (20), gorse, furze, is native to Europe; *U. europaeus* is grown for showy yellow flowers. *Dalbergia* (100) is a genus of tropical trees with valuable timber; *D.*

nigra, Brazil, is rosewood; *D. melanoxylon,* Africa, is blackwood; *D. retusa,* Central America, is cocobolo, with showy orange heartwood. *Derris* (50), a tropical genus, includes *D. elliptica,* Borneo, derris root, yielding rotenone, an insecticide. *Pterocarpus* (30), is a group of tropical trees with winged fruits; *P. marsupium,* East Indies, yields kino, an astringent resin; *P. santalinus,* East Indies, is red sandalwood; *P. officinalis,* bloodwood, Central America, yields red resin.

Ononis (70), rest-harrow, occurs in the Mediterranean region. *Trigonella* (100) is mostly Mediterranean, but also in South Africa and Australia; *T. foenumgraecum* is fenugreek (Greek hay), the seeds used in India as flavoring. *Medicago* (50) occurs especially in the Mediterranean; *M. sativa,* lucerne, alfalfa, is one of the world's leading hay plants; *M. lupulina,* black medic, is a widespread weed; *M. hispida,* bur clover, is a weed and also a valuable forage plant in arid regions. *Melilotus* (20), in Eurasia and North Africa, yields good pasture and hay; *M. officinalis* is sweet clover. *Trifolium* (300), clover, occurs in temperate and subtropical regions. Well-known species are *T. repens,* white or Dutch clover; *T. pratense,* red clover; *T. hybridum,* alsike clover; *T. agrarium,* yellow-hop clover; *T. incarnatum,* crimson clover. *Anthyllis* (30) occurs in Europe, North Africa, and western Asia; *A. vulneraria* is woundwort and *A. barba-jovis,* Jupiter's beard. *Lotus* (100), of temperate Europe and Asia and South Africa, includes *L. corniculatus,* bird's foot trefoil, a good pasture plant.

Amorpha (20), in North America, includes *A. frutescens,* bastard indigo. *Indigofera* (350) is a genus of the tropics; *I. tinctoria,* East Indies, yields indigo, formerly "king of the dyestuffs." *Psoralea* (100), mostly of tropical and subtropical regions, includes *P. physodes,* California tea, which was used to make a beverage by early Californians; and *P. esculenta,* prairie turnip, with an edible tuberous root. *Wistaria* (6), a genus of decorative lianas, occurs in eastern Asia and eastern North America. *Sesbania exaltata,* Colorado River hemp, yields a strong fiber once extensively utilized by Indians of western North America. *Robinia* (20), in the United States and Mexico, includes *R. pseudoacacia,* black locust, with useful wood. *Gliricidia* (5), of tropical America, includes trees with ornamental flowers. *Colutea* (10) ranges from southern Europe to the Himalayas; *C. arborescens,* central Europe, is bladder senna, an ornamental shrub. *Caragana* (50) is a genus of central Asia, including *C. arborescens,* Siberia, Siberian pea-tree, planted in the United States as a wind-break in "shelter-belts." *Astragalus* (1600), milk vetch, is a vast genus, one of the largest in the plant kingdom, mostly north temperate but with an extension along the Andes to Patagonia. Many species are on prairies and steppes, and many are xerophytes, often thorny; *A. gummifera,* yields gum-tragacanth from the wounded stem. *Oxytropis* (150) is common in grasslands of north temperate regions. *O. lamberti,* locoweed, in central North America, causes cattle poisoning. *Glycyrrhiza glabra,* Mediterranean, has roots that yield commercial licorice.

Hedysarum (100) is a genus of north temperate regions. *Ornithopus* has 8 species of the Mediterranean and South America, including *O. sativus,* seradella or serratella, Portugal, a forage plant. *Onobrychis* (100), mostly of the Mediterranean, includes *O. sativa,* sainfoin, holy clover, a good pasture plant. *Coronilla* (20) occurs mostly in the Mediterranean region; *C. varia* is crown vetch. *Alhagi* (3), camelthorn, ranges from the Mediterranean to India. *Arachis hypogaea,* peanut, a native of Brazil, has fruits with valuable edible seeds ripening underground (**geocarpy**). *Desmodium* (170) is a genus of tropical and temperate regions; many species, called sticktights, are common weeds in the United States. *D. gyrans,* telegraph plant, India, is a common weed with leaflets exhibiting tropisms. *Lespedeza* (60), of temperate regions, includes many species grown as forage plants and to arrest soil erosion.

Abrus precatorius, rosary pea, tropical, produces hard red seeds with black tips, often strung in necklaces. *Cicer arietinum,* chickpea, of the Mediterranean, is cultivated for food. *Vicia* (150), vetch, a genus of the north temperate region and South America, includes *V. villosa,* Eurasia, *V. sativa,* Europe, grown for pasture. *V. faba* is the broad bean, the only edible bean of Europe before 1492. *Lens culinaris,* lentil, of the Mediterranean region, is a food plant of great antiquity; the seeds from their shape gave the name to the magnifying lens. *Lathyrus* (100), a genus of the north temperate zone and mountains of tropical Africa and South America, includes *L. sativus,* cultivated for hay, *L. odoratus,* Italy, sweet pea, *L. latifolius,* everlasting pea, the two latter cultivated as ornamentals. *Pisum* (6), mostly of the Mediterranean, includes *P. sativum,* garden pea, an important food plant.

Glycine (25), of the Old World tropics, includes *G. soja,* soy bean, an important food in Manchuria and Japan and, recently, elsewhere. *Erythrina* (30) is a genus of the tropics; *E. cristagalli* is coral-tree, cultivated for red flowers; *E. caffra,* South Africa, is Kaffir boom, producing light timber. *Mucuna* (50) is a genus common on tropical coasts; *M. urens* is cowitch, with stinging hairs on pods. *Canavalia* (12) is a genus of mostly tropical vines; *C. ensiformis* is horse bean or jack bean, useful for food and forage. *Pueraria lobata,* Kudzu-vine, southeastern Asia, is grown as a porch vine and on roadbanks to control erosion in the southern United States. *Phaseolus* (150), of the tropics and warm temperate regions, includes *P. vulgaris,* South America, kidney bean, with many varieties, as the common pole bean, navy bean, and bush bean; *P. lunatus,* lima bean; *P. multiflora,* Mexico, scarlet runner bean. *Vigna* (50), of tropical regions, includes *V. sinensis,* cowpea, or black-eyed pea. *V. sesquipedalis* is yardlong bean, with pods 1-3 feet long. *Dolichos* (30), a genus of warm climates, includes *D. lablab*, hyacinth bean or lablab, cultivated in the tropics for edible pods. *Cajanus indicus*, tropical Africa, is pigeon pea or cajan bean, grown for forage. *Clitoria* (30), of tropical and subtropical regions, includes *C. ternatea*, butterfly pea, grown as an ornamental.

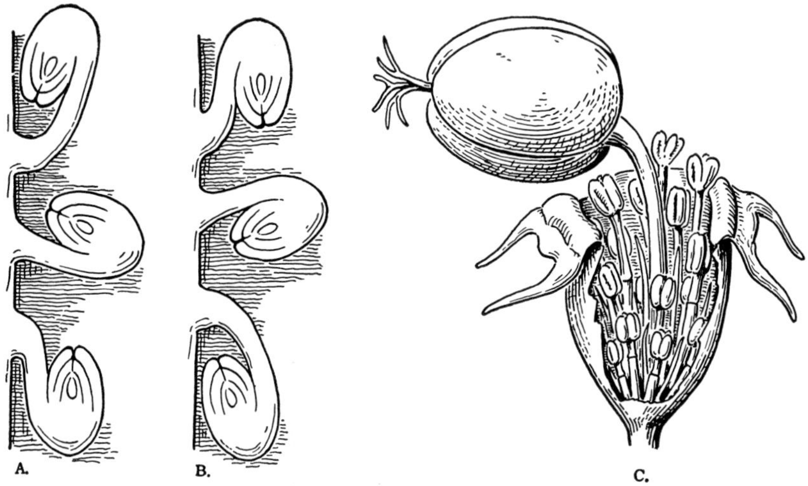

Figure 113. Schematic drawings to show modes of suspension of ovules: *A*, in the Geraniales; *B*, in the Sapindales. *C*, cyathium of spurge, *Euphorbia commutatus*.

Order 19. Geraniales. The evidence indicates that the order Geraniales, as set up by Engler, is not a natural group and that the families here included may actually comprise 4 or 5 different orders. As here regarded, the order is characterized by having the stamens typically in 2 whorls, and the ovules pendulous, with the raphe ventral (Figure 113).

a. Flowers bisexual
  b. Without secretory cells or passages
    c. Flowers regular
      d. Carpels at maturity splitting apart as separate fruitlets
        e. Carpels splitting apart elastically from the central axis as mericarps . . . . *Geraniaceae*
        e. Carpels often splitting apart as tuberculate or spiny nutlets . . . . *Zygophyllaceae*
      d. Carpels at maturity not splitting apart
        e. Leaves compound; juice sour . . . . *Oxalidaceae*
        e. Sap not sour
          f. Locules 4-5, all fertile . . . . *Linaceae*
          f. Locules 3-4, only 1 fertile . . . . *Erythroxylaceae*
    c. Flowers irregular
      d. Anthers opening longitudinally
        e. Leaves alternate . . . . *Tropaeolaceae*

e. Leaves opposite . . . . *Malpighiaceae*
d. Anthers opening by pores . . . . *Polygalaceae*
b. With secretory cells or passages
c. Herbage covered with glandular dots . . . . *Rutaceae*
c. Herbage not covered with glandular dots . . . . . . *Meliaceae*
a. Flowers unisexual
b. Flowers not reduced
c. Ovules usually 1 in each cell . . . . *Simaroubaceae*
c. Ovules usually 2 in each cell . . . . *Burseraceae*
b. Flowers usually much reduced
c. Terrestrial; carpels 3 . . . . *Euphorbiaceae*
c. Aquatic; carpels 2 . . . . *Callitrichaceae*

Linaceae. Flax Family.

HABIT. Herbs and shrubs, sometimes climbing, or arborescent.

LEAVES. Entire, alternate, simple.

INFLORESCENCE. Cymose.

FLOWERS. Perfect, regular; sepals 5, petals 5, stamens 5, 10, or more, carpels 2-5, joined, the ovary superior.

FRUIT. A capsule or drupe.

The family includes 9 genera with 300 species, primarily in temperate and subtropical regions of both hemispheres. Its phylogenetic position has been a matter of considerable dispute. The principal economic importance is for the fiber produced by the flax plant; a few species are grown as ornamentals.

Hugonia (32) is a genus of lianas of the Old World tropics, especially of the African rain forest. *Linum* (200), flax, is widely distributed, particularly abundant in southwestern United States. *L. usitatissimum,* Eurasia, is one of the oldest known textile fibers, the source of linen; the seeds yield linseed oil. *L. grandiflorum,* Algeria, red flax, and *L. perenne,* Europe, are cultivated as ornamentals. *Radiola linoides,* all-seed, occurs in Europe, temperate Asia, North Africa, and the mountains of tropical Africa.

Oxalidaceae. Oxalis Family.

HABIT. Perennial herbs or shrubs, often with fleshy rhizomes or tubers.

LEAVES. Alternate, typically compound, without stipules; the leaflets are often photeolic.

INFLORESCENCE. Cymose, racemose, or the flowers solitary.

FLOWERS. Regular, perfect; sepals 5, petals 5, stamens 10, carpels 5, united, the ovary superior.

FRUIT. A capsule or berry.

A family of 7 genera with 1000 species, mostly tropical and subtropical. Most authors agree that this family is closely related to the Geraniaceae. Economically it is of little importance.

Oxalis (850) is the principal genus, widely distributed but with 3 main centers, South Africa, the Andes, and Mexico-Central America. *O. acetosella,* wood sorrel, is circumboreal in spruce forests; *O. oregana,* redwood sorrel, is in California and Oregon; *O. corniculata* and *O. stricta* are widespread weeds; *O. tuberosa,* oca, of the Andes, has edible tubers. *Biophytum* (50), of the tropics, has sensitive leaflets and an explosive aril on the seeds, expelling them from the capsule; *B. sensitivum* is a common roadside weed of the tropics. *Averrhoa* (2) is a genus of small trees of tropical Asia; *A. bilimbi,* bilimbi, is grown for its acid fruits, used in relish; *A. carambola,* carambola, is cultivated for edible fruits produced on old wood (**cauliflory**).

Geraniaceae. Geranium Family.

HABIT. Mostly herbs, sometimes shrubs.

LEAVES. Alternate or opposite, compound, or simple and lobed or divided, stipulate.

INFLORESCENCE. Cymose or umbellate.

FLOWERS. Regular or irregular, perfect, protandrous; sepals 5, petals 5, stamens 5-15, carpels 3-5, joined, the ovary superior.

FRUIT. A capsule, or a schizocarp splitting into mericarps.

The family includes 11 genera with 850 species, widely distributed in temperate and subtropical regions. They are important chiefly as ornamentals.

Geranium (300), cranesbill (from the shape of the fruit), includes *G. robertianum,* herb Robert, circumboreal, *G. maculatum,* wild geranium, eastern North America. *Erodium,* heronsbill, has 60 species, especially of the Mediterranean, including *E. cicutarium,* alfilaria, grown for pasture. *Pelargonium* (250), storksbill, "geranium," mostly of South Africa, includes many cultivated varieties and hybrids, among the most widely grown house-plants in the United States; they are mostly aromatic.

Tropaeolaceae. Nasturtium Family. A small family of herbs, usually climbing by sensitive petioles, with 1 genus, *Tropaeolum* (80), from Chile to Mexico. The flowers are irregular, with 5 sepals, 5 petals, 8 stamens, 3 united carpels, and a superior ovary; the fruit is a schizocarp. *T. majus,* nasturtium (Figure 63), *T. peregrinum,* canary-bird flower, are cultivated ornamentals; *T. tuberosum* is grown in the Andes for edible tubers, cubios.

Erythroxylaceae. Coca Family. A family of 3 genera and 200 species, principally of the American tropics. The flowers are perfect and regular, with 5 sepals, 5 petals, 10 stamens, and 3-4 joined carpels. The chief genus is *Erythroxylum* (200). *E. coca,* Peru and Bolivia, is coca, a shrub with leaves which are chewed by natives, enabling them to undergo fatigue. It is the source of cocaine, and an extract is used, with cola (page 358), in the manufacture of soft drinks.

Zygophyllaceae. Caltrop Family.

HABIT. Perennial herbs or shrubs, many xerophytes or halophytes.

LEAVES. Opposite, often fleshy or leathery, mostly compound, stipulate.

INFLORESCENCE. Cymose, or the flowers solitary.

FLOWERS. Regular, perfect; sepals and petals usually 5, stamens 5, 10, or 15, carpels 4-5, joined, the ovary superior.

FRUIT. A capsule or berry.

A family of 27 genera including 250 species, mostly of warm lands, especially abundant in the Mediterranean. Most systematists include the family in the Geraniales. There are some useful timber trees and a few are grown as ornamentals.

Zygophyllum (80) is a genus of fleshy plants on Old World deserts and steppes. *Guaiacum* (6), of tropical America, includes *G. officinale* and *G. sanctum,* Florida, West Indies, and northern South America, yielding lignum-vitae, one of the hardest and heaviest of commercial woods (sp. gr., .95-1.25), also guaiacum, medicinal. *Larrea tridentata,* creosote-bush, southwestern United States, binds drifting sand; its strong odor protects it from animals. *Tribulus* (20), caltrops, occurs in Asia, Africa, and America, but chiefly in the Mediterranean. The mericarps have sharp rigid spines that may penetrate the feet of animals or tires of automobiles; *T. terrestris,* puncture weed, extends from the Mediterranean to Tibet (a weed in many other lands). *Balanites* (20), of Africa and Asia, includes *B. aegyptiaca,* thornwood, of African savannas.

Rutaceae. Rue Family.

HABIT. Herbs, shrubs, and trees, often xerophytic, aromatic.

LEAVES. Usually compound, glandular-dotted, aromatic, without stipules.

INFLORESCENCE. Cymose.

FLOWERS. Perfect, regular or irregular; sepals 4-5, petals 4-5 (sometimes none), stamens 3-10 or indefinite, attached at base or rim of an elevated development of the receptacle (the **disk**); carpels typically 4-5, joined, the ovary superior.

FRUIT. A capsule, hesperidium (Figure 87, E), schizocarp, berry, drupe or samara.

This is a large family, of 140 genera including 1300 species, widely distributed in temperate and tropical regions, but most abundant in South Africa and Australia. The development of glands producing an aromatic oil is a characteristic feature. By some botanists this family, with the next two, is placed in a separate order, the Rutales.

Zanthoxylum (20) is a genus of temperate East Asia and North America; *Z. americanum,* eastern North America, is prickly-ash or toothache tree; *Z. flavum* is West Indian satinwood, used for making furniture. *Ruta* (60), ranging from the Mediterranean to eastern Siberia, includes *R.*

graveolens, rue, a strongly scented shrub, yielding an oil, narcotic and stimulating. *Dictamnus albus,* gas-plant, candle-plant, Moses' burning bush, of Europe and western Asia, yields a volatile and inflammable oil which may be ignited around the plant on hot calm evenings. *Correa* (7) occurs in temperate Australia; some are cultivated ornamental shrubs, "Australian fuchsia." *Agothosma* (150), and *Diosma* (15), heath-like xerophytes, are characteristic of South Africa; *D. ericoides* is buchu. *Calodendron* (2) occurs in South Africa, including *C. capense,* Cape chestnut, an ornamental. *Cusparia* (25), in Brazil and Colombia, includes *C. febrifuga,* Angostura bark, or Cusparia bark, a substitute for quinine. *Pilocarpus* (20), in tropical America, includes *P. perinatifolius,* of southern Brazil, yielding pilocarpine, a medicinal alkaloid. *Chloroxylon swietenia,* of Indonesia, is East Indian satinwood, with useful timber. *Phellodendron amurense,* corktree, East Asia, with a thick corky bark, is planted as an ornamental. *Ptelea* (10), in temperate North America, includes *P. trifoliata,* hoptree, a cultivated ornamental shrub.

Poncirus trifoliata, hardy orange, of northern China, has a very sour fruit; the plants withstand frost. *Feronia elephantum,* elephant-apple, Java to India, has useful wood and gum and edible fruits. *Aegle* (3), of Indonesia, includes *A. marmelos,* ball fruit or wood-apple, a valuable remedy for dysentery. *Citrus* (10) is a genus yielding some of the world's most important fruits, widely cultivated in warm lands, including *C. sinensis,* sweet orange, native of China and Indo-China; *C. limon,* lemon, southeastern Asia; *C. aurantifolia,* lime, East Indies; *C. reticulata,* mandarin orange or tangerine, Philippines and southeastern Asia; *C. paradisi,* grapefruit, a hybrid or sport that apparently originated in the West Indies; *C. medica,* citron, China, India and Indonesia; *C. grandis,* pummelo, southeastern Asia and East Indies; *C. aurantium,* sour orange, Seville orange, bigarade, southeastern Asia. *Fortunella,* kumquat, is a closely related genus with 6 Asiatic species; the genus was named for Robert Fortune (p. 85), who introduced it into Europe.

Simaroubaceae. Quassia Family. A family of tropical trees and shrubs with 32 genera and 200 species. The leaves are alternate, the flowers small, regular, perfect or imperfect, with 3-7 sepals, 3-7 petals, 6-14 stamens, and 4-5 united carpels. *Suriana maritima* is a characteristic strand shrub from Florida to Brazil, in East Africa, tropical Asia, and Micronesia. *Simarouba* (9), ranging from Florida to Brazil, yields bitters from the bitter bark. *Quassia amara,* quassia wood, of Brazil, has very bitter wood, yielding the drug quassia; formerly the wood was made into cups in which water was allowed to stand for several minutes, then imbibed as a blood tonic. *Ailanthus* (15) ranges from India and China to Australia; *A. altissima,* tree of heaven, China, is planted as an ornamental, and has widely escaped from cultivation in America and elsewhere.

Burseraceae. Balsam Family.

HABIT. Aromatic shrubs and trees.

LEAVES. Alternate, deciduous, usually compound, exstipulate.

INFLORESCENCE. Flowers solitary or in panicles.

FLOWERS. Small, regular, generally unisexual; sepals 3-5, petals 3-5, stamens 3-5, carpels 2-5, joined; ovary superior.

FRUIT. A drupe or capsule.

A family of 20 genera including about 600 species, with greatest development in tropical America and northeastern Africa. There are resin ducts in the bark which yield gums, balsams, and resins of considerable commercial value.

Boswellia (25) occurs in tropical Africa and Asia; *B. carteri,* Somaliland, yields frankincense. *Bursera* (100) is a genus of tropical and subtropical America, especially Mexico; *B. gummifera,* gommier, yields balsam known as chibou or cachibou. *Commiphora* (170), of Asia and Africa, includes trees characteristic of savannas; *C. erythraea* yields the myrrh of antiquity, *C. mokul,* bdellium, *C. opobalsamum,* Mecca balsam. *Canarium* (150), occurs in tropical Asia and Africa; *C. luzonicum,* pili tree, has an edible seed and furnishes Manila elemi, a resin; *C. strictum,* of Malabar, yields black dammar.

Meliaceae. Mahogany Family.

HABIT. Shrubs and trees, often with fragrant wood.

LEAVES. Usually alternate, compound, exstipulate.

INFLORESCENCE. Cymose.

FLOWERS. Regular, perfect; sepals 4-5, joined; petals 4-5; stamens 8-10, monadelphous; carpels 2-5, joined; ovary superior.

FRUIT. A berry, capsule, or drupe.

This is primarily a tropical family, with 50 genera including about 1000 species. The plants lack the resin ducts of the closely related family Burseraceae. A few yield important timber and some are grown ornamentally.

Cedrela (40), in tropical America, includes *C. odorata,* West Indian cedar, the principal wood used in cigar boxes; it is insect repellent. *Swietenia* (3) occurs in tropical and subtropical America; *S. mahogani,* mahogany, yields a valuable hard, red-brown timber, one of the most highly esteemed in the world for cabinet making. *Khaya senegalensis,* African mahogany, tropical Africa, produces a valuable cabinet wood. *Melia azedarach,* beadtree, chinaberry tree, or pride of India, of tropical Asia, is cultivated as an ornamental tree.

Malpighiaceae. Malpighia Family.

HABIT. Shrubs or trees, usually climbing, sometimes with stinging hairs.

LEAVES. Usually opposite, stipulate, simple.

INFLORESCENCE. Racemose.

FLOWERS. Perfect, regular or irregular; sepals 5, petals 5, stamens 10, carpels 3, united; ovary superior.

FRUIT. A schizocarp, samara, capsule, berry, or drupe.

A tropical family of 60 genera including 850 species, primarily American. Members of the family are marked features among tropical lianas. Most botanists include them with the Geraniales. Few species are of economic importance.

Banisteria (80) ranges from the West Indies to Bolivia and Brazil; the plants are lianas with showy yellow flowers. *Malpighia* (30) is a genus of shrubs ranging from Texas and Mexico to the West Indies, some with stinging hairs; *M. glabra* is Barbados-cherry, the fruits used in making preserves. *Byrsonima* (100) is a genus of shrubs and trees in Central and South America and the West Indies; *B. crassifolia,* nance, is a very common and distinctive tree of Central America.

Polygalaceae. Milkwort Family.

HABIT. Herbs, shrubs, or trees, sometimes twining.

LEAVES. Usually alternate, simple, exstipulate.

INFLORESCENCE. Spicate or racemose, or the flowers solitary.

FLOWERS. Irregular, bisexual with 5 sepals, the inner 2 often large and petal-like, usually 3 petals, 3-10 stamens, and 2-5 united carpels, with a superior ovary.

FRUIT. A capsule, nut, samara, or drupe.

A family of 10 genera including 700 species, nearly cosmopolitan. Despite the implication in the name, the plants do not produce latex; some of them were formerly reputed to increase lactation. There is little agreement with respect to the phyletic position. They have slight economic importance.

Polygala (500) is the largest genus; most of the showiness of the pretty flowers is from 2 red, white, blue, or yellow sepals; *P. senega,* Seneca snakeroot, eastern North America, is medicinal; *P. vulgaris* is in Europe and Asia; *P. paucifolia,* gaywings, eastern North America; *P. chinensis* is a common weed in southern Asia. *Xanthophyllum* (50), from India to northeastern Australia, includes *X. flavescens,* gundhi, a large tree of northern India.

Euphorbiaceae. Spurge Family.

HABIT. Herbs, shrubs, trees, some xerophytic, heath-like or cactus-like, or lianas; often with a milky latex.

LEAVES. Mostly alternate, stipulate, often variously reduced.

INFLORESCENCE. Various, often condensed so as to give the appearance of a single flower (**cyathium;** see Figure 113).

FLOWERS. Unisexual (the plants monoecious or dioecious), regular, hypogynous; sepals 5 or none, petals 5 or usually none, staminate flowers with 1 to many stamens, pistillate flowers usually with 3 united carpels.

FRUIT. A schizocarp or capsule.

This is a very large and widely distributed family, of 283 genera including 7300 species, almost world-wide in distribution. Much difference of opinion exists as to the phyletic position. Many are of great economic importance, providing food, drugs, rubber and other products.

Phyllanthus (500) is tropical and subtropical in range; many tropical species have flat green phylloclades with flowers on the margins (hence the generic name); *P. emblica,* India, myrobalan, and *P. acidus,* India, gooseberry-tree, have fruits made into preserves.

Croton (600) is tropical and subtropical, most common in America; *C. tiglium,* tropical Asia, yields croton oil, a purgative; *C. cascarilla,* Florida and the Bahamas, yields cascarella bark; many are grown for colored foliage, while others are common weedy shrubs. *Aleurites* (5) is a genus of eastern Asia and Malaysia; *A. moluccana* is candlenut; *A. fordii,* much cultivated in China and America, yields tung oil, used in varnishes. *Hevea* (12) is a genus of Brazil, especially of the Amazon Valley. The plants yield latex and *H. brasiliensis,* Pará or Brazilian rubber tree (p. 77), is the source of the rubber of commerce; it is extensively cultivated in Malaysia. *Mercurialis* has 8 species in Europe and Asia; *M. perennis* is mercury, a weed, also yielding a drug. *Acalypha* (430), tropical and subtropical, includes *A. hispida,* and *A. wilkesiana,* copperleaf, cultivated for variegated leaves. Several species as *A. virginica,* 3-seeded mercury, are common weeds. *Ricinus communis,* a native of tropical Africa, now widespread, is the source of castor oil (from the seeds). *Codiaeum variegatum,* Java to Fiji to Queensland, is cultivated in the tropics for its colored leaves. *Jatropha* (150), tropical, includes *J. curcas,* coquillo, a common shrub of Central America. *Cnidoscolus* (50), includes herbs and shrubs chiefly of tropical America, armed with stinging bristles; *C. stimulosus,* tread-softly, is a weed of the southern United States. *Manihot* (160), is a genus of tropical America. *M. glazioviana,* Brazil, yields Ceara rubber. *M. esculenta,* bitter cassava, manioc, yuca, is extensively cultivated for its starchy tuberous roots; next to sweet potato it is the most important tropical root crop; tapioca is made from the roots by a special preparation. *Hippomane mancinella,* manchineel, of the West Indies, is a common seashore tree, with poisonous latex. *Sapium* (100) is tropical and subtropical; *S. sebiferum,* China and Formosa, Chinese tallow-tree, has a waxy seed covering used for candles; *S. biloculare* is one of the species producing "Mexican jumping beans"; the propelling agent is the larva of a moth. Another "jumping bean" is produced by *Sebastiana pavoniana,* also in this family. *Hura* (2), of tropical America, includes *H. crepitans,* sandbox tree; the explosive fruit was formerly used for sandboxes for blotting ink; the trees sometimes reach 9 feet in diameter, and yield useful timber (possumwood).

Euphorbia (1600) is a vast genus of subtropical and warm temperate regions; the small naked unisexual flowers are grouped into a cyathium, the plants are latex-bearing; many are cactus-like and are among the commonest of Old World desert succulents; *E. splendens*, Madagascar, is crown-of-thorns; *E. marginata*, is snow-on-the-mountain; *E. pulcherrima*, Central America, poinsettia, is grown as an ornamental, especially for Christmas decoration; *E. cyparissias*, cypress spurge, is often seen in old cemeteries. *Pedilanthus* (30) occurs in tropical America; the plants are grown as ornamentals (redbird-cactus, slipper-flower, or Jew-bush); the red involucre is slipper-shaped.

Callitrichaceae. Water-starwort Family. A family of 1 genus, *Callitriche*, with about 40 species, of aquatic plants, distributed generally from the arctic to subantarctic regions, except for South Africa. The leaves are both submerged and floating; the flowers are unisexual and naked, with 1 stamen in the staminate, and 2 united carpels in the pistillate.

Order 20. Sapindales. This order, as here understood, differs from the Geraniales in having the ovules pendulous with the raphe dorsal, or erect with the raphe ventral (see Figure 113). By many phylogenists the families included here are distributed in 3 to 6 separate orders.

a. Flowers regular
  b. Petals none
    c. Stamens 2-3; low heath-like shrubs .... *Empetraceae*
    c. Stamens 4-many; woody plants .... *Buxaceae*
  b. Petals usually present
    c. Herbs .... *Limnanthaceae*
    c. Woody plants
      d. Stems bearing resin-passages .... *Anacardiaceae*
      d. Resin-passages not usually present
        e. Leaves alternate
          f. Leaves often evergreen
            g. Flowers bisexual .... *Cyrillaceae*
            g. Flowers unisexual .... *Aquifoliaceae*
          f. Leaves usually deciduous
            g. Flowers usually cymose .... *Celastraceae*
            g. Flowers paniculate .... *Icacinaceae*
        e. Leaves opposite
          f. Carpels 5-10, free at maturity .... *Coriariaceae*
          f. Carpels united
            g. Leaves simple
              h. Fruit usually a capsule or berry . *Celastraceae*
              h. Fruit a samara .... *Aceraceae*

g. Leaves compound
h. Fruit a capsule . . . . *Staphyleaceae*
h. Fruit a samara . . . . *Aceraceae*
a. Flowers usually irregular
b. Woody plants
c. Leaves opposite . . . . *Hippocastanaceae*
c. Leaves usually alternate
d. Stamens usually 8; carpels 2-3 . . . . *Sapindaceae*
d. Stamens 4-5, or 10
e. Carpels 4-5 . . . . *Melianthaceae*
e. Carpels 2 . . . . *Sabiaceae*
b. Herbs . . . . *Balsaminaceae*

Buxaceae. Box Family. A family mostly of evergreen shrubs with leathery leaves, 6 genera, 30 species, temperate and subtropical. The flowers are in heads or spikes, unisexual (the plants monoecious or dioecious), regular, apetalous, or naked. Sepals 4, stamens 4 to indefinite, carpels usually 3, united. *Buxus* (20) is the principal genus, occurring in Eurasia, Africa, and the West Indies; *B. sempervirens,* box, western and southern Europe, is much cultivated for hedges. *Pachysandra* (5), in eastern Asia and eastern North America, includes *P. procumbens,* of the southern Appalachians.

Empetraceae. Crowberry Family. A family of heath-like shrubs with 3 genera including 5 species, of the north and south temperate regions. The leaves are incurved, forming a cavity partly filled with hairs, into which the stomata open. The inflorescence is racemose and the plants are often dioecious. The regular flowers have 3 sepals, 3 petals, 3 stamens, and 2-9 united carpels. The fruit is a drupe. *Corema,* broom crowberry, includes 2 species, in southwestern Europe and northeastern United States. *Empetrum* (2) has an unusual range, with *E. nigrum,* crowberry, circumboreal on moors, and *E. rubrum* in the southern Andes, Tierra del Fuego, Falkland Islands, and Tristan da Cunha (see map, Figure 24). This is perhaps more closely allied to the Coriariaceae than to any other family, and they may constitute relics of ancient groups.

Coriariaceae. Coriaria Family. A family mostly of shrubs with opposite leaves, with 1 genus, *Coriaria* (10), from the Mediterranean to Japan, New Zealand, and Chile to Mexico. The flowers are racemose and inconspicuous, with 5 sepals, 5 petals, 5-10 stamens, and 5-10 distinct carpels. The petals ripen with and enclose the carpels, forming a pseudo-drupe.

Limnanthaceae. False-mermaid Family. A family of herbs with alternate leaves, 2 genera and 8 species, of North America. The flowers are regular, perfect, and 3-5-merous. The fruit is a schizocarp. *Limnanthes* has 7 species in western North America, including *L. douglasii,* meadowfoam, ornamental. *Floerkea proserpinacoides* of eastern North America is false mermaid weed.

Anacardiaceae. Sumac Family.

HABIT. Trees and shrubs, with a milky sap.

LEAVES. Alternate, exstipulate, simple or compound.

INFLORESCENCE. Paniculate.

FLOWERS. Typically 5-merous, regular, hypogynous; stamens typically 10, arising from a disk; carpels 1-3, united.

FRUIT. Usually a drupe.

The family includes 73 genera with about 600 species, chiefly tropical, but extending into the Mediterranean region, eastern Asia and North America. Systematists agree in placing it in the Sapindales. The presence of resin ducts is a distinguishing character. The family is important for edible fruits and nuts.

Mangifera indica, mango, East Indies, is widely cultivated in the tropics for the large edible drupe, derived from a single carpel; it is one of the most popular of tropical fruits. *Anacardium occidentale,* cashew, of the West Indies, is cultivated for the edible kidney-shaped cashew-nut, and the cashew-apple, a pear-shaped, fleshy, edible structure developing from the flower stalk and receptacle (Figure 88, G). *Spondias* (6), of the tropical regions, has edible drupes developing from the 3 united carpels; *S. purpurea* is ciruelo, Spanish plum, or red mombin; *S. mombin* is hogplum or yellow mombin. *Pistacia* (9) ranges from the Mediterranean to eastern Asia, and in Mexico; *P. vera,* pistachio, Mediterranean, produces edible nuts; *P. terebinthus,* terebinth, yields Chian turpentine. *Schinus molle,* Mexico to Chile, peppertree, is much grown for the graceful drooping branches and red fruits. *Cotinus* (2) ranges from southern Europe to eastern Asia; *C. coggygria,* smoke-tree, is a cultivated ornamental. *Rhus* (150) is a genus of subtropical and warm temperate regions. *R. coriaria,* Sicilian sumac, is cultivated for tannin. *R. vernicifera,* lacquer-tree, is the principal source of natural lacquer; the art of lacquering originated in China and reached its highest development under the Ming dynasty (1368-1644). *R. glabra, R. typhina, R. copallina,* sumac, are common in eastern North America. *R. vernix,* poison sumac, *R. radicans,* poison-ivy (Figure 42) of eastern North America, and *R. diversiloba,* poison-oak, of California, cause ivy poisoning, a dermatitis. *R. trilobata,* of western North America, is skunkbush. *Semecarpus* (40) occurs in Indomalaysia; *S. anacardium,* markingnut, has young fruits which yield a marking ink. *Schinopsis* (5) includes *S. lorentzii,* Paraguay, quebracho, at present the world's most important source of tannin. *Metopium* (3), poisonwood, West Indies, Florida, yields a resin causing dermatitis, like poison-ivy.

Cyrillaceae. Cyrilla Family. A family of usually evergreen shrubs, with 3 genera including 5 species of warm temperate and tropical America. The leaves are alternate; the flowers are racemose, perfect, regular, with

5 sepals, 5 petals, 5-10 stamens, and 2-5 united carpels. *Cliftonia monophylla,* of the southeastern United States, buckwheat tree, or titi, is cultivated as an ornamental shrub. *Cyrilla racemosa,* southern leatherwood, black titi, growing in swamps in warm temperate America, is also cultivated as an ornamental.

Aquifoliaceae. Holly Family.

HABIT. Shrubs and trees.

LEAVES. Alternate, simple, deciduous or persistent.

INFLORESCENCE. Cymose.

FLOWERS. Regular, bisexual or unisexual (the plants dioecious or polygamo-dioecious).

FRUIT. A drupe.

The family comprises 3 genera including about 300 species, widely distributed. Most phylogenists separate this family and the next, with several others from the Sapindales. Some of them are important for their wood or ornamental nature.

Ilex (280), holly, is widely distributed; *I. aquifolium,* Europe, and *I. opaca,* eastern North America, are grown for evergreen leaves and red fruits, especially for Christmas decoration. *I. paraguariensis,* southern Brazil, Paraguay, Uruguay, northern Argentina, is yerba maté or Paraguay-tea; the leaves are much used in South America to make a beverage. *I. cassine,* dahoon, *I. vomitoria,* yaupon, are in southeastern United States. *Nemopanthus mucronata,* of eastern North America, is wild holly.

Celastraceae. Stafftree Family.

HABIT. Trees and shrubs, often climbing.

LEAVES. Simple, alternate or opposite, persistent or deciduous.

INFLORESCENCE. Cymose.

FLOWERS. Small, regular, usually perfect; sepals 4-5, free or united; petals 4-5, stamens 4-5, carpels 2-5, united.

FRUITS AND SEEDS. Fruit a capsule, samara, drupe, or berry; seeds usually with a brightly colored aril.

The family includes 45 genera with about 500 species, widely distributed. The small greenish flowers and the brightly colored arils are distinctive. The plants are of slight economic importance.

Euonymus (100) is the largest genus; *E. europaea,* Europe to Central Asia, is spindletree; *E. atropurpureus,* wahoo, *E. americanus,* strawberry-bush, are in eastern North America; *E. alatus,* China, Japan, has corky-winged branches, and is grown as an ornamental. *Celastrus* (30) includes mostly lianas, of tropical and subtropical regions; *C. scandens,* climbing bittersweet, eastern United States, is sometimes grown for the decorative fruits and seeds. *Maytenus* (70) is a genus of South America and the West Indies, *M. boaria,* mayten, is a characteristic evergreen tree from central Chile to northern Patagonia, planted as an avenue tree. *Catha edulis,* of Arabia, Abyssinia, and East Africa, is used to make Khat-tea, an important beverage of Arabians. *Pachystima* (2) includes *P. canbyi,* Canby's mountain-lover, in the Alleghenies, and *P. myrsinites* in western North America.

Staphyleaceae. Bladdernut Family. A family of shrubs and trees, with 6 genera including 25 species, chiefly of the northern hemisphere. The leaves are opposite or alternate and compound. The flowers are racemose or paniculate, regular, with a cup-shaped disk; sepals 5, petals 5, stamens 5, carpels 2-3, united; fruit a capsule, often inflated. *Staphylea* (11), bladdernut, includes plants grown as ornamental shrubs; *S. pinnata* is found from Central Europe to Asia Minor; *S. colchica* is in the Caucasus; *S. trifolia* is in eastern North America; *S. bolanderi* is in California.

Icacinaceae. Icacina Family.

HABIT. Trees or shrubs (often climbing).

LEAVES. Alternate, simple, exstipulate.

INFLORESCENCE. Paniculate.

FLOWERS. Regular, perfect; sepals 4-5, united; petals 4-5; stamens 4-5; carpels 2, 3, or 5, united.

FRUIT. A drupe or samara.

This is a family of pantropical distribution, with about 38 genera including 225 species. Few of the species have economic value. *Icacina* (5) is a genus in the rain forest of tropical West Africa.

Aceraceae. Maple Family.

HABIT. Trees and shrubs, sometimes with milky latex.

LEAVES. Opposite, simple or sometimes compound, usually lobed.

INFLORESCENCE. Corymbose, racemose, or paniculate.

FLOWERS. Regular, bisexual or unisexual, the plants monoecious, polygamous or dioecious; sepals 4-5, petals 4-5 or none, stamens 4, 8, or 10, carpels 2, united.

FRUIT. A double samara.

The family includes 2 genera with about 150 species, of the northern hemisphere, mainly in temperate regions and on tropical mountains. They are distinguished by the characteristic fruit. Some are important for lumber and many are grown ornamentally. Maple syrup is another important product.

Acer (150), maple, occurs in Europe, eastern Asia, North America, and on mountains of Java and Sumatra. *A. platanoides,* Norway maple, is found from Europe to Asia Minor. Other Old World species are *A. campestre,* hedge maple, central and southern Europe, *A. pseudoplatanus,* sycamore maple, Central Europe to Asia Minor, *A. tataricum,* Tatarian maple, southeastern Europe to Asia Minor, and *A. palmatum,* Japanese maple, Japan, Korea. *A. saccharum,* sugar maple, of the eastern United

States, yields good timber (hard maple) and a sugary sap from which maple syrup is made. *A. negundo,* boxelder, North America, has compound leaves. Other species are *A. saccharinum,* silver maple, North America, *A. rubrum,* red maple, eastern North America, *A. macrophyllum,* bigleaf maple, western North America. *Dipteronia* (2), in China, has fruits with wings all around.

Hippocastanaceae. Horsechestnut Family.

HABIT. Trees and shrubs.

LEAVES. Opposite, palmately compound, exstipulate (Figure 62).

INFLORESCENCE. Flowers in terminal thyrses.

FLOWERS. Bisexual, irregular; sepals 4-5, united, petals 4-5, stamens 5-8, carpels 3, united.

FRUIT. A leathery capsule with 1 or more large seeds.

The family includes 2 genera with about 25 species, of the north temperate zone and South America (see map, Figure 23). The family is united to the Sapindaceae by some authorities, but the thyrsoid inflorescence, the leathery capsule, and the opposite leaves, are distinctive. Several species are cultivated as ornamentals.

Aesculus (23) is the principal genus. *A. hippocastanum,* horsechestnut, is a native of the Balkans and Caucasus, but widely cultivated as an ornamental. American species include *A. octandra,* sweet buckeye, eastern United States, *A. glabra,* Ohio or fetid buckeye, *A. pavia,* red buckeye, southeastern United States, and *A. californica,* California buckeye. *Billia* (2) ranges from Mexico to Colombia.

Sapindaceae. Soapberry Family.

HABIT. Trees or shrubs, in some cases tendril-bearing vines.

LEAVES. Alternate, simple or pinnately compound.

INFLORESCENCE. Racemose, paniculate, or cymose.

FLOWERS. Bisexual or unisexual (the plants commonly polygamo-dioecious), regular or irregular; sepals 5, petals 5, stamens 4-10, or many, carpels usually 3, united.

FRUIT. A capsule, nut, berry, drupe, schizocarp, or samara.

The family includes 130 genera and 1100 species, primarily tropical. Some species are important for edible fruits, timber, or as ornamentals.

Serjania (200) is a genus of tropical America, including lianas with tendrils; the fruit is a 3-winged schizocarp. *Paullinia* (150) is mostly in tropical America but with 1 species in tropical Africa and Madagascar. *P. cupana,* Amazonas, yields quarana, the most stimulating of all caffeine; it is cultivated in Brazil as a beverage plant. *Sapindus* (20) is a genus of tropical and subtropical regions; the berries of *S. saponaria,* soapberry, Mexico to Argentina, form a lather in water and are used for soap. *Cardiospermum halicacabum,* balloon vine, with bladdery fruits, is a common tropical weed, sometimes cultivated as an ornamental climber. *Litchi chinensis,* leechee, of China and the Philippines, is cultivated for the edible juicy fruit (also eaten dried, as leechee nuts). *Pappea capensis,* wild preume, South Africa, yields edible fruits, oil, and timber. *Blighia* (6) occurs in tropical Africa; *B. sapida,* akee, vegetable brain, is grown for its edible fruit; the genus was named for the captain of the "Bounty" (see page 46).

Koelreuteria (6) is a genus of shrubs in China and Formosa; the capsule is large and bladdery. *K. paniculata,* goldenrain-tree, is grown for the profusion of yellow flowers and attractive winged fruits. *Dodonaea* has 52 species in Australia, 1 in Hawaii, and 1 in Madagascar; *D. viscosa,* hopbush is now a very widespread tropical and subtropical shrub, with winged fruits. *Melicocca bijuga,* Spanish lime, genip, tropical America, is grown for the edible fruit.

Sabiaceae. Sabia Family. A family of trees and shrubs (some lianas), 4 genera, about 90 species, tropical, mostly in southeastern Asia. The leaves are alternate. The flowers are paniculate and perfect, with 3-5 united sepals, 4-5 petals, the inner 2 much smaller than the others, stamens 3-5, opposite the petals, and 2 united carpels. The fruit is a berry. The principal genera are *Sabia* (20) in southeastern Asia, and *Meliosma* (60), of tropical Asia and America; species of the latter are cultivated as ornamental trees in Florida.

Melianthaceae. Melianthus Family. A family of trees and shrubs, 3 genera, 38 species, tropical and South Africa. The leaves are alternate. The flowers are racemose, perfect or imperfect, irregular, with 5 sepals, 4-5 petals, 4, 5, or 10 stamens and 4-5 united carpels. The fruit is a capsule. *Melianthus* (5), in South Africa, has flowers very rich in nectar; *M. major,* honeybush, is grown as a decorative shrub.

Balsaminaceae. Jewelweed Family.

HABIT. Herbs with watery stems, sometimes succulent, rarely epiphytic.

LEAVES. Alternate, opposite, or whorled, simple.

INFLORESCENCE. The flowers solitary, or in axillary clusters.

FLOWERS. Perfect, irregular; sepals 3-5, the 2 anterior very small, the posterior 1 spurred, large and petal-like; petals 5, distinct, or united and appearing as 3; stamens 4-5; carpels 5, united.

FRUIT. A fleshy capsule, dehiscing explosively, thus distributing the seeds.

The family includes 2 genera with about 450 species, widely distributed, but most abundant in the tropics of Asia and Africa. The elastic dehiscence of the capsule is characteristic. The relationships of the family are uncertain, some botanists placing it with the Geraniales. A few species are grown as ornamentals.

Impatiens (420) is a genus of tropical and north temperate regions, especially abundant in the mountains of India and Ceylon; *I. noli-tangere,* Europe to Japan, is touch-me-not; *I. balsamina* is garden balsam. *I. pallida, I. capensis,* jewelweed, occur in eastern United States.

Order 21. Rhamnales. The order differs from the Geraniales and Sapindales by having the stamens in a single whorl, opposite the petals. A disk surrounds the ovary.

a. Woody plants, trees, shrubs or lianas; fruit dry or a drupe *Rhamnaceae*
a. Climbing shrubs; fruit a berry . . . . *Vitaceae*

Rhamnaceae. Buckthorn Family.

HABIT. Trees or shrubs, sometimes climbing.

LEAVES. Simple, mostly alternate, stipulate.

INFLORESCENCE. Cymose or corymbose.

FLOWERS. Inconspicuous, perfect or imperfect, regular, sometimes apetalous; sepals 4-5, petals 4-5, stamens 4-5, arising from a disk, carpels 2-4, united.

FRUIT. A capsule, samara, or drupe.

This family is of almost cosmopolitan distribution, comprising 45 genera with 550 species. A distinguishing feature is the position of the stamens, opposite the petals. Several are of economic value, for drugs, fruits, or ornamental planting.

Paliurus (6) ranges from southern Europe to eastern Asia; *P. spina-Christi* is Christ's-thorn, with stipular thorns. *Zizyphus* (60) occurs in warm lands; *Z. jujuba,* East Indies and southern China, jujubes, is cultivated for the edible fruits; *Z. chloroxylon,* cogwood, Jamaica, has valuable hard wood. *Rhamnus* (100) is mostly north temperate. *R. cathartica,* purging buckthorn, from Europe to Altai and in North Africa, has purgative berries. *R. frangula,* alder buckthorn, Europe and the Caucasus, produces frangula bark, purgative. *R. purshiana,* western North America, is cultivated for the bark, which yields cascara sagrada; *R. californica,* coffee-berry, is a common shrub in California. *Hovenia dulcis,* Japanese raisin-tree, ranging from the Himalayas to Japan, has an edible fruit stalk. *Ceanothus* (50) is a genus of North America, particularly common in the west portion, especially in the chaparral. *C. americanus,* eastern North America, is redroot, New Jersey tea. *Krugiodendron ferreum,* leadwood, black ironwood, of Florida and West Indies, is one of the heaviest of woods, with a specific gravity of 1.3.

Vitaceae. Grape Family.

HABIT. Climbing (rarely erect) shrubs.

LEAVES. Alternate, simple or compound.

INFLORESCENCE. Cymose.

FLOWERS. Regular, small, perfect or imperfect; sepals 4-5, united, small, petals 4-5, often united at the tips and falling off as a hood, stamens 4-5, arising from a disk, carpels 2, united.

FRUIT. A berry.

The family includes 11 genera with 600 species, widely distributed in the tropics and subtropics and extending into temperate regions. They have terminal buds that develop into apparently lateral tendrils as they are subordinated by the more vigorous growth of the axillary branch in the opposite leaf axil. Economically the family is of great importance for the edible fruits, and the juice, from which wine is made.

Vitis (60) occurs mostly in the northern hemisphere. *V. vinifera,* European grape, is one of the oldest and most valuable of cultivated fruits, the source of wine; the dried fruits are raisins; currants (from Corinth) are the dried fruits of a Greek variety. *V. aestivalis,* summer grape, *V. riparia,* frost grape, *V. vulpina,* winter grape, *V. labrusca,* fox grape, *V. rotundifolia,* muscadine, are found in eastern North America. *Parthenocissus* (15) occurs in temperate Asia and North America; *P. tricuspidata,* China, Japan, is an ornamental wall vine, known as Boston ivy; *P. quinquefolia,* eastern North America, is Virginia creeper. *Ampelopsis* (20) occurs in Asia and North America, including *A. arborea,* pepper-vine, southern United States.

Order 22. Malvales. Most phylogenists are in accord with Engler's treatment of these families. The order was first named Columniferae by Eichler, with reference to the column of stamens in the Malvaceae.

a. Mucilage cells absent .... *Elaeocarpaceae*
a. Mucilage cells usually present
  b. Sepals free
    c. Stamens numerous, free or in separate bundles ... *Tiliaceae*
    c. Stamens with filaments united into a column
      d. Carpels 5 to many; pollen rough; mostly herbs or shrubs .... *Malvaceae*
      d. Carpels 2-5; pollen smooth; tropical trees .... *Bombacaceae*
  b. Sepals united .... *Sterculiaceae*

Elaeocarpaceae. Elaeocarpus Family. A family of trees and shrubs, with 7 genera including 125 species, tropical and subtropical. The leaves are alternate or opposite. The flowers have 4-5 sepals, 4-5 petals (rarely none), numerous stamens, and 2 to many carpels. The fruit is a capsule or drupe. *Elaeocarpus* (70), of Indonesia, Australia, Madagascar, Japan, has some species grown as ornamentals. *Aristotelia* (7), of Australia, New Zealand and Chile, includes *A. maqui* of central and southern Chile.

Tiliaceae. Linden Family.

HABIT. Trees or shrubs, rarely herbs.

LEAVES. Alternate, simple, stipulate, often oblique.

INFLORESCENCE. Cymose.

FLOWERS. Perfect, regular; sepals 5, petals 5 (rarely none), stamens numerous, carpels 2 to many.

FRUIT. A berry, drupe, capsule or nut.

The family comprises mostly woody plants, with 41 genera including 400 species, mostly tropical, but with extensions into temperate regions. They are distinguished by the nearly distinct stamens. Some are important for lumber and many are ornamental.

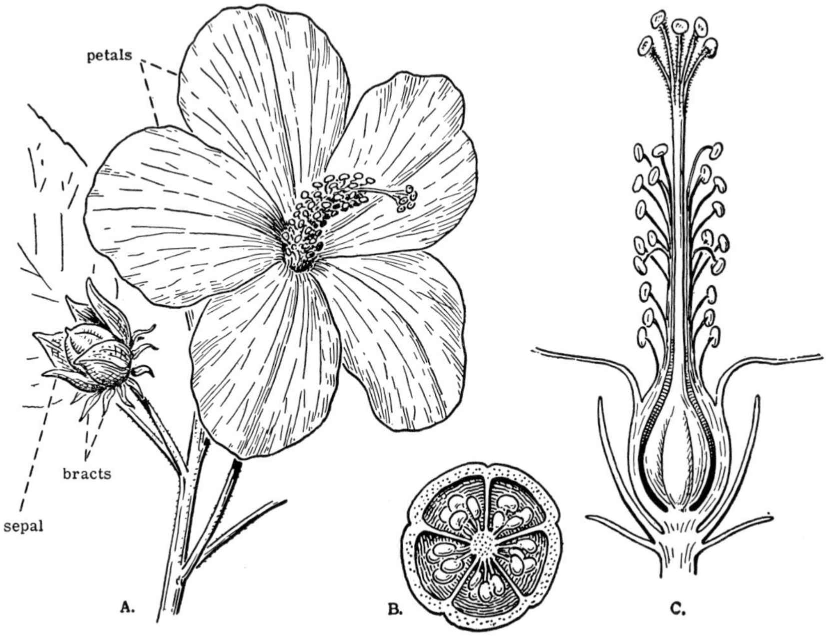

Figure 114. A mallow, *Hibiscus palustris*. *A*, flower; *B*, cross-section of ovary; *C*, section of staminal tube (column), exposing gynoecium.

Tilia (12) is a genus of the north temperate zone; the bracts are adnate to the axes of the inflorescences arising in their axils; the flowers are a valuable source of nectar, and the wood is extensively used in the manufacture of bee-keepers' supplies; *T. cordata, T. platyphyllos,* Europe, lime or linden, are often planted as shade trees as, for example, along the avenue Unter den Linden in Berlin. *T. americana, T. heterophylla,* basswood, are in eastern North America; *T. japonica* is Japanese linden; *T. mongolica* is Mongolian linden. Some species were formerly utilized as a source of fibers, hence the name basswood (bast wood). *Corchorus* (30), a genus of tropical annuals, includes *C. capsularis* and *C. olitorius*, pat or koshta, the chief source of the fiber jute or gunny, mainly grown in the Ganges and Brahmaputra valleys. *Sparmannia* (3), in Abyssinia and

South Africa, includes S. *africana* (rumslind), of Cape Colony. *Grewia* (120), of the Old World tropics; includes G. *asiatica,* phalsa, planted in India for its edible berries. *Triumfetta* (50) is a genus of tropical regions; the fruits bear hooked spines; many are common tropical weeds. *Heliocarpus* (10), ranging from Mexico to Paraguay, includes *H. popayanensis,* majaguillo, a common tree of the northern Andes.

Malvaceae. Mallow Family.

HABIT. Herbs, shrubs, or trees.

LEAVES. Alternate, simple, stipulate.

INFLORESCENCE. Cymose, or the flowers solitary.

FLOWERS. Perfect, regular; sepals 5, petals 5, stamens numerous, all united below into a tube (**column,** see Figure 114), carpels 1 to many, often 5, united.

FRUIT. A capsule, schizocarp, or berry.

The family is composed of 82 genera including 1500 species, widely distributed over the earth, especially abundant in the American tropics. They are characterized by the distinctive column of stamens. Economically the family is of great importance for cotton fibers, while many species are cultivated ornamentals.

Abutilon (100), is a genus of tropical and subtropical regions; *A. theophrasti,* velvetleaf, southern Europe and Asia, is cultivated for the fiber, China jute, used in rugmaking, and is a widespread weed. *Lavatera* (20), tree-mallow, is a genus mostly of the Mediterranean, but also in Asia and Australia; *L. arborea,* England to the Canaries, is tree mallow. *Althaea* (15) occurs in Europe and Asia; *A. rosea,* Balkans, Crete, hollyhock, is a popular ornamental; *A. officinalis,* marsh mallow, has roots used in confections (the original marshmallow). *Malva* (30) occurs in the north temperate zone; *M. moschata,* musk mallow, *M. alcea,* are ornamentals; *M. rotundifolia* is roundleaf mallow, a widespread weed. *Malvaviscus* (12), of tropical and subtropical America, includes *M. grandiflorus,* Turk's-cap, much grown as an ornamental hedge. *Malvastrum* (100) occurs in America and South Africa. *Sida* (130), of tropical and subtropical regions, includes *S. rhombifolia,* China jute, a fiber plant and a very common tropical weed of both hemispheres. *Urena* (6), of the tropics, includes *U. lobata,* aramina, Brazil, a common weed, which yields a fiber used for making coffee sacks. *Hibiscus* (200) is mostly tropical and subtropical; *H. rosa-sinensis,* rose of China, shoeflower, is conspicuous in cultivation as an ornamental throughout the tropics. *H. syriacus,* shrubby althaea, rose of Sharon, is a common ornamental shrub. *H. sabdariffa,* rozelle, has fruits used for jelly. *H. esculentus* is okra, gumbo, or bandakai, with fruits used for food. *H. trionum,* Central Africa, is flower-of-an-hour, a widespread weed. *H. oculiroseus* is crimsoneye mallow, of eastern North America. *Thespesia* (8), of the tropics, includes *T. populnea,* portia-tree, an Old World strand tree. *Gossypium* (30) is a genus of tropical and subtropical regions. The seeds are covered with long hairs, forming the cotton of commerce, first used by the Hindus before 1800 B.C., also domesticated in America before 1492. Important species are *G. herbaceum,* Levant cotton, *G. arboreum,* tree cotton, of India, *G. hirsutum,* upland cotton, America, *G. punctatum,* Jamaica cotton, *G. barbadense,* sea-island cotton, America. Egyptian cotton is thought to be derived from *G. peruvianum.* The invention of the cotton-gin in 1793, and the industrial revolution, made cotton the world's greatest textile fiber. Crushing the seeds yields cottonseed oil, and the resulting oil-cake is fed to cattle.

Sterculiaceae. Sterculia Family.

HABIT. Trees, shrubs, and herbs.

LEAVES. Alternate, simple, stipulate.

INFLORESCENCE. Of various types, usually axillary, often cauliflorous.

FLOWERS. Perfect, regular; sepals 5, united; petals 5, often small or absent; stamens 10, the outer whorl sterile, all united into a tube; carpels 5, united.

FRUIT. Leathery, fleshy, or woody.

A subtropical and tropical family of 50 genera with 750 species. They are distinguished by the monadelphous stamens, the outer whorl of staminodes being united to the fertile stamens. Economically the family is important as the source of chocolate; several species are cultivated ornamentals.

Waltheria (30), of tropical America, includes *W. americana,* friegaplato, mala sombra, a common weed of tropical America. *Theobroma* (20), in tropical America, includes *T. cacao,* cacao or chocolate, the "food of the gods." The flowers are produced by cauliflory. The cacao is secured from the seeds after roasting, and cocoa-butter is obtained by pressing. The tree was domesticated by the Aztecs. *Fremontia* (3) is a genus of evergreen shrubs of California and Mexico; *F. californica,* flannel-bush, is planted as an ornamental. *Sterculia* (100) is a genus of the tropics, with apetalous, unisexual flowers; *S. apetala* is Panamá tree, which gave the name to the isthmus of Panama. *Brachychiton* (11), bottle-tree, in Australia, includes *B. populneum,* kurrajong, Queensland to Victoria, planted as an ornamental. *Guazuma ulmifolia,* guacimo, is one of the commonest trees of Central America and northern South America. *Firmiana* (10) occurs in Asia; *F. platanifolia,* Chinese parasol-tree, is often planted; the fruit opens into 5 leaf-like structures, with seeds on the edges. *Cola* (50) occurs in tropical Africa; *C. acuminata* is source of cola nuts of West Africa. They contain caffeine, which, when chewed, confers the power to endure fatigue, and are imported into the United States for use with coca in manufacture of soft drinks. *Hermannia* (120), chiefly African, is one of the largest genera.

Bombacaceae. Bombax Family.

HABIT. Trees, often of vast girth and with enormous buttresses.

LEAVES. Alternate, deciduous, simple or compound, stipulate.

INFLORESCENCE. Flowers solitary, or fascicled in leaf axils.

FLOWERS. Perfect, often large, usually regular; sepals 5, united, petals 5, stamens 5 to many, distinct or monadelphous, carpels 2-5, united.

FRUIT. A capsule; seeds often embedded in hairs.

The family is tropical, primarily American, with 22 genera including 140 species. Staminodes are frequent and characteristic. Economically the plants are important as a source of kapok, lumber, and ornamental plants.

Adansonia (10) occurs in Africa, Madagascar, and northern Australia. *A. digitata,* baobab, tropical Africa, reaches 30 feet or more in thickness of the trunk, although the height is not great (Figure 115). It is a characteristic tree of the savanna, the large woody tomentose fruit being known as monkey-bread. *Chorisia* (3) includes trees characteristic of the Brazilian caatinga; *C. speciosa,* paina de deda, samohu, yields cotton from the pods. *Bombax* (60) is a genus of tropical regions; *B. malabaricum,* cotton-tree, East Indies to Australia, flowers in January while leafless; the cotton is used for pillows. *Ceiba* (20) occurs in tropical America; *C. pentandra,* silk-cotton, has seeds covered with silky hairs, yielding kapok, the most valuable of all stuffing materials, used in cushions and mattresses. *Ochroma lagopus,* balsa, of tropical South America, produces the lightest commercial wood in the world, with a specific gravity of 0.12. *Durio zibethinus,* durian, Indomalaysia, produces a fruit with a delicate flavor, although a disagreeable odor ("like French custard passed through a sewer pipe"). *Pachira* (4), in tropical America, includes *P. aquatica,* provisiontree, a small tree with large flowers and enormous fleshy fruits. *Cavanillesia platanifolia,* cuipo, is a remarkably tall tree of Colombia, with a very thick trunk.

Order 23. Parietales. This large order is now generally regarded as an artificial taxon, and the families are variously re-distributed by many authors. A characteristic feature is the parietal placentation (see Figure 113).

a. Ovary superior
  b. Endosperm oily
    c. Leaves opposite or whorled
      d. Leaves compound .... *Caryocaraceae*
      d. Leaves simple .... *Guttiferae*
    c. Leaves alternate
      d. Petals separate
        e. Gynoecium of separate carpels ...... *Dilleniaceae*
        e. Gynoecium of united carpels
          f. Flowers with a tubular axis and a gynophore .... *Passifloraceae*

- f. Not as above
  - g. Fruit conspicuously winged ..... *Dipterocarpaceae*
  - g. Fruit not as above
    - h. Plants with a colored juice .... *Cochlospermaceae*
    - h. Juice watery
      - i. Aromatic .... *Canellaceae*
      - i. Usually not aromatic
        - j. Lateral nerves usually parallel .... *Ochnaceae*
        - j. Lateral nerves not conspicuously parallel
          - k. Placentas axile ...... *Theaceae*
          - k. Placentas parietal
            - l. Flowers often imperfect .... *Flacourtiaceae*
            - l. Flowers perfect
              - m. Flowers often irregular .... *Violaceae*
              - m. Flowers regular . *Turneraceae*

- d. Petals often somewhat united
  - e. Fruit winged .... *Dipterocarpaceae*
  - e. Fruit not winged
    - f. Plants with latex .... *Caricaceae*
    - f. Without latex
      - g. Cactus-like desert plants .... *Fouquieraceae*
      - g. Not cactus-like
        - h. Leaves stipulate .... *Caryocaraceae*
        - h. Leaves exstipulate .... *Theaceae*

- b. Endosperm starchy
  - c. Leaves alternate
    - d. Leaves scale-like; juice watery .... *Tamaricaceae*
    - d. Leaves larger; juice colored .... *Bixaceae*
  - c. Leaves opposite or whorled
    - d. Leaves with glandular hairs and volatile oil. *Cistaceae*
    - d. Not as above
      - e. Placentas axile; hydrophytes .... *Elatinaceae*
      - e. Placentas parietal; halophytes .... *Frankeniaceae*

- a. Ovary inferior
  - b. Plant clothed with rough, stinging, or barbed hairs *Loasaceae*
  - b. Not as above
    - c. Flowers in racemes; leaves exstipulate ...... *Datiscaceae*
    - c. Flowers in cymes; leaves stipulate .... *Begoniaceae*

Dilleniaceae. Dillenia Family.

Habit. Trees or shrubs, sometimes climbing.

Leaves. Alternate, usually leathery, simple, stipulate.

Inflorescence. Cymose.

Flowers. Regular, perfect or imperfect; sepals 3-5, or indefinite, persistent; petals 5; stamens indefinite (rarely 10 or less); carpels 1 to indefinite, free or slightly united.

Fruit. A follicle or berry.

A family of 15 genera including 560 species, of tropical regions, well represented in Australasia and America. Some phylogenists regard the family as allied with the Ranales, because of the free carpels. Economically the species are of little importance; a few are grown ornamentally and a few are minor food plants.

Curatella (2), of tropical America, includes *C. americana,* sandpaper tree, Central America; the leaves, containing silica, are sometimes used for sandpaper. *Dillenia* (20), of Indomalaysia, is found in the monsoon region; the fruit is often enclosed in a fleshy calyx; *D. indica,* chalta, is grown for its handsome white fragrant flowers.

Saurauia (250) is the largest genus, its members occurring in tropical Asia and America, where they are common trees and shrubs. *Actinidia* (23) is a genus of eastern Asia, often grown for attractive foliage; *A. chinensis,* yangtao, has edible fruits with flavor of gooseberries.

Ochnaceae. Ochna Family.

HABIT. Trees and shrubs, rarely herbs.

LEAVES. Alternate, simple, leathery, stipulate.

INFLORESCENCE. A panicle, raceme, or cyme.

FLOWERS. Perfect, regular; sepals 4-5, petals 4-5, stamens 5, 10, or indefinite, carpels 2, 5, 10, or 15, united.

FRUIT. Berrylike, at maturity separating into drupe-like carpels, borne on a fleshy receptacle.

The family includes 21 genera with 375 species, in the tropics of both hemispheres, most abundant in northern South America. A distinctive feature is the deeply lobed ovary, which at maturity separates into the individual carpels. The plants are of little importance economically.

Ochna (90), of the Old World, includes *O. multiflora,* sometimes grown as an ornamental. *Lophira* (2), an African genus, includes *L. alata,* a small tree of the Sudan savanna, with a winged fruit. *Ouratea* (200) is the largest genus. *Godoya* (4), in Peru, Colombia, and Brazil, includes *G. antioquiensis,* caunce, of the northern Andes.

Caryocaraceae. Caryocara Family. A family of trees and shrubs with 2 genera including 18 species, in tropical America. The leaves are compound and opposite or alternate. The flowers are racemose, perfect, with 5-6 united sepals, 5-6 united petals, numerous united stamens, and 4, 8, or 20 united carpels. The fruit is a drupe. *Caryocar* (14) occurs in tropical America; the wood of some species, as *C. villosum,* piquia, is durable and sometimes used in shipbuilding; the fruit has an oily mesocarp and woody endocarp; the seeds are souari-nuts, yielding a non-drying oil.

Theaceae. Tea Family.

HABIT. Trees or shrubs.

LEAVES. Alternate, simple, exstipulate, often persistent.

INFLORESCENCE. Flowers solitary in the axils or fascicled.

FLOWERS. Perfect, regular, with 5, 6, or 7 persistent sepals, 4, 5, or 9 (or numerous) petals, usually numerous stamens, and 2-10 united carpels.

FRUIT. A capsule.

The family includes 30 genera with 500 species, of tropical and subtropical regions, in both the Old and New Worlds. A distinctive feature is the androecium, with several whorls of stamens. Economically the family is important because of the tea plant, while many species are grown as ornamentals.

Camellia (40) is a genus of India, China, and Japan, including *C. japonica,* and others, cultivated for ornamental flowers. *Thea* (16), ranging from India to Japan, includes *T. sinensis,* tea. The young shoots are snipped off and either dried immediately to form green tea (Gunpowder, Hyson) or fermented and then dried to form black tea (Pekoe, Orange Pekoe). *Stewartia* (6) has a bicentric distribution, with 4 species in eastern Asia, and 2, including S. *malachodendron,* silky camellia, in the southeastern United States. *Gordonia* (30) ranges mostly from India to China, with 1 species, *G. lasianthus,* loblolly-bay, an ornamental tree, in the southeastern United States. *Ternstroemia* includes 25 species of tropical Asia, 60 species of tropical America, and 1 in West Africa. *Franklinia alatamaha,* lost camellia, was discovered by Bartram in Georgia in 1765, but has not been seen wild since 1790, although preserved in cultivation.

Guttiferae. Garcinia Family.

HABIT. Trees, shrubs, and herbs, with resinous sap.

LEAVES. Opposite (sometimes whorled or alternate), simple, entire, exstipulate.

INFLORESCENCE. Flowers solitary or cymose.

FLOWERS. Regular, unisexual or bisexual, sepals 2-10, petals 4-12, stamens indefinite, often grouped in bundles, carpels 3-5, united.

FRUIT. A capsule, berry, or drupe.

The family includes 43 genera with about 820 species, chiefly of tropical regions, except for *Hypericum,* which, with its related genera, is sometimes separated as the family Hypericaceae. The tropical species are of some value for timber and edible fruits, while *Hypericum* includes noxious weeds.

Ascyrum (5) occurs in North America, the West Indies, and the Himalayas; *A. hypericoides,* eastern North America, is St. Andrew's cross. *Hypericum* (300), St. John's wort, is a genus of herbs of the temperate regions, usually with dotted leaves; *H. perforatum, H. punctatum,* are widespread noxious weeds. *Mesua* (3), of tropical Asia, includes *M. ferrea,* Na or ironwood, with valuable timber. *Mammea* has 1 species in

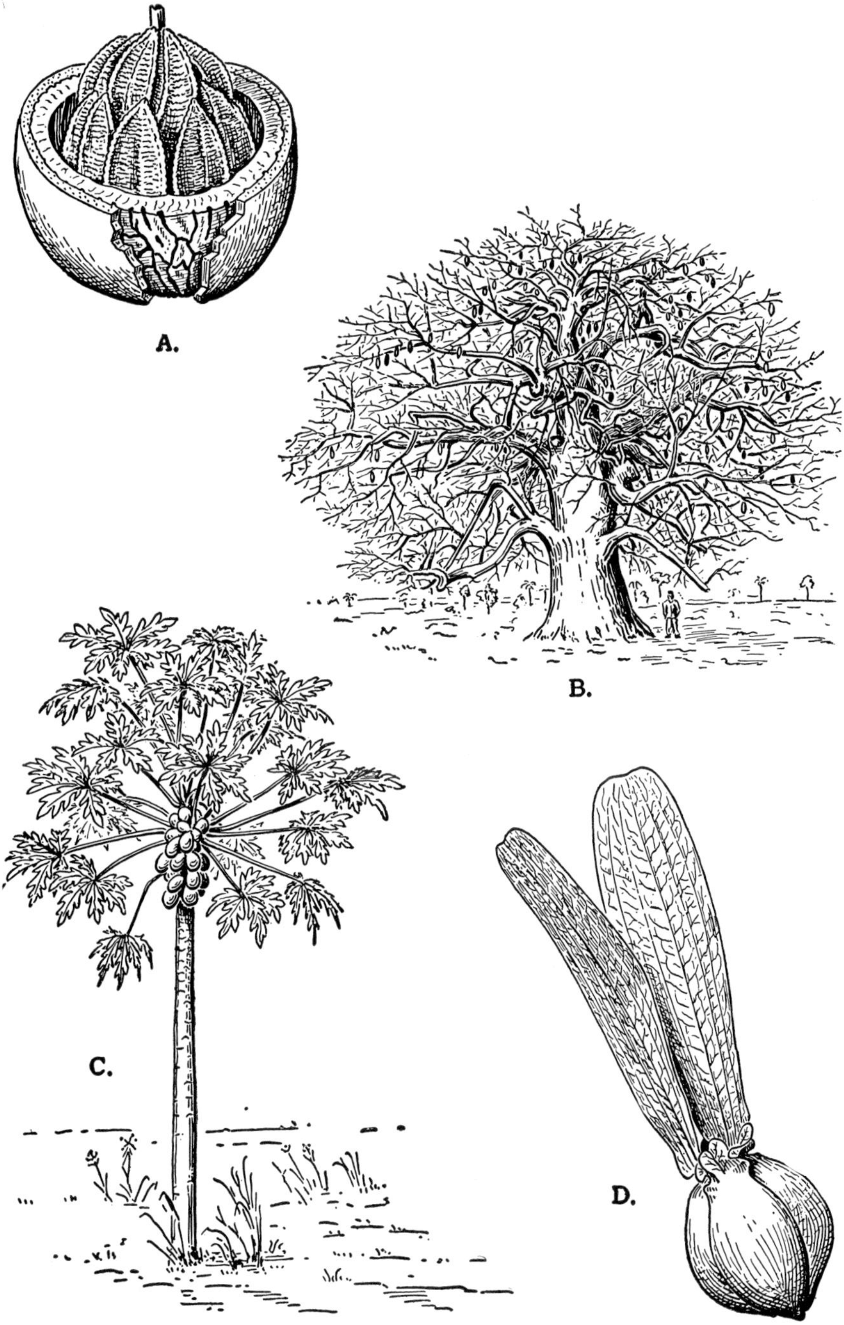

Figure 115. *A,* fruit of Brazil-nut, *Bertholletia excelsa,* sectioned to show seeds; *B,* baobab tree, *Adansonia digitata; C,* papaya, *Carica papaya; D,* fruit of a dipterocarp, *Dipterocarpus.* (Redrawn from Engler and Prantl.)

West Africa, and 1, *M. americana,* in the West Indies, cultivated for its edible fruit, mamey or St. Domingo apricot. *Calophyllum* (70) occurs chiefly in the Old World tropics; *C. inophyllum,* punnag, laurelwood, a coast tree from Africa to Polynesia, is planted for its beautiful leathery leaves. *Clusia* (100) includes trees and shrubs abundant in forests of tropical America; some species are climbing epiphytes with thick heavy leaves, often strangling the host. *Garcinia* (200) includes plants of the Old World tropics; *G. mangostana,* mangosteen, East Indies, is one of the most highly prized edible fruits of the tropics.

Dipterocarpaceae. Dipterocarp Family.

HABIT. Tall, little-branched trees.

LEAVES. Alternate, entire, evergreen, leathery.

INFLORESCENCE. Racemose.

FLOWERS. Perfect, regular; sepals 5, petals 5, stamens 5, 10, 15 or more, carpels 3, united.

FRUIT. A 1-seeded nut enclosed in the calyx, with some (often 2) of the sepals enlarged, forming wings.

A family of 25 genera including 375 species, in the Old World tropics from India to New Guinea and the Philippines. A distinctive feature, suggesting the name of the family, is the winged fruit (Figure 115). The trees furnish valuable timber, and resin used in varnishes.

Dipterocarpus (75) is a group of trees of the monsoon region of southern Asia; they yield Gurjun balsam, used in varnish, also valuable timber; *D. tuberculatus,* Burma, is "eng." *Drybalanops* (7), in Borneo and Malaya, includes *D. aromatica,* the source of Borneo or Sumatra camphor. *Hopea* (55), ranging from India to New Guinea, includes *H. micrantha,* which yields the valuable dammar, mata kuching. *Shorea* (100) ranges from India to the Philippines; *S. robusta,* saul tree, is a large and valuable timber tree and a source of dammar for varnish. *Vatica* (45) is a genus of Indomalaysia, producing resins and useful timbers. *Vateria* (3) occurs in the Seychelles and India; *V. indica* yields a gum resin, Indian copal or white dammar.

Elatinaceae. Waterwort Family. A family of 2 genera including 30 species of shrubs or herbs, tropical and temperate, often aquatic. The leaves are opposite or whorled. The flowers are perfect, with 3-5 sepals, 3-5 petals, 3-5 (or 6-10) stamens, and 3-5 united carpels. *Elatine* (10), of tropical and temperate regions, includes *E. hexandra, E. hydropiper,* waterpepper. *Bergia* (20) is almost exclusively tropical and subtropical, except for *B. texana,* Missouri to California.

Frankeniaceae. Frankenia Family. A family of 4 genera with 48 species, mostly halophytic herbs, of tropical and temperate regions. The flowers are regular and perfect, with 4-7 united sepals, 4-7 petals, 6 stamens, and

3 united carpels. *Frankenia* (45) occurs on coasts of the Mediterranean, Asia, America, and Australia; *F. grandiflora,* alkali heath, is sometimes cultivated as an oddity.

Tamaricaceae. Tamarisk Family. A family of 4 genera with 100 species, temperate and tropical, desert, shore, and steppe plants, often heathlike. The minute flowers are perfect and regular, with 4-5 united sepals, 4-5 petals, 4-5, 8-10, or numerous stamens, and 2, 4, or 5 united carpels. *Tamarix* (80), of Europe and Asia, has several species grown as ornamentals, such as *T. gallica,* French tamarisk. *T. mannifera,* Egypt to Afghanistan, produces manna of the Bedouins, a white substance exuded through insect punctures. *Myricaria germanica,* false tamarix, western Europe to the Caucasus, is cultivated as an ornamental.

Fouquieraceae. Candlewood Family. A family of 2 genera with 8 species, of northern Mexico and southwestern United States, mostly shrubs or small trees. The leaf-blades are deciduous, the petioles persisting, becoming thorny. The flowers are perfect, regular, and showy, with 5 sepals, 5 united petals, 10-15 stamens, and 3 united carpels. In recent treatments the family is included in the Tubiflorales because of the united petals. *Fouquiera* (7), of Mexico and southwestern United States, includes *F. splendens,* ocotillo, coachwhip, one of the most distinctive shrubs of southwestern deserts.

Cistaceae. Rockrose Family.

HABIT. Herbs and shrubs, with volatile oils and glandular hairs.

LEAVES. Leaves mostly opposite, simple.

INFLORESCENCE. Flowers solitary, cymose, or racemose.

FLOWERS. Perfect, regular, with 3-5 sepals, 3-5 petals (or none), numerous stamens, and 3, 5, or 10 united carpels.

FRUIT. A capsule.

The family includes 8 genera with about 200 species, mostly of the north temperate zone. Economically they are of slight importance.

Cistus (16), rockrose, is a genus of the Mediterranean region. Some species are cultivated ornamentals. *C. ladaniferus,* of Spain and Morocco, yields the resin ladanum. *Helianthemum* (80) occurs in the Mediterranean region and in North America; *H. vulgare* is sunrose; *H. canadensis* is frostweed; in cold weather crystals of ice shoot from the cracked bark at the base of the stem. *Hudsonia* (3) is a genus of heathlike herbs of eastern North America. *Lechea* (15), pinweed, occurs in North America and the West Indies.

Bixaceae. Bixa Family. A family of small trees or shrubs with reddish sap, 1 genus, *Bixa,* and 2 species, of tropical South America. The flowers are paniculate, perfect, regular, with 5 sepals, 5 petals, numerous stamens, and 2 united carpels. *B. orellana,* arnotto, annatto, urucu, is grown for its showy fruit and for the orange dye yielded by the testa of the seed, used to color butter, cheese, and other foods; it has run wild throughout the tropics.

Cochlospermaceae. Cochlospermum Family. A family of trees and shrubs, 3 genera with 25 species, tropical and subtropical. The sap is reddish-orange. The leaves are palmately lobed. The flowers are racemose, large, perfect, regular, with 4-5 sepals, 4-5 petals, numerous stamens, and 3-5 united carpels. *Cochlospermum* (15) is a genus of tropical regions, mostly xerophytic; *C. vitifolium* is cultivated for the yellow flowers; *C. gossypium,* white silk-cotton, India, is the source of Bassora gum.

Canellaceae (*Winteranaceae*). *Canella Family.* A family of 5 genera including 11 species of aromatic trees having a remarkable discontinuous distribution in both the Old and New World. The leaves are alternate, leathery, and dotted. The flowers are perfect and regular, with 4-5 sepals, 4-5 petals (or none), numerous monadelphous stamens, and 2-5 united carpels. *Canella* (2), in the West Indies and tropical America, includes *C. winterana,* wild cinnamon, which yields medicinal canella bark.

Violaceae. Violet Family.

HABIT. Annual or usually perennial herbs or shrubs, rarely climbing.

LEAVES. Alternate or opposite, simple.

INFLORESCENCE. Flowers solitary, or with various types of arrangement; cleistogamous flowers sometimes present (Figure 83).

FLOWERS. Perfect, zygomorphic, or actinomorphic; sepals 5, persistent; petals 5, the anterior one spurred; stamens 5; carpels 3, united.

FRUIT. A capsule.

The family includes 16 genera with 850 species, of wide distribution on all the continents. A distinctive feature is the zygomorphic corolla, and the nectar-secreting horn that projects backward into the spur of the lower petal. The phylogenetic position is uncertain. Economically the species are important mainly as ornamentals.

Rinorea (260) is a genus of trees or shrubs of the tropical rain forest, especially in Africa. *Hybanthus* (90) is a genus mostly of tropical and subtropical regions; *H. concolor,* of eastern North America, is green violet. *Viola* (400) includes herbs especially common in the north temperate zone, but also on tropical mountains in Mexico, the Andes, Brazil, and tropical Africa; also in Cape Colony. There are 75 species in Europe and over 60 in the United States. Representative species are *V. biflora,* circumboreal; *V. odorata,* English violet; *V. tricolor,* Eurasia, pansy or heart's ease; *V. canina,* dog violet; *V. pedata,* bird's foot violet; *V. papilionacea,* common blue violet, eastern United States; *V. canadensis,* Canada violet; *V. scandens,* in the Andes.

Flacourtiaceae. Flacourtia Family.

HABIT. Trees and shrubs, sometimes climbing.

LEAVES. Alternate, leathery, simple, stipulate, persistent.

INFLORESCENCE. Cymose.

FLOWERS. Regular; sepals 2-15, petals 2-15 (or none); stamens numerous; carpels 2-10, united, superior or more or less inferior.

FRUIT. A capsule or berry.

The family includes 84 genera with 850 species, of tropical and subtropical regions. A distinctive feature is the variously modified disk and the often enlarged receptacle. The phyletic position is a matter of uncertainty. Some species produce medicinal oils, others are grown for edible fruits or ornamental flowers.

Hydnocarpus (43) is a genus of Indomalaysia; *H. kurzii,* of Burma and Assam, yields chaulmoogra oil, formerly an important remedy for leprosy. *Pangium* (2) occurs in the Malay Archipelago; seeds of *P. edule,* pangi, are eaten after long boiling to remove hydrocyanic acid. *Azara* (20) ranges from Mexico to South America; several species are characteristic of the rain forest of southern Chile. *Flacourtia* (20) is most common in tropical Asia; *F. indica,* governor's plum, batoko plum, or ramontchi, has edible fruits.

Turneraceae. Turnera Family. A family of 6 genera with 110 species of trees, shrubs, and herbs, chiefly of tropical Africa and America. The leaves are alternate. The flowers are perfect, regular, and perigynous, with 5 sepals, 5 petals, 5 stamens, and 3 united carpels. *Turnera* (60) ranges from Mexico to Argentina; dried leaves of *T. diffusa,* damiana, have been used as an aphrodisiac.

Passifloraceae. Passion-flower Family.

HABIT. Shrubs and herbs, mostly climbers, with axillary tendrils.

LEAVES. Alternate, stipulate, simple or compound.

INFLORESCENCE. Flowers axillary, usually in pairs.

FLOWERS. Perfect or imperfect, regular, with a petaloid corona produced as an outgrowth of the androperianth; sepals 5; petals 5 (or more); stamens 5; carpels 3, united.

FRUIT. A capsule or berry.

A family of 11 genera with 600 species, chiefly of tropical America. They are distinguished by the climbing habit and the variously modified corona. Economically they are important as ornamentals and for edible fruits. The unusual flower parts have been fancied to resemble the instruments of the crucifixion, whence the name.

Passiflora (400), passion-flower, is a genus mainly of South America. Edible fruits are produced by *P. quadrangularis,* giant granadilla, with fruits 10 inches long, *P. maliformis,* sweet calabash, *P. laurifolia,* waterlemon, *P. edulis,* purple granadilla, *P. mollissima,* curuba. Many species are grown as ornamentals, including *P. incarnata,* eastern United States, and *P. caerulea,* Brazil.

Caricaceae. Papaya Family.

HABIT. Small trees, soft-wooded, with a milky sap.

LEAVES. Alternate, palmately lobed, large, long-petioled, in a terminal crown.

INFLORESCENCE. Flowers solitary, or in racemes or corymbs.

FLOWERS. Unisexual or bisexual, the staminate with 10 stamens, the pistillate with 5 united carpels; calyx very small, 5-lobed; petals 5, united or distinct; ovary superior.

FRUIT. A large berry.

The family includes 4 genera with 50 species, chiefly of tropical America. The plants are readily distinguished by the unbranched trunks with the terminal crown of leaves (Figure 115). The papaya is one of the most highly prized fruits of the tropics.

Carica (40) is especially abundant in the Andes from Peru to Colombia. *C. papaya,* papaya, papaw, is cultivated throughout the tropics for its large edible melon-like fruits, "the melon that grows on a tree." *C. candamarcensis,* mountain papaya, is cultivated in tropical mountains.

Loasaceae. Loasa Family.

HABIT. Herbs or shrubs, sometimes climbing, often with rough, sometimes stinging hairs.

LEAVES. Opposite or alternate, simple or pinnately divided, exstipulate.

INFLORESCENCE. Cymose.

FLOWERS. Usually yellow, perfect, regular; sepals 5, petals 5, stamens 5 to many, carpels 3-7, united, the ovary inferior.

FRUIT. A capsule.

A family of 15 genera including 250 species, most abundant in the Andes. They are characterized by the peculiarly shaped, often stinging hairs. A few species are grown as ornamentals.

Mentzelia (60), in tropical and subtropical America, includes *M. laevicaulis,* blazing star, of arid regions of western North America. *Blumenbachia* (3) occurs in temperate South America; the fruit is very light and covered with barbed hairs which attach to animals. *Loasa* has 80 species from Mexico to Patagonia; the plants have stinging hairs.

Datiscaceae. Datisca Family. A family of perennial mostly dioecious herbs or small trees, with 3 genera including 5 species, of tropical and temperate regions. The flowers are regular, with 3-9 united sepals, 8 petals, numerous stamens, and 3 united carpels, with an inferior ovary. *Datisca* (2), a group of plants resembling hemp (*Cannabis*), includes *D. cannabina* in southeastern Asia, and *D. glomerata,* Durango root, from Mexico to California.

Begoniaceae. Begonia Family.

HABIT. Perennial herbs with thick rhizomes or tubers, sometimes shrubby.

LEAVES. Alternate, simple, oblique (one side larger than the other; Figure 58). The plants are easily reproduced by buds which form on the cut leaves.

INFLORESCENCE. In terminal dichasia.

FLOWERS. Unisexual (the plants monoecious), the staminate with 2 petal-like sepals, 2 smaller petals, and numerous stamens, the pistillate with 2-5 perianth parts (undifferentiated) and 2-3 united carpels, with an inferior ovary.

FRUIT. A capsule; the ovary is usually winged, with the wings persistent on the capsule.

The family includes 5 genera with more than 800 species, widely distributed in the tropics but with the greatest development in northern South America. They are characterized by the unisexual flowers and the angled or winged inferior ovary. The family is important economically for the many ornamentals.

Begonia (800) is a genus of tropical regions, with centers of development in Colombia, Ecuador, Hawaii, and New Guinea. Many species are in cultivation, including *B. semperflorens,* Brazil, *B. subpeltata,* India, *B. dregei,* Cape Colony, *B. socotrana,* Sokotra, *B. pearcii,* Bolivia, and *B. metallica,* Bahia. There are many hybrids, including "Gloire de Lorraine," *B. tuberhybrida,* tuberous begonias, and *B. rex-cultorum,* rex begonias.

Order 24. Opuntiales. The order includes but a single family. Conventionally it has been regarded as derived from the Parietales but some systematists treat it as allied to the Centrospermales.

Cactaceae. Cactus Family.

HABIT. Xerophytes of the most pronounced sort, fleshy, herbaceous, or woody, sometimes branched and tree-like, usually bearing spines and bristles at a pit or raised spot (**areole**) in the axils; stems modified for photosynthesis and water storage (Figure 116).

LEAVES. Ordinarily scale-like; flat and fleshy in 2 genera.

INFLORESCENCE. Flowers usually solitary.

FLOWERS. Usually large, brightly colored, perfect, regular or irregular; perianth parts indefinite, showing a gradual transition from sepals to petals; stamens indefinite, epipetalous; carpels 4 to many, united; ovary inferior.

FRUIT. A berry.

The family includes 120 genera with perhaps 1700 species, probably restricted to America in the indigenous state. They are characterized by the fleshy habit, with spines and bristles, and large, solitary flowers. Economically they are important as ornamentals. A few have edible fruits.

Pereskia (20) occurs in Mexico, West Indies, and tropical South America; the species have a habit most nearly like that of ordinary plants, with fully developed leaves and paniculate flowers; *P. aculeata,* Barbados-gooseberry, is climbing.

Rhipsalis (60) occurs mostly in Brazil and Argentina; the plants are epiphytes forming dense pendent masses on trees. *R. cassytha* is found in Ceylon, Madagascar, Mauritius, and Africa, the only cactus native outside America; some botanists believe even it was introduced. *Epiphyllum* (20) ranges from Mexico to Brazil; *E. crenatum* is cultivated for showy flowers. *Phyllocactus* (25), blade-cactus, occurs in Mexico and Central America. The plants are flat-stemmed and often epiphytic. *Echinocactus* (9) of Mexico, includes *E. grusonii,* golden ball cactus, grown as an oddity. *Melocactus* (20) ranges from Mexico and the West Indies to Brazil; the stems are ribbed and the flowers produced at the top, suggesting the name Turk's-head. *Ferocactus* (30), of southwestern United States and Mexico, is barrel cactus, so-called from its shape. *Echinopsis* (40), hedgehog cactus, of South America, is grown as an oddity. *Echinocereus* has 60 species in North America, sometimes grown for showy flowers. *Mammillaria* (215) is a genus of North and Central America; they are small plants of a very condensed form, often almost spherical, with well-marked leaf cushions (**mammillae**). *M. bocasana,* powder-puff cactus, and *M. hahniana,* old-woman cactus, are grown as oddities. *Cereus* (200) ranges from southern North America and the West Indies to Central Chile and Argentina. The stems are fleshy, erect, cylindrical, and ribbed; *C. giganteus,* saguaro, 70 feet high, is the largest of the cacti; it occurs in Arizona (the state flower) and Sonora. *C. grandiflorus* is night-blooming cereus; *C. marginatus* is organ-pipe cactus; *C. variabilis* and others have edible fruits, pitahayas. *Zygocactus truncatus,* of Brazil, has bright showy flowers in winter and is grown as Christmas cactus.

Opuntia (350), prickly-pear, includes plants widespread in arid regions in warm parts of America. They have a fleshy, flattened, branched stem. Some have become troublesome weeds when introduced into Australia. *O. humifusa* is found throughout the eastern United States from Massachusetts to South Carolina. *O. ficus-indica,* Indian fig, tuna, with edible fruits, of Central America, is widely naturalized, in the Mediterranean region, the Canaries, Australia, Hawaii, and South America. *Nopalea* (8) occurs in Mexico, the West Indies, and Central America. The plants have fleshy, flattened stems, and no thorns. The cochineal insect, which produces a red dye, is cultivated chiefly on *N. coccinellifera,* cochineal cactus.

Order 25. Myrtales. The families here included by Engler have been variously re-distributed by numerous other phylogenists. As here treated they show a transition from perigyny to epigyny.

a. Flowers perigynous
  b. Petals usually present
    c. Leaves with 3-9 equal conspicuous longitudinal veins .... *Melastomaceae*
    c. Leaves not as above .... *Lythraceae*
  b. Petals usually none
    c. Plants covered with silvery scales .... *Elaeagnaceae*
    c. Plants not covered with scales .... *Thymaealaceae*
a. Flowers epigynous
  b. Aquatic or marsh herbs
    c. Petals reduced or none .... *Haloragaceae*
    c. Petals present .... *Hydrocaryaceae*
  b. Terrestrial
    c. Locules of ovary superposed .... *Punicaceae*
    c. Locules of ovary not superposed
      d. Leaves alternate
        e. Stamens 4-8 .... *Onagraceae*
        e. Stamens numerous
          f. Tall tropical trees; stamens not in bundles; fruit often woody .... *Lecythidaceae*
          f. Trees or shrubs, often aromatic; stamens often in bundles; fruit usually not woody *Myrtaceae*
      d. Leaves opposite
        e. Often lianas .... *Combretaceae*
        e. Not usually lianas
          f. Sea-coast plants, forming tangled thickets; often viviparous .... *Rhizophoraceae*
          f. Not as above
            g. Stamens 4-8 .... *Onagraceae*
            g. Stamens numerous .... *Myrtaceae*

Thymelaeaceae. Mezereum Family.

Habit. Mostly shrubs or trees, rarely herbs.

Leaves. Alternate, or opposite, simple, entire, exstipulate.

Inflorescence. Racemose or umbellate (or the flowers sometimes solitary).

Flowers. Perfect, regular, with a deep androperianth tube; sepals 4-5, petaloid, petals 4-12 (or none), stamens 4-5, 8-10, or reduced to 2; carpel typically 1; ovary superior.

Fruit. An achene, berry, drupe, nut, or capsule.

The family includes 40 genera with 500 species, nearly cosmopolitan in distribution, with centers of development in South Africa, Australia, the Mediterranean region, and central and western Asia. A distinctive feature is the androperianth tube, with petals reduced to appendages upon it. The phyletic position is uncertain. Some species are grown as ornamentals.

Daphne (50) occurs in temperate Eurasia, and includes *D. mezereum*, mezereon, and *D. laureola*, spurge-laurel, cultivated as ornamental shrubs. *Dirca*, leatherwood, with very tough bark, includes *D. occidentalis*, of California, and *D. palustris*, of eastern North America. *Lagetta* (3), lacebark, occurs in the West Indies; the inner bark is lace-like and used in dress-making.

Elaeagnaceae. Oleaster Family. A family of shrubs and trees, sometimes thorny, with 3 genera including 45 species, chiefly on steppes and seacoasts of the northern hemisphere. The leaves are entire, often leathery, and covered with silvery or golden-brown peltate or stellate scales. The flowers are racemose, perfect or imperfect, 2-4-merous, apetalous, with 1 carpel. The presence of the androperianth tube seems to indicate its relationship to the Thymelaeaceae. *Hippophaë* (2) is a genus of the Old World; *H. rhamnoides*, sea-buckthorn, is sometimes cultivated as an ornamental. *Elaeagnus* (40) occurs in Asia, Europe, and North America; *E. angustifolia*, oleaster, *E. commutata*, silverberry, and others are cultivated as ornamentals. *Shepherdia* (3) occurs in North America; *S. argentea*, buffaloberry, is cultivated ornamentally, and the fruit is edible.

Lythraceae. Loosestrife Family.

HABIT. Herbs, shrubs, or trees.

LEAVES. Usually opposite, or whorled, simple, entire.

INFLORESCENCE. The flowers solitary or variously clustered.

FLOWERS. Perfect, regular or irregular; sepals 4, 6, or 8; petals the same number or absent; stamens usually twice as many as the petals; sepals, petals, and stamens arise from the rim of the androperianth tube; carpels usually 2-6, united, the ovary superior.

FRUIT. A capsule.

A family of 23 genera including 475 species, widely distributed, but most abundant in the American tropics. The androperianth tube is a distinguishing feature. Several species are grown as ornamentals and a few produce useful timber.

Lythrum (25) occurs in the northern hemisphere, and includes *L. salicaria*, purple loosestrife, grown as an ornamental. *Cuphea* (200) is a genus mostly of tropical and subtropical America; some plants are covered with sticky hairs, as *C. petiolata*, tarweed; *C. ignea*, cigar-flower, has a bright red corolla tube, white at the mouth, and is grown as an ornamental. *Lagerstroemia* (30), of the Old World tropics, is a group of ornamental flowering shrubs and trees, some producing useful timber; *L. indica*, crape myrtle, is a shrub grown for showy flowers. *Lawsonia inermis*, ranging from East Africa to India and Australia, is the source of henna, an orange dye used for personal adornment, especially by

Mohammedans. *Decodon verticillatus,* of North America, is swamp loosestrife.

Punicaceae. Pomegranate Family. A family of trees, with 1 genus, *Punica,* including 2 species, from the Balkans to the Himalayas and Sokotra. The flowers are perfect and regular, with 5-8 sepals, 5-8 petals, numerous stamens, and generally 8-12 carpels. The fruit is generally termed a berry (or balausta), although the fleshy part around the seeds is really part of the seed coats. *P. granatum,* pomegranate, granada, is widely cultivated in warm regions for the edible fruit.

Lecythidaceae. Brazilnut Family.

HABIT. Trees, some very tall.

LEAVES. Alternate, simple, exstipulate, clustered at the ends of twigs.

INFLORESCENCE. Flowers solitary or racemose.

FLOWERS. Perfect, regular or irregular, with 4-6 sepals, 4-6 petals, numerous stamens, and 2-6 (or more) united carpels; ovary inferior.

FRUIT. A berry or woody capsule, often with a dehiscent lid, where the embryos emerge (Figure 115).

The family includes 18 genera with 315 species, of tropical regions. The woody capsule is a distinctive feature of many species. Some produce good timber, or edible nuts (or both).

Couroupita (18) ranges from the West Indies to Brazil; *C. guianensis,* cannonball tree, has large woody capsules and produces good timber. *Lecythis* (50) ranges from the West Indies to Brazil; the capsule, monkeypot, is said to have been used with sugar to catch monkeys, which cannot withdraw their closed hand. *Bertholletia* (2) occurs in tropical South America and the West Indies. *B. excelsa,* Brazilnut, "nigger-toes," an important commercial nut, has a woody capsule and seeds with a woody testa. The fruit is indehiscent and must be opened with an ax. The tree is one of the tallest of the Amazon region, reaching 160 feet. *Grias* (4) occurs in South America and the West Indies; *G. cauliflora,* anchovy-pear, is cultivated for fruits used in pickles. *Barringtonia* (100) occurs in the Old World tropics, characteristic of the beach-jungle; several produce useful wood; *B. asiatica* is common on coasts from Madagascar to southern Asia, northern Australia, and Polynesia. *Napoleona* (18) occurs in tropical west Africa; the flowers bear a crown somewhat like that of *Passiflora* and the fruit is a berry.

Rhizophoraceae. Mangrove Family. A family of tropical trees and shrubs with 17 genera including 70 species, principally on muddy tidal flats and shore lines. The leaves are opposite. The flowers are perfect and regular, with 4-8 sepals, 4-8 petals, 8 to numerous stamens, and 2-5 united carpels. *Rhizophora mangle,* mangrove, America, West Africa, in muddy swamps, forms extensive dense thickets with much-branched aerial roots growing downwards from branches. Seed germination is **viviparous** (that is, while still on the parent plant), the hypocotyl projecting at the micropyle and elongating before falling from the tree.

Combretaceae. Combretum Family.

HABIT. Trees and shrubs, often lianas.

LEAVES. Alternate or opposite, simple, exstipulate.

INFLORESCENCE. Racemose, spicate, or paniculate.

FLOWERS. Perfect, regular; calyx-lobes 4-8, petals 4-8, or none, stamens usually 2-5; carpel 1, with an inferior ovary.

FRUIT. Leathery, 1-seeded, winged at the angles.

The family includes 18 genera with 500 species, of tropical and subtropical regions. The winged fruits are distinctive. They are of little value except for ornamental planting.

Terminalia (200), of tropical regions, has many species yielding good timber and tan bark; *T. catappa,* tropical, country or Indian almond, has an edible seed. *Combretum* (260), of warm climates, includes *C. butyrosum,* Africa, which yields chiquito, a butter-like substance, from the fruits. *Quisqualis* (4), occurs in tropical Africa and Asia; *Q. indica,* Rangoon-creeper, is planted for red flowers; Linnaeus applied the curious generic name, which means *who, what. Conocarpus* (2) of tropical Africa and America, includes *C. erecta,* button mangrove, one of the characteristic species of mangrove swamps. *Laguncularia racemosa,* of tropical Africa and America, is white mangrove.

Myrtaceae. Myrtle Family.

HABIT. Shrubs and trees.

LEAVES. Usually opposite, simple, mostly entire, leathery, dotted, exstipulate.

INFLORESCENCE. Cymose, racemose, or paniculate, or the flowers solitary.

FLOWERS. Perfect, regular; sepals usually 4-5, petals usually 4-5, stamens numerous (rarely few), carpels 3 or more; ovary inferior.

FRUIT. A berry, drupe, nut, or capsule.

The family includes 80 genera with 3000 species, of warm climates, with 2 chief centers of distribution, in America and Australia. They are distinguished by the glandular-dotted leaves, containing volatile oils. Economically they are of considerable importance for fruits, spices, oils, timbers, and so forth.

I. Fruit fleshy (a berry or drupe). *Myrtus* (75) is a genus of tropical and subtropical regions, especially in America; *M. communis,* the classical myrtle, of the Mediterranean region, is an ornamental strong-scented shrub. *Psidium* (100) is a genus of tropical America. *P. guajaba,* guava, West Indies, is cultivated throughout the tropical regions for its edible fruits. *Pimenta* (5) occurs in tropical America; the dried unripe fruits of *P. dioica* form allspice; *P. racemosa* is bay tree, yielding an oil used in making bay rum. *Eugenia* (1000) is a vast genus of tropical and subtropical regions, especially of America. The dried flower buds of *E. caryophyllata* are cloves, among the most important of spices; the trees are grown mostly on islands, since they must "see the sea." *E. uniflora* is pitanga or Surinam cherry, producing a crimson edible fruit; *E. jambos* is pomarrosa, rose-apple, the edible fruit with the odor of roses; *E. jambolana*, kala-jam; *E. malaccensis*, jamrool, Malay-apple; these four produce edible fruits and are beautiful shade trees. *Myrciaria* (75) occurs in tropical America; *M. cauliflora*, jaboticaba, has edible purple fruits.

II. Fruit dry. *Metrosideros* (25) occurs in Polynesia, especially Hawaii, Australia, Sunda Islands, Cape Colony; some species produce valuable timber. *Eucalyptus* (600) is a large genus of Australia, New Guinea, and the Sunda Islands. They are tall trees known by many different names, such as ironbark, stringy-bark, bloodwood, gum, or mallae, and comprise one of the most characteristic genera of the Australian flora (Figure 29). Some are of tremendous size, as *E. regnans*, New South Wales, Victoria, Queensland, which has a height of 326 feet and a diameter of 25 feet. *E. diversicolor*, karri, *E. marginata*, jarrah, and *E. redunca*, wandoo, are valuable timber trees. *E. globulus*, bluegum, New South Wales, Victoria, Tasmania, has been introduced in many parts of the world because of its rapid growth. The plants produce medicinal oil of eucalyptus. *Leptospermum* (30) occurs in Malaya, Australia, New Zealand; *L. laevigatum*, Australian tea-tree, is extensively planted for reclamation of moving sand. *Tristania conferta*, Brisbane-box, of Australia, is an ornamental tree to 150 feet high. *Callistemon* (12), bottle-brush, occurs in Australia; the plants are cultivated ornamental shrubs with conspicuous stamens. *Melaleuca* (100), bottle-brush, includes plants mostly of Australia; some yield useful timber. Leaves of *M. leucadendron*, cajeput tree, punk tree, Sunda Islands to Australia, yield cajeput oil, a universal remedy in the Orient.

Melastomaceae. Melastoma Family.

HABIT. Herbs, shrubs, trees; erect or climbing, terrestrial, epiphytic, or aquatic.

LEAVES. Commonly opposite, usually with 3-9 veins palmately diverging from the base, no mid-rib.

INFLORESCENCE. Cymose.

FLOWERS. Perfect, regular; sepals 3-6, usually 5; petals mostly 5; stamens mostly twice as many as the petals, usually with curious appendages; carpels 4-14; ovary inferior.

FRUIT. A capsule or berry.

The family includes 150 genera with 4000 species, mostly of the American tropics. The plants are distinguished by the characteristic leaf venation and by the connective of the stamens, which is usually provided with curious sickle-form appendages (Figure 116). Many of them are grown as ornamentals but otherwise this large family is of remarkably little economic value.

Meriania (30) occurs in the West Indies and tropical South America; *M. nobilis* is a beautiful tree of the Andes. *Tibouchina* (200) occurs in tropical America; *T. longifolia* is a very common plant of Central

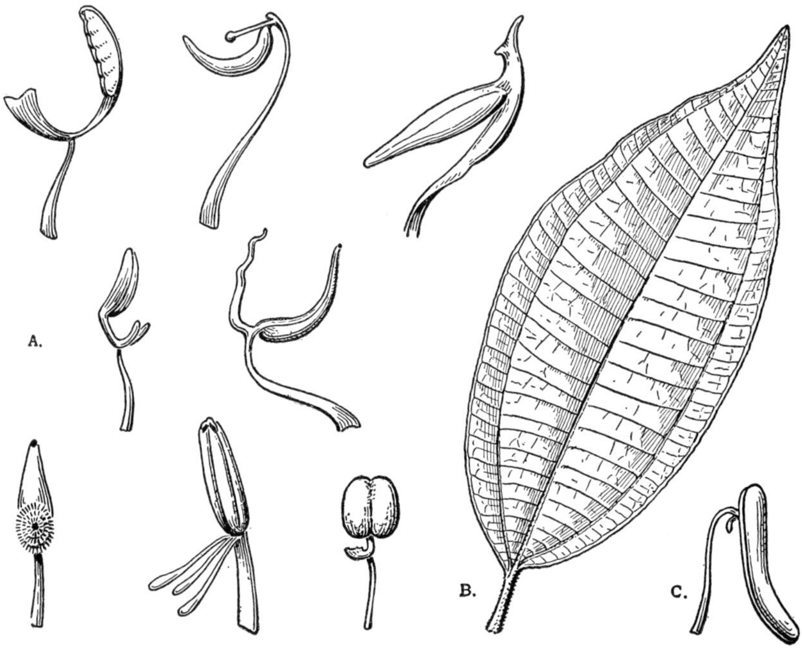

Figure 116. Characteristic structures of the Melastomaceae. *A*, miscellaneous examples of curiously shaped stamens, all after Engler and Prantl; *B*, leaf of *Miconia*, showing distinctive venation; *C*, stamen of meadow beauty, *Rhexia virginica*.

America; *T. semidecandra,* glory-bush, Brazil, is cultivated. *Melastoma* (50) is a genus of the Old World tropics. *Rhexia* (15) occurs mostly in eastern United States; *R. virginica* is meadow beauty. *Memecylon* (100), of the Old World tropics, sometimes produces leaves with long drip-tips. *Miconia* (600) is the largest genus in the family, occurring in tropical America; *M. argentea,* Central America, is doscaras (two faces), the leaves green above, white below.

Onagraceae. Evening-Primrose Family.

Habit. Herbs, shrubs, or trees.

Leaves. Alternate or opposite, simple.

INFLORESCENCE. Spicate, racemose, or paniculate, or the flowers solitary.

FLOWERS. Perfect; sepals usually 4, persistent or deciduous; petals mostly 4, sometimes none; stamens the same number as the petals or twice as many; carpels typically 4; ovary inferior.

FRUIT. A capsule (Figure 85, F), nut, or berry.

A family of 20 genera including 650 species, cosmopolitan in distribution, especially abundant in temperate regions of North America. Members of the family are distinguished by the usually 4-merous, epigynous flowers. Several are grown as ornamentals.

Jussieua (50), primrose-willow, is a genus of water and marsh plants, especially of tropical Brazil. *Epilobium* (200) is a genus of temperate and arctic regions; *E. angustifolium,* fireweed, *E. latifolium,* willow-herb, are circumboreal. *Oenothera* (100) ranges from North America to Patagonia; *O. biennis,* evening-primrose, is now a widespread weed; *O. lamarckiana* is a hybrid "species" associated with deVries' mutation theory (p. 92). *Ludwigia* (30) is cosmopolitan; *L. palustris* is water purslane, *L. alternifolia,* seedbox. *Clarkia* (8), of western North America, includes plants cultivated for ornamental flowers, especially *C. pulchella* and *C. elegans. Godetia* (25) is a genus of western North America, particularly California; *G. amoena,* farewell-to-spring, summer's darling, is a cultivated ornamental. *Fuchsia* (75) is a genus of shrubs or trees, mostly in Central and South America, with 2 in New Zealand. Many species are cultivated as ornamentals, including *F. magellanica,* indigenous from Peru to the Strait of Magellan, *F. fulgens,* Mexico, and *F. hybrida,* the common garden fuchsia, of hybrid origin. *Circaea* (9), enchanter's nightshade, is a group of north temperate and arctic plants with hooked fruits; *C. alpina, C. quadrisulcata,* are in North America.

Hydrocaryaceae. Water-Chestnut Family. A family of aquatic herbs, 1 genus, *Trapa,* 3 species, of Europe and Asia. The flowers are 4-merous, the fleshy seed is large, in a horned nut. *T. natans,* water-caltrops, horn-nut, or water-chestnut, is eaten in Europe and Asia.

Haloragaceae. Water Milfoil Family. A family of 9 genera including 150 species, widely distributed, but especially abundant in Australia, terrestrial or aquatic. The flowers are usually imperfect, regular, epigynous, usually 4-merous. They are thought to be reduced relatives of the Onagraceae, or by some authorities as allied to the Ranales. *Haloragis* (70) occurs in Australia, New Zealand, Tasmania, southeastern Asia, Rapa, and Juan Fernandez. *Myriophyllum* (40), water milfoil, is cosmopolitan in distribution; the genus includes submerged plants with whorled much-divided leaves; *M. brasiliense,* parrot's feather, is often grown in aquaria. *Proserpinaca* (4), mermaid-weed, occurs in North America; the flowers are tri-merous. *Gunnera* (30) occurs in South America, Central America, Mexico, Hawaii, Java, New Zealand, Tasmania, and Juan Fernandez; the plants are enormous herbs with leaves several feet across; some are cultivated ornamentals, as *G. chilensis*, of southern Chile. *Hippurus vulgaris*, mare's-tail, is a submerged aquatic of cool temperate regions of both the northern and southern hemisphere.

Order 26. Umbellales. This order is characterized by having the flowers in determinate umbels, and is generally regarded as constituting a natural taxon.

a. Sepals, petals, and stamens 5
  b. Carpels 2-5; fruit a drupe or berry .... *Araliaceae*
  b. Carpels 2; fruit a schizocarp .... *Umbelliferae*
a. Sepals, petals, and stamens 4 .... *Cornaceae*

Araliaceae. Ginseng Family.

Habit. Herbs, shrubs, or trees, sometimes lianas, often prickly.

Leaves. Alternate, compound, or sometimes simple, often very large.

Inflorescence. Capitate or umbellate.

Flowers. Small, bisexual or unisexual (the plants dioecious or polygamo-dioecious), regular, with 5 minute sepals, 5-10 petals, usually 5 stamens, usually 5 united carpels; ovary inferior.

Fruit. A berry or drupe.

The family includes 65 genera with 800 species, primarily tropical, with 2 principal centers of distribution, in Indo-Malaysia and tropical America. They are distinguished by the usually umbellate flower cluster, 5-merous flowers, and fleshy fruit.

Fatsia japonica, of Japan, is cultivated for its ornamental foliage. *Tetrapanax papyrifera*, of Formosa, is rice-paper tree, used for making rice-paper. *Echinopanax* (3), in western North America and East Asia, includes *E. horridus*, devil's-club, Alaska to California, an obstacle to travelers. *Pseudopanax* (8) has a bicentric distribution, in New Zealand and southern Chile. *Tieghemopanax* (26), of Australia and New Caledonia, includes *T. murrayi*, pencil-wood, one of lightest woods of Australia. *Hedera* (5), ranging from Europe to Japan, is a group of root-climbers; *H. helix* is English ivy, often grown against walls. *Acanthopanax* (20) is a genus of the Himalayas and East Asia; *A. sieboldianus*, eastern Asia, is planted for shrubbery. *Oreopanax* (80) occurs in tropical America; *O. argentata, O. trianae*, cinco-dedos (five-fingers) are common shrubs in high Andean forests.

Aralia (30) is a genus mainly of the northern hemisphere; *A. spinosa* is Hercules'-club, *A. nudicaulis*, wild sarsaparilla, *A. racemosa*, American spikenard, all of eastern North America; *A. elata*, Japanese angelica-tree, is in temperate eastern Asia. *Panax* (6) occurs in tropical and eastern Asia and North America; *P. schinseng*, ginseng, Manchuria, is much used medicinally by the Chinese; *P. quinquefolius*, American ginseng, eastern North America, was formerly exported to China as a substitute.

Umbelliferae. Carrot Family.

HABIT. Mostly biennial or perennial herbs, rarely shrubs; stem often stout, with hollow internodes.

LEAVES. Alternate, sheathing, pinnately or palmately compound, sometimes simple.

INFLORESCENCE. A simple or more often compound umbel, usually subtended by an involucre.

FLOWERS. Perfect, regular; sepals 5, very small; petals 5, white or yellow; stamens 5; carpels 2, united; style swollen at the base (**stylopodium**); ovary inferior (Figure 77, C).

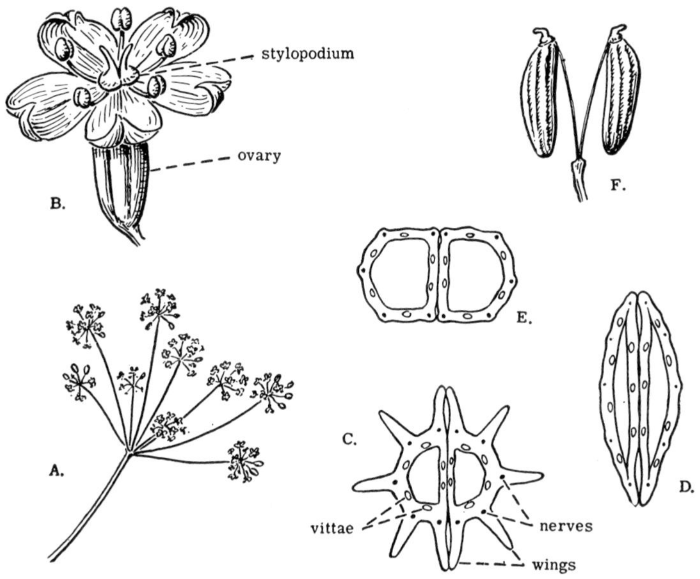

Figure 117. Features of the Umbelliferae. *A,* compound umbel of *Pseudotaenidia montana; B,* flower of *Chaerophyllum procumbens; C,* cross-section of fruit of *Thaspium; D,* cross-section of winged fruit of *Pastinaca,* flattened parallel to the commissure; *E,* cross-section of fruit of *Carum,* flattened at right angles to the commissure; *F,* splitting fruit of *Carum.*

FRUIT. A dry schizocarp composed of 2 **mericarps,** coherent and splitting at their faces (**commissure**), suspended after splitting on the thin **carpophore;** each mericarp is 1-seeded and has 5 ridges, sometimes winged, with **vittae** or oil tubes in the furrows between them; the fruit is flattened dorsally (parallel to the commissure) or laterally (at right angles to the commissure).

A vast family, of 125 genera including 2900 species, mostly of the north temperate zone, but represented on all the continents. They are characterized by the aromatic foliage, sheathing petioles, and the umbellate inflorescence. It is generally accepted as a natural taxon.

Economically members of the family are important as foods, condiments, drugs or ornamentals. Some species are poisonous.

Hydrocotyle (80), water pennywort, includes plants of tropical and temperate regions; they have peltate leaves and simple umbels. *H. americana* is a low herb of eastern North America. *Azorella* (100) includes plants of the south temperate zone, especially in the southern Andes; they are densely tufted xerophytes; *A. caespitosa,* balsam-bog, is endemic to the Falkland Islands.

Eryngium (200) is a large genus of tropical and temperate regions; the flowers are in cymose heads, and the plants are often prickly; *E. maritimum,* eryngo, sea-holly, is an Atlantic-Mediterranean strand plant; *E. yuccifolium,* eastern United States, is rattlesnake-master, reputed to cure the bite of rattlesnakes. *Astrantia* (10), in Europe and Asia, includes *A. major,* masterwort, central and southern Europe, a border plant. *Sanicula* (40), black snakeroot, cosmopolitan in distribution, has hooked fruits; *S. marilandica, S. canadensis,* are in eastern North America.

Myrrhis odorata, myrrh, of southern Europe, is grown for its pleasing odor. *Chaerophyllum* (26), chervil, is a genus of the north temperate zone; *C. procumbens* is in eastern North America; *C. bulbosum,* Europe, is grown for its edible root. *Anthriscus* (10) occurs in Europe, Asia, and Africa; *A. cerefolium,* salad chervil, Mediterranean, is cultivated as a garden vegetable for edible foliage. *Scandix* (45) in the Mediterranean region, includes *S. pecten-veneris,* Venus'-comb.

Torilis has 23 species of the Mediterranean region; *T. anthriscus* is hedge-parsley.

Coriandrum (3) occurs in the Mediterranean region; the fruits of *C. sativum,* coriander, have been used in flavoring since prehistoric times. *Cuminum cyminum,* Mediterranean, cumin, has fruits used in flavoring.

Smyrnium (7) occurs in Europe; *S. olusatrum,* alexanders, was formerly used like celery. *Conium* (2), of the Old World, includes *C. maculatum,* poison hemlock, very poisonous; used in ancient Greece to execute criminals; a famous example was the philosopher Socrates, accused of corrupting the Athenian youth.

Bupleurum (70), buplever, hare's-ear, is mainly in the north temperate zone; *B. rotundifolium,* thoroughwax, has entire perfoliate leaves. *Apium* (20) is cosmopolitan in distribution; *A. graveolens,* celery, is cultivated for edible petioles; the seeds are used in flavoring; var. *rapaceum,* turnip-rooted celery, is celeriac, with an edible root. *Petroselinum* (5) of southern Europe, includes *P. sativum,* parsley, cultivated for its herbage used for garnishing. *Cicuta* (3) is circumboreal in distribution, including *C. maculata,* water-hemlock, eastern North America, with very poisonous roots. *Carum* (25) is a genus of temperate and subtropical regions. *C. carvi* is cultivated for its fruits, caraway seeds, used in flavoring; they are the most important of umbelliferous fruits. *Pimpinella* (90) ranges from southern Europe to the Orient; *P. anisum,* anise, eastern Mediterranean, used in flavoring, is one of the earliest aromatics mentioned in literature. *Aegopodium* (2) occurs in Europe and Asia; *A. podograria,* goutweed, was formerly used in treatment of gout. *Sium* (10) is a genus of the north temperate region and tropical Africa; *S. sisarum,* skirret, southeastern Europe, is grown for edible roots.

Seseli (60) is a genus of the north temperate zone; *S. libanotis,* Eurasia, is meadow-saxifrage. *Foeniculum* (3) occurs in Europe; *F. vulgare,* fennel, has young leaves eaten like celery, the fruits used as a relish. *Anethum* (2), of the eastern Mediterranean, includes *A. graveolens,* dill (Figure 5), used in flavoring, especially pickles. *Arracacia* (45) ranges from Peru to Mexico; *A. xanthorhiza,* arracacha, is much cultivated in the Andes for its edible roots. *Ligusticum* (50) occurs in the north temperate zone and in Chile and New Zealand; *L. scoticum,* lovage, is a circumboreal strand plant, sometimes cooked for greens.

Levisticum officinale, lovage, of southern Europe, is grown for aromatic fruits. *Angelica* (50) is a genus of the north temperate region and New Zealand; aromatic petioles of *A. archangelica,* subarctic, alpine, the source of angelica oil, were used in confections.

Ferula (60) ranges from the Mediterranean to central Asia and Abyssinia; *F. assa-foetida,* Iran, Afghanistan, yields asafoetida, a very ill-scented drug used as a condiment and stimulant. *Peucedanum* (115) occurs in Europe, Asia, and Africa; *P. ostruthium* is masterwort. *Pastinaca* (14), ranging from Europe to the Altai, includes *P. sativa,* parsnip, widely cultivated for its edible roots.

Heracleum (60) is a genus of the north temperate region; *H. lanatum* is cow-parsnip.

Daucus (60), a genus of the north temperate region, includes *D. carota,* carrot, widely cultivated for its edible roots, also a widespread weed (Queen Anne's lace).

Cornaceae. Dogwood Family.

HABIT. Trees and shrubs.

LEAVES. Opposite or alternate, simple, exstipulate (Figure 60).

INFLORESCENCE. Cymose, corymbose, umbellate, or capitate, sometimes with showy involucres.

FLOWERS. Perfect or imperfect, regular, with 4-5 sepals, 4-5 petals, 4-5 stamens, and usually 2 united carpels; ovary inferior.

FRUIT. A drupe or berry.

The family includes about 18 genera with 125 species, of the north and south temperate zones and tropical mountains. They are characterized by the woody habit, 4-5-merous flowers and inferior ovary. *Nyssa* and its relatives are separated by some systematists as the Nyssaceae and placed in the Myrtales. There is strong evidence, however, that the group is closely allied to the Cornaceae.

Cornus (40), cornel, includes trees and shrubs of the north temperate region and tropical mountains. Many are cultivated ornamentally as *C. sanguinea,* blood-red dogwood, Europe; *C. alba,* Tatarian dogwood, eastern Russia to Siberia and Korea. Trees with a showy involucre surrounding the flowers are *C. mas,* cornelian cherry, central and southern Europe and western Asia, *C. nuttallii,* Pacific dogwood, British Columbia to California, and *C. florida,* flowering dogwood, eastern North America and eastern Mexico. *C. canadensis,* bunchberry, North America, and *C. suecica,* circumboreal, are low subshrubs. *Aucuba* (3), ranging from the Himalayas to eastern Asia, includes *A. japonica,* Japan laurel, Japan, cultivated as an ornamental.

Nyssa (6) occurs in India, eastern Asia, and North America; *N. sylvatica,* United States, is sour gum, black gum, or tupelo; *N. aquatica,* United States, is water tupelo; both are of timber value. *Davidia involucrata* is dove tree, of Tibet and western China, cultivated as an interesting ornamental.

20

Angiospermae. Dicotyledoneae. Sympetalae

Order 27. Ericales. Members of the primitive families of the Ericales have distinct petals but the more advanced families have petals united at least at the base.

a. Stamens free from the corolla
  b. Corolla essentially polypetalous
    c. Shrubs with deciduous leaves .... *Clethraceae*
    c. Low perennial herbs .... *Pyrolaceae*
  b. Corolla distinctly sympetalous .... *Ericaceae*
a. Stamens borne on the corolla
  b. Plants with green leaves
    c. Stamens 4-5; carpels 5 .... *Epacridaceae*
    c. Stamens 5-10; carpels 3 .... *Diapensiaceae*
  b. Non-green parasites .... *Lennoaceae*

Clethraceae. White-Alder Family. A family of 2 genera including about 30 species of trees and shrubs, mostly tropical American, but some in temperate North America, Madeira, the Sunda Islands and Japan. The flowers are in racemes or panicles, perfect, regular, with 5 sepals, 5 petals, 10 stamens and 3 united carpels. *Clethra alnifolia,* sweet pepper-bush, is on the eastern coastal plain of the United States, and *C. acuminata,* white-alder, in the Appalachians from West Virginia to Georgia; both are grown as ornamentals.

Pyrolaceae. Pyrola Family. A family of 10 genera including 70 species of perennial evergreen herbs and non-green saprophytes, mostly of the north temperate and arctic regions. The flowers are perfect with 4-5 sepals, 4-5 petals, 8-10 stamens, and 4-5 united carpels. *Pyrola* (30), wintergreen, occurs in the north temperate and arctic regions; *P. elliptica,* shinleaf, and *P. rotundifolia,* wintergreen, are North American, while *P. uniflora, P. secunda,* and *P. minor* are circumboreal. *Chimaphila* (5), of Japan and North America, includes *C. maculata,* spotted wintergreen, and *C. umbellata*, pipsissewa, prince's pine. *Monotropa* (4) is a genus of yellowish or white saprophytes, in the north temperate zone; *M. uniflora* is Indian pipe and *M. hypopitys* is pinesap. *Sarcodes sanguinea*, snow plant, is a red saprophyte in the Sierra Nevadas of California (often seen under bigtrees). Some authors separate the saprophytic genera under the Monotropaceae.

Lennoaceae. Lennoa Family. A family of parasitic herbs, with 3 genera including 4 species of the southwestern United States and Mexico to Colombia. The flowers are perfect and regular, typically 5-merous, with 6-14 united carpels. *Lennoa* has 2 species in Mexico and Colombia. *Pholisma arenarium* occurs in southern California and Baja California. *Ammobroma sonorae*, sand food, occurs in Arizona, California and Mexico; the tubers are eaten by Gulf Indians. The family has been placed by many taxonomists in the Tubiflorales.

Ericaceae. Heath Family.

HABIT. Shrubs and trees, rarely trailing or scrambling.

LEAVES. Alternate, sometimes opposite or whorled, deciduous or persistent.

INFLORESCENCE. Racemose, or the flowers solitary.

FLOWERS. Perfect, regular or slightly irregular; sepals 4-5, persistent; petals 4-7, joined; stamens 8-10; carpels 4-5, joined; ovary superior or inferior.

FRUIT. A capsule, drupe, or berry.

A family of 70 genera including 1900 species, forming the characteristic features of the vegetation of many regions of acid soils, particularly in moors, swamps, and mountain slopes, throughout the temperate regions of both hemispheres; also, to a lesser extent, on tropical mountains and in the arctic. The family is generally divided into 4 subfamilies. The genera having the ovary inferior are sometimes separated in the family Vacciniaceae. They are economically valuable for ornamental planting and for edible fruits.

I. Fruit a septicidal capsule; corolla deciduous; ovary superior. *Ledum* (5) is a genus of evergreen shrubs of sphagnum bogs in arctic and north temperate regions, including *L. groenlandicum*, Labrador tea. *Befaria* (20), Andes rose, of tropical and subtropical America, constitutes a conspicuous feature of the vegetation of the Andes. *Rhododendron* (850) is a vast genus distributed in the arctic and north temperate regions, also on tropical mountains; especially concentrated in Asia, from Yunnan and Szechuan to the eastern Himalayas, with extensions through the Sunda Islands and New Guinea to Australia, also in Europe and North America. Many species are popular cultivated ornamentals. *R. lapponicum* is in Scandinavia, Greenland, and northeastern North America. *R. maximum* is in eastern North America, the state flower of West Virginia (Figure

118). *R. catawbiense,* rose bay, is in the southern Appalachians. *R. californicum* is the state flower of Washington. Most species are evergreen, but in the section Azalea the leaves are deciduous; here are included *R. flavum,* of the Caucasus, *R. molle,* China, *R. japonicum,* Japan, *R. canadense,* rhodora, from Newfoundland to Pennsylvania; *R. nudiflorum,* pinxter-flower, and *R. calendulaceum,* flame azalea, in the Appalachians; *R. occidentale,* California, Oregon. *Kalmia* (8) ranges from Canada to Cuba; *K. angustifolia,* sheep-laurel, is poisonous to sheep; *K. latifolia,* mountain-laurel, is the state flower of Pennsylvania. *Phyllodoce* (10) is a

Figure 118. ***Rhododendron maximum.*** **(Photograph by Jesse F. Clovis.)**

genus of subarctic regions and in the Pyrenees. *Daboecia polifolia,* St. Dabeoc's heath, of northern Spain, southwestern France, and Ireland, is cultivated in rock gardens.

II. Fruit a berry or loculicidal capsule; ovary superior. *Arbutus* (20) is a genus of the Mediterranean and North and Central America; *A. unedo,* strawberry-tree, is Mediterranean; *A. menziesii,* madroño, western North America, yields timber; the bark is smooth and red, peeling in thin strips. *Arctostaphylos* (50) is a genus of north temperate and arctic regions; *A. uva-ursi,* bearberry, is circumboreal and alpine. Various species, including *A. pungens,* manzanita, are characteristic of the chaparral of southern California. *Pernettya* (30) has a bicentric range, from Mexico to Tierra del Fuego and in Tasmania and New Zealand. *Gaultheria* (100) occurs in America from Alaska and Newfoundland to Tierra del Fuego, also in Australia and New Zealand. *G. procumbens,* eastern North America, is wintergreen or mountain-tea; *G. shallon,* northwestern North America, shallon, is sold as "lemon leaf." *Cassiope* (12) is especially abundant in central and eastern Asia; *C. hypnoides* is in arctic Europe and America; *C. tetragona* is circumpolar, extending north in Greenland to 83°. *Andromeda* (2), bog rosemary, of north temperate and arctic regions, includes *A. polifolia,* circumboreal, and *A. glaucophylla,* from Labrador to West Virginia. *Pieris* (8), a genus of the Himalayas, eastern Asia, and North America, includes *P. floribunda,* of the Allegheny Mountains, cultivated as an ornamental. *Chamaedaphne calyculata,* leatherleaf, occurs in bogs of circumboreal regions. *Leucothoë* (35) occurs in America, Madagascar, the Himalayas, and Japan, and includes *L. catesbaei,* of the southern Appalachians. *Oxydendrum arboreum,* sourwood, of eastern North America, has deciduous leaves. *Epigaea* (2) includes *E. asiatica* in Japan, and *E. repens,* trailing arbutus, mayflower, in eastern North America, the floral emblem of Massachusetts and of Nova Scotia.

III. Fruit a berry or loculicidal capsule; ovary inferior. *Vaccinium* (200) is a genus of the north temperate region and tropical mountains, such as the Andes, especially well developed in tropical Asia and New Guinea, also in Madagascar and Polynesia; many species produce edible fruits. *V. myrtillus,* Europe, northwestern Asia, North America, is blueberry, whortleberry, or bilberry. *V. uliginosum, V. vitis-idaea,* arctic, circumpolar, are called whinberries. *V. corymbosum* is the cultivated blueberry of eastern North America. *V. stamineum* is deerberry, of eastern North America. The commercial cranberry is *V. macrocarpon,* northeastern North America, grown in bogs. *Cavendishia* (40), of tropical America, includes *C. quereme,* quereme, a fragrant shrub of the Andes. *Gaylussacia* (40) occurs in North and South America, chiefly in Brazil, including *G. baccata,* black huckleberry, and *G. brachycera,* box-huckleberry, both of eastern North America.

IV. Fruit a septicidal or loculicidal capsule or nut; corolla persistent;

ovary superior. *Calluna vulgaris,* of western Asia, Europe, Greenland, and Newfoundland to Massachusetts, is ling, a low evergreen shrub covering large areas. *Erica* (500) is a large genus mostly in Europe and South Africa, especially the latter. *E. arborea,* bruyere, tree heath, of the Mediterranean area, grows to a height of 65 feet, furnishes wood for briar pipes. *E. cinerea* and *E. vagans,* heaths, are in western Europe, common on moors; *E. tetralix,* heath, western Europe, is characteristic of vast areas of moors.

Epacridaceae. Epacris Family.

HABIT. Shrubs or small trees.

LEAVES. Alternate, narrow, entire, rigid, often sheathing, exstipulate.

INFLORESCENCE. Racemose or spicate.

FLOWERS. Usually white or red, perfect, regular; sepals 5, united, petals 5, united; stamens 5, epipetalous; carpels 5, united; ovary superior.

FRUIT. A capsule or drupe.

A family of 23 genera with 350 species, mainly in Australia and Tasmania, but also in India, Hawaii, New Zealand, and South America. The family may be regarded as the Australian counterpart of the Ericaceae, differing from that family in having epipetalous stamens. A few species are cultivated as ornamentals.

Epacris (40), Australian heath, occurs in southeastern Australia, Tasmania, New Caledonia, and New Zealand; some species are cultivated as decorative shrubs. *Styphelia* (180) is the largest genus, occurring in Australia, New Zealand, New Caledonia, Malaya, and Hawaii. *Leucopogon* (130), of Australia and Malaysia, includes *L. glacialis,* beard-heath.

Diapensiaceae. Diapensia Family. A family of alpine and arctic evergreen undershrubs, with 6 genera including 13 species. The leaves are in rosettes. The flowers are solitary or racemose, perfect, and regular, with 5 sepals, 5 slightly joined petals, 5 epipetalous stamens, and 3 united carpels, with an inferior ovary. *Diapensia* (3) has 1 species in central Asia and 1 *D. lapponica,* circumpolar, growing in very dense tussocks. *Shortia* has 3 species in eastern Asia, and 1, *S. galacifolia,* Oconee-bells, in the southern Appalachians (page 69). *Galax aphylla,* ranges from West Virginia to Georgia; the leaves are collected for ornamental use by florists, especially about Galax, Virginia.

Order 28. Primulales. Recent phylogenetic studies indicate that the Primulales are derived from ancestors related to the Caryophyllales. The plants are characterized by a single whorl of stamens, opposite the petals, and by free-central placentation.

a. Style 1
    b. Herbs; fruit a capsule .... *Primulaceae*
    b. Trees or shrubs; fruit a drupe or berry .... *Myrsinaceae*
a. Styles 5; fruit an achene or utricle .... *Plumbaginaceae*

Myrsinaceae. Myrsine Family.

Habit. Trees and shrubs.

Leaves. Alternate, often in rosettes, usually leathery, with resin-passages, exstipulate.

Inflorescence. Racemose.

Flowers. Perfect or imperfect, regular; sepals 4-6, distinct or united, corolla-lobes 4-6, stamens 4-6, opposite the corolla-lobes, carpels 4-6; ovary usually superior.

Fruit. A drupe.

A family of 32 genera with about 1000 species, tropical and subtropical. They are closely related to the Primulaceae, differing in their woody habit. The family is of little economic value; a few species are grown as ornamentals.

Aegiceras (2), of the Old World tropics, includes *A. majus,* India, which grows in mangrove swamps and exhibits features of mangroves, including vivipary. *Ardisia* (250) is a genus of warm climates, mostly of tropical Asia and America; *A. crispa,* tropical Asia, is a popular greenhouse plant, grown for its brilliant red fruits. *Oncostemon* (60), in Madagascar and the Mascarenes, is said to be the largest genus of seed plants endemic to oceanic islands. *Myrsine* (4), of the Old World tropics, includes *M. africana,* from the Azores through Africa to eastern Asia.

Plumbaginaceae. Leadwort Family.

Habit. Perennial herbs or shrubs, sometimes climbing.

Leaves. Narrow, alternate, sometimes with water- or chalk-glands on the surface.

Inflorescence. Capitate, spicate, racemose or paniculate.

Flowers. Regular, perfect; calyx 5-lobed; corolla 5-lobed, sometimes lead-colored; stamens 5; carpels 5, united; ovary superior.

Fruit. A utricle.

A family of 10 genera including 300 species, most common in semi-arid regions of the Old World, especially of the Mediterranean and central Asiatic regions. Members of the family are distinguished by the 5 styles of the pistil. A few species are grown as ornamentals.

Plumbago (10), leadwort, is a genus mostly of tropical and subtropical regions; *P. capensis,* South Africa, and *P. rosea,* southern Asia, are cultivated ornamentals. *Limonium* (150) is more or less cosmopolitan, chiefly in steppes and salt marshes; *L. vulgare,* sea-lavender, is on coasts of western Europe. *Armeria* (50) is a genus of the north temperate zone and the Andes; *A. maritima,* thrift, sea-pink, is circumboreal. *Acantholimon* (90), prickly-thrift, is characteristic of arid and semi-arid lands from Greece to Tibet.

Primulaceae. Primrose Family.

Habit. Usually perennial herbs, sometimes annual, rarely subshrubs.

LEAVES. Opposite or whorled, sometimes all basal.

INFLORESCENCE. Of various types, terminal and axillary.

FLOWERS. Often on scapes, usually regular, perfect; sepals 5, united; petals 5, united; stamens 5, opposite the petals; carpels typically 5, with 1 locule, and free-central placentation; ovary superior.

FRUIT. A capsule.

A family of 28 genera including 800 species, on all continents, but most abundant in the north temperate zone. It is distinguished from other families of the order by the herbaceous habit. Economically the plants are of little importance except as ornamentals.

Primula (500), primrose, is a genus of the northern hemisphere, especially in the Alps, Caucasus, Asia Minor and Himalayas to western China. *P. veris,* Eurasia, is cowslip; *P. elatior,* central and eastern Europe, is oxslip; *P. vulgaris,* Mediterranean, is European primrose. Among other cultivated forms are *P. auricula,* of the Alps; *P. bulleyana,* western China; *P. denticulata,* western Himalayas; *P. japonica,* Japan; *P. rosea,* Himalayas; *P. juliae,* Caucasus; *P. sikkimensis,* Himalayas; *P. sinensis, P. malacoides,* fairy primrose, and *P. obconica,* China. *Douglasia* has 6 species, 5 in North America, 1, *D. vitaliana,* in the Pyrenees and Alps; the genus was named for David Douglas. *Androsace* (100) is a genus of tufted xerophytes of arctic, circumboreal, and alpine regions; *A. septentrionalis,* rock-jasmine, is in temperate Europe, Asia, and North America.

Soldanella (8) occurs in the Alps; the flowers expand at very low temperatures. *Hottonia* (2), featherfoil, is a group of floating water plants with finely divided leaves; *H. inflata* occurs in eastern North America. *Dodecatheon* (30), shooting star, occurs in North America and northeastern Asia; *D. meadia,* is in eastern North America. *Cyclamen* (13) occurs in Europe, mostly in the Alps; *C. europaeum,* Alp's-violet, ranges from France to the Caucasus; *C. persicum,* ranging from Greece to Syria, is grown for ornamental flowers. *Lysimachia* (110) is cosmopolitan in range; *L. nummularia,* moneywort, is native of Europe, but naturalized in Japan and North America; *L. vulgaris,* Eurasia, is yellow loosestrife; *L. ciliata,* eastern North America, fringed loosestrife. *Trientalis* (3) occurs in north temperate regions; *T. europaea* is in Europe, Asia, northwestern North America; *T. americana,* eastern North America, is starflower. *Glaux maritima,* sea-milkwort, is a circumboreal strand plant with fleshy leaves. *Anagallis* (50) is cosmopolitan; *A. arvensis,* pimpernel, poor-man's weatherglass, has flowers that close upon the approach of bad weather. *Centunculus minimus,* chaffweed, is in Europe, Asia, Africa, and North America. *Samolus* (10) is widely distributed, including *S. parviflorus,* brookweed, widespread in America. *Coris* (2), of the Mediterranean, is the only genus in the family with irregular flowers.

Order 29. Ebenales. As regarded by Engler, the order is characterized by having 2 or 3 whorls of stamens. There is evidence that the order is not a natural group and the families included here are differently distributed by some phylogenists.

a. Ovary superior
  b. Stamens the same number as the lobes of the corolla ... *Sapotaceae*
  b. Stamens twice as many as the lobes of the corolla
    c. Styles 2-8; flowers mostly imperfect .... *Ebenaceae*
    c. Style 1; flowers perfect .... *Styracaceae*
a. Ovary inferior
  b. Ovary completely chambered; stamens in 1-3 whorls .. *Symplocaceae*
  b. Ovary incompletely chambered; stamens in 1 whorl .. *Styracaceae*

Sapotaceae. Sapodilla Family.

HABIT. Mostly trees, some shrubs, with a milky sap.

LEAVES. Entire, leathery, alternate, simple.

INFLORESCENCE. Cymose, or the flowers solitary.

FLOWERS. Perfect, often regular; sepals 4-12, basally united; petals united, the same number as the sepals; stamens in 2 or 3 whorls but usually only 1 whorl functional, the others reduced to staminodes; carpels typically 4 or 5; ovary superior.

FRUIT. A berry.

A family of 40 genera including 600 species of primarily tropical trees. The plants are distinguished by the milky sap and completely septate superior ovary. Many yield valuable latex or edible fruits.

Palaquium (50) is a genus of Indomalaysia; *P. gutta* was formerly the chief source of gutta-percha. *Achras zapota,* of tropical America, yields chicle for chewing gum, and the rusty-brown fruit, sapodilla, is edible. *Calocarpum* (15) occurs in tropical America; *C. sapota* is sapote or marmalade-plum; the russet-brown fruit is one of the well-known edible fruits of tropical America. *Lucuma* (35) occurs in tropical America, including *L. nervosa,* canistel, vegetable egg, a popular fruit. *Chrysophyllum* (80), a genus of the American tropics, includes *C. cainito,* starapple, of the West Indies, with edible fruits, and *C. olivaeforme,* satinleaf, yielding cabinet wood. *Butyrospermum* (2) occurs in tropical Africa; seeds of *B. parkii* yield shea butter. *Sideroxylon* (100), ironwood, occurs in the Old World tropics. *Manilkara bidentata,* bulletwood, northern South America, yields balata, a commercially important latex.

Ebenaceae. Ebony Family.

HABIT. Trees or shrubs, without latex, the heartwood often black.

LEAVES. Simple, leathery, entire, alternate, exstipulate.

INFLORESCENCE. Cymose, or the flowers solitary.

FLOWERS. Regular (the plants usually dioecious); calyx 3-7-lobed, persistent; corolla 3-7-lobed; stamens the same number as the corolla lobes or 2-3 times as many; carpels 2-16, united; ovary superior.

FRUIT. A berry.

A family of 5 genera with 325 species, widely distributed in tropical and subtropical regions, but best developed in Indomalaysia. Members of this family are distinguished from related families by the unisexual flowers. Some are of importance as a source of timber or edible fruits.

Diospyros (250) is the principal genus, chiefly of warm climates. *D. ebenum,* Ceylon, and *D. reticulata,* Mauritius, yield ebony wood, hard and intensely black. *D. lotus,* Chinese date-plum, and *D. kaki,* Japanese persimmon, have edible fruits. *D. virginiana,* persimmon, eastern United States, also has edible fruits. *Euclea* (20) occurs in Africa; *E. pseudebenus,* Orange River ebony, produces good timber.

Styracaceae. Storax Family.

HABIT. Trees and shrubs.

LEAVES. Alternate, simple, leathery, exstipulate.

INFLORESCENCE. Racemose or paniculate.

FLOWERS. Perfect, regular; sepals 4-5, united; petals 4-6, united; stamens twice as many as the petals; carpels 3-5, united; ovary superior.

FRUIT. A drupe, with a stony endocarp and a fleshy or dry mesocarp.

A family of 8 genera and 125 species, from Brazil to Peru and Mexico, in the southeastern United States, eastern Asia, and in the Mediterranean region. It is separated from the Ebenaceae by the perfect flowers, and by stellate pubescence. A few species are grown as ornamentals and some yield medicinal products.

Halesia (4) occurs in the southeastern United States and in Japan and China. *H. carolina,* snowdrop tree, or silver-bell, is an ornamental shrub; the fruits are winged. *Pterostyrax* (3) occurs in eastern Asia; *P. hispida,* epaulette-tree, resembles *Halesia. Styrax* (100) is tropical and subtropical. *S. officinalis,* snowdrop bush, of the Mediterranean, yields storax, a resin formerly much used. *S. benzoin,* of Indomalaysia, yields aromatic benzoin gum, used in soap, lotions, toothpaste. *S. americana,* southeastern United States, is snowbell, grown as an ornamental.

Symplocaceae. Sweetleaf Family.

HABIT. Shrubs and trees.

LEAVES. Alternate, simple, leathery, exstipulate.

INFLORESCENCE. Racemose or paniculate.

FLOWERS. Perfect, regular; sepals 5, united; petals 5-10, united; stamens 5, 10, 15, or more; carpels 2-5, united; ovary inferior.

FRUIT. A berry or drupe.

A family of 1 genus, *Symplocos,* including 300 species of tropical and subtropical Asia and America. Members are distinguished by the inferior or half-inferior ovary. A few are cultivated as ornamental shrubs. *S. paniculata,* sapphire-berry, Himalayas to Japan, has showy fragrant flowers. *S. tinctoria,* southeastern United States, is sweetleaf or horse-sugar.

Order 30. Gentianales. These plants are characterized by having the corolla lobes convolute in the bud (whence the name Contortae, sometimes used). The arrangement of these families by different authors varies widely.

a. Plants without a milky latex
  b. Trees or shrubs
    c. Stamens fewer than the lobes of the corolla ...... *Oleaceae*
    c. Stamens as many as the lobes of the corolla ..... *Loganiaceae*
  b. Herbs
    c. Style simple, stigma entire or 2-lobed .... *Gentianaceae*
    c. Style 2-cleft .... *Loganiaceae*
a. Plants with a milky latex
  b. Filaments distinct; style 1 .... *Apocynaceae*
  b. Filaments united; styles 2 .... *Asclepiadaceae*

Oleaceae. Olive Family.

HABIT. Shrubs and trees, sometimes climbing.

LEAVES. Opposite, simple or compound, stipulate.

INFLORESCENCE. Axillary or terminal, racemose, or paniculate.

FLOWERS. Perfect (sometimes imperfect), regular; calyx usually 4-lobed; corolla usually 4-lobed (sometimes absent); stamens usually 2; carpels 2; ovary superior.

FRUIT. A berry, drupe, capsule, or samara.

A family of 22 genera including 500 species, of tropical and warm temperate regions. Members of the family are distinguished by the androecium typically of 2 stamens. The family is regarded by some authors as not constituting a natural taxon. Fruits, timber, and ornamentals make it of economic importance.

Fraxinus (65), ash, is a genus of north temperate regions, including trees with pinnate leaves, winged fruits (Figure 85, G), and useful timber. *F. excelsior,* European ash, ranges from Europe to Asia Minor; *F. ornus,* flowering ash, Mediterranean, has showy white petals, unlike most ashes. North American species are apetalous; they include *F. americana,* white ash, *F. nigra,* black ash, *F. pennsylvanica,* red ash, *F. quadrangulata,* blue ash, and *F. latifolia,* Oregon ash. *Forsythia* (4), goldenbells (Figure 48), is a genus of shrubs of the temperate regions of the Old World, including *F. suspensa,* China, and *F. europaea,* Albania, a Tertiary relic; they are cultivated for the early yellow flowers. *Syringa* (25), lilac, occurs in Europe and Asia; several cultivated as ornamentals. Common in cultivation are *S. vulgaris,* southeastern Europe, *S. josikaea,* Galicia, Hungary, *S. persica,* Iran to northwestern China, and *S. reflexa,* western China. *Osmanthus* (10) occurs in southern and eastern Asia, Polynesia, and North America; *O. americana* is devilwood, a shrub of the southeastern states. *Olea* (35) occurs in the Mediterranean, South Africa, Indomalaysia, New Zealand, and Polynesia. *O. europaea,* olive, one of man's most important trees, has been cultivated in the Mediterranean region since ancient times for edible fruits and oil. *O. capensis* is a characteristic tree of Cape Colony. *Ligustrum* (50), privet, includes plants of the Old World, often grown for hedges. *L. vulgare* is a native of the Mediterranean region; *L. ovalifolium*, "California" privet, is a native of Japan. *Jasminum* (200), jasmine, is a genus mostly of tropical regions, best developed in Indomalaysia; they are ornamental vines or erect shrubs. Common in cultivation are *J. fruticans*, Mediterranean, *J. officinale*, Persia to Cashmir and China, white jasmine, and *J. nudiflorum*, China, winter jasmine. *Chionanthus* (3) occurs in North America and China; *C. virginica*, eastern United States, is fringetree, an ornamental shrub. *Nyctanthes arbor-tristis*, Indomalaysia, is sheuli, a cultivated ornamental.

Loganiaceae. Logania Family.

HABIT. Trees, shrubs, and herbs, many climbers.

LEAVES. Opposite (sometimes alternate or whorled), simple, stipulate.

INFLORESCENCE. Usually cymose.

FLOWERS. Usually regular, perfect; sepals 4-5, united; petals 4-5, united; stamens 4-5; carpels 2, united; ovary superior.

FRUIT. A capsule, berry, or drupe.

A family of 32 genera including 800 species of tropical and subtropical regions. Distinctive features are the opposite leaves and (usually) bicollateral bundles. Many species are cultivated ornamentals and several are sources of drugs and poisons.

Logania (25) is a genus of Australia and New Zealand. *Spigelia* (35) ranges from southern North America to Brazil. *S. splendens*, Central America, is often cultivated for its ornamental flowers. *S. marilandica*, Indian pink or pinkroot, ranges from New Jersey to Texas. *Gelsemium* (2) includes *G. sempervirens*, Carolina yellow jessamine (or jasmine), in southern United States, grown as a porch vine; it is the state flower of South Carolina. *Strychnos* (150) is a genus of tropical regions, erect trees or climbing shrubs with exceedingly poisonous seeds. *S. nux-vomica*, India, Ceylon, is the source of strychnine. *S. toxifera* and *S. castelnaei*, Guiana, Amazonas, and *S. tieute*, Sunda Islands, yield curare, used to poison arrows. *Buddleja* (90) is a genus of tropical and subtropical regions; some species are grown as ornamentals, including *B. alternifolia*, northwest China, butterfly-bush, with lilac-colored flowers.

Gentianaceae. Gentian Family.

HABIT. Herbs, rarely shrubs.

LEAVES. Opposite, entire, simple, exstipulate.

INFLORESCENCE. Cymose.

FLOWERS. Regular, perfect; sepals usually 5, united; petals usually 5, united; stamens usually 5, epipetalous; carpels 2, united; ovary superior.

FRUIT. A capsule.

A family of 70 genera including 800 species, of wide distribution, most abundant in the north temperate zone; many are arctic or alpine. Members of the family are distinguished by the opposite leaves and the (usually) 1-celled ovary with parietal placentation. Several species are grown as ornamentals.

Erythraea (30) includes *E. centaurium*, centaury, Europe, its medicinal properties reputedly discovered by the centaur, Chiron. *Gentiana* (500) is found in most parts of the world, but is chiefly alpine; some species are among the most striking features of the flora of the Alps. *G. campestris* is in north and central Europe; *G. amarella*, Europe to Mongolia; *G. przewalskii*, China, discovered by Przewalski (page 88); *G. pneumonanthe*, temperate Eurasia; *G. tenella*, subarctic, alpine; *G. nivalis*, subarctic and alpine, Europe and North America; *G. lutea*, Spain to the Balkans and Asia Minor, the source of gentian root tonic; *G. acaulis*, of the Alps, is one of the most beautiful. *G. crinita*, fringed gentian, eastern North America. *Swertia* (80) occurs in Asia, Africa, and America; *S. perennis*, from the Pyrenees to Japan, is often cultivated. *Nymphoides* (20), water snowflake or floating heart, of tropical and temperate regions, is a group of water plants with the habit of *Nymphaea*. *Menyanthes trifoliata*, buckbean, is a plant of sphagnum bogs, circumboreal in range.

Apocynaceae. Dogbane Family.

HABIT. Trees, shrubs, or herbs, with many large tropical lianas; sap milky.

LEAVES. Simple, opposite (sometimes alternate or whorled), entire, exstipulate.

INFLORESCENCE. Racemose or cymose, or the flowers solitary.

FLOWERS. Perfect, regular; sepals 5, united; petals 5, united; stamens 5, epipetalous; carpels 2, united; ovary superior or half-inferior.

FRUIT. A capsule, follicle, berry, or drupe.

A family of 300 genera including 1300 species, widely distributed but most abundant in the tropics. These plants are closely related to the Asclepiadaceae but differ in the nature of the pollen and in the absence of the corona. They are important as ornamentals, while some yield drugs, tannin, latex, and similar substances.

Allamanda (12) occurs in tropical America; *A. cathartica*, cup of gold, is a liana cultivated for its very showy yellow flowers. Plants which have been used as a source of rubber are *Landolphia* (35), in Africa, Madagascar, South America; *Clitandra* (15), in Africa; *Hancornia speciosa*, in Brazil; and *Funtumia elastica*, in West Africa. *Plumeria* (50) occurs in tropical America; several species, including *P. rubra*, temple tree or frangipani, are cultivated for their perfumed flowers. *Aspidosperma* (50) ranges from the West Indies to Argentina; *A. quebracho-blanco*, Argentina, produces medicinal quebracho blanco bark; *A. cruentum*, mylady,

Central America, produces useful timber. *Lochnera* (3) is a genus of the tropics; *L. rosea,* princesa, is one of the commonest tropical weeds. *Vinca* (5) ranges from Europe to the Orient; *V. minor,* periwinkle, running myrtle, western Europe to Asia Minor, is often grown decoratively as a ground-cover. *Catharanthus* (3), of tropical regions, includes *C. roseus,* much grown as ornamental ground-cover in the southern United States. *Tabernaemontana* (50), in tropical America, includes *T. coronaria,* crape-jasmine. *Thevetia* (8) in America, includes *T. neriifolia,* yellow oleander,

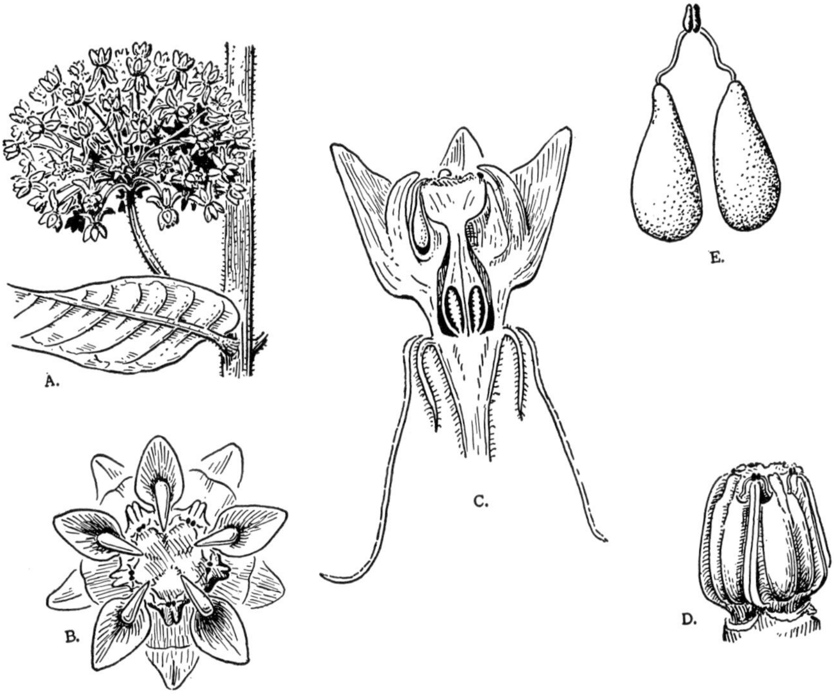

Figure 119. Milkweed, *Asclepias syriaca. A,* inflorescence; *B,* top view of a single flower; *C,* longitudinal section of a flower; *D,* flower with hoods and horns removed, showing androecium surrounding gynoecium and translator arching over the slit between anthers; *E,* translator with pollinia.

from Mexico to Brazil. *Pachypodium* (10), a genus of grotesque succulents, occurs in South Africa (p. 80) and Madagascar. *Apocynum* (25), dogbane, of the north temperate zone, includes *A. androsaemifolium* and *A. cannabinum,* Indian hemp; because of its name it is sometimes confused with *Cannabis* (page 298). *Strophanthus* (43) is a genus of Asia and Africa; seeds of *S. hispidus* and others yield the drug strophanthin, a heart stimulant, and precursor of cortisone, used for arthritis. *Nerium* (3) is a genus of the Mediterranean region; *N. oleander,* oleander, ranges from Portugal to Mesopotamia and in North Africa. It is widely cultivated in warm lands for its white or red flowers, and is much planted along highways in California and Florida.

Asclepiadaceae. Milkweed Family.

HABIT. Perennial herbs, shrubs, or rarely trees, sometimes cactus-like, or epiphytic; many lianas; sap usually milky.

LEAVES. Simple, opposite, entire, stipulate.

INFLORESCENCE. A cyme, raceme, or umbel.

FLOWERS. Perfect, regular, with an elaborate corona, sepals 5; petals 5, united; stamens 5; carpels 2; ovary superior; the stamens and carpels are united into a complex organ, the **gynostegium;** the carpels are free below and united to a common stigma; the pollen grains are often coherent, forming masses or **pollinia,** carried on legs of insects by a curious mechanism known as a **translator;** seeds usually bearing a coma of long silky hairs.

FRUIT. A follicle (Figure 85, D).

The family includes perhaps 100 genera with 1700 species, although estimates of these numbers vary widely; the species are mostly tropical, with a few in temperate regions. The curious corona and translators are distinctive features (see Figure 119). Some species are grown decoratively and others have been used as a source of natural rubber.

Periploca (12) is a genus of southern Europe, Asia, and Africa; unlike most members of the family, the pollen is in tetrads; *P. graeca,* Mediterranean, is silk-vine, planted for ornament. *Asclepias* (90), milkweed, is a genus of Africa and America, especially in the United States. Insects accidentally catch their legs in the slits between the anthers and remove the translators. *A. curassavica,* blood-flower, tropical America, is a common tropical weed. Species of eastern North America are *A. tuberosa,* butterfly-weed; *A. syriaca,* common milkweed; *A. incarnata,* swamp milkweed. *Cynanchum* (200) occurs in temperate and tropical regions; there are many climbers and xerophytes with fleshy stems and reduced leaves; *C. vincetoxicum* ranges from central Europe to central Asia. *Sarcostemma* (12) is a genus of bizarre xerophytic shrubs, in Africa, India, and Australia, sometimes grown as oddities. *Oxypetalum* (100) ranges from the West Indies to Argentina; *O. caeruleum,* blue milkweed, is grown as an ornamental. *Hoya* (80), of Asia and Australia, is a genus of climbers with fleshy leaves; *H. carnosa,* southern China, wax-flower, is cultivated as an ornamental. *Dischidia* (50), of Indomalaysia, Polynesia, and Australia, is a genus of epiphytes, climbing by aerial roots; *D. rafflesiana,* pitcher-plant, has pitcher-leaves containing rainwater and debris carried in by nesting ants, while adventitious roots grow into each pitcher and absorb water. *Ceropegia* (100) occurs in the tropical Old World, a genus of herbs or under-shrubs, somewhat xerophytic; some species have tuberous rootstocks, some are leafless, some have fleshy stems. *Stapelia* (100) includes the carrion-flowers, of South Africa, xerophytes with swollen stems, reduced leaves, and flowers with the odor of carrion; some species are cultivated as oddities. *Cryptostegia* (2), of tropical Africa and Madagascar, includes *C. grandiflora,* which has been used as a source of rubber.

Order 31. Tubiflorales.

a. Corolla regular
  b. Style terminal
    c. Leaves generally alternate
      d. Trees or shrubs; fruit a drupe .... *Myoporaceae*
      d. Herbs, shrubs, or trees; fruit usually not a drupe
        e. Mostly herbs or shrubs, usually climbing; fruit a capsule .... *Convolvulaceae*
        e. Erect herbs or shrubs
          f. Ovary usually 3-celled .... *Polemoniaceae*
          f. Ovary not usually 3-celled
            g. Ovary separating at maturity into four 1-seeded nutlets
              h. Stamens 5
                i. Carpels two .... *Boraginaceae*
                i. Carpels five .... *Nolanaceae*
              h. Stamens 4 or 2 .... *Verbenaceae*
            g. Ovary not separating into 4 nutlets at maturity
              h. Style usually deeply 2-cleft .... *Hydrophyllaceae*
              h. Style not deeply 2-cleft .... *Solanaceae*
    c. Leaves opposite .... *Acanthaceae*
  b. Style gynobasic; ovary deeply lobed .... *Boraginaceae*
a. Corolla irregular
  b. Ovary separating at maturity into 1-seeded nutlets
    c. Stamens 5 .... *Boraginaceae*
    c. Stamens 4 or 2
      d. Style terminal .... *Verbenaceae*
      d. Style gynobasic .... *Labiatae*
  b. Ovary not separating into nutlets at maturity
    c. Ovary superior
      d. Parasitic or carnivorous plants
        e. Non-green root parasites .... *Orobanchaceae*
        e. Carnivorous aquatics .... *Lentibulariaceae*
      d. Green plants, not carnivorous and seldom parasitic
        e. Carpels usually 2
          f. Fruit a drupe .... *Myoporaceae*
          f. Fruit a capsule, nutlet, or berry
            g. Fruit commonly spiny or with hooked prongs
              h. Placentas axile .... *Pedaliaceae*
              h. Placentas parietal .... *Martyniaceae*

g. Fruit not commonly spiny
h. Fruit a nutlet enclosed by the calyx . . . . *Globulariaceae*
h. Fruit a capsule or berry
i. Stamens 5 . . . . *Solanaceae*
i. Stamens usually 2 or 4
j. Anthers generally free
k. Placentas axile
l. Usually herbs . . . . *Scrophulariaceae*
l. Woody plants . . . . . . *Bignoniaceae*
k. Placentas parietal . . . . . *Bignoniaceae*
j. Anthers connivent or connate in pairs
k. Seeds attached to curved outgrowths of the placentas . . . . *Acanthaceae*
k. Seeds not attached as above . . . . *Gesneriaceae*
e. Carpel 1; stamens 4 . . . . *Phrymaceae*
c. Ovary inferior . . . . *Gesneriaceae*

Convolvulaceae. Morning-glory Family.

HABIT. Herbs, shrubs, or trees, commonly twining; some thorny xerophytes; sap often milky; some are non-green parasites (these sometimes separated as the Cuscutaceae).

LEAVES. Alternate, simple, variously lobed or entire, exstipulate.

INFLORESCENCE. An axillary dichasium, or racemose or paniculate, or the flowers solitary.

FLOWERS. Perfect, regular, usually large and showy; sepals 5; corolla 5-lobed; stamens 5, epipetalous; carpels 2, united; ovary superior (Figure 79).

FRUIT. A berry, nut, or capsule.

A family of 50 genera including 1200 species, primarily of the tropics and subtropics, with extensions into temperate regions. The twining habit is a distinctive feature. The family is important for the sweet potato and for numerous ornamentals.

Convolvulus (200) is mostly in the temperate zone; *C. arvensis*, bindweed, southern Europe, is now a cosmopolitan weed; *C. japonicus*, of Japan, is California rose; *C. sepium*, widespread in temperate regions, is Rutland beauty. *Ipomoea* (300) is a genus of the tropics and subtropics; *I. batatas*, sweet potato, of tropical America, is the most important tropical root crop, cultivated by Aztecs from ancient times. *I. pes-caprae* is characteristic of tropical and subtropical beaches. *I. purpurea* is morning-glory; *I. pandurata*, North America, is wild sweet potato or potato-vine, a common weed. *I. leari*, blue dawn-flower, is a handsome ornamental. *Calonyction* (6), in tropical America, includes *C. aculeatum*, moonflower, cultivated for large white flowers. *Quamoclit* (12), of tropical America, includes *Q. pennata,* cypress vine, *Q. sloteri,* cardinal climber, cultivated for red flowers.

Cuscuta (160), dodder, is a genus of leafless parasites, twining around host plants (Figure 45). *C. europaea* extends from Europe and North Africa to the Himalayas; *C. epilinum,* parasitic on flax, extends from Europe and North Africa to Iran; *C. epithymum* ranges from Europe to Altai; *C. gronovii* is in eastern North America.

Polemoniaceae. Phlox Family.

HABIT. Mostly herbs, rarely shrubs, small trees, or vines.

LEAVES. Alternate or opposite, simple or compound, exstipulate.

INFLORESCENCE. Cymose, corymbose, or capitate, or the flowers solitary.

FLOWERS. Perfect, regular; sepals 5, united; corolla 5-lobed, bell-shaped, funnel-shaped or salver-shaped; stamens 5, epipetalous; carpels 3, united; ovary superior.

FRUIT. A capsule.

The family includes 13 genera with 265 species, chiefly in the western United States. The tricarpellate pistil is a distinctive feature. The phylogenetic position is most uncertain. Several species are grown as ornamentals.

Polemonium (30) is chiefly in North America, but also in Eurasia and Chile; *P. caeruleum,* charity, is in Europe; *P. van-bruntiae,* eastern North America, is Jacob's ladder; *P. reptans,* eastern North America, is Greek valerian. *Phlox* (50) occurs in North America with 1 species in northeastern Siberia; many are cultivated ornamentals, as *P. paniculata,* summer phlox, *P. divaricata,* wild sweet william, *P. douglasii, P. drummondii,* annual phlox, *P. subulata,* moss-pink. *Gilia* (100) occurs in temperate and subtropical America; *G. aggregata,* foxfire, *G. tricolor,* birds'-eyes, and others, are ornamental. *Collomia* (20) occurs in California and Chile; many are ornamental. *Navarettia* (40) occurs in California; *N. squarrosa* is skunk-weed, the herbage ill-scented. *Cobaea* (9) occurs in tropical America; *C. scandens* is a cultivated ornamental climber of very rapid growth.

Hydrophyllaceae. Waterleaf Family.

HABIT. Herbs, rarely shrubs.

LEAVES. Radical, alternate or opposite.

INFLORESCENCE. Cymose, or the flowers solitary.

FLOWERS. Perfect, regular; sepals 5, united; corolla of 5 united petals, rotate, bell-shaped or funnel-shaped; stamens 5, epipetalous; carpels 2, united; ovary superior.

FRUIT. A capsule.

The family includes 20 genera with 265 species, widely distributed, especially abundant in western North America. There is a tendency toward development of helicoid cymes (Figure 69). The family is closely related to the Polemoniaceae and the Boraginaceae. Several species are cultivated as ornamentals.

Hydrophyllum (7), waterleaf, is a genus of forest herbs of North America. *Nemophila* (20) occurs in North America, including *N. menziesii,* baby blue-eyes, California, and others, cultivated as ornamentals. *Phacelia* (115) ranges from North America south to Tierra del Fuego; *P. tanacetifolia* and others, are ornamental flowers. *Eriodictyon* (4), of western North America, includes *E. californicum,* yerba santa, a very common glutinous shrub of the chaparral.

Boraginaceae. Borage Family.

Habit. Mostly herbs, but also shrubs or trees, or lianas.

Leaves. Generally alternate, simple, entire, exstipulate, often covered with rough bristly hairs (hence the name, Asperifoliaceae, formerly used).

Inflorescence. Cymose, glomerate-racemose or spicate, usually "scorpioid" or "boragoid," appearing to uncoil as the flowers open.

Flowers. Perfect, usually regular; calyx of 5 united sepals; corolla of 5 united petals, funnel-form or tubular, often changing color (pink to blue) as the flowers advance in age; stamens 5, epipetalous; carpels 2, united; ovary superior; style usually **gynobasic,** that is, arising from the depression between the lobes of the ovary (Figure 120).

Fruit. Often deeply 4-parted into 1-seeded nutlets (apparent achenes); sometimes a drupe.

The family includes 100 genera with 2000 species, of wide distribution, but especially abundant in the Mediterranean region. Distinctive features are the apparently coiled inflorescences and the 4-parted fruits. Several are cultivated as ornamentals.

Cordia (250) is a group of plants of warm climates, mostly trees and shrubs with edible fruits (drupes). *C. sebestena,* geiger-tree, tropical America, has handsome orange-red flowers and medicinal fruit. Some species produce good timber, as *C. alliodora,* tropical America, laurel blanco. *Tournefortia* (120) is a genus of trees and shrubs, especially in America; *T. argentea* occurs in the Old World tropics. *Heliotropium* (250) occurs in tropical and subtropical lands, including *H. arborescens,* heliotrope, Ecuador, Peru, cultivated for perfumed flowers; *H. indicum* is a common tropical roadside weed.

Omphalodes (25), navel-wort, occurs in Europe, Asia, and Mexico, including *O. linifolia,* southwestern Mediterranean, and *O. verna,* southern Alps. *Cynoglossum* (50), hound's tongue, occurs in temperate and subtropical lands; *C. officinale,* Europe, is introduced elsewhere as a common weed (Figure 120). *Lappula* (50), stickseed, beggar's-lice, is mostly boreal, including *L. deflexa,* circumboreal. *Cryptanthe* (125), nievitas, occurs in western America, from California to Chile. *Symphytum* (17) is a genus mostly of the eastern Mediterranean; S. *officinale,* middle and eastern Europe, is comfrey, a medicinal herb. *Borago* (3) occurs in the Mediterranean; *B. officinalis,* borage (Figure 4), is cultivated in Europe as a source of nectar for bees. *Anchusa* (40) occurs in southern Europe, western Asia, and Cape Colony; *A. officinalis,* alkanet or bugloss, is an ornamental. *Alkanna* (40) of the Mediterranean region, includes *A. tinctoria;* the roots yield alkanet, a red dye. *Pulmonaria* (12) ranges from Europe to Siberia; *P. officinale* is lungwort. *Myosotis* (30), of north tem-

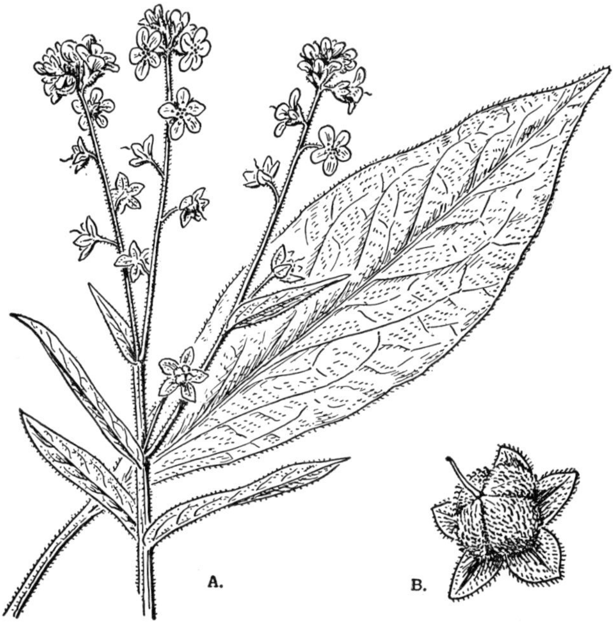

Figure 120. *Cynoglossum officinale. A,* general view of portion of the plant; *B,* ripe fruit, showing four nutlets.

perate regions, is scorpion-grass or forget-me-not; *M. sylvatica, M. scorpioides,* and others, are cultivated ornamentals; *M. alpestris* is the floral emblem of Alaska. *Lithospermum* (50), of temperate regions, includes *L. arvense,* gromwell, and *L. canescens,* puccoon. *Cerinthe* (10) of central and southern Europe, and western Asia, is honeywort; the flowers yield much nectar. *Mertensia* (50), of north temperate regions, especially North America and Asia, includes *M. virginica,* bluebells, *M. maritima,* along coasts. *Echium* (50) is a genus of Europe, Asia, and Africa; the flowers are irregular. *E. vulgare,* Central Europe, naturalized elsewhere, is blue thistle, viper's bugloss, blue devil; it is a widespread weed, especially on limestone soils.

Verbenaceae. Vervain Family.

HABIT. Herbs, shrubs, or trees, many lianas, some xerophytes, often thorny.

LEAVES. Usually opposite, rarely alternate or whorled, simple or compound, exstipulate.

INFLORESCENCE. Racemose or cymose, often with an involucre of colored bracts.

FLOWERS. Perfect, usually irregular; calyx usually 5-parted; corolla 5-parted, often 2-lipped; stamens usually 4, didynamous; carpels usually 2, united; ovary superior.

FRUIT. A drupe, capsule, or schizocarp.

The family includes 98 genera with 2600 species, mostly of tropical regions, with extensions into temperate lands. Members of the family differ from the Boraginaceae in the 4 stamens and from the Labiatae in the undivided ovary. Some species yield valuable timber, and some are cultivated as ornamentals.

Verbena (230) is a genus of tropical and temperate regions; *V. officinalis,* vervain, was a sacred herb of the Romans and Druids; *V. hybrida,* of hybrid origin, is the common garden vervain. *Lantana* (155), a genus of tropical and subtropical regions, mostly of shrubs, is often used for hedges; *L. camara,* a common tropical weed, is cultivated for yellow or red flowers in warm lands. *Lippia* (120) is mostly of tropical America and Africa; leaves of *L. citriodora* yield verbena-oil; *L. lanceolata* is fogfruit, along streams in the eastern United States. *Priva* (10), a tropical genus, includes *P. lappulacea,* a common tropical weed. *Petraea* (29), of tropical America, is climbing; some species, including *P. volubilis,* purplewreath, are cultivated for ornamental flowers.

Vitex (270), of tropical and temperate lands, includes *V. agnus-castus,* chaste tree, Spain to Central Asia, an ornamental shrub with blue or white flowers. *Tectona* (3) occurs in Indomalaysia; *T. grandis,* teak, produces a hard timber used in shipbuilding, one of the most durable woods known. *Callicarpa* (40), beauty-berry, of tropical and subtropical regions, includes *C. americana,* French-mulberry, and *C. purpurea,* grown for ornamental fruits. *Clerodendron* (380), glorybower, of tropical and subtropical regions, has some species cultivated, as *C. indicum,* Turk's-turban; *C. thompsonae* is grown for ornamental flowers with red calyx and white corolla; *C. infortunatum* is believed in India to have power over evil spirits causing itch. *Avicennia* (4) is a group of tropical plants, constituents of the mangrove vegetation; *A. nitida* is black mangrove.

Labiatae. Mint Family.

HABIT. Usually herbs, sometimes shrubs or trees, or lianas, usually with epidermal glands secreting characteristic aromatic oils; stem square.

LEAVES. Opposite, simple (rarely compound), exstipulate.

INFLORESCENCE. Usually composed of axillary pairs of cymes forming an apparent whorl (**verticillaster**), or the flowers solitary.

FLOWERS. Usually perfect, zygomorphic; calyx 5-parted, usually conspicuously ribbed; corolla 5-parted, 2-lipped; stamens 4, **didynamous** (that is, in two pairs of different lengths), or 2, epipetalous; carpels 2, united; ovary superior (Figure 121).

FRUIT. Usually a group of 4 nutlets each with 1 seed.

The family consists of 200 genera including 3200 species, cosmopolitan in distribution, but centering in the Mediterranean region. Distinctive features are the square stem, opposite leaves, aromatic herbage, 2-lipped

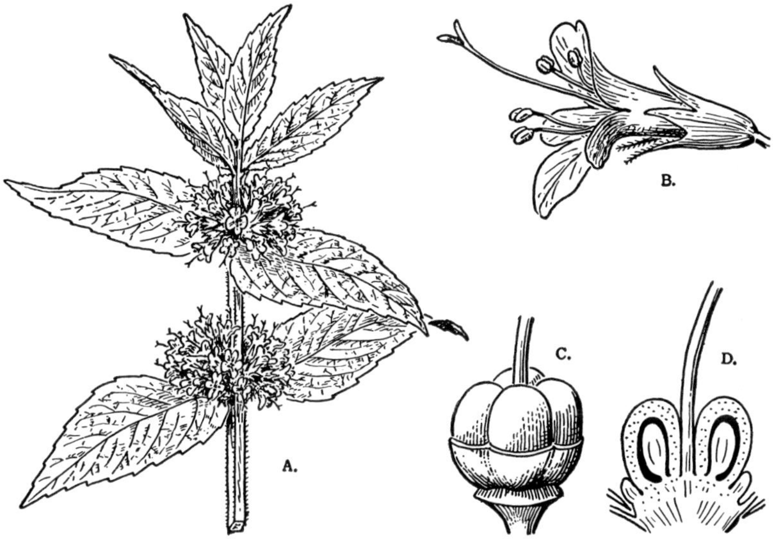

Figure 121. Characteristic features of the Labiatae. *A, Mentha arvensis,* showing square stem, opposite leaves, and verticillasters of flowers; *B, Thymus* flower, showing bilabiate corolla; *C,* ovary, deeply four-lobed; *D,* Ovary sectioned, showing gynobasic style. (*C* and *D* adapted from Engler-Gilg.)

flowers, and 4-parted ovary. They are important as a source of volatile aromatic oils, and several are ornamental garden plants.

Ajuga (50), of the temperate Old World, includes *A. pyramidalis,* blue bugle, and *A. reptans,* bugleweed. *Teucrium* (100), germander or woodsage, is widely distributed; *T. scordium* ranges from western Europe to Central Asia; *T. canadense* is in North America. *Scutellaria* (190), skullcap, is cosmopolitan; the calyx is closed in fruit, resembling a skull cap. *Lavandula* (26) ranges from the Mediterranean and Abyssinia to the East Indies; *L. officinalis,* lavender, yields oil of lavender from the flowers. *Rosmarinus officinalis,* rosemary, a xerophytic shrub of the Mediterranean region, yields oil of rosemary, used in perfumery. *Marrubium*

(30) occurs in Europe, Asia, and North Africa; *M. vulgare,* horehound, is native from the Canaries to Central Asia, naturalized elsewhere. It is much used in confections (horehound candy) and medicines. *Nepeta* (160) is a genus of temperate Eurasia; *N. cataria,* catnip, catmint, ranges from southern Europe to central Asia, but is widespread as a weed. *Glechoma* (5), of Eurasia, includes *G. hederacea,* groundivy, a cosmopolitan weed. *Dracocephalum* (40), dragonhead, of central Asia, includes *D. ruyschiana,* eastern Europe to central Asia, grown as an ornamental. *Prunella vulgaris,* self-heal, heal-all, is a cosmopolitan weed. *Phlomis* (75) ranges from southern Europe to China; *P. fruticosa,* Jerusalem sage, and *P. lychnitis,* lampwick plant, grown in gardens. *Lamium* (40), in Europe, Asia, and North Africa, includes *L. maculatum,* Europe, spotted deadnettle, *L. album,* white deadnettle, cultivated as ornamentals, *L. amplexicaule,* henbit, a common weed. *Galeopsis tetrahit,* hempnettle, a widespread weed, is a species that may be created experimentally by polyploidy (see p. 94). *Leonurus* (9) in Europe and Asia, includes *L. cardiaca,* motherwort, formerly regarded as useful in childbirth. *Micromeria* (130), cosmopolitan, includes *M. chamissonis,* yerba buena, of California. *Stachys* (200) is almost cosmopolitan; *S. sieboldii,* east Asia, crosnes or Chinese artichoke, has edible tubers; *S. palustris,* woundwort, is in North America and Eurasia; *S. sylvatica* ranges from western Europe to central Asia; *S. aspera,* North America, is hedge-nettle. *S. (Betonica) officinalis,* betony, of western Europe, central Asia, and northern Africa, was formerly very highly regarded as a drug plant (hence the expression, "as good as betony"). *Salvia* (550), of tropical and temperate regions, includes *S. officinalis,* Europe, garden sage, an important culinary herb, used in meat packing. *S. splendens,* Brazil, scarlet sage, is common in cultivation. Other species are *S. verbenacea,* sage; *S. pratensis,* clary; *S. carduacea,* thistle sage, California. *Monarda* (20), in North America, includes *M. didyma,* Oswego tea, bee balm; *M. fistulosa,* wild bergamot, horsemint. *Melissa officinalis,* lemon balm, bee balm, is grown in flower gardens. *Satureja* (150), of temperate and tropical regions, includes *S. acinos,* Europe, North Africa; *S. vulgaris,* basil; *S. montana,* Europe, grown for greens. *Hyssopus officinalis,* of the Mediterranean, is hyssop, grown for drugs and as ornamentals. *Majorana hortensis,* sweet marjoram, of the Mediterranean region, is cultivated for the aromatic herbage. *Thymus* (40), of Eurasia and Africa, includes *T. serpyllum,* Eurasia, North Africa, garden thyme, used in flavoring. *Origanum vulgare,* wild marjoram, Europe to the Himalayas, is grown for aromatic herbage. *Lycopus* (9), mostly north temperate, is water horehound, a common herb of wet places. *Mentha* (15), of Eurasia and North America, includes *M. piperita,* peppermint; *M. spicata,* spearmint, *M. arvensis,* wild mint; *M. pulegium,* European pennyroyal. *Hyptis* (350) is a genus mostly of tropical America and especially Brazil; some species

are shrubs, or trees to 40 feet high, while others are common tropical weeds. *Coleus* (120), of the Old World tropics, includes *C. blumei,* widely grown for its variegated foliage. *Collinsonia* (3), in eastern North America, includes *C. canadensis,* horsebalm. *Ocimum* (60) occurs in the tropics; *O. basilicum,* basil, tulsi, is used in seasoning and is sacred to Hindus.

Nolanaceae. Nolana Family. A family of 2 genera with 60 species of herbs or shrubs of Chile and Peru. The leaves are simple and often covered with glandular hairs. The flowers are axillary, solitary, perfect and regular, with a 5-parted calyx, 5-parted corolla, 5 stamens, and 5 carpels, free or united. The fruit is composed of 1-7 mericarps. *Nolana paradoxa* is grown as a garden annual.

Solanaceae. Potato Family.

HABIT. Herbs, shrubs, or trees, sometimes lianas.

LEAVES. Alternate, usually simple, exstipulate.

INFLORESCENCE. Cymose.

FLOWERS. Perfect, usually regular; calyx 5-parted, persistent; corolla 5-parted, rotate to tubular; stamens usually 5; carpels 2, united; ovary superior.

FRUIT. A berry (Figure 87, B) or capsule.

A large family of 85 genera including 2200 species in tropical and temperate regions, primarily in Central and South America. It is most closely related to the Scrophulariaceae. The regular corolla is a distinctive feature. Economically the family is of very great importance, yielding foods, drugs, and ornamentals.

Nicandra physalodes, of Peru, is apple-of-Peru, an old-fashioned flower-garden plant. *Lycium* (100) includes many thorny plants; *L. halimifolium* is matrimony vine; *L. afrum,* Kaffir thorn, is used for hedges in South Africa. *Atropa* (2) occurs in the Mediterranean; *A. belladonna,* deadly nightshade, contains atropine, basis of the drug belladonna. *Hyoscyamus* (11) ranges from the Canaries to Siberia; *H. niger,* henbane, Europe to the East Indies, was formerly cultivated as a narcotic. *Physalis* (50) is cosmopolitan, but chiefly in America; the edible berry is enclosed in a bladdery persistent calyx, sometimes colored, as in *P. alkekengi,* Chinese lantern; *P. peruviana* is gooseberry-tomato; *P. ixocarpa* is tomatillo; *P. heterophylla* is ground-cherry. *Mandragora* (4) ranges from the Mediterranean to the Himalayas; *M. officinarum,* mandrake, has a thick root forked and somewhat resembling a miniature human being; it was formerly used in magic and medicine and has many interesting old superstitions associated with it. *Capsicum* (30) is native in Central and South America. *C. frutescens* is the most important American spice (Figure 5); various forms yield red or green peppers, paprika, pimiento, tabasco, chili; *C. frutescens* and *C. fastigiatum* yield Cayenne pepper.

Solanum (1700) is one of the largest genera of plants, mostly of tropical and temperate regions, especially in America. *S. dulcamara,* bittersweet, Eurasia, is cultivated for flowers and colored fruits; *S. nigrum* is nightshade; *S. melongena,* East Indies, eggplant, is cultivated for edible fruit. *S. tuberosum,* potato, originated in the temperate Andes (Figure 2); it is cultivated for the edible tubers, one of most important food plants of the world. *S. quitoense,* lulo, Andes, yields a refreshing beverage from the fruits. *S. sodomoeum* is apple-of-Sodom, of Palestine. *S. giganteum,* Andes, is a tree up to 50 feet or more high. *Lycopersicon* (10), of

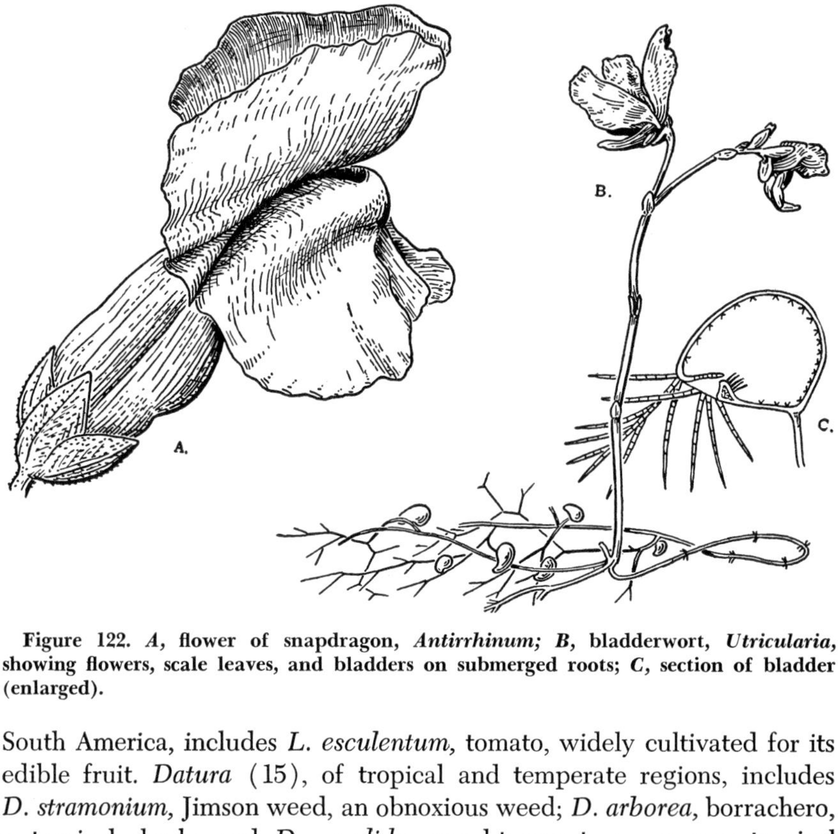

Figure 122. ***A,* flower of snapdragon, *Antirrhinum; B,* bladderwort, *Utricularia,* showing flowers, scale leaves, and bladders on submerged roots; *C,* section of bladder (enlarged).**

South America, includes *L. esculentum,* tomato, widely cultivated for its edible fruit. *Datura* (15), of tropical and temperate regions, includes *D. stramonium,* Jimson weed, an obnoxious weed; *D. arborea,* borrachero, a tropical shrub; and *D. candida,* angel-trumpet, a common tropical ornamental. *Cyphomandra* (30) occurs in tropical America; *C. betacea,* tree-tomato, Andes, grows 10 feet high, and produces edible fruits. *Cestrum* (250) occurs in tropical and subtropical America; some species are cultivated ornamentals, as *C. diurnum,* day-jessamine, and *C. nocturnum,* night-jassamine, fragrant by day or by night, respectively. *Nicotiana* (100) has its distribution in America and Australia to Polynesia. *N. tabacum,* tobacco, is grown in enormous quantities for smoking, snuffing and chewing (p. 63); ornamentals are *N. alata,* southern Brazil,

N. sylvestris, Argentina, *N. glauca,* Argentina, Uruguay. *Petunia* (15), in tropical America, includes *P. violacea, P. hybrida,* and others, cultivated as ornamentals. *Salpiglossis* (8), in Chile, includes *S. sinuata,* painted-tongue, and others, cultivated as ornamentals. *Schizanthus* (8), butterfly flower, Chile, has zygomorphic flowers; some species are cultivated for their ornamental flowers. *Brunfelsia* (20), in tropical America, includes *B. americana,* lady-of-the-night, very sweet-fragrant.

Scrophulariaceae. Figwort Family.

HABIT. Mostly herbs or undershrubs, rarely trees, several climbers, some parasitic on roots (green or non-green).

LEAVES. Alternate, opposite, or whorled, simple, exstipulate.

INFLORESCENCE. Variable, determinate or indeterminate; bracts sometimes brightly colored.

FLOWERS. Perfect, irregular; calyx usually 5-parted; corolla 5-parted, typically 2-lipped, sometimes nearly regular; stamens sometimes 5, or 4 and didynamous, the 5th stamen sometimes represented by a staminode, or sometimes only 2; carpels 2, united; ovary superior (Figure 122).

FRUIT. A capsule, rarely a berry.

A large family of 200 genera including 2600 species, represented on all the continents. They are separated from the Solanaceae by the zygomorphic corolla and from the Labiatae by the undivided ovary. Economically they are important chiefly as ornamental plants and for the drug digitalis.

Verbascum (260), native of the north temperate Old World, has flowers almost regular, with 5 stamens; *V. thapsus,* Europe, is common mullein; *V. blattaria* is moth mullein (Figure 67). *Celsia* (75), ranging from Cape Verde to China, includes *C. arcturus,* Crete, Cretan bear's-tail, resembling *Verbascum.*

Calceolaria (200), slipperwort, from Mexico to Tierra del Fuego, is especially abundant in Chile; many species are cultivated as ornamentals, including *C. integrifolia* and *C. crenatiflora; C. ridiculoides,* of the Colombian páramos, is ridiculos. *Jovelliana,* a closely related genus, has a bicentric range, with 2 species in Peru and Chile, and 4 in New Zealand. *Antirrhinum* (30) occurs in the north temperate zone, especially in the Mediterranean region; *A. majus,* snapdragon, Mediterranean, is a popular ornamental. *Linaria* (100) mostly Eurasian, with 1 species in North America, includes *L. vulgaris,* butter-and-eggs, toadflax, *L. cymbalaria,* Kenilworth ivy, a vine on walls, *L. alpina,* Pyrenees to Balkans, *L. minor,* Middle Europe, all cultivated ornamentals. *Scrophularia* (150), figwort, is a genus of the north temperate zone, especially in Asia; *S. marilandica* is in eastern North America; European species were reputed to cure scrofula. *Penstemon* (250), beardtongue, of North America, has 4 functional stamens and 1 bearded staminode; about 50 species are cultivated as ornamentals, as *P. gentianoides* and *P. hartwegii. Chelone* (4), turtlehead, is a group of North American plants with white or purple flowers. *Collinsia* (20) North America, includes *C. bicolor, C. grandiflora,* ornamentals, and *C. verna,* blue-eyed Mary. *Paulownia* (10), of China and Japan, includes *P. tomentosa,* imperial tree, up to 40 feet high, often planted in parks, sometimes escaping freely. *Mimulus* (60), monkey-flower, is cosmopolitan, including *M. moschatus,* muskplant, *M. ringens,* eastern North America, *M. luteus,* North America to Chile. *Mazus* (6) is a genus of low herbs of Indonesia and Australia grown as ground-cover and escaping in the United States. *Gratiola* (25), of the north and south temperate zones, includes *G. officinalis,* hedge-hyssop, a folk-remedy, and *G. virginiana,* eastern North America; there are 2 stamens.

Veronica (150), speedwell, is a genus of small herbs of north temperate regions, as *V. chamaedrys,* Europe, northern and western Asia; *V. officinalis,* Europe, Asia Minor, northeastern North America; *V. anagallis,* circumboreal; *V. serpyllifolia,* circumboreal; *V. montana,* central and southern Europe; *V. alpina,* circumpolar and alpine; *V. fruticans,* sub-arctic and alpine Europe, Greenland. *Hebe* (140) is Australasian; *H. cupressoides* and others are xerophytic shrubs or small trees with cypress-like branches; they play a dominant role in the New Zealand flora, with a large number of endemic species. *Digitalis* (25) ranges from the Canary Islands to Central Asia; *D. purpurea,* foxglove, western Europe, introduced in many lands, is the source of the drug digitalin. *Gerardia* (40), of North America, is false foxglove, with yellow or pink flowers. *Euphrasia* (100) includes herbs of north and south temperate regions, called eyebright, from the former use of some species as a source of eye wash; the plants are semi-parasites. *Castilleja* (50), paintbrush or paintedcup, is a genus of North and South America, mostly western North America; the upper leaves and bracts are brightly colored. *Bartsia* (30) occurs in Europe, North Africa, and on mountains of South America; the plants are semi-parasites; *B. alpina* is circumpolar and alpine. *Rhinanthus* (12), yellow rattle, occurs in Greenland, North America, Eurasia; the plants are semi-parasites. *Pedicularis* (350), lousewort, is arctic-alpine, circumboreal, Andean; *P. sceptrum-carolinum,* King Karl's sceptre, ranges from Europe to Japan; *P. groenlandica* (*Elephantella g.*), arctic and alpine North America, is little red elephants. *P. lapponicum* is circumpolar; *P. canadensis,* wood-betony, eastern North America; farmers once thought the presence of these plants in fields would cause sheep to have lice. *Melampyrum* (14) of Europe, Siberia, East Indies, eastern Asia, and eastern North America, includes *M. nemorosum,* Central Europe to western Asia, Swedish soldiers, and *M. lineare,* eastern North America, cow-wheat.

Lentibulariaceae. Bladderwort Family

HABIT. Herbs, mostly aquatic or in moist places, predominantly carnivorous.

Leaves. Alternate, or in rosettes, often bladder-like or pitcher-like or covered with glands secreting a sticky fluid (Figure 122).

Inflorescence. Racemose, or the flowers solitary.

Flowers. Perfect, zygomorphic; calyx 2-5-lobed; corolla 5-lobed, 2-lipped; stamens 2, epipetalous; carpels 2, united; ovary superior, with free-central placentation.

Fruit. A capsule.

The family includes about 6 genera with 260 species, on all the continents, in marsh and aquatic habitats. The carnivorous habit is distinctive. They have no economic importance except for growing as curiosities in aquaria.

Pinguicula (40), butterwort, occurs in the north and south temperate zones and on mountains of tropical America. Insects adhere to the sticky radical leaves and are digested. Examples are *P. vulgaris,* Europe, northeastern Asia, northern North America; *P. alpina,* subarctic Eurasia; *P. villosa,* subarctic Eurasia, Alaska; *P. antarctica,* Chile, Tierra del Fuego. *Utricularia* (250), bladderwort, is tropical and temperate, especially in South America and the East Indies. The finely divided submerged leaves bear bladders in which small animals (daphnids and the like) are caught and digested. *U. vulgaris, U. intermedia, U. minor,* occur in temperate Asia and North America.

Orobanchaceae. Broomrape Family.

Habit. Fleshy, non-green, root parasites.

Leaves. Alternate, scale-like.

Inflorescence. Terminal, the flowers each solitary in the axil of a bract.

Flowers. Perfect, zygomorphic; calyx 2-5-parted; corolla 5-parted, 2-lipped; stamens 4, didynamous, epipetalous; carpels usually 2, united; ovary superior.

Fruit. A capsule.

The family includes 13 genera with 140 species, mostly of the north temperate zone. The non-green appearance is a distinctive feature. The taxonomic evidence indicates that the family has been derived from the Scrophulariaceae. There is no special economic importance, although some do slight damage as parasites on crop plants.

Orobanche (100), broomrape, is temperate and subtropical. Examples are *O. lucorum, O. reticulata, O. ramosa, O. minor, O. uniflora,* parasitic on various hosts, as broom (*Cytisus*). *Epifagus virginiana,* beechdrops, of eastern North America, Mexico, is parasitic on beech. *Conopholis americana,* cancerroot or squawroot, of North America, somewhat resembles a pine cone in general appearance.

Bignoniaceae. Bignonia Family.

Habit. Trees and shrubs, commonly lianas.

LEAVES. Opposite, simple or compound, exstipulate.

INFLORESCENCE. Cymose.

FLOWERS. Perfect, zygomorphic, often showy; calyx 5-parted; corolla 5-parted, campanulate or funnel-form; stamens 4, epipetalous, didynamous; carpels 2, united; ovary superior.

FRUIT. A capsule, often woody, with winged seeds, sometimes fleshy and indehiscent.

The family includes 110 genera with 750 species, mostly of tropical regions, especially abundant in northern South America, where the climbers form an important feature of the forest vegetation. It is generally regarded as allied to the Scrophulariaceae. The lianous habit, winged seeds, and absence of endosperm are distinctive features. Many are ornamental and some produce useful wood.

Bignonia (150) is a genus of mostly tropical American lianas; *B. unguis-cati,* cat's-claw, ranges from the West Indies to Argentina; *B. capreolata,* crossvine, is in eastern United States. *Catalpa* (10) is in North America, West Indies, and East Asia. *C. bignonioides, C. speciosa,* of North America, and *C. bungei,* of Asia, are cultivated as ornamental trees and yield useful wood. *Campsis* (2) has 1 species in eastern North America, *C. radicans,* trumpet-creeper, and 1, *C. grandiflora,* in China. *Tecoma* (100) is a genus of trees and shrubs of tropical America, especially in Brazil. *Jacaranda* (40), in the West Indies and Brazil, includes handsome trees with showy blue or purple flowers, one of the world's most beautiful trees. *Spathodea* (8), of tropical Africa, includes *S. campanulata,* tulipan, African tulip, one of the showiest of tropical trees. *Parmentiera* (2) occurs in Mexico and Central America; *P. cerifera,* candletree, Panama, has candle-shaped caulifloral fruits used as food for cattle. *Crescentia* (5), is a genus of tropical American trees; *C. cujete,* calabash-tree, has gourd-like caulifloral fruits, with a woody exocarp that forms a calabash after removal of the pulp. *Kigelia* (3), of tropical Africa and Madagascar, is sausage-tree; the large sausage-shaped woody fruits hang on long stalks. *Chilopsis linearis,* desert willow, is a well-known shrub of the southwestern United States and northern Mexico.

Pedaliaceae. Pedalium Family.

HABIT. Herbs, rarely shrubs.

LEAVES. Opposite, with glandular hairs, simple, exstipulate.

INFLORESCENCE. Flowers usually solitary, or in axillary dichasia.

FLOWERS. Perfect, zygomorphic; calyx 5-parted; corolla 5-parted; stamens 4, didynamous; carpels 2, united; ovary superior.

FRUIT. A capsule or nut, sometimes spiny or with wings or hooks.

The family includes 16 genera with 60 species, mostly seashore or desert plants. The beaked or barbed fruits are distinctive. Economically the family is important as the source of sesame oil.

Pedalium murex ranges from Madagascar and tropical Africa to India. *Harpagophytum procumbens,* grapple-plant, of South Africa, has the fruit covered with woody hooks an inch long, very troublesome to sheep and other grazing animals. *Sesamum* (16) occurs in tropical Africa and Asia. *S. indicum,* til, gingelly, yields sesame oil, a substitute for olive oil. It is the chief oil plant of India, with 3 million acres devoted to its cultivation.

Martyniaceae. Martynia Family. A family of viscid-pubescent herbs, 5 genera, 10 species, of tropical and subtropical America. The flowers are racemose, perfect, zygomorphic, with a 5-parted calyx, a 5-parted corolla, 4 epipetalous, didynamous stamens, and 2 united carpels, with a superior ovary. The fruit is a woody capsule, the tip forming a long proboscis-like hooked or curved process, splitting at maturity into 2 parts. *Martynia* (7), unicornplant, occurs in subtropical America; *M. louisiana,* and others, are sometimes grown as oddities.

Gesneriaceae. Gesneria Family.

HABIT. Mostly herbaceous, sometimes shrubs or trees, a few lianas or epiphytes.

LEAVES. Usually opposite, often purplish.

INFLORESCENCE. Cymose or the flowers solitary.

FLOWERS. Perfect, zygomorphic; calyx 5-parted; corolla 5-parted, 2-lipped; stamens usually 4, didynamous, sometimes 2 or 5; carpels 2, united; ovary superior or inferior.

FRUIT. A capsule.

A large family of 85 genera including 1200 species, tropical and subtropical, among the most common herbaceous plants of the tropical American forests. The plants may be distinguished by the 1-celled ovary, with parietal placentas. Economically they are important chiefly as ornamentals.

Streptocarpus (50), of Africa and Madagascar, is Cape primrose; *S. dunnii, S. polyanthus, S. rexii,* are ornamentals. *Mitraria coccinea,* of Chile, a shrub, is near the family's southern limit. *Ramonda* has 1 species in the Pyrenees, 2 in Serbia, often grown in rock gardens; the flowers are almost regular. *Saintpaulia* (3) of East Africa, includes *S. ionantha,* African-violet, a popular ornamental, one of the commonest house plants in the United States. *Columnea* (100), in tropical America, includes *C. gloriosa,* Costa Rica, ornamental. *Sinningia* (20), in Brazil, includes *S. speciosa,* gloxinia, propagated by planting the leaves on soil. *Achimenes* (25), ranging from Mexico to Brazil, includes *A. longiflora,* ornamental. *Gesneria* (50) is a genus of tropical America and the West Indies.

Globulariaceae. Globularia Family. A family of herbs or shrubs with 3 genera including 25 species, chiefly of the Mediterranean region. The leaves are alternate and simple. The flowers are perfect, with a 5-parted, persistent calyx, a 5-parted zygomorphic corolla, 4 didynamous, epipetalous stamens and 1 carpel. *Globularia trichosantha,* globe-daisy, is an ornamental herb. *G. alypum* is a characteristic shrub of the Mediterranean bush formation.

Acanthaceae. Acanthus Family.

HABIT. Mostly herbs or shrubs, rarely trees; some climbers, xerophytes, hydrophytes; many are thorny.

LEAVES. Opposite, simple, exstipulate.

INFLORESCENCE. A cyme, often with large and colored bracts.

FLOWERS. Perfect, zygomorphic; calyx 4-5 parted; corolla 4-5-parted, commonly 2-lipped; stamens usually 4, didynamous; carpels 2, united; ovary superior.

FRUIT. A capsule, often elastically dehiscent with the seeds thrown out by hook-like growths known as **jaculators.**

This is a large family, of 240 genera including over 2200 species, chiefly tropical, with centers of distribution in Indomalaysia, Africa, Brazil, and Central America. Most botanists are agreed that it is derived from the Scrophulariaceae. Distinctive features are the 2-lipped corollas, the 2-loculed ovaries, and the elastically dehiscent capsules. Economically members of the family are of little importance except as ornamentals.

Thunbergia (100), of the tropical Old World, includes *T. alata,* clock-vine, East Africa, grown for showy flowers. *Strobilanthes* (200) is a genus of plants of Indomalaysia and Madagascar; the plants occur in vast numbers, forming almost the only undergrowth in some forests. *S. dyerianus* is grown in greenhouses for its purplish iridescent leaves. *Ruellia* (200), tropical, warm temperate, includes *R. ciliosa,* eastern North America. *Acanthus* (25) includes plants of the tropical Old World, mostly xerophytes with thorny leaves. *A. spinosus* is said to have formed the pattern for the decoration of capitals of ancient Corinthian columns. *A. montanus,* bear's-breech, is cultivated as an ornamental. *Justicia* (300), mostly tropical, includes *J. americana,* water-willow, eastern North America. *Beloperone* (30) occurs in tropical America; *B. guttata,* shrimp-plant, is an ornamental.

Myoporaceae. Myoporum Family. A family of 5 genera including 110 species, shrubs or trees, chiefly in Australia, eastern Asia, and Polynesia. The leaves are opposite or alternate, often covered with woolly or glandular hairs. The flowers are perfect, regular or irregular, with a 5-parted calyx, a 5-parted corolla, 4 didynamous stamens, and 2 united carpels. *Myoporum* has 30 species in Australia (where known as boobyalla), eastern Asia, Mauritius, and Hawaii. Some species produce useful timber.

Phrymaceae. Lopseed Family. A family of herbs with a single genus and species, *Phryma leptostachya,* having a bicentric range, in eastern Asia and eastern North America. The leaves are opposite. The flowers are axillary, small, zygomorphic, at first erect, then spreading, finally (in fruit) abruptly reflexed against the axis; calyx and corolla bilabiate, stamens 4, didynamous, carpel 1. Some botanists have placed this species in the Verbenaceae.

Order 32. Plantaginales. The order includes but a single family, of uncertain phylogenetic position.

Plantaginaceae. Plantain Family.

HABIT. Herbs, rarely subshrubs.

LEAVES. All basal or nearly so, commonly alternate, exstipulate.

INFLORESCENCE. Scapose, capitate or spicate.

FLOWERS. Inconspicuous, usually perfect, regular; calyx 4-parted, corolla 4-parted, the lobes scarious; stamens 4; carpels 2, united; ovary superior.

FRUIT. A circumscissile capsule (pyxis).

A family of 3 genera including 200 species, cosmopolitan in range. The rosettes of leaves and the scapose, capitate or spicate inflorescences are distinctive. Several species are noxious weeds.

Plantago (200), is a cosmopolitan genus, largely weedy; examples are *P. major, P. rugelii,* broadleaf plantain, *P. lanceolata,* English plantain or buckhorn plantain, *P. maritima,* seaside plantain, with fleshy leaves. *P. psyllium,* fleawort, is cultivated in Spain and France for psyllium seeds, reputedly laxative. *Littorella* has 2 species, 1 in South America, 1, *L. lacustris,* shore-weed, in Europe. The plants have the appearance of *Isoetes.*

Order 33. Rubiales. This order, regarded by most recent systematists as a natural group, includes plants characterized by opposite leaves and an inferior ovary.

- a. Stamens the same number as the lobes of the corolla or fewer
  - b. Stamens as many as the lobes of the corolla
    - c. Leaves opposite and stipulate or apparently whorled and without stipules .... *Rubiaceae*
    - c. Leaves opposite or perfoliate, not stipulate .... *Caprifoliaceae*
  - b. Stamens fewer than the lobes of the corolla
    - c. Ovary 3-celled, with 2 cells empty .... *Valerianaceae*
    - c. Ovary 1-celled; flowers in dense involucrate heads .. *Dipsacaceae*
- a. Stamens twice as many as the lobes of the corolla .... *Adoxaceae*

Rubiaceae. Madder Family.

HABIT. Trees, shrubs, and herbs.

Leaves. Opposite, entire, stipulate; stipules often united and as large as the ordinary leaves, so that the leaves seem to be whorled.

Inflorescence. Cymose.

Flowers. Perfect, regular; calyx 4-5-parted, the lobes often obsolete; corolla 4-5-parted; stamens 4-5, epipetalous; carpels 2, united; ovary inferior.

Fruit. A capsule, berry, or schizocarp.

A family of 400 genera including 5000 species, mostly in tropical and subtropical regions. The stipulate leaves and epigynous flowers are distinctive features. Several important tropical crops belong to this family, as well as numerous ornamentals.

Cinchona occurs in cool cloud forests of the Andes; the bark (fever-bark, Peruvian bark, Jesuit bark) yields quinine, one of the most specific of drugs, used in treatment of malaria. It was used by the Incas and discovered by the Spanish in Peru about 1650, being exploited by early Jesuit missionaries. Many species have been described, most of which may be variants of *C. pubescens* or *C. officinalis*. The tree was introduced into India in 1860 (see page 77), and later into Java, where most commercial quinine is now produced in plantations. *Cephalanthus* (6) occurs in North America, Africa, and Asia; *C. occidentalis*, buttonbush or Spanish pin-cushion, is North American. *Gardenia* (100), of the Old World tropics, has several species, among them *G. jasminoides*, China, cultivated for ornamental perfumed flowers. *Houstonia* (20) is a genus of herbs of North America; *H. caerulea* is bluets, innocence, or Quaker ladies. *Elaeagia* (2), of the Northern Andes, includes *E. utilis*, varnish of Pasto, Colombia, which yields a resin useful in paint manufacture.

Coffea (45), of the Old World tropics, occurs mostly in Africa and Madagascar; *C. arabica*, Abyssinia, East Africa, Arabian coffee, is the world's most important beverage plant; also largely cultivated in Brazil, Colombia, Java. The fruit is a 2-seeded red drupe ("berry"), the seeds (beans) are ground for the beverage. *Pavetta* (350), of the Old World tropics, and *Plectronia* (100), of the same region, are shrubs in forests. *Psychotria* (500), the largest genus of the family, includes shrubs in tropical forests. *Palicourea* (100) is a genus of shrubs in forests of tropical America. *Cephaelis* (150), occurring in tropical forests, includes *C. ipecacuanha*, Brazil, ipecac, the root used in medicine. *Myrmecodia* (20) is a genus of Malaysian epiphytes; the plants have galleries inhabited by ants. *Nertera* (8) is a genus of the Andes, New Zealand, Australia, Hawaii, and Malaya; *N. gratensis*, beadplant, a low herb, is widespread in the southern hemisphere. *Mitchella* (2), in North America and Japan, includes *M. repens*, partridge-berry, turkey-berry. *Asperula* (90) occurs in Europe, Asia, and Australia; *A. odorata*, Mediterranean, woodruff, and *A. cynanchica*, squinancy-wort, are grown in rock gardens. *Galium* (300) is almost cosmopolitan; some species, called bedstraw, were formerly used for filling mattresses because of the pleasant odor. *G. aparine* is goosegrass. *Rubia* (40) occurs in Europe, Asia, America; *R. tinctorium*, madder, was formerly cultivated for the red dye (turkey red) obtained from the roots; for centuries madder was a most important item of commerce, largely controlled by the Dutch.

Caprifoliaceae. Honeysuckle Family.
HABIT. Trees or shrubs, sometimes lianas.
LEAVES. Opposite, usually simple, exstipulate.
INFLORESCENCE. Cymose.

Figure 123. ***Cinchona ledgeriana.*** **(Courtesy Chicago Natural History Museum.)**

FLOWERS. Perfect, regular or irregular; calyx 5-parted; corolla 5-parted; stamens 5, epipetalous; carpels 2-5, united; ovary inferior.

FRUIT. A berry, drupe, or capsule.

A family of 18 genera including 275 species, primarily of the northern hemisphere. The inferior ovary, and opposite, exstipulate leaves are distinctive features. It is closely related to the Rubiaceae, from which it can usually be separated by the absence of stipules. Its economic importance is chiefly owing to the large number of hardy ornamental shrubs.

Sambucus (20), elder, is a genus of trees and shrubs in temperate and tropical regions, including S. *pubens,* North America, red elder; S. *nigra,* black elder, Denmark to North Africa and western Asia; S. *canadensis,* North America. *Viburnum* (120) is temperate and subtropical, especially in Asia and North America. V. *opulus,* cranberry-bush, Eurasia, North Africa, is often cultivated, especially its var. *sterile,* snowball, or guelder-rose. V. *lantana,* Europe to North Africa, is wayfaring tree, also cultivated. V. *cassinoides,* eastern North America, is wild raisin; V. *lentago,* eastern North America, nannyberry; V. *prunifolium,* eastern North America, blackhaw; V. *acerifolium,* eastern North America, dockmackie. V. *carlesii,* Korea, is grown for perfumed flowers. *Lonicera* (180) is a genus of the northern hemisphere; the flowers are zygomorphic, in pairs, the 2 producing separate berries or the berries fused into 1. L. *xylosteum,* ranging from Europe to the Amur, is fly honeysuckle; L. *caerulea,* circumboreal; L. *tatarica,* southern Russia to Central Asia, Tartarian honeysuckle; L. *periclymenum,* woodbine, western Europe to North Africa and Asia Minor; L. *caprifolium,* southern and southeastern Europe, Italian honeysuckle; L. *sempervirens,* southern United States; L. *japonica,* Japanese honeysuckle, much planted along roadsides in eastern United States, often becoming a serious weed; these and numerous others are cultivated as ornamentals. *Diervilla* (3), in North America and eastern Asia, includes D. *lonicera,* bush honeysuckle, northern and eastern North America. *Weigela* (12), eastern Asia, includes showy shrubs; W. *florida,* W. *praecox,* and others, are cultivated ornamentals. *Symphoricarpos* (15), of North America and China, includes S. *albus,* snowberry, S. *orbiculatus,* Indian-currant, coralberry, S. *occidentalis,* wolfberry. *Linnaea borealis,* twinflower, Linnaeus'-wort, circumboreal, was the favorite flower of Linnaeus (see his portrait, Figure 8).

Adoxaceae. Moschatel Family. A family of a single genus and species, *Adoxa moschatellina,* moschatel, north temperate. It is a perennial herb with a few radical leaves, 2 opposite cauline ones, and a small head of greenish flowers. The flowers are perfect and regular, with a 3-parted calyx, a 5-parted corolla, 5 stamens, and 2-5 united carpels. The fruit is a drupe.

Valerianaceae. Valerian Family.

HABIT. Herbs, rarely subshrubs.

LEAVES. In basal rosettes or opposite, exstipulate.

INFLORESCENCE. A cyme, or capitate.

FLOWERS. Perfect or imperfect, irregular; calyx little developed at time of flowering, later often forming a pappus as in the Compositae; corolla usually 5-parted; stamens 1-4, epipetalous; carpels 3, and locules also often 3, but only 1 locule is fertile, the others empty.

FRUIT. An achene.

The family includes 10 genera with 370 species, mostly of the north temperate zone and in the Andes. The tricarpellate ovary, with 2 abortive locules, is a distinctive feature. Economically the family is of little value, except for ornamentals.

Nardostachys (2) occurs in the Himalayas and China; *N. jatamansi*, nard, spikenard, has a very fragrant rhizome used medicinally. *Valerianella* (50) is mostly of the Mediterranean region. *V. olitoria*, *V. chenopodifolia*, corn salad, are grown for greens. *Valeriana* (200) is circumboreal and alpine; *V. officinalis*, *V. excelsa*, valerian, Eurasia, are somewhat used medicinally. *Fedia cornucopiae*, African valerian, is grown ornamentally for red flowers. *Centranthus* has 12 species in the Mediterranean, including *C. ruber*, red valerian, a cultivated ornamental.

Dipsacaceae. Teasel Family.

HABIT. Mostly herbs.

LEAVES. Opposite or whorled, exstipulate.

INFLORESCENCE. A dense involucrate head or a spike.

FLOWERS. Perfect, irregular; calyx small, cuplike, or of 5-10 pappus-like divisions; corolla 4-5-lobed; stamens 4, epipetalous; carpels 2, with 1 locule; ovary inferior.

FRUIT. An achene, enclosed in an epicalyx.

The family includes 9 genera with 160 species, primarily of the north temperate Old World and tropical and South Africa. The 1-celled inferior ovary and the dense flower heads are distinctive. There are a few ornamentals and some are noxious weeds.

Morina (12) ranges from the Mediterranean to China; *M. longifolia*, whorl-flower, of the Himalayas, is ornamental. *Dipsacus* (12) occurs in southern Europe, North Africa, Abyssinia, Caucasus, and India. *D. fullonum*, fuller's teasel, has hooked bracts (teasels) and the fruit heads are used with machinery in "fulling" cloth (raising the nap). *D. sylvestris*, wild teasel, is a widespread weed. *Scabiosa* (80), sweet scabious, mourning bride, pincushion flower, mostly of the Mediterranean, includes several ornamentals. Some species were once used medicinally for itch (scabies), whence the Latin name.

Order 34. Campanulales. This order, as here constituted, includes plants characterized by connate or coherent stamens. However, many phylogenists separate the Cucurbitaceae as a separate order (the Cucurbitales), the systematic position of which is uncertain.

a. Flowers not in involucrate heads
  b. Flowers usually imperfect .... *Cucurbitaceae*
  b. Flowers usually perfect
    c. Stamens 5
      d. Flowers regular .... *Campanulaceae*
      d. Flowers irregular
        e. Ovules numerous in each cell .... *Lobeliaceae*
        e. Ovules 1-4 in each cell .... *Goodeniaceae*
    c. Stamens 2-3 .... *Stylidiaceae*
a. Flowers in involucrate heads .... *Compositae*

Cucurbitaceae. Gourd Family.

HABIT. Chiefly climbing or prostrate annual herbs, monoecious or dioecious, making extremely rapid growth; climbing by tendrils (Figure 52).

LEAVES. Alternate, entire or lobed.

INFLORESCENCE. Axillary, cymose.

FLOWERS. Imperfect, rarely perfect; calyx and corolla typically 5-parted, regular; stamens typically 5, but often, by union of parts, only 4, 3, or 2, or sometimes all united into a column; carpels 1-10, usually 3, united; ovary inferior.

FRUIT. Fleshy, berry-like (commonly called a *pepo,* Figure 87, D), or dry, sometimes one-seeded.

The family includes 100 genera with 850 species, primarily tropical and subtropical. Members of the family are distinguished by the tendril-bearing stems and unisexual flowers with inferior ovaries. Economically they are quite important for food and as ornamentals.

Dendrosicyos (2) occurs in Sokotra and tropical Africa; unlike most members of the family, these are arborescent. *Acanthosicyos horrida,* narras, of Southwest Africa, is a bizarre plant growing on sand dunes, with a root up to 40 feet long; it is a thorny shrub with long tendrils. *Luffa* (7) is a genus of tropical regions; *L. cylindra* is dishcloth gourd, loofah; the vascular bundle network of the pericarp is used as a bath sponge. *Bryonia* (8), Mediterranean, includes *B. alba* and *B. dioica,* bryony, grown as cover vines. *Ecballium elaterium,* squirting cucumber, of the Mediterranean, has a fruit becoming very turgid; when ripe, the seeds are squirted out through a hole in the end. *Citrullus* (4) is indigenous in Africa and India; *C. vulgaris* is watermelon and its var. *citroides* is citron or preserving melon. *C. colocynthis* is colocynth or bitter-apple, the dried pulp yielding a powerful laxative. *Cucumis* (30) is a genus of tropical and subtropical regions. *C. melo* is muskmelon, native of tropical Africa and Asia; its var. *cantalupensis* (from Cantaluppi, Italy), a hard-rinded form, is the true cantaloupe; in North America that name is often improperly applied to muskmelons in general; the var. *conomon* is Oriental pickling melon. *C. sativus,* cucumber, cultivated in the Levant since ancient times, is now world-wide; it was highly regarded in the hot, dry Mediterranean climate. *Lagenaria siceraria,* calabash-cucumber, bottle-gourd, of the Old World tropics, has a pericarp used for a flask. *Trichosanthes* (50), of Indomalaysia, includes *T. anguina,* serpent or snake gourd; the fruit is 1-6 feet long and very slender. *Momordica* (40), tropical Africa and Asia, includes *M. balsamina,* balsam-apple, and *M. charantia,* balsam-pear, grown as ornamentals and sometimes for food.

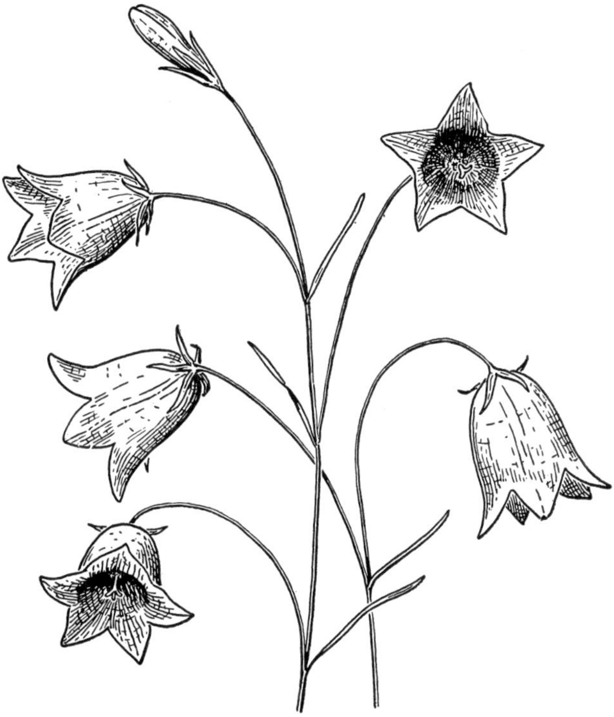

Figure 124. Bluebell, *Campanula rotundifolia.*

Cucurbita (10) is a genus of tropical America; *C. pepo,* pumpkin, vegetable marrow, summer squash, has been cultivated so long that no wild forms are known. *C. maxima* is autumn and winter squash, with edible fruits which may weigh over 100 pounds. *C. foetidissima,* calabazilla, is common in arid regions of the southwestern United States. *Sechium edule,* chayote, tropical America, was cultivated for root tubers and edible fruit by the ancient Incas and Mayas and cultivation is now beginning in the United States. *Sicyos* (40) bur cucumber, occurs in tropical America, Australia, and Polynesia, especially Hawaii. *Echinocystis* (25), North and South America, includes *E. lobata,* wild cucumber

(Figure 52). *E. fabacea,* manroot, southern California, has a root as large as and somewhat the shape of a man's body.

Campanulaceae. Bellflower Family.

HABIT. Herbs, shrubs, or trees, with milky sap.

LEAVES. Alternate, simple, exstipulate.

INFLORESCENCE. Cymose or racemose.

FLOWERS. Usually regular, bisexual, calyx-lobes usually 5; corolla-lobes usually 5; stamens as many as the corolla-lobes; carpels typically 5 or 2, united; ovary inferior.

FRUIT. A capsule.

A family of 50 genera with 650 species, widely distributed over the earth. Members of the family are distinguished by the milky juice, inferior ovary and united stamens. Economically they are important for the large number of ornamentals.

Campanula (250) occurs principally in north temperate regions. *C. rotundifolia* is harebell, "bluebell of Scotland"; *C. persiciflora,* Eurasia, is an old garden favorite; *C. medium,* southern Europe, is Canterbury bells; *C. pyramidalis,* eastern Mediterranean, is chimney bellflower; *C. carpatica,* central Europe, is tussock bellflower; *C. elatines,* Italy, Balkans, is Adria bellflower; *C. rapunculus,* Europe, is rampion; *C. rapunculoides,* rover bellflower, Eurasia, is now a widespread weed; many species are grown as ornamentals. *Phyteuma* (40), horned rampion, occurs principally on mountains of middle and southern Europe; some species are cultivated. *Specularia* (10), Venus' looking-glass, of the Mediterranean and in North America, includes *S. speculum,* middle and southern Europe, and *S. perfoliata,* eastern North America. *Adenophora* (30), ladybell, from eastern Asia, has several species in cultivation. *Ostrowskya magnifica,* giant bellflower, is a native of Bokhara; it attains a height of 8 feet, and is grown as an ornamental in the Puget Sound region. *Wahlenbergia* (100), tuftybells, is a genus chiefly of south temperate regions, and especially in South Africa, but with outposts in North Africa, southern Europe, St. Helena, and Juan Fernandez; *W. hederacea* is ivyleaf bellflower. *Jasione* (13) is a genus of middle and southern Europe; *J. montana* is sheep's-bit scabious, ranging from Scandinavia to North Africa. *Platycodon grandiflorum,* of eastern Asia, Chinese bellflower, balloonflower, is cultivated as an ornamental.

Lobeliaceae. Lobelia Family.

HABIT. Herbs, shrubs, and trees, usually with latex.

LEAVES. Alternate, simple, exstipulate.

INFLORESCENCE. Cymose.

FLOWERS. Irregular, perfect or imperfect, mostly 5-merous, ovary inferior.

FRUIT. A capsule or berry.

The family includes 20 genera with 700 species, chiefly tropical, but also in temperate regions. It is distinguished from the Campanulaceae by the irregular flowers, although by many phylogenists it is united to that family. Several are cultivated ornamentally.

Lobelia (250) is a genus of tropical and temperate regions. *L. erinus,* South Africa, is often grown in borders of flower beds, one of the commonest edging plants. North American species are *L. inflata,* Indian tobacco; *L. cardinalis,* cardinal-flower; *L. syphilitica,* blue lobelia. In tropical highlands, as Hawaii, Indomalaysia, Africa, some locally endemic species grow to heights of 10 feet or more, as *L. leschenaultiana,* Ceylon, *L. keniensis,* Kenya. *Centropogon* (100) occurs in tropical America, especially in Colombia. *Siphocampylos* (125) occurs in tropical America, chiefly in the Andes and Brazil.

Goodeniaceae. Goodenia Family.

HABIT. Herbs and shrubs.

LEAVES. Radical or alternate, rarely opposite, simple, exstipulate.

INFLORESCENCE. Cymose, racemose, capitate, paniculate, or the flowers solitary.

FLOWERS. Perfect, zygomorphic; calyx 5-lobed; corolla 5-lobed; stamens 5; carpels 2; united; ovary usually inferior.

FRUIT. A capsule, berry, nut, or drupe.

A family of 13 genera including 300 species, primarily Australian, but also in New Zealand, Polynesia, and along other tropical coasts. The absence of latex and the smaller number of ovules are features distinguishing these plants from the Lobeliaceae. They are of no special economic importance.

Goodenia (100) occurs in Australia. *Scaevola* (90) occurs in Australia, Polynesia, and tropical coasts; *S. frutescens,* Pacific and Indian Oceans, and *S. plumierii,* Indian and Atlantic Oceans, are characteristic shrubs of the tropical beach jungle.

Stylidiaceae. Stylidium Family. A family of 3 genera with 125 species of Australia, New Zealand, South America, and tropical Asia, perennial herbs or shrubs, more or less xerophytic. The leaves are simple, grass-like, often in radical rosettes. The flowers are perfect or imperfect, usually zygomorphic, with 5 united sepals, 5 united petals, 2 stamens united with the style to form a column, and 2 united carpels with an inferior ovary. *Stylidium* (100) occurs in Australia and tropical Asia, including *S. adnatum,* sometimes cultivated as an ornamental.

Compositae. Composite Family.

HABIT. Mostly herbs, but also shrubs or rarely trees.

LEAVES. Alternate, rarely opposite, simple or compound, sometimes much reduced, exstipulate.

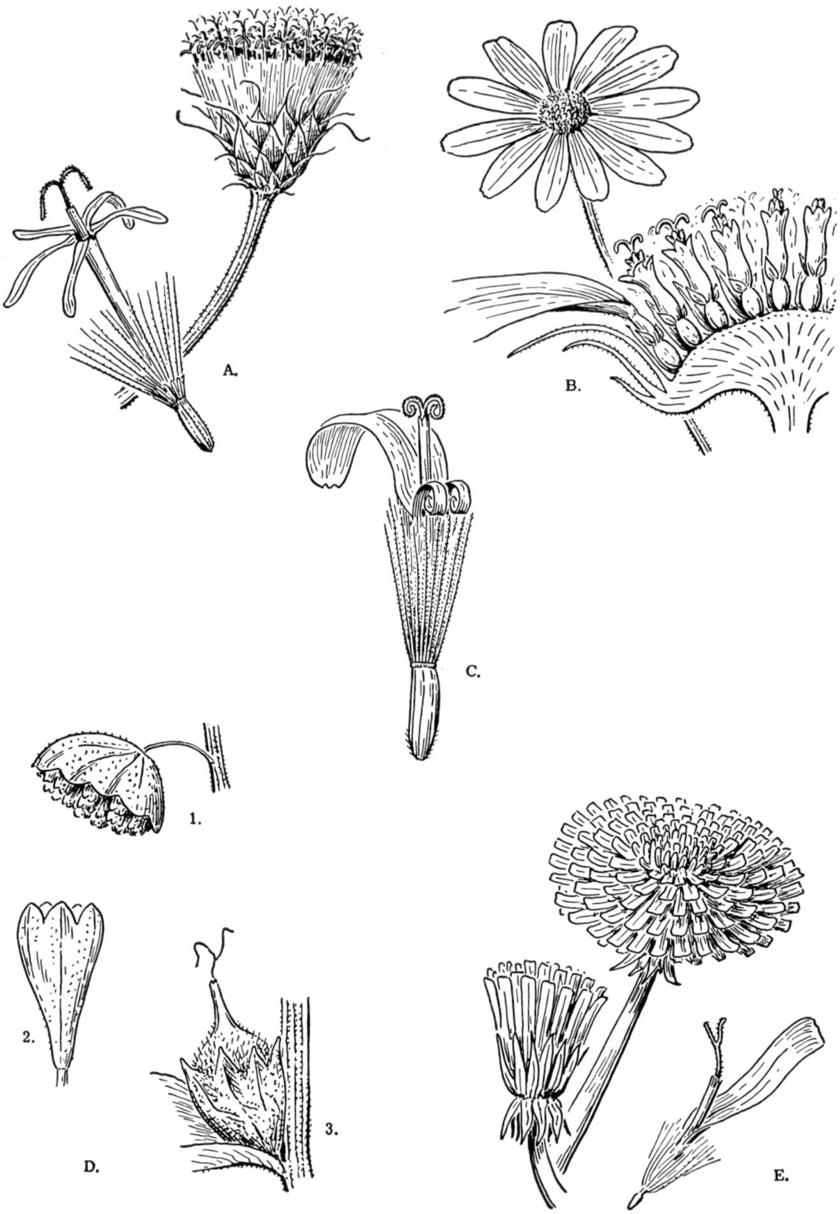

Figure 125. Types of composite flowers. *A,* ironweed, *Vernonia noveboracensis,* capitulum bearing only tubular flowers, and a single flower enlarged; *B,* sunflower, *Helianthus,* capitulum with both ligulate (radiate) and tubular (disk) flowers, also a portion of a capitulum showing phyllaries, a single ligulate flower and several tubular flowers; *C, Nassauvia,* single flower, showing two-lipped corolla; *D,* ragweed, *Ambrosia artemisiifolia,* showing imperfect flowers: *1,* capitulum with involucre and several staminate flowers, *2,* a single staminate flower, *3,* capitulum with involucre and its single pistillate flower, maturing into a fruit; *E,* dandelion, *Taraxacum,* capitulum (open, and closed) with only ligulate flowers, and a single ligulate flower enlarged.

INFLORESCENCE. A **capitulum,** with few or many flowers on a common receptacle or **disk** subtended by an involucre of **phyllaries;** the capitula are then arranged in spikes, racemes, corymbs, panicles, heads.

FLOWERS. Perfect or imperfect, regular or irregular; calyx usually represented by the extremely variable **pappus;** corolla gamopetalous, composed of 5 united petals, usually either a 5-lobed tubular corolla, a ligulate corolla with 3-5 apical teeth, or a 2-lipped corolla, with a 3-lobed upper lip and a 2-lobed lower lip; stamens 5, epipetalous, the anthers united (**syngenesious**); carpels 2, united; ovary inferior. The tubular (or disk) flowers may occupy the entire receptacle (the capitulum then **discoid;** Figure 125, A), or all except the margin; the ligulate (or ray) flowers may cover the entire receptacle (the capitulum then **ligulate;** Figure 125, E), or only the margin (Figure 125, B). The tabular flowers are usually perfect, but sometimes imperfect; the ligulate flowers when comprising the entire capitulum are usually perfect; when occupying only the margin they are usually neuter or pistillate. The bilabiate flowers characterize a single tropical tribe, *Mutisia* and its relatives (Figure 125, C).

FRUIT. An achene.

This is the largest family of flowering plants, with 950 genera including 20,000 species, widely distributed over the earth, in practically all habitats. The plants are easily recognized by the involucrate capitulum and the presence of a pappus. Some authors regard the two subfamilies as distinct families, the first being called the Compositae (or Asteraceae or Carduaceae), the second the Cichoriaceae. Economically the family is of considerable importance, but, for its size the importance is not as great as might be expected. There are numerous food and drug plants, many are ornamentals, and several are noxious weeds.

Subfamily Tubuliflorae. Tubular disk-flowers present; ligulate flowers if present marginal (Figure 125, A, B). No latex.

Vernonia (500) is tropical and subtropical, in America, Africa, and Asia, very common in grasslands. Some species furnish timber in Africa, and may be the world's largest composites. *V. noveboracensis,* eastern North America, is ironweed. *Elephantopus* (20), of tropical and subtropical regions, includes *E. scaber,* elephant's foot, eastern North America, an abundant and troublesome weed. *Stokesia laevis,* Stokes' aster, of the southern United States, is a cultivated ornamental.

Eupatorium (450) is found mostly in America. In eastern North America are *E. purpureum,* Joe-Pye weed; *E. perfoliatum,* boneset; *E. rugosum,* white snakeroot; *E. coelestinum,* mistflower. *Mikania* (150) is a genus of tropical America, twining herbs or shrubs with opposite leaves; *M. scandens,* of eastern United States, is climbing hempweed. *Ageratum* (30) occurs in tropical America; *A. conyzoides,* goatweed, is a common weed in the tropics; *A. mexicana* is a cultivated ornamental.

Liatris (15) occurs in North America; *L. spicata,* blazing star, and others, are cultivated as ornamentals.

Chrysothamnus (50), a genus of American shrubs, is well represented in arid regions of the western United States, where known as rabbitbrush. *Solidago* (90), goldenrod, is distributed chiefly in North America, very common in grasslands; *S. leavenworthii* contains rubber in form of granules; *S. canadensis, S. rugosa,* and so forth are in eastern North America. *Bellis* (10) occurs in middle and southern Europe; *B. perennis,* true or English daisy, is cultivated as an ornamental. *Grindelia* (35), an American genus, includes *G. squarrosa,* gumweed, stickyheads. *Montanoa* (35) is a genus of trees and shrubs in tropical America; *M. quadrangularis,* Venezuela and Colombia, reaches 40 feet in height, the largest composite in America, and yields strong timber. *Callistephus chinensis,* Chinese aster, of China and Japan, is a very widely cultivated ornamental, the common aster of flower gardens. *Aster* (600), aster, Michaelmas daisy, frostflower, occurs in America, Asia, Africa, and Europe, especially abundant in North America. Examples are *A. novae-angliae,* New England aster; *A. amellus,* Italian aster, Central Europe to Asia Minor and Siberia; *A. novi-belgii,* New York aster, eastern North America. Many are cultivated ornamentals. *Erigeron* (170) is cosmopolitan in distribution, but most abundant in North America; *E. uniflorus* is arctic-alpine; *E. speciosus,* in the Rocky Mountains; *E. pulchellus,* eastern North America, is robin's plantain; *E. ramosus,* also of eastern North America, is daisy fleabane; *E. canadensis,* colt's tail, is a semi-cosmopolitan weed. *Olearia* (125), tree aster, daisy-bush, a genus of trees and shrubs, replaces *Aster* in Australia, New Zealand, and New Guinea. *Brachycome* (50), of Australia, New Zealand, Africa, and North America, includes *B. iberidifolia,* Australia, Swan River daisy. *Baccharis* (300) occurs in America, from Massachusetts (*B. halimifolia,* groundsel-bush) to Tierra del Fuego. Members of the genus are shrubs, especially common on campos, while some are leafless xerophytes with green stems. *B. pilularis,* coyote brush, chaparral broom, is common on hills in California. *Haastia* (4), in New Zealand, includes *H. pulvinaris,* vegetable sheep, growing closely on the ground and forming large cushions. *Chrysopsis* (20), of North America, is golden aster.

Filago (*Gifola*) (12) occurs in Europe, Asia, America, and North Africa; *F. germanica* is herba impia. *Antennaria* (25), pussytoes, is arctic and boreal, with 1 species (*A. alpina*) subantarctic; many species occur in eastern North America. *Gnaphalium* (150) is cosmopolitan; *G. luteo-album* is everlasting; *G. macounii,* cudweed, oldfield balsam. *Leontopodium* (40) of Eurasia, includes *L. alpinum,* edelweiss, in high mountains from the Alps to the Himalayas. *Helichrysum* (000) is a genus of the Old World, chiefly of South Africa and Australia. Many are cultivated for the dried flower clusters, everlasting or strawflower, as *H. bracteatum,*

H. arenarium. Anaphalis (30) is chiefly in tropical and temperate Asia; *A. margaritacea,* northeastern Asia, North America, is pearly everlasting. *Inula* (120) a genus of Eurasia and Africa, includes *I. helenium,* Central Asia, elecampane. *Odontospermum* (12), of the Mediterranean, includes *O. pygmaeum,* North Africa to Iran, Jericho-rose.

Espeletia (30), a genus of the tropical Andes, includes characteristic plants of the páramos, called frailejones, from fancied resemblance of the plants to monks in capes. *Parthenium argentatum,* guayule, southwestern United States, has latex in solid particles in suspension in the cell sap. It was used by the Aztecs for making footballs and has recently become a source of rubber. *Echinacea* (5), North America, is purple coneflower. *Silphium* (23) occurs in eastern North America, chiefly on grasslands; *S. laciniatum* is compass-plant, rosinweed; *S. perfoliatum,* cup-plant; *S. terebinthinaceum,* prairie-dock, with large basal leaves. *Zinnia* (12) occurs in southern North America. Some species, as *Z. elegans,* youth-and-old-age, are cultivated as ornamentals. *Rudbeckia* (35) is characteristic of prairies in North America; *R. hirta,* black-eyed Susan, is the state flower of Maryland; *R. laciniata* is coneflower. *Helianthus* (60) occurs in North America, especially in southern United States and Mexico. *H. annuus,* sunflower, bears enormous numbers of flowers in each capitulum, and is much grown for the seeds, rich in oil. Kansas is known as the sunflower state. *H. tuberosus,* Jerusalem artichoke, girasole, was cultivated by North American Indians for edible tubers (to 4 in. long), and is now being revived as a garden vegetable. *Balsamorhiza* (10), of western North America, is balsam root, with scented roots. *Wyethia* (12), of western North America, is common on open plains. *Dahlia* (9), in Mexico, includes *D. pinnata,* garden dahlia, from which have been derived more than 10,000 different varieties grown as ornamental flowers. *Coreopsis* (115) occurs in America, Africa, and Hawaii, chiefly in North America; *C. major,* eastern North America, is tickseed; many species are cultivated as ornamentals. *Cosmos* (25) is a genus of tropical America; *C. bipinnatus,* Mexico, and others, are cultivated as ornamentals. *Bidens* (240), Spanish-needle, burr-marigold, beggarticks, is widely distributed over the world; *B. tripartitus,* is in Eurasia and North Africa; *B. bipinnata,* eastern North America.

Baeria (20), goldfields, is a Californian genus of yellow-flowered plants. *Helenium* (40), a genus of North America, includes *H. autumnale,* sneezeweed, eastern North America. *Tagetes* (20), marigold, includes plants from the southern United States to Argentina, often cultivated as ornamentals. *Gaillardia* (12), a genus of southwestern North America, has many species cultivated as ornamentals (blanket-flower).

Anthemis (100) ranges from southern Europe and North Africa to Iran; *A. tinctoria* is golden marguerite; *A. arvensis,* corn chamomile; *A. cotula,* dogfennel, *A. nobilis,* garden chamomile. *Achillea* (100), of north temperate regions, includes *A. millefolium,* milfoil, yarrow; *A. ptarmica,* sneezewort; in Greek mythology the plants were used by Achilles for healing wounds. *Matricaria* (70), matricary, ranges from the Mediterranean to the East Indies and is also in South Africa; *M. chamomilla,* chamomile, is medicinal; *M. suaveolens* is pineapple-weed. *Chrysanthemum* (150) includes plants of Europe, Asia, Africa, America, of major ornamental value. *C. leucanthemum,* ox-eye daisy, Eurasia, is a widespread weed. *C. parthenium* is feverfew, of the Balkans and Asia Minor. *C. morifolium,* a cultigen from East Asiatic species, is extensively cultivated, the florets becoming all ligulate and the heads of fantastic shapes and sizes; this is the chrysanthemum of commerce. *C. coccineum,* pyrethrum, yields Persian insect flower; *C. cinerariaefolium* yields Dalmatian insect flowers, used to make insect powder. *Tanacetum* (50) occurs in the north temperate zone; *T. vulgare,* tansy, Eurasia, was formerly grown medicinally and for seasoning. *Artemisia* (200) occurs in Europe, North America, South America, South Africa; the plants are common on arid soil of steppes or salt plains. *A. tridentata,* sagebrush, is very abundant in semi-deserts of the western United States; it is the state flower of Nevada. *A. stelleriana,* dusty miller, is a cultivated ornamental. *A. absinthium,* absinthium, southern Europe to central Asia, is used to flavor absinthe.

Tussilago farfara, colt's foot, a native of northern Eurasia, is a widespread weed in northern lands. *Petasites* (15), of north temperate regions, includes *P. frigidus,* circumpolar; *P. hybridus,* butterbur, Europe, western Asia, is medicinal; *P. fragrans,* winter heliotrope, is cultivated for perfumed flowers which appear in February. *Arnica* (18) occurs in north temperate and arctic regions, including *A. montana,* Europe, western Asia; *A. alpina,* circumpolar; some species yield tincture of arnica. *Doronicum* (34), leopard's-bane, occurs in Eurasia. *Senecio* (1300), of tropical and temperate regions, is one of the largest genera of flowering plants. Examples are *S. aureus, S. obovatus,* eastern North America, ragwort; *S. vulgaris,* groundsel, Europe; *S. jacobaea,* stinking Willie, Europe; *S. glabellus,* butterweed, eastern North America; *S. clivorum,* China, *S. cruentus,* Canaries, florists' cineraria; *S. cineraria,* dusty miller, Mediterranean. *S. keniodendron* is a remarkable tree of cloud forests on mountains of Kenya, attaining a height of 20 feet or more. *Emilia* (12) occurs in tropical Africa and Asia, including *E. sagittata,* tassel-flower.

Dimorphotheca (25) cape-marigold, of South Africa, includes *D. pluvialis,* ornamental. *Calendula* (20) is native of the Mediterranean; *C. officinalis,* pot-marigold, was formerly used for flavoring; it is now a common ornamental, flowering "through the calendar."

A group that is mostly South African, includes *Ursinia* (75), *Arctotis* (60), cultivated ornamentals, and *Venidium* (18), Namaqualand daisy, monarch-of-the-veldt.

Xeranthemum (6) occurs in the Mediterranean region; *X. annuum,* immortelle, one of the oldest and best known "everlasting," is grown as an ornamental. *Carlina* (20), ranging from the Canaries to Central Asia, includes *C. vulgaris*, carline thistle; *C. acaulis* is the weather thistle of the Alps, the phyllaries closing up at the approach of bad weather. *Arctium* (6) is native in temperate Eurasia; *A. nemorosum, A. lappa, A. minus*, burdock, are widespread noxious weeds. *Saussurea* (130) is north temperate, especially characteristic of mountains of Asia; some species ascend the Himalayas to great heights. *Carduus* (120), occurring principally in the Mediterranean region, includes *C. nutans*, musk thistle. *Cirsium* (150), thistle, is a genus of the north temperate region; many species are noxious weeds, as *C. palustre*, Europe; *C. heterophyllum*, Eurasia; *C. arvense*, Europe to Japan, "Canada" thistle (naturalized in North America); *C. lanceolatum*, Eurasia, Africa, *C. vulgaris*, Eurasia, pasture thistle; *C. horridulum*, southeastern United States, yellow thistle; *C. pumilum*, eastern United States, bull thistle. *Cnicus benedictus*, blessed thistle, of the Mediterranean region, is medicinal. *Onopordum* (25), of Europe, includes *O. acanthium*, "Scotch" thistle, ornamental. *Cynara* (11), of the Mediterranean region, includes *C. cardunculus*, cardoon, with the blanched leaves edible; and *C. scolymus*, true artichoke, with edible phyllaries. *Silybum* (2) occurs in the Mediterranean region and as a weed elsewhere; *S. marianum* is Lady's thistle or milk-thistle. *Centaurea* (500) occurs in most parts of the world, many species ornamental. Examples are *C. nigra*, knapweed, western Europe; *C. jacea, C. scabiosa*, star thistle, Europe to Siberia; *C. cyanus*, bluebottle, cornflower, southern Europe; *C. cineraria*, dusty miller, Europe; *C. calcitrapa*, caltrops, Europe, with spiny phyllaries; *C. solstitialis*, Barnaby's thistle, Europe. *C. melitensis*, Napa thistle, Europe, is one of the worst weeds in California. *Carthamnus* (20) ranges from Europe to East Africa and India; *C. tinctorius*, safflower, is one of the great tropical crops, grown for flowers used in dyeing; over a million acres are under cultivation in India. *Echinops* (70), globe thistle, extends from southern Europe to Japan; some are grown for the ornamental foliage.

Mutisia (70), in South America, is a genus of showy shrubby climbers, dedicated to the founder of the Expedición Botanica (page 74). *Gerbera* (35), of Africa and Asia, includes a number of cultivated ornamentals as *G. jamesonii*, Transvaal daisy, Barberton daisy. *Nassauvia* (50) is an Andean genus (Figure 125, C).

Ambrosia (20) is mostly in America, but with 1 species in the Mediterranean; the heads are unisexual (Figure 125, D). *A. artemisiifolia, A. trifida*, ragweed, eastern North America, cause hay fever. *Xanthium* (25), in Europe, Asia, and America, includes *X. spinosum*, and others, cocklebur, widely distributed noxious weeds.

Subfamily Liguliflorae. All flowers ligulate (Figure 125, E). Latex present.

Scolymus (3), in the Mediterranean, includes *S. hispanicus,* golden thistle, Spanish oyster-plant, somewhat grown for edible root. *Cichorium* (9), of the Mediterranean region, includes *C. intybus,* chicory, succory; the roots are used to adulterate coffee. *C. endivia,* endive, is grown for edible leaves. *Catananche* (5), cupid's-dart, of the Mediterranean region, was used anciently in making love philters. *Crepis* (200), principally of the northern hemisphere, has been much studied genetically. *Hieracium* (2000), hawkweed, is an extremely large genus, the species (perhaps biotypes; see p. 97), separated by minute morphologic characters. It is circumboreal and alpine, in northern Asia, North America, South Africa, and on the Andes of South America. Examples are *H. aurantiacum,* devil's paintbrush, Alps; *H. pratense,* king-devil, Europe, widespread noxious weeds. *Hypochaeris* (70), of Europe and the Andes, includes *H. radicata,* Europe, cat's-ear. *Leontodon* (45), ranging from Europe and North Africa to Central Asia, includes *L. autumnalis,* fall dandelion. *Taraxacum* (300 "micro-species") is common in temperate regions. *T. officinale,* dandelion, is a well-known weed. *T. kok-saghyz,* Russian dandelion, is a potential source of rubber. *Lactuca* (100) is a genus of temperate regions. *L. sativa,* lettuce, widely grown for edible leaves, is one of the most important composites. *L. canadensis,* North America, is wild lettuce; *L. serriola,* Canaries, southern Europe, Siberia, is compass-plant, the foliage oriented to point in a north-south direction. *Prenanthes* (28) extends from the Canaries to Japan and North America; *P. alba,* eastern North America, is lion's-foot. *Sonchus* has 70 species, paleotropical and temperate; *S. oleraceus, S. asper,* sow thistle, are widespread weeds. *Tragopogon* has 45 species in Eurasia and Africa; *T. pratensis* is goat's beard, also called John-go-to-bed-at-noon, from flower heads closing at midday. *T. porrifolius,* salsify, oyster-plant, has edible roots. *Scorzonera* (100) ranges from Europe to Central Asia; *S. hispanica,* black salsify, has edible roots.

Glossary of Common Greek and Latin Roots

a-, an-, without
acanthus, thorn
aciculus, needle
acris, sharp
acutus, sharp-pointed
aestivus, summer
agrarius, of fields
agrestis, pertaining to fields
alatus, winged
albus, white
alpinus, alpine
altus, tall, high
amabilis, lovely
amarus, bitter
amoenus, charming
amplus, large
anceps, two-edged
andros, man, male
angustus, narrow
applanatus, flattened
arbor, tree
arcuatus, bowed
arenarius, of sand
argenteus, silvery
argutus, sharp-pointed
aristatus, awned
armatus, armed
arvensis, of cultivated fields
asper, rough
ater (*atro-*), black
aurantiacus, orange-red
aureus, golden
auricula, ear
australis, southern
autumnalis, autumnal
azureus, sky-blue
bacca, berry
barba, beard
bellus, beautiful
bi-, two
blandus, mild
bonus, good
borealis, northern
bracteatus, bearing bracts
brevis, short
brunneus, deep brown
bufonius, of a toad (*Bufo*)
bulbus, bulb
calcareus, pertaining to lime
caespitosus, tufted, growing in low dense clumps
calcareus, pertaining to lime
calvus, bald, without hair
campana, bell (*campanula*, a little bell)
campestris, of fields
canaliculatus, channelled
candidus, white
capillus, hair
capreolus, tendril
cardia, heart
carina, keel
carnis, flesh
carpos, fruit
cauda, tail
caulos, stem
cephalo-, head
cera, wax

cernuus, drooping
chloros, green
chrysos, gold
cilium, eyelid (hence, a structure with fringes like the eyelashes)
cinis, ashes
clandestinus, concealed
clava, a club
coccineus, scarlet
coelestinus, sky-blue
collinus, pertaining to a hill
coloratus, colored
coma, hair
communis, common, general
concinnus, neat, well-made
confertus, crowded
contortus, twisted
cordis, heart
cornu, horn
corona, crown
costatus, ribbed
crassus, thick
crista, crest
croceus, saffron-colored, yellow
crucis, cross
cucullus, cap, hood
cuneus, wedge
cyaneus, blue
dactylos, finger
debilis, weak
decem, ten
declinatus, bent downwards
decorus, elegant
decumbens, reclining at base, with tips upright
deltoideus, triangular (like a delta)
dens, dentis, tooth
depauperatus, starved, dwarfed
dis, twice, two
didymus, in a pair
digitus, finger
discolor, of different colors
distans, distant, separate, remote
diurnus, relating to the day
drupaceus, like a drupe
dulcis, sweet
dumetorum, of hedges
e-, ex-, out, out of, from, without
echinatus, bristly, prickly (like *echinus,* a hedgehog)
edulis, edible
elatus, tall
elegans, elegant
ensis, sword
entomon, insect
equus, horse
erion, wool
erythros, red
esculentus, edible
exiguus, little, poor, small
exsertus, protruding from
falcatus, sickle-shaped
farinosus, mealy, powdery
fascicularis, clustered
femella, woman, female
-fer, to bear or carry
ferrum, iron
filum, thread
flagellum, a whip
flavus, yellow
floris, flos, flower
fluvius, river
foetidus, bad-smelling
folium, leaf
frutex, fruticis, shrub
fulvus, tawny
furcatus, forked
geminus, twin
gibbus, humped
glaber, smooth
glaucus, with a bloom, grayish
glutinosus, gluey, sticky
gracilis, slender
gramen, graminis, grass
grandis, large
gratus, pleasing
graveolens, heavy-scented
guttatus, spotted
gymnospermos, naked seed
gyno-, women, female
hastatus, spear-shaped
hebe-, downy, pubescent
helios, the sun
heteros, other
hexa-, six
hibernalis, pertaining to winter

hiems, winter
hirsutus, hirsute, hairy
hispidus, hispid, bristly
hortus, garden
humilus, low, dwarf
hyemalis, of winter
hyper-, over, above
hypo-, under, beneath
igneus, fiery
imbricatus, overlapping
immaculatus, immaculate, spotless
inaequalis, unequal
incanus, hoary
incarnatus, flesh-colored
inermis, without thorns
inodorus, without odor
integer, entire
intumescens, swollen
ion-, violet
isos-, equal
jubatus, with a mane
labium, lip
laciniatus, laciniate, torn
lactis, milk
lacus, lake
laevis, smooth
lanuginosus, woolly
lasios, hairy
latus, broad, wide
laxus, open, loose
leios, smooth
leptos, small, slender, weak
leucos, white
lignum, wood
limosus, of muddy places
linea, line
lithos, stone
littoralis, of the seashore (*littus*)
lividus, bluish
lobatus, lobed
longus, long
lucidus, bright, clear
lunatus, moon-shaped
luteus, yellow
macros, large, great
maculatus, spotted
magnificus, magnificent
majalis, of May
major, greater
margarita, a pearl
marginalis, marginal
maritimus, of the sea
mas, male
matronalis, pertaining to matrons
maximus, largest
mega-, great
melas, black
mellis, honey
micros, small
mille, a thousand
minimus, least
minor, smaller
mirabilis, wonderful
mitis, mild, gentle
mollis, soft
monos, one
montanus, pertaining to mountains
multus, much, many
muralis, pertaining to a wall
myrios, countless
nanus, dwarf
natans, floating, swimming
nemoralis, of shady places
nervosus, nerved
nictitans, blinking
niger, black
nitens, shining
nivalis, snowy
nobilis, noble
nocturnus, relating to the night
nodosus, jointed
notatus, marked
novus, new
nubes, cloud
nucis, *nux*, a nut
nudus, nude
nutans, nodding
nyctos, night
obconicus, obconical
obcordatus, obcordate
oblongatus, oblong
obtusatus, obtuse
occidentalis, western
ochros, pale yellow
octo, eight
odontos, tooth

odoratus, odorous, fragrant
officinalis, of the apothecaries
-oides, like, resembling
oligo-, few, scanty
orbicularis, round
orientalis, eastern
ornatus, ornate, adorned
ornitho-, bird
ovalis, oval
ovum, egg
ovis, sheep
oxys, sharp, acid
pachys, thick
pallens, pale
paludosus, marshy
palus, marsh
papilla, nipple
parvus, small
patens, spreading
paucus, few
pecten, *pectinis*, a comb
pedatus, pedate, footlike
pendulus, hanging
penta-, five
peregrinus, foreign, travelled
petro-, stone
philo-, loving
phlogos, flame
-phoros, to bear
phyllon, leaf
pictus, painted
pilus, a hair
planus, flat
platy-, broad, wide
plenus, full, plenty
plicatus, folded lengthwise
plumatus, plumed
poly-, many, much
prae-, *pre-*, before
pratensis, of meadows
prince, *princeps*, first
prolificus, fruitful
pruinosus, with a frost-like bloom
pseudo-, false
pubens, downy
pubescens, pubescent
pudicus, modest
pulcher, beautiful
pulvinus, cushion
pumilus, dwarf
punctatus, dotted
pungens, sharp-pointed
puniceus, purplish-red
purpura, purple
pusillus, very small
pycnos, compact, dense
quadri-, four
quinqu-, five
racemosus, racemed
radicans, rooting
ramus, branch
rarus, uncommon
reclinatus, reclined
recurvus, recurved
reflexus, reflexed
refractus, broken
remotus, with parts distant
renis, kidney
repens, creeping
reticulatus, netted
rhiza, root
rhodon, rose
ringens, open-mouthed
riparius, of river banks
rivularis, of brooks
robustus, robust
rostratus, beaked
rotundus, rotund, round
ruber, red
rufus, reddish
rugosus, wrinkled
runcinatus, backwardly incised
rupestris, of rocky places
saccus, a sack
saccharum, sugar
sagittalis, of an arrow
salinus, salt
sanctus, holy
sanguineus, blood-red
saponaceus, soapy
sarcos, flesh
sarmentosus, bearing runners
sativus, cultivated
saxum, rock
scaber, rough
scandens, climbing

schizo-, to split
scleros, hard
scutum, shield
sebaceus, fatty
secundus, one-sided
semi-, half
semper, always, ever
senilis, old, white-haired
sensibilis, sensitive
sepium, of hedges
septem, seven
sericeus, silky
serotinus, late
serratus, saw-toothed
sesqui-, one and a half
setaceus, bristle-like
siliceus, pertaining to sand
silvaticus, pertaining to woods
silvestris, pertaining to woods
simplex, unbranched
sinuatus, wavy
somnus, sleep
sordidus, dirty
sparsus, scattered, few
speciosus, showy
sphaero-, sphere
spheno-, wedge
spinosus, spiny
squamosus, with scales
stans, standing
stella-, star
stenos, narrow, little
stramineus, straw-colored
streptos, twisted
striatus, striped
strigosus, with straight appressed hairs
suavis, sweet
sub-, under, below, beneath
suffrutescens, slightly shrubby
sulcatus, furrowed
superbus, proud, superb
sylvaticus, pertaining to woods
tardus, slow
taurus, a bull
tectorum, of roofs
tenax, strong
tenebrosus, of shaded places
tener, slender
tenuis, slender, thin
teres, circular in cross section
ter-, three
terrestris, of the earth
tetra, four
tinctus, dye
torosus, cylindrical with contractions at intervals
tortus, twisted
toxicus, poisonous
tri-, three
tristis, sad, dull
trivialis, common, ordinary
tumidus, swollen
uliginosus, of marshy places
umbellatus, having umbels
umbonatus, having an umbo
umbrosus, shade-loving
undulatus, wavy
unguiculus, finger nail
uni-, one
urceolatus, pitcher-shaped
urens, stinging
usitatissimus, exceedingly useful
uva, grape
vaginatus, sheathed
validus, strong
vegetus, vigorous
velutinus, velvety
venosus, veiny
venustus, handsome
vernalis, pertaining to spring
verticillatus, whorled
verus, true
vestitus, clothed
villosus, covered with fine hairs
vinum, wine
violaceus, violet
virens, green
virginalis, virgin
viridis, green
volubilis, twining
vulgaris, common
vulpinus, pertaining to a fox
xanthinus, yellow
zonalis, banded

Index to Technical Terms

Pages are given on which definitions or illustrations appear.

General Index